ISBN 978-1-331-15287-3
PIBN 10151256

BIENNIAL REPORT

OF THE

ATTORNEY GENERAL

OF THE

STATE OF NORTH CAROLINA

VOLUME 26

1940-1942

HARRY MCMULLAN
ATTORNEY GENERAl

T. W. BRUTON
GEORGE B. PATTON
W. J. ADAMS, JR.*
ASSISTANT ATTORNEYS GENERAl

*Succeeded L. O. Gregory, deceased, October 18, 1941.

LIST OF ATTORNEYS GENERAL SINCE THE ADOPTION OF CONSTITUTION IN 1776

	Term of Office
Avery, Waightsill	1777-1779
Iredell, James	1779-1782
Moore, Alfred	1782-1790
Haywood, J. John	1791-1794
Baker, Blake	1794-1803
Seawell, Henry	1803-1808
Fitts, Oliver	1808-1810
Miller, William	1810-1810
Burton, Hutchins G.	1810-1816
Drew, William	1816-1825
Taylor, James F.	1825-1828
Jones, Robert H.	1828-1828
Saunders, Romulus M.	1828-1834
Daniel, John R. J.	1834-1840
McQueen, Hugh	1840-1842
Whitaker, Spier	1842-1846
Stanly, Edward	1846-1848
Moore, Bartholomew F.	1848-1851
Eaton, William	1851-1852
Ransom, Matt W.	1852-1855
Batchelor, Joseph B.	1855-1856
Bailey, William H.	1856-1856
Jenkins, William A.	1856-1862
Rogers, Sion H.	1862-1868
Coleman, William M.	1868-1869
Olds, Lewis P.	1869-1870
Shipp, William M.	1870-1872
Hargrove, Tazewell L.	1872-1876
Kenan, Thomas S.	1876-1884
Davidson, Theodore F.	1884-1892
Osborne, Frank I.	1892-1896
Walser, Zeb V.	1896-1900
Douglas, Robert D.	1900-1901
Gilmer, Robert D.	1901-1908
Bickett, T. W.	1909-1916
Manning, James S.	1917-1925
Brummitt, Dennis G.	1925-1935
Seawell, A. A. F.	1935-1938
McMullan, Harry	1938-

LETTER OF TRANSMITTAL

1 November, 1942

To His Excellency
J. MELVILLE BROUGHTON, *Governor,*
Raleigh, North Carolina.

DEAR SIR:

In compliance with statutes relating thereto, I herewith transmit the report of the Department of Justice for the biennium 1940-1942.

Respectfully yours,

HARRY MCMULLAN,
Attorney General.

EXHIBIT I

CIVIL ACTIONS DISPOSED OF OR PENDING IN THE COURTS OF NORTH CAROLINA AND IN OTHER COURTS

PENDING IN SUPERIOR COURTS OF NORTH CAROLINA

American Tobacco Company v. Maxwell, Commissioner of Revenue.
Caswell Training School v. T. A. Loving Company.
Church, William J. v. Insurance Companies.
Commissioners of Chowan County v. State Board of Assessment, et al.
Harris, M. D., et al. v. Maxwell, Commissioner of Revenue.
Hyde County v. A. D. McLean Estate, et al.
Lewis and King v. Johnson, State Treasurer.
Morrison v. Williams, et al.
N. C. Mortgage Corporation v. Maxwell, Commissioner of Revenue.
Plummer, et al. v. H. E. King, Trustee.
Pure Oil Company v. Maxwell, Commissioner of Revenue.
Southern Dairies, Inc. v. Maxwell, Commissioner of Revenue.
State ex rel. Johnson, State Treasurer v. Wachovia Bank and Trust Company.
State ex rel. Corporation Commission v. Southern Railway Company.
State ex rel. Beaufort County v. Henry P. Webster, et al.

DISPOSED OF IN SUPERIOR COURTS OF NORTH CAROLINA

Atlanta & Charlotte Air Line Ry. Company v. Maxwell, Commissioner of Revenue.
Bridges, N. W., et al. v. City of Charlotte, et al.
Brown, A. C. v. W. B. Bruce.
Cary, Francis, et al. v. Unemployment Compensation Commission, et al.
Chadwick, I. M., Admr. v. State Dept. of Conservation and Development.
Champion, H. M. v. Board of Health, et al.
Clover Brand Dairies v. J. A. Hart.
Cochran, Gus., et al. v. Security National Bank, et al.
Forsyth County v. E. M. Johnson, University, et al.
Forsyth County v. J. W. Stovall, University, et al.
Gilmore, et al. v. Hoke County Board of Education, School Commission, et al.
Gregory, Leslie v. Department of Revenue.
Mann, C. L., Trustee v. T. C. Mann, Jr., et al.
Metcalf, M. M. v. Dept. of Conservation and Development.
McLean, Dan W. v. Durham County Board of Elections.

Norden, Eric v. State Board of Education.
N. C. Midland Railroad Company v. Maxwell, Commissioner of Revenue.
N. C. Railroad Company v. Maxwell, Commissioner of Revenue.
Richwip Corporation v. Scott, Commissioner of Agriculture.
Slaughter, Vaye v. Kiser, et al.
State ex rel. State School for Blind v. J. F. Bost.
State ex rel. Corporation Commission v. Railway Company.
State ex rel. R. Bruce Etheridge, Director v. W. M. Bryan.
Steliondakis v. Maxwell, Commissioner of Revenue.
In Re: Tourist Traveltons, Inc.

Pending Before Industrial Commission

Hill, L. O. v. Forsyth County Board of Education, et al.
Smith, Wilhelmina H. v. Thomasville Board of Education and State School Com.

Disposed of Before Industrial Commission

Casey, S. E. v. Board of Education, et al.
Gilmore, et al. v. Hoke County Board of Education, School Commission, et al.
Metcalf, M. M. v. Dept. of Conservation and Development.
McDonald, Dr. Ralph v. University of North Carolina.
Pittman, Leroy v. Dept. of Conservation and Development.
Yates, Henry Wade v. State School Commission.

Pending in North Carolina Supreme Court

Gilmore, et al. v. Hoke County Board of Education, School Commission, et al.
McLean, Dan W. v. Durham County Board of Elections.
Norden, Eric v. State Board of Education.
Pue, et al. v. Hood, Commissioner of Banks.

Disposed of in North Caorlina Supreme Court

Bridges, N. W. v. City of Charlotte, et al., 221 N. C. 472.
Chadwick, I. M., Admr. v. Dept. Conservation and Development, 219 N. C. 766.
Champion, H. M. v. Board of Health, 221 N. C. 96.
State ex rel. Utilities Com. v. Carolina Scenic Coach Company, 218 N. C. 233.
Wachovia Bank and Trust Company v. Maxwell, Commissioner of Revenue, 221 N. C. 528.

Pending in United States Supreme Court

Steele, Eldon v. State of North Carolina.
Williams and Hendrix v. State of North Carolina.

Disposed of in United States Supreme Court

Chalk, Commissioner, et al. v. United States, 312 U. S. 679.
United States v. Appalachian Electric Power Company, 311 U. S. 377.

Pending in United States District Court

United States of America v. Southern States Power Company.
United States of America v. on relation of Tennessee Valley Authority v. George Whitcomb, et al.
United States of America v. 1028.238 Acres of Land in Onslow County, et al.
United States of America v. 166.77 Acres of Land in Buncombe County, et al.
United States of America v. State of North Carolina ex rel. Condemnation of Test Farm Site at Swannanoa.

Disposed of in United States District Court

Noel, Jeannette A. v. Edson B. Olds, Jr., et al. (Ackland Will Case).
United States of America and Credit Commodity Corp. v. W. Kerr Scott, et al.
United States of America v. 248.88 Acres of Land in Brunswick County, et al.

Pending in District Court of Appeals

Noel, Jeannette A. v. Edson B. Olds, Jr., et al.

Pending Before Federal Power Commission

In Re: Declaration of Intention of Nantahala Power and Light Company, etc. (Fontana Project).

Disposed of in Circuit Court of Appeals

In Re: Application of Carolina Aluminum Company, etc.

EXHIBIT II

LIST OF CRIMINAL CASES ARGUED BY THE ATTORNEY GENERAL AND HIS ASSISTANTS BEFORE THE NORTH CAROLINA SUPREME COURT: FALL TERM, 1940; SPRING TERM, 1941; FALL TERM, 1941; SPRING TERM, 1942.

FALL TERM, 1940

State v. Abbott, et al., from Wake; violation of slot machine laws; appeal by defendant Laing; affirmed; 218 N. C. 470.

State v. Barnett, from Franklin; A. D. W., etc.; defendant appealed; affirmed; 218 N. C. 454.

State v. Brackett, from Cleveland; seduction; defendant appealed; no error; 218 N. C. 369.

State v. Brown, et al., from Rowan; sci. fa; appeal by respondent; affirmed; 218 N. C. 368.

State v. Brown, Azor, from Catawba; murder first degree; defendant appealed; no error; 218 N. C. 415.

State v. Brown, W. M., et al., from Wake; violation of slot machine laws; appeal by defendant Laing; affirmed; 218 N. C. 480.

State v. Cannon, et al., from Wake; breaking, entering, larceny and receiving; defendant Cannon appealed; reversed on second count; venire de novo on third count; 218 N. C. 466.

State v. Chambers, from Lenoir; burglary first degree; defendant appealed; new trial; 218 N. C. 442.

State v. Cotton, from Wake; murder first degree; defendant appealed; new trial; 218 N. C. 577.

State v. Cureton, from Mecklenburg; murder first degree; defendant appealed; no error; 218 N. C. 491.

State v. Dale, from Mecklenburg; conspiracy to defraud; defendant appealed; no error; 218 N. C. 625.

State v. Davis, et al., from Wake; violation of slot machine laws; appeal by defendant Finch; affirmed; 218 N. C. 482.

State v. Eller, et al., from Rowan; sci. fa; appeal by respondent; error and remanded; 218 N. C. 365.

State v. Finch, et al., from Wake; violation of slot machine laws; appeal by defendant Finch; reversed; 218 N. C. 511.

State v. Finch, et al., from Wake; violation of slot machine laws; appeal by defendant Finch; reversed; 218 N. C. 512.

State v. Greer, from Forsyth; A. D. W., etc.; defendant appealed; new trial; 218 N. C. 660.

State v. Helms, from Union; breaking, entering and larcency; defendant appealed; new trial; 218 N. C. 592.

State v. Henderson, Mrs. J. E., from Gaston; violating liquor laws; defendant appealed; no error; 218 N. C. 513.

State v. Howell, from Wayne; murder first degree; defendant appealed; new trial; 218 N. C. 280.

State v. Hudson, from Northampton; murder first degree; defendant appealed; no error; 218 N. C. 219.

State v. Jackson, et al., from Sampson; larceny and receiving; defendant Wooten appealed; reversed; 218 N. C. 373.

State v. Johnson, from Robeson; burglary first degree; defendant appealed; no error; 218 N. C. 604.

State v. Jones, from Durham; possession of gambling devices; defendant appealed; judgment arrested; 218 N. C. 734.

State v. Mills, et al., from Wake; violation of slot machine laws; appeal by defendant Finch; affirmed; 218 N. C. 482.

State v. Moseley, et al., from Wake; violation of slot machine laws; appeal by defendant Laing; affirmed; 218 N. C. 481.

State v. Rogers, et al., from Wake; violation of slot machine laws; appeal by defendant Laing; affirmed; 218 N. C. 481.

State v. Samia, from Craven; violating liquor laws; defendant appealed; no error; 218 N. C. 307.

State v. Shu, from Iredell; breaking and entering; defendant appealed; reversed; 218 N. C. 387.

State v. Smith, from Sampson; murder first degree; defendant appealed; no error; 218 N. C. 334.

State v. Starnes, from Mecklenburg; murder first degree; defendant appealed; new trial; 218 N. C. 539.

State v. Stephenson, from Johnston; obtaining money from insurance company under false pretense; defendant appealed; reversed; 218 N. C. 258.

State v. Wagstaff, from Alamance; rape; defendant appealed; no error; 219 N. C. 15.

State v. Wall, from Anson; murder first degree; defendant appealed; no error; 218 N. C. 566.

State v. Webster, from Durham; possession of gambling devices; defendant appealed; no error; 218 N. C. 692.

State v. Wilson, from Yancey; assault upon female, etc.; defendant appealed; modified and affirmed; 218 N. C. 556.

State v. Wilson, from Orange; reckless driving; defendant appealed; no error; 218 N. C. 769.

State v. Woodard, from Wayne; murder first degree; defendant appealed; no error; 218 N. C. 572.

State v. Wyont, from Gaston; carnal knowledge; defendant appealed; new trial; 218 N. C. 505.

Docketed and Dismissed on Motion

State v. Nichols, from Mecklenburg.
State v. Reavis, from Forsyth.
State v. Rigsbee, from Surry.
State v. Smith, from Avery.

SPRING TERM, 1941

State v. Blue, from Robeson; murder first degree; defendant appealed; new trial; 219 N. C. 612.

State v. Calcutt, from Wake; violation of slot machine laws; defendant appealed; first count, judgment affirmed; second count, error and remanded; 219 N. C. 545.

State v. Cash, from Durham; murder first degree; defendant appealed; no error; 219 N. C. 821.

State v. Gardner, from Buncombe; abandonment and non-support; defendant appealed; reversed; 219 N. C. 331.

State v. Inscore, from Forsyth; manslaughter; defendant appealed; no error; 219 N. C. 759.

State v. Jessup, from Bladen; seduction; defendant appealed; no error; 219 N. C. 620.

State v. Johnson, from Guilford; rape; defendant appealed; no error; 219 N. C. 757.

State v. King, from Granville; hit and run driving; defendant appealed; no error; 219 N. C. 667.

State v. McDaniels, from Forsyth; operating car without driver's license; defendant appealed; reversed; 219 N. C. 763.

State v. Mann, from Dare; perjury; defendant appealed; no error; 219 N. C. 212.

State v. Melvin, from Wayne; murder first degree; defendant appealed; no error; 219 N. C. 538.

State v. Miller, from Mecklenburg; murder first degree; defendant appealed; no error; 219 N. C. 514.

State v. Muse, from Haywood; doing business without license; defendant appealed; error and remanded; 219 N. C. 226.

State v. Powell, from Rockingham; violating lottery laws; defendant appealed; no error; 219 N. C. 220.

State v. Roddey, from Mecklenburg; manslaughter; defendant appealed; new trial; 219 N. C. 532.

State v. Sheek, from Forsyth; murder second degree; defendant appealed; new trial; 219 N. C. 811.

State v. Smith, from Lenoir; false pretense; defendant appealed; reversed; 219 N. C. 400.

State v. Wells, from Polk; conspiracy to burn; defendant appealed; new trial; 219 N. C. 354.

State v. Williams, from Harnett; petty larceny; defendant appealed; no error; 219 N. C. 365.

Docketed and Dismissed on Motion

State v. Graham, from Columbus.

State v. Shaw, from Columbus.

FALL TERM, 1941

State v. Abernethy, from Wayne; violation of election laws; defendant appealed; no error; 220 N. C. 226.

State v. Absher, from Wilkes; murder second degree; defendant appealed; new trial; 220 N. C. 126.

State v. Ayres, from Avery; reclamation of confiscated automobile; appeal by petitioner Dessie Ayres; new trial; 220 N. C. 161.

State v. Batson, from New Hanover; barratry; defendant appealed; no error; 220 N. C. 411.

State v. Beachum, from Sampson; mans aughter; defendant appealed; no error; 220 N. C. 531.

State v. Clarke, from Catawba; failure to support illegitimate child; defendant appealed; error and remanded; 220 N. C. 392.

State v. Eurell, from Robeson; embezzlement; defendant appealed; reversed; 220 N. C. 519.

State v. Floyd, from Robeson; murder first degree; defendant appealed; new trial; 220 N. C. 530.

State v. Goodman, from Cabarrus; violating gambling laws; defendant appealed; reversed; 220 N. C. 250.

State v. Hayworth, et al., from Guilford; conspiracy to violate prohibition laws; defendants appealed; affirmed; 220 N. C. 534.

State v. Horne, from Robeson; aiding and abetting in prostitution; defendant appealed; no error; 220 N. C. 712.

State v. Howley, et al., from Avery; false pretense; defendants appealed; no error; 220 N. C. 113.

State v. Johnson, from Iredell; violating liquor laws; defendant appealed; no error; 220 N. C. 252.

State v. Johnson, from Robeson; aiding and abetting in prostitution; defendant appealed; no error; 220 N. C. 773.

State v. Levy, from Durham; violating bad check law; defendant appealed; no error; 220 N. C. 812.

State v. McAlhaney, from Swain; assault, causing serious damage; defendant appealed; no error; 220 N. C. 387.

State v. McDaniels, from Robeson; disposing of mortgaged property; defendant appealed; no error; 220 N. C. 820.

State v. Miller, from Forsyth; manslaughter and operating car intoxicated; defendant appealed; affirmed; 220 N. C. 660.

State v. Moore, from Columbus; non-support of illegitimate child; defendant appealed; error and remanded; 220 N. C. 535.

State v. Parker, from New Hanover; operating car while drunk, C. C. W., larceny; defendant appealed; affirmed; 220 N. C. 416.

State v. Peacock, from Wilson; larceny and receiving; State appealed; reversed; 220 N. C. 63.

State v. Penry, from Randolph; violating liquor laws; defendant appealed; reversed; 220 N. C. 248.

State v. Shepherd, from Wilkes; manslaughter; defendant appealed; no error; 220 N. C. 377.

State v. Starnes, from Mecklenburg; murder first degree; defendant appealed; new trial; 220 N. C. 384.

State v. Thomas, from Surry; murder second degree; defendant appealed; no error; 220 N. C. 34.

State v. Turner, from Moore; violating liquor laws; defendant appealed; no error; 220 N. C. 437.

State v. Williams, et al., from Caldwell; bigamous cohabitation; defendants appealed; no error; 220 N. C. 445.

State v. Williams, from Person; violating liquor laws; defendant appealed; reversed; 220 N. C. 724.

State v. Willis, from Robeson; aiding and abetting in prostitution; defendant appealed; no error; 220 N. C. 712.

DOCKETED AND DISMISSED ON MOTION

State v. Caudle, from Forsyth.

State v. Morrow, from Union.

State v. Peele, from Bertie.

State v. Sturdivant, from Bladen.

State v. Westcott, from New Hanover.

SPRING TERM, 1942

State v. Brown, et al., from Guilford; public nuisance; special verdict; defendant appealed; affirmed; 221 N. C. 301.

State v. Cagle, from Henderson; violating liquor laws; defendant appealed; affirmed; 221 N. C. 131.

State v. Chapman, from Craven; rape; defendant appealed; no error; 221 N. C. 157.

State v. Fields, from Jones; manslaughter; reckless driving; A. D. W.; defendant appealed; no error; 221 N. C. 182.

State v. Gibson, from Buncombe; carnal knowledge, etc.; defendant appealed; no error; 221 N. C. 253.

State v. Isley, from Rockingham; carnal knowledge, etc.; defendant appealed; new trial; 221 N. C. 213.

State v. Lefevers, from Burke; manslaughter; defendant appealed; no error; 221 N. C. 184.

State v. McFalls, from Buncombe; larceny and receiving; defendant appealed; new trial; 221 N. C. 22.

State v. Manning, from Bertie; murder first degree; defendant appealed; no error; 221 N. C. 70.

State v. Miller, from Robeson; A. D. W.; defendant appealed; new trial; 221 N. C. 356.

State v. Mitchell, from Alamance; violating liquor laws; defendant appealed; affirmed; 221 N. C. 460.

State v. Norden, from Harnett; violating liquor laws; defendant appealed; no error; (per curiam); 221 N. C. ....

State v. Patton, from McDowell; setting fire to woods; defendant appealed; remanded; 221 N. C. 117.

State v. Pelley, from Buncombe; violation Capital Issues Law; defendant appealed; affirmed; 221 N. C. 487.

State v. Potter, from Greene; Accessory after the fact (secret assault); defendant appealed; no error; 221 N. C. 153.

State v. Richardson, from Franklin; involuntary manslaughter; defendant appealed; affirmed; 221 N. C. 209.

State v. Rogers, from Forsyth; assault; defendant appealed; reversed; 221 N. C. 462.

State v. Smith, from Wayne; murder first degree; defendant appealed; no error; 221 N. C. 278.

State v. Smith, et als., from Guilford; conspiracy to burn, etc.; defendants appealed; no error; 221 N. C. 400.

State v. Wells, from Polk; conspiracy to commit arson; defendant appealed; no error; 221 N. C. 144.

State v. Wilson, from Buncombe; bawdy house and prostitution; defendant appealed; no error; 221 N. C. 365.

Docketed and Dismissed on Motion

State v. Baldwin, from Durham.
State v. Blue, from Buncombe.
State v. Cockrell, from Nash.
State v. Shaw, from Currituck.

SUMMARY

Affirmed on defendant's appeal	68
Reversed on State's appeal	1
New trial or reversed on defendant's appeal	32
Error and remanded	5
Judgment arrested	1
Appeal dismissed	15
	122

Fees Transmitted by Attorney General to State Treasurer since February Term, 1940, through February Term, 1942

State v. Smith	$ 10.00
State v. Hargrove	10.00
State v. Rodgers, et al.	10.00
State v. Samia	10.00
State v. Oliver	10.00
State v. Oliver	10.00
State v. Abbott, et al.	10.00
State v. Brown, et al.	10.00
State v. Rogers, et al.	10.00
State v. Moseley, et al.	10.00
State v. Davis, et al.	10.00
State v. Mills, et al.	10.00
State v. Reavis	10.00
State v. Webster	10.00
State v. Wilson	10.00
State v. Barnett	10.00
State v. Henderson	10.00
State v. Williams	10.00
State v. Mann	10.00
State v. King	10.00
State v. Jessup	10.00
State v. Shepherd	10.00
State v. McDaniels	10.00
State v. Williams	10.00
State v. Howley, et al.	10.00
State v. Miller	10.00
State v. Levy	10.00
State v. Parker	10.00
State v. McAlhaney	10.00
State v. Abernethy	10.00
State v. Hayworth, et al.	10.00
State v. Wells	10.00
State v. LeFevers	10.00
State v. Johnson	10.00
State v. Fields	10.00
State v. Johnson	10.00
State v. Potter	10.00
State v. Nordan	10.00
State v. Brown, et al.	10.00
State v. Smith, et al.	10.00
State v. Cagle	10.00
State v. Pelley	10.00
	$420.00

SUMMARY OF ACTIVITIES

Staff Personnel

The sudden and untimely death of Assistant Attorney General Lee Overman Gregory on October 18, 1941, was a sad shock to the entire staff of this office. Mr. Gregory was appointed as Assistant Attorney General in June, 1938, and assigned to the Revenue Department under the provisions of the statute. In his work in this capacity, as well as in the performance of other duties assigned to him, he rendered a splendid service to the State. He was devoted to his work and untiring in his efforts. During the time that the Commissioner of Revenue, A. J. Maxwell, was on leave of absence, Mr. Gregory served as Acting Commissioner of Revenue and at the same time carried on the work of his office as Assistant Attorney General. In the capacity of Acting Commissioner of Revenue he demonstrated his full understanding of problems of taxation, with which he had to deal, and by his fairness in his contacts with the public secured fine cooperation in the performance of these important duties. His death is recorded with great sorrow.

Mr. W. J. Adams, who had theretofore acted as Director of the Division of Legislative Drafting and Codification of Statutes, was promoted to fill the vacancy caused by Mr. Gregory's death. Mr. Adams continued to have oversight and general direction of the work being done on the North Carolina Code. Mr. Harry McGalliard, who was a member of the staff of the Division of Legislative Drafting and Codification of Statutes, was placed in the immediate charge of the office and the work of this division. The work is now going forward under his supervision.

The war had made heavy demands upon the young men serving as part of the personnel in this office. Mr. J. B. McMillan of McDonald, North Carolina, after having served from September, 1940, to April, 1942, was called into service. Mr. Kemp P. Yarborough of Louisburg, North Carolina, who served from November, 1941, to February, 1942, was likewise called. Mr. W. W. Speight of Spring Hope, North Carolina, served from January, 1940, until called into service in May, 1942.

Mr. T. W. Bruton and Mr. George B. Patton, Assistant Attorneys General, served throughout the biennium.

Division of Legislative Drafting and Codification of Statutes

During the 1941 Session of the General Assembly the Division of Legislative Drafting and Codification of Statutes, as well as other members of the staff, assisted the members of the General Assembly and State and local officials in the drafting of bills which were presented at that session. This office was particularly gratified on account of the extent to which the facilities of this office were used in this connection by the members of the General Assembly. It would reasonably follow that the drafting of legislation by members of the staff of this office should tend to improve the form and legal requirements of legislation which is presented for enactment. Appreciation is here expressed for Joint Resolution No. 30, adopted by the General Assembly, expressing approval of the work of this office in this respect. The facilities of this office will be fully available to the members of the next General Assembly, and State and local officials, in carrying out the provisions of the statute with respect to the preparation of bills to be presented to the General Assembly.

The General Assembly of 1941 made satisfactory provisions for carrying on the work of recodification. It enacted Chapter 35 of the Public Laws of 1941, authorizing the printing and distribution of a legislative edition of the new Code and appropriated sufficient funds to pay for the cost of same. During the biennium work has gone forward in the preparation of the legislative edition which will be placed in the hands of the members of the General Assembly as much in advance of the convening of the 1943 Session as may be possible, in order that the members may fully acquaint themselves with its contents.

The General Assembly of 1941 adopted Joint Resolution No. 33, providing for a Commission on Recodification to coöperate with the Attorney General and the Division of Legislative Drafting and Codification of Statutes, naming on this Commission the following persons:

Representatives F. E. Wallace, J. A. Pritchett, Hubert C. Jarvis, Irving Carlyle, Rupert T. Pickens, Julian R. Allsbrook, J. Q. LeGrand, O. L. Richardson, Arch T. Allen, John Kerr, Jr., George R. Uzzell, W. Frank Taylor, S. O. Worthington, J. T. Pritchett, Forrest A. Pollard, and T. E. Story; Senators Jeff D. Johnson, Jr., E. T. Sanders, J. C. Pittman, Wade B. Matheny, John W. Wallace, John D. Larkins, Jr., Thomas J. Gold, Archie C. Gay, Herbert Leary, and Hugh G. Horton.

The Commission organized shortly after the adjournment of the Legislature and elected Mr. F. E. Wallace as Chairman.

Plans were adopted by the Commission under which each chapter in the revised Code has been submitted to and approved by the Commission. It is anticipated that a full report of the activities of the Commission will be made to the General Assembly. Acknowledgment is here made for the full coöperation which this office has received from the Commission in this difficult and laborious task. It has necessarily involved a great deal of time and effort on the part of the members of the Commission.

There will be made a part of this Biennial Report a report from the Director of the Division of Legislative Drafting and Codification of Statutes in which in more complete detail the work of this division will be reviewed.

Division of Criminal and Civil Statistics

The work of this division has been during the biennium in charge of Mr. Clifton Beckwith. A report of the activities of this division is contained in a statement from Mr. Beckwith which is made a part of this Biennial Report. There is also included and made a part of the Report the compilation of the statistics covering the activities of the criminal courts, other than courts of justices of the peace, and civil cases tried in our Superior Courts.

Recommendation

At the last General Assembly a bill was presented authorizing the inclusion of ten cents in the bill of costs in each criminal and civil case, to be paid to the reporting officers of the inferior and Superior Courts as compensation for their services in making the required reports. This bill failed to pass in the rush of business at the end of the session. It is recommended that an act of this character be passed at the next session. The clerks of the inferior and Superior Courts are required to give a great deal of time and attention to the making of the necessary reports. Some method of just compensation should be provided to take care of this service.

State Bureau of Investigation

There is included in this Biennial Report a report made by Mr. Frederick C. Handy, Director of the Bureau of Investigation, covering fully the activities of his division during the biennium.

The facilities for criminal investigation provided by this division, as appears from this Report, have been widely used by State and local officers during the period covered by this Report. It has been an effective organization in the detection and prosecution of many criminals in cases of importance. We have been fortunate in having in this division a personnel of high type men who are well trained in the work which they are required to carry on. Without the facilities for this character of investigation, numerous crimes committed in North Carolina would have gone unpunished. The existence of this division has been thoroughly justified in the results accomplished.

Assistant Attorney General Assigned to the Revenue Department

Under the provision of the statute, one Assistant Attorney General is assigned to the Revenue Department and paid from the funds of that department. An office is maintained in the Revenue Department for this purpose. With the expanding tax system of the State and the increasing tax revenue, a very heavy burden has been placed upon the Assistant Attorney General assigned to this work. It is earnestly recommended that provision be made in the appropriation for the Revenue Department to take care of the employment of a Research Assistant to the Assistant Attorney General carrying on this work. The volume of work is just more than one person can carry. With the proposed assistant, it is anticipated that the work can be turned out with reasonable promptness and with greater satisfaction to all concerned.

Office Conferences and Consultations with State Officers and Departmental Officials

As required by the State Constitution, Article III, Section 14, this department has continued to serve as legal adviser for the Executive Department. In addition to numerous questions raised and decided by correspondence, frequent conferences in the office of the Attorney General and in the offices of the various State agencies have been held. C. S. 7694 requires the Attorney General to represent all State institutions whenever requested so to do by the official head of such institution, and to give, when requested, his opinion upon all questions submitted to him by the General Assembly, or either branch thereof, or by the Governor, Auditor, Treasurer, or any other State officer.

This office has, therefore, acted as a clearing house for the legal problems arising in the various State offices and agencies. We have received the finest possible cooperation from all State officials in the discharge of these duties. The extension of the State's activities has necessarily made the problems more numerous and complicated. In this connection there should be especially mentioned the Teachers' and State Employees' Retirement System of North Carolina.

Teachers' and State Employees' Retirement System of North Carolina

Chapter 25 of the Public Laws of 1941 created the Teachers' and State Employees' Retirement System of North Carolina. Section 10 of this Act specially provided that the Attorney General should act as the legal adviser of the Board of Trustees.

This office coöperated in the drafting of the complicated legislation setting up this very important system. A member of the staff of this department, at the request of the committee having the bill in charge, sat with the committee during its deliberations. Since the system has been set up under the provisions of the Act, frequent conferences have been held with the officials of the system and advice has been given on the many problems which have arisen in connection with this organization. It may be reasonably anticipated that with the progress of time in the operation of the plan, legal questions of importance will constantly arise. Reference is made elsewhere in this Report to the suit brought to contest the constitutionality of the Act. This office intervened for the purpose of contesting the challenge made to the constitutionality of the law.

The adoption of this Act represented a new policy of the State towards school teachers and its officers and employees, and will continue to involve complicated questions of a legal nature as to the application and effect of the Act.

Unemployment Compensation Law

The Unemployment Compensation Commission has a legal department appointed independent of the Department of Justice and paid by administrative funds provided by the Federal Government. This office, however, when requested, advises with the attorneys appointed by the Commission and will continue to do so as the need may arise.

Social Security Laws

This office has continued to act as the adviser to the State Board of Charities and Public Welfare and the State Commission for the Blind in the administration of the Social Security Laws committed to their charge. Whenever requested to do so, the Attorney General's office has rendered such legal assistance as was necessary to these important agencies of the State Government.

The Eugenics Board

By law the Attorney General is made a member of the State Eugenics Board which meets monthly in the office of the State Board of Charities and Public Welfare. During the past biennium the agency has considered and passed upon 396 cases in open hearings. A member of the staff of this office has been present at all the meetings which have been held.

ADVISORY OPINIONS TO LOCAL OFFICIALS

During the biennium the office has continued the time-honored policy of furnishing, when properly requested, advisory opinions to municipal, county and other local officials. Administrative problems arise with local governments which frequently have been solved by advisory opinions furnished by this office. These opinions, while not legally binding upon the local authorities, are generally accepted in settlement of controversies and questions which arise. Some idea of the extent of the volume of this service is indicated by opinions and partial digests of opinions whch will be found elsewhere in this Report. It is the desire of the Attorney General to continue to furnish this service to the local governments, although it does require a large amount of time and effort to respond to the many requests which we receive. It is realized that but for this method of ironing out the local administrative problems, no other convenient method of solution could be found. In order that the service might be made available to the public as much as possible, the digests of the opinions of general interest have been, from time to time, furnished to the State press and published by many newspapers of the State. The Institute of Government at Chapel Hill publishes periodically a digest of these opinions. The North Carolina League of Municipalities has recently begun sending out in mimeographed form to its membership digests of opinions affecting municipalities.

SUMMARY OF THE CONSTITUTIONAL AND STATUTORY DUTIES OF THE ATTORNEY GENERAL

References are herein given to provisions of the Constitution of North Carolina, and laws enacted in pursuance thereto, prescribing the duties and functions of the Attorney General.

As legal adviser to the Council of State and as a member of the various boards and commissions hereinafter listed, the participation of the Attorney General in the consideration of matters coming before meetings of the Council of State and such boards and commissions will be disclosed in the reports made therefrom. It is not required that they should be further detailed in this Report.

The Constitution of North Carolina, Article III, Section 13, provides that the duties of the "Attorney General shall be prescribed by law." Pursuant to this section, the General Assembly has vested in the Department of the Attorney General the following powers, obligations, and duties:

> C. S. 7694. "Duties.—It shall be the duty of the attorney general—
>
> "1. To defend all actions in the supreme court in which the state shall be interested, or is a party; and also when requested by the governor or either branch of the general assembly to appear for the state in any court or tribunal in any cause or matter, civil or criminal, in which the state may be a party or interested.
>
> "2. At the request of the governor, secretary of state, treasurer, auditor, corporation commissioners, insurance commissioner or

superintendent of public instruction, he shall prosecute and defend all suits relating to matters connected with their departments.

"3· To represent all state institutions, including the state's prison, whenever requested so to do by the official head of any such institution.

"4. To consult with and advise the solicitors, when requested by them, in all matters pertaining to the duties of their office.

"5· To give, when required, his opinion upon all questions of law submitted to him by the general assembly, or by either branch thereof, or by the governor, auditor, treasurer, or any other state officer.

"6· To pay all moneys received for debts due or penalties to the state immediately after the receipt thereof into the treasury.

"7· To compare the warrants drawn by the auditor on the state treasury with the laws under which they purport to be drawn."

In addition to these duties, the following ones are prescribed:

To institute actions to recover taxes due under the Revenue Act (C. S. 7880 (167)), and to approve all tax refunds made by the State (C. S. 7979 (a)).

To enforce the statutes relative to monopolies and trusts (C. S. 2567-2573).

To institute actions to prevent ultra vires acts on the part of corporations, or to dissolve corporations for certain offenses (C. S. 1143, 1185, 1187).

To institute quo warranto proceedings to oust persons who have usurped, who unlawfully hold, or who have forfeited public offices, and to begin actions to protect State lands (C. S. 870).

To see that the solicitors prosecute violations of the act relating to the practice of medicine (C. S. 6625).

To enforce charitable trusts (C. S. 1143).

To prescribe the rules of practice for land registration under the Torrens Act (C. S. 2379).

To institute proceedings for the dissolution of fraternal insurance societies (C. S. 6524-6525).

To appear on behalf of the court or other officers on appeal in contempt proceedings (C. S. 980).

To investigate extradition cases, at the request of the Governor (C. S. 4556 (d)).

To institute actions to enforce the rulings and orders of the Utilities Commission, and to represent said Commission in the enforcement of intrastate rates before the Interstate Commerce Commission and in federal or state courts (C. S. 1062 and 1065).

To give advice to the State Board of Elections as to the form of ballots (C. S. 6046).

To institute action against persons, firms, or corporations who violate the terms of the act regulating the quality of agricultural seeds. This duty may be delegated to the solicitor (C. S. 4828).

To approve deeds and grants to the State of property given to, or purchased by, it for park purposes (C. S. 6124).

To collect from inmates of state institutions the cost of their upkeep, provided they are able to pay (C. S. 7534 (k)).

To approve the grant of easements by state institutions to public-service corporations (C. S. 7525).

To act as legal adviser and institute necessary condemnation proceedings for the North Carolina Cape Hatteras Seashore Commission (Ch. 257, P. L. 1939).

To enforce rules and regulations adopted by the Commissioner of Labor relating to safety devices (Ch. 398, P. L. 1939).

To witness the burning of cancelled State bonds and coupons (Ch. 28, P. L. 1941).

To collect the delinquent taxes due the State Board of Health (Ch. 340, P. L. 1935).

The Attorney General is a member of, or adviser to, the following boards, councils, and commissions: Legal adviser to the Executive Department (Const., Art. III, S. 14); member of the State Board of Education (C. S. 5394), of the State Board of Assessments (C. S. 7971 (3)), of Advisory Board of Paroles (C. S. 7757), of State Banking Commission (Ch. 91, P. L. 1939), of the State Text-Book Purchase and Rental Commission (C. S. 5754 (1)), of Board of Public Buildings and Grounds (Ch. 224, P. L. 1941), of Municipal Board of Control (C. S. 2779), of the Eugenics Board (C. S. 2304(q)), the Board of Advisors of the World War Veterans Loan Fund (Ch. 155, P. L. 1925); and legal adviser to the Soldier's Settlement Board (C. S. 7508).

World War II

In common with other agencies of the State, this office has felt the impact of war conditions. The Attorney General is a member of the State Council of Defense. The Attorney General and members of the staff have, from time to time, advised with the Governor and various groups set up to deal with conditions brought about by the war and the voluntary coöperation of the people of the State in the war effort. The treacherous attack of the Japanese at Pearl Harbor having occurred after the adjournment of the last Legislature, no emergency war legislation has been enacted to provide for the emergency conditions brought on by these grave events. The need for emergency war powers on the part of the Governor has become evident, recommendations as to which will be made from other sources. The location of many important bases for soldiers, sailors, and marines in North Carolina has brought thousands of members of the armed forces of the United States within our borders. Harmonious coöperative plans have been worked out between the military and civil officers, which plans have adequately cared for these emergency conditions.

Appeals in Criminal Cases

In Exhibit II will be found a list of criminal cases which were argued by the Attorney General and his Assistants before the Supreme Court for the Fall Term, 1938, Spring Term, 1939, Fall Term, 1939, and Spring Term, 1940.

Summary of Important Litigation

Exhibit I contains a list of the civil cases pending or disposed of in the various courts, and also a list of all cases in the courts of the United States in which this office has participated. The volume of civil litigation affecting the State, its agencies and departments has been less during this biennium than the preceding one. Litigation has been avoided in many instances by consultation and adjustments. Following is a short statement of cases closed during the past biennium and those which are now pending.

Civil Actions

Leslie Gregory v. North Carolina Department of Revenue, Division of Highway Safety

This was a petition to the Superior Court by the plaintiff following action of the Highway Safety Division in revoking the petitioner's driver's license. The matter was heard in the Superior Court of Perquimans County in November, 1940, and the petitioner was allowed to take a nonsuit at his cost. No further action has been taken by the petitioner.

Vaye Slaughter v. L. S. Kiser and the Training School

This action was instituted in the Superior Court of Cabarrus County against L. S. Kiser and Stonewall Jackson Training School. This was an action for damages instituted against L. S. Kiser, the operator of an automobile owned by Stonewall Jackson Training School, which the plaintiff incurred when she was knocked down and thrown to the pavement at a highway crossing in Cabarrus County. The plaintiff alleged negligence on the part of the driver and the school and claimed damages in the amount of $3,000.00. A demurrer was filed to the complaint by the Stonewall Jackson Training School and this demurrer as to the school was sustained by Judge Olive at the November Term, 1941, of the Cabarrus Superior Court. The case was not further prosecuted by the plaintiff against the institution.

Gus Cochran, et al., v. Security National Bank, Trustee, and Treasurer of the State of North Carolina

This was an action instituted to restrain the foreclosure of a deed of trust executed by the plaintiff to the Treasurer of the State of North Carolina, the deed of trust having been given to secure money borrowed by the plaintiff from the World War Veterans Loan Fund. The case came on for trial in Haywood Superior Court. The plaintiff paid in full his indebtedness to the fund and took a nonsuit.

Best & Company v. Maxwell, 311 U. S. 454, 85 Law ed. 275

The Supreme Court of North Carolina in this case, reported in 216 N. C. 114, upheld the validity of a tax imposed by the Revenue Act of 1937, Chapter 127, Section 121, subsection (e). This subsection imposed a tax of $250.00 for the display of goods in any hotel room, or in any house rented or occupied temporarily for the purpose of securing orders for the retail sale of such goods. On appeal to the Supreme Court of the United States, the decision of the Supreme Court of North Carolina was reversed upon the ground that the statute imposed a burden upon interstate commerce as applied to the plaintiff in this case.

North Carolina Railroad v. Maxwell;
North Carolina Midland Railroad v. Maxwell;
Atlantic and Charlotte Air Line Railroad v. Maxwell

In these three cases the identical question as to income tax liability of the Railroads was involved. Three plaintiff railroads leased their property to the Southern Railway Company and an income tax was levied upon the rentals received by the three railroads from the Southern Railway Company, lessee. The plaintiffs contended that since the Southern Railway Company, in filing its income tax return, was not permitted to deduct therefrom rentals paid for the use of the railroad equipment and that in reality a tax was paid on such rentals by Southern Railway Company, that, under the Revenue Act, there would be no income tax liability by the three railroads, lessors, involved in the case. The case was instituted in 1938 after the total amount of approximately $30,000.00 had been paid by the railroads under protest. The case was calendared for trial a number of times and after numerous conferences the plaintiffs in each case took voluntary nonsuits in April, 1941.

Richwip Corporation v. W. Kerr Scott, Commissioner of Agriculture

In this case plaintiff, a corporation engaged in the business of manufacturing and selling condensed milk, had a large quantity of its products embargoed by the Department of Agriculture because the containers were improperly labeled in violation of the Pure Food and Drug Act of this State. Plaintiff obtained a temporary restraining order in Wake County Superior Court in April, 1941. The case came on for hearing upon the temporary restraining order. A consent judgment was signed conditioned upon the plaintiff withdrawing its mislabeled products from the State and upon payment of the costs.

In Re Steele, 220 N. C. 445

In *Tumey v. Ohio,* 273 U. S. 210, the Supreme Court of the United States held that an Ohio mayor was disqualified to try criminal cases and that his judgments in such cases were void because he was entitled to compensation only if a defendant were convicted. A conviction by a judge having such a pecuniary interest in the case was held to amount to a denial of due process. After this decision there was much speculation in North Carolina as to whether our fee system for the compensation of justices of the peace in criminal cases is valid. The question was brought before the Supreme Court of North Carolina in In re Steele. One Eldon Steele, having pleaded guilty to a criminal offense before a justice of the peace in Richmond County, was released from imprisonment on writ of habeas corpus, it being held by the Superior Court that the judgment of the justice of the peace was void because of his pecuniary interest in fees which would accrue to him in case of a conviction. The Attorney General's petition to have the case reviewed by writ of certiorari was granted by the North Carolina Supreme Court, and the judgment of the Superior Court was reversed. The Supreme Court held that Steele had waived his right to object to the constitutionality of proceedings before justices of the peace by pleading guilty and, further, procedure before justices of the peace in North Carolina is distinguishable from that condemned in the *Tumey Case* because a defendant is entitled to a trial de novo on appeal to the Superior Court. Attorneys for Eldon Steele petitioned the United States Supreme Court for a writ of certiorari to review the decision of the North Carolina Supreme Court. On May 25 petition for certiorari was denied.

State of North Carolina ex rel. Utilities Commission v. Carolina Scenic Coach Company

This was an appeal from the order of the Utilities Commission denying the petition of Carolina Scenic Coach Company for removal of restrictions contained in its franchise for operating a bus line between points south of the North Carolina State Line and Asheville, N. C. At the May-June Term, 1939, of Henderson County Superior Court, the appeal was dismissed. On appeal to the Supreme Court the action of the lower court was reversed, 216 N. C. 325. The case was again heard at the April-May Term, 1940, of Henderson County Superior Court. The Utilities Commission, through the Attorney General and the protestant, Atlantic Greyhound Corporation, through its counsel, made a motion that the matter be heard before the Presiding Judge in chambers. The motion was over-ruled and an issue submitted to the jury which was answered in favor of the Coach Company. The Utilities Commission and Atlantic Greyhound Corporation gave notice of appeals to the Supreme Court, the participation of the Utilities Commission being confined to an effort to protect its jurisdiction and to secure a proper interpretation of the statutes governing the procedure in matters of this kind. It was deemed advisable that the appeal be abandoned. The Atlantic Greyhound Corporation perfected its appeal and the judgment of the lower court was affirmed. *Utilities Commission v. Coach Company*, 218 N. C. 233.

Francis C. Carey and Gladys M. Carey v. The North Carolina Unemployment Compensation Commission, et al.

This was an action instituted by plaintiffs in the Superior Court of Macon County to restrain the Unemployment Compensation Commission, a State agency, from proceeding to collect the amount represented by a judgment entered under the provisions of the Act creating the North Carolina Unemployment Compensation Commission. The Attorney General participated in the hearing on the injunction on account of the fact that the administrative procedure used by the Unemployment Compensation Commission and certain other State agencies in the collection of taxes was being attacked. At the hearing before the Resident Judge of the 20th Judicial District the court held that the Sections of the Unemployment Compensation Act providing for the docketing and collection of judgments were constitutional and valid. The restraining order was dissolved and the action dismissed. Plaintiffs excepted and gave notice of appeal to the Supreme Court but the appeal was not perfected.

Standard Oil Company of New Jersey v. Allen J. Maxwell, Commissioner of Revenue

This is a case which was instituted in Wake County in September, 1937, in which the plaintiff sued to recover franchise taxes additionally assessed against the plaintiff for the year 1934, amounting to $5,349.75, which had been paid by the plaintiff under protest on September 28, 1934; and for the recovery of franchise taxes for the year 1935 in the sum of $4,766.69 additionally assessed against the plaintiff for the year 1935, which the plaintiff paid under protest on or about February 24, 1936; and for the recovery of franchise taxes for the year 1936 in the sum of $4,088.54 paid by the plaintiff under protest on April 8, 1937.

This litigation was predicated upon the contention of the plaintiff that in additionally assessing franchise taxes against the plaintiff, the Department of Revenue had improperly included investments in affiliated companies for the year 1934, amounting to $80,592,389.47, and miscellaneous stocks and bonds amounting to $171,686.70. A similar contention was made for franchise taxes of 1935, the plaintiff claiming the exclusion of $53,409,-205.58 of investments in affiliated companies not doing business in North Carolina, and miscellaneous stocks and bonds. For the year 1936 a similar contention was made with reference to company assets amounting to $50,362,115.66.

A nonsuit was taken in this case on account of a decision of the Supreme Court of the United States in the case of *Ford Motor Company v. Beauchamp*, 308 U. S. 331, 84 Law ed. 304, in which the principle upon which the plaintiff relied was decided adversely to the plaintiff. This case held that the Texas allocation formula which included in the base all of the assets of the Ford Motor Company might be validly applied to that company, the Ford Motor Company contending that a large part of its assets were unrelated to the business carried on by it in that State.

Jeannette A. Noel v. Edson B. Olds, et al.

By a will executed November 10, 1938, William Hayes Ackland of the District of Columbia, who is now dead, bequeathed certain property, the bulk of which is personal property, to trustees with directions that they have erected on the campus of Duke University, according to plans and specifications already drawn up by the University architect, a building in the form of a gallery or museum, to be known as the William Hayes Ackland Memorial. The will provides that the remains of the testator shall be interred in an apse in this building and within a marble sarcophagus beneath a recumbent statue. Provision is made for the display in the building of certain writings and objects of art belonging to the testator and for the maintenance of the building and the purchase of objects of art selected by the University governing body with the income from the trust estate.

Duke University has refused to accept the benefits and responsibilities imposed upon it by the will. The next-of-kin of the testator contend that the trust has failed and that the property should be distributed as if the testator had died intestate with respect to it.

The University of North Carolina contends that the trust property should be administered *cy pres*, and that the general charitable purpose of the testator can best be approximated by having an art gallery such as that contemplated by the will erected on its campus at Chapel Hill, North Carolina. A similar claim is made on behalf of Rollins College in Florida.

In a previous will executed by William Hayes Ackland on May 4, 1936, provision was made for the erection of a memorial art gallery similar to that contemplated in the 1938 will. However, the trustees were directed to have the building erected at Duke, if the University would accept it; at the University of North Carolina, if Duke should decline it; and at Rollins College, if it should be declined by the University of North Carolina.

In August of 1941 Jeannette A. Noel, Catherine A. Brown, Pauline A. Landis and Robert L. Acklen, all children of a brother of the decedent, filed a complaint in the District Court of the United States for the District of Columbia for construction of the decedent's will. In their prayer for relief the plaintiffs ask that the court adjudge and decree that the dispositions attempted to be made by the testator pursuant to the provisions of Item VII of his last will are null and void. The plaintiffs allege that the attempted dispositions are in contravention of the rule against perpetuities, and that the trust provisions of Item VII are incapable of fulfillment and execution because the trust provisions are vague and uncertain and because Duke University has not consented and cannot lawfully consent to the erection of the William Hayes Ackland Memorial on its campus in accordance with the terms and conditions prescribed in the will. The executors and trustees under the will, Duke University, Pauline Lockett Kaiser, Pauline Hyatt Kaiser Everett, Frank Kaiser and Rollins College, were all joined as defendants in the action.

The executors and trustees filed an answer to the plaintiffs' complaint and, in addition, interposed a counter-claim and cross-claim for instructions and for specification of a trustee in place of Duke University. In their pleading, the executors and trustees allege that on September 6, 1941, the executive committee of Duke University adopted a resolution declining all the benefits, burdens, responsibilities and provisions of the will of the decedent with respect to said institution, that the decedent had formulated a general intention of dedicating his estate to educational and charitable purposes, and that, notwithstanding the fact that Duke University had declined to be the medium through which the general charitable and educational purposes of the decedent should be carried out, the court should give effect to the decedent's purposes and appoint the University of North Carolina, or Rollins College, or some other southern state university or adequately endowed southern university, to administer the educational and charitable trust provisions of the decedent's will.

Following this, the University of North Carolina made a motion in the cause to intervene in order that it might present its claim to the trustees and ask the court to substitute it as beneficiary under the will of Ackland. The trust set up by Mr. Ackland was in the amount of $1,400,000.00. The case came on for hearing in the United States District Court of the District of Columbia and in May, 1942, a formal judgment was signed denying the motion to intervene on the part of the University, from which judgment the University of North Carolina has appealed to the

Court of Appeals of the District of Columbia. The case is now pending in that court.

Eric Norden v. State Board of Education

This action was instituted to set aside a deed and release executed by the plaintiff to the State Board of Education in December, 1935. The plaintiff, prior to that time, had a contract with the State Board of Education to locate, survey, and market certain swamp lands in Eastern North Carolina owned by the Board. At the solicitation of the plaintiff an agreement was reached whereby the plaintiff was to be paid the sum of $5,000.00 in full settlement for all his right, title, and interest in the lands claimed to have been located and surveyed by him and all services rendered the State Board of Education. Pursuant to this agreement and upon the payment of the $5,000.00, the deed and release were executed and delivered by the plaintiff to the State Board of Education. After the complaint to set aside the deed and release was filed, the Attorney General, representing the State Board of Education, filed a motion to strike certain allegations from the complaint and also filed a demurrer on the ground that the complaint failed to state a cause of action. The hearing on the motion to strike was had at the October Term, 1941, of New Hanover Superior Court. The court being of the opinion that the case could not be tried on the complaint as filed, allowed the plaintiff sixty days from October 17, 1941, in which to file a new complaint which would clearly and concisely set forth the facts upon which he based his alleged cause of action. The new complaint was filed within the time allowed and a demurrer was filed to this complaint on the ground that it failed to state a cause of action. The hearing on the demurrer was had at the March Term, 1942, of New Hanover Superior Court, at which time the demurrer was sustained and the case dismissed. The plaintiff gave notice of appeal to the Supreme Court and the appeal is now pending in the Supreme Court.

N. W. Bridges, on Behalf of Himself and All Other Citizens and Taxpayers of the City of Charlotte, N. C., v. City of Charlotte, et al.

This action was instituted in the Superior Court of Mecklenburg County by the plaintiff on behalf of himself and all other citizens and taxpayers of the City of Charlotte to restrain the City of Charlotte and certain other defendants from collecting and paying over to the State Retirement System certain funds realized from a tax levy made by the tax levying authorities of the City of Charlotte to meet employers' contributions to the State Retirement System. The plaintiff also attacked the constitutionality of the acts creating the Teachers' and State Employees' Retirement System. The Attorney General made a motion that the Board of Trustees of the Teachers' and State Employees' Retirement System be made a party defendant due to the fact that the constitutionality of the whole retirement system was attacked. This motion was allowed by the Presiding Judge. On the 23rd day of March, 1942, the case came on to be heard in the Superior Court of Mecklenburg County before His Honor Hubert E. Olive, Judge Presiding, and on the 24th day of March, 1942, the Presiding Judge entered a judgment upholding the constitutionality of the acts creating the Teachers' and State

Employees' Retirement System and validating the tax levy made by the City of Charlotte to meet employers' contributions to the Retirement System. Plaintiff gave notice of appeal to the Supreme Court of North Carolina. The case was heard in the Supreme Court and judgment of the lower court was affirmed, 221 N. C. p. 472.

CRIMINAL ACTIONS

State v. Williams and Hendrix, 220 N. C. 445

A series of North Carolina decisions hold that a divorce decree obtained from a North Carolina defendant in a state in which only the plaintiff is domiciled and in which the defendant is not personally served with process and makes no appearance will be treated as void in North Carolina. It has been thought that these decisions are sanctioned by the decision of the United States Supreme Court in *Haddock v. Haddock,* 201 U. S. 562, but the constitutionality of the North Carolina rule was challenged in *State v. Williams and Hendrix.* The defendants, convicted of bigamous cohabitation in Caldwell County, had obtained in Nevada divorces from their North Carolina spouses on service by publication, married, and lived together in North Carolina. Their contention that the Nevada divorce decrees were entitled to full faith and credit under Article IV, Section 1, of the United States Constitution, was rejected by the North Carolina Supreme Court. A writ of certiorari was granted by the United States Supreme Court, and the case will be heard by that Court at the October Term, 1942.

State v. Brown, et al., 221 N. C. 301

In this case, it was found by a special verdict that defendants operated an establishment at which bets on horse races were received by the defendants and transmitted to race tracks outside the State for acceptance. It was adjudged in the Superior Court that the defendants were guilty of maintaining a criminal nuisance in violation of C. S., Section 3180. The defendants appealed to the Supreme Court, contending that under the special verdict they were not guilty of any criminal offense inasmuch as betting on horse races is not a crime in North Carolina and, if it is, the bets in this case were consummated outside the State. Judgment of the lower court was affirmed by the Supreme Court in an opinion in which it was held that betting on horse races is a criminal offense under C. S., Section 4430. The court intimated, in addition, that the operation of premises at which gambling takes place is a criminal nuisance even though the actual bets are not criminal and even though the bets are ultimately accepted outside the State.

State v. Joe Calcutt, 219 N. C. 545

The defendant was indicted in the Superior Court of Wake County on a two-count bill of indictment charging the ownership, sale, lease and transportation of certain slot machines and devices prohibited by law and with the operation and possession of certain slot machines and gambling devices. The defendant entered a plea of guilty to both counts contained in the bill of indictment. On the first count the defendant was sentenced to 12 months in the Wake County Jail to be assigned to work on the roads. On the second count the defendant was given a two-year sentence suspended upon the payment of a $10,000.00 fine and the compliance with certain other conditions contained in the judgment. On appeal to the Supreme Court the judgment on the first count was affirmed. Error was found in the judgment as to the second count and the cause remanded to the Wake County Superior Court for further consideration of this count. Upon the matter being remanded to the Superior Court of Wake County, the defendant was sentenced to 12 months in jail to be assigned to work the public roads, suspended on the payment of a fine of $10,000.00. This judgment was complied with by the defendant and he was imprisoned on the judgment entered on the first count in the bill of indictment.

State v. Batson, 220 N. C. 411

The defendant in this case was convicted of an attempt to commit barratry in the Superior Court of New Hanover County. Common barratry, the offense of frequently exciting and stirring up suits and quarrels, was a criminal offense at common law. The defendant appealed to the Supreme Court, contending that barratry is not a criminal offense in North Carolina. The Supreme Court affirmed the decision of the lower court, holding that inasmuch as the common law remains in effect in North Carolina, except as modified by statute or inconsistent with the form of government in this State, barratry is still a criminal offense.

State v. Wm. Dudley Pelley, 221 N. C. 487

The defendant was convicted at the January Term, 1935, of Buncombe County Superior Court on two counts in a bill of indictment charging a violation of the Capital Issues Law of the State of North Carolina. Prayer for judgment was continued until the February Term, 1935, at which term a prison sentence of not less than one nor more than two years was imposed on the first count contained in the bill of indictment and the prison sentence was suspended for a period of five years on certain conditions, including the payment of a fine of $1,000.00 and that the defendant be and remain continuously of good behaviour during the five-year period. On the second count, prayer for judgment was continued for five years. At the October Term, 1939, a capias was issued for the arrest of the defendant. On February 10, 1940, the defendant was arrested in the District of Columbia and upon extradition proceedings being instituted for his return to the State of North Carolina, the defendant resisted extradition and applied to the United States District Court of the District of Columbia for a writ of habeas corpus. An order was issued by the United States District Court discharging the writ of habeas corpus and remanding petitioner to the custody of the Marshal for delivery to the agent of the State of North Carolina. The defendant appealed from this order to the United States Court of Appeals for the District of Columbia and on April 14, 1941, an opinion was handed down by the United States Court of Appeals for the

District of Columbia affirming the judgment of the lower court. See 122 F. (2d) 12. The defendant then filed a petition for a writ of certiorari in the United States Supreme Court, which petition was denied on October 20, 1941. On October 24, 1941, the defendant returned to the State of North Carolina and surrendered himself to the Sheriff of Buncombe County, North Carolina. At the January Term, 1942, of Superior Court of Buncombe County, the Solicitor of the Nineteenth Judicial District moved that the suspended sentence theretofore imposed upon the defendant be put into effect and also prayed for judgment under the second count in the bill of indictment on which the defendant was convicted. Upon the evidence introduced at the hearing, the suspended sentence was ordered put into effect and a prison sentence of not less than two nor more than three years was imposed on the second count in the bill of indictment, this sentence to run concurrently with the sentence put into effect on the first count. On the same date a hearing was had on the petition for a writ of habeas corpus filed by the defendant after he returned to the State of North Carolina. Judgment was entered denying the prayer of the defendant for his discharge. From the judgment on the merits and the judgment on the habeas corpus proceedings, the defendant appealed to the Supreme Court of North Carolina. Thereafter, a petition for a writ of certiorari was filed by the defendant in the Supreme Court of North Carolina which was allowed by the court and the case was set for argument at the end of the appeals from the Tenth and Eleventh Judicial Districts. The judgment of the lower court was affirmed by the Supreme Court of North Carolina. State vs. Pelley, 221 N. C., p. 487.

Industrial Commission Cases

Horace Champion v. Vance County Board of Health, et al., and State Board of Health

This was an action instituted by the plaintiff against Vance County Board of Health, et al., and State Board of Health, et al. The action was originally instituted before the Industrial Commission and in June, 1938, the Industrial Commission granted an award to the plaintiff against the Vance County Board of Health for injuries received by him in an accident arising out of and in the course of his employment. The award was not paid by the Vance County Board of Health. Thereafter, the plaintiff instituted mandamus proceedings in the Superior Court against the Vance County Board of Health and the State Board of Health, alleging that, among other things, the State Board of Health was liable for the award of the Industrial Commission against Vance County Board of Health because the County Board of Health was a subsidiary of and acting under the direction and for the benefit of the State Board of Health. The State Board of Health, through the Attorney General, demurred to the complaint in the Superior Court of Vance County and the demurrer was upheld. The Action was dismissed as to the defendant State Board of Health upon the demurrer. The demurrer as to the State Board of Health was not taken up on appeal to the Supreme Court. This case is reported in 221 N. C. 96.

Henry W. Yates v. State School Commission

This was a case before the Industrial Commission. The plaintiff instituted action against the State School Commission and Randolph County Board of Education for injuries received as a result of a wreck which he had while driving a school bus. The plaintiff incurred severe head injuries at the time of the accident for which compensation and doctor's bills were paid him during the period of his recovery. Some time later the claimant, through counsel, made further claim for continuing illness. The matter came on for trial before the Industrial Commission and after hearing evidence of expert medical authority, the Commission ruled that the claimant had no loss of earnings subsequent to the determination of the total disability which was due to the original injury and denied any further compensation. No appeal was taken to the Superior Court from this holding.

Metcalf v. Department of Conservation and Development

This was an Industrial Commission case brought by the plaintiff against the Department of Conservation and Development. The plaintiff alleged that he was injured while acting as a temporary fire fighter during a forest fire in Western North Carolina. The action came on for trial before the trial commissioner in Buncombe. Compensation was denied on the ground that the plaintiff was not an employee of the Department. An appeal was taken to the full commission which affirmed the trial commissioner's findings and on appeal to the Superior Court Judge Pless affirmed the finding of the Full Commission and dismissed the case. No appeal was taken to the Supreme Court.

S. E. Casey v. Board of Education of the City of Durham and the State School Commission

This was an action instituted before the Industrial Commission against the Board of Education of the City of Durham and the State School Commission for injuries received by the plaintiff in an accident arising out of and in the course of his employment. The Industrial Commission made an award against the Board of Education of the City of Durham and its insurance carrier but denied recovery against the State School Commission. The case was appealed to the Full Commission where the award made by the individual Commissioner was adopted and confirmed. Upon an appeal to the Superior Court of Durham County the award of the Full Commission was affirmed. The case was appealed to the Supreme Court of North Carolina and the judgment of the lower court affirmed. *Casey v. Board of Education,* 219 N. C. 739.

REPORT OF DIVISION OF LEGISLATIVE DRAFTING AND CODIFICATION OF STATUTES TO THE ATTORNEY GENERAL FOR THE PERIOD FROM JULY 1, 1940, TO JUNE 30, 1942

The Division of Legislative Drafting and Codification of Statutes during the past biennium has been engaged in performing two principal functions: (1) The preparation of bills to be presented to the General Assembly at the request of State officials and agencies and members of the General Assembly, and (2) the recodification of the general statutes of North Carolina.

The drafting of legislation, elsewhere described in this Report, occupied almost the entire time of this Division for some four months during the biennium, the weeks immediately preceding the convening of the legislature and the time the legislature was in session. The remainder of the time has been devoted exclusively to the work of recodification.

In the fall of 1940 it became apparent that it would be desirable to extend until 1943 the time for final action on recodification of the statutes. This was true for two reasons: (1) It was thought to be increasingly important to print a legislative edition of the proposed recodification, particularly in view of the decision to submit a recodification designed to be adopted as an official code; and (2) additional time was needed to redraft many sections which could not otherwise be effectively codified and to review and discuss many chapters with the various State agencies charged with the administration of those chapters, and to permit a legislative committee to review the recodification work.

In the absence of any authorization for the preparation and publication of the legislative edition it would have been necessary to submit the proposed code in the form of a single manuscript and it was thought that the magnitude and bulk of the work would prevent its adequate examination and consideration unless it could be submitted in printed form, with a sufficient number of copies for the examination and consideration of the legislators, the interested committees, the judiciary, and the heads of State departments and agencies. The Advisory Subcommittee on Recodification unanimously recommended that the final action on recodification be deferred until the 1943 session of the General Assembly, in order to make available enough time for the necessary redrafting of statutes and consultations with State agencies to insure preparation of a thorough, effective code. In December, 1941, the Advisory Committee on Recodification unanimously recommended that the proposed code be submitted to the General Assembly in a printed edition of 500 volumes. This is in accordance with all previous practice in that legislative editions of prior proposed codes were submitted in printed form.

Pursuant to these recommendations, the General Assembly of 1941 (Public Laws, Chapter 35) determined on the preparation and printing of a legislative edition of the proposed code to be submitted to the General Assembly of 1943. The statute provided that, "Such legislative edition shall set forth all the general public laws of North Carolina found by the division to be intended to be in effect, together with any supplemental or implementing legislation recommended by the division as essential to make a complete and clear statement of said laws, in such form and with such arrangement, numbering system, tables of contents, and editorial aids as said division shall determine, and with a complete and effective index. The legislative edition need not contain annotations or supplementary material."

The Commission was advised of the appropriations that would be necessary to publish the final code with new and larger type, but it instructed the Division to proceed under a contract for publication by the Michie Company, inasmuch as it was concluded that the cost of an entirely new, State-owned annotated code would be prohibitive.

In accordance with the terms of this 1941 Act, a contract was entered into with the same publisher who will publish the final edition of the code to print a legislative edition in one volume without any supplementary materials except an index and comparative tables, and without any annotations except "Local Modifications" citing relevant local statutes.

VOLUME AND CHAPTER ARRANGEMENT

The arrangement of chapters in the proposed code has proceeded on the basis that such code will in its final form, together with annotations and other supplementary materials, be printed in four volumes. Once the idea of a one-volume final code was abandoned it became necessary to devise a new classification and arrangement of statutes since a purely alphabetical arrangement of chapters would be most inconvenient in that all too frequently it would be necessary to resort to all volumes in order to consult several related sections appearing in different chapters. Therefore, an effort was made to group related chapters in larger "divisions" and to place related divisions together in each volume. At the same time it is necessary to maintain a balance so that all four volumes will be as nearly uniform in size as is conveniently possible. Within each division the chapters are arranged alphabetically. Under present plans Volume I will contain the chapters on *Civil Procedure, Courts,* and related matters, *Criminal Laws and Procedure* and related matters, *Motor Vehicles,* and *Commercial Laws.* Volume 2 will contain the divisions relating to *Decedents' Estates, Fiduciaries, Real and Personal Property, Domestic Relations, Corporations and Associations, Regulations in the Exercise of the Police Power, Occupations, Employer and Employee, Taxation* and a few miscellaneous chapters. Volume 3 will consist exclusively of divisions containing the chapters relating to *State Government and Agencies, County and City Government, and Election Laws.* Volume 4 will contain the index, appendices, and other supplementary materials. The space required for printing the index will be much greater than that used for this purpose at present because (1) the index is being expanded considerably as to number of titles and index lines; (2) the size of the type in which it is to be printed will be increased from 6-point to 8-point; and (3) it will be printed two columns to the page instead of three. The Legislative Commission on Recodification has approved this chapter arrangement.

NUMBERING SYSTEM

The change in the arrangement of the chapters has necessitated a change in section numbers, and the entire code, therefore, is being renumbered. The choice of a satisfactory numbering system for the new code was carefully studied. The following systems were considered: (1) A decimal numbering system, (2) a purely consecutive numbering system, and (3) a modified form of the consecutive numbering system. It was thought that the decimal system of numbering, although in use in the newer codes, would cause entirely too much confusion, outweighing any theoretical advantage with respect to unlimited expansion. On the other hand, consecutive numbering throughout from section one to the end of the code, as practiced in many older codes, would be open to the objection that it is cumbersome and permits of no addition of new sections without immediately introducing variations in the numbering scheme, resulting ultimately in such a number as "6055(a27½)" or "7880(156)uuu," appearing in the present unofficial code.

It was finally decided that a modified form of consecutive numbering would be the most satisfactory system to adopt, and such a system was approved by the Legislative Commission on Recodification. This system will consist of: (1) numbering the *chapters* of the code consecutively, (2) using the *chapter number* as the first part of each code section number, and (3) numbering the *sections in each chapter* consecutively from "one" on through the end of the chapter. The code section number will consist of the chapter number, a dash, and the number of the section in the chapter. Thus, the sections in Chapter One will be numbered "1-1, 1-2, 1-3, 1-4, etc."; the sections in Chapter Two will be numbered "2-1, 2-2, 2-3, 2-4, etc.," the sections in Chapter Three, "3-1, 3-2, 3-3, 3-4, etc." To illustrate further, Section 27 of Chapter Nine will be "9-27." This system will have two advantages. The fact that the numbers in front of the dash in the code section number will also be the chapter number should be helpful in immediately locating a section. Further, new sections may be added indefinitely at the end of each chapter without disturbing the numbering system. The old Consolidated Statutes section number will be carried forward in the section history as has been the practice heretofore in placing prior official code references in section histories. Furthermore, comparative tables translating the new section numbers to the Consolidated Statutes will be included in an appendix.

Method of Work

While the character of examination, review and study of the statutes for recodification purposes has not been changed in any essential, the decision to print a legislative edition to be submitted to the General Assembly necessarily changed some of the methods of work. A prime consideration in contracting for the printing of the legislative edition was the preparation of a manuscript which would contain the maximum number of changes when first printed so that the same type could be used with a minimum of additional changes in the printing of the final code and so that superseded and obsolete sections would not be needlessly printed. So long as only the submission of a *single manuscript* to the General Assembly was contemplated it would have been feasible to submit an exact copy of each statute with detailed notes as to every type of change proposed, from the correction of a grammatical error to the redrafting and consolidation of related, partially duplicating statutes, leaving to the last moment any decision as to the exact action to be taken with respect to such recommendation. However, Chapter 35 of the Public Laws of 1941, as set forth above, directed that the legislative edition should set forth a proposed code and that *in it should be incorporated such changes as were desirable for codification purposes* without, of course, changing the substance or effect of any law. Resolution 33 of the 1941 General Assembly created a Commission on Recodification consisting of ten Senators and sixteen Representatives to advise with the Attorney General and the Division in the preparation of the legislative edition: "To that end the Commission shall review and examine the recodification work and consult with and advise the Attorney General and the Division in the revision of the statutes . . . ."

The Division has worked closely with the Legislative Commission and every matter of policy such as the terms of the contract for the legislative edition, the chapter arrangement of the Code, the numbering system, as well as every change made in any section for the legislative edition, has been approved by the Commission.

Certain changes which could not possibly affect the meaning of the statutes have been made without making detailed explanations such as (1) conforming the proof to the Consolidated Statutes or to session laws appearing since, (2) correcting section histories, (3) improving section catch lines so that they will more accurately indicate the contents of the sections, (4) correcting spelling and (5) making purely formal changes for recodification purposes such as changing "act" to "section" or to specifically inclusive sections or to "article" or "chapter" as might be appropriate under the different circumstances.

Any changes in any law beyond those of the purely formal nature described above are carefully explained in a detailed section-by-section report. Even in this field no change is made which it is thought would change existing law but rather only such changes as are necessary to set forth the laws "found by the Division to be intended to be in effect, together with any supplemental or implementing legislation . . . essential to make a complete and clear statement of said laws . . ." These changes which will be illustrated in some detail below have been submitted to and approved by the Legislative Commission. There are no hidden or buried changes. Every alteration is spotlighted with an explanation calling attention to the specific change made and setting forth the reasons for it. Full copies of these explanatory reports will be submitted to the members of the General Assembly and other interested persons along with copies of the legislative edition to the end that all may study in such detail as they may choose, each change, with the result that the proposed code will not have to stand or fall on the basis of objections to any one change, but rather, any change made by the Division and the Legislative Commission may, if found unsatisfactory, be individually corrected to conform to the views of the General Assembly.

These changes which are accompanied by explanatory remarks consist of those made:

(1) *To modernize references.*

To illustrate: There are frequently references in the Code to "the preceding section." But since the enactment of the original section a new section has been inserted between the section containing the reference and the section to which reference is made, thus rendering the reference inaccurate. Such a reference is corrected to refer to the proper section (e.g., Section 427 where the correct reference therein is Section 425 instead of "the preceding section").

(2) *To correct improper wording resulting from clerical errors or inadvertence.*
To illustrate: "Affected" is often used when "effected" is obviously intended, and vice-versa. Such wording is corrected. To illustrate further, in Section 7150, second paragraph, line five, the word "pilotage" is used when "postage" was obviously intended. Here, the correct word is substituted.

(3) *To delete statutes expressly repealed.* (Self-explanatory)

(4) *To delete superseded statutes.* (Self-explanatory)

(5) *To delete statutes having only a temporary usefulness, and being without prospective significance.*
To illustrate: Section 4269(a) providing for certain types of refunds by the Governor and Council of State directs that the power granted therein to make such refunds shall not be exercised after July 1, 1927.

(6) *To delete statutes unconstitutional under the decisions of the North Carolina Supreme Court.*
To illustrate: Section 218(v) purports to authorize depositors in banks in certain enumerated counties to assign their claims to debtors of the banks and to permit such debtors to set off such assigned claims against the debts owed by them to the banks. This statute was held unconstitutional in *Edgerton v. Hood,* 205 N. C. 816.

(7) *To delete statutes unconstitutional under the decisions of the United States Supreme Court.*
To illustrate: The Alien Registration Act, Sections 193(a)-193(h), required aliens to register with the Clerk of the Superior Court of the counties where they resided. Under the decision of *Hines v. Davidowitz,* 312 U. S. 52 (1940) such a statute is clearly unenforceable.

(8) *To incorporate in the Code hitherto uncodified statutes which should be codified.*
To illustrate: Chapter 155 of the Public Laws of 1925, the "World War Veterans Loan Act of 1925" is being codified as an article in the chapter dealing with State Departments, Institutions and Commissions.

(9) *To restore to the Code in proper form statutes erroneously deleted.*
To illustrate: Section 3891 prescribed solicitors' fees. Chapter 157 of the Public Laws of 1923 placed solicitors on an exclusively salary basis. Section 3891 subsequently was deleted from the code. This was erroneous in that the same Chapter 157 of the Public Laws of 1923 did not abolish the solicitors' fees but merely diverted them, with certain exceptions, to certain county purposes. There-

fore, the section should be restored to furnish the list of fees and to indicate proper application.

(10) *To redraft sections to eliminate obsolete or superseded provisions in the sections.*

To illustrate: Section 2617, relating to the meeting and passing of motor vehicles, has been deleted because it has been superseded as to meeting of vehicles by Section 2621(295), as to overtaking by Sections 2621(296) and 2621(298), as to turning at intersections by Sections 2621(300) and 2621(301); and persons riding or driving animals are made subject to vehicle traffic laws by Section 2621(317)a. The penalty provision for violating the superseding sections is found in Section 2621(322).

(11) *To redraft a section where imperfect expression and ungrammatical construction render sections or portions of sections awkward although there is no ambiguity and the meaning intended can be perceived.*. (Self-explanatory)

(12) *To redraft and consolidate related sections or parts of sections dealing with the same aspects of the same subjects.*

To illustrate: Sections 1112(n) and 1112(z), both relating to the adoption and use of a seal by the Utilities Commission, have been combined into a single section.

Recommendations

In addition to making the types of changes listed above for the purpose of the legislative edition, the work of recodification has naturally uncovered a variety of situations which should be improved by express legislative action but which are beyond the authority of the Division to incorporate in the proposed code since they would effect changes in the law. They include generally such matters as the necessity for express repeal of outmoded statutes, redrafting to clarify ambiguity and to resolve conflicts between different sections, and the enactment of implementing or supplemental legislation. In all cases the defects in the statutes have been pointed out in some detail, but it has not always been possible to make a recommendation as to the specific action which should be taken. When a statute is ambiguous and there is no means of determining which possible meaning expresses the legislative intent, or even where the more likely intended meaning is clear, it has been felt that it was beyond the scope of the power of the Division to choose under such circumstances and to incorporate such choice in the legislative edition, but, rather, it was thought desirable to set out the problem and to indicate which course seemed advisable along with the reasons therefor. Therefore, these recommendations along with the explanatory reports described above have also in every case been submitted to the Legislative Commission on Recodification for approval, and it is hoped that they will furnish the basis for the drafting of supplemental legislation, in addition to an official code, in order to produce the most effective final code.

Even if none or only a few of the "recommendations" are acted on by the 1943 General Assembly, the material will still be available for consideration at some future date, and failure to iron out all the difficulties presented by the sections on which "recommendations" have been made will not prevent the adoption in 1943 of a vastly improved official code.

The Index

A great deal of attention has been devoted to the index in a section-by-section analysis, designed (1) to delete inapplicable index references, (2) to correct inaccurate index references, and (3) to add new index references where sections or portions of sections are found to be indexed inadequately or not at all. At the same time, index lines will be repeated as often as the limitations of space and utility permit to the end that "Cross References" or "See" references may be reduced to a minimum, and where they cannot be entirely eliminated, the section numbers are also being listed along with the Cross Reference. Frontal tables, furnishing a key to each section in a chapter, are being placed at the beginning of each chapter and should be of great assistance in locating any section desired.

The publisher is now engaged in printing the legislative edition of the code and it will be placed in the hands of the legislators and other interested parties as soon as possible before the 1943 General Assembly convenes.

OPINIONS TO GOVERNOR

SUBJECT: INSANE PERSONS AND INCOMPETENTS COMMITTED WITHOUT BEING TRIED FOR CRIME; HOW DISCHARGED

7 August, 1940.

It is not clear from your letter of August 6, 1940, together with the judgment of Honorable E. H. Cranmer, whether the defendant was actually put on trial on a charge of murder or whether the issue of his sanity was separately inquired into.

It seems more reasonable to me to conclude that he was not put on trial at all, since the State introduced no evidence, but that the sole issue inquired into was as to his sanity at the time he was supposed to stand trial. Since it was decided that defendant was insane at the time of the hearing, he was not then put on trial. It would, therefore, seem to me that the hospital authorities would be the judges of whether he has been restored to his proper mind, and his release would be governed by Section 6237. Section 6239 applies only to cases where a person has been acquitted of a crime on the grounds of insanity. Such section would have no application here, because the defendant has never been tried for crime.

SUBJECT: COSTS; PAROLE BEFORE SERVICE OF SENTENCE; LIABILITY OF DEFENDANT FOR COSTS

14 August, 1940.

I have your letter of August 8, 1940, in which you request a ruling on the following question:

> "When a prisoner is given a sentence in the penitentiary and certain court costs are taxed against him in the judgment, including witness fees, etc., and before the prisoner is committed for the service of said sentence the Governor issues a parole, is the prisoner liable for the costs above referred to?"

You point out that the parole order makes no reference to the costs.

I am of the opinion that the prisoner is liable for the costs in this case. C. S. 1267 provides that "every person convicted of an offense, or confessing himself guilty, or submitting to the court, shall pay the costs of prosecution." The Supreme Court decided this question in the early case of State v. Mooney, 74 N. C. 98. It was there held that costs and fees due officers of the court are vested rights by law, and, after conviction and sentence, a defendant is not discharged from liability for their payment, even though he receive an unconditional pardon from the Governor of the State. The reason for this holding is stated as follows at page 98:

> "By Art. III, sec. 6, of the Constitution, the Governor is invested with power to grant reprieves, commutations and pardons, after conviction, for all offenses except in cases of impeachment. In the State v. Underwood, 64 N. C., 599, it was held that where the pardon is pleaded after verdict and before judgment, it will discharge the defendant from the costs. How it would be if the pardon had been granted after judgment, was left an open question, and it is now presented for our decision.

> "The costs and fees in criminal prosecutions are regulated by statute, Bat. Rev., ch. 105, and the Acts of 1873-'74, ch. 175. It is expressly provided in ch. 33, sec. 80, Bat. Rev., that 'every person convicted of an offense, or confessing himself guilty, or submitting to the Court, shall pay the costs of the prosecution.'
>
> "The legal effect of a conviction and judgment is to vest the right to the costs in those entitled to receive them. The judgment, though nominally in the name of the State, is, in effect, in favor of those performing services in the case for which fees are given as a compensation. An absolute pardon discharges a fine imposed, because that goes to the public, and the Governor represents the public, but the costs belong to private persons, and the pardon can no more discharge the costs than it can discharge a debt due by the defendant to a third person . . ."

This case has not been overruled or questioned by our Court subsequently, and was cited with approval in State v. Crook, 115 N. C. 760, at page 765. It clearly represents the weight of authority in this country. See: Note, 15 L. R. A. 395; 20 R. C. L. 568; 29 Cyc. 1566; 46 C. J. 1195; and authorities there cited.

I am enclosing the copy of the parole order issued in this case and the letter of the Clerk of the Superior Court, as you requested.

RE: STATE HIGHWAY PATROL; DETERMINATION OF THE NUMBER OF PATROLMEN

13 August, 1940.

Section 3846, Michie's North Carolina Code, provides that the State Highway Patrol shall consist of one person to be designated as Major and such additional subordinate officers and men as the Commissioner of Revenue, with the approval of the Governor and Advisory Budget Commission, shall direct.

This is in confirmation of my statement to you over the telephone on yesterday to this effect.

ELECTIONS; PRESIDENTIAL ELECTORS; MEETINGS; NOTICE OF

26 November, 1940.

As requested by you, I have prepared a proclamation as to the Presidential Electors, which I enclose herewith. I also enclose copies which you may wish to deliver to the press.

The statute, C. S. 6012, requires that the Governor shall "immediately issue his proclamation" after receipt of the certificate from the Secretary of State and "cause the same to be published in such daily newspapers as may be published in the City of Raleigh," setting forth the names of the persons duly elected as electors, and warning each of them to attend at the Capitol in the City of Raleigh at Noon on the first Monday after the second Wednesday in December next after his election.

The statute further requires that the electors shall meet, and in case of the absence or ineligibility of any elector chosen, or if the proper number of electors shall for any cause be deficient, those present shall therewith elect from the citizens of the State so many persons as will supply the deficiency, and the persons so chosen shall be Electors to vote for the President and Vice-President of the United States.

I mention this part of the statute, as I understand possibly Mr. V. B. Jurney, who is already holding a public office, may not desire to hazard the title to it by attending the meeting and accepting his election. It will, therefore, be necessary for the Electors to select someone else in his place, which, under the statute, they have a right to do.

The Act further provides that the Governor shall on or before the first Monday after the second Wednesday in December make out six lists of the names of the said persons so elected and appointed Electors and cause the same to be delivered to them, as directed by the Act of Congress. I have prepared the form for this list, to be signed by you, making six copies of it as required by statute, in order that this may be ready at the time you are required to file it.

I will also prepare the other forms required to comply with the Federal Constitution and Acts of Congress in certifying the results of the action of the meeting of the North Carolina Electors in time to be used on the 16th of December, which I assume you desire me to do. I shall retain all of these papers here until it is time to have them filed.

SUBJECT: ELECTION LAW; MEMBERS OF GENERAL ASSEMBLY—FILLING VACANCIES

6 February, 1941.

I have an inquiry from you as to the law relating to filling the vacancy in the Senate caused by the death of Dr. T. W. M. Long.

Our Constitution, Article II, Section 13, provides as follows: "If vacancies shall occur in the General Assembly by death, resignation, or otherwise, writs of election shall be issued by the Governor under such regulations as may be prescribed by law."

Our election law, C. S. 5975, provides: "Every election held in pursuance of a writ from the Governor shall be conducted in like manner as the regular biennial elections, so far as the particular case can be governed by general rules * * *."

C. S. 5919 provides that when a vacancy occurs in the General Assembly by death, resignation, or otherwise, while the General Assembly shall be in session, it shall be the duty of the Presiding Officer in the House in which the vacancy occurs to notify the Governor of the same, "who shall thereupon issue a writ of election to the chairman or chairmen of the district or county represented by the late member, said election to be held at such time as the Governor may designate, and in such manner as may be prescribed by law."

Under the section of our Constitution and the above referred to sections of the election law, I am of the opinion that upon notice to you by the Lieutenant Governor, as President of the Senate, of the death of Senator Long, you "shall thereupon issue a writ of election." This language, I think, is mandatory and requires that the writ be issued under these circumstances.

Under our law above quoted, I am further of the opinion that you are authorized to fix the day on which the election is to be held and that there is no requirement as to length of time after the writ is issued before the election can be held, provided, of course, that reasonable opportunity is given for notice of the election and the organization of the election machinery.

If I can be of further service in this respect, I shall be glad to do so.

SUBJECT: NOTARIES PUBLIC

19 February, 1941.

I have your letter of February 18, wherein you state that Mrs. Irene Wilson was first commissioned a notary public on February 9, 1937; that she was married on November 1, 1937, and that without advising your office of her marital status, she, on January 14, 1939, had her commission as a notary public renewed for the usual two year period; that this last commission expired on January 14, 1941, and she failed to apply for a renewal thereof until the 9th of February of this year, but that she continued to act as a notary public until February 9 of this year, at which time she applied for a renewal of her commission in her maiden name, and you inquire, first, as to the legal status of papers which she has notarized between January 14 of this year, the time her old commission expired, and February 9 of this year, the time her commission was renewed; and, second, if the commission dated February 9, 1941, should be reissued and dated January 14, 1941.

The commission which was issued to this notary public, dated February 9, 1937, expired on February 9, 1939; however, her commission which was dated January 14, 1939, would not hold over and be effective, in my opinion, until February 9, 1941, since the second commission was issued January 14 and ran only for a period of two years; that is to say, until January 14, 1941.

I advise that the commission dated this year would necessarily have to be dated on the day which it was issued, February 9, 1941.

As to the validity of the papers or instruments which she notarized between the dates of January 14 and February 9, 1941, I am rather of the opinion that some validating act should be enacted at this session of the Legislature, in order to protect any such instruments which she notarized between these two dates.

SUBJECT: COURTS—RECORDER'S; SUSPENDED SENTENCE; MODIFICATION OF JUDGMENT

13 March, 1941.

You inquire as to whether, in my opinion, under the provisions of Section 5 of Chapter 96 of the Public Laws of 1939, the Judge of the Recorder's Court of Durham County would have the power to change, alter or modify a sentence previously imposed and suspended and which was later placed in effect, more than thirty days having elapsed between the date of the imposition of the original sentence and the attempt to change or modify such sentence, and no appeal having been taken to the Superior Court.

Section 5 of Chapter 96 of the Public Laws of 1939 provides:

"Sec. 5. The Recorder of the Recorder's Court of Durham County shall not change, alter, or modify any judgment rendered or sentence pronounced by him, after the expiration of thirty days from the date of rendering said judgment or pronouncing said sentence, except that in those cases in which there shall be a failure or refusal to comply with a judgment requiring the payment of a fine, costs, or other sum of money, or failure to comply with the terms of a suspended judgment, the Recorder may pronounce sentence on such defendant: Provided, however, that nothing in this section shall be construed as conferring upon the Recorder any authority to change, alter, or modify any judgment or sentence prior to the expiration of thirty days from the date of the rendition of said judgment or sentence in cases in which an appeal has been taken and the appeal docketed in the Superior Court."

Under the provisions of this section, I am of the opinion that the exception in this section relative to cases in which there is a failure or refusal to comply with a judgment requiring the payment of a fine, costs or other sum of money or failure to comply with the terms of a suspended judgment was intended to give the Judge of the Recorder's Court the power to put in effect a judgment carrying a prison sentence suspended on certain conditions in so far as it relates to suspended judgments.

When the judgment is pronounced and at a later date the prison sentence is put in effect, I do not believe the Judge of the Recorder's Court would have any right to change the original sentence if more than thirty days had elapsed since the original sentence was pronounced.

SUBJECT: OFFICERS; ELECTION LAWS; FILLING VACANCIES CAUSED BY DEATH, ETC.—CONGRESSMEN

2 May, 1941.

In response to your request, I have examined the constitutional provisions and the statutes with reference to the filling of the vacancy of Member of Congress of North Carolina caused by the accidental death of Honorable A. D. Folger.

Our statute, C. S. 6007, in accordance with the provision of the Federal Constitution, Article I, Section 4, provides as follows:

"Special Election for Congressmen. If at any time after the expiration of any congress and before another election, or if at any time after an election, there shall be a vacancy in the representation in congress, the governor shall issue a writ of election, and by proclamation shall require the voters to meet in the different townships in their respective counties at such times as may be appointed therein, and at the places established by law, then and there to vote for a representative in congress to fill the vacancy, and the election shall be conducted in like manner as regular elections."

C. S. 6008 provides as follows:

"Certificate of Election for Congressmen. Every person duly elected a representative to congress, upon obtaining a certificate of his election from the secretary of state, shall procure from the governor a commission certifying his appointment as a representative of the state, which the governor shall issue on such certificate being produced."

You inquire, also, as to whether or not any provision is made in our law for the nomination of candidates who may desire to run in such special election.

I regret to advise you that our law is silent on this subject in the case of a vacancy under the circumstances occasioned by the death of Mr.

Folger. C. S. 6053 makes provision for filling of vacancies occurring after the primary and before the ensuing general election. A similar provision may be found in Section 52 of the Democratic Party Plan of Organization. I am not informed as to whether the minority party has any rule covering the situation.

This question was presented to this office in June 1923, upon the death of the Honorable Claude Kitchin. At that time, the then Attorney General James S. Manning expressed the opinion in a letter to Mr. T. B. Ward, Chairman of the Executive Committee of the Second Congressional District, that our primary law made no provision whatever for the nomination of candidates under such circumstances. Mr. Kitchin died after the general election and while he was a Member of Congress, presenting the exact question which has arisen on account of the death of Mr. Folger. There has been no change in our law in this respect since that time.

The opinion was expressed by Attorney General Manning that there were three methods by which a candidate might be selected: first, by vote of the Executive Committee of the party to which the candidate belongs; second, by a Congressional District Convention called by the Congressional Executive Committee of the party calling the same; or, third, by a voluntary primary, called by the Executive Committee of the particular party calling the same. I concur in the views expressed by Attorney General Manning, which I believe are correct.

It is my opinion that the party congressional committees of a party would have whatever authority there exists for determining the method of selection of the party candidates. The candidates so selected would doubtless be recognized as the party candidates, although the selection as such could not be attributed to any statutory provision.

I find no authority in the statutes for paying the expense of a primary, if any should be called, out of public funds. This expense would have to be provided for in some other manner.

For your information, I am sending you herewith copy of the letter written by Attorney General Manning on June 15, 1923, to which I refer in this letter.

In Re: Armstead Clifton; Remedy of Prisoner Who Has Received Punishment in Excess of Statutory Limitation

27 May, 1941.

I have your letter of May 22 in which you ask my opinion as to the remedy available to a prisoner who has received punishment imposed by a court of competent jurisdiction in excess of the punishment permissible under the controlling statute. You inquire specifically whether a writ of habeas corpus would be proper or would his only remedy be to apply to the Governor for executive clemency.

In the case of In Re: Holley, 154 N. C. 163, the Court held (quoting from the syllabus, which is supported by the text):

> "The term, 'competent jurisdiction,' used by the Revisal, sec. 1822, in making an exception to the power of this Court to review a judgment in habeas corpus proceedings, means that where a committed criminal is detained under a sentence not authorized by law, he is entitled to be heard, and where, though authorized in kind, it extends beyond what the law expressly permits, he may be relieved

> from further punishment after serving the lawful portion of the sentence; and a different construction would render the statute unconstitutional."

In this case, conviction was sustained upon the ground that the punishment inflicted by the court was not in excess of that permitted by law, so that the conclusion in the respects above referred to was not necessarily involved and might be considered obiter dicta. The authorities, however, stated and relied upon by the Court in stating the proposition amply sustained the view stated by the Court. In my opinion our Court would so hold.

I find nothing in the case of Ex Parte McCown, 139 N. C. 96, which challenges this position or militates against the view expressed by the Court in the Holley case. I find no other State decision in which the question has been directly considered.

Mr. Whitley, Attorney at Law of Plymouth, discussed this matter with me and had before him at the time the Holley and McCown cases. Mr. Whitley is a very able and careful lawyer and was of the opinion that the exclusive remedy for the prisoner was executive clemency. After careful consideration, however, I cannot bring myself to agree with Mr. Whitley's conclusion and I believe that the language found in the Holley case would be followed by our Court.

I am enclosing an extra copy of this letter which you may, if you so desire, send to Mr. Whitley, as I discussed the question with him.

SUBJECT: NOTARIES PUBLIC; ELIGIBILITY FOR APPOINTMENT—RESIDENCE REQUIREMENTS

21 June, 1941.

I have your letter of June 20, enclosing a letter from Lieutenant-Colonel C. W. Woodward relative to the appointment of Mr. Dan R. Browning as a Notary Public. Colonel Woodward asks that you reconsider Mr. Dan R. Browning's application for appointment as a Notary Public.

Under date of June 12, 1941, Mr. Thomas A. Banks advised Mr. Browning that due to the fact that he had not been a resident of this State for one year, he was ineligible for appointment as a Notary Public. Mr. Banks is correct in his opinion in this regard. Our Supreme Court held in the case of Harris v. Watson, 201 N. C. 661, that the office of Notary Public is a public office within the meaning of Article XIV, Section 7, of the Constitution, which prohibits double office holding.

One of the requirements for eligibility to public office is that a person be a qualified elector in this State. In order to be a qualified elector, one must have been a resident herein for a period of one year. Since Mr. Browning has not been a resident of this State for the required length of time, he is ineligible for appointment as a Notary Public.

SUBJECT: NOTARIES PUBLIC; POWERS AND DUTIES

23 July, 1941.

I have your letter of July 22, enclosing a letter from Miss Nell Bowen, a Notary Public of Burgaw, North Carolina. She asks if she has authority as a Notary Public of Mecklenburg County to take acknowledgments and administer oaths in any other county in the State.

Consolidated Statutes 3176 provides that "notaries public have full power and authority to perform the functions of their office in any and all counties of the State, and full faith and credit shall be given to any of their official acts wheresoever the same shall be made and done." Under this statute she has authority to perform her official duties in any of the counties in the State.

Miss Bowen also states that there is no space designated in the forms which she is required to fill out for a seal.

The seal which she has should be impressed either over or beside the place where she signs the instrument in her official capacity, regardless of whether any space is provided therefor or not. In the place for her address as a Notary Public, she should give her present address; that is, the place where she resides at the time the Oath is administered.

As to the address of applicants for employment, this should perhaps show the present address of such applicant.

SUBJECT: UNIFORM DRIVERS LICENSE ACT; RESTORATION OF LICENSE

24 July, 1941.

I have examined the letter of Mr. Walter E. Johnston, Jr., relative to the case of Jack R. Landis. It appears from the judgment in this case that this man was charged with the illegal transportation of intoxicating liquor.

Upon receiving a record of this conviction and a copy of the judgment entered in the case, wherein one of the conditions for a suspended sentence was that the defendant be deprived of the privilege of operating an automobile upon the highways of the State for a period of eighteen months, the Highway Safety Division suspended his license under Section 11(a) (8) of Chapter 52 of the Public Laws of 1939. This section of the drivers license act provides that the Department of Highway Safety shall have authority to suspend the license of any operator or chauffeur without preliminary hearing, upon a showing by its records or other satisfactory evidence that the license has been convicted of the illegal transportation of intoxicating liquor.

Under Section 18(b) of the Act, it is provided that every court having jurisdiction over offenses committed under the Act, or any other Act of this State regulating the operation of motor vehicles on the highways, shall forward to the Department a record of the conviction of any person in said court for a violation of any of said laws, and may recommend the suspension of the operator's or chauffeur's license of the person so convicted.

The Highway Safety Division having received a copy of the judgment in this case, proceeded to act under Section 11(a) (8), referred to above, and suspended the chauffeur's license of this defendant.

The only authority which the Governor has with regard to the power to pardon is under Article III, Section 6, of the Constitution. The Constitution gives the Governor power to pardon criminals and commute sentences imposed upon them which have been imposed incidental to the conviction of crime. The decisions uniformly hold that the revocation or suspension of a license under the terms of the Uniform Drivers License

Act is not a punishment for crime. The state has power to grant operator's licenses upon reasonable conditions, or to revoke or suspend such licenses upon a violation of these conditions. The fact that the violation of these conditions may also be a criminal offense is not material.

The law requiring or authorizing the Highway Safety Division to take up a driver's license when the driver has been convicted of a violation of the provisions of the Act, does not impose a penalty, but, on the contrary, it is entirely disconnected with any punishment or burden to be imposed upon a convicted person because of the crime he has committed. It proceeds purely as a police measure under authority of the police power of the State and for the protection of the public.

In the case of Commonwealth v. Funk, 186 Atlantic Reporter 65, the Court, in interpreting a very similar statute of Pennsylvania to the North Carolina law, said:

> "The plenary power of the legislature over the highways of the Commonwealth is of ancient standing and seldom, if ever, has been questioned.
>
> "The permission to operate a motor vehicle upon the highways of the Commonwealth is not embraced within the term 'civil rights' nor is a license to do so a contract or right of property in any legal or constitutional sense, although the privilege may be a valuable one, it is no more than a permit granted by the State, its enjoyment depending upon compliance with the conditions prescribed by it and subject always to such regulation and control as the State may see fit to impose."

The Supreme Court of New York, in the case of People v. Cohen, 217 N. Y. S. 726-728, said:

> "In passing I state my opinion that no constitutional right of the applicant has been invaded. His license to operate and his certificate of registration conferred upon him a privilege and not a right to operate his automobile. It was competent for the legislature to prescribe the conditions under which such privilege was conferred."

To the same effect, see Hendrick v. Maryland, 235 U. S. 610-632.

From the above authorities and other not cited here, it is my opinion that the Governor does not have, under the pardoning power granted him by the Constitution, power to restore a driver's license which has been either suspended or revoked under the terms of the Uniform Driver's License Act, Chapter 52 of the Public Laws of 1935.

I wish to call your attention, however, to the fact that this defendant's driver's license was suspended under Section 11 of the Act and not revoked under Section 12.

Section 13 of the Act provides that the Department shall not suspend a license for a period of more than one year, and, upon revoking a license, shall not in any event grant application for a new license until the expiration of one year.

There is nothing in the statute which would prohibit the restoration of a driver's license by the Highway Safety Division if it has been suspended by reason of a violation of Section 11 of the Act, and I think the Division has authority, upon a proper showing, to restore the driver's license of a person which has been suspended under the terms of Section 11. It seems to me that a full pardon granted by the Governor to the defendant in this case would have great weight with the Highway Safety Division, should this defendant make application for the restoration of his suspended license.

SUBJECT: INSTITUTIONS; ERECTION OF ADDITIONAL BUILDINGS; COOPERATION WITH FEDERAL DEFENSE COUNCIL

4 September, 1941.

I have before me your letter of September 3 with reference to the erection of an additional building or unit at the Industrial Farm Colony for Women at Kinston or at the State Home and Industrial School for Girls at Eagle Springs by these institutions, in coöperation with the Federal Defense Council, to deal with girls and young women who have been apprehended in the defense areas and committed by the courts to these institutions. You advise that it is anticipated that the girls committed will range in age between twelve and twenty-five years. You ask my opinion as to whether there are legal barriers to the erection of such a unit at either of the above mentioned institutions, both of which have indicated a willingness to coöperate and participate in the program.

Our statute with reference to Samarcand provides in C. S. 7334 that any girl who may come or shall be brought before any court of the State, and may either have confessed herself guilty or have been convicted of being an habitual drunkard or being a prostitute, or of frequenting disorderly houses or houses of prostitution, or of vagrancy, or of any other misdemeanor, may be committed by the court for confinement to this institution; provided, such person is not insane or mentally or physically incapable of being substantially benefited by the discipline of the institution. The person is committed for an indefinite term, subject to being paroled or discharged at any time by the board of managers, but in no case shall be detained longer than three years. By C. S. 7331 the board of managers is authorized to secure by gift or purchase suitable real estate for the institution, and with such money as it may receive, either by donations or from individuals, or by appropriation from the State, is authorized to erect such buildings as may be suitable for carrying out the purposes of the institution, which is made a body corporate under the name of State Home and Industrial School for Girls.

I am of the opinion, therefore, that the institution would have the authority to coöperate with the Federal Defense Council in the erection of additional buildings to carry out the object and purposes for which the corporation is formed, as recited in the Code section above referred to, which I understand to be the purpose intended by the plan under consideration.

The Industrial Farm Colony for Women was created by Chapter 219 of the Public Laws of 1927, Michie's Code 7343(d), et seq. Michie's Code Section 7343(k) provides that women sixteen years of age and over, belonging to the following classes, and who are not eligible for admission to Samarcand, may be committed by any court of competent jurisdiction to this institution, to-wit: Persons convicted of or who plead guilty to the commission of misdemeanors, including prostitution, habitual drunkenness, drug using, or disorderly conduct. The board of directors may in its discretion receive and detain as an inmate of the institution any woman or girl, not otherwise provided for, who may be sentenced by any court of the United States within this State. Conditions are attached to admissions which are not necessary to be mentioned here. Commitments are for an indefinite period, not to exceed three years; inmates may be paroled by the Governor upon recommendation of the board of directors. General management of the affairs of the institution, including the erection of buildings, is placed in the hands of the board of directors, appointed by the Governor.

After an examination of this statute, I am of the opinion that this institution would have the authority to erect an additional building or unit on its property in coöperation with the Federal Defense Council for the purposes mentioned in your letter, provided funds were made available for this purpose.

As stated above, the statute confines admissions to the Industrial Farm Colony for Women to women sixteen years of age and older. You state in your letter of September 3 that the ages of the girls who may be committed will range from twelve to twenty-five years. Admissions to the Industrial Farm Colony for Women at Kinston, under the statute, are limited to those who are sixteen years of age and over.

Subject to the limitation as to admissions contained in the statute, either or both of these institutions would be authorized, in my opinion, to coöperate with the Federal Defense Council in carrying out the contemplated plan.

SUBJECT: DOUBLE OFFICE HOLDING; POSTMASTER AND NOTARY PUBLIC

27 October, 1941.

This office has held that the positions of Postmaster and Notary Public are both offices within the meaning of Article XIV, Section 7, of the Constitution, which prohibits double office holding, and that one person could not hold both of these offices at the same time. Under the decisions of our Court, where a person qualifies for a second office, he automatically vacates the first.

SUBJECT: DOUBLE OFFICE HOLDING; NOTARY PUBLIC—
COLLECTOR AND TOWN ACCOUNTANT

7 November, 1941.

The office of town accountant and tax collector, as well as that of notary public, are both offices within the meaning of Article XIV, Section 7, of the Constitution, which prohibits double office holding, and one person may not hold both these offices at one and the same time.

Our Court has held that where an officeholder accepts another office and qualifies, that action ipso facts has the effect of vacating the former office.

SUBJECT: OFFICERS; STATE HIGHWAY PATROL; GOVERNOR'S GRANTING
GENERAL POLICE POWER TO CONSTABLES; STATE POLICE POWER

11 December, 1941.

You inquire if the power is vested in you as Governor of North Carolina, during the present emergency, to declare that an emergency exists to the extent that you have authority by proclamation to extend to members of the State Highway Patrol general police power throughout the State.

Consolidated Statutes 3846(ooo) provides, among other things, that "the State Highway Patrol or any member or members thereof shall have full power and authority to perform such additional duties as peace officers as may from time to time be directed by the Governor . . ."

This, in my opinion, gives you the power, by order directed to the State Highway Patrol, to require that organization to perform such duties as peace officers as in your judgment the emergency now existing, both in the State and in the Nation, would require. I do not think that any special emergency would have to exist to enable you to order the State Highway Patrol to perform duties other than those prescribed by statute, if, in your judgment, the best interests of the State required such action on your part.

You further inquire as to whether or not you have authority to extend the jurisdiction of sheriffs, deputy sheriffs, chiefs of police and other peace officers from their respective local jurisdictions so as to enable them to operate on a state-wide basis.

I know of no statute which would give you this power. Local officers have jurisdiction only within the limits of their respective public local subdivisions; that is to say, in the absence of legislation authorizing it, sheriffs and other county peace officers have jurisdiction only within the limits of the county in which they are officers, and municipal peace officers would have jurisdiction only within the limits of the municipality in which they are appointed to office.

Subject: School Law; Use of School Buses

15 January, 1942.

I have your letter of January 14, enclosing a letter from Mr. J. A. Forney, Manager of the Duke Power Company, who is Sub-chairman of the Transportation Committee of the Mecklenburg Chapter of the American Red Cross, and who is also Sub-chairman of the Mecklenburg County Civilian Defense Council, wherein he inquires if school buses may be used for the purpose of evacuating school children and other people in the event of an emergency which might arise in case of invasion by enemy forces.

Prior to the enactment of the School Machinery Act of 1933, there was no limitation upon the use of school buses except that the same were to be operated under the supervision of the local authorities, and, under the law as it then existed, school buses owned by the various political subdivisions of the State were used for various purposes other than actually carrying children to and from schools.

In 1933 the control and management of school buses was taken over by the State of North Carolina and the State School Commission was given direction and supervision over the same, and was also required to make rules and regulations as were necessary for the efficient and economical operation of the school transportation system. Section 26, Chapter 562, Public Laws of 1933.

In 1935 the Legislature, for some reason, perhaps to confine the operations more strictly to the transportation of school children to and from schools, amended the section relating to the operation of school buses by rewriting the same and including the following language:

> "The use of school buses shall be limited to the transportation of children to and from school for the regularly organized school day: Provided, that in the discretion of the county superintendent and the principal of the school, buses may be used to transport children entitled to attend commencement exercises."

In 1939 the Legislature rewrote this same section into the permanent School Machinery Act, Chapter 358 of the Public Laws of 1939, and eliminated therefrom the proviso appearing in the 1935 Act, which permitted such buses to be used, in the discretion of the superintendent and principal of the school, to transport children entitled to attend commencement exercises. This section was not amended by the 1941 Legislature.

Under the law as it is now written, I do not think that the school buses could be legally used for the purpose of evacuating school children or other people from any congested area in the case of an emergency. Of course, I think they could be used for the purpose of evacuating school children in case an emergency arose during school hours on a regularly organized school day, to the same extent that they are now used to carry children to and from school on such days.

I know of no law which would permit the use of school buses for any other purpose than that outlined in the statute, but I have no doubt that in the case of an emergency, such as suggested by Mr. Forney, such school buses would be used by the local authorities without any such authority, should the necessary occasion arise in this regard.

Subject: Hospitals for the Insane; Investigations

4 February, 1942.

In your letter of February 3, you state that circumstances have arisen which in your judgment make it necessary to conduct a very full investigation of the management and conditions at the State Hospital for the Insane at Morganton. You inquire as to what procedure may be appropriately followed under the law for conducting such investigation.

The Constitution, Article XI, Section 7, is as follows:

> "Beneficent provisions for the poor, the unfortunate and orphan, being one of the first duties of a civilized and Christian state, the General Assembly shall, at its first session, appoint and define the duties of a board of public charities, to whom shall be entrusted the supervision of all charitable and penal state institutions, and who shall annually report to the Governor, with suggestions for their improvement."

Under the provisions of C. S. 6168, the State Board of Charities and Public Welfare and Members of the General Assembly are ex-officio visitors of all hospitals for the insane, and it is there provided that it shall be the duty of the State Board of Charities to visit the hospitals from time to time as they may deem expedient to examine into their condition and make report thereon to the General Assembly, with such suggestions and remarks as they may think proper.

C. S. 6173 provides that the Board of Directors of each of the institutions for the insane shall appoint a superintendent for each of said institutions and prescribe his duties. His term of office is fixed at six years from and after his appointment, unless sooner removed by said board, who may for infidelity to his trust, gross immorality or incompetency to discharge the duties of his office, fully proved and declared, and the proofs thereof recorded in the book of their proceedings, remove and appoint another in his place.

C. S. 5008 provides that the State Board of Charities and Public Welfare has, among others, the power to inspect all institutions of a penal or charitable nature and to require reports from responsible officials of such institutions. Under C. S. 5011, the Board may require the Superintendent or other officers of the several charitable and penal institutions of the State to report to them any matter relating to the inmates of such institutions, their manner of instruction and treatment, with structure of their buildings, and to furnish them any desired statistics, upon demand. C. S. 5013 provides that it shall be a misdemeanor for any official of such institution to fail to furnish said Board with information in this regard.

You will also find under C. S. 5006 that, among other powers, the Board has authority to investigate through and by its own members, or its agents or employees, the whole system of charitable and penal institutions of the State and to recommend such changes and additional provision as it may deem needful for their economical and efficient administration. This statute extends this power also to private institutions of this character, and gives the Board power to issue subpoenas, compel attendance of witnesses, administer oaths, and to send for persons and papers whenever it deems it necessary in making such investigations, and in the other discharge of its duties, and to give such publicity to its investigations and findings as it may deem best for the public welfare.

Under the grant of powers to the Governor of this State, C. S. 7636, you will find the following:

> "He is to supervise the official conduct of all executives and ministerial officers; and when he shall deem it advisable, he shall visit all state institutions for the purpose of inquiring into the management and needs of the same . . ." Also under this section "he is to see that all offices are filled, and the duties thereof performed, or in default thereof, apply such remedy as the law allows, and if the remedy is imperfect, acquaint the General Assembly therewith."

From the above it will be seen that the State Board of Charities and Public Welfare is primarily charged under the Constitution and the law with the supervision of all charitable and penal institutions of the State, and is required to report to the Governor and to the General Assembly as to the conditions under which said institutions are operated, and to make recommendations upon their findings. Of course, the Governor is given general supervision under the statute above referred to, C. S. 7636, but it seems to me that the primary duty lies with the State Board of Charities and Public Welfare.

Nowhere have I been able to find that the Attorney General has any independant authority to conduct such investigation. Of course, however, under the statute prescribing the duties for the Attorney General, he is required to render legal services to all departments, agencies and institutions of the State, when requested to do so by such agencies or departments.

The State Hospital at Morganton, as well as other state institutions of similar character, are charitable institutions within the meaning of the constitutional provision above referred to. See State v. Security National Bank, 207 N. C. 697.

SUBJECT: NOTARIES PUBLIC; WOMEN; MARITAL STATUS

26 February, 1942.

In your letter of February 25, you state that on January 11, 1942, a Notary Public commission was issued to one Katherine VanEschop; that very recently she married and she is now Mrs. Katherine DeBruhl, and you inquire if it is necessary that a new commission be issued to her and a fee charged therefor, or if Mrs. DeBruhl could use the original commission issued to her in her maiden name until its expiration.

The fact that this Notary Public was married shortly after the commission was issued to her in her maiden name would not, in my opinion, invalidate any official acts, should she continue to notarize papers by signing all papers in her maiden name, appending thereafter her married name; for example, in this case, signing "Katherine VanEschop," and under or after that, "now Katherine DeBruhl."

I do not think that any official acts attested in her maiden name as indicated above would be held by the courts of this State to be invalid. Neither do I think that she should be required to have a new commission issued in her married name and be required to pay the $5 fee therefor.

SUBJECT: SPECIAL POLICE; CORPORATIONS; JURISDICTION OF SPECIAL POLICE; POWER OF ARREST

10 March, 1942.

You inquire as to the jurisdiction of special policemen appointed by you under authority of C. S. 3484, and their power to make arrests, regardless of county lines, when acting in the capacity of such policemen for railroads, utilities and manufacturing concerns within the contemplation of the Act.

C. S. 3484 provides in effect that railroad companies, public utilities or manufacturing companies may apply to you, as Governor, to commission such persons as the corporation or company may designate to act as policemen for it. The statute also empowers you, upon such application, to appoint such persons or so many of them as you may deem proper to be such policemen and authorizes you to issue to the person so appointed a commission to act in such capacity.

C. S. 3485 provides in part as follows:

> "Every policeman so appointed shall, before entering upon the duties of his office, take and subscribe the usual oath. Such oath, with a copy of the commission, shall be filed with the corporation commission and a certificate thereof by its clerk shall be filed with the clerk of each county through or into which the railroad for which such policeman is appointed may run or in which the company may be engaged in work, and in which it is intended he shall act, and such policemen shall severally possess within the limits of the county all the powers of policemen in the several towns, cities and villages in which they shall be so authorized to act as aforesaid: . . ."

From the quoted portion of C. S. 3485, it would appear that the jurisdiction of such special policemen would be limited to that area "in which the company may be engaged in work, and in which it is intended he shall act."

From the wording of the above statute, it is my opinion that such special policemen have the power of arrest only in those counties in which the company for which they were appointed is engaged in business. As stated in Butler v. Manufacturing Co., 185 N. C. 250-253, a damage suit arising out of a suit for false arrest by a nightwatchman of a cotton mill:

> "On such an inquiry the authorities are to the effect that if the defendant's night watchman, while acting within the scope and course of his duties as such employee, wrongfully caused the arrest and imprisonment of the plaintiff, liability on the part of defendant would not be prevented because the employee had been clothed with authority as special policeman for the purpose. On the other hand, if the night watchman at the time held such authority, and for the purpose stated, the company would be entitled to have the issues considered and determined in reference to that fact, and he is only to be regarded and dealt with as such and within the area designated if any such restriction is established."

SUBJECT: SPECIAL POLICEMEN; APPOINTMENT BY THE GOVERNOR

27 March, 1942.

I have your letter of March 26, enclosing a letter from Mr. Milton B. Dworsky, wherein he requests that you appoint special state officers in the towns of Oxford and Creedmoor; that these men will serve without pay, and that they are seriously needed, due to the close proximity of the army camp which is being constructed in that area. He further states that these additional policemen are necessary during the present emergency, but that for the towns concerned to employ them would be to incur an added expense which would amount to more than the towns could afford to pay.

The only statute which permits you as Governor to appoint special policemen, aside from your authority to appoint State Highway Patrolmen, is to be found as C. S. 3484. Under this, however, you can appoint such policemen only upon the application of a railroad corporation or any public utility or manufacturing company, and, after such appointment, such special policemen have authority and jurisdiction to act only in the area in which such utility or manufacturing company may be engaged in work.

I know of no authority for you to appoint the special policemen requested by Mr. Dworsky.

SUBJECT: HIGHWAY PATROL; LIMITATION AS TO NUMBER APPOINTED

21 April, 1942.

You inquire if there is any limitation upon the number of highway patrolmen you may appoint under the law as it now exists.

The statute governing the number of state highway patrolmen formerly had a limitation upon the number of men who might have been employed. However, the Legislature of 1937, by enacting Chapter 313, amended the act so that it now reads, in part, as follows:

"The State Highway Patrol, created and existing by virtue of Chapter 218 of the Public Laws of 1929, as amended, shall consist of one person to be designated as Major, and such additional subordinate officers and men as the Commissioner of Revenue, with the approval of the Governor and the Advisory Budget Commission, shall direct."

Of course, the 1941 Legislature placed the duties theretofore placed upon the Commissioner of Revenue upon the Motor Vehicle Commissioner authorized by Chapter 36 of the Public Laws of 1941.

As the law now stands, there is no limit upon the number of highway patrolmen who may be appointed, should funds be available to pay the additional expense thereof and should the Governor, in his discretion, think that public need demands an increase in the patrol.

SUBJECT: CRIMINAL LAW; JUDGMENTS; LENGTH OF SENTENCE; CORRECTION OF ERROR

4 May, 1942.

You state in your memorandum that one Jess Hall was convicted at the February, 1941, Term of the Superior Court of Caldwell County for nonsupport, and that the judgment of the court provides that the defendant be confined in the common jail of Caldwell County and assigned to light labor only and pay the costs on or before the first day of November, 1941, and with certain other conditions attached thereto. The judgment fails to state the length of the sentence.

You further state that subsequent to the entry of the judgment the defendent violated the provisions set out in the judgment referred to and that at the November Term, 1941, the Solicitor requested that the suspended judgment be invoked, and motion was allowed by the presiding judge. The prisoner was then committed to prison for a term of eighteen months.

You have now been requested to investigate the case for parole, and you desire to know whether the remedy of the defendant is by application for writ of habeas corpus rather than an application to your department for parole.

Of course, the term of imprisonment must be fixed by the trial judge within certain limits. State v. Gaskins, 65 N. C. 320; State v. Vickers, 184 N. C. 676 (678). From an inspection of the judgment referred to in your memorandum, it appears to me that it is possible the trial judge sentenced the defendant to a definite term and the clerk in copying the judgment in the minutes failed to insert the length of the sentence. Certainly when the clerk issued the commitment he must have had some record which showed that the sentence to be served by the defendant was eighteen months.

It is my thought that on a proper motion by the Solicitor and at a proper legal hearing at which the prisoner is present, the court would have the power to amend the minute docket so as to make it speak the truth. State v. Swepson, 84 N. C. 827; State v. King, 27 N. C. 203; State v. Craton, 28 N. C. 164; 16 C. J. 1322.

In 1 Freeman on Judgments, 5th ed., page 322, section 165, it is said:

> "All courts have inherent power independent of statute, to correct clerical errors at any time and to make the judgment entry correspond with the judgment recorded. . . . It exists in criminal prosecutions as well as in civil cases."

It is true that with the record in its present state the remedy of the defendant would be by petition for writ of habeas corpus rather than an application for a parole. However, it is my thought that the Solicitor of the district in which the defendant was tried and the trial judge should be notified as to the present state of the record so that they may, if they so desire, take steps to have the record corrected to speak the truth.

Our Supreme Court has held that on appeals where the sentence in a criminal case is void for indefiniteness the case will be remanded in order that a correct sentence may be imposed. State v. Satterwhite, 182 N. C. 892; State v. Shipman, 203 N. C. 325. It is entirely possible that if the defendant applied for a writ of habeas corpus and the true facts should be brought out, the judge hearing the application for a writ might remand the prisoner to Caldwell County for a proper sentence.

OPINIONS TO SECRETARY OF STATE

SUBJECT: CORPORATIONS; MERGER; FEES

20 July, 1940.

You have asked this office for an opinion on the proper fees to be charged by you when two corporations merge, as provided in North Carolina Code, Annotated (Michie's, 1939), Section 1224(a), et seq.

Your attention is called to a part of Section 1224(f), which reads in part as follows:

> "Providing that the only fees that shall be collected from said merging corporations shall be office or filing fees and charter fees upon any increase in the authorized capital stock of the merged corporations in excess of that provided for in the charters of the merging corporations when the authorized capital stock of said merging corporations shall be added."

It is felt that the above statute will give you the desired information.

SUBJECT: ENTRIES; DOMESTIC AND FOREIGN CORPORATIONS—RIGHT TO MAKE

14 August, 1940.

You have requested that I advise you whether under C. S. 7554 an entry may be made by a corporation and, if so, would such entry be confined to a domestic corporation or whether it would include a foreign corporation; also, the further question if a grant could be made to a corporation, who would be the proper officers of the corporation to make the entry and sign the necessary papers in connection with it.

I regret to state that an examination of the authorities in this State does not provide a definite answer to these questions, except, I may say, in my opinion a foreign corporation could not under any circumstances enter land in North Carolina. 14a Corpus Juris, 1224, Title, Corporations; Ballentine on Corporations, Section 7.

In the case of Wallace v. Moore, 178 N. C. 114, involving the validity of an entry and grant made to the Atlantic and North Carolina Railroad Company, the Court, speaking through Judge Hoke, said:

> "It is contended for defendant that although the charter and general law applicable to railroads may not confer the power to acquire this property, it arises to the company by virtue of the very general terms of the statute authorizing the issuance of grants for the State lands (Rev., ch. 37, sec. 1692), to the effect that any citizen of this State and all persons who shall have come into this State with the *bona fide* intent of becoming citizens thereof shall have the right and privilege of making entries and obtaining grants for vacant and unappropriated lands. Although it is held that corporations are to be regarded as citizens under the statutes conferring jurisdiction on the Federal courts by reason of diversity of citizenship, they are not so considered within the meaning of the constitutional and statutory provisions guaranteeing the privileges and immunities of citizenship, nor do they come generally within this meaning of that term. Orient Ins. Co. v. Daggs, 172 U. S., 55-7; Ins. Co. v. Commonwealth, 5 Bush, 68 (Ky.). And while the word 'person' is more usually held to extend to corporations, this may depend largely on the context and the extent and purpose of the particular law. 7 R. C. L., citing Overland Cotton Mills v. People,

> 32 Col., 263, and other cases. A perusal of the statute in question here will disclose that it applies primarily to natural persons, having general capacity to take and hold real estate, and if it extends to corporations at all, it is subject to the restrictions and limitations established by the charter or the general law."

Thus, it is seen that the Court has thrown very strong doubt upon the right of a corporation to enter land.

In the case of Wilson v. Land Company, 77 N. C. 445, our Court upheld the validity of a grant to a corporation, which was entered, however, by an individual and transferred after entry to the corporation.

The statute, C. S. 7554, makes the same provision as to an entry as to a grant in providing that "any citizen of this State and all persons who come into the State with the *bona fide* intent of becoming residents and citizens thereof have the right and privilege of making entries of and obtaining grants for vacant and unappropriated lands."

The cases, therefore, leave me in doubt as to the correct answer. In the absence of a direct decision by our Court, I would hesitate to express an opinion. I would suggest that if an entry is attempted to be made by a corporation, the question should be presented to the court and decided in some properly constituted case. Authorities in other states do not afford us a satisfactory answer to the problem.

SUBJECT: CORPORATIONS; FOREIGN; DOMESTICATION; DOING BUSINESS UNDER A TRADE NAME

21 August, 1940.

I have your letter of August 17, in which you ask my opinion as to whether or not a foreign corporation domesticated in this State can conduct its business here under any name other than its corporate name, and, if so, whether you should incorporate this authority in the certificate of domestication to be issued by your office. You state that you permitted the domestication of a foreign corporation by its corporate name only, without any reference in your certificate to the manner in which it desires to conduct its business under a trade name in this State.

I am of the opinion that this corporation could do business in this State under its corporate name only. Although there is no statute specifically covering this situation, Section 1131, subsection 2, of the Code, sets out the statutory method whereby a corporation may change its name. This would seem to indicate that this is the exclusive manner in which a corporation doing business in this State can acquire a new name under which it may conduct its business here.

It is well settled that a corporation has no right or power, of itself, and without statutory or other legal authorization to abandon its corporate name originally selected and stated in its charter, and take on a new and different name.

Bellows v. Hallowell, 2 Mason 31, Fed. Cas. No. 1, 279;
American Elementary Elec. Co. v. Normandy, 46 App. Cas. 329;
Pilsen Brewing Co. v. Wallace, 291 Ill. 59, 125 N. E. 714;
Sykes v. People, 132 Ill. 32, 23 N. E. 391;
Glass v. Tipton, T & B Turnpike Co., 32 Ind. 376;
McGrary v. People, 45 N. Y. 153.

Fletcher, in his recent work on Corporations, Cyclopedia Corporation, Volume 6, states at page 89:

> "This legal name and title which the law confers upon a corporation is the one which it should use. It may not, without authority of law expressed or implied, use any other name, particularly where the statute directly prohibits corporations from transacting any business under any other or different name than that conferred upon them by their articles of incorporation."

While it does not appear that our Court has passed upon the precise point here under consideration, in view of the reasons and authorities outlined above, and as a matter of public policy, I am inclined to believe that the foreign corporation you refer to would have to do business in this State under its corporate name, and would not be warranted in assuming another.

SUBJECT: ENTRIES; GRANTS; BOARD OF TRUSTEES OF OCRACOKE METHODIST CHURCH—CAPACITY TO TAKE

21 October, 1940.

In conference with you today, you submitted to me copy of the entry, No. 749, made in the name of the Board of Trustees of the Ocracoke Methodist Church by H. J. Williams, Chairman, E. S. Tolson, Member, and Wheeler Howard, Member. The question has occurred to you whether or not the grant for this land could be made to the Board of Trustees of the Ocracoke Methodist Church.

It is provided in Michie's N. C. Code, 1939, Section 1013 (a), that voluntary organizations and associations of individuals, when organized for purposes which are not prohibited by law, are authorized and empowered to acquire real estate and to hold the same in their common or corporate names. Provision is made in subsequent sections for conveyance of such property so acquired and held.

The trustees all being resident individuals and the church itself an association of residents of the State, I am inclined to the opinion that you would not be prohibited from issuing the grant on account of the provisions of Code Section 7554, providing that any citizen of the State and all persons who come into the State with the bona fide intent of becoming residents and citizens thereof are permitted to make entries and obtain grants for vacant and unappropriated lands. I believe, for the purpose of the law, that the Board of Trustees of the Ocracoke Methodist Church would be considered as within the requirements of the above mentioned section. In any event, the title could be questioned only by the State, which doubtless never would be done. Johnson v. Eversole Lumber Company, 144 N. C. 717.

I, therefore, am of the opinion that you would be justified in issuing the grant to the Board of Trustees of the Ocracoke Methodist Church, and that under the statute cited it would be capable of taking title of the land.

SUBJECT: CAPITAL ISSUES LAW; APPLICATION; SALE OF UNDIVIDED INTEREST IN OIL LEASE ROYALTIES

11 July, 1941.

Receipt is acknowledged of your letter of July 11, requesting my opinion as to the application of the Capital Issues Act, Chapter 149, Public Laws of 1927, to sales which Mr. C. E. Robertson proposes to make in North Carolina.

Mr. Robertson, with the Honorable Walter Murphy, called at this office and I examined the form to be used by him in the business which he proposes to transact, a copy of which is attached to your letter. The transaction purports to be a sale of an undivided interest in all of the oil, gas and other minerals to be found on a certain tract of land in Logan County, Okalahoma, within a period of years. The paper further provides that the sale is made subject to any rights now existing to any lessee or assigns under any valid subsisting oil and gas lease of record heretofore executed. The grantee is to receive the undivided interest in and to all bonuses, rents, royalties and other benefits which may accrue under the terms of the said lease, to the extent of the undivided interest transferred to the grantee.

I am informed from the attached papers that the land has been leased and that it is proposed to sell an undivided interest in landowners reserved royalties of one-eighth. I understand from the conference and the file that the thing proposed to be offered for sale is actually an undivided interest in the oil lease royalties reserved by the landowner.

Our statute defines securities or security to include, "transferable certificate or interest in participation, certificate of interest in a profit sharing agreement, certificate of interest in an oil, gas or mining lease . . ."

It seems to me that the thing which is proposed to be offered for sale is a certificate of interest in an oil, gas or mining lease, and, therefore, is such a security as requires registration with you under the Capital Issues Act.

The offering is to be distinguished from the proposed sales of a definite leasehold or interest in land, which the Court had before it in the case of State v. Allen, 216 N. C. 621. I, therefore, advise in my opinion you are correct in your conclusion that the proposed securities are subject to the terms of this Act. I find no exemption in the statute in favor of such offerings.

SUBJECT: TRADE-MARKS; REGISTERABILITY OF EMBLEM "A. A. A."

21 July, 1941.

I am of the opinion that, under our trade-mark statute, C. S. 3971, et seq., the American Automobile Association is not entitled to have its emblem "A.A.A." registered as a trade-mark.

Our trade-mark law provides for the registration of any label, trade-mark, term or design that has been used or is intended to be used for the purpose of designating, making known or distinguishing any "*goods, wares, merchandise, or products of labor.*" It is apparent that the emblem "A.A.A." is not used for the purpose of designating any goods, wares, merchandise, or products of labor. This emblem is evidence of membership in the American Automobile Association, and of the service and protection afforded by that organization to its members. The items listed in the application for the registration of this emblem as a trade-mark seem to be incidentals of the service rendered by the association, and not articles of merchandise.

A definition of the word "merchandise" which has been accepted by the Supreme Court of this State appears as follows, at p. 187, in Rubber Co. v. Morris, 181 N. C. 184:

> "Objects of commerce; whatever is usually bought and sold in trade or market or by merchants; wares, goods, commodities. . . . all those things which merchants sell, either at wholesale or retail, as dry goods, hardware, groceries, drugs, etc."

The generally recognized definition of the term "trade-mark" limits the use of the mark or design to designating or marking vendible or marketable articles of trade. The function of a trade-mark is to indicate the ownership of goods or wares to which it is attached, or to which it relates. Trade-marks are applicable only to articles of traffic, that is, articles which may be bought and sold in the market. Mendez v. Holt, 128 U. S. 514, 9 Sup. Ct. 143, 32 L. Ed. 526; Scandanavian Belt Co. v. Asbestos & Rubber Works of America, 257 F. 937; Commonwealth v. Kentucky Distilleries, 132 Ky. 521, 116 S. W. 766; Nicholson v. William Stickney Cigar Co., 158 Mo. 158, 39 S. W. 121; Fisher v. Star Co., 231 N. Y. 414, 132 N. E. 133; Wisconsin White Lily Butter Co. v. Safer, 182 Wis. 71, 195 N. W. 700; 38 Cyc. 693; 63 C. J. 308; 42 Words and Phrases (Perm. Ed.) 176. As was stated by Mr. Justice Holmes in the case of Beech-Nut Packing Co. v. P. Lorillard Co., 273 U. S. 629, 47 S. Ct. 48, 71 L. Ed. 810: "Primarily it is a distinguishable token devised or picked out with the intent to appropriate it to a particular class of goods and with the hope that it will come to symbolize good will."

Clearly, the emblem submitted by the American Automobile Association does not meet the requirement of these authorities that the design or mark must relate to goods, wares, or articles of commerce before it is to be accepted as a trade-mark. The Illinois Court of Appeals had occasion to pass upon the question of whether or not an emblem of the type here under consideration was a trade-mark. Yellow Cab Co. v. Ensler, 214 Ill. App. 607. It was held in this case, under a trade-mark registration statute similar in all respects to the North Carolina statute, that a device used by a taxicab service corporation did not relate to trade in articles of commerce or their containers, and was therefore not a valid trade-mark. The Court made the following observation and distinction at p. 609:

> "If complainant's device is a valid trade-mark and the complainant obtained an exclusive property right in it by the registration thereof, we think it would be entitled to a decree. However, we think it is apparent from the statute, Hurd's Rev. St. ch. 140, p. 2935 (J. & A. p. 11391), as well as decisions of the courts, that complainant's device cannot be considered a trade-mark as applied to its business.
>
> " 'Service is not trade in articles of commerce, and * * * trade-marks * * * must actually be upon articles of commerce or their containers.' Searchlight Gas Co. v. Prest-O-Lite Co., 215 Fed. 695."

Although the good will and service of the American Automobile Association as represented by the emblem "A.A.A." would probably be protested by our Court from infringement and unfair competition, Cab Co. v. Creasman, 185 N. C. 551, I do not believe that under our trade-mark statute and the authorities cited above, this emblem is entitled to be registered as a trade-mark.

SUBJECT: SECURITIES LAW; R. L. SWAIN TOBACCO COMPANY

15 October, 1941.

I received your letter of October 14, enclosing letter of the same date from the First Securities Corporation referring to the listing with you of the Class B Common Stock of the R. L. Swain Tobacco Company.

You call my attention to the fact that the fourth paragraph of the application for listing provides that the selling group, in addition to ten per cent commission, is to be granted an option for a three-year period to purchase the Class B Common Stock at $5.00 per share, such purchase to be limited in an amount not to exceed ten per cent of the number of shares sold by the selling group. Your question is whether or not this provision excludes the listing under the phraseology of the Act, which provides in Code Section 3924(i) in part as follows:

> "With respect to securities required to be registered by qualification under the provisions of this section, the commissioner may by order duly entered fix the maximum amount of commission or other form of remuneration to be paid in cash or otherwise, directly or indirectly, for or in connection with the sale or offering for sale of such securities which shall in no case exceed ten per cent of the actual sale price of the security."

Providing the selling group with an option to purchase Class B Common Stock as set out above would, in my opinion, constitute additional consideration to the selling group for selling the stock and, therefore, would be contrary to the section of the law above quoted. The option to purchase the stock at $5.00 per share has a contingent value which obviously is an additional consideration; otherwise, it would be eliminated from the proposal.

SUBJECT: AMENDMENT TO CORPORATE CHARTERS; CORPORATIONS; TAX

5 November, 1941.

You state that the records of your office disclose that the present total authorized capital stock structure of the Henderson Cotton Mills is $125,000, and the total authorized capital stock structure of the Harriet Cotton Mills is $450,000. No amendment or amendments have been filed, according to your records, indicating that the total authorized capital stock of either of these companies has ever been increased in excess of these figures; that these corporations, through their attorney, Mr. Bennett H. Perry, have submitted to you certificates of amendment to their charters which recites that the outstanding capital stock of each of these corporations has been, by a proper action of the stockholders, reduced from approximately $1,000,000 to approximately $500,000; that is to say, the par value of the outstanding capital stock, according to the books and records of the corporations, has been by a proper action of the board reduced in one instance from $50 to $25, and in the other from $100 to $50.

You further state that your records do not disclose that any amendment has been filed in your office which would have the effect of increasing the original authorized capital stock of either of these corporations to the amounts which the books disclose, being the amounts which these corporations now desire to file amendments reducing the same by approximately fifty per cent.

You inquire as to the amount of tax you should charge these corporations upon filing the amendments to the charters under these circumstances.

C. S. 1131 provides the method by which corporations may amend their charters. After setting out in detail the manner in which charters many be amended by action of the board of directors and stockholders, you will find that a certificate of such proceedings "shall be signed by the president and secretary, under the corporate seal, acknowledged as in the case of deeds to real estate, and this certificate, together with the written consent, in person or by proxy, of said stockholder, shall be filed and recorded in the office of the Secretary of State. Upon such filing the Secretary of State shall issue a certified copy thereof, which shall be recorded in the office of the clerk of the Superior Court in the county in which the original certificate of incorporation is recorded, and thereupon the certificate of incorporation is amended accordingly . . ."

From the above, you will see that so far as your records are concerned, there has been no amendments to the charters of these corporations since they were originally organized. Even though the amendments in the instant case purport to be a reduction of the capital stock of these corporations, the actual effect of the amendments, so far as the records of your office disclose, is an increase from the original authorized capital stock to the amounts which, according to the wording of the amendments and no doubt the records of the corporations themselves, purports to be a reduction.

I advise, therefore, that the proper tax which you should charge for this amendment would be calculated under C. S. 1218 at the rate of forty cents for each thousand dollars of the difference between the original authorized capital stock and the figures to which the amendment purports to reduce the same, this figure being in excess of that originally authorized in the charters of these corporations.

SUBJECT: LAND GRANTS; CORRECTION OF CALLS IN GRANTS

26 February, 1942.

Since the error in the call in the grant to which you refer in your letter of February 25 was made in 1924 and the statute of limitations set out in C. S. 7587 and C. S. 7588 has run, I do not think that court proceedings authorized by these statutes could now be availed of, but that the only method by which these calls could be corrected would be by a special act of the General Assembly.

RE: LIABILITY FOR DOMESTICATION OF FOREIGN CORPORATIONS (1) SELLING AND INSTALLING WATER AND OIL TANKS AND (2) ENGAGED IN CONSTRUCTION WORK FOR THE UNITED STATES GOVERNMENT

9 April, 1942.

You request my opinion concerning the liability of certain foreign corporations to domesticate in North Carolina under the provisions of Section 1181 of the Consolidated Statutes, as amended.

The situation about which you inquire and my opinion with regard to them are as follows:

(1) A foreign corporation fabricates outside of North Carolina large steel water and oil tanks and other steel plate structures and ships these structures knocked down and ready for assembly into North Carolina where they are assembled by crews of laborers sent by the corporation into North Carolina for the express purpose of installing the structures. The structures are so complicated in design that their installation requires the specialized skill and experience of the manufacturers. The crews sent in are supplemented to some extent by local labor.

I am of the opinion that this corporation is not rendered liable for domestication in North Carolina by the activity referred to. It is the general rule that a transaction of the type referred to retains the character of interstate commerce since the installation requires a skilled and expert knowledge which make the installation merely a necessary incident to the agreement for the purchase of the structure or equipment and such transaction was an interstate transaction. See York Mfg. Company v. Collie, 247 U. S. 19, and discussion and cases cited in Paragraph 7151, Prentice-Hall, State and Local Tax Service.

(2) A foreign corporation has entered into a cost-plus-a-fixed-fee contract with the United States Navy Department for the construction of a naval air station in Virginia. As a supplement to this original contract, the contractor undertook to erect a few igloos on Navy property in North Carolina and to perform this operation transported the necessary material and personnel from Virginia to the site of the work. The contractor contends that since this activity involves only work for the Federal Government on Federal-owned property, it is not liable for domestication. However, I am of the opinion that the mere fact that the work is being performed under a contract with the federal government, and upon property owned by the federal government, would not exempt the corporation from liability for domestication.

(3) From the correspondence which you enclose, it appears that the activity of the Chattanooga Boiler and Tank Company is substantially similar to that of the Chicago Bridge and Iron Company, and if this is so, domestication would not be required.

I return herewith the correspondence from Chicago Bridge and Iron Company, Virginia Engineering Company, Inc., and Taber, Chambliss and Swafford, and a copy of this opinion for your use.

OPINIONS TO STATE AUDITOR

SUBJECT: FIREMEN'S RELIEF FUND

17 October, 1940.

I have your letter of October 15, in which you ask my opinion as to the disposition of the appropriation of $1750 made by the Maintenance Appropriation Bill of 1939 to the Firemen's Relief Fund. You call attention to the fact that prior to 1925, C. S. 6057 provided that the appropriation for the Firemen's Relief should be paid one-fourth to the Treasurer of the N. C. State Volunteer Firemen's Association and three-fourths to the Treasurer of the N. C. Firemen's Association, but that this section was repealed by Chapter 275, subsection 10, Public Laws of 1925.

The Maintenance Appropriation Act, Chapter 185, Public Laws of 1939, provides, under the heading "State Aid and Obligations," for the following appropriation:

"7. Firemen's Relief."

No provision is made in the act directing to whom this appropriation is to be paid. Since the repeal of C. S. 6056 and 6057 by the General Assembly of 1925, the remaining sections, C. S. 6058 to and including 6062 found in Chapter 98, entitled "Firemen's Relief Fund," deal with a fund designated as "Firemen's Relief Fund" and refer to the money paid into the hands of the Treasurer of the N. C. Firemen's Association, and provide for the distribution of said fund for the relief of firemen, members of the Association, etc., who have been injured or rendered sick by disease contracted in the discharge of their duties as firemen, and to widows and children, etc., of firemen.

I note from the Budget for the current biennium submitted by the Advisory Budget Commission to the General Assembly of 1939, on page 503, under the title "Firemen's Relief Fund," and sub-head "Purposes and/or Objects," the following entries:

"For Annual Payment to the Following Organizations, Consolidated Statutes, Section 6057:

"1. North Carolina State Volunteer Firemen's Association, Recommended for 1939-41 .... $1,312

"2. North Carolina State Firemen's Association, Recommended for 1939-41 .... $ 438."

The legislative history of the appropriation found in the Budget might be resorted to for the purpose of clarifying the intention of the General Assembly in making the appropriation and definitely fixing the objects for which the appropriation was intended. In conference with you and Mr. Deyton, however, it was pointed out as obvious that a mistake was made in the Budget by reversing the appropriations, making the one intended for the North Carolina State Volunteer Firemen's Association, and *vice versa*. This conclusion is based upon the provision of C. S. 6057 and the manner in which these appropriations have heretofore been made, in keeping with the language of that section, which was repealed in 1925.

In view of this confusion and uncertainty, I am of the opinion that it would be desirable to withhold the current payment until the next General Assembly could be given an opportunity to clarify the law with reference to the appropriation and make more certain the ones to whom it should be paid. As the law is now written, there are omissions which make it necessary to resort to inferences to reach any conclusion, and these are clouded with the apparent error in the Budget provisions.

SUBJECT: E. L. HIGHT, PRISON CAMP SUPERVISOR; RIGHT OF WIDOW TO BE PAID BENEFITS UNDER CHAPTER 6, PUBLIC LAWS OF 1939

17 December, 1940.

I received your letter of December 16, with attached file, relating to the death of Captain E. L. Hight, Prison Camp Supervisor, and note that the Commissioners of the Law Enforcement Officers Benefit and Retirement Fund would wish my opinion as to whether or not the widow of Captain Hight is entitled to be paid benefits on account of his death.

I understand the only question submitted to me is whether or not Captain Hight was killed in line of duty within the meaning of the Act referred to. The Act provides in Section 3(i), in part, as follows:

> "The Board of Commissioners herein created shall have the power and authority to promulgate rules and regulations and to set up standards under and by which it may determine the eligibility of officers for the benefits under this Act, payable to peace officers who may be killed or become seriously incapacitated *while in the discharge of their duty* * * * such rules, regulations and standards shall include the amount of benefits to be paid to the recipient in case of incapacity to perform their duty, as well as the amount to be paid such officer's dependents in case such officer is killed *while in the discharge of his duty*, * * *."

The Act provides in Section 3(d) that the Board of Commissioners "shall have the power to make decisions on applications for compensation or retirement benefits, and its decision thereon shall be final and conclusive and not subject to review or reversal, except by the Board itself."

Under the Workmen's Compensation Law, it is very generally held that a workman injured by accident while going and returning to and from his place of employment is not entitled to compensation. This determination as to the workmen's compensation benefits is based upon the statute which requires that the accident to be compensable must arise out of and in the course of the employment.

Under the Act governing the distribution of the fund controlled by your Commissioners, the statute requires that the death or injury should occur while the officer is in the discharge of his duty. From the file which you submitted to me, it appears that Captain Hight was on twenty-four hour duty and subject to call at any time. The accident occurred while Captain Hight was going across the highway to his home, which was located a short distance from the prison camp. Mr. Oscar T. Pitts, Superintendent of Prisons, in his letter of November 23, attached to the file, states that on this occasion Captain Hight's intentions were to return to the camp immediately, that he still had on his holster with his pistol, which ordinarily if he were going off duty, he would have left in the locker at the camp.

I believe that this question is one which the Commissioners have the right to decide and cannot be determined as a matter of law. If in view of all the circumstances presented to them, they found that the death occurred while Captain Hight was in the discharge of his duty, his widow would be entitled to the death benefits fixed by the rules and regulations. On the other hand, if they should not so find, then such conclusion would not be reviewable. In other words, I think it is a case which is entirely in the hands of the Commissioners.

OPINIONS TO STATE TREASURER

SUBJECT: ISSUANCE OF 4% PERMANENT IMPROVEMENT AND REFUNDING BONDS; LEGALITY

28 August, 1940.

You request an opinion as to the legality of the issue of 4% Permanent Improvement and Refunding Bonds of the State of North Carolina, in the amount of $1,142,500, authorized by Chapter 102 of the Public Laws of the Regular Session, 1913.

I have examined this statute and advise that it authorizes and directs the State Treasurer to issue bonds of the State of North Carolina, payable forty years after the first day of July, 1913, to an amount not to exceed $1,142,500, and that such bonds shall bear an interest rate not in excess of 4% per annum, payable semi-annually on the first days of January and July of each year so long as any portion of the bonds shall remain unpaid.

The purpose of the issuance of said bonds is set out in the Act and according to the terms thereof is ". . . for the purpose of relieving the present deficit in the State Treasury, for furnishing, painting and heating the new State buildings, for rearranging and furnishing the Supreme Court building and for installing new equipment in the office of the State Treasurer, and for meeting the appropriations made for permanent improvements for the several State institutions . . ."

Following the above quoted portion of the Act is set out in detail the amounts which are required to be allocated for the various purposes set out in the Act from the proceeds of the sale of the bonds authorized thereby.

I have examined the House and Senate Journals of the Regular Session of the General Assembly of 1913 and find that the Act was passed by both the House and Senate in the manner prescribed by the laws and the Constitution of this State in such cases made and provided.

The records now on file in the office of the State Treasurer disclose that pursuant to the direction and authority contained in the above Act, the State Treasurer duly issued and sold $1,142,500 bonds of the State of North Carolina, dated July 1, 1913, maturing July 1, 1953, and consisting of eight hundred bonds of $1,000 each, numbered one to eight hundred, inclusive, and six hundred eighty-five bonds of $500 each, numbered one to six hundred eighty-five, inclusive, with interest coupons attached, and that the State Treasury received the full proceeds of said bonds.

From the above, I am of the opinion that the bonds referred to are valid and binding obligations of the State of North Carolina.

SUBJECT: GUARDIANSHIP; FATHER OF MINOR CHILD EXECUTING POWER OF ATTORNEY TO STATE TREASURER; TRANSFER OF BONDS

5 December, 1940.

In your letter of December 3 you inquire if the father of a minor child could execute a power of attorney as a natural guardian of such child to the State Treasurer, which would authorize the Treasurer to transfer bonds which are now registered in such minor child's name to another owner.

I do not think that the father of such child has such authority unless he is the duly appointed legal guardian of such child and has been given such authority by a proper court order authorizing him, as guardian, to invade his ward's estate, under the laws of the State in which he holds his letters of guardianship. The fact that the father is the natural guardian of such minor child would not, in my opinion, in itself, clothe him with the power to dispose of his ward's estate; certainly, he could not under the laws of this State.

SUBJECT: TEACHERS' AND STATE EMPLOYEES' RETIREMENT SYSTEM; EMPLOYEES' CONTRIBUTION; DEDUCTIONS FROM SALARIES OF MEMBERS AFTER SUCH MEMBERS REACH THE AGE OF SIXTY

27 June, 1941.

You inquire as to whether, under the Teachers' and State Employees' Retirement Act, deductions should be made from salaries of members of the System who have attained the age of sixty years.

In undertaking to answer this question, it is necessary to look first to the provisions of the Act itself in order to ascertain whether there is any language contained therein which would tend to settle the question.

In Subsection 1(a) of Section 8 of the Act the following language is found:

> "Each employer shall cause to be deducted from the salary of each member on each and every payroll of such employer for each and every payroll period four per centum of his earnable compensation."

There is no limitation as to age contained in the provision above referred to and the clear inference seems to be that deductions from the compensation of members will continue so long as membership in the System is retained, regardless of the age of such members.

Subsection 2 of Section 5 provides:

> "Upon retirement from service a member shall receive a service retirement allowance which shall consist of:
>
> (a) An annuity which shall be the acturial equivalent of his accumulated contributions at the time of his retirement, and
>
> (b) A pension equal to the annuity allowable at age of sixty years computed on the basis of contributions made prior to the attainment of age sixty; and
>
> (c) If he has a prior service certificate in full force and effect, an additional pension which shall be equal to the annuity which would have been provided at the age of sixty years by twice the contributions which he would have made during such prior service had the system been in operation and he contributed thereunder."

Considering the language used in this subsection, it clearly appears that the contribution of the employer stops when the member reaches the age of sixty, but as the service retirement allowance is based in part on an annuity, which is the actuarial equivalent of the accumulated contributions of the member,—not at the age of sixty, but at the time of retirement—, it is difficult to see any justification for saying that the member's contribution stops at the same time as that of the employer. Considerable argument could be advanced that the Legislature in setting up the Retirement System did not intend to engage in the insurance business, as such, and that the member's contribution should end at the same time as that of the employer.

Of course, the object of all interpretation and construction of statutes is to ascertain the meaning and intention of the Legislature. This meaning and intention must be sought first of all in the language of the statute itself, for it must be presumed that the means employed by the Legislature to express its will are adequate to the purpose and do express that will correctly. A statute must be interpreted literally if the language used is plain and free from ambiguity. This is true even though the court should be convinced that some other meaning was really intended by the law-making power and even though the literal interpretation should defeat the very purpose of the enactment. The explicit declaration of the Legislature is the law.

I am unable to find any language in the Retirement Act which, to my mind, would justify me in concluding that a member of the System should cease to contribute at age sixty if the member continues in service. I am, therefore, of the opinion that deductions should be made from salaries of members of the Retirement System so long as such members continue in active service.

SUBJECT: COURT COSTS; STATE TREASURER; DUTY OF COLLECTING

7 August, 1941.

You inquire of this office as to whose duty it is to collect the one dollar additional court cost provided for by Chapter 349 of the Public Laws of 1937, as amended by Chapter 6 of the Public Laws of 1939, as further amended by Chapter 157 of the Public Laws of 1941.

Section 9 of the Act, as amended, provides that "the local custodian of such costs shall monthly transmit such moneys to the State Treasurer with a statement of the case in which the same has been collected.

Since the statute provides that the money shall be transmitted to you as State Treasurer, it is my opinion that the responsibility of seeing that the money is properly collected and remitted to you rests in your office.

RE: ESCHEATS; FUNDS HELD BY TREASURER—
SIR WALTER RALEIGH MONUMENT

16 September, 1941.

I understand that you have on hand a sum of money, approximately $2100, which was paid over to you as dividends on a claim filed by you in the liquidation of the North Carolina Bank and Trust Company for funds which had been deposited in this bank by a voluntary association, which secured contributions for the purpose of erecting in Raleigh a monument to Sir Walter Raleigh. The funds, I understand, had originally been deposited in the Citizens National Bank of Raleigh, and upon consolidation, were transferred to the North Carolina Bank and Trust Company. The funds raised by this association apparently were insufficient to erect the monument, and were permitted to remain unused in the bank for many years prior to the liquidation. The organization raising the funds apparently became inactive. A claim was filed by you, as State Treasurer, for the funds, and they were paid over to you during and prior to 1934. I understand from you that you do not hold these funds as Treasurer under any statutory authority to receive them as such, but the receipt of the funds by you was a voluntary act upon your part.

Our statute, C. S. 5786, provides as follows:

> "OTHER UNCLAIMED PERSONALTY TO UNIVERSITY. Personal property of every kind, including dividends of corporations, or of joint-stock companies or associations, choses in action, and sums of money in the hands of any person, which shall not be recovered or claimed by the parties entitled thereto for five years after the same shall become due and payable, shall be deemed derelict property, and shall be paid to the University of North Carolina and held by it without liability for profit or interest until a just claim therefor shall be preferred by the parties entitled thereto; and if no such claim shall be preferred within ten years after such property or dividend shall be received by it, then the same shall be held by it absolutely."

I am of the opinion that the funds would come within the purview of this section and that you would be authorized by this section to pay them over to the University of North Carolina, to be held by it under the terms of the statute. If any claimant appears within ten years, the University would be required, under this statute, to pay them over to the claimant if the claim were legally sustained. I would suggest as an additional precaution on account of the unusual nature of the transaction that you could require an agreement from the University of North Carolina, stipulating that if a legal and just claim were presented for the funds at any time, without reference to the ten year period, they would be paid over to the claimant, but without interest on the funds. I am quite sure the University would be willing to make such an agreement.

SUBJECT: BONDS ISSUED BY THE STATE DURING CIVIL WAR; VALIDITY

14 November, 1941.

You submit to this office a bond issued by this State on the first day of March, 1862, bearing No. 3455, in the amount of $1,000, signed by Z. B. Vance, Governor of North Carolina at that time, wherein it appears that the State of North Carolina promises to pay to bearer the sum of $1,000 "in good and lawful money of the Confederate States at the office of the Treasurer of the State of North Carolina, in the City of Raleigh." This bond has been presented to you for redemption by one H. T. Tudor, of Bennington, Vermont.

This bond not being among those mentioned and contemplated in Chapter 98 of the Public Laws of 1879, the same being an Act to compromise, commute and settle the State debt, in my opinion you have no authority to redeem the same and I advise that the bond is of no value in the hands of any person.

Article I, Section 6, of the Constitution provides that "the State shall never assume or pay, or authorize the collection of any debt or obligation, express or implied, incurred in aid of insurrection or rebellion against the United States." You will see also that this section of the Constitution would prohibit the redemption of the bond presented here for consideration. Attention is also called to the fact that the face of the bond calls for payment in "lawful money of the Confederate States," and since Confederate States currency is no longer legal tender, in my opinion it would be impossible to fill the obligation of this bond, even in the absence of the constitutional provision above referred to and the 1879 Act compromising the State debt..

This bond was no doubt issued under authority of Ordinance No. 35, enacted on the 26th day of March, 1862. This Ordinance was passed at the Third Session of the General Assembly of North Carolina in 1862 and may be found in Laws of North Carolina 1862-1863. It is an amendment to "An Ordinance to Provide for the Assumption and Payment of the Confederate Tax" and provides for the funding of treasury notes authorized by the State Convention on the first day of December, 1861, and is without question an obligation within the meaning of Article I, Section 6, of the Constitution, which prohibits the payment of the same by this State.

OPINIONS TO STATE SUPERINTENDENT OF PUBLIC INSTRUCTION

SUBJECT: CONVEYANCE OF LAND; WINSTON-SALEM COLLEGE TO THE CITY OF WINSTON-SALEM

26 July, 1940.

You have sent me a letter to you dated July 22 from Mr. F. L. Atkins, President of the Winston-Salem Teachers College, with a deed conveying in the name of the State Board of Education to the City of Winston-Salem several tracts of land described in this deed. I understand you wish my approval as to the form of the deed.

Under Chapter 143, Public Laws of 1929, Michie's Code Sections 7524(a) to 7524(e), the deed should be made in the name of the State of North Carolina, signed in the name of the State by the Governor and attested by the Secretary of State. You will note that Section 5 of the Act, C. S. 7524(e), provides that it shall not be held or considered to apply to the State Board of Education in so far as it relates to authority to convey lands held by the State Board of Education, but when the State Board of Education shall have determined to convey any real property in accordance with the statutes now or hereafter applying to lands held by the State Board of Education, then the method of conveying same shall be as provided in this Act.

This is a bit confusing, but I am of the opinion that the conveyance should be executed in conformity with the Act. As a matter of precaution, the deed might be executed in the name of the State Board of Education and the State of North Carolina.

I would also suggest that the deed should contain recitals of the resolution of the State Board of Education authorizing the conveyance and the execution of the deed by the proper officials. The deed should recite that it is made in consideration of public benefits and should omit the acknowledgment of consideration of $1.00, as this would require the officers executing the deed to account for this consideration.

I have not, of course, attempted to check the descriptions.

The deed should omit any warranty of title. The State does not give a warranty deed and is not authorized to execute such a conveyance.

IN RE: SCHOOLS; CAPITAL OUTLAY; PER CAPITA DISTRIBUTION

8 August, 1940.

With your letter of July 29 you sent me a letter from Mr. C. W. Davis, Superintendent Roanoke Rapids Public Schools, requesting that I answer the questions submitted by Mr. Davis.

I am not entirely clear as to what questions Mr. Davis intended to ask, except he says "We should like to know whether or not the Capital Outlay Fund in all instances is distributed per capita by law."

The School Machinery Act of 1939 in Section 15(c) provides: "All county-wide capital outlay school funds shall be apportioned to county and city administrative units on the basis of budgets submitted by such units to the County Commissioners for the amounts and purposes approved by the Commissioners."

Therefore, Capital Outlay funds are not distributed on a per capita basis at all, but on the basis of need as approved by the Board of Commissioners.

If there are other questions which Mr. Davis intends to ask, I think it would be desirable to have them submitted through the attorney for his Board.

SUBJECT: SCHOOL FUNDS; CITY ADMINISTRATIVE UNIT—TRANSFER APPROPRIATION FOR CAPITAL OUTLAY TO BUILD ARMORY

14 August, 1940.

I have your letter of August 13 referring to the action of the Board of School Trustees of Roanoke Rapids City Administrative Unit with reference to the capital outlay item of $8,930 "for repairs to auditorium of the Roanoke Rapids High School building," as to which you ask the following questions:

1. "May the Board of Commissioners of Halifax County now apply the $8,930.00, which was approved for 'repairs to auditorium of the Roanoke Rapids High School building,' on the construction of an armory?"

In my opinion, the Board of Commissioners of Halifax County would not have a right to apply this appropriation for the construction of an armory. C. S. 1334(64) prohibits the transfer of any appropriation made by the appropriation resolution, except an appropriation for general county expenses, and no appropriation for general county expenses shall be transferred to any fund or any subdivision of the county, or *vice versa*. The capital outlay fund of the City Administrative Unit, approved by the County Board of Commissioners on the basis of need as provided by Section 15 of Chapter 358, Public Laws of 1939, the School Machinery Act, should not be diverted to any other purpose.

2. "If the $8,930.00 for the above mentioned repairs is duly made available to the Board of Trustees of the Roanoke Rapids School, may this Board properly release these funds to the Board of Commissioners, or to any other agency, to be used in construction of the aforesaid armory?"

It is my opinion that the Board of Trustees of the Roanoke Rapids School would have no authority to release these funds to the Board of County Commissioners, or to any other agency, to be used in the construction of an armory, but when funds are provided, they should be applied to the purposes designated in the budget approved by the Board of County Commissioners.

SUBJECT: DOUBLE OFFICE HOLDING; MEMBER COUNTY BOARD OF EDUCATION—MEMBER BOARD OF TRUSTEES OF SCHOOL DISTRICT

26 September, 1940.

Since a member of a county board of education is an office and a member of a board of trustees of a school district is also an office, I do not think that one person could serve in both these capacities at the same time without violating the provisions of Article XIV, Section 7, of the Constitution, which prohibits double office holding.

SUBJECT: SCHOOL LAW; FIRE INSURANCE

16 October, 1940.

The question raised by J. C. Colley in his letter to you of September 16 is whether the County Board of Education is responsible for the purchase of insurance on school buildings situated within city administrative units.

Section 9 of Chapter 358, Public Laws of 1939, provides that maintenance of plant and fixed charges are supplied by funds required by law to be placed to the credit of the public school funds of the county and derived from fines, forfeitures, penalties, dog taxes, and poll taxes, and from all other sources except State funds, provided that when necessity shall be shown and upon approval of the County Board of Education or the trustees of any city administrative unit, the State School Commission may approve the use of such funds in any administrative unit to supplement any object or item of the current expense budget.

C. S. 5596 provides that insurance is included under current expense as a fixed charge.

Section 15(c) provides that all county-wide current expense funds shall be apportioned to county and city administrative units and distributed monthly by the county treasurer to each unit located in said county on a per capita enrollment basis. County-wide expense funds shall include all funds for current expenses levied by the Board of County Commissioners in any county to cover items for current expense purposes, and including also all fines, forfeitures, penalties, dog taxes, and funds for vocational subjects.

Section 5 of Chapter 358, Public Laws of 1939, provides in part that in all city administrative units as now constituted, the trustees of said special charter districts included in said city administrative unit and their duly elected successors shall be retained as the governing body of such district and the title to all property of the said special charter district shall remain with such trustees or their duly chosen successors; and the title to all school property hereinafter acquired or constructed within the said city administrative unit shall be taken and held in the name of the trustees of said city administrative unit. It is also provided in this section that city administrative units as now constituted shall be dealt with by the State school authorities in all matters of school administration, in the same way and manner as are county administrative units. You will also find in this section that in cases where title to property has been vested in the trustees of a special charter district which has been abolished and has not been reorganized, title to such property shall be vested in the County Board of Education of the county embracing such special charter district.

From the above it follows that all property situated in city administrative units should be insured by a governing body of such administrative unit, and property situated outside of such unit should be provided for by the County Board of Education of the county in which such property is situated. Should there be other property situated in a city administrative unit which is actually owned by the County Board of Education but is being used by the city administrative unit in the administration of the school system therein, such property should be insured by the city administrative unit's trustees, in the name, however, of the County Board of Education.

SUBJECT: SCHOOLS; COMPULSORY ATTENDANCE—PAROCHIAL AND OTHER NON-STATE SCHOOLS—REPORTS OF ATTENDANCE

16 October, 1940.

In conference with me on yesterday, you handed me a letter to you from Mr. B. L. Smith, Superintendent of the Greensboro Public Schools, under date of October 9, asking whether there is any existing legislation or regulation whereby the superintendent in a given administrative unit can find out about the attendance of pupils in parochial schools to the end of enforcing the compulsory attendance laws.

C. S. 5758 provides, in substance that it is the duty of the State Board of Education to formulate such rules and regulations as are necessary for the proper enforcement of the compulsory attendance law. C. S. 5757 provides that all private schools receiving and instructing children of compulsory school age shall be required to keep such records of attendance and render such reports on the attendance of such children as are required of public schools; and attendance upon such schools, if the school or tutor refuses or neglects to keep such records or to render such reports, shall not be accepted in lieu of attendance upon the public schools of the district, etc.

I am not informed as to whether or not the Board of Education has adopted regulations appropriate to this end, but under the authority of the statute, the Board is given ample power to do so.

SUBJECT: SCHOOLS; TEXTBOOK ADOPTION; NUMBER OF BASAL PRIMERS AND READERS REQUIRED TO BE ADOPTED FOR THE FIRST, SECOND AND THIRD GRADES

7 December, 1940.

Receipt is acknowledged of your letter of December 5. Careful consideration has been given to the question presented by you.

C. S. 5730 provides, in part, as follows:

> "The State Board of Education is hereby *authorized* to adopt * * * textbooks and publications * * *. And six months before the expiration of the contracts now in force *shall* adopt for a period of five years from a multiple list submitted by the Textbook Commission, as hereinbefore provided, two basal primers for the first grade and two basal readers for each of the first three grades, and one basal book or series of books on all other subjects contained in the outline course of study for elementary grades where a basal book or books are recommended for use * * *."

Further provisions are made which are not pertinent here.

You inquire whether under this language it is mandatory that two basal primers and two basal readers for each of the first three grades be adopted, or whether the language found in the statute is directory and not mandatory.

Ordinarily, the word "shall," when used in a statute, is mandatory. It will always be presumed by the Court that the Legislature intended to use a word in its usual and natural meaning. If such meaning leads to absurdity or great inconvenience, or for some other reason is clearly contrary to the obvious intention of the Legislature, the courts might construe the word "shall" as directory or *vice versa.* Crawford, Statutory Construction, Paragraph 262.

In the case of Davis v. Board of Education, 186 N. C. 227, our Court was called upon to construe the use of the word "shall" in an act of the General Assembly, and held that it was mandatory and not directory, as used in the statute referred to. The general rule outlined above was said to be applicable. To the same effect is the case of Battle v. Rocky Mount, 156 N. C. 329.

In reading the whole statute, with a view of seeking the legislative intent, I have been unable to find in it anything that would support the view that the use of the word "shall" in the particular connection was intended to be directory rather than mandatory. You will observe that the Legislature, apparently conscious of the distinction to be made in the use of the words shall and may, later on in the same section used the word "may" in connection with the adoption of three basal books on the subject of North Carolina History and with reference to adoption of rules and regulations as to the use of the books, and with reference to the period of time for which the contract should be made.

The only language found in the section which would point towards a construction of a directory character is the word "authorize" in the first part of the section, with reference to the adoption by the State Board of Education.

Upon reading the entire law, it seems to me that the Legislature imposed a positive requirement by the use of the word shall as to the adoptions of the basal primers for the first grade and the readers for the first three grades. By the same token, I am of the opinion that we would not be permitted to have a multiple adoption of other books for which the State Board is authorized to adopt.

I regret to reach this conclusion, as you indicate that it would be, in your opinion, an advantage to the State if we could avoid multiple adoptions, as apparently is required by the statute. This can be cured only by legislative action, assuming the correctness of my view.

SUBJECT: SCHOOL LAW; FINES AND FORFEITURES; CONFISCATED LIQUOR

10 January, 1941.

This office has formerly held that proceeds from the sale of confiscated whiskey is a forfeiture, and, under the School Machinery Act, Section 9 of Chapter 358 of the Public Laws of 1939, should be paid out in the same way and manner and for the same objects as are funds derived from fines, forfeitures, penalties, dog taxes and poll taxes. This section of the School Machinery Act designates the expenditure of such funds under Maintenance of Plant and Fixed Charges.

In no event should the proceeds derived from the sale of such confiscated whiskey be paid into the general fund.

SUBJECT: SCHOOLS; CONVEYANCE OF COUNTY PROPERTY TO CITY ADMINISTRATIVE UNIT

14 January, 1941.

I have your letter of January 10, enclosing a letter from Mr. J. O. Bowman, Superintendent of Anson County Public Schools, in which the question is submitted as to whether or not the County Board of Education can convey to the Board of Trustees of the City Administrative Unit school property owned by the County Board of Education within the City Administrative Unit.

The only statutory authority for conveyance of school property of which I am informed is C. S. 5470(a), which authorizes the public sale of school property not required for school purposes. I find nothing in the School Machinery Act which authorizes a conveyance of the character referred to. I would suggest that if it is considered as a desirable thing to be done, the School Machinery Act should be amended at this Session of the General Assembly to authorize conveyance in such cases.

SUBJECT: SCHOOL LAW; COUNTY-WIDE CURRENT EXPENSE FUND; APPORTIONMENT

12 February, 1941.

You state that a good many counties and cities in this State receive gifts or donations from private sources, and, in addition to this, they also receive specific allotments from State and Federal funds for vocational subjects and for other purposes, and you inquire if these items are subject to per capita distribution under Section 15 of the School Machinery Act. The portion of the Act in question is as follows:

> "All county-wide current expense school funds shall be apportioned to county and city administrative units and distributed monthly by the county treasurer to each unit located in said county on a per capita enrollment basis. County-wide expense funds shall include all funds for current expenses levied by the Board of County Commissioners, in any county to cover items for Current Expense purposes, and including also all fines, forfeitures, penalties, poll and dog taxes and funds for vocational subjects."

I do not think that the above portion of Section 15 applies to funds received from the sources above referred to, but the per capita distribution within the meaning of this paragraph of Section 15 applies only to taxes which go into this fund, and, of course, fines, forfeitures, penalties, poll and dog taxes. I quite agree with you in your conclusion on this subject.

SUBJECT: SCHOOLS; TAXES; TAX SALES CERTIFICATES; APPLICATION OF SCHOOL TAXES AFTER TAX SALES HAVE BEEN MADE

17 February, 1941.

I have your letter of February 14, in which you advise that a question has arisen in several counties as to the rights of the schools in the distribution of the proceeds of land sales. By this, I understand you mean the right of the schools to receive the part of the tax levy included in certificates of sale of land for taxes.

You are certainly entirely correct in your statement, and taxes levied for school purposes cannot legally be paid into the general fund and should be applied only for the purpose for which they are levied. The schools are entitled to receive that part of the taxes included in the land sale certificate which was levied for school purposes. The fact that the sale has been made does not in any sense alter this situation. Of course, you will understand that in no event should there be paid over to the school fund any amount in excess of the approved budget. It sometimes happens that the money necessary to meet the budget for a current year is advanced from other funds held by the county or from borrowings. In such a case, the amount of the tax levy involved in land sales certificates could be held to reimburse such advances.

If I can be of any further service in this connection, please advise.

SUBJECT: SCHOOL MACHINERY ACT; APPOINTMENT OF SCHOOL COMMITTEES

13 March. 1941.

You inquire as to whether a board of education appointed in 1941 would have the authority to remove members of a district school committee who were appointed by the preceding board of education and whose terms had not expired.

Section 7 of the School Machinery Act of 1939 provides that at the first regular meeting during the month of April, 1939, or as soon thereafter as practicable, and biennially thereafter, the county boards of education shall elect and appoint school committees for each of the several districts in their counties, consisting of not less than three nor more than five persons for each school district, whose terms of office shall be for two years.

This section also contains a proviso that in units desiring the same, by action of the county board of education and subject to the approval of the State School Commission, one-third of the members may be selected for a term of one year, one-third of the members for a term of two years, and one-third of the members for a term of three years, and thereafter all members for a term of three years from the expiration of said terms.

Under the provisions of this section, if a county board of education prior to the appointment of the district school committees during the month of April, 1939, passed an order in accordance with the proviso above referred to, and this order was approved by the State School Commission, the one-third of the school committee appointed for three years would continue to hold office during their full term.

You will note that there would be some difficulty in applying the provisions contained in this section where a school committee consisted of five members, as it would be impossible to appoint one-third of a committee of five for a term of three years. It would seem to me that the only practical solution would be to appoint two members of the committee for a period of one year, two members for a period of two years, and one member for a period of three years, and thereafter all members for a term of three years from the expiration of said terms.

SUBJECT: LOTTERY, CONTESTS; PUBLICATION IN SCHOOL NEWSPAPERS

15 March, 1941.

I have examined the letter of Mr. Bault to you. Unless there is some element of chance connected with the awarding of the prizes referred to in Mr. Bault's letter, I do not think that a contest between the three newspapers published in the three high schools in his county would be a violation of the lottery laws; that is to say, if there is a contest between these three newspapers as to the best issue or article gotten out by them and a prize awarded for this, there would not, in my opinion, be any violation of the lottery laws of this State.

SUBJECT: SCHOOL LAW; BOARD OF EDUCATION; VACANCIES IN OFFICE

27 March, 1941.

Your letter of March 25 enclosing a letter from Honorable P. G. Gallop, Superintendent of Schools of Hyde County, raises two questions.

The first question is whether the present members of the Board of Education of Hyde County will remain in office until all the new members appointed by the General Assembly of 1941 qualify by taking the oath of office. It is stated in Mr. Gallop's letter that the entire membership of the Board of Education of Hyde County was changed by the 1941 General Assembly; that two of the three new members will qualify on April 7 by taking the oath of office, but that the third member will likely resign or fail to take the oath of office.

It is my opinion that if two of the new members appear on April 7 and qualify by taking the oath of office, these two members (being a majority of those appointed by the General Assembly of 1941) would constitute the Board of Education of Hyde County until the vacancy caused by the failure of the third member to qualify could be filled. It is also my opinion that the Board could, if the members see fit, organize and proceed with the transaction of business without waiting for the appointment of a third member to fill the vacancy.

The second question relates to filling the vacancy caused by the failure of the third member of the new Board to qualify by taking the oath of office.

Section 5416 of Michie's N. C. Code of 1931 provides that all vacancies in the membership of the Board of Education caused by death, resignation or otherwise shall be filled by the action of the County Executive Committee of the political party of the member causing such vacancy until the meeting of the next regular session of the General Assembly. This section further provides that all vacancies not filled by the County Executive Committee within thirty days from the occurrence of such vacancy shall be filled by appointment by the State Board of Education. Of course, the County Executive Committee would have no right to attempt to fill a vacancy until such vacancy clearly existed, and unless there is some action taken by the member of the new Board who has expressed an intention to resign or fail to qualify, the County Executive Committee could do nothing. If this member actually does not intend to serve as a member of the County Board of Education, it seems to me that he could submit his resignation in writing and that the County Executive Committee could proceed to fill the vacancy so that the member chosen to fill the vacancy could qualify on April 7 at the time the other two members qualify. If this is not done, there will be no vacancy until April 7, after which time, if this member fails to qualify, there would be automatically created a vacancy.

SUBJECT: SCHOOLS; ELECTION OF VOCATIONAL TEACHERS—NOTIFICATION

31 March, 1941.

Section 12 of the School Machinery Act of 1939, as amended in 1941, provides as follows: "It shall be the duty of such county superintendent or administrative head of a city administrative unit to notify *all* teachers and principals now or hereafter employed, by registered letter, of his or her rejection *prior to the close of the school term,* subject to the allotment of teachers made by the State School Commission."

In your letter of March 28, attaching a letter from Mr. G. B. Harris, Superintendent of Franklinton Public Schools, you ask if the above statute is applicable to vocational teachers. I note that you are of the opinion that it is applicable, subject to approval of the State Department of Vocational Education, as well as the allotment of teachers made by the State School Commission. I agree with you in the conclusion which you have reached.

The fact that vocational teachers are employed on a different basis from other teachers, their salaries being paid from State, Federal, and local funds, would not, in my opinion, do away with the requirement that they be notified of their rejection prior to the close of the school term in which they are employed. The fact that home economics and agricultural teachers are elected and serve for a period longer than the regular school term, I do not think would change the requirement of the statute above quoted.

As all vocational teachers are elected subject to the final approval of the State Department of Vocational Education, I am of the opinion that the action or inaction of the local authorities would be subject to the final approval of the State Department of Vocational Education.

Unfortunately, the statute, as amended, does not make this matter as clear as it should be. I therefore think that it would be very desirable for the State Department of Vocational Education to advise the local authorities prior to the expiration of the school term whether or not it will approve the rejection of a vocational teacher, the absence of which would be equivalent to a reelection under the present terms of the statute. I believe the State authorities should notify the local authorities whether or not they wish to approve the continuance of such a vocational teacher in the school for the next year. This would avoid questions which might otherwise arise under the statute.

SUBJECT: SCHOOL LAWS; NOTICE TO PRINCIPALS AND TEACHERS OF REJECTION

3 April, 1941.

You enclose a letter from Honorable W. L. Lathan, Superintendent of Swain County Public Schools, in which he inquires if it is necessary, under the law, for the County Board of Education to approve or reject election of principals and teachers prior to the close of the school term.

The General Assembly of 1941 amended Section 7 of the School Machinery Act of 1939 by providing that contracts of teachers and principals shall continue from year to year until said teachers or principals are notified as provided in Section 12 of the School Machinery Act of 1939, as amended. Section 12 of the School Machinery Act of 1939 was amended so as to eliminate notification of election. That portion of Section 12 relating to notification of principals and teachers now reads as follows:

> "It shall be the duty of such county superintendent or administrative head of a city administrative unit to notify all teachers and/or principals now or hereafter employed, by registered letter, of his or her rejection prior to the close of the school term subject to the allotment of teachers made by the State School Commission."

Thus, you will see that the law now requires notice to the principals or teachers only in case of rejection and no approval of the County Board of Education is required prior to the close of the school term.

SUBJECT: SCHOOLS; WORKMEN'S COMPENSATION INSURANCE FOR TEACHERS AND EMPLOYEES, PAID FROM LOCAL FUNDS

3 April, 1941.

You inquire as to whether local school units are required to carry insurance with commercial companies or whether they may act as self-insurers.

Section 22 of the School Machinery Act provides that county and city administrative units shall be liable for Workmen's Compensation for school employees whose salaries or wages are paid by such local units from local funds, and that such local units shall likewise be liable for Workmen's Compensation on school employees employed in connection with teaching vocational agriculture, home economics, trades and industrial vocational subjects, supported in part by State and Federal funds. This section further provides that local units are authorized and empowered to provide insurance to cover such compensation liability and to include the cost of such insurance in their annual budgets.

I know of no reason why local units should not, with the approval of the Industrial Commission, become self-insurers. The liability to the employees is definitely fixed by the School Machinery Act, but the method of providing for the payment of claims is a matter more or less in the discretion of the governing bodies in local units.

SUBJECT: SCHOOLS; SCHOOL COMMITTEES; LIABILITY IN CASE OF ACCIDENT TO PUPILS ASSIGNED TO DIRECT TRAFFIC

22 April, 1941.

The following question is presented by your letter of April 3, 1941:

> "Does a School Board have the authority to assign school age pupils to traffic duty on city streets, and in case of an accident to a pupil assigned to direct traffic or an accident to a pupil being directed by one assigned to such duty, would school officials face any personal responsibility or liability?"

I am not aware of any statute which gives school committees authority to assign pupils to traffic duty on city streets; and, in my opinion, they do not have such authority. The principal function of a school committee is the employment of teachers. It has no control over pupils except that which indirectly results from the choice of teachers.

In case of injury to a pupil assigned to direct traffic or to a pupil being directed by him, the members of the committee would not be liable in their *official* capacity. The committee, being an agency of the State, is not liable in tort. Benton v. Board of Education, 201 N. C. 653.

The general rule as to the *personal* liability of public officers for injuries caused by their official acts is that such liability will attach when the cause of action is based on failure to perform or the negligent performance of a *ministerial* duty, but when the duty is discretionary the officer's conduct must be corrupt and malicious if there is to be any liability.

Betts v. Jones, 203 N. C. 590;

Moffitt v. Davis, 205 N. C. 565.

These principles, however, would not be applicable if recovery for an injury to a pupil assigned to direct traffic were sought. Assigning pupils to direct traffic being unauthorized, the act of the committee would be neither ministerial or discretionary.

In Gurganious v. Simpson, 213 N. C. 613, a coroner was held personally liable for performing an unauthorized autopsy on a deceased person when there was no suspicion of foul play. In the opinion Justice Devin observed at page 616:

> "The general rule is that when an officer goes outside the scope of his duty he is not entitled to protection on account of his office, but is liable for his acts like any private individual."

If a pupil of reasonable maturity should voluntarily agree to direct traffic, his consent would probably preclude any recovery from school committeemen. However, if the school committeemen under color of their office should require a pupil to direct traffic or should exert strong pressure upon pupils to do so and an injury should result, it is possible that under the rule stated in the Gurganious Case they might be held liable.

SUBJECT: SCHOOL LAWS; PAYMENT OF EMPLOYER'S CONTRIBUTION TO TEACHERS' AND STATE EMPLOYEES' RETIREMENT SYSTEM

24 April, 1941.

Receipt is acknowledged of your letter of April 22, enclosing letter from Honorable W. A. Graham, Superintendent of Schools in Kinston.

It is not very clear from Mr. Graham's letter what question he wishes to raise. I assume that his question is whether the school authorities of the Kinston administrative unit would be authorized to pay the employer's contribution for teachers, whose salaries are paid from local funds, from funds realized from a tax levied as a result of an election held under the provisions of Section 14 of the School Machinery Act.

It is necessary under the provisions of Subsection (a) of Section 15 of the School Machinery Act that the request for funds to supplement State school funds be filed with the tax levying authorities in each county and city administrative unit on or before the 15th day of June of each year, and the tax levying authorities are authorized to approve or disapprove this supplemental budget in whole or in part. If approval is given, it must be submitted to the State School Commission, which has authority to approve or disapprove any object or item contained therein.

Paragraph (c) of Subsection (1) of Section 8 of the Retirement System Act authorizes, empowers and directs the tax levying authorities in each city or county administrative unit to provide the necessary funds for the payment of the employer's contribution for teachers who are paid from sources other than appropriations of the State of North Carolina.

As the purpose of the supplement voted under the provisions of the School Machinery Act is to supplement the funds received from the State, which includes the payment of teachers' salaries, I can see no reason why the employer's contribution for teachers paid from local funds should not be paid from taxes collected as a result of voting the supplement, provided the request for funds for this purpose has been approved by the tax levying authorities and by the State School Commission. This position is strengthened by the fact that the tax levying authorities are authorized, empowered and directed to provide funds for the payment of the employer's contribution. Of course, in no event could the total amount of funds requested for any year exceed the maximum rate voted at the election held on the question of voting a supplement.

SUBJECT: PER CAPITA DISTRIBUTION; COUNTY EXPENSE FUNDS INCLUDING RETIREMENT FUNDS

3 May, 1941.

I have your letter of May 2 adverting to the fact that under the law establishing the Teachers' and State Employees' Retirement Fund, Chapter 25 of the Public Laws of 1941, it may be necessary for a local tax to be levied for the payment of retirement costs for local employees. You inquire whether or not such items, when included in a local budget, are subject to per capita distribution as are other current expense funds.

Our School Machinery Act, Section 15, requires that "all county-wide current expense school funds shall be apportioned . . ." This requirement, I think, would include an item in the current expense budget for the purpose above mentioned.

SUBJECT: TEACHERS; CONTINUING CONTRACTS; NOTICE OF REJECTION; EFFECT OF FAILURE TO SEND

8 May, 1941.

I have your letter of May 5. The failure of a County Superintendent to notify a teacher of her rejection, by registered letter, before the end of the school term, as required by Section 12 of the School Machinery Act, read in connection with the provisions of Section 7 of the School Machinery Act, would continue the teacher's contract, notwithstanding that failure to give such notice was due to inadvertence on the part of the Superintendent.

The amendment of 1941 provides "that such contract shall continue from year to year until said teacher or principal is notified as provided in Section 12 of this Act * * *." Section 12 requires that the notice be given by the Superintendent by registered letter prior to the close of the school term.

SUBJECT: TEACHERS; REQUIREMENT AS TO PLACE OF RESIDENCE

22 May, 1941.

I received your letter of May 20 enclosing a letter from Mr. Hunter Huss, County Superintendent of Public Schools in Gaston County, in which he inquires as to the right of the school authorities to require teachers to live in the community in which they teach during the school term.

There is nothing in the school law, so far as I have been able to discover, which gives the school authorities the right to require the teachers to live in any particular place. The school authorities, however, do have a right to require that teachers in our schools shall at all times be in position to render the service as teachers which they are employed to perform. C. S. 5513 provides that the County Superintendent shall have authority to suspend any teachers who shall fail or who may be incompetent to give instruction in accordance with the directions of the Superintendent, or who shall wilfully refuse to cooperate in teachers meetings, provided the teacher may appear before the County Board of Education or the courts to review such action. Provisions are further made in C. S. 5534 for dismissal of teachers by a school committee when a teacher is guilty of misconduct or who may persistently be neglectful of the duties as a teacher.

The place of residence of a teacher may be involved in the capacity of a teacher to properly perform duties as a teacher, and if it is necessary to the proper performance of the duties as a teacher that the teacher shall reside in the community in which the school is operated, it is probable that the Superintendent or trustees of the school would have the right to make such requirement. This would depend upon the circumstances in a particular case and the reasonableness of the requirement in connection with the efficiency of the teacher in the school.

SUBJECT: SCHOOL LIBRARIES—NECESSARY EXPENSE

22 May, 1941.

I have your letter of May 20 enclosing a letter from Mr. A. S. Webb, Superintendent of Schools in Concord. In your letter you also enclosed a circular letter issued by you under date of July 14, 1939, copying the opinion rendered by me on July 13, 1939, holding that school libraries are for a necessary school purpose and taxes levied for the purpose of providing the funds therefor would not have to be sanctioned by a vote of the people, and that the appropriations therefor should be classified as capital outlay and not current expense. You inquire whether or not the Acts of the General Assembly of 1941 change or add to the opinion rendered on July 13, 1939.

I find no change in the School Machinery Act which would affect this matter. I think my opinion is strengthened by the enactment of Chapter 93 of the Public Laws of 1941, which provides an appropriation of $100,000 annually for promoting, aiding and equalizing the public library service in North Carolina. The preamble to this Act contains the following recitals:

> "WHEREAS, it is provided in the Constitution of the State that religion, morality and knowledge being necessary to good government and happiness of mankind, schools and means of education shall forever be encouraged, and that the people have the right

to the privilege of education, and it is the duty of the State to guard and maintain that right; and

"WHEREAS, the establishment and maintenance of public libraries is an integral part of the educational program of a great State."

These recitals constitute legislative recognition of the principle involved in my opinion to the effect that the establishment of libraries is an integral part of an educational program. I therefore see no reason to change in any respect the opinion which was heretofore rendered.

SUBJECT: TORTS; LIABILITIES OF LOCAL OFFICERS IN DAMAGES FOR INJURIES

23 May, 1941.

Our Supreme Court has held, in the case of Betts v. Jones, 203 N. C. 590, that a public officer is not ordinarily personally liable for the exercise of his official discretion in matters within the scope of his authority, but he may be personally liable if he acts in such matters corruptly or maliciously.

Under the facts outlined in your letter of May 21, I do not think that the County Board of Education could in any wise be either officially or personally liable, in the absence of gross negligence or maliciousness, in the employment of its personnel; certainly, the Board, either in its official capacity or individually, would not be liable in damages where the secretary of the board had an accident resulting in the injury or death of any person, even if the secretary was on official business of the board at such time.

SUBJECT: SCHOOL LAW; APPOINTMENT OF DISTRICT COMMITTEES

23 May, 1941.

You enclose a letter from Mr. R. B. Griffin, Superintendent, Person County Schools, in which Mr. Griffin raises the question as to the appointment of the school committee for the Roxboro School District.

From the information contained in Mr. Griffin's letter, it appears that prior to the year 1933 there existed what was known as the Roxboro Special Charter District, which was abolished by the School Machinery Act of 1933. I assume that what was formerly the Roxboro Special Charter District is now a part of the county administrative unit and was not converted into a city administrative unit. If this is true, I am of the opinion that the school committee for the Roxboro School District should, under the provisions of the School Machinery Act of 1939, be appointed by the county board of education of Person County. There is no authority, so far as I am able to ascertain, for the appointment of the school committee of a district which is a part of the county administrative unit by the governing body of a city or town. When the State took over the operation of the schools in 1933, all special charter districts were abolished in so far as the operation of the schools was concerned, and only retained their identity for the purpose of retiring the outstanding indebtedness of such special charter districts.

SUBJECT: TEACHERS' AND STATE EMPLOYEES' RETIREMENT SYSTEM OF NORTH CAROLINA—RAISING FUNDS FOR PARTICIPATION; CONTRIBUTIONS FROM LOCAL BOARDS; VOTE OF THE PEOPLE

23 June, 1941.

I have your letter of June 5 asking for an opinion relative to Section 8(c), Chapter 25, Public Laws of 1941. This section provides that City Boards of Education and County Boards of Education in every county and city which have employees whose salaries are supplemented by such local boards from funds other than the State appropriation shall pay to the State Retirement System "the same per centum of the salaries that the State of North Carolina pays * * *." Your inquiry is directed specifically to the proviso at the end of this section, which is as follows:

> "Provided, that for the purpose of enabling the County Boards of Education and the Boards of Trustees of City Administrative Units to make such payment, the tax levying authorities in each such city or county administrative unit are hereby authorized, empowered and directed to provide the necessary funds therefor."

Your question concerning this proviso is: "Can the City Council, the tax levying authorities of Charlotte, levy a special tax over and above the 25c levy, which has been approved by a vote of the people for the purpose of meeting the requirements of the State Retirement System?"

The Supreme Court of this State has never reversed its ruling that the expense of establishment and maintenance of schools is not a necessary expense within the meaning of Article VII, Section 7, of the Constitution. Graded School v. Broadhurst, 109 N. C. 228; Bear v. Commissioners, 124 N. C. 204; Smith v. School Trustees, 141 N. C. 143; Wharton v. Greensboro, 146 N. C. 356; Perry v. Commissioners, 148 N. C. 521; Ellis v. Trustees, 156 N. C. 10; Stephens v. Charlotte, 172 N. C. 564; Hill v. Lenoir County, 176 N. C. 572; Frazier v. Commissioners, 194 N. C. 49.

The Court has placed the expenditure for public schools, however, in a class by itself. It has held that such an expense, where the tax is levied for the support of and is necessary for a six months school term, which is required by another Article of the Constitution, Article IX, Section 3, does not require a vote of the people before the debt is incurred or the tax is levied. Collie v. Commissioners, 145 N. C. 170; Lacy v. Bank, 183 N. C. 373; Frazier v. Commissioners, 194 N. C. 49; Hall v. Commissioners, 194 N. C. 768. Brogden, J., states this conclusion as follows in Hall v. Commissioners, supra, at p. 771:

> "We therefore hold that the board of commissioners of any county in the State, upon compliance with the provisions of the County Finance Act, has authority and is empowered to issue bonds or notes of the county for the purpose of erecting and equipping schoolhouses, and purchasing land necessary for school purposes, and to levy taxes for the payment of said bonds or notes, with interest on the same, without submitting the question as to whether said bonds or notes shall be issued or said taxes levied, in the first instance, to the voters of the county, where such schoolhouses are required for the establishment or maintenance of the State system of public schools in accordance with the provisions of the Constitution."

In view of these decisions, I am of the opinion that our Court would be justified in holding that the levying of a special tax to provide the required contribution of local school boards, proportionate to the amount the salaries of school employees are supplemented and paid from local funds, for six months of the school term, would not have to be submitted to a vote of the qualified voters, if the Supreme Court should deem the salaries supplemented and paid from local funds reasonably essential and necessary to the State operated six months school term. Although the question has not been passed upon in this State, the authorities elsewhere are in accord in holding that contributions of governing boards to a retirement system, in order that their employees might participate and receive the benefits therefrom, are considered as part of the compensation of such employees. Cobbs v. Home Ins. Co., 18 Ala. App. 206, 91 So. 627; Whitehead v. Davie, 189 Cal. 715, 209 PAG. 1008; People v. Abbott, 274 Ill. 380, 113 N. E. 696; State v. Lane, 89 Neb. 149, 131 N. W. 196; 5 McQuillin on Municipal Corporations 95th Ed. Sec. 2422.

Hence, if the Supreme Court should decide that it was necessary for the support of the constitutionally required six months school term that the salaries of school employees and teachers be supplemented and paid from local funds for six months of the term, then it would follow that the supplementary tax to provide the employer's contribution to the State Retirement System would fall into the same category, and as such, would not require a vote of the people. However, it should be pointed out that this question has not yet been presented to the Supreme Court for consideration. It is also clear that any expenditure, in order to escape the requirement of an election on the question of pledging the faith of, or levying a tax by, a city or county therefor, must be reasonably *essential* and *necessary* for the operation of the public schools and the minimum constitutional term of six months in that particular district. Greensboro v. Guilford County School district, 209 N. C. 655.

The question of whether or not a tax to supplement or pay the salaries of, or to provide the necessary contributions to the State Retirement System for, teachers and school employees beyond the constitutionally required six months school term would have to be submitted to a vote of the qualified voters is more difficult of solution. The constitutional provision, Article IX, Section 3, on which the Supreme Court has relied in reaching the conclusion that a levy necessary for the support of a six months school term need not be submitted to a vote does not place a limit as to the maximum number of months public schools shall be maintained in the counties of the State. It states that: "Each county of the State shall be divided into a convenient number of districts, in which one or more public schools shall be maintained *at least six months in every year;*" (Emphasis added). This section leaves it within the discretionary power of the Legislature to fix terms in excess of that period. For this reason, the court might very well hold that a tax levy necessary for the support of a longer term than six months (now established by the Legislature at eight or nine months, as the case may be), would also not have to be submitted to a vote of the people. An intimation to this effect appears in the following language of Clarkson, J., in the case of Fuller v. Lockhart, 209 N. C. 61, at p. 68:

> "In Julian v. Ward, 198 N. C., 480 (482), it is said: 'Under these (N. C. Const., Art. Ix, secs. 1, 2, and 3) and other pertinent sections of the Constitution, it has been held in this jurisdiction that

these provisions are mandatory. It is the duty of the State to provide a general and uniform State system of public schools of at least six months (now eight months—Public Laws 1935, ch. 455) in every year wherein tuition shall be free of charge to all children of the State between the ages of six and twenty-one. It is a necessary expense and a vote of the people is not required to make effective these and other constitutional provisions in relation to the public school system of the State. Under the mandatory provision in relation to the public school system of the State, the financing of the public school system of the State is in the discretion of the General Assembly by appropriate legislation either by State appropriation or through the county acting as an administrative agency of the State. Lacy v. Bank, 183 N. C. 373; Lovelace v. Pratt, 187 N. C. 686; Frazier v. Commissioners, 194 N. C. 49; Hall v. Commissioners of Duplin, 194 N. C. 768; Elliott v. Board of Equalization, 203 N. C. 749."

Again, however, it should be pointed out that the court has been consistent in requiring that the levy must be reasonably essential and necessary for the support of the constitutionally required six months term. Julian v. Ward, 198 N. C. 480; Greensboro v. Guilford County, 209 N. C. 655; School District v. Alamance County, 211 N. C. 213, and cases there cited. In view of these cases, and the earlier decisions cited in the first part of this letter, holding that any expenditure for schools is not a necessary expense within the meaning of Article VII, Section 7, there is, of course, a probability that the Supreme Court might hold that a vote is required in this case. The determination of this question rests ultimately with that tribunal.

In the light of the authorities holding that a contribution from the governing body of the employing agency is part of the compensation of the employee, I believe that part of the levy which has already been approved by a vote to supplement and pay the salaries of teachers from local funds could be used for the purpose of contributions to the Retirement System for these employees, if necessary. I do not believe that such would be a variance from the purpose for which the levy was made.

SUBJECT: SCHOOL LAW; TEACHING BIBLE IN PUBLIC SCHOOLS

18 July, 1941.

I have your letter of June 18, enclosing a letter from Mr. G. R. Wheeler, wherein he inquires if the Sanford Graded School District, which has voted a supplementary tax for the purpose of providing a twelfth grade and a ninth month to the schools in that district, has the legal authority to employ and pay from the supplementary funds a part of all of the teacher's salary to teach Bible in the school.

The North Carolina statute does not contain any provisions dealing with the reading of the Bible or teaching thereof in the common schools of the State. The Constitution, Article I, Section 26, provides as follows:

> "26. Religious liberty.—All men have a natural and inalienable right to worship Almighty God according to the dictates of their own consciences, and no human authority should, in any case whatever, control or interfere with the rights of conscience."

There is no prohibition in the statute against teaching courses in Bible in the public schools of this State as an elective course, nor is there any statute which would have the effect of prohibiting the using of public money to defray the expense involved in teaching such a course, in the same way and manner as other courses in the public schools are taught. The only statute relating to compulsory courses which must be taught in our public schools is C. S. 5440. Here it will be seen that the Superintendent of Public Instruction is charged with the duty of preparing courses of study in spelling, reading, writing, grammar, language and composition, English, arithmetic, drawing, geography, histories of the State of North Carolina and the United States, Americanism; elements of agriculture, health, education, and the nature and effect of alcoholic drinks and narcotics, and fire prevention.

As stated above, these are the only compulsory courses required by law to be taught in our public schools. Other subjects may be taught as elective courses.

No doubt, it was because of the constitutional provision above quoted that courses in Bible were left out of the compulsory courses of study required by law. The language of the Constitution, with regard to freedom of religious worship, is very broad in its terms and if elective courses of study of the Bible are made a part of the curriculum of any of the public schools of this State, great care should be taken in the selection of such courses and in the manner in which the courses are taught, that there is no violation of this section of the Constitution.

From a practical standpoint, due to the great variety of religious beliefs and sects in this State, it seems to me that it would be very difficult to prescribe a curriculum which includes a course in the study of the Bible, to select one which would not in some instance infringe upon the inalienable right to worship Almighty God according to one's own dictates, or interfere in some manner, however small, with the rights of one's conscience in this regard.

SUBJECT: SCHOOL LAW; MODIFICATION OF BOUNDARY LINES OF CITY ADMINISTRATIVE UNITS

13 August, 1941.

In your letter of August 13, you inquire if the State School Commission has the right to make alterations and modifications in the boundary lines of city administrative units after said units have been set up by authority of law.

Under the 1933 School Law, Chapter 562 of the Public Laws of 1933, the State School Commission was authorized to establish county and city administrative units and proceeded to carry out this authority.

Upon the adoption of the permanent School Machinery Act, Chapter 358 of the Public Laws of 1939, you will find in Section 5 that "the State School Commission, in making provision for the operation of schools, shall classify each county as an administrative unit and shall, with the advice of the county board of education; make a careful study of the existing *district organization in each county administrative unit, and may modify such district organization* when deemed necessary for the economical administration of the State school system . . . ." You will further find in this section that city administrative units "as now constituted" shall be dealt with by the State school authorities in matters of school administration in the same way and manner as are county administrative units.

I do not think that the Legislature intended to give authority to the State School Commission to alter the boundary lines of either the county or city administrative units once they had been established. Of course, the district organizations within such units might be modified or altered in the discretion of the State School Commission, when such modification or alteration is deemed necessary for the economical administration and operation of the school system.

SUBJECT: SCHOOL BUILDINGS; AUTHORITY OF CITY ADMINISTRATIVE UNIT AS TO BUILDING CONTRACT

17 September, 1941.

I have your letter of September 15, enclosing letter to you from Mr. A. B. Gibson, Superintendent of Laurinburg City Schools. Mr. Gibson asks the question as to who will "administer" the funds which may be allocated from the bond issue recently voted in Scotland County for the building of a new school building in the East Laurinburg City Administrative Unit.

Chapter 353, Public Laws of 1937, amended Section 60 of Chapter 136, Public Laws of 1923, by adding thereto the following:

> "PROVIDED, HOWEVER, that in the building of all new schoolhouses and the repairing of all old schoolhouses which may be located in a special charter district (as such district is defined by subsection three of section three of Chapter one hundred thirty-six of the Public Laws of one thousand nine hundred and twenty-three), the building of such new schoolhouses and the repairing of such old schoolhouses shall be under the control and direction of and by contract with the board of education or the board of trustees having jurisdiction over said special charter district."

I believe this enactment answers the question which you have in mind. The statute uses the term "special charter district," which, in my opinion, is the equivalent and is intended to mean a city administrative unit comprising what was at one time, at least in part, and is for certain purposes, a special charter district.

SUBJECT: SCHOOL LAW; EMPLOYMENT OF TEACHERS; ALLOTMENTS

2 October, 1941.

In your letter of September 30, you state that one school district in Robeson County lost one teacher in the allotment provided by the State School Commission, but the County Superintendent of Schools failed to notify this teacher of her rejection in accordance with Section 12 of the School Machinery Act, and you inquire if this teacher would have a contract of employment to the extent that the County Board of Education would be required to place her in another district of the county for the ensuing school year; that is to say, the question is whether the limitation in the Machinery Act refers to districts or to the entire county-wide school organization.

Section 7 of the School Machinery Act is in part as follows:

"The principles of the district shall nominate and the district committee shall elect teachers for all the schools of the districts subject to the approval of the county superintendent of schools and the county board of education. The distribution of the teachers between the several schools of the district shall be subject to the approval of the county board of education."

Section 12 of the Act provides in part that:

"It shall be the duty of the county superintendent or administrative head of a city administrative unit to ratify all teachers and/or principals now or hereafter employed, by registered letter, of his or her rejection prior to the close of the school term, *subject to the allotment of teachers made by the State School Commission; . . .*"

Fom the language of the portions of the above quoted sections of the Machinery Act, it is my opinion that the distribution of teachers applies only to the districts of the county, and, the State School Commission having withdrawn the allotment from the district about which you inquire of this one teacher because she nor her school were no longer needed in that district, she would have no contract of employment for the ensuing school year, because the continuing contract is, under Section 12, "subject to the allotment of teachers made by the State School Commission."

SUBJECT: PRIVATE ELEMENTARY SCHOOLS; JURISDICTION AND RESPONSIBILITY OF COUNTY SUPERINTENDENT OF PUBLIC SCHOOLS

8 October, 1941.

You inquire as to what is the responsibility of the school authorities, including county superintendent of public instruction, as to the establishment and maintenance of private elementary schools.

I am able to find only three sections of the Annotated Code which refer to private schools,—Section 5440, which is as follows:

"5440. Subjects taught in the elementary schools.—The county board of education shall provide for the teaching of the following subjects in all elementary schools having seven grades or seven years: Spelling, reading, writing, grammar, language and composition, English, arithmetic, drawing, geography, the history and geography of North Carolina, history of the United States, elements of agriculture, health education, including the nature and effect of alcoholic drinks and narcotics, and fire prevention.

"It shall be the duty of the state superintendent of public instruction to prepare a course of study outlining these and other subjects that may be taught in the elementary schools, arranging the subjects by grades and classes, giving directions as to the best methods of teaching them, and including type lessons for the guidance of the teachers. The board of education shall require these subjects in both public and private schools to be taught in the English language, and any teacher or principal who shall refuse to conduct his recitations in the English language shall be guilty of a misdemeanor, and may be fined or imprisoned in the discretion of the court."

Section 5537, which is as follows:

"5537. Power to contract with private schools.—In any school district where there may be a private school regularly conducted for at least six months in the year, unless it is a sectarian or denominational school, the school committee with the approval of the county superintendent may contract with the teacher of such private school to give instruction to all pupils of the district between the ages of six and twenty-one years in the branches of learning taught in the public schools, as prescribed by law, without charge to pupils and free tuition. The amount paid such private school for each pupil in the public school branches, based on the average daily attendance, shall not exceed the regular tuition rates in such school for branches of study."

Section 5757, which is as follows:

"5757· Parent or guardian required to keep child in school; exceptions.—Every parent, guardian or other person in the state having charge or control of a child between the ages of seven and fourteen years shall cause such child to attend school continuously for a period equal to the time which the public school in the district in which the child resides shall be in session. The principal, superintendent, or teacher who is in charge of such school shall have the right to excuse the child from temporary attendance on account of sickness or distance of residence from the school, or other unavoidable cause which does not constitute truancy as defined by the state board of education. The term 'school' as used in this section is defined to embrace all public schools and such private schools as have tutors or teachers and curricula that are approved by the county superintendent of public instruction or the State Board of Education.

"All private schools receiving and instructing children of compulsory school age shall be required to keep such records of attendance and render such reports of the attendance of such children as are required of public schools; and attendance upon such schools, if the school or tutor refuses or neglects to keep such records or to render such reports, shall not be accepted in lieu of attendance upon the public school of the district, town or city which the child shall be entitled to attend: Provided, instruction in a private school or by private tutor shall not be regarded as meeting the requirements of the law unless the courses of instruction run concurrently with the term of the public school in the district and extend for at least as long a term."

Unless I have overlooked some pertinent statute, it would appear that the school authorities, including the county superintendents, would only have the jurisdiction authorized in the sections above referred to.

If you are aware of any other provisions in the law which would have any application, please advise me and I will give the matter further consideration.

SUBJECT: SCHOOL MACHINERY ACT; TEACHERS; NOTICE OF RESIGNATION.

14 October, 1941.

You inquire as to whether, in my opinion, a teacher under the provisions of the School Machinery Act of 1939, as amended, may resign during the school term on thirty days' notice without suffering the penalty prescribed in Section 12 of the School Machinery Act:

Section 7 of the School Machinery Act of 1939, as amended, provides that teachers' contracts shall continue from year to year until such teachers are notified as provided in Section 12 of the Act. Section 12 provides in part:

> "It shall be the duty of such county superintendent or administrative head of a city administrative unit to notify all teachers and/or principals now or hereafter employed, by registered letter, of his or her rejection prior to the close of the school term subject to the allotment of teachers made by the State School Commission: Provided, further, that principals and teachers desiring to resign must give not less than thirty days' notice prior to opening of school in which the teachers or principal is employed to the official head of the administrative unit in writing. Any principal or teacher violating this provision may be denied the right to further service in the public schools of the State for a period of one year unless the county board of education or the board of trustees of the administrative unit where this provision was violated waives this penalty by appropriate resolution."

It seems to me that the School Machinery Act as now written undertakes not only to protect teachers by providing for a continuation of their contracts from year to year until notified as required by the Act, but also to protect the units employing these teachers by requiring them to give the proper notice in case they intend to resign.

You will note that the section requiring the notice and prescribing the penalty for the failure to give the proper notice uses the word "must" when referring to the notice, but uses the word "may" when referring to the denial of the right to further service in the public schools of the State for a period of one year. It is my thought that a teacher undertaking to resign during a school term might be subject to the penalty prescribed in this section, but the penalty could be waived by appropriate resolution passed by the governing board of the employing unit, and even in event the governing board did not pass such resolution, it would not be mandatory on the school authorities to deny the teacher the right to teach in the public schools for a period of one year.

Of course, the safest course for a teacher to pursue is to comply with his or her contract unless something unforeseen occurs which would justify the governing board of the employing unit in releasing such teacher from his or her contract.

SUBJECT: SCHOOLS; AUTHORITY OF BOARD OF EDUCATION OF COUNTY TO DESIGNATE SCHOOLS FOR CHILDREN TO ATTEND

1 November, 1941.

In your letter of October 28 you raise the question as to the authority of the County Board of Education to designate the school in the county administrative unit which a child shall attend.

This office, in a letter to you dated June 12, 1940, supplementing a letter of May 31, 1940, answered this question in the following language:

> "I agree with the view expressed by you in conference on Monday that the County Board of Education has the right to designate the schools in the county administrative unit which shall be attended by children in the county administrative unit, subject to the right of the State School Commission, whenever it shall appear to be more economical for the efficient operation of the schools, to transfer children living in one administrative unit or district to another administrative unit or district, subject to the proviso that sufficient space is available in the buildings of such unit or district to which said children are transferred."

I think the above view is amply supported by the School Machinery Act of 1939, as amended, and the other statutes governing the operation of the Public School System in North Carolina.

SUBJECT: SCHOOL LAW; CONDUCT OF PUPILS; DISCIPLINE

6 November, 1941.

I have your letter of November 5, with which you enclosed a letter from Mr. J. E. Allen, Principal of the school at Minneapolis. Mr. Allen inquires as to the authority of a school principal to discipline students, particularly what jurisdiction such a school principal has over a pupil after school hours and off the premises of school property.

There is no question but that a school principal has authority to discipline school students while on the premises of the school, but, in my opinion, this jurisdiction and authority ends when such students are off the premises of school property. In the specific instances to which Mr. Allen refers, I would think that a school principal has authority to maintain discipline on a school bus transporting children to and from school, but when such students leave the bus and are on their way home, I would think that the parents of such children would be responsible for their good conduct.

SUBJECT: SCHOOLS; DISBURSEMENT OF STATE FUNDS

26 November, 1941.

You inquire as to whether it is necessary for the county accountant or county auditor to sign vouchers for the disbursement of State school funds.

Subsection 1 of Section 20 of the School Machinery Act of 1939, as amended, provides that State school funds shall be released only on warrants drawn on the State Treasurer, signed by the chairman and the secretary of the county board of education for county administrative units, and by the chairman and the secretary of the board of trustees for city administrative units, and countersigned by such officer as the county government laws may require. The County Fiscal Control Act provides for warrants on the county treasurer or county depository to be countersigned by the county accountant or county auditor, as the case may be. Section 19 of the School Machinery Act provides in detail for the disbursement of the State funds necessary to the operation of the eight months school term in the various county and city administrative units. Under the provisions of Section 19 the State School Commission, from a certified statement from the local authorities, certifies to the State Superintendent the amounts due and necessary to be paid, and the State Superintendent in turn draws a requisition on the State Auditor for this amount and same is placed to the credit of the local unit with the State Treasurer. The receipts and disbursements are audited by the State School Commission.

It is my opinion that under the above state of facts it is unnecessary for the county accountant or county auditor to countersign warrants drawn on the State Treasurer for the disbursement of State school funds.

SUBJECT: STATE INSTITUTIONS; LAUNDRIES DOING OUTSIDE WORK

17 December, 1941.

In your letter of December 16, you inquire if East Carolina Teachers College is permitted under the law to do laundry work for the soldier and marine camps located in eastern North Carolina, during the present emergency, provided this additional work does not interfere with the laundry work to be done for that institution.

Under the provisions of C. S. 5863, the East Carolina Teachers College is a corporation and by that name is authorized to sue and be sued, make contracts, acquire real and personal property by gift, purchase, or devise, and exercise such other rights and privileges incident to corporations of like character as are necessary for the proper administration of the College.

I know of no prohibition in the statute which would prohibit this institution from carrying on this business. Similar work is done by the University of North Carolina, both at Chapel Hill and here in Raleigh. No doubt these institutions are engaging in this business under their general corporate powers.

SUBJECT: COUNTY BOARD OF EDUCATION; VACANCIES IN OFFICE

13 January, 1942.

You state that on April 7, 1941, a member of the County Board of Education of Graham County resigned his office to take effect when accepted by the Chairman of the Board, and that on December 2, 1941, the resignation was accepted by the Chairman. Since that time the Democratic Executive Committee has held a meeting and reappointed this member to the Board of Education, and inquiry is made as to whether or not the proceedings for the reappointment of this member of the Board should be certified to you in order that this member may be legally reinstated.

Consolidated Statutes 5416 provides in part as follows:

> "All vacancies in the membership of the board of education in such counties by death, resignation, or otherwise shall be filled by the action of the county executive committee of the political party of the member causing such vacancy until the meeting of the next regular session of the General Assembly and then for the residue of the unexpired term by that body . . ."

Apparently, the statute has been followed in this case. I think that a certificate by the Secretary of the County Board of Education to you, to the effect that this member has been reappointed to fill the vacancy caused by his resignation, would be sufficient compliance with the statute.

SUBJECT: SCHOOL LAW; CONTRACT TRANSPORTATION OF SCHOOL CHILDREN

23 January, 1942.

In your letter of January 22, you refer to Section 28 of the School Machinery Act, which provides the conditions under which contract transportation may be provided for school children in the various schools of the State where school children are not transported by publicly-owned buses. This section of the Act provides that the tax levying authorities in the various counties shall provide additional funds from the capital outlay budget to pay their share of the additional cost of such transportation.

You inquire if the Board of Education may pay this additional fee from donations received from private sources for this purpose, and if, in the contract made by the Board of Education in such counties with the State School Commission for contract transportation, payment for this additional cost could be made from this source.

Should there be any private donation to meet the payments for this extra expense, I see no reason why the Board of Education could not legally execute a contract with the State School Commission and make payment for its part of the cost of this contract transportation from such sources.

SUBJECT: TEACHERS' AND STATE EMPLOYEES' RETIREMENT SYSTEM; EMPLOYMENT OF TEACHERS WHO HAVE REACHED THE AGE OF SIXTY-FIVE YEARS

19 February, 1942.

Receipt is acknowledged of your letter of February 16, enclosing letter from Hon. N. F. Steppe, Superintendent of Public Instruction of McDowell County.

The question you raise is whether, under the provisions of the Teachers' and State Employees' Retirement Act, the State Board of Education is authorized to issue a certificate to an applicant who has reached the age of sixty-five and has not heretofore been granted a teaching certificate by the State of North Carolina, and whether a board of education may legally employ such person if he is otherwise qualified?

There is nothing appearing in the Teachers' and State Employees' Retirement Act which would prohibit the State Board of Education from issuing a certificate to an applicant who has reached the age of sixty-five and has not heretofore been granted a certificate by the State of North Carolina, if such party is otherwise qualified. Likewise, there is no provision contained in the Act which would prohibit a county board of education from employing such an applicant for a teaching position.

Section 5 of the Teachers' and State Employees' Retirement Act provides that any member in service who has attained the age of sixty-five years shall be retired at the end of the year unless the employer requests such person to remain in the service and notice of this request is given in writing thirty days prior to the end of the year. This section further provides that any member in service who has attained the age of seventy years shall be retired forthwith, with the proviso that with the approval of his employer he may remain in the service until the end of the year following the date on which he attains the age of seventy years, and with the further proviso that with the approval of his employer and the Board of Trustees, any member who has attained, or shall attain, the age of seventy years may be continued in service for a period of two years following each such request.

Section 13 of the Retirement Act provides that no payment of benefits shall become effective or begin to accrue until the end of one year following the date the System is established, and that no compulsory retirement shall be made until one year after the establishment of the System. The System was established as of July 1, 1941 and, therefore, the compulsory retirement provision would not become effective until after July 1, 1942. After July 1, 1942, it will be necessary that employers strictly comply with the provisions of Section 5 of the Retirement Act where they desire to retain employees who have attained the age of sixty-five years.

SUBJECT: SCHOOL LAW; TEACHERAGES; DEDUCTIONS FROM SALARY FOR RENT

2 March, 1942.

I have your letter of February 23, enclosing a letter from Mr. Frank B. Aycock, Jr., Superintendent of Schools in Currituck County. Mr. Aycock inquires if the Board of Education has authority to make the payment of rent by teachers in a teacherage a condition of their employment prior to the time they sign a contract, regardless of whether or not such teacher lives at the teacherage during the school year.

There is no law which would require a teacher to live in a teacherage; neither is there any law which would authorize the Board of Education to deduct from a teacher's salary rent on quarters in a teacherage, regardless of whether or not such teacher elected to live at the teacherage during the school year. I seriously doubt if the courts would uphold any such deductions, especially in those cases where a teacher does not live at the teacherage.

It is possible that as a matter of policy in the interest of the schools, the County Board of Education might make it a condition of employment prior to the signing of a contract with a teacher that such teacher live either at a teacherage or at some place near enough to the school to enable such teacher to be in close contact with the school and its students and constituents. However, this is a matter which is perhaps more administrative than legal.

SUBJECT: TEXTBOOKS; BASAL—ELEMENTARY; REQUIREMENT FOR USE IN EXTRA GRADE

5 March, 1942.

I have your letter of March 4, in which you submit the following question:

> "Is there anything in the law relating to the adoption of textbooks, or in any other law with which you are familiar, which would prevent the use of supplementary books for general use in connection with the establishment of an additional grade in the public schools of the State as provided in Chapter 158, Public Laws of 1941?"

Chapter 158 of the Public Laws of 1941 provides for the extension of the public school system to embrace twelve grades in those school districts requesting the same "in accordance with such plans as may be promulgated by the State Superintendent of Public Instruction." There is nothing in the Act which attempts to determine whether or not the additional grade will be considered as a part of the elementary school or the high school. It would, therefore, seem that under the authority granted to the State Superintendent to promulgate plans for such additional grade, the plans might provide for classification of the extra grade or year as a part of the high school term rather than the elementary school term, pending such time as the twelfth grade system becomes permanently established as a part of the school system; or the State Superintendent might, if he saw fit, make a plan contemplating that the extra grade would be an extension of the elementary school, as I understand probably will actually be done when the system is established generally throughout the State, as it is more logically a part of the elementary school.

This feature is mentioned, as our law deals separately with the requirements of textbooks to be used in the elementary schools and in the high schools.

C. S. 5730, dealing with the subject of textbooks for the elementary grades, provides that the State Board of Education is authorized to adopt "for the exclusive use in the public elementary schools * * * textbooks and publications, including instructional materials, to meet the needs of such schools in each grade and on each subject matter in which instruction is required to be given by law." This section further provides that the State Board of Education shall adopt basal books from the multiple list submitted by the Textbook Commission as provided in the law.

C. S. 5734 provides as follows: "The State Board of Education is hereby authorized to select and adopt all supplementary books and instructional material necessary to complete the courses of study for all schools. *Such supplementary books shall neither displace nor be used to the exclusion of basal books.*"

The underscored portion of the section above quoted would prohibit the use of supplementary books to displace the basal books required by law to be used in the elementary schools. It was apparently the intent of the General Assembly that there should be an adoption of a basal book for each subject to be taught in the elementary schools and that no supplementary book should be permitted to be used except, as the term implies, to complement the course of study based upon the books adopted for that purpose.

C. S. 5749(a) authorizes the State Board of Education to adopt textbooks for use in all the public high schools of the State. C. S. 5749(d) provides that it shall be the duty of the State Board of Education to select one book in each field of instruction for exclusive use in the public high schools of the State. C. S. 5749(g) provides that the textbooks for high school instruction adopted under the provisions of this law shall be for the exclusive use of the high schools of the State.

C. S. 5734 above referred to, which authorizes the State Board of Education to adopt all supplementary books and instructional material necessary to complete the course of study of all schools, expressly provides that such adoptions shall not displace or be used to the exclusion of the basal books.

It, therefore, seems to me that whether or not the extra term shall be considered as a part of the elementary or high school term, the law contemplates that the books to be used shall be basal books, plus such supplementary books as may be found necessary to enrich or amplify the course of study built around the basal books.

I have examined the provisions of Chapter 158 of the Public Laws of 1941, and in it I find nothing which would justify us in disregarding the law with reference to the adoption and use of basal and supplementary textbooks in our schools in view of your suggestion that the expansion of the school system to include twelve grades will be on an experimental basis, making it unwise to make adoptions of basal books for exclusive use in the additional grade. The statute authorizes the operation of a school system embracing twelve grades "in accordance with such plans as may be promulgated by the State Superintendent of Public Instruction," but this language, in my opinion, is not broad enough to justify you in failing to follow the provisions of the statute with regard to the use of basal or supplementary textbooks. It may be unfortunate that the Act did not allow some latitude in prescribing the books to be used in the courses of study fixed by you for the extra grade.

SUBJECT: SCHOOLS; TITLE TO PROPERTY; CITY ADMINISTRATIVE UNITS; COUNTY BOARD OF EDUCATION

25 March, 1942.

Receipt is acknowledged of your letter of March 23, enclosing letter from Superintendent J. N. Hauss of Thomasville, North Carolina, in which the question is raised as to the title of the property of city administrative units acquired prior to the enactment of the School Machinery Act of 1939. It is stated in the letter from Superintendent Hauss that there are two buildings in the Thomasville city administrative unit which were erected by the County in 1936, and that the title to this property still remains in the County Board of Education. It is further stated that the insurance policies on these buildings were taken out in the name of the County Board of Education and that certain damage was recently done to one of these buildings by fire, and you desire to know whether the trustees of the city administrative unit have the authority to adjust the damages with the insurance company.

Section 5 of the School Machinery Act of 1939, as amended, provides that the title to all school property acquired or constructed after the enactment of the School Machinery Act of 1939 within a city administrative unit shall be taken and held in the name of the trustees of the city administrative unit, and that in all city administrative units as constituted at the time of the enactment of the statute above referred to the trustees of the special charter district included in city administrative units and their duly elected successors are to be retained as the governing body of the district, and that the title to all property of said special charter district is to remain with the trustees or their duly chosen successors. This section further provides that the boards of county commissioners of the various counties shall provide funds for the erection or repair of necessary school buildings on property the title to which is held by these boards of trustees.

In the case about which you inquire, the title to the property was in the County Board of Education on or prior to the year 1936, and I am unable to find anything in the School Machinery Act or elsewhere which would authorize a conveyance of this property by the Board of Education of the County to the trustees of your city administrative unit. As it is the duty of the County to furnish the funds to erect and repair the school buildings in the city administrative unit, and as the property is insured in the name of the County Board of Education, it is my opinion that it would be necessary to secure the consent of the County authorities before any adjustment could be made as to the loss or damage by fire. It is my opinion that the title to the property would remain in the County Board of Education unless and until the General Assembly of North Carolina sees fit to change the law so as to authorize a conveyance to the board of trustees of the city administrative unit.

SUBJECT: SCHOOLS; TEACHERS; REJECTION; NOTICE

31 March, 1942.

Receipt is acknowledged of your letter of March 30, enclosing letter from Honorable T. T. Murphy, Superintendent of Schools, Pender County, in which he raises the question as to the method to be used in rejecting and notifying teachers who are not to be employed during the next school year.

Section 7 of the School Machinery Act of 1939, as amended, provides that contracts of teachers shall continue from year to year until said teachers are notified as provided in Section 12 of the Act, as amended. Section 12 of the School Machinery Act, as amended, provides that it is the duty of the county superintendent or administrative head of a city administrative unit to notify all teachers now or hereafter employed by registered letter of his or her rejection prior to the close of the school term, subject to the allotment of teachers made by the State School Commission. This office, in a letter to Honorable Worth McKinney of Asheville, North Carolina, dated April 25, 1941, in construing the method to be used in rejecting teachers and notifying the teachers of such rejection, said:

> "As to a teacher or principal who was heretofore employed and who was serving under contract during the current year, it is my opinion that such teacher or principal has a continuing contract and that the contract can be terminated only by action of the District Committee in rejecting the teacher or principal. If the local or District Committee rejects the teacher or principal, the County or City Superintendent should be notified by the local or District Committee in order that the Superintendent may comply with the statute and give timely notice to the teacher or principal rejected."

This seems to answer Mr. Murphy's question as to the method to be used in disposing of teachers who are not to be retained during the next school year.

SUBJECT: SCHOOL LAW; COMPETITIVE BIDDING; PUBLIC CONSTRUCTION CONTRACTS

2 April, 1942.

You state in your letter of March 31 that it is becoming more and more difficult to get bona fide competitive bids on school construction work and that it is almost impossible to obtain priorities on certain materials except in emergency situations. You desire to know whether, in my opinion, the replacement of burned buildings and much of your other construction work during this period of emergency cannot be classed work involving the health and safety of the people and thereby come within the exception contained in Section 7534(o) (1) of Michie's N. C. Code of 1939, Annotated.

The section above referred to requires competitive bids after advertisement for at least one week before the time specified for opening of the proposals in a newspaper having circulation in the State of North Carolina. This rule applies except in cases of special emergency involving the health and safety of the people or their property.

An emergency is a condition of things appearing suddenly or unexpectedly,—that is, it is an unforeseen occurrence. Mere necessity for quick action does not always constitute an emergency. In the case of United States v. Southern Pacific Company, 209 Fed. 562 (565), the Court defines the word "emergency" as a sudden or unexpected happening, an unforeseen occurrence or condition. In the case of United States v. Atlantic Coast Line Co. 224 Fed. 160 (166), the Court, defining the word "emergency," said:

> "We find that the English word 'emergency' is derived from the Latin 'emergo', to arise out of, as something which arises suddenly out of the current of events."

The term "emergency" as it relates to exemption of emergency contracts from the requirement of competitive bidding implies sudden or unexpected necessity requiring speedy action.

In the case of Safford v. City of Lowell, 151 N. E. 111 (113), the Court, in discussing a statute practically identical with the one under consideration. said:

> "It would be to misuse language to describe the condition which existed April 15 as 'a special emergency involving the health or safety of the people or their property'. Without attempting an exact or all-inclusive definition, it is manifest that that language does not apply to a condition which may clearly be foreseen in abundant time to take remedial action before serious damage to the health or to the safety of person or property is likely to occur. Without doubt, lack of foresight and failure to take proper precaution to meet contingencies which any prudent person would anticipate might occasion a condition which would jeopardize public health and safety, and to which the words of the statute would be applicable. It would be remarkable, however, if the legislators used them to describe such a situation. It is not to be supposed that they intended to make it possible for municipal officers to avoid advertising for bids for public work by merely delaying to take action to meet conditions which they can foresee until danger to public health and safety has become so great that the slight further delay caused by advertising will entail public calamity. No such imminent danger of calamity existed here.
>
> "In so far as it was question of fact, the master's finding must stand. As matter of law no special emergency within the language of the statute confronted the defendants on April 15, 1925. See Merrill v. Lowell, 128 N. E. 862, 236 Mass. 463, 466."

It is said in the case of Los Angeles Dredging Co. v. City of Long Beach, 291 Pac. 839, that to state what constitutes an emergency is not an easy task. The term depends greatly upon the special circumstances of each case and the authorities are not very helpful in the present inquiry.

You can readily see from what has been said above that it is almost impossible to lay down a rule which would apply in all cases which might be thought to come within the purview of the exception hereinbefore referred to. It seems, rather, that it would depend upon the facts and circumstances appearing in each case. In a matter of this kind, where the statute provides that a certain procedure is to be followed in letting contracts and the statute also contains an exception, the one who claims the benefit of the exception in the statute has the burden of showing that he comes within the exception. Moore v. Lambeth, 207 N. C. 23 (26).

The case of Moore v. Lambeth also holds that where public funds are wrongfully, wilfully and knowingly disbursed by municipal officers without adequate consideration moving to the municipality and with intent to evade the law, those responsible for such illegal withdrawal of said funds may be required to make good the loss to the public treasury.

You can readily see that there is a possibility of personal liability on the part of public officials who let contracts without first complying with the provisions of the statute above referred to, unless the contract is one which would clearly come within the exception, with the burden being on the public officials to show that the contract was one which could be justified under the exemption. I have very grave doubts as to whether there is any great amount of construction work done in connection with the school program in which the school authorities would be justified in claiming the exemption in Section 7534(o) (1). The cases in which it seems to me the Court would most likely uphold the action of public officials in claiming the benefit of the exception would be where school equipment or other facilities are suddenly destroyed by fire, or otherwise.

However, I would not recommend that the officials let contracts without first complying with the statute as to advertisement except in cases in which it clearly appears that the health and safety of the people are involved. The advertising period required by the statute is so short that in my opinion public officials should comply with the statute except in extreme emergencies, about which there can be no question. There is no question as to the diffculty which public officials are now encountering in the attempt to secure the necessary materials for the construction of buildings, etc., but this within itself would not bring contracts within the exception set out in the statute.

After officials have complied with the provisions of the statute and are then unable to secure reasonable bids, they would be justified in proceeding with the work, provided the same could be done for an amount less than the lowest bid offered in response to the advertisement for bids.

SUBJECT: SCHOOL LAW; APPOINTMENT OF COMMITTEES; TERM OF OFFICE; INCREASE IN MEMBERSHIP; CALL OF MEETINGS

23 April, 1942.

Receipt is acknowledged of your letter, enclosing letter from Honorable A. H. Hatsell, Superintendent of Onslow County Schools, in which he raises the question as to whether a county board of education may increase the membership on a local school committee during the biennium, and whether the principal, who had been elected by a majority of the original committee, could be deprived of his position by a vote taken by the enlarged committee.

Section 7 of the School Machinery Act of 1939, as amended, provides that at the first regular meeting during the month of April, 1939, or as soon thereafter as practicable, and *biennially thereafter*, the county boards of education shall elect and appoint school committees for each of the several districts in their counties, consisting of not less than three nor more than five persons for each school district, whose term of office shall be for two years.

It is my opinion that if a board of education appointed a school committee for a certain school district, consisting of three persons, at the time required by the School Machinery Act, the membership of the school committee could not be increased from three to five until the end of the biennium. The only changes provided for in the statute during the biennium are as to appointments to fill vacancies in case of death or resignation of a member or members of the committee. An individual member of the county board of education would have no authority to take action, even in case of filling a vacancy, unless authorized by action of the committee.

Section 7 of the School Machinery Act also provides that the district committee shall elect the principals of the schools of the district, subject to the approval of the county superintendent of schools and the county board of education. If the district committee had elected a principal by a majority vote of the committee of three, and his election had been approved by the county superintendent of schools and the county board of education, the district committee would have no authority to take any further action, and the person elected would be entitled to the position of principal of the school. However, if the principal who was elected had not been approved by the county superintendent of schools and the county board of education, the original committee of three could have rescinded its election of the principal and have elected some other person.

It occurs to me that the duty of calling a meeting of the committee rests primarily with the chairman. However, it is my thought that a meeting called by any duly qualified and acting member of the committee, where notice was served on all the members constituting the committee, would be held to be a legal meeting. A person who is not a member of the committee or who was placed on the committee without authority of law would, in my opinion, have no right to call a meeting.

SUBJECT: SCHOOL LAW; NOTIFICATION OF REJECTION OF TEACHERS; TIME OF

9 June, 1942.

Receipt is acknowledged of your letter of June 6, enclosing letter from Honorable J. Shepard Bryan, Attorney at Law of Dunn, North Carolina, in which he inquires whether a registered letter placed in the mail on the afternoon of the last day of the school term, notifying a teacher of his or her rejection, will be sufficient compliance with the provision of Section 12 of the School Machinery Act of 1939, as amended.

Section 12 of the School Machinery Act of 1939, as amended, provides in part:

> "It shall be the duty of such county superintendent or administrative head of a city administrative unit to notify all teachers and/or principals now or hereafter employed, by registered letter, of his or her rejection prior to the close of the school term subject to the allotment of teachers made by the State School Commission."

To my mind, this provision means that notification by registered letter of a teacher's rejection must be placed in the mail prior to the close of the school term. It is, therefore, my opinion that if the county superintendent or head of the city administrative unit places a registered letter in the mail on the last day of the school term, notifying the teacher of his or her rejection, it would be a sufficient compliance with the provisions of the School Machinery Act relating to notification of teachers of their rejection.

SUBJECT: SCHOOLS; TEACHERS; CONTRACTS; NOTICE OF REJECTION; TEACHERS' AND STATE EMPLOYEES' RETIREMENT ACT; RETIREMENT OF MEMBERS WHO HAVE ATTAINED THE AGE OF SIXTY-FIVE YEARS

22 June, 1942.

In your letter of June 15, you enclose letter from Mr. J. W. Paisley of Winston-Salem, North Carolina, which raises the question as to whether a teacher who is now sixty-six years of age would have a continuing contract under the provisions of the School Machinery Act unless notified of rejection prior to the close of the school term, or whether such teacher would be automatically retired and his or her contract terminated under the provisions of the Teachers' and State Employees' Retirement Act.

Section 7 of the School Machinery Act of 1939, as amended, provides that all principals and teachers shall enter into a written contract upon forms to be furnished by the State Superintendent of Public Instruction and that such contract shall continue from year to year until said teacher or principal is notified as provided in section 12 of the Act, as amended.

Section 12 provides that it shall be the duty of the county superintendent or administrative head of a city administrative unit to notify all teachers and/or principals now or hereafter employed by registered letter of his or her rejection prior to the close of the school term, subject to the allotment of teachers made by the State School Commission.

It appears from these sections that a teacher's contract continues from year to year unless such teacher is notified by registered mail of his or her rejection prior to the close of the school term provided such teacher within ten days after the close of school notifies the superintendent of schools of the administrative unit in which he or she is employed of the acceptance of employment for the following year. All these provisions are subject to the allotment of teachers made by the State School Commission.

A teacher who is sixty-six years of age would be on the same basis as any other teacher unless, under the provisions of the Teachers' and State Employees' Retirement Act, such teacher would have been automatically retired at the close of the last school term. Section 5(1) (b) of the Teachers' and State Employees' Retirement Act provides:

> "Any member in service who has attained the age of sixty-five years shall be retired at the end of the year unless the employer requests such person to remain in the service, and notice of this request is given in writing thirty days prior to the end of the year."

Section 2 of the Act provides that the Retirement System shall be established as of July 1, 1941. Section 13 provides that no payment of benefits shall become effective or begin to accrue until the end of one year following the date the System is established, and that no compulsory retirement shall be made during such period.

Thus, the automatic retirement provisions applying to members who have attained the age of sixty-five years and who are less than seventy would not become operative until after July 1, 1942, and would not affect contracts of teachers who are over sixty-five years of age and less than seventy until the end of the school term beginning in 1942 and ending in 1943. The provisions of the Retirement Act as to the retirement of members over sixty-five years of age are automatic and have the effect, when they become operative, of terminating the contract of employment unless some affirmative action is taken by the employer.

There is nothing in the Retirement Act which prohibits local school authorities from rejecting a teacher under the provisions of the School Machinery Act, but such local school authorities are not authorized to use provisions of the Retirement Act which have not yet become effective as a basis for rejecting teachers they do not desire to continue in their employment.

OPINIONS TO COMMISSIONER OF REVENUE

RE: INHERITANCE TAXES; FAMILY SETTLEMENT; PROPERTY PASSING BY AS BASIS OF TAX; ESTATE OF ERNEST A. OGLE, BUNCOMBE COUNTY, FILE #11-772

5 July, 1940.

As requested in your letter of July 2, I have reviewed the file in this matter, including the brief of Mr. Kester Walton of the Law Firm of Harkins, Van Winkle and Walton, and am of the opinion that Mr. Walton is correct in his contention that the inheritance tax should be based upon the property transferred by the family settlement entered into by the heirs and next of kin of the decedent rather than upon the transfers that, but for the settlement, would have passed under the intestate laws of this State.

Mr. Walton's brief sets forth the facts and fully details the situation out of which the settlement arose, his statement of facts being verified by his oath and the oath of the widow and administratrix of the decedent. It is conceded that the statement fully and correctly sets forth the substance of all the facts bearing upon the question.

The settlement does not involve a mere transfer for convenience of the property of the estate so that the North Carolina heir should take the North Carolina property and the other heirs the Tennessee property. There was very substantial doubt and uncertainty as to what the rights of the heirs were as between themselves, and real and bona fide disputes and contentions between them with respect to their interests both under the North Carolina law and the law of Tennessee.

Under these circumstances, I am clearly of the opinion that Section 1 of the Revenue Act of 1939 requires the tax to be based upon the transfers effected by the family settlement. See my opinion given to you on June 17, 1939.

SUBJECT: INHERITANCE TAX; DEDUCTIONS FOR TAXES UNDER SECTION 7 OF THE REVENUE ACT

17 July, 1940.

A change in our law found in Section 1401 of the Machinery Act of 1939, makes it necessary to reconsider the opinion which was expressed to Commissioner Maxwell in a letter from this office under date of July 26, 1937.

Section 1401 provides that the lien of taxes levied on property and polls, listed pursuant to the Act, shall attach to real estate as of the day as of which property is listed, regardless of the time at which liability for the tax may arise or the amount thereof be determined.

This change in our statute was referred to by the Supreme Court in the case of Lumber Co. v. Graham County, 214 N. C. 167, in which the Court disapproved the decision in State v. Fibre Co., 204 N. C. 295, and, in this connection said:

> "The tax on property is a visitational tax, and is the taking of a part of the taxpayer's wealth, represented by the property he owns, for the needs of Government. Under our present statute it is taken as a percentage of the ascertained value 'according to ownership', as of the day of the visitation—1 April. It is not an excise tax for the privilege of owning property for the period of the fiscal year, or any other period.
>
> "Logically, therefore, the liability for the tax arises on the day the lien attaches to the property, and on the day the taxpayer is found to be in ownership thereof 1 April—and we so hold. The purpose and effect of the statute above quoted was to reinstate the law in this respect as it existed prior to S. v. Fibre Co., supra, here considered."

Under Section 302 of the Machinery Act of 1939, all property real and personal shall be listed, or listed and assessed, as the case may be, in accordance with ownership and value as of the first day of April, 1939, and thereafter all property shall be listed, or listed and assessed, in accordance with ownership and value as of the first day of January of each year.

Our Revenue Act of 1939, in Section 7, provides in part as follows:

> "In determining the clear market value of property taxed under this article, or schedule, the following deductions, and no others, shall be allowed:
>
> "(a) Taxes that have become due and payable and the pro rata part of taxes accrued for the fiscal year that have not become due and payable."

Considering these sections of the law, together with the decision of our Court in the Graham County case, it is my opinion that the proper construction of our law is that a deduction for ad valorem taxes should be allowed for a decedent who dies in the year 1939 on or after the first day of April, one-twelfth of the amount of taxes for each month up to October first, and, after October first, the full amount of taxes.

To illustrate what I mean, I will say that if decedent died in the month of April in the year 1939, one-twelfth of the amount of the taxes should be allowed; if the decedent died in the month of May, two-twelfths of the amount of taxes should be allowed as the deduction; if the decedent died after the first day of October, 1939, the full amount of taxes should be allowed as a deduction. If the decedent died on or after the first day of January, 1940, and any subsequent year, a similar amount of deduction should be allowed for each month after the first day of January, which is the listing date for that year and thereafter. To illustrate this, I would explain that if the decedent died in the month of January, one-twelfth of the amount of taxes should be allowed as a deduction; if the death occurred in the month of February, two-twelfths; if the death occurred on or after the first day of October, the full amount of taxes should be allowed.

RE: INCOME TAXES; INCLUDING IN GROSS INCOME OF TAXPAYER THE INCOME FROM STOCKS HELD UNDER A REVOCABLE TRUST PREVIOUSLY CREATED BY HIM AND OTHERS

22 July, 1940.

I reply to your letter of July 9 relating to the 1936 and 1937 income tax liability of Mr. Charles D. Owen, Jr., Biltmore, N. C.

The question presented is whether there should be included in Mr. Owen's gross income for these years the dividends from certain stocks received by trustees under a revocable trust.

It appears from a copy of the trust indenture that in 1932 Mr. Owen's father transferred 600 shares of the stock of the Dalton Investment Company, a Delaware Corporation, to "Charles D. Owen, Jr., Stephen C. Owen and Mary C. Owen, as joint tenants and not as tenants in common, with right of survivorship," and 200 shares of said stock to "Charles D. Owen, Jr., and Stephen C. Owen, as joint tenants and not as tenants in common, with the right of survivorship." On July 31, 1936, Charles D. Owen, Jr., Stephen C. Owen and Mary C. Owen transferred and assigned these 800 shares to themselves in trust to hold and receive the dividends therefrom, with full powers of management and sale. The trust was to continue for 15 years after the death of Mrs. Alice E. Owen, the settlors' mother, unless sooner revoked. During the period in which all of the settlors should be living, one-half of the net income of the trust was to be paid to the mother of the settlors, though it was provided that in their discretion they might pay her the entire income, any of the income not paid to her to be divided between the settlors in proportion to their contribution to the corpus of the trust.

The trust indenture is a very elaborate document of twenty legal size pages and makes detailed provisions for numerous contingencies that might occur after the death of any of the settlors, the trust to end, in any event, 21 years after certain lives in being. It reserves to the settlors a full joint power of written revocation during their joint lives, but if any one or more of the settlors should die, the power to revoke extended only to the shares or contributions of the survivor or survivors of the settlors. All of the settlors were living on December 28, 1937, and on that day they duly revoked the indenture by a written instrument under seal.

The question is whether, during the period from July 31, 1936, to December 28, 1937, Charles D. Owen, Jr., is liable for an income tax on all of the income received by said trustees from his original 3/8ths of the 800 shares of said stock or whether he is liable for an income tax only upon that part of such income actually received by him under the provisions of the trust. The settlors were brothers and sister. Before the execution of the indenture, they owned 600 of the shares as joint tenants with right of suvivorship, and two of them similarly owned the remaining 200 shares. The indenture reserved to them substantially the same power and control over the stock which they would have had had it not been executed. The power of revocation gave them full and effectual command and control over both the corpus and the income.

The taxpayer was required to pay to the United States an income tax upon 3/8ths of the entire income. He suggests that this was because of the provisions of Section 166 and 167 of the Federal Revenue Act of 1936, taxing to settlor the income from a revocable trust, and contends that inasmuch as there were no similar provisions in our Revenue Acts of 1935 and 1937, therefore, he is liable for a tax only upon the income actually received by him.

In a prior letter of October 15, 1937, the taxpayer cites and relies upon the opinion of Seth T. Cole, Deputy N. Y. Tax Commissioner, Prentice-

Hall's State and Local Tax Service, New York, Paragraph No. 57,300, upholding his contention. This opinion was rendered April 5, 1927, and was based upon the then Federal Law.

Section 317(1) of the Revenue Acts of 1935 and 1937 define "gross income" as follows:

> "The words 'gross income' mean the income of a taxpayer derived from salaries, wages, or compensation for personal service, of whatever kind and in whatever form paid, or from professions, vocations, trades, business, commerce or sales, or dealings in property, whether real or personal, located in this or any other State or any other place, growing out of the ownership or use of or interest in such property, also from interest, rent, dividends, securities, or the transactions of any business carried on for gain or profit, or gains or profits, and income derived from any source whatever and in whatever form paid."

The same definition, word for word, was set forth in Section 22(a) of the Federal Revenue Act of 1934. Its effect upon the taxability of the settlor of a revocable trust was considered by the United States Supreme Court on February 26, 1940, in Helvering v. Clifford, 60 S. Ct. 554, and in holding him liable for an income tax upon the trust income the court said:

> " . . . The broad sweep of this language indicates the purpose of Congress to use the full measure of its taxing power within those definable categories. . . . Hence our construction of the statute should be consonant with that purpose. Technical considerations, niceties of the law of trusts or conveyances, or the legal paraphernalia which inventive genius may construct as a refuge from surtaxes should not obscure the basic issue. That issue is whether the grantor after the trust has been established may still be treated, under this statutory scheme, as the owner of the corpus. . . . And where the grantor is the trustee and the beneficiaries are members of his family group, special scrutiny of the arrangement is necessary lest what is in reality but one economic unit be multiplied into two or more by devices which, though valid under state law, are not conclusive so far as Section 22(a) is concerned.
>
> "In this case we cannot conclude as a matter of law that respondent ceased to be the owner of the corpus after the trust was created. Rather, the short duration of the trust, the fact that the wife was the beneficiary, and the retention of control over the corpus by respondent all lead irresistibly to the conclusion that respondent continued to be the owner for purposes of paragraph 22(a).
>
> "So far as his dominion and control were concerned it seems clear that the trust did not effect any substantial change. In substance his control over the corpus was in all essential respects the same after the trust was created, as before. The wide powers which he retained included for all practical purposes most of the control which he as an individual would have. There were, we may assume, exceptions, such as his desirability to make a gift of the corpus to others during the term of the trust and to make loans to himself. But this dilution in his control would seem to be insignificant and immaterial, since control over investment remained. If it be said that such control is the type of dominion exercised by any trustees, the answer is simple. We have at best a temporary reallocation of income within an intimate family group. . . . It is hard to imagine that respondent felt himself the poorer after this trust had been executed or, if he did, that it had any rational foundation in fact. For as a result of the terms of the trust and the intimacy of the familial relationship respondent retained the substance of

> full enjoyment of all the rights which previously he had in the property. . . .
>
> "The bundle of rights which he retained was so substantial that respondent cannot be heard to complain that he is the 'victim of despotic power when for the purpose of taxation he is treated as owner altogether.' . . .
>
> "We should add that liability under paragraph 22(a) is not foreclosed by reason of the fact that Congress made specific provision in paragraph 166, 26 U. S. C. A. paragraph 166, for revocable trusts, . . . Rather, on this evidence it must be assumed that the choice was between a generalized treatment under paragraph 22(a) or specific treatment under a separate provision (such as was accorded revocable trusts under paragraph 166); not between taxing or not taxing grantors of short term trusts. In view of the broad and sweeping language of paragraph 22(a) a specific provision covering short term trusts might well do no more than to carve out of paragraph 22(a) a defined group of cases to which a rule of thumb would be applied. The failure of Congress to adopt any such rule of thumb for that type of trust must be taken to do no more than to leave to the triers of fact the initial determination of whether or not on the facts of each case the grantor remains the owner for purposes of paragraph 22(a). . . ."

Much has been written in recent years on the effect of such revocable trusts upon the settlor's income tax liability, for the trust device has been widely used in an attempt to avoid taxes. See Magill, Taxable Income, Ch. 8, Section III, Revocable Trusts, p. 274; 7 Law and Contemporary Problems, Duke University Law School, "The Problem of Personal Income Tax Avoidance," p. 243; 4 Paul and Mertens, Law of Federal Income Taxation, Section 34.144, et seq; "The Income Tax on Short Term and Revocable Trusts," 53 Harvard Law Review, p. 1322 (June, 1940).

The foregoing authorities discuss the subject fully and cite many decisions showing that even prior to Helvering v. Clifford it was settled that the provisions of Sections 166 and 167 of the Federal Act were merely declaratory of existing law, particularly Section 22(a). For example, in O'Donnell v. Commissioner, (CCA 9), 64 Fed. (2d) 634, 12 A.F.T.R. 435, certiorari denied 290 U. S. 699, Judge Wilbur, formerly Secretary of the Interior, said:

> "We think that as the income received by the trustee was at all times under the control of petitioner by reason of his power of revocation, the petitioner is liable for the tax thereon."

And in McCauley v. Commissioner, (CCA 5) 44 F. (2d) 919, 9 A.F.T.R. 462, the court said:

> "We are of opinion that petitioners, by reserving to themselves the power to sell the minerals and to revoke their agreement at will, failed to accomplish their purpose. . . . An owner of property is liable for the income which the property earns, and the tax cannot be escaped by anticipatory arrangement or contract."

These and the other cases referred to related to tax years before 1924, the year when what is now Section 166 was enacted and when only Section 22(a) affected the liability.

Because the special statute (Sec. 166) is merely declaratory, as aforesaid, cases arising under or authorities dealing with it are pertinent to the question here dealt with.

Magill says at page 276 of his "Taxable Income":

> "Although the possibility of reducing taxes through the use of trusts for the benefit of one's self or one's family afforded the general underlying reason for the enactment of all of these provisions, the further legal justification of the respective clauses rests upon distinctive grounds. The revocable trust provisions are mainly based upon the proposition that an individual may realize income in the legal sense by virtue of his control over the property producing the income, even though he actually receives no money during the year. The taxation to a settlor of the income of a trust which, in his discretion, may be distributed to him or accumulated for future distribution to him, rests upon a similar basis."

In dealing with a revocable trust case in Corliss v. Bowers, 281 U. S. 376, the court said through Judge Holmes:

> "But taxation is not so much concerned with the refinements of title as it is with actual command over the property taxed—the actual benefit for which the tax is paid. If a man directed his bank to pay over income as received to a servant or friend, until further orders, no one would doubt that he could be taxed upon the amounts so paid. It is answered that in that case he would have a title, whereas here he did not. But from the point of view of taxation there would be no difference. The title would merely mean a right to stop the payment before it took place. The same right existed here although it is not called a title but is called a power. The acquisition by the wife of the income became complete only when the plaintiff failed to exercise the power that he reserved. . . . The income that is subject to a man's unfettered command and that he is free to enjoy at his own option may be taxed to him as his income, whether he sees fit to enjoy it or not."

This decision was followed in Reinecke v. Smith, 289 U. S. 172, and the court said:

> "A settlor who at every moment retains the power to repossess the corpus and enjoy the income has such a measure of control as justifies the imposition of the tax upon him. . . . As declared by the Committee reporting the Section in question, a revocable trust amounts, in its practical aspects, to no more than assignment of income. This court has repeatedly said that such an assignment, where the assignor continued to own the corpus, does not immunize him from taxation upon the income. . . . A contrary decision would make evasion of the tax a simple matter. There being no legally significant distinction between the trustee and a stranger to the trust as joint holder with the grantor of a power to revoke, if the contention of the respondents were accepted, it would be easy to select a friend or relative as co-holder of such a power and so place large amounts of principal and income accruing therefrom beyond the reach of taxation upon the grantor, while he retained to all intents and purposes control of both."

The fact that the power to revoke here involved required the unanimous consent of all of the settlors, does not, under the circumstances here presented, change the fact that the control reserved gave them such command over the property as to make each of them liable for the income from their original shares of the stock. See Reinecke v. Smith, supra; N. H. Boynton, 11 B. T. A. 1352; Cleveland Trust Co., Executor, 24 B. T. A. 132, 140.

In Bowler v. Helvering, (CCA 2), 80 F. (2d) 103, 16 A.F.T.R. 1383, the power of revocation was lodged in a committee of three who were neither trustees or beneficiaries and of whom the settlor was not one, the trust indenture providing that no exercise of the power would be valid unless consented to in writing by the settlor. The case involved the years 1926 through 1929 and arose prior to the amendment of 1932 in which Congress provided that the income should be taxable to the settlor if the power to revoke was held by any person, other than the settlor, "not having a substantial adverse interest." In holding the settlor liable upon the trust income, the court said with respect to the argument that his veto power gave him no substantial command or control:

> "'We cannot see that this makes any difference save in form. All donees of a joint power must concur in its exercise; the refusal of any one is an effective veto. It is true that in form any change in the limitations of the trusts at bar had to originate with the committee; at least, we may assume that they are first to decide and then submit their decision to the settlor for his approval, while in the case of a joint power any of the donees may suggest an exercise of the power to the others. But such a difference is of no practical moment whatever; if the settlor wishes to modify any of these trusts, he need only persuade two of the committee to his mind, exactly as he would have had to do if he had been a member. Nothing prevents his taking the affirmative; his power is as much and as little as it was in Reinecke vs. Smith, supra, except that here he has two persons to convince, while there he had only one. The constitutional apology for the doctrine is that unless the income is regarded as the settlor's, it will always be easy for him to induce complaisant trustees to qualify and practically to control the income, resuming it when he chooses. That reasoning applies equally well to these trusts."

The power to amend and revoke in John H. Fulham, 40 B. T. A. 48, was lodged in a Committee of three, no one of whom was settlor, trustee or beneficiary. After the Congressional Amendment of 1932, the Committee amended the indenture to provide that the power to revoke could not be validly exercised during the life of the settlor's wife without her written consent. While the decision that the settlor was liable on the trust income rested in part on the fact that any payment of income to the wife was discretionary with the trustees, he being one of them, the remark of the Board that "one who may legally refuse the request of another is not subject to an adverse interest" would seem equally applicable to a case where there is a right to revoke. The decision was affirmed by the First Circuit Court of Appeals on April 10, 1940, Magruder, J., saying:

> "The evident policy of the Revenue Act is to tax the income of grantor of a trust when he retains the substantial mastery over the corpus. Even though in form he lodges the power in someone other than himself, Section 166 is founded on the reasonable premise that the grantor still retains substantial mastery when the power is given to someone having no stake in the trust, or a stake so insubstantial that the holder of the power would not improbably be amenable to the grantor's wishes. This calls for a realistic appraisal."

Morton v. Commissioner, 4 P. H., 1940 Fed. T. S., Paragraph No. 62,368, decided by the Seventh Circuit Court of Appeals on January 9, 1940, dealt in part with a case where the power to revoke was lodged in the corporate trustee and a like result was reached.

If the owner of property is to insulate himself from liability for a tax upon the income it produces, his surrender of ownership, command and control over it must be substantial, real and bona fide. Impermanent, indefinite, revocable transfers of property and its fruits, leaving him with substantial incidents of ownership, also leave him with its tax burdens. While this is not new doctrine, recent commentators and recent decisions of the courts have emphasized it to a degree and with a frequency not previously observed, and particularly with regard to efforts to give up enough control over property to avoid income taxes upon its fruits and yet not part with its substantial ownership. For example, Paragraph No. 3127, P. H. 1940, Federal Tax Service, states:

> "Although, as pointed out at Paragraphs 3001-3101, there are many methods of saving taxes which are both sound and practicable, it is becoming increasingly evident that there is one type of plan which holds very little hope of success. This involves transactions whereby the taxpayer transfers property for the purpose of obtaining a tax benefit, but does not give up control thereof . . . Decisions of the courts are becoming more and more strict, not only in interpreting the statutes, but also in cases not covered by express statutory provisions. The most recent decision, Morton vs. Commissioner, (62,368, C. C. A. 7) agrees with the Commissioner and the Board of Tax Appeals that when a trust may be terminated at any time by the trustee, the income thereof is taxable to the grantor under Section 166. . . . While it perhaps cannot be stated categorically that all sales to controlled corporations, trustees, or to relatives, will hereafter be disregarded by the courts, nevertheless, the recent decisions add substantially to the ammunition with which the Bureau may attack such transfers, and taxpayers who are unwilling to fight a long battle in the courts may do well to eliminate such sales from their lists of tax saving methods, not only when the sales result in losses, but also where they are part of a plan to shift the taxable gain to the purchaser."

The recent cases are discussed in "The Problem of Personal Income Tax Avoidance," 7 Law and Contemporary Problems, p. 243, Spring 1940. It is pertinent, I think, to refer briefly to the "intimations" of these decisions, to use a word taken from the opinion in the Morton Case.

Lucas v. Earl, 281 U. S., 111, decided in 1930, was one of the earliest of these decisions and gives the first indication of judicial hostility to "anticipatory arrangements and contracts however skillfully devised . . . by which the fruits are attributed to a different tree from that on which they grew."

The next is Corliss v. Bowers, 281 U. S. 376, discussed above, where Justice Holmes laid it down that where a man has command over property, as by a power to revoke a trust, its income "may be taxed to him as his income, whether he sees fit to enjoy it or not."

In Gregory v. Helvering, 293 U. S. 465, the entire Court, speaking through Justice Sutherland, took the position that "mere devices . . . nothing more than a contrivance . . . an elaborate and devious form of masquerading" would be disregarded, and that the courts would not "exalt artifice over reality" in cases affecting the public revenue, at least where the contrivance has no "business" use or purpose.

Griffiths v. Helvering, 308 U. S. 355, was another unanimous opinion where the court turned its face against "technically elegant arrangements whereby an intricate outward appearance is given to the simple" and said:

> "We cannot too often reiterate that 'taxation is not so much concerned with the refinements of title as it is with actual command over the property taxed—the actual benefit for which tax is

paid'. Corliss vs. Bowers, 281 U. S., 376, 378, 50 S. Ct. 336, 74 L. Ed. 916. And it makes no difference that such 'command' may be exercised through specific retention of legal title or the creation of a new equitable but controlled interest, or the maintenance of effective benefit through the interposition of a subservient agency. Cf. Gregory vs. Helvering, 293 U. S. 465, 55 S. Ct. 266, 79 L. Ed. 596, 97 A. L. R. 1355. 'A given result at the end of a straight path', this Court said in Minnesota Tea Co. vs. Helvering, 302 U. S. 609, 613, 58 S. Ct. 393, 395, 82 L. Ed. 474, 'is not made a different result because reached by following a devious path'. . . . Taxes cannot be escaped by 'anticipatory arrangements and contracts however skilfully devised . . . by which the fruits are attributed to a different tree from that on which they grew'. Lucas vs. Earl, 281 U. S. 111, 115, 50 S. Ct. 241, 74 L. Ed. 731."

On January 8, 1940, a majority of the court reiterated in Higgins vs. Smith, 308 U. S. 473, that "it is command of income and its benefits which marks the real owner of property."

The last case in the line is Helvering v. Clifford, 60 S. Ct. 554, decided February 26, 1940, discussed above.

In considering this matter of the sweep of tax statutes and the effect to be given to a taxpayer's acts and devices which are relied on as reducing or avoiding the tax, it is well to recall the following words of Justice Holmes in Bullen v. Wisconsin, 240 U. S. 625:

"We do not speak of evasion because when the law draws a line, a case is on one side of it or the other, and if on the safe side, is none the worse legally that a man has availed himself to the full of what the law permits. When an act is condemned as an evasion, what is meant is that it is on the wrong side of the line indicated by the policy if not the mere letter of the law."

In the light of the foregoing authorities, it is my opinion that the control over his original three hundred shares of stock and its dividends left Mr. Owen by the trust indenture makes him liable for an income tax upon such dividends for the years in question. It puts him on the "wrong side of the line."

RE: INHERITANCE TAXES; ESTATES BY ENTIRETY; DEDUCTIBILITY OF MORTGAGE INDEBTEDNESS

24 July, 1940.

I reply to your letter of July 2 enclosing a letter from Mr. J. G. Merrimon, Attorney, with respect to the Estate of Roy F. Ebbs, late of Buncombe County, who died in December, 1939.

The decedent was a tenant by the entirety of real estate valued at $5,280.00. Prior to his death, he and his wife had executed a mortgage on the real estate upon which there was due at his death $4,296.00. The entire debt was paid out of the personalty of the deceased.

You ask whether or not the entire debt of $4,296.00 is deductible in "determining the clear market value" of the property transferred at his death, or whether only one-half of the debt is deductible. You suggest the latter is correct, while Mr. Merrimon contends the former is correct.

The decedent having died in 1939, the Revenue Act of 1939 controls. Section 1(7) of that Act provides:

> "Where real property is held by husband and wife as tenants by the entirety, the surviving tenant shall be taxable on one-half of the value of such property."

In Tyler vs. United States, 281 U. S. 497, 8 A.F.T.R. 10912, it is held that the death of the husband effects a transfer of property and economic benefits that may be taxed without violating the Constitution. That, I understand, is now settled law.

Section 7(d) of the Act provides that in "determining the clear market value of property taxed" the "debts of decedent" may be deducted. This, of course, includes secured as well as unsecured debts.

I am not able to find any basis in the Act for your suggestion that since only half of the property is to be included in the taxable estate, therefore only half of the mortgage indebtedness upon that property is deductible. The Act does not provide that mortgages upon property are to be deducted from its value, either entirely or in the proportion that the property is taxable. It simply provides that the value of the property shall be the measure of the tax on the succession, and from that value there may be deducted, among other things, the debts of the decedent, secured or unsecured.

The real question presented seems to be whether the debt was, in whole or in part, the debt of the decedent. As between the decedent and his wife, on the one hand, and the holder of the note, on the other, each maker was, of course, jointly and severally liable, and in that sense the debt was the debt of the decedent. But I do not think that all obligations upon which the decedent is bound are to be allowed as deductions.

I think the Act refers to debts for which the decedent is primarily bound, or debts for which he is secondarily liable and the burden of which his estate must ultimately bear in whole or in part. He may, for instance, be a joint maker of a note; in that case, as between him and his co-maker, the liability is, in the absence of a contract to the contrary, equal and joint and only one-half the debt is deductible. Raleigh Trust Co. v. York, 199 N. C. 624. In re Parrott's Estate, 199 Calif., 107, 248 Pac. 248; Parrott v. Commissioner, (CCA 9), 30 F. (2d) 792, cert. den. 279 U. S. 780, 49 S. Ct. 512, 73 L. Ed. 1007, 7 Am. Fed. Tax Reports 8501. Or he may be only secondarily liable, in which case the debt is deductible only if and to the extent that his estate will be called on to bear the ultimate burden of the obligation, settlement of the estate to await the determination of that contingency. See Annotation on the subject, 113 A. L. R. 368.

As stated in Kidder State Inheritance Tax, etc., page 378:

> "Any contingent liability of a decedent is to be suspended until the happening of the contingency determines whether there is actual liability. If the decedent is the endorser of a note or the guarantor of any obligation, the determination of whether or not the note or other obligation should be allowed as a deduction is to be suspended until it is determined whether or not the estate of the decedent must pay it."

Estate of Wormser, 28 Misc. 608, 59 N. Y. S. 1088; Estate of Wormser, 36 Misc. 434, 73 N. Y. S. 718. As ultimate burden is the test, it follows that the deduction is to be allowed in cases where the debt is satisfied by foreclosure of a lien upon the property of decedent or by the application of collateral posted by him, as well as where it is paid in due course of administration.

In Parrott v. Commissioners, supra, the court said:

> "The estate of the testatrix was subject to the payment of a mortgage. Her brother was jointly liable for the payment of the same mortgage. Looking through the form of the instrument to the substance of the obligation created thereby, the makers thereof, as between themselves, were each liable only for the payment of one-half the mortgage debt, for the property of each was sufficient for the payment of that half, and, if either were required to pay more than one-half, the excess so paid was recoverable from the other. Such was the nature of the obligation created between the makers of the instrument at the time when it was executed. Clearly, for taxation purposes under the Revenue Act, but one-half of the total mortgage debt was deductible in arriving at the amount of the tax upon the estate of the testatrix. It is no answer to this to say that, since the testatrix had not paid the entire obligation in her lifetime, no liability on the part of her brother to reimburse her existed at the time of her death, which could be said to be property to be included in her gross estate. At the time of the death of the testatrix her brother was under contractual obligation to her to pay his half of the debt, and to repay to her any sum that she might pay in excess of one-half of the amount of their joint debt, and that obligation existed from the date of the execution of the note and mortgage and was property."

Infinitely varied forms and sources of liability may arise and it is hardly possible to lay down a general rule for the solution of all cases. It can only be said that you should ascertain the facts and determine the primary obligation or ultimate burden in each case, remembering that the controlling factor is not the liability of the decedent and his co-obligors to the payee or holder of the debt, but the obligation or ultimate burden as between the latter, that is between the decedent and his co-obligors.

We now come to the particular facts here presented. Insufficient facts are stated to enable me to express an opinion as to the primary obligation of the mortgage debt, as between the decedent and his wife. I can only say that if the debt was the primary obligation of the decedent, all of it is deductible. If it was the primary obligation of the wife, then none of it is deductible. If it was for their joint use or benefit, or for the purchase price of the property, then they are equally liable and only half of the debt is deductible. The foregoing propositions, I think, are established by the decisions in this State and elsewhere.

In Wachovia Bank and Trust Company v. Black, 198 N. C. 219, a husband and wife bought land, taking title by the entireties and executing a mortgage for the purchase price. Upon the death of the husband the court held that as between the husband's estate and wife they were equally liable, saying:

> "This is an adjudication of the liability of the makers of the note as between themselves, not an adjudication of their liability to the payees. . . . If the note in question had been reduced to judgment against the makers an execution could have been issued against the estate which they held by the entirety. . . . But it does not follow that the judgment could have been collected only out of the estate by the entirety. . . . The makers were primarily liable jointly and severally. C. S., 458, 3041, 3166; Roberson vs. Spain, 173 N. C. 23. The unity of person is an incident of the estate

created by the conveyance to Black and his wife; it is not incident to the note. As the makers were jointly and severally liable, payment of the whole amount by either would entitle the other, or his representative, to contribution—an equity which arises when one of several parties who are liable on a common debt discharges the obligation for the benefit of all. It results that as between themselves each party is liable for one-half the debt, although the whole title is vested in the defendant as the survivor."

The same rule is laid down in Husband and Wife, 26 American Jurisprudence, Section 79, page 704, as follows:

> "A presumption exists of the equal liability of husband and wife as principals in consequence of their joint execution of a mortgage on an estate purchased or held by them by the entireties, including liabilities on covenants for the payment of the purchase money or other debts thereby secured. The right of proportionate contribution exists, however, between them as joint and equal principals, and such right is assertible against the estate of the deceased spouse. Such right is superior to the rights of heirs of real estate of the deceased spouse to have mortgages thereon paid ratably out of the deceased spouse's personalty. Payments made on such mortgage indebtedness by one spouse are to be regarded as gifts to the other to the extent to which they relieve the latter of an equality of contribution, and not as evidence of a purpose to place him or her in the position of a surety. The spouse to whom an estate by the entireties remains by right of survivorship, not taking by descent, has no right to exoneration of encumbrances thereon out of the personal property of the deceased spouse, and this applies to a purchase-money mortgage."

Cunningham v. Cunningham, 158 Md. 372, 148 Atl. 444, 67 A.L.R. 1177, holds that in such case the wife is not entitled to have the mortgage paid in full out of the husband's personal estate, but is entitled to have one-half of it paid by virtue of her right to contribution, they being equally liable. Other cases holding likewise are cited in the annotation.

Wilson v. Freeland, 176 N. C. 504, holds that where husband and wife are co-makers of a note their liability, as between themselves, is for one-half of the full amount, nothing else appearing, the court saying the husband "was not legally bound to his wife for the payment of her half, though he was so bound to the creditors." See also Taft v. Covington, 199 N. C. 51 and Newhart v. Peters, 80 N. C. 167.

In these cases our court apparently did not regard the right of the husband to contribution as any violation of C. S. 2515, regulating contracts between husband and wife. This would seem to be sound and correct for the right is not a conventional right of contract, but an equitable right or obligation created and imposed by law out of the situation and obligation of the parties. The evils and dangers guarded against by the constitutional and statutory provision for the protection of married women are not present in such a case.

In conclusion, I would say that it is your duty to ascertain what the facts are with respect to the debt in question and make your decision rest upon your finding as to whether the wife was the primary obligor, in which case no part of the debt should be allowed as a deduction, or whether the husband was the primary debtor, in which case all of the debt should be allowed as a deduction, or whether, as between themselves, the debt was their joint affair and obligation, in which event half of it is deductible.

As shown above, presumably, nothing else appearing, they are, between themselves, equally liable; but you should not rest upon that presumption but should find the truth of the matter and act accordingly.

In view of the fact that the land is security for the debt, the ultimate burden of the debt cannot fall upon the estate of the decedent, in whole or in part, even though the decedent was only secondarily liable for all or half of the obligation as between himself and his wife. If the estate has been called on to satisfy an obligation for which it is only secondarily bound, it has the right to have the land sold for its exoneration. See Wachovia Bank and Trust Company v. Black, supra, and Parrott v. Commissioner, supra.

It is, therefore, not conclusive that the estate has already paid the entire debt nor would the State be bound if it should appear that in the Probate Court the debt was allowed or its payment approved. (Re Parrott's Estate, 199 Calif. 107, 248 Pac. 248, Kidder, State Inheritance Tax, etc., page 377; Taxation, 61 Corpus Juris Section 2597 p. 1706) just as the State is not bound by the local assessor's valuation of property in ascertaining value for inheritance tax purposes. Re: Davis Estate, 190 N. C. 372.

RE: INHERITANCE TAXES; DEDUCTIONS; COMMISSIONS

26 July, 1940.

I reply to your letter of July 11 with reference to the Estate of J. Ward Powell, late of Lenoir, North Carolina.

You state that the court having jurisdiction over the estate allowed the administrators $225.00 per month for one year for their services, the same to be in lieu of commissions. This amount was substantially in excess of the five per cent commissions provided by law for the maximum allowance to executors and administrators for their services.

Section 7(g) of the Revenue Acts of 1937 and 1939 authorizes "commissions of executors and administrators actually allowed and paid" to be deducted in determining the value of the taxable estate.

It is, of course, well settled that all deduction and exemptions from taxation are to be strictly construed and are not to be allowed except where and to the extent plainly authorized by statute.

It is my opinion that the proper construction of the Act is that the maximum deduction that may be allowed is five per cent of the lawful receipts and disbursements. In many cases the full maximum allowance is neither asked for nor allowed. For this reason, the Act limits the deduction, within the maximum allowance, to the total which is "actually allowed and paid." But it is still "commissions" that are deductible and as they are limited to five per cent, as stated, you are not authorized to allow a deduction which exceeds that sum, properly calculated. You are no more bound by a greater allowance than five per cent than you are, for example, by a local tax assessor's valuation of property. Re Davis' Estate, 190 N. C. 372. The ex parte or interlocutory allowance of commissions is not conclusive. Overman v. Lanier, 157 N. C. 544. See also

Rose v. Bank of Wadesboro, 217 N. C. 600, where allowed but unlawful commissions were recovered.

The burden is upon the executor or administrator and they must satisfy you that the amount of deductions claimed is lawful and proper, that is, is such as is allowed by the Revenue Act.

RE: INCOME TAXES; LIABILITY OF MUTUAL OR COOPERATIVE ASSOCIATIONS ORGANIZED UNDER CHAPTER 93, SUB-CHAPTERS IV AND V OF THE CONSOLIDATED STATUTES

31 July, 1940.

I reply to your letter of July 29 with respect to the liability of the Woodland Cooperative Bonded Warehouse Company, Woodland, N. C.

You have demanded that this Corporation file with you income tax returns for the years 1937, 1938, and 1939, and they have claimed exemption under the laws of this State. I have examined a copy of the original and amended charter of the corporation and it appears therefrom that it was organized under Chapter 93, Sub-chapter V of the Consolidated Statutes.

Section 314(9) of the Revenue Acts of 1937 and 1939 exempts from income taxes "mutual associations formed under Consolidated Statutes five thousand two hundred and fifty-five, et seq. (Chapter one hundred forty-four, Public Laws of one thousand nine hundred fifteen and amendments), formed to conduct agricultural business on the mutual plan; or to marketing associations organized under Sub-chapter five, Chapter ninety-three, Consolidated Statutes, Article XVI, Section five thousand two hundred fifty-nine (a) and following."

Inasmuch as the Woodland Cooperative Bonded Warehouse Company was formed under the provisions of the Consolidated Statutes mentioned in this exemption clause, they are exempt from income taxes.

RE: INCOME TAXES; REFUND OF TAXES PAID BY RESIDENT BENEFICIARY ON INCOME OF NONRESIDENT ESTATE WHERE INCOME WAS NON-DISTRIBUTABLE AND ESTATE PAID NO TAX THEREON

1 August, 1940.

I reply to your oral request for an opinion whether Mrs. Florence Chapin Tyler, 210 West Devine Street, Dunn, N. C., is entitled to a refund of the income taxes paid by her in 1936 and 1937 on certain income of the estate of her father received by her in these years.

Your file in the matter, including correspondence with Mr. Henry M. Tyler, shows that during these years the Estate of the late Mr. William E. Chapin, of Atlanta, Georgia, was being administered by his Executor, the Trust Company of Georgia, at Atlanta, and certain income from the property of the Estate was received. Item Five of Mr. Chapin's will directed that his residuary estate be divided equally among his five nieces and nephews at the expiration of two years from his death. He died in January, 1936, and the income in question was received during the two-year period. The Executor distributed the income among the five nieces and nephews, Mrs. Tyler being one of them, and they included it in their Federal income tax return. Thereafter the Federal authorities took the position that the income was not distributable under the terms of the will and therefore the entire income was taxable to the Estate. Although the Executor did not fully agree with that view, it nevertheless paid the tax and the nieces and nephews were refunded the taxes paid by them on such income to the United States.

Mrs. Tyler included the income in her returns for 1936 and 1937 and her claim is based upon the ground that as it was not "distributable," therefore it was not taxable to her. She did not refund the payments to the Executor and it paid the income taxes assessed against the Estate out of corpus.

Non-distributable income received by a non-resident estate or fiduciary for a resident of this State is taxed by this State under Section 315 of the Revenue Acts of 1935 and 1937, which provides as follows:

> "The tax imposed by this article shall be imposed upon . . . a non-resident fiduciary having in charge funds or property for the benefit of a resident of this State, which tax shall be levied, collected and paid annually with respect to:
>
> "(a) That part of the net income of estates or trusts which has not become distributable during the income year."

Under Section 318(4) such income is taxable to the beneficiary if it is "received by him or distributable to him during the income year."

In view of these Sections it would seem to be clear that the income received by Mrs. Tyler is taxable whether or not the income was "distributable." The language of Section 318(4) is in the alternative and taxes the estate income to Mrs. Tyler if it was "received . . . *or* . . . distributable." Since it was "received," in any event, she is not entitled to a refund even though it be admitted that it was not "distributable."

If it be admitted or assumed that the income was not "distributable," then Mrs. Tyler's share of it was taxable to the Executor and it should have returned and paid the taxes upon it, as is expressly provided in Section 315. Subsection 315(d) makes the tax a charge against the estate or trust which would include any part of it received by Mrs. Tyler.

A closely similar question was dealt with by the United States Supreme Court in Stone v. White, 301 U. S. 532, 57 S. Ct. 851, 81 L. Ed. 1265, rehearing denied, 302 U. S. 639, 58 S. Ct. 260, 82 L. Ed. 897, where distributable income had been improperly assessed against a trustee which ought to have been assessed against the beneficiary, and the court held the trustee not entitled to a refund even though an assessment against the beneficiary was barred by the statute of limitations. The court took the view that since a tax upon the particular income was due, it was no matter that it may have been paid by the wrong person, that is, by the trustee for the beneficiary rather than by the beneficiary himself. The language of the opinion clearly indicates that the result should be the same in a case where the income is paid by the beneficiary when it should have been paid by the trustee.

For the foregoing reasons, I am satisfied that Mrs. Tyler is not entitled to the refunds and return your file herewith.

SUBJECT: MOTOR VEHICLE OWNER HOLDING LICENSE FOR OPERATION OF PRIVATE HAULER VEHICLE; GROSS WEIGHT IN EXCESS OF LEGAL WEIGHT

August 3, 1940.

You have informed me that a certain motor vehicle owner in Person County holds a license for the operation of a private hauler vehicle, the license being to haul a gross weight, including load, not in excess of 11,000 pounds. He was apprehended with a load and gross weight of 14,400 pounds and has been indicted for not having proper license plates.

The question is whether or not he is guilty of criminal violation of the motor vehicle laws of this State.

Section 52(b) of the Motor Vehicle Act of 1937, N. C. Code 1939, Section 2621(238), provides for the licensing of property hauling vehicles according to 100 pounds of gross weight. The application for and obtaining of a license under that Section authorizes the holder to operate a vehicle, which, with load, shall have a gross weight not in excess of the limits of his license. Section 60 of the Motor Vehicle Act of 1937, N. C. Code 1939, Section 2621(246) authorizes the Commissioner of Revenue to issue a permit for the over loading of a motor vehicle upon payment of the additional fee therein prescribed and provides that "it is the intent of this Section that every owner of a motor vehicle shall procure license in advance to cover any overload which may be carried." One of the penalties provided for the violation of the Section is the levying of an additional tax of $3.00 for each one thousand pounds in excess of the license weight of the vehicle. Section 137 of the Motor Vehicle Act of 1937, N. C. Code 1939, Section 2621(322), provides: "It shall be unlawful and constitute a misdemeanor for any person to violate any of the provisions of this article unless such violation is by article or other law of this State declared to be a felony." This latter Section is plain in its provisions and makes any violation of the Act a misdemeanor, except as stated.

It is my opinion that the person above referred to is guilty of the crime of operating an overloaded property hauling motor vehicle without procuring in advance a license to cover such overload and paying the additional fee prescribed therefor.

RE: MOTOR VEHICLES; REGISTRATION AND LICENSE TAXES; "HIGHWAYS"; PORTIONS UNDER CONSTRUCTION OR REPAIR

8 August, 1940.

You have orally advised me that certain road contractors are engaged with trucks in the repair of portions of the highways of the State, some of the portions being of considerable length. Some portions are, during the repairs, open to limited and controlled use by the public, while other portions are wholly closed until completion of the repairs.

Section 15 of the Motor Vehicle Act of 1939, Chapter 407, Public Laws of 1937, provides that "every owner of a vehicle intended to be operated upon any highway of this State" shall register the same and pay the taxes required by other Sections of the Act.

Section 2(cc) defines a street or highway as "the entire width between property lines of every way or place of whatever nature, when any part thereof is open to the use of the public as a matter of right for the purposes of vehicular traffic."

Section 61 provides that the motor vehicle taxes levied by the Act are "compensatory taxes for the use and privileges of the public highways of this State."

The question presented is whether, under these Sections, such portions under repair are parts of the "highways" of the State and open to the use of the public. If so, the contractors are liable for motor vehicle registration and licenses taxes.

The Open Portions of The Highways

In my opinion the trucks used by the contractors in repairing those portions of the highways which, during such repairs, are open to public use are liable for the proper registration and license taxes.

This view seems to be required by the Sections referred to and is further supported by Section 16(b), exempting vehicles "driven or moved upon a highway only for the purpose of crossing such highway from one property to another." Any other vehicular use of the highways renders the vehicle owner liable for the tax.

The Closed Portions of The Highways

I think it equally clear that the contractors are not liable for such taxes when their trucks are used only upon portions of the highways which are not "open to the use of the public as a matter of right for the purposes of vehicular traffic." Such portions are not parts of "the public highway" as that term is defined in Section 2(cc).

However, if the trucks are driven under their own power or "pulled by a self-propelled vehicle" (Section 2-p) to the scene of the work and pass over open portions of the highways, there is liability for the taxes. Liability for the taxes can be avoided in such case only if the trucks are placed upon and transported to the scene of work by another "property hauling vehicle" which must be licensed and tax paid as set forth in Section 52.

RE: INCOME TAXES; DEDUCTIBILITY OF GIFTS MADE TO FAIR ASSOCIATION ORGANIZED AND OPERATING FOR SCIENTIFIC AND EDUCATIONAL PURPOSES

August 12, 1940.

You have handed me a letter from Mr. Monroe M. Redden, Attorney at Law, Hendersonville, N. C., and a copy of the charter of the Western North Carolina Agriculture and Industrial Fair Association, Inc., and requested my opinion whether gifts to this Association are deductible from the gross income of the individual donors under Section 322 (9) of the Revenue Act of 1939, which provides that "contributions or gifts made by individuals within the income year to corporations or associations operated exclusively for . . . scientific or educational purposes . . . no part of the net earnings of which inures to the benefit of any private stockholder or individual to an amount not in excess of ten per cent of the taxpayer's net income, etc."

The Association in question is organized under Chapter 84, Article 21 of the Consolidated Statutes. Section 4941 provides that the object of such associations shall be "to encourage and promote agriculture, domestic manufactures, and the mechanic arts," and Section 4945 provides that the moneys subscribed by the incorporators, after necessary expenses are paid, shall be "annually paid for premiums awarded by such societies . . . on such live animals, articles of production, and agricultural implements and tools, domestic manufactures, mechanical improvements, tools and productions as are of the growth and manufacture of the county, and also such experiments, discoveries, or attainments as are made within the county wherein such societies are respectively organized."

The charter sets forth that the purpose of the Association is "to encourage and promote agriculture, domestic manufactures and the mechanic arts," to spread the enjoyment "to be derived from the benevolent, educational, experimental, and entertainment advantages and benefits provided by the Association," to gather and disseminate "statistics, reports, trade news and any and all other information relative to the encouragement and promotion of agriculture." It provides that the Association shall be non-stock but for $10.00 each may issue certificates of membership "of no monetary value," all of which may be used only to promote and pay the expenses of the Association and provide for "premium awards." It also provides for the charging of rents, exhibition and other fees which may be used only for like purposes.

The Association is operated for the purposes and within the limitation of its charter and the law under which it is organized and no part of its net earnings inures to the benefit of any stockholder or individual. The exclusive aim of its operation is the promotion and improvement of agriculture, principally by the dissemination of information and the awarding of excellence and achievements in the field.

Such associations are themselves exempt from income taxes by Section 314(7) of the Revenue Act.

Under these facts, it is my opinion that this Association is organized and operated for "scientific or educational purposes" and gifts to it are deductible from the gross income of the donors as provided in Section 322 (9) of the Revenue Act.

RE: INHERITANCE TAXES; WORKMEN'S COMPENSATION BENEFITS; TAXABILITY

13 August, 1940.

You have asked my opinion whether workmen's compensation benefits received by the dependents of a deceased employee are includible in his taxable estate.

Section 21 of the Workmen's Compensation Act exempts its benefits "from taxes." This exemption is broad and all inclusive, and, in my opinion, includes inheritance taxes. To hold otherwise would be to interpolate the words "except inheritance taxes," and violate the liberal rule of construction universally followed in the interpretation of such laws. Blassingame v. Southern Asbestos Company, 217 N. C. 223.

It might be suggested that this exemption, enacted in 1929, is repealed by the taxing provisions of the Inheritance Tax Act of 1939 or by the general repeal of prior exemptions contained in Section 919 of that Act. I do not think it necessary to attempt to find the answer to that question for I think it plain that the benefits under consideration are not taxable under the Inheritance Tax Act.

The decedent had no "property" in the award. It was made after his death. Therefore, there was no "transfer" of "property" at his death within the meaning of Section 1 of the Inheritance Tax Act. The benefits are clearly not "the proceeds of life insurance" within the meaning of Section 11 of the Act. The system of compensation for damages or losses suffered from the injury or death of employed persons established by the Workmen's Compensation Act is no more "insurance" than was the prior system under which such damages or losses were recoverable by ordinary legal action, and, so far as I am informed it never yet has been suggested that damages recovered for wrongful death are subject to inheritance taxes, at least without a special statute.

For these reasons, I am of the opinion that workmen's compensation benefits are not includible in the taxable estate of a deceased employee.

SUBJECT: UNIFORM DRIVERS LICENSE ACT; AGRICULTURAL OR INDUSTRIAL TRACTORS; EXEMPTION

13 August, 1940.

Since the Uniform Drivers License Act, Chapter 52 of the Public Laws of 1935, specifically exempts agricultural or industrial tractors, I am of the opinion that no operator's or chauffeur's license is required of a person who operates the same.

RE: INHERITANCE TAXES; CONVEYANCE BY TENANTS BY ENTIRETIES TO WIFE FOR LIFE, REMAINDER TO NEPHEW. INCLUSION OF HALF OF VALUE OF LAND IN WIFE'S TAXABLE ESTATE

21 August, 1940.

I comply with your oral request for my opinion on the following facts appearing in the Estate of Dora Lee Kearns, late of Forsyth County.

In 1920 the decedent and her husband, owning lands by the entireties, conveyed the same to the wife for life, remainder to their nephew. The wife died July 3, 1940, and the question has arisen between you and the decedent's Executors as to whether the value of the land should be included in the wife's taxable estate.

The conveyance by the husband and wife to the wife for life, remainder to the nephew, extinguished the estate by the entireties. Moore v. Greenville B. and T. Co., 178 N. C. 118, 121; Davis v. Bass, 188 N. C. 200, 208; Turlington v. Lucas, 186 N. C. 283, 286. Even where the husband alone conveys to the wife land held by entireties, the conveyance takes effect and estops the husband. Capps v. Massey, 199 N. C. 196; Willis v. Willis, 203 N. C. 517.

Certainly the joint conveyances to the nephew was good and vested in him a remainder upon execution of the deed. The deed having extinguished the estate by entireties, the unity was severed and the remainder is, in my opinion, to be taken as a transfer from the husband and wife equally. Since a life estate was reserved to the wife, her half came into the nephew's possession and enjoyment at her death and hence is taxable under Section 1(3) of the Revenue Act and the value of that half should be included in her taxable estate.

Under the law of this State, if the wife furnished the consideration for the original purchase of the land, or was solely entitled thereto for any reason, no estate by entireties was created. If that is true here, the entire value of the land is includible. You no doubt will want to ascertain what the facts are with regard to that point. In writing the foregoing I have assumed that the husband furnished the consideration or at least half thereof.

RE: INCOME TAXES; INCOME REALIZED BY DISCHARGE OF TAXPAYER'S INDEBTEDNESS AT A DISCOUNT

28 August, 1940.

I reply to your letter of August 20, 1940, with respect to the 1939 income tax of the Jennings Furniture Company, Lenoir, North Carolina.

I am not able to understand clearly from your letter and the enclosure what the facts are. However, in my conference today with Mr. Johnson it was understood that I should state the rule applicable to income received from the discharge at a discount of a taxpayer's indebtedness and you would apply it to the facts after they were ascertained.

Apparently the taxpayer received a cancellation of indebtedness in the sum of $6,556.29. It contends that inasmuch as thereafter it had a deficit of $56,680.22 no taxable income resulted. The file indicates that in arriving at the deficit the taxpayer's common and preferred stock was included as a liability.

This general subject was dealt with in my letters to you dated December 15, 1938, February 15, 1939, April 28, 1939 and October 20, 1939, and pertinent authorities were cited.

In such cases "gain is realized to the extent of the value of the assets freed from the claims of creditors." Lakeland Grocery Company v. Commissioner, 36 B. T. A. 289. The amount of the gain is to be computed by deducting the taxpayer's total indebtedness from its total assets and the taxable income resulting from the cancellation is the amount of its net worth not in excess, however, of the amount of the debts cancelled. The example given in my letter of December 15, 1938, was of a corporation owing $140,000.00 which settled debts of $100,000.00 by the payment of $50,000.00; after the cancellation it had assets of $50,000.00 and debts of $40,000.00. Its net gain by the transaction is not $50,000.00, the book-saving by the cancellation, but $10,000.00, the amount of its worth over and above its indebtedness to creditors. In such cases the corporation and its stockholders have gained to the extent of the $10,000.00 and have realized a taxable gain only to that extent.

In this case, apparently, the deficit was arrived at by including the corporation's common and preferred stock as liabilities. This was not correct. For the purpose of computing the taxable gain from the cancellation its stock liability should not be included in liabilities. Only its indebtedness to creditors should be included in the deduction from its assets. See Lakeland Grocery Company v. Commissioner, supra. For treatments of the general subject see Magill, Taxable Income, Chapter 7, page 207; 1 C. C. H. 1940 Standard Federal Tax Service, Paragraph No. 77; 1 Prentice-Hall, 1940 Federal Tax Service, Paragraph No. 7252.

RE: WESTERN UNION TELEGRAPH COMPANY; FRANCHISE TAXES; YEARS 1937 AND 1939

30 August, 1940.

I have considered the protests and briefs filed by the above taxpayer with respect to the proposed additional assessment of franchise taxes for the years 1937 and 1939 and am of the opinion that they should be sustained.

In both years the taxpayer objects to the use as a tax base or measure sums received by it for the relaying of messages sent by the United States Government. The cases cited in its brief sustain its position that the State is without power to lay a tax upon such receipts or to measure a tax by their gross amount. It is true that the cases were decided a good many years ago and that recently the decisions of the United States Supreme Court have brought about fundamental changes in the construction of the Constitution, yet nevertheless the cases relied on were apparently affirmed by the decision in James v. Dravo Contracting Company, 302 U. S. 134, decided December 6, 1937, and it cannot now be said that they are no longer law. The trend of the decisions seem definitely away from them, however, and notice should be given that this disposition of the matter is not to be taken as a precedent and is without prejudice to reconsideration of the matter with respect to the taxpayer's liability in any future year.

The second objection with respect to 1939 is to basing any tax upon the taxpayer's receipts from its messenger or errand boy service. Without admitting the correctness of the arguments contained in the brief as to other matters, I think this objection should be sustained on the ground that when the Budget Revenue Bill of 1939 was introduced Section 206(2) expressly provided that the taxpayer's gross receipts from, among other things, "messenger services" should be included in the tax base, and, upon objection by the taxpayer and a hearing before the Joint Finance Committee, the words quoted were stricken from the Bill and it was later enacted without them. It is argued that this legislative history, often resorted to by the courts in the construction of statutes, shows an intention that such services shall be excluded from gross receipts. Since it does not appear that the deletion of the words was because it was argued to the Committee, or the General Assembly, that the general words of the Section were sufficient to include such services (Helvering v. Clifford, 60 S. Ct. 554), the argument is sound and must be accepted. What the General Assembly has put asunder let no man join together.

RE: INCOME TAXES; BANKS—(1) LOANS CHARGED OFF TO SURPLUS OR LOSS BY ORDER OF BANKING AUTHORITIES—LATER RECOVERY OF AS TAXABLE INCOME. (2) ARTICLE V, SECTION 3, NORTH CAROLINA CONSTITUTION, AS AUTHORIZING ONLY A NET INCOME TAX

24 September, 1940.

I write you with reference to the matters of the Bank of Belmont and the Roanoke Bank and Trust Company, and other banks represented by George G. Scott and Company, Certified Public Accountants, Charlotte, N. C.

In years past, these banks had made loans which the banking authorities later ordered them to charge off. In some cases they were charged to the surplus account and in other instances they were charged to profit and loss or to an undivided profit and loss account. The loans were thereafter collected, in whole or in part, in the tax years involved and the question is whether such collections constitute taxable income.

The banks argue that it is the settled rule that the State will and should follow the Federal rule as to what is or is not "taxable net income," except when some express provision of our Revenue Acts require otherwise, and that this is particularly true with respect to the deduction of bad debts and the taxation of recoveries. It is believed that this is a correct statement when applied to general income tax decisions and the construction of statutes similar to ours but not to the Regulations, although, as stated below, on September 13, 1939, this office refused to accept as sound G. C. M. 20,854.

The taxpayers rely on G. C. M. 20,854, C. B. 1939, page 102, which holds that recoveries of debts previously charged off do not constitute taxable income unless the deductions in prior years resulted in a reduction of tax liability. This decision made the rule applicable to all taxpayers, though the prior ruling of Counsel to the same effect had been restricted to Banks and to debts charged off by direction of the banking examiners or authorities.

In 1939 this ruling and other Federal authorities based upon it were relied upon by a taxpayer in a case where debts previously charged off were later collected and it was contended that income was not realized since the previous deductions in its income tax returns did not result in a tax saving. I was unable to see how the fact that there was no tax saving in prior years could prevent the realization of income in the year in which the debt was recovered and in my letter to you of September 13, 1939, I stated that it was my opinion that the soundness and correctness of G. C. M. 20,854, C. B. 1939, page 102, was "subject to grave doubt" and refused to follow it. That this view was correct is shown by G. C. M. 22,163, Prentice Hall 1939, F. T. S., Paragraph No. 66,252, (July, 1940), revoking G. C. M. 20,854, and holding, on authority of Burnet v. Sanford and Brooks Company, 282 U. S. 359, 75 L. Edition, 383, and Lake View T. and S. Bank v. Commissioner, 27 B. T. A. 209, that the question of the tax saving had nothing to do with the fact that the recovery of the debt was a realization of income in the year of recovery. See, also, Prentice Hall, supra, Paragraph No. 60,132.

The taxpayers are, therefore, not entitled to prevail because the prior deduction resulted in no tax savings.

But the banks further contend that the recoveries of the loans were merely recoveries or returns of capital and, therefore, do not constitute taxable income, and say that this is particularly true in those instances where the loans were charged off to surplus.

The statement and files clearly show that the banking authorities concluded that the loans in question were of such worthless or doubtful value as to require them to be "charged off" and definitely removed from the list of assets of the banks. This was done and undoubtedly entitled the banks to deductions in the years in which the banking examiners required the charge-offs to be made. It is not material that, as frankly stated, no deductions were taken in the income tax returns of the banks in such years because the banks then had no income subject to tax. In United States v. Ludey, 274 U. S. 295, 47 S. Ct. 608, 71 L. Ed. 1054, 6 A. F. T. R. 6754, it was held that in computing gain or loss on a sale, the original basis must be reduced by the depreciation allowable during the years the property was held regardless of whether deduction had actually been claimed. It is stated in G. C. M. 22,163, P. H., 1940, Fed. T. S., Paragraph No. 66,252, that this case stands for the proposition that "a taxpayer is to be charged with having recovered his capital to the extent that the Statute permits deductions from gross income on account thereof, regardless of whether the taxpayer took advantage of the deduction privilege provided in the Revenue Acts."

The Memorandum further states that inasmuch as all of the Federal Regulations since 1921 provided that recovery of a debt previously charged off would not constitute taxable income unless it had been "allowed as a deduction for income tax purposes," such recoveries would not be taxed unless the deductions had been taken and allowed. This would seem to be contrary to the Ludey Case and as the Revenue Acts of this State contain no such modification or requirement, I do not think you are bound by the effect of the Regulations referred to. It has long been the settled view that you can neither take advantage of nor be bound by a rule that has its only origin and authority in a Federal Regulation.

It appears to me that the only question here is whether or not the loans that were charged to surplus were actually "charged off" so as to constitute a reduction or destruction of basis. The books admit that such destruction occurs when the loans are deducted in an income tax return. But any logic and substance that G. C. M. 20,854 might have had disappeared when it was recognized in G. C. M. 22,163 that the requirement of a tax-saving was unsound. To require thereafter that to be taxable the recovery must be of a debt theretofore taken as a deduction would seem to be wholly arbitrary and purposeless, at least in a state where there never was any legal requirement to that effect. At most, such a deduction would seem to be merely evidential, proof that the loans were as of the time of the charge-off, no longer regarded as capital or assets, and here the action of the banking authorities would seem to be sufficient for that purpose.

A "charge-off" of a bad debt is the elimination of the item from the book assets of the taxpayer. See P. H. 1940, Federal T. S., Paragraph No. 13,895, Paul and Mertens, Law of Federal Income Taxation, Section 28.25, et seq., and cases cited. Charging the debt to surplus effects a "charge-off." Western Plumbing Supply Company v. Reinecke, 17 A. F. T. R. 1020. No further citations on this point are believed to be necessary in view of the plain effect to be given to the action of the banking authorities.

In Burnett v. Sanford and Brooks Co., 282 U. S. 359, 75 L. Ed. 383, 9 A. F. T. R. 603, the court held that if operations under a contract extend over a period of years, a return must be filed for each of the years and losses in prior years cannot be used to offset income received in the last, Stone, J,. saying:

> "The Sixteenth Amendment was adopted to enable the government to raise revenue by taxation. It is the essence of any system of taxation that it should produce revenue ascertainable, and payable to the government, at regular intervals. Only by such a system is it practicable to produce a regular flow of income and apply methods of accounting, assessment, and collection capable of practical operation. It is not suggested that there has ever been any general scheme for taxing income on any other basis. The computation of income annually as the net result of all transactions within the year was a familiar practice, and taxes upon income so arrived at were not unknown, before the Sixteenth Amendment. While, conceivably, a different system might be devised by which the tax could be assessed, wholly or in part, on the basis of the finally ascertained results of particular transactions, Congress is not required by the amendment to adopt such a system in preference to the more familiar method, even if it were practicable. It would not necessarily obviate the kind of inequalities of which respondent complains. If losses from particular transactions were to be set off against gains in others, there would still be the practical necessity of computing the tax on the basis of annual or other fixed taxable periods, which might result in the taxpayer being required to pay a tax on income in one period exceeded by net losses in another. . . .

See, also, Magill's Taxable Income, page 324, et seq., and Paul and Merten's Law of Federal Income Taxation, Section 11.03 and Chapter 40:

> "The exigencies of a tax determined on the annual basis may lead to the inclusion as income of items which might be shown to involve no gain if the transactions were viewed as a whole over several years." Brandeis, J., in Helvering v. Midland Mutual Life Ins. Co., 300 U. S. 216, 81 L. Ed. 612, 18 A. F. T. R. 1144.

While it is entirely true as a general rule that cost or capital must first be restored before there can be taxable income, yet, as said in Doyle v. Mitchell Brothers Company, 247 U. S. 179, 62 L. Ed. 1054, 3 A. F. T. R. 2979, it is "the capital that existed at the commencement of the period under consideration," namely, the tax year or annual accounting period, that must be looked to, and at that time we find that the loans in question were no longer capital; they had previously been lost and charged off by order of the banking examiners. It is not guaranteed to taxpayers that capital lost or charged off in prior years may be recouped before they will be required to pay an income tax on recoveries in subsequent years. Under the annual system of taxation in force here, they are entitled to no more than a deduction in the year of loss and if that be no benefit to them, it cannot affect taxability of the recovery in a later year. We have here no statute allowing such charge-offs to be carried over to another year, nor any statute or regulation which requires you to look back to see if, in a prior year, the deduction was claimed and allowed in a tax return. The case may be summed up shortly by saying that the charge-off destroyed the banks' "basis" and there is nothing applicable to the recovery to reduce it as taxable income.

The taxpayers also contend that Article V, Section 3 of the Constitution of North Carolina, provides in terms for only an annual net income tax and suggest that all costs and expenses must therefore be allowed. A reading of the Section does not prove this. Its terms indicate that deductions lie in the discretion of the Legislature. It is the general rule that deductions are a matter of legislative grace, Deputy vs. DuPont, 60 S. Ct., 363, and I do not think our Constitution provides otherwise, certainly not as to losses suffered and charged off in prior years.

RE: INCOME TAXES; DEDUCTIONS; (1) BAD DEBTS; BANK FORECLOSING MORTGAGE AND TAKING TITLE SUBJECT TO DOWER; CHARGE-OFF IN LATER YEAR. (2) DEDUCTION OF DEBTS ONLY PARTIALLY WORTHLESS

24 September, 1940.

I reply to your letter with respect to the 1938 return of the Bank of Ahoskie.

Prior to 1934 the Bank made a loan to W. J. Vaughn which was secured by a mortgage executed by Vaughn and wife. In that year the Bank advertised the property for sale under power and thereupon Vaughn and wife enjoined the sale and it was judicially determined that the conveyance of the wife was void for failure of the Notary to take her private examination, as required by law. In August, 1934, the property was sold subject to the wife's dower or home site right and bought in by the Bank which set it up as "Other Real Estate." In December, 1938, pursuant to action of the banking examiners, the Bank charged the loan off as a loss.

The taxpayer contends that it is entitled to a deduction of $3,425.00 "for loss on real estate," which, I presume, is the amount of the loan. In another paragraph of its claim the Bank relies on the provision for the deduction of bad debts.

I do not think the Bank is entitled to a deduction with respect to the land until it has sold it for less than the bid at which the land was bought at foreclosure. Until then, there is, under the law of this State, no closed or completed transaction.

The question presented is, I think, whether the Bank is entitled to a deduction under Section 322(7) of the Revenue Act of 1937, which allows a deduction of "debts ascertained to be worthless and actually charged off within the income year."

Under the language of the Section two things must occur within the tax year, (a) the debt must then be ascertained to be worthless and (b) it must be actually charged off. A charge-off cannot be deducted if made in a year following that in which the debt was ascertained to be worthless. 1 Prentice-Hall, 1940, Fed. T. S., Paragraph No. 13,880.

If the taxpayer ascertained, or a reasonable person would have ascertained, that the debt was worthless in a year prior to that in which the charge-off occurred, the deduction must be disallowed. 1 Prentice-Hall,

1940 F. T. S., Paragraph No. 13,880-A. The year in which the banking authorities ordered the charge-off does not of itself establish that the debt was then ascertained to be worthless, especially in cases where other circumstances indicate that ascertainment ought to have occurred in a prior year. 3 Paul and Merten's Law of Fed. Inc. Taxation, Sec. 28.76. When foreclosure follows default and unsuccessful efforts to collect, the year in which it occurs is to be taken as the time of ascertainment in the absence of convincing evidence to the contrary. 1 Prentice-Hall, 1940 F. T. S., Paragraph Nos. 13,890 and 13,904, et seq.

Here, in 1934, the Bank had been able to collect neither principal nor interest and its foreclosure purchase in that year was subject to the dower or home site rights of the wife. No evidence appears that the maker of the note was then able to pay the deficiency, if any, or that he might thereafter be reasonably expected to be able to make any payment or that he owned other property from which payment might be expected. In my opinion, the Bank has not shown itself entitled to the deduction in 1938.

If, as may well be the case, the Bank bid in the property at the amount of the loan, then the property takes the place of the debt and the deduction could not be allowed for two reasons. First, because under our law, the transaction is not closed and completed until the property is sold and until then it cannot be ascertained whether or not it will suffer a loss. Helvering v. Midland Mutual Life Ins. Company, 300 U. S. 216, 81 L. Ed. 612. Second, irrespective of whether the property was bid in at the amount of the loan or at a lesser figure, and assuming a closed transaction, the land is of some value, therefore, there is no more than a partial loss. Where the statute provides merely for the deduction of "debts ascertained to be worthless," a partially worthless debt is not deductible. Spring City Foundry Co. v. Comm., 292 U. S. 182, 78 L. Edition 1200; Paul and Merten's Law of Fed. Inc. Taxation, Sec. 28.33. We have no statute here like the Federal Regulation, which provides that the action of the banking authorities conclusively establishes the worthlessness of the debt, but even such a statute would not seem to give to the action of the bank examiners the effect of establishing the worthlessness of the land, which has, in whole or in part, taken the place of the debt.

In my opinion, you properly disallowed the deduction.

SUBJECT: MOTOR VEHICLE LAWS; SPEED LIMITS; RESIDENTIAL DISTRICTS

27 September, 1940.

Under the provisions of C. S. 2621(288) (d), whenever the State Highway and Public Works Commission shall determine upon the basis of an engineering and traffic investigation that any prima facie speed thereinbefore set out is greater than is reasonable or safe under the conditions found to exist at any intersection or other place, or upon any part of a highway, the Commission is required to determine and declare a reasonable and safe prima facie speed limit thereat, which limits shall be effective only after appropriate signs giving notice of such prima facie limits have been erected at such place or part of the highway.

In my opinion, the definition of a residential district applies to those areas both within and without the corporate limits of a municipality, and, even in the absence of signs posted by the State Highway and Public Works Commission, the operator of a motor vehicle is required to observe the prima facie speed limits prescribed in C. S. 2621(288) in those residential districts which are defined in C. S. 2621(187)(w-1), even though such residential district is without the corporate limits of any municipality in this State. Of course, if the Highway Commission wanted to reduce the speed limit in such residential districts to a lower prima facie speed than that prescribed in C. S. 2621(288), before such lower prima facie limits would be effective, signs would have to be erected notifying the public of such reduced prima facie speed limits.

RE: FRANCHISE TAXES; MASSACHUSETTS OR BUSINESS TRUSTS; LIABILITY FOR TAX

27 September, 1940.

I reply to your letter of the 20th with respect to the American Optical Company, Southbridge, Massachusetts.

It appears that this organization is what is known in the law as a Massachusetts or Business Trust, organized in 1912 under the laws of Massachusetts. It has been doing business in this State since 1923 and regularly files income and intangible tax returns with the proper officials of the State.

The questions you present are whether it is required to domesticate under the provisions of Sections 1181 and 1181(b) of the Code of 1939 and to file the returns and pay the taxes required of corporations by Section 210 of the Revenue Act.

Sections 1181 and 1181(b) merely use the words "foreign corporations." These words are not defined, there or in any other applicable law of this State. Section 1113 define "corporation" to mean "a corporation which may be created or organized under this Chapter, or under any other general or any special act:" The Chapter on corporations nowhere refers to organizations created under a trust indenture. It would seem to follow from this, in the absence of other definition, that a foreign corporation would be a corporation created under the laws of some jurisdiction other than North Carolina. The only requirement in our law with respect to such trusts, in any way related or similar to the acts of domestication required of foreign corporations, are those found in Section 3288 of the Code providing for registration in the office of the Clerk of Court of those doing business under an assumed name. They, of course, do not affect your questions.

I, therefore, conclude that a Massachusetts or Business Trust is not a "foreign corporation" and is not required to domesticate under the provisions of the Code referred to.

In Hemphill v. Orloff, 277 U. S. 537, 72 L. Edition, 978, 48 S. Ct., the law of Michigan defined "corporations" so as to include "associations." A Business Trust is an "association," under the laws of Massachusetts, as well as other states, and, therefore, the court held that it was required to domesticate in Michigan in the same manner as a corporation, properly so called.

Section 210 of the Revenue Act does no more than lay a franchise tax upon "Corporations, domestic and foreign." The Franchise Tax Article of the Revenue Act does not define the word "corporation" and nowhere indicates that it is to be taken as including associations or Massachusetts or Business Trusts. For this reason, the American Optical Company is not required to file the franchise returns or pay the franchise taxes provided in Section 210 of the Revenue Act.

Massachusetts or Business Trusts were discussed by our court in Roberts v. Aberdeen-Southern Pines Syndicate, 198 N. C. 381, and it was there said that such an organization is "admittedly not a corporation, for although it has some of the characteristics of a corporation, it was not organized under or pursuant to the law of this State or of any other state, as a corporation." See, also, State v. Thomas, 209 N. C. 722.

SUBJECT: TAXATION; INHERITANCE TAX; EXEMPTIONS; WAR RISK INSURANCE

5 October, 1940.

I have your letter of September 23, 1940, in which you inquire whether certain funds in the hands of the administrator of Anna Leak Ledbetter, representing proceeds of a War Risk Insurance Policy on the life of H. S. Ledbetter, the insured, are subject to an inheritance tax. For the purposes of this letter it is assumed that, as the proceeds were paid to the estate of Anna Leak Ledbetter, the beneficiary, the policy was one of converted insurance and, therefore subject to the provisions of 38 U. S. C. A. (Supp. 1939), Section 512, requiring that "if the designated beneficiary survives the insured and dies before receiving all of the installments of converted insurance payable and applicable, then there shall be paid to the estate of such beneficiary the present value of the remaining unpaid monthly installments."

It is my opinion that the proceeds of this insurance policy may be subjected to a North Carolina inheritance tax under either Section 11 or Section 1 of the Revenue Act, unless they are expressly exempted by Act of Congress or State law.

The present Federal statute regulating exemption of War Risk Insurance from taxation is 38 U. S. C. A. (Supp. 1939), Section 454(a), which provides, in part, as follows:

> "Payments of benefits due or to become due shall not be assignable, and such payments made to, or on account of, a beneficiary under any of the laws relating to veterans shall be exempt from all taxation . . ."

This provision has been construed by the United States Supreme Court in United States Trust Co. v. Helvering, 307 U. S. 57, 59 Sup. Ct. 692, 83 L. ed. 1104. In that case it was held that the inclusion of the proceeds of such insurance in the gross assets of the insured for purpose of computing the Federal estate tax, was proper, the rationale of the opinion being that the estate tax is really a tax on the transfer of the proceeds rather than a tax on the actual property constituting the proceeds of the insurance policy. A State inheritance Tax, like the Federal estate tax, may be considered a tax on the transfer of property rather than on the property itself, and, therefore, it follows from United States Trust Co. v. Helvering, supra, that the exemption under consideration does not preclude the collection of an inheritance tax.

Section 2 of the Revenue Act, paragraph (d), exempts from inheritance taxes: "and also proceeds of all policies of insurance and the proceeds of all adjusted service certificates paid by the United States Government to the beneficiary or beneficiaries or heirs-at-law of any deceased soldier . . ." Exemptions of this type are construed strictly. Plummer v. Coler, 178 U. S. 115, 20 Sup. Ct. 829, 44 L. ed. 998. As this provision provides for an exemption only when the proceeds are payable to a beneficiary named in the policy or to the heirs-at-law of a deceased soldier, I am of the opinion that it would have no application in a situation where, as in that under consideration, the proceeds are payable to the estate of a deceased beneficiary to be distributed among his next of kin or legatees.

In the absence of an applicable statutory exemption, it would seem that an inheritance tax based on this insurance may be collected from the estate of Anna Leak Ledbetter.

Re: Income Taxes; Dividends from the North Carolina Railroad

8 October, 1940.

You have shown me the letter written to you under date of October 4 by Mr. Thomas ZumBrunun, in which he contends that dividends received by the stockholders of the North Carolina Railroad, a North Carolina corporation, are not taxable.

Dividends are expressly included in "gross income," as that term is defined in Section 317 of the Revenue Act. Section 322(5) provides that "dividends from stock in any corporation, the income of which shall have been assessed, and the tax on such income paid by the corporation, under the provisions of this article," are deductible. The Section further provides for a proportionate deduction in case the corporation has paid an income tax to this State on only part of its income.

Under Section 312, the North Carolina Railroad is exempt from income taxes in this State inasmuch as all of its income is in the form of rents received from the Southern Railway.

Under these circumstances, it is my opinion that individual stockholders of the North Carolina Railroad Company are required to include in their gross income dividends received from the North Carolina Railroad Company. Mr. ZumBrunun suggests that the Southern Railway Company is not allowed to deduct from its gross income the rental which it pays to the North Carolina Railroad Company and contends that, therefore, it would appear that the income tax has been paid to the State of North Carolina on the income earned by the North Carolina Railroad Company, even though that tax is not paid directly by the said Railroad Company. I am not able to agrēe to this suggestion. Exemptions and deductions from taxes are strictly construed and are never allowed unless the claimant can bring himself within the literal languages of a statute granting such exemption or deduction. In this matter, we find that the statutes of this State allow dividends to be deducted only when the issuing corporation has paid a tax on its income to this State.

I think you are correct in taking the position that dividends from the North Carolina Railroad Company, received by its individual stockholders, are taxable in this State.

RE: FRANCHISE TAXES; ELECTRIC POWER COMPANIES; TAX MEASURED BY SIX PER CENT OF GROSS RECEIPTS FROM NORTH CAROLINA SALES

17 October, 1940.

I write you in compliance with your request for my opinion on the constitutional validity of the additional franchise taxes proposed against the Virginia Electric and Power Company for the years 1937, 1938, and 1939. This Company is a Virginia Corporation. It is domesticated in this State under its laws and is engaged here both in interstate and intrastate commerce, it being licensed under the laws of this State to carry on its business here generally and unrestrictedly.

The Facts

The Company maintains in this State the lines and plants usually maintained by electric power companies. It brings electric current into this State from Virginia which it sells both to consumers and to distributors. The current enters North Carolina at 110,000 volts. At the Company's Winfall, N. C., substation it is reduced to 33,000 volts. It goes thence at that voltage to the towns of Elizabeth City, Edenton, and Hertford in this State. It is then delivered to the municipal distribution systems of these towns for sale to their customers. Before the power is delivered to the municipalities, it is reduced by the Company in its substations to 2,300 volts. Reduction of the voltage is necessary in order to make the current available for use by the distributors and the consumers.

Section 203 of the Revenue Acts of 1937 and 1939 imposes a franchise tax upon electric power companies at the rate of or measured by six per cent "of the total gross receipts derived from such business in this State." The gross receipts from distributors selling to the public and paying a tax on their receipts are excluded from the tax base, but gross receipts from sales to municipal distribution systems are required to be included, they not being required to pay any franchise tax for engaging in such business.

The Question Presented

The question presented is whether the gross receipts of the Company from the current brought in from Virginia and sold to the municipalities can be included in the tax measure or base without a violation of the Commerce Clause.

The Nature of The Tax

In its brief the Company contends that the tax imposed by Section 203 is a tax of six per cent of the gross receipts and is not a franchise tax measured by six per cent of such receipts. In my opinion, this is not a correct view of the nature of the tax. Section 203(3) expressly declares that the tax is "an annual franchise or privilege tax." It is true that it also states that the tax is a "tax of six per cent . . . of the total gross receipts," but the Section must be construed as a whole, and in connection with related

Section, to learn its true nature. It is a part of Article III, Schedule C, of the Revenue Act. The Schedule itself is entitled "Franchise Tax" and Section 201 declares in terms that "the taxes levied and assessed in this Article or Schedule shall be paid as specifically herein provided, and shall be for the privilege of engaging in or carrying on the business or doing the act named; and, if a corporation, shall be a tax also for the continuance of its corporate rights and privileges granted under its charter, if incorporated in this State, or by reason of any act of domestication if incorporated in another State."

In Safe Bus Company v. Maxwell, 214 N. C. 12, the tax is described as a "franchise tax" and the court said that "Section 203 is primarily intended to fix the basis of taxation and to impose the rate to be paid by public utilities." In Stagg v. Nissen Company, 208 N. C. 285, it is held that our corporate franchise tax is a tax not on the doing of business, but on the privilege or right to do business.

It is my opinion that the tax is a privilege tax for engaging in this State in the business of "furnishing electricity, electric lights, current, or power," and also a corporate franchise tax, measured by six per cent of "the total gross receipts derived from such business within this State."

The Power of the State to Lay a Franchise Tax on Interstate Corporations

I assume that the business of selling to local distributors electric current brought in from Virginia is interstate and that the reduction of current is incidental to such business and not within the "broken package" doctrine. State Tax Commission of Mississippi v. Interstate Natural Gas Company, 284 U. S. 41, 76 L. Ed. 156; Public Utilities Comm. v. Landon, 249 U. S. 236, 63 L. Ed. 577; and East Ohio Gas Company v. Tax Comm. of Ohio, 283 U. S. 465, 75 L. Ed. 1171.

In Southern Natural Gas Company v. Alabama, 301 U. S. 148, 81 L. Ed. 970, the facts were in some respects similar to those here involved. There, a gas company piped gas in from other states under high pressure. After reducing the pressure, it sold the gas to four purchasers, three of whom were local distributors, the fourth being a consumer. It was held that Alabama could impose upon the company a franchise tax based on the capital employed in the state.

In Stone v. Interstate Natural Gas Company, (CCA 5) 103 F(2d) 544, similar facts were involved except there the entire business in the state was interstate inasmuch as the only sales were to three local distributors and the court held the company liable for the state franchise tax based on capital employed in the state. The decision was affirmed per curiam in 307 U. S. 620, 83 L. Ed. 1499. See also Ficklen v. Shelby County Taxing District, 145 U. S. 1, 36 L. Ed. 601.

In view of these cases, and many others to like effect, it would seem to be quite clear that this State has power to impose a franchise tax on the Virginia Electric and Power Company and would have such power even if all of the Company's sales were to local distributors and none were to consumers.

Measuring the Tax by Interstate Gross Receipts

This brings us to the real question presented. May the tax be measured by sales of current in this State, to distributors selling only to local consumers, when the sales by the company to such distributors are interstate in character?

Until very recently, it was long a notorious fact that under the afflatus of the Commerce Clause the decisions of the Supreme Court afforded interstate business a haven from State taxation and an unfair advantage over local but competing commerce. In its endeavor to protect interstate commerce from multiple or discriminatory taxation, the Court very nearly freed it of any State taxes whatsoever. That this was unsound and unnecessary is shown by the decisions of the Court at its last three terms.

The use of gross receipts or sales prices from interstate commerce as the measure of a State tax has recently been considered by the Supreme Court of the United States in a case of far reaching importance. The decision itself lays down no new rule; its significance lies in the emphasis which it places upon the fact that the tax is so measured or conditioned as to avoid the danger that it may be repeated in other states. Such taxes, the case holds, are valid. Western Live Stock v. Bureau of Revenue, 303 U. S. 250, 82 L. Ed. 823. The tax there was a privilege tax laid on a trade journal publisher measured by two per cent of his gross receipts from advertising space, the magazine having an interstate circulation and the advertisements being received from other states. In his opinion Stone, J., said, citations omitted:

> "It was not the purpose of the commerce clause to relieve those engaged in interstate commerce from their just share of state tax burden even though it increases the cost of doing business. 'Even interstate business must pay its way,' . . .
>
> "On the other hand, local taxes, measured by gross receipts from interstate commerce, have often been pronounced unconstitutional. The vice characteristic of those which have been held invalid is that they have placed on the commerce burdens of such a nature as to be capable in point of substance, of being imposed, . . . with equal right by every state which the commerce touches, merely because interstate commerce is being done, so that without the protection of the commerce clause it would bear cumulative burdens not imposed on local commerce. . . . The multiplication of state taxes measured by the gross receipts from interstate transactions would spell the destruction of interstate commerce and renew the barriers to interstate trade which it was the object of the commerce clause to remove. . . .
>
> "Taxation measured by gross receipts from interstate commerce has been sustained when fairly apportioned to the commerce carried on within the taxing state, . . . and in other cases has been rejected only because the apportionment was found to be inadequate or unfair, . . . Whether the tax was sustained as a fair means of measuring a local privilege or franchise, . . . or as a method of arriving at the fair measure of a tax substituted for local property taxes, . . . it is a practical way of laying upon the commerce its share of the local tax burden without subjecting it to multiple taxation not borne by local commerce and to which it would be subject if gross receipts, unapportioned, could be made the measure of a tax laid in every state where the commerce is carried on. A tax on gross receipts from tolls for the use by interstate

trains of tracks lying wholly within the taxing state is valid, . . . although a like tax on gross receipts from the rental of railroad cars used in the interstate commerce both within and without the taxing state is invalid. . . . *In the one case the tax reaches only that part of the commerce carried on within the taxing state; in the other, it extends to the commerce carried on without the state boundaries, and, if valid, could be similarly laid in every other state in which the business is conducted.*

"In the present case the tax is, in form and substance, an excise conditioned on the carrying on of a local business, that of providing and selling advertising space in a published journal, which is sold to and paid for by subscribers, some of whom receive it in interstate commerce. The price at which the advertising is sold is made the measure of the tax. This Court has sustained a similar tax said to be on the privilege of manufacturing, measured by the total gross receipts from sales of the manufactured goods both intrastate and interstate. American Manufacturing Co. vs. St. Louis, supra, 250 U. S. 459, 462, 39 S. Ct. 522, 63 L. Ed. 1084. The actual sales prices which measured the tax were taken to be no more than the measure of the value of the goods manufactured, and so an appropriate measure of the value of the privilege, the taxation of which was deferred until the goods were sold. Ficklen vs. Shelby County Taxing District, supra, sustained a license tax measured by a percentage of the gross annual commissions received by brokers engaged in negotiating sales within for sellers without the state.

"Viewed only as authority, American Manufacturing Co. vs. St. Louis, supra, would seem decisive of the present case. But we think the tax assailed here finds support in reason, and in the practical needs of a taxing system which, under constitutional limitations, must accommodate itself to the double demand that interstate business shall pay its way, and that at the same time it shall not be burdened with cumulative exactions which are not similarly laid on local business.

"Experience has taught that the opposing demands that the commerce shall bear its share of local taxation, and that it shall not, on the other hand, be subjected to multiple tax burdens merely because it is interstate commerce, are not capable of reconciliation by resort to the syllogism. Practical rather than logical distinctions must be sought. . . .

"But there is an added reason why we think the tax is not subject to the objection which has been leveled at taxes laid upon gross receipts derived from interstate communication or transportation of goods. So far as the value contributed to appellants' New Mexico business by circulation of the magazine interstate is taxed, it cannot again be taxed elsewhere any more than the value of railroad property taxed locally. The tax is not one which in form or substance can be repeated by other states in such manner as to lay an added burden on the interstate distribution of the magazine. As already noted, receipts from subscriptions are not included in the measure of the tax. It is not measured by the extent of the circulation of the magazine interstate. All the events upon which the tax is conditioned—the preparation, printing and publication of the advertising matter, and the receipts of the sums paid for it—occur in New Mexico and not elsewhere. All are beyond any control and taxing power which, without the commerce clause, those states could exert through its dominion over the distribution of the magazine or its subscribers. The dangers which may ensue from the imposition of a tax measured by gross receipts derived directly from interstate commerce are absent. . . ."

The decision points out that it is supported by American Manufacturing Co. v. St. Louis, 250 U. S. 459, 63 L. Ed. 1084, upholding a manufacturer's tax measured in part by gross receipts from interstate sales.

The importance of this case is referred to in a Case Comment in 52 Harvard Law Review, page 502, and by Professor C. L. B. Lowndes in an article in 88 Univ. Pa. Law Review 1, at 8. It has been extensively and favorably commented upon also in other legal periodicals.

Maine v. Grand Trunk R. Co., 142 U. S. 217, 35 L. Ed. 994, sustains a gross receipts percentage franchise tax on an interstate railroad, the tax being proportioned according to the relation which the mileage in the state bears to the total mileage both within and without the state.

Ficklen v. Shelby County Taxing District, 145 U. S. 1, 36 L. Ed. 601, upholds a tax of "2½ per cent on their gross yearly commissions" on commercial agents or merchandise brokers engaged in the state principally in interstate commerce but licensed to do business generally.

W. and M. Railway Co. v. Powers, 191 U. S. 379, 48 L. Ed. 229, sustains a tax upon the property and business of an interstate railroad, which provided that the gross income taxable should be the income earned from the intrastate business and that proportion of the interstate income which the mileage in the state bore to the total mileage in and out of the state.

In Adams Mfg. Company v. Storen, 304 U. S. 307, 82 L. Ed. 1365, it was held that a gross income tax of the State of Indiana, not conditioned upon any necessarily local activity, could not be laid by the state of the *seller* upon the gross receipts from interstate sales, the tax being attempted to be imposed upon the gross receipts of a local manufacturer, eighty per cent of whose sales were interstate or foreign. The Court emphasized the fact that the tax was not based upon, or apportioned according to, any essentially local act or business but taxed acts and business done beyond the boundaries of the state, and that, if valid, it could be levied by every state in which the seller did business. It said:

> "The vice of the statute as applied to receipts from interstate sales is that the tax includes in its measure, without apportionment, receipts derived from activities in interstate commerce . . . It is because the tax, forbidden as to interstate commerce, reaches indiscriminately and without apportionment, the gross compensation for both interstate commerce and intrastate activity that it must fall in its entirety as applied to receipts from sales interstate."

Gwin, White and Prince v. Henneford, 305 U. S. 434, 83 L. Ed. 272, invalidated the application of the Washington "business activities" tax to the gross income of a domestic corporation. The corporation, with headquarters in Washington, was engaged in a general marketing business selling products of Washington and Oregon fruit growers in other states and foreign countries and receiving a commission on each box sold. Numerous out of state agents of the corporation negotiated sales and made deliveries and collections which were remitted to Washington. The tax was held invalid because "not apportioned to the activities carried on in the state." It was a tax laid in the *seller's* state and is thus like that involved in the Storen Case. The court cited the Powers, Grand Trunk and Ficklen Cases, supra, to show that had the tax been conditioned upon or apportioned according to necessarily local events, it would have been sustained. With respect to the tax upheld in the Ficklen Case, the court said:

> "Although the tax, measured by gross receipts, to some extent burdened the commerce, it was held that the burden did not infringe the Commerce Clause. Since it was apportioned exactly to the activities taxed, all of which were intrastate, the tax was fairly measured by the value of the local privilege or franchise."

Here the tax is "apportioned exactly to the activities taxed," namely, the "furnishing" of electric current "within this State."

In his address before the 1939 Session of the National Tax Association, Professor Roger John Traynor of the University of California Law School, recently appointed to the Supreme Court of California, points out that the opinion in the Gwin Case lends "forceful support to the apportionment theory." National Tax Association Proceedings, 1939, Page 27, 38. In the same address, he also noted that the decision in Puget Sound Stevedoring Co. v. Tax Comm., 302 U. S. 90, 82 L. Ed. 68, is not inconsistent with the recent apportionment cases for there the tax was on the very act of engaging in interstate commerce, "a privilege which the state does not grant, regardless of the measure."

In Southern Pacific Co. v. Gallegher, 306 U. S. 167, 83 L. Ed. 587, appellant, an interstate carrier, brought into California rails, tools, equipment and supplies purchased by it in other states for immediate or future use in its interstate business and it was held that California properly applied its "use" tax to such property, the court laying down its now famous "taxable moment" theory and pointing out that the levy involved no danger of multiple taxation. The Court said:

> "Where a similar levy by other states may be imposed, with consequent multiplicity of exaction on commerce *for the same taxable event,* local tax of a privilege, measured by total gross receipts, is considered identical with an exaction on the commerce itself. This rule is applicable to . . . a tax upon gross receipts from (interstate) commerce without apportionment. The measurement of a tax by gross receipts where it cannot result in a multiplication of the levies it upheld," citing the Western Live Stock decision and cases there cited.

Here no other state can tax the "furnishing" of electric current "within this State," nor lay any tax on the exercise of its corporate functions and domestication here, as above pointed out. See also Felt and Tarrant Mfg. Co. v. Gallegher, 306 U. S. 62, 83 L. Ed. 488, and Pacific Tel. and Tel. Co. v. Gallegher, 306 U. S. 182, 83 L. Ed. 595.

The development of the new doctrine was carried a step farther in McGoldrick v. Berwind-White Coal Mining Company, 60 S. Ct. 388, McGoldrick v. Felt and Tarrant Mfg. Co., 60 S. Ct., 404, McGoldrick v. A. H. Du Grenier, Inc., 60 S. Ct. 404, and McGoldrick v. Campagnie Gemrab Transatlantique, 60 S. Ct. 670. These latter cases hold that the city of the *buyer* may collect from the interstate seller a sales tax measured by two per cent of the gross receipts from all sales for consumption in the city with respect to which title or possession was there transferred. The tax was upheld although the sales were clearly of an interstate character. In the first case, the court pointed out numerous instances where state taxes upon interstate commerce had been invalidated because of discrimination or the possibility of multiple levies and said, citations omitted:

"Finally it is said that the vice of the present tax is that it is measured by the gross receipts from interstate commerce and thus in effect reaches for taxation the commerce carried on both within and without the taxing state. . . . It is true that a state tax upon the operations of interstate commerce measured either by its volume or the gross receipts derived from it has been held to infringe the commerce clause, because the tax if sustained would exact tribute for the commerce carried on beyond the boundaries of the taxing state, and would leave each state through which the commerce passes free to subject it to a like burden not borne by intrastate commerce. . . .

"In Adams Manufacturing Co. vs. Storen, supra, . . . a tax on gross receipts, so far as laid by the state of the seller upon the receipts from sales of goods manufactured in the taxing state and sold in other states, was held invalid because there the court found the receipts derived from activities in interstate commerce, as distinguished from the receipts from activities wholly intrastate, were included in the measure of the tax, the sales price, without segregation or apportionment. *It was pointed out, . . . that had the tax been conditioned upon the exercise of taxpayer's franchise or its privilege of manufacturing in the taxing state, it would have been sustained, despite its incidental effect on interstate commerce since the taxpayer's local activities or privileges were sufficient to support such a tax, and that it could fairly be measured by the sales price of the goods. . . .*

"The rationale of the Adams Manufacturing Company Case does not call for condemnation of the present tax. Here the tax is conditioned upon a local activity delivery of goods within the state upon their purchase for consumption. It is an activity which apart from its effect on the commerce, is subject to the state taxing power. The effect of the tax, even though measured by the sales price, as has been shown, neither discriminates against nor obstructs interstate commerce more than numerous other state taxes which have repeatedly been sustained as involving no prohibited regulation of interstate commerce."

Few changes in the attitude of the Court have elicited greater or more favorable comment in the legal periodicals and by tax and constitutional experts than the new emphasis and approach found in its decisions at the last three terms, beginning with the Western Live Stock Case. Those that are available I have read and they appear to me to sustain fully my opinion that the proposed additional taxes are not prohibited by the Commerce Clause. Traynor, "Tax Decisions of the Supreme Court, 1937," National Tax Association Proceedings, 1937, 22; Traynor, "Tax Decisions of the Supreme Court, 1938," National Tax Association Proceedings, 27; Professor Thomas Reed Powell, "New Light on Gross Receipts Taxes—The Berwind-White Case," 53 Harvard Law Review, 909; Professor W. B. Lockhart, "State Barriers to Interstate Trade," 53 Harvard Law Review, 1253; Lockhart, "The Sales Tax in Interstate Commerce," 52 Harvard Law Review, 617; Professor C. L. B. Lowndes, "Taxation and the Supreme Court, 1938," 88 Univ. of Pa. Law Review, 1; Comment, 52 Harvard Law Review, 502; Comment, 34 Illinois Law Review, 989; Comment, 25 Cornell Law Quarterly, page 423. See, also, Perkins, "The Sales Tax and Transactions in Interstate Commerce, 12 N. C. Law Review, 99.

In the excellent discussion found in the Note in 34 Illinois Law Review, page 989, it is pointed out that in the Berwind-White Case the taxable event or condition, consummation of the sale in New York, could occur nowhere else and that therefore the tax was necessarily and automatically "apportioned" and multiple taxation was impossible, especially in view of the Storen and Gwin Cases forbidding an unapportioned tax in the seller's state. Other cases where the tax was "self-apportioned" in this manner are the Ficklen, Western Live Stock, American Manufacturing Company, and Southern Pacific Company Cases. Accordingly, I repeat that the tax we are here dealing with likewise is automatically apportioned for it is measured by the gross proceeds from the "furnishing" of electric current "within this State."

Summarizing, we have the Western Live Stock and Gwin Cases holding that interstate commerce may be subjected to a non-discriminatory State franchise or privilege tax measured by gross receipts when it is conditioned upon a local activity not occurring in other states. We have the Storen, Southern Pacific, Ficklen, Grand Trunk, and Powers Cases holding that the State of the interstate seller cannot lay on him a general gross income tax not based upon or apportioned according to any localized act or business. And, finally, we have the McGoldrick Cases holding that the jurisdiction of the interstate buyer may impose a gross sales tax upon his gross sales receipts when the tax is based upon an essentially local act, the passage of title or possession. In the McGoldrick Case and in the Western Live Stock Case, citing American Manufacturing Co. v. St. Louis, 250 U. S. 459, 63 L. Ed. 1084, the Court pointed out that a franchise or privilege tax laid on local acts could be measured by gross receipts from interstate commerce, the decisions so holding being referred to above.

In the matter at hand, we are concerned with a privilege or franchise tax laid at the same time on two things, (a) the "furnishing" of electric current "within this State," and (b) "the continuance of its corporate rights and privileges . . . by reason of" the domestication of the Virginia Electric and Power Company in this State, the tax being measured by six per cent "of the total gross receipts from such business within this State." Thus, the tax is laid on definitely localized activities not occurring in other states, and it is measured solely by the electric current "furnished within this State." It is very clear that it could not be measured by any current "furnished" in any other state. This could not be done for two reasons, first, because of the provisions of the Statute, and, second, because of the Storen and Gwin Cases and the other recent cases cited above.

In my opinion, the proposed additional franchise taxes are valid and would not be in violation of the Commerce Clause.

RE: INCOME TAXES; FEDERAL EMPLOYEES FROM OTHER STATES ASSIGNED TO DUTY HERE; TAXABILITY OF THEIR SALARIES

9 December, 1940.

The administrative decision made last winter that the above referred to persons should not be taxed for 1939 was not based on the view that they were not legally liable. It was based on the fact that it was understood that there were pending before the Committees of Congress certain proposed amendments which might have the effect of limiting State taxation of such salaries. In view of this information and of the fact that only during the tax year of 1939 had Congress authorized State taxation of such salaries, it was felt that it would be best to await the outcome of Congressional action.

In October, Congress enacted the Buck Act, which in effect supplements the Public Salary Tax Act of 1939, and permits federal salaries to be taxed by the States even though the federal employee resides in a federal area within the State. It applies only to income received after December 31, 1940. It fails to restrict the right of the State granted in the Act of 1939.

Thus it now appears that for 1940 each State has full Congressional assent to tax the salaries of federal employees or officers, the same as other income subject to State taxation. It further appears that in 1941 income received by such an employee will be taxable even though the employee is not a resident of this State and resides or works on a federal area over which the United States has exclusive jurisdiction, including Fort Bragg.

There is no doubt that the Income Tax Article of this State is broad enough to include all such salaries in the gross income required to be returned here for taxation.

The possible application of Section 325 to any such case is not presented by your inquiry.

RE: MOTOR VEHICLE SAFETY RESPONSIBILITY ACT; JUDGMENT RECOVERED IN ANOTHER STATE; RECOVERY ON JUDGMENT HERE; APPLICABILITY OF ACT

30 January, 1941.

I reply to your request for my opinion with respect to the case of Charles M. Dixon, Guilford College, North Carolina.

Judgment was recovered against Mr. Dixon in a New York Court for damages suffered by the plaintiff therein as a result of an automobile collision. Suit was then brought on the New York judgment in the Superior Court of Beaufort County by the New York plaintiff and the latter court rendered judgment against Mr. Dixon on the recovery in New York. The judgment in Beaufort County was rendered more than thirty days ago and has not been paid.

The Safety Responsibility Act, Chapter 116, Public Laws of 1931, provides that thirty days failure to satisfy a final judgment rendered by "a court of competent jurisdiction in this State" for damages resulting from the use of a motor vehicle shall result in suspension of the operator's license and registration certificates of the person against whom the judgment is rendered. The question is whether the judgment rendered in Beaufort County is such a judgment as is included in the Act. I am of opinion that it is not and that you should therefore return Mr. Dixon's license and registration certificates.

The question involved is solely one of statutory construction. If the Act is construed to include judgments recovered and unpaid in other States, it would not be void for extra-territoriality. See, for instance, Osborne v. Oglin, 310 U. S. 53, 84 L. Ed. 1074, 60 S. Ct. 758.

The act is patterned after the Uniform Act drawn by the National Conference of Commissioners on Uniform State Laws recommended by the American Automobile Association. See 9 N. C. L. R. 384. Section 11 of the Uniform Act provides in terms for suspension on failure to pay any judgment rendered against him by a court of competent jurisdiction in this or any other State, etc. Section 1 of our Act is the counterpart of Section 11 and the judgments it refers to are those rendered by "a court of competent jurisdiction in this State." The difference, I think, is significant and conclusive and forces the conclusion that our Act was not intended to apply to judgments rendered in any other State. The absence of a reciprocity provision with other states is referred to in 9 N. C. L. R., page 386. The settled maxim of statutory construction, expressio unius est exclusio alterius, supports this conclusion. The decisions of our Court make it clear that the Act would be "strictly construed," which means that it would not include in its terms any judgment, not expressly included therein, particularly in view of the difference between it and the Uniform Act referred to.

It may be suggested that a judgment has been rendered in this State and therefore the Act operates upon it. But the cause of action was not the original cause of action for damages growing out of the collision. That cause of action was merged in the judgment and the cause of action here sued on was one in contract, not tort. Therefore, the case is not brought within the terms of the Act. This is a rather technical and unsatisfactory ground, and I prefer to rest my opinion more upon the intentional exclusion of judgments recovered in other States. To hold that the act applies to such judgments later sued on in this State would amount to an extension of the Act to foreign judgments, which is the very thing that was intended to be excluded. Compare Nichols v. Maxwell, 202 N. C. 38.

SUBJECT: COSTS; ARREST FEES; STATE HIGHWAY PATROLMEN

19 February, 1941.

You state in your letter that it has recently been brought to your attention by the patrolman stationed in Iredell County that his warrants sworn out before magistrates have been signed by some officer other than the patrolman himself, for the purpose of collecting the arrest and witness fees, and that the magistrate claims that some officer must take such fees.

C. S. 3893 provides, in part, that any sheriff, deputy sheriff, chief of police, police, patrolmen, State Highway patrolmen, and/or any other law enforcement officer who receives a salary or compensation for his services from any source or sources other than the collection of fees, shall prove no attendance, and shall receive no fee as a witness for attending any superior or inferior criminal court sitting within the territorial boundaries in which such officer has authority to make an arrest. This provision was written into the above section by authority of Ch. 40 of the Public Laws of 1933.

Section 8 of Ch. 218, Public Laws of 1929, being C. S. 3846 (fff), provides that all fees for arrest or service of process that may be taxed in the bill of costs for the various courts of the State on account of the official acts of the members of the State Highway patrol shall be remitted to the general fund in the county in which said cost is taxed.

It is my opinion that highway patrolmen should sign the warrants in all cases instituted by such patrolmen, and this applies to prosecutions instituted in Iredell County, as well as the other counties of the State, unless there is some local statute applicable to Iredell County, of which I am unaware. It is extremely doubtful that there is a local statute containing the provisions set out in your letter. If the patrolman who is now located in Iredell County will secure from the magistrate a reference to the law under which he claims to operate, I will be glad to investigate the matter and advise you further.

RE: INCOME TAXES; OFFICERS AND ENLISTED MEN IN THE MILITARY AND NAVAL FORCES OF THE UNITED STATES; GROSS INCOME; RENTAL VALUE OF QUARTERS AND PAYMENTS MADE IN COMMUTATION OF QUARTERS AND SUBSISTENCE

27 February, 1941.

In your letter of the 17th you ask my advice on the question whether the rental value of quarters and payments in cash made to officers and enlisted men in the military and naval forces of the United States in commutation of quarters and subsistence constitute income includible in their returns of gross income to this State.

The general problem involved in your inquiry is to determine whether such items are furnished or paid as "compensation," for if that be their nature, they are income and taxable. But if they are furnished because necessary to the performance of the government service and not by way of payment for services rendered, they are not income and are not taxable.

There can be no question that the furnishing of general living quarters and meals by an employer to an employee constitutes gross income where it is compensatory and not done solely in the interest and for the convenience of the employer. Prentice-Hall 1941 Federal Tax Service, Paragraph No. 7704, et seq. C. C. H. 1941 Federal Tax Service, Paragraph No. 53, et seq. Such items are included in the broad sweep of the definition of "gross income" found in Section 317 of the Revenue Act of 1939, notwithstanding that they may not have been paid in cash. But the presence and movement of officers and enlisted men in the military and naval forces of the United States is a matter of such unique and constant interest and convenience to the Government that quarters and subsistence furnished them and payments made in commutation thereof have been treated separately and constitute an exception to the rule. Accordingly, as to them, such items do not constitute gross income and are not required to be reported as a matter of law. It is so provided by Section 19.22(a)-3, Regulations 103 of the United States Bureau of Internal Revenue. See, also, Mim. 3413, V-1 CB 29; IT 2219, IV-2CB41; IT 2232, IV-2CB144; IT3420, P-H. 1941 Fed. Tax Service, Paragraph No. 66007.

The question is thoroughly discussed and the reasons for the exception fully set forth in the very able opinion of Judge Booth in Jones v. U. S., 60 Ct. Cls, 552, 5 A. F. T. R. 5297, 1 U. S. T. C. 129.

The general problem being that of determining what is and what is not "compensation" and that being a question of general law as to which the Regulation is merely declaratory, it is my opinion that the Federal rule should be followed here. I think it not only correct on principle but that it is indirectly supported by Section 323(h) of the Revenue Act of 1939, which provides: "In computing net income no deduction shall in any case be allowed in respect of . . . (h) Commutation expenses." In U. S. v. Phistner, 94 U. S. 224, 24 L. Ed. 116, it was said: "Quarters are expected to be furnished by the government to its officers; when it cannot thus furnish, it allows them to be obtained otherwise and pays a money compensation therefor called commutation." In Jaegle v. U. S. 28, Ct. Cls., 133, the court said: "Commutation in the military service is money paid in substitution of something to which an officer, sailor, or soldier is entitled by law or regulations or general orders of the Commander in Chief."

Section 323(h) provides that such expenses cannot be deducted because reimbursement therefor has been or will be made. The necessary effect of this is to treat proper commutation expenses as items of proper expense, deductible but for the prohibition based on the reimbursement. To classify commutation payments or allowances as income would seem to require that the moneys paid out be allowed as deductions. The Section seems to recognize that such payments or allowances are not in the nature of compensation.

RE: MOTOR VEHICLE TAXES; FOR HIRE PASSENGER VEHICLES; EXCLUSION OF "NEIGHBOR FELLOW WORKMEN"

26 February, 1941.

Section 2(2) of the Motor Vehicle Act, Chapter 407, Public Laws of 1937, provides:

> "*For Hire Passenger Vehicles.* Passenger motor vehicles engaged in the business of transporting passengers for compensation; but this classification shall not include motor vehicles of seven-passenger capacity or less operated by the owner where the cost of operation is shared by neighbor fellow workmen between their homes and the place of regular daily employment, when operated for not more than two trips each way per day."

You ask my opinion whether or not this exclusion of "neighbor fellow workmen" is confined to workmen living in the same neighborhood and who are employed by the same employer.

The words "fellow workmen" constitute a term that has been well known in the law for over a hundred years. If they did not originate in, they were at least given greater currency by the case of Priestly v. Fowler, 3 M. and W. 1, an English Case, decided in 1837. See Mordecai Law Lectures, 2nd Edition, page 148, et seq. They mean persons employed by the same master in the same work or enterprise. See the Restatement of the Law of Agency, American Law Institute, Section 475.

In my opinion the term "neighbor fellow workmen" as used in Section 2(2) means workmen living in the same general neighborhood and who are employed by the same employer in the same work or enterprise. That this is true I think appears from the language used in the Section. When reference is made to the "homes of the workmen" the plural is used but the term "the place of regular daily employment" is in the singular. When a term or phrase which has a well understood meaning is used in a statute, the courts construe it as carrying that meaning. For these reasons, I do not think that the exclusion applies to a case where the workmen are not all employed by the same employer.

I call your attention to the fact that the wisdom or fairness of the provision is not for us to decide. We must take the language as we find it in the statute and give it the meaning which the words were understood to carry at the time of the enactment.

RE: INCOME TAXES; GROSS INCOME; PURCHASE BY CORPORATION OF ITS OWN BONDS FOR LESS THAN ISSUED PRICE

10 March, 1941.

You state that a Delaware corporation purchased its own bonds for less than the issued price; some of the bonds were kept alive and carried on the corporation's books as "treasury bond investment," while the other bonds were cancelled. You ask my opinion whether, in these instances, the corporation received taxable income.

In my opinion the corporation received taxable income in both instances. The difference between the purchase price and the issuing price, adjusted for amortized discount of premium and selling expense, is income to the corporation when the latter exceeds the former, and this is true whether or not the bonds are cancelled within the income year. I know of no period when the contrary was deemed to be the law of this State. See Magill, Taxable Income, pages 222-231; United States v. Kirby Lumber Company, 284 U. S. 1; 52 Harvard Law Review 977; 49 Yale Law Journal 1153; 37 Michigan Law Review 1353.

SUBJECT: PROCESS TAXES

26 March, 1941.

Section 157(a) of the Public Laws of 1939 is as follows:

> "In every indictment or criminal proceeding finally disposed of in the Superior Court, the party convicted or adjudged to pay the cost shall pay a tax of two dollars ($2.00): Provided, that this tax shall not be levied in cases where the county is required to pay the cost."

I advise from the above that unless a criminal case reaches the Superior Court, there is no liability for process tax in such a case; that is to say, there is no liability for the tax in those criminal cases which are begun and end in recorders courts.

In those recorders courts which have civil jurisdiction, there is a liability for the tax because of the wording of subsection (b) of this section, which is in part as follows:

> "At the time of suing out the summons in a civil action in the Superior Court *or other court of record*, or the docketing of an appeal from the lower court in the Superior Court, the plaintiff or the appellant shall pay a tax of two dollars ($2.00)."

Since county recorders courts are courts of record, it is my opinion that the process tax should be collected in those recorders courts which have civil jurisdiction.

RE: (1) INCOME TAXES; EXEMPTION OF INCOME; INTEREST FROM BONDS ISSUED BY NORTH CAROLINA HOUSING AUTHORITIES. (2) INTANGIBLE TAXES; EXEMPTIONS; BONDS OF LOCAL HOUSING AUTHORITIES

8 May, 1941.

In your letter of the 2nd you ask my opinion whether interest from bonds issued by a Housing Authority organized in this State under Chapter 456, Public Laws of 1935, is exempt from taxation.

Section 317(2)d of the Revenue Act exempts "interest upon the obligations of . . . the State of North Carolina, or of a political subdivision thereof." Our Supreme Court has held that Housing Authorities organized under Chapter 456, Public Laws of 1935, are political subdivisions of the State. Wells v. Housing Authority, 213 N. C. 744.

Section 26 of the Housing Authority Act, supra, is in part as follows:

> "Bonds, notes, debentures and other evidences of indebtedness of an authority are declared to be issued for a public purpose and to be public instrumentalities and, together with interest thereon, shall be exempt from taxes when same are held by the Federal Government or by any purchaser from the Federal Government or anyone acquiring title from or through such purchaser."

Thus, in Section 317(2)d of the Revenue Act we have a general law broad enough to grant a total exemption of such interest, while in Section 26 of the Housing Authority Act we have a special provision dealing particularly with such interest and providing a more limited exemption. Section 317(2)d of the Revenue Act of 1939 was contained in the Revenue Act of 1935 and prior Revenue Acts and is therefore to be regarded as simply a continuation of the earlier provisions. Under such circumstances, our court has repeatedly held that the special provision governs, it being regarded as an exemption of the general provision. State v. Johnson, 170 N. C. 685; Branham v. Durham, 171 N. C. 196; Rankin v. Gaston County, 173 N. C. 683; Young v. Davis, 182 N. C. 200; Blair v. Board of Commissioners of New Hanover County, 187 N. C. 488; State v. Baldwin, 205 N. C. 174.

It is therefore my opinion that such interest is exempt only when the bonds are held by "the federal government or by any purchaser from the federal government or anyone acquiring title from or through such purchaser."

Your correspondent asks also whether such bonds are exempt from our intangibles tax.

Section 704 of the Revenue Act exempts from the intangibles tax bonds issued by "political subdivisions of this State." Section 26 of the Housing Authority Act grants to bonds issued by local Housing Authorities the same exemption granted to interest on such bonds. Therefore, for the same reasons, it is my opinion that the bonds themselves are exempt from the tax only when held by "the federal government or by any purchaser from the federal government or anyone acquiring title from or through such purchaser."

RE: INCOME TAXES; DEDUCTIONS; INTEREST PAID ON LOANS TO PAY LIFE INSURANCE PREMIUMS

15 May, 1941.

You have handed me the letter written to you on May 12, 1941, by Mr. Clayton L. Burwell, Charlotte Attorney, with attached memorandum on the question whether certain interest is deductible for income tax purposes.

Mr. Burwell states the facts as follows: "In the instant case, an insured proposes to pay up life insurance policy 'A' by using the cash value of policy 'B' as collateral and remitting to the insurance company the proceeds of the loan." It is not stated whether the loan is to be made by the issuing insurance company or by a bank. However, I do not think that important for it would seem that in either event the answer must be the same, for the important and controlling point is that the proceeds of the loan are to be used to pay life insurance premium or premiums.

Section 317(2) (a) and (b) of the Revenue Act are as follows:

> "(a) The proceeds of life insurance policies and contracts paid upon the death of the insured to beneficiaries or to the estate of the insured.
>
> "(b) The amount received by the insured as a return of premium or premiums paid by him under life insurance endowment contracts, either during the term or at the maturity of the term mentioned in the contracts or upon surrender of the contract."

In the statement of facts submitted it is said that the insurance policy to be paid up will yield no current income and that the returns that will be received will be in the nature of a return of premiums.

It thus appears that the loan is to be obtained and used for the purchase of a policy or contract which will yield no taxable income and the proceeds of which, upon maturity, will also not constitute taxable income.

It is an established principle that interest paid on loans to purchase tax-exempt securities or to purchase property, the income of which is not taxable, is not deductible. Denman v. Slayton, 282 U. S. 514, 75 L. Ed. 500; Prentice-Hall, Fed. Tax Service, 1941, Paragraph No. 13,018-A; 3 Paul and Merten's Law of Federal Income Taxation, Section 24.15. See also Deputy v. Dupont, 308 U. S. 488, 84 L. Ed. 416.

It is upon this principle that Section 322(3) of our Revenue Act provides that "interest paid or accrued in connection with the ownership of real or personal property, the current income from which is not taxable under this Article." For the same reason, Section 323(c) prohibits the deduction of "premiums paid on any life insurance policy."

In my opinion interest paid on loans obtained to pay life insurance premiums may not be claimed as a deduction from gross income, and I think this is true not only with respect to loans obtained from a bank but also with respect to policy loans made by the insurance company.

If the loan is obtained from the insurance company and the interest is merely charged against the credits or values attaching to the policy, the deduction must be disallowed for the additional reason that in such case no interest is "paid". Alsberg v. Comm'r. of Int. Rev., 42 B. T. A. 61; Hirsch v. Comm'r. of Int. Rev., 42 B. T. A. 566; 1 CCH 1941 Fed. Tax Ser., Paragraph No. 171.208.

RE: LICENSE TAXES; CONTRACTORS; LIABILITY OF CONTRACTOR FOR UNITED STATES POST OFFICE

16 May, 1941.

In our recent conference you requested my opinion whether J. M. Gregory, Raleigh Contractor, is liable for the contractor's project tax levied by Section 122(b) of the Revenue Act of 1937 under the following facts.

In 1938 the United States awarded him the contract for the construction of the new annex to the United States Post Office at Raleigh, N. C., for a price of $289,000.00. The annex was constructed on land belonging to the United States. Section 8059 of the Consolidated Statutes cedes to the United States exclusive jurisdiction over lands in this State acquired by the United States for post offices, pursuant to the power granted in Article I, Section 8, Clause 17 of the Constitution of the United States.

Section 122(b) of the Revenue Act of 1937 provides that a contractor "who, for a fixed price, commission, fee or wage, undertakes or executes a contract for the construction, or who superintends the construction of any (building) shall, before or at the time of entering into such project, and/or such contract, apply for and procure from the Commissioner of Revenue a State-wide license, and shall pay for such license" a tax based on the contract price of the project. The tax in question amounts to $300.00.

In performing the contract with which we are concerned the contractor blocked off and took exclusive possession of the sidewalks and a portion of the streets adjoining the work. In addition, it is understood that he stored materials for the work at places in or near the City not owned by the United States and used the streets of the City in transporting materials for the project. It is also understood that he supervised the work, in part, from his local office which was not on Federal property.

It is further understood that the contract for the annex provided that the contractor would comply with the Workmen's Compensation Law of this State.

The contractor contends that as the annex was constructed on land over which the State had ceded exclusive jurisdiction to the United States, it therefore follows that jurisdiction is lacking to support the tax.

Under the same facts, a similar contention was made in Ralph Sollitt and Sons Const. Co. v. Virginia, 161 Va. 584, 172 S. E. 290, 91 A. L. R. 774, the appellant being an Illinois Corporation whose sole business in Virginia was the performance of a contract with the United States for the construction of the Post Office at Lynchburg, the tax being, as here, a contractor's project tax measured by five per cent of the contract price. In holding that the tax was not invalid for want of territorial jurisdiction, Chief Justice Campbell said:

> "The basis of the tax, however, is found in the distinction between general use and sole appropriation of the highway. In its last analysis it conclusively appears that the company is not performing its contract solely upon government property; it is in no sense an instrumentality of the government . . . A case directly in point is Ohio River Contract Co. vs. Gordon, 244 U. S., 68, 37 S. Ct., 599, 600, 61 L. Ed. 997. In that case Chief Justice White said:
>
> " 'The Contract Company was a corporation organized under the laws of Indiana, and had its principal place of business in that state. At the time in question it was engaged within the geograph-

> ical limits of the State of Kentucky in constructing, under a contract with the United States government, a canal with locks and dam on the Ohio River on a piece of land known as the Canal Reservation, acquired by the United States by purchase or condemnation from the State of Kentucky with the consent of its legislature. While most of the work under the contract was performed on the land thus acquired, the earth and rocks excavated in the construction of the canal were hauled over railroad tracks laid by the defendant company on land outside of the Canal Reservation, and, through an arrangement with the Kentucky and Indiana Terminal Railway Company, were dumped on its property in the state of Kentucky. The accident which gave rise to the injuries complained of occurred in the course of the work on the Canal Reservation. In conformity with a statute of Kentucky the company had designated an agent in the state upon whom process might be served in the event suits were brought against it in the state. The summons issued in the cause was served on the designated agent when he was on the land of the United States, but subsequently an alias summons was served on him at his home in Louisville. . . .
>
> " 'Conceding, for the sake of the argument only, that the Canal Reservation was within the exclusive legislative jurisdiction of Congress, it is clear from the facts we have stated that the business carried on by the corporation was not confined to the land owned by the United States, since it is admitted that, in order to dispose of the material excavated in the construction of the canal, a line of railway was built which extended beyond the reservation and connected with the tracks of the Kentucky and Indiana Terminal Railway, upon whose property all of the earth and rocks were dumped. This clearly constituted the doing of business within the state and subjected the corporation to the jurisdiction of the Kentucky courts. . . ."

From this decision Sollitt appealed to the United States Supreme Court which dismissed his appeal "for the want of a substantial federal question," 292 U. S. 599, 78 L. Ed. 1463, and denied a rehearing, 292 U. S. 604, 78 L. Ed. 1466. In so doing the court cited the Gordon Case which had been relied on by the Virginia Court.

A closely similar decision is found in Atkinson v. State Tax Commission, 303 U. S. 20, 82 L. Ed. 621, where part of the work of constructing a dam for the United States was done on Federal land and part on land over which the State had jurisdiction, namely the bed of a navigable river, which would seem not different from the streets and sidewalks in the Sollitt Case.

Another distinct ground for upholding the tax is found in Silas Mason Company v. State Tax Commission, 302 U. S. 186, 82 L. Ed. 187, and in the Atkinson Case, supra. In both it is held that a state statute granting exclusive jurisdiction to the United States over federal areas in the state, such as Section 8059 of our Consolidated Statutes, does not preclude state taxes with respect to acts done or business carried on in such areas if the United States has not accepted such grant. Non-acceptance of an exclusive jurisdiction was found in these cases in the fact that the contracts provided that the contractors should comply with State Compensation and other like laws. The effect of this, the court held, was necessarily to preclude an exclusive jurisdiction in the United States, the consequence of which was that State taxes might be levied against the contractor. The contract in this matter required the contractor to comply with our Workmen's Compensation Act.

On the same principle, James Stewart and Company v. Sadrakula, 309 U. S. 94, 84 L. Ed. 596, upheld a judgment awarding damages for wrongful death of the employee of a contractor building the New York Post Office, the basis of the award being a violation of a New York building regulation which caused the death.

These cases and other recent decisions of the court show a marked tendency and practice to seize upon any point, however unreal and unconvincing it may be, to avoid striking down State taxes on federal contractors on the fictitious and technical ground of territoriality. In the Sollitt Case it supported the tax on the ground that the contractor used the city streets and sidewalks, while in the Silas Mason and Atkinson Cases the taxes were upheld on the fact that the contracts provided that the contractor should comply with State Workmen's Compensation Laws. This trend is seen in the following excerpt from Chief Justice Hughes' opinion in James v. Dravo Cont. Co., 302 U. S. 134, 148, 82 L. Ed. 155, 166, likewise upholding a State license tax against a federal contractor:

> "The possible importance of reserving to the State jurisdiction for local purposes which involve no interference with the performance of governmental functions is becoming more and more clear as the activities of the Government expand and large areas within the States are acquired."

While it was passed subsequent to the transactions here involved and its provisions are not literally applicable, the new Federal policy to preserve State jurisdiction over Federal areas, when its exercise will not interfere with Federal functions, is shown by the Buck Act, Public No. 819, Chapter 787, 3rd Series, 76th Congress, authorizing the levying and collection of State sales, use and income taxes in such areas.

I do not discuss the question whether a Federal contractor is a Federal instrumentality and therefore exempt from State taxes. Numerous recent decisions have thoroughly established that he occupies no such status and is liable for non-discriminatory taxes to the same extent as others similarly engaged. See the Silas Mason, Dravo, and Atkinson Cases, supra, and those cited therein.

Wisconsin v. J. C. Penney Company, Prentice-Hall's State and Local Tax Service, Paragraph No. 92,045, decided by the United States Supreme Court December 16, 1940, is an extremely illuminating revelation of the new attitude of the court toward State taxes and the Constitution. To fully appreciate this change we must look back to Baldwin v. Missouri, 281 U. S. 586, 74 L. Ed. 1057, where, dissenting against the invalidation of State taxes on fictitious and arbitrary territorial grounds, Justice Holmes said that he saw "hardly any limit but the sky to the invalidating of (State taxing) rights if they happen to strike a majority of this court as for any reason undesirable."

In the Penney Case the court said:

> "The simple but controlling question is whether the State has given anything for which it can ask return. The substantial privilege of carrying on business in Wisconsin, which has here been given, clearly supports the tax and the state has not given the less merely because it has conditioned the demand of the exaction upon hap-

penings outside its own borders. The fact that the tax is contingent upon events brought to pass without a state does not destroy the nexus between such a tax and transactions within a state for which the tax is an exaction. . . . Nothing can be less helpful than for our courts to go beyond the extremely limited restrictions that the Constitution places upon the states and to inject themselves in a merely negative way into the delicate processes of fiscal policy-making."

So here it is obvious that the State has given the contractor much for which it can ask return. It is wholly inconceivable that he could have constructed the annex on the small plot upon which it stands without doing much of the work without its bounds. It is safe to say that most of the planning and preparation, the purchasing and storing of materials and supplies, and the removal of excavated dirt all occurred in large part outside of the Federal land. There is no doubt that he took exclusive possession of the adjoining sidewalks and a portion of the streets during the period of construction. These things were held enough to give the tax jurisdictional support in the Sollitt Case, and I have no doubt that they are enough here.

For the reasons and upon the authorities above stated, it is my opinion that the contractor is liable for the project tax with respect to his contract for the Raleigh Post Office Annex.

A similar opinion upon the same question was expressed by the Attorney General of Utah on March 17, 1941, CCH, State and Local Tax Service, Utah, Paragraph Number 7897.

RE: INCOME TAXES; EMPLOYEES THRIFT PLAN; THE STANDARD OIL COMPANY; TAXABILITY (1) OF DEDUCTIONS FROM EMPLOYEES ANNUAL SALARY AND (2) OF CONTRIBUTIONS MADE TO THE PLAN BY THE COMPANY

23 May, 1941.

I reply to your letter of May 19 and return herewith the letters which you have received from Mr. C. E. Motte, Charlotte, North Carolina.

It is stated that Mr. Motte, an employee of the Standard Oil Company of New Jersey, is a participant in the Company's Employees Thrift Plan. Under this plan the employee can authorize the Company to deduct from his current compensation up to 13 per cent of the amount thereof. These deductions are credited to the account of the employee with the plan fund. In addition to these deductions, the Company itself makes certain contributions to the employee's account. The questions presented are whether or not the employee must include in his income tax returns (a) that part of his annual compensation deducted during the year under the plan, and (b) the contribution made by the Company.

In my letter of November 4, 1939, I advised you that in my opinion contributions of an employer to an employees thrift or benefit plan or system were not taxable for the reason that they were not available to the employee. However, I stated further that such sums would be taxable when withdrawn by the employee. That opinion is applicable here to the contributions made by the company to the thrift plan.

I think it quite clear that the employee is not entitled to deduct from gross income the amount of his stated annual compensation which is deducted and credited to his plan account. Section 317 of the Revenue Act defines gross income very broadly and expressly includes compensation for personal services of all kinds. The full amount of the annual compensation accrues to the taxpayer and is available to him. When paid, it is a discharge of the company's obligation and it is no matter that under a collateral agreement a part of the compensation is deducted for the purpose of the plan. Section 322 of the Act governs the deductions that may be made from the defined gross income and none of its provisions authorize a taxpayer to deduct his own contributions to the plan which are charged against his salary.

SUBJECT: UNIFORM DRIVERS LICENSE ACT; REVOCATION OF LICENSE; NONRESIDENTS

29 May, 1941.

I have examined the letter of Mr. A. W. Graham, Jr., Clerk of the Superior Court of Granville County, wherein he raises the question as to the constitutionality of Section 18 of Chapter 52 of the Public Laws of 1935 when applied to the drivers license of a nonresident which has been issued to him by the state of his residence and forwarding the same to the Highway Safety Department of this State.

I do not think our statute contemplates the actual taking up of such a nonresident's license and forwarding the same to your Department. Section 16 of the Act relates only to the suspension of the privilege of operating a motor vehicle upon the highways of this State by nonresidents who have been convicted of a violation of the laws of this State, the conviction of which requires either the suspension or revocation of such license.

It seems to me that as far as the Department could go in such a case would be to suspend or revoke the license of such nonresidents to operate a motor vehicle upon the highways of this State, and, under subsection (b) of Section 16, upon receiving record of the conviction in this State of a nonresident driver of a motor vehicle of any offense under the motor vehicle laws, to forward a copy of such record to the motor vehicle administrator in the state wherein the person so convicted is a resident. This would enable the authorities of the foreign state to take such action as to the drivers license issued by it in such a case as the laws of that state authorize and permit.

I think that under subsection (a) of Section 18, the court in which a conviction is had might enter a notation upon a nonresident's license or any violation of the motor vehicle laws of this State at the time of conviction of an offense in this State which would require suspension or revocation of such operator's or chauffeur's license.

The question, therefore, raised by Mr. Graham would perhaps not arise because, under the Act, such a foreign license is not authorized to be taken up at the time of conviction by the authorities of this State.

RE: INCOME TAXES; EXEMPTIONS; HEAD OF HOUSEHOLD; MARRIED WOMEN AS

7 June, 1941.

I reply to your letter of June 6 with respect to the 1939 and 1940 income tax returns of Mrs. Phoebe B. Summers, Salisbury, N. C.

Mrs. Summers is married and lives with her husband. During the income year in question her husband was competent and engaged in business activities but his income was insignificant. Mrs. Summers, having income of her own, furnished funds for the operation and maintenance of the home and without which it could not have been maintained. She has two children under 18 years of age. She claims to be entitled to the $2,000.00 exemption under Section 324 (1) (b) of the Revenue Act of 1939. You have denied this claim for exemption, relying upon the opinion of Attorney General Brummitt, dated June 29, 1933. My opinion is requested whether you were correct in refusing the exemption.

In my opinion, it is clear that Mrs. Summers, under the circumstances stated, is entitled to this exemption. The question of who is the head of the household is economic and practical. It is not to be decided upon archaic and antiquated views as to the inferior status of the wife. Under the law of today, if she is competent to furnish the money for the maintenance of the household, she is also competent to demand the exemption allowed to those who maintain and support households.

SUBJECT: SCRAP TOBACCO TAX LAW

10 July, 1941.

In your letter of June 17 you submitted four questions with reference to the Scrap Tobacco Tax Law, Chapter 414 of the Public Laws of 1937, as amended by Chapter 389 of the Public Laws of 1939 and by Chapter 246 of the Public Laws of 1941. I will attempt to answer your questions as submitted:

> "1. Will a redrying plant, located in one county, be permitted to buy scrap tobacco, in another county, from a licensed warehouse or redrying plant without being subject to a license tax, for the county in which the tobacco is bought?"

Section 2 of Chapter 246, Public Laws of 1941, is as follows:

> "Provided, that the tax herein levied shall not apply in cases where the producer delivers his scrap or untied tobacco to a tobacco warehouse or tobacco redrying plant."

This proviso is added at the end of Section 1 of the 1937 Act, as amended. I would conclude, therefore, that a redrying plant, wherever located, purchasing scrap tobacco from a licensed warehouse or redrying plant would not be required to pay the tax imposed by Section 1, if the scrap tobacco so purchased had been delivered by the producer to the tobacco warehouse or redrying plant which made the sale. If, on the other hand, the redrying plant, wherever located, was engaged in the business of buying scrap tobacco and purchased from a redrying plant or tobacco warehouse, scrap tobacco which had not been delivered to such seller by the producer, the tax would be applicable.

> "2. What is your definition of a tobacco warehouse?"

In my opinion, a tobacco warehouse within the meaning of the section is a tobacco warehouse which is subject to the tax imposed by Section 142 of the Revenue Act of 1939. In using the words "tobacco warehouse" in this statute, the General Assembly undoubtedly intended to refer to tobacco warehouses in which auction sales of tobacco are regularly conducted throughout the tobacco belts in North Carolina. In the absence of some statutory definition to the contrary, the words would be given the meaning of the general and accepted use and would refer to that type of tobacco auction warehouse so well known in this State.

> "3. Will a person or a redrying plant be subject to a scrap tobacco license, if the said person or redrying plant were to open a tobacco warehouse in an adjoining county, to engage in the business of buying leaf or scrap tobacco, such tobacco not being sold at auction?"

The answer to this question, in my opinion, is yes, unless the tobacco warehouse is in fact a bona fide place where tobacco is bought and sold at auction, or has the general characteristics of tobacco warehouses such as are generally conducted in this State. In my opinion, the exemption provided by the 1941 Act in favor of tobacco delivered by the producer to a tobacco warehouse or a tobacco redrying plant would not be applicable and the tax should be collected.

> "4. Will a pick-up-station, having paid tax for buying scrap tobacco in a county, other than the county in which the parent establishment is located, be liable for agents licenses, if they employ agents to solicit business and buy scrap tobacco for them in the county in which the pick-up-station is located?"

Yes, in my opinion any person, firm or corporation which carries on the business described in this statute through agents, representatives, solicitors or peddlers, other than those named on the original license issued, are required to pay the additional license of $250 for each additional agent, representative, solicitor or peddler for each county in which such business is carried on, as required by Section 3(a) of the amended Act.

SUBJECT: AD VALOREM TAXATION; POWERS OF BOARD OF EQUALIZATION AND REVIEW AFTER DATE FIXED BY STATUTE FOR ADJOURNMENT; POWERS OF COUNTY COMMISSIONERS WITH RESPECT TO RECORDS AFTER ADJOURNMENT OF BOARD OF EQUALIZATION AND REVIEW

12 July, 1941.

Receipt is acknowledged of your letter of July 11, enclosing correspondence with Mr. H. Armfield, Tax Supervisor of Stanly County.

It appears from the correspondence with Mr. Armfield that the County Commissioners of Stanly County, when they met as a Board of Equalization and Review, appointed a committee under the provisions of Paragraph (d) of Subsection 7 of Section 1105 of the Machinery Act of 1939, and that this committee did not finish its work and make its report until after the date fixed by statute for the adjournment of the Board of Equalization and Review had passed. The question raised is whether either the Board of Equalization and Review of Stanly County or the County Commissioners of Stanly County would have the right to validate the actions of the committee, and order the changes made on the tax books in compliance with the committee's report.

Subsection 5 of Section 1105 of the Machinery Act of 1939 provides that the Board of Equalization and Review shall hold its first meeting on the eleventh Monday following the day on which tax listing began, and may adjourn from time to time as its duties may require; but it shall complete its duties not later than the third Monday following its first meeting. The primary reason for fixing a definite time for the final adjournment of the Board of Equalization and Review is to require the completion of the duties of this Board in time for the valuations to be settled when the county budget is adopted in accordance with the statute. In many instances Boards of Equalization and Review have found it impossible to complete their duties within the time specified in Section 1105 of the Machinery Act of 1939, and have followed the procedure of adjourning from time to time until their duties have been completed.

This office has heretofore given as its opinion that although the provisions of the Machinery Act relative to the date for the first meeting and final adjournment of Boards of Equalization and Review appear to be mandatory, if a Board of Equalization and Review holds its first meeting on the date specified in the statute and is absolutely unable to complete its duties prior to the time set by the statute for its final adjournment, it can find as a fact that it has been unable to complete its work within the prescribed time, and upon entering such finding upon its minutes, can adjourn from time to time until it has finally completed its duties.

However, if a Board of Equalization and Review fails to enter an order adjourning from time to time and allows the time to elapse or enters an order of final adjournment, it would then have no right to reconvene for the purpose of reconsidering the tax list. See Commissioners of Cleveland v. Railroad, 86 N. C. 541, and Wolfenden v. Commissioners of Beaufort, 152 N. C. 83.

If the Board of Equalization and Review of Stanly County allowed the date for final adjournment to pass without taking any action toward continuing its sessions beyond the statutory time, or has entered an order of final adjournment, I am of the opinion that it would have no right to reconvene for the purpose of further considering the tax list of Stanly County; but if the Board of Equalization and Review on or prior to the date fixed by statute for its final adjournment found as a fact that it has been unable to complete its duties and has continued its sessions from time to time, the Court, in my opinion, would hesitate to invalidate any action taken by the Board, even though the action is taken after the date fixed by statute for the final adjournment of the Board.

If the Board of Equalization and Review is not in position to take action on the report of the committee appointed by such Board, it is possible that the matter may be taken care of under the provisions of Section 1108(6) of the Machinery Act of 1939. This section provides that after the Board of Equalization has finished its work and the changes effected by it have been given effect on the tax records, the Board of County Commissioners may not authorize any changes to be made on said records, with certain exceptions, one of these exceptions being "To reassess property when the supervisor reports that, since the completion of the work of the Board of Equalization, facts have come to his attention which render it advisable to raise or lower the assessment of some particular property of a given taxpayer: Provided, that no such reassessment shall be made unless it could have been made by the Board of Equalization had the same facts been brought to the attention of said Board of Equalization: Provided further, that this shall not authorize reassessment because of events or circumstances not taking place or arising until after the tax listing day."

This provision first appeared in the Machinery Act in 1937. The Supreme Court of North Carolina, prior to the time the above quoted provision was placed in the Machinery Act, held in the case of Buncombe County v. Beverly Hills, Inc., 203 N. C. 170, that where the value of lands listed by the taxpayer has been increased and the taxpayer duly files complaint before the Board of County Commissioners sitting as a Board of Equalization and Review, and the matter of reassessment is referred to the County Tax Supervisor, who makes a reduction of the tax value and the reassessment is approved by the County Commissioners at a regular meeting after the date prescribed by statute for action thereon, the approval of the reassessment is not void and the taxpayer is entitled to the benefit of the reduced assessment. I call your attention specifically to the following excerpt from the opinion:

> "The spirit of the act in controversy never intended, under the facts in this case, to confiscate any part of defendant's property by an exorbitant and excessive tax, when it used due diligence and relied on plaintiff's chairman, whose act was afterwards ratified by plaintiff corporation. The provisions of the statute relied on by plaintiff is not like the 'law of the Medes and Persians, which altereth not'."

Of course, Commissioners should be very careful in attempting to exercise the powers contained in Section 1108(6), especially as to reducing valuations, as Section 7976 of the Consolidated Statutes might render them personally liable to the amount of the taxes involved.

Subject: Scrap Tobacco Tax Law

23 July, 1941.

In your letter of July 21 you submit four questions with reference to the scrap tobacco tax law, Chapter 414 of the Public Laws of 1937, as amended by Chapter 389 of the Public Laws of 1939, and by Chapter 246 of the Public Laws of 1941. I will answer the questions in the order presented:

> "1. When redrying plants buy scrap tobacco from a licensed warehouse, will the redrying plant be subject to a license tax?"

Section 2 of Chapter 246 of the Public Laws of 1941 is as follows:

> "Provided, that the tax herein levied shall not apply in cases where the producer delivers his scrap or untied tobacco to a tobacco warehouse or tobacco redrying plant."

This proviso is added at the end of Section 1 of the 1937 Act, as amended. I would conclude, therefore, that a redrying plant, wherever located, purchasing scrap tobacco from a licensed warehouse or redrying plant would not be required to pay the tax imposed by Section 1, if the scrap tobacco so purchased had been delivered by the producer to the tobacco warehouse or redrying plant which made the sale. If, on the other hand, the redrying plant, wherever located, was engaged in the business of buying scrap tobacco and purchased it from a redrying plant or tobacco warehouse, scrap tobacco which had not been delivered to such seller by the producer, the tax would be applicable.

> "2(a). Will a redrying plant be subject to scrap tobacco dealer's license tax, if a pick-up-station is opened in a county, other than the county in which the parent establishment is located? In this pick-up-station, scrap tobacco will be bought only from the producer."

In order to escape liability for the payment of the tax provided in Section 1, the scrap tobacco must originally have been delivered by the producer to a tobacco warehouse or tobacco redrying plant. If such tobacco is delivered to a pick-up-station, it does not come within the exemption because the statute specifically says that it must be delivered by the producer to a tobacco warehouse or redrying plant. Delivery by the producer to a pick-up-station would not, in my opinion, be delivery to a tobacco warehouse or redrying plant. This pick-up-station would also be liable for the solicitor's or agent's license prescribed by Section 3(a) of the amended Act, in the amount of $250.

> "2(b). Will a redrying plant be liable for scrap tobacco dealer's license tax, if scrap tobacco is bought from the operator of a pick-up-station, if the operator of said pick-up-station delivers the scrap tobacco to the door of the redrying plant?"

Delivery by the operator of a pick-up-station of scrap tobacco to the door of a redrying plant would not, in my opinion, be delivery by the producer to the extent that such a sale would be exempt from the Act, and a redrying plant which purchased from such a pick-up-station would be subject to the payment of the tax prescribed, as a scrap tobacco dealer.

> "3. Will a redrying plant be subject to the scrap tobacco dealer's license tax, if scrap tobacco is bought from another redrying plant?"

A redrying plant, wherever located, purchasing scrap tobacco from a licensed warehouse or redrying plant would not be required to pay the tax imposed by Section 1, if the scrap tobacco so purchased had been delivered by the producer to the tobacco warehouse or redrying plant which made the sale. If, on the other hand, the redrying plant, wherever located, was engaged in the business of buying scrap tobacco and purchased it from a redrying plant or tobacco warehouse, scrap tobacco which had not been delivered to such seller by the producer, the tax would be applicable.

If, however, one redrying plant purchases scrap tobacco from another redrying plant, such scrap having been processed, redried or manufactured, such sales would be exempt from the Act under the last clause in Section 4½.

> "4. Will a redrying plant, located in an adjoining state, be subject to the scrap tobacco dealer's license tax, if it opens a pick-up-station in North Carolina? At this station tobacco will be bought only from producers."

In my opinion, the pick-up-station only in this case would be subject to the payment of the tax imposed. You could not tax the redrying plant if it is located outside the State. In this case it is the pick-up-station operator who would be subject to the tax and such sales would not be exempt even though delivered to such pick-up-station by the producer, since a pick-up-station is not, as I understand it, a tobacco warehouse or tobacco redrying plant, but merely a point located and established solely for the purpose of engaging in the business of buying and selling scrap tobacco.

RE: INCOME TAXES; CITIZENS OF NORTH CAROLINA; TAXABILITY IN THIS STATE OF INCOME TAXED IN ANOTHER STATE

1 August, 1941.

You have shown me the letter of March 3, 1941, written to you by Judge N. A. Townsend with respect to his income tax liability to this State for the year 1939. Judge Townsend states that his income for this year was taxed in the District of Columbia where he resided and that he feels that therefore he should not be taxed on the same income here.

His letter shows that he considers himself a North Carolinian, as do most citizens of this State temporarily residing and working in the District of Columbia. Citizens of this State, even though temporarily residing elsewhere, are taxable here on their entire income. It has been authoritatively determined on numerous occasions that the power of the domiciliary state to tax the income of its citizens, even though earned elsewhere, is not affected by the fact that such income is taxed by another state or taxing jurisdiction. See, for example, Shaffer v. Carter, 252 U. S. 37, 64 Law. Edition 445; Guaranty Trust Co. v. Virginia, 305 U. S. 19, 83 L. Ed. 16, and cases cited.

The cases of District of Columbia v. Murphy and District of Columbia v. DeHart were decided by the United States Court of Appeals for the District of Columbia on March 24, 1941. They held that persons in the situation of Judge Townsend are not liable for an income tax to the District of Columbia. But had they held otherwise, the power of this State to tax would not be affected. While it is clear that the double taxation of income is not unconstitutional, yet the ordinary person feels that double taxation is unfair and should be avoided. In recognition of this popular feeling, the General Assembly of 1941 provided that the compensation for personal services of citizens of this State should not be taxed here if they are "required" to pay an income tax thereon to another State. This provision was made applicable to the income year 1940 and subsequent years. Chapter 204, Public Laws of 1941, Section 1(b).

In view of the Murphy and DeHart cases, it would seem to be clear that no citizens of this State can be "required" to pay an income tax to the District of Columbia. Therefore, payment of such a tax is no defense to the tax due this State. Payment without legal compulsion or requirement is voluntary and not "required."

It is, therefore, my opinion that Judge Townsend is liable to this State for income taxes for the years 1939 and 1940.

RE: INHERITANCE TAX; INTEREST OF DECEDENT IN A PARTNERSHIP CONDUCTED IN ANOTHER STATE

1 August, 1941.

You have shown me the letter of Hon. James P. Bunn, Attorney for the W. E. Fenner Estate. Mr. Bunn raises the question whether or not $13,677.34 interest of the decedent in a partnership is taxable in this State. The partnership was conducted and operated in the State of Georgia and all of the money earned by it, and represented by the value stated, was earned and kept in that State and was deposited in banks there at the time of the death of the decedent. It is suggested that under these facts this State does not have jurisdiction to tax the interest of the decedent in such partnership.

The applicable rule is set forth in paragraph 1615, Volume 4, of the Inheritance, Estate, and Gift Tax Service, Commerce Clearing House, where it is stated:

> "Intangible personal property of resident decedents has been subjected to inheritance and estate taxes in practically every state statute and in the Federal statute. This view is supported by numerous decisions of the United State Supreme Court including Blodgett vs. Silberman, (1928) 277 U. S. 1; Farmers Loan and Trust Co. vs. Minnesota, (1930) 280 U. S., 204; Baldwin vs. Missouri, (1930), 281 U. S., 586; Beidler vs. South Carolina Tax Commission, (1930) 282 U. S. 1; and First National Bank of Boston vs. Maine, (1932) 284 U. S., 312. Indeed, the right of the state of domicile to levy a death tax measured by the value of a decedent's intangibles is so firmly rooted that the power to levy the tax remains in the domiciliary state even though the intangibles have acquired a taxable situs elsewhere. Curry, et al vs. McCanless, (1939) 307 U. S., 357, and Graves, et al, vs. Elliott, et al, (1939) 307 U. S., 383. These cases are reviewed at paragraph 1675, and following, in connection with the discussion of the validity of inheritance or estate taxes upon the intangibles of nonresident decedents.
>
> "Intangibles taxable in estates of resident decedents include, of course, stocks and bonds, accounts receivable, claims, partnership interest, good will, etc. As to inclusion of good will of a foreign partnership in the estate of a resident decedent for inheritance tax purposes, see Est. of H. Deutz, (1930) 105 N. J. Eq. 671, 148 Atl. 257."

The decisions referred to make it clear that the Constitution does not prohibit an inheritance tax upon the transfer of such property. There cannot be any doubt that it is taxed by the terms of Section 1 of the Revenue Act.

It is, therefore, my opinion that the partnership interest referred to should be included in the gross taxable estate of the decedent.

RE: INTANGIBLES TAX; TAXABILITY OF AMOUNTS DEDUCTED FROM WAGES OR SALARIES BY EMPLOYERS AND DEPOSITED IN A COMMON BANK ACCOUNT, IN TRUST, FOR THE BENEFIT OF THE SEVERAL EMPLOYEES

4 August, 1941.

On July 9 I wrote you a letter with regard to salary or wage deductions from the salaries of employees of the Atlantic Coast Line Railroad Company. The deductions are made under a coöperative arrangement with the United States Treasury and are for the purpose of creating funds for purchase by the employees of United States Savings Bonds. I indicated in the letter that the facts were not definitely stated and that a more accurate and specific statement might raise questions other than those discussed by me.

I have just conferred with Mr. E. A. Wayne, Secretary of the North Carolina Bankers Association, and with Mr. I. M. Bailey, General Counsel for the Association, and they have given me information with respect to the matter that was not previously presented. That information is this: That after the Company deducts the specific amounts from the wages or salaries of the employees, the amounts are deposited in trust in a common bank account; that at no time does the amount equitably due any particular employees exceed the sum of $100.00.

This new information, I think, leads me to the conclusion that no tax is due upon these deposits.

Section 701 of the Revenue Act provides that bank "accounts having an average of quarterly balances for the year of less than $100.00 may be disregarded," for the purpose of the intangible tax on bank accounts. You have construed "may" as meaning "shall" and have not taxed accounts having average quarterly balances of less than $100.00 and in so doing I think you are correct.

The total of the common deposit will exceed, of course, the sum of $100.00, but I am of the opinion that in a common trust account with several beneficiaries, the deposit, for tax purposes, must be treated as though there was a deposit for each separate beneficiary. This was the view taken by the United States Supreme Court at the last term with respect to the Federal gift tax where the gift was made in trust for several beneficiaries. Helvering v. Hutchins, 61 Sup. Ct. 653; Ryerson v. U. S., 61 Sup. Ct. 656; U. S. v. Pelzer, 61 Sup. Ct. 659.

You are, therefore, advised that, in my opinion, the interest of none of the beneficiaries being in excess of $100.00, no tax is due. I am informed that under the arrangement the interest of no beneficiary would ever exceed $100.00 for the reason that when that interest reaches $75.00, it is withdrawn and a bond is purchased.

RE: INTANGIBLES TAX; FOREIGN CORPORATIONS; TAXABILITY OF STOCK HELD IN OTHER FOREIGN CORPORATIONS; HARVEY C. HINES CO., INC., KINSTON, N. C.

5 August, 1941.

You have referred to me the letter written to you on July 29, 1941, by Honorable F. E. Wallace, Attorney for Harvey C. Hines Company, Inc., Kinston, N. C., in support of the Company's claim for a refund of intangible taxes for the years 1938, 1939 and 1940 levied upon the stock of other foreign corporations held by the Company. The claim is based on the fact that the corporation is a foreign corporation, chartered in Delaware but domesticated here. It is said that because the corporation is chartered in Delaware "such stocks do not have a situs in the State of North Carolina" and hence the tax is invalid.

The business of the corporation is wholly conducted in this State and is confined to an area within sixty miles from Kinston, N. C., where its office and place of business is located. It has no other office, although the Corporation Trust Company is its statutory agent in Delaware and lists its name there with thousands of other like corporations. Its only connection with Delaware is that its corporate charter was issued by that State.

All of the corporation's officers and directors are residents of Kinston; all its operations are carried on from there; all of its books and records are kept there; and the dividends from the stocks were received and deposited there.

Under these circumstances, it is difficult to see how the stock could have a business or commercial situs in any state other than North Carolina. No facts are pointed out as showing such a situs in any other state. Apparently, the claim for refund is based upon the mere fact that the corporation is chartered in Delaware.

This position cannot be maintained. The Supreme Court of the United States has held that under the facts appearing here such stocks may be taxed by this State. Wheeling Steel Corp. v. Fox, 298 U. S. 203, 80 L. Ed. 1143; First Bank Stock Corporation v. Minnesota, 300 U. S. 635, 81 L. Ed. 853, and cases cited. The question was also determined against the taxpayer in Mecklenburg County v. Sterchi Brothers Stores, 210 N. C. 79.

It is therefore my opinion that the claims for refund should be denied.

RE: USE TAXES; INTERSTATE COMMERCE; CORPORATION HAVING NO PLACE OF BUSINESS IN THE STATE BUT SOLICITING ORDERS IN STATE THROUGH SALESMEN, WHICH ARE ACCEPTED AT HOME OFFICE IN ANOTHER STATE; CONSTITUTIONALITY OF REQUIREMENT THAT CORPORATIONS REGISTER AND COLLECT AND REMIT TAX; STANDARD REGISTER COMPANY, DAYTON, OHIO

12 August, 1941.

You have shown me the correspondence which you have recently had with the Standard Register Company of Dayton, Ohio, and with their attorneys, E. H. and W. B. Turner, of that City.

The Standard Register Company is not qualified to do business in North Carolina and has no office or place of business in this State. Its business is obtained by orders solicited by its traveling salesmen in this State and these orders are sent to the home office for acceptance or rejection. If the orders are accepted, they are filled by an interstate shipment, F. O. B. Dayton, Ohio.

You have demanded that the Company register as a retailer under the Use Tax Act and that it collect and remit the use tax on sales made to persons and corporations in this State. The Company and its counsel state that they are willing to collect and remit the tax but suggest that they cannot constitutionally be required to register under the Act, particularly since, as they say, such registration might be deemed a waiver of the interstate character of their business.

Section 801(j) of the Use Tax Act of 1941 expressly provides that any seller operating in this State through salesmen shall be deemed to be "engaged in business in this State." Section 805 requires the seller to collect the use tax notwithstanding the fact that orders obtained by the salesman are mailed to the home office seller outside of this State and is there accepted and filled by an F. O. B. Shipment to the seller in this State.

The Attorneys for the taxpayer contend that the Commerce Clause places the above described business of their Company beyond the power of this State. It seems pretty plain to me that the above referred to provisions of the Use Tax Act in terms require such a seller to register as a retailer and to collect and remit the use tax. The question presented is whether such provisions violate the Commerce Clause.

In Felt and Tarrant Manufacturing Co. v. Gallagher, 306 U. S. 62, 83 L. Edition 488, appellant sold only in interstate commerce through agents. It is true that the agent maintained offices in the state but they were used only in connection with the interstate business. In an opinion written by Justice McReynolds the court held appellant was subject to the provisions of the California Use Tax Act. A like decision was made in McGoldrick v. Berwind-White Coal Mining Co., 309 U. S. 33, 84 L. Ed. 565, and in McGoldrick v. Felt and Tarrant Mfg. Co. and McGoldrick v. A. H. DuGrenier, Inc., (2 cases) 309 U. S. 70, 84 L. Ed. 584, and Jagels "A Fuel Corporation" v. Taylor, 309 U. S. 619, 84 L. Ed. 983, affirming 280 N. Y. 766. In these cases orders were obtained by salesmen in the State, were accepted out of the State and filled by interstate shipments F. O. B. the point of shipment.

In Nelson v. Sears Roebuck and Co., 61 S. Ct. 586, and Nelson v. Montgomery Ward Co., 61 S. Ct. 593, it was held that even mail order sales could be subjected to the use tax.

In the Sears Roebuck Case the court said that "the fact the buyer employs agencies of interstate commerce in order to effectuate his purchase is not material, since the tax is 'upon the privilege of use after commerce is at an end'. . . . The fact that respondent could not be reached for the tax if it were not qualified to do business in Iowa would merely be a result of the 'impotency of State power'." This is a plain statement, it seems to me, that the State has the power to make any seller collect the tax, even though he is an interstate operator, but if the seller is physically beyond the reach of the State, the power is impotent, and impotent for physical and geographic reasons and not because of the Commerce Clause.

In the Montgomery Ward Case the court said:

> "There is a further fact in this record which makes a reversal of this judgment necessary. It was stipulated that 'advertisements have been caused to be printed by the retail stores of the petitioner (Montgomery Ward and Company) in the State of Iowa, advertising not only retail merchandise, but the ability to complete service through the use of the catalog'. This stipulation clearly means that respondent has collected mail order sales in Iowa. The fact that that solicitation was done through local advertisements rather than directly by local agents as in Felt and Tarrant Mfg. Co. vs. Gallagher, 306 U. S., 62, 59 S. Ct., 376, 83 L. Ed., 488, is immaterial. Nor is it material that the orders were filled by direct shipments from points outside the state to purchasers within the state. For that method of delivery also obtained in case of some of the orders involved in Felt and Tarrant Mfg. Co. vs. Gallagher, supra."

It is difficult to understand why this is not a direct and express holding that the solicitation of orders in the State by salesmen or by advertisement or catalog is sufficient to bring the seller within the power of State Use Tax Acts. It would seem that if it does not mean that, it does not mean anything, an obviously unacceptable conclusion.

In United Autographic Register Co. v. McGoldrick, decided by the N. Y. Supreme Court, Appellate Division, 1st Dept. on June 28, 1940, the seller was held liable although it operated precisely as does the taxpayer here, except that it maintained a local office for its salesmen and its interstate business, a thing apparently not done here. That is equally true of all the cases cited other than the Sears Roebuck and Montgomery Ward Cases. But that would not seem to be important for an office maintained solely for interstate business does not deprive the operator of the protection afforded by the Commerce Clause. Cheney Brothers v. Massachusetts, 246 U. S. 147, 62 L. Ed. 632, Alpha Portland Cement Company v. Massachusetts, 368 U. S. 203, 69 L. Edition 916.

The point of the cited cases is that the use tax is, as the court said in the Sears Roebuck Case, "upon the privilege of use after commerce is at an end." The cases hold that even if the seller does no more than solicit by advertisement, the State has power to require it to comply with the Act, though that power may be impotent if the seller is beyond the physical reach of the State. That is in line with Wisconsin v. J. C. Penney Co., 61 S. Ct. 246, where it was said that "the simple but controlling question is whether the State has given anything for which it can ask return." Here it has given protection to the salesmen; it has enabled them to travel over the State and obtain orders, and has protected the shipment and receipt of the goods.

That those selling only through salesmen are, under the cited cases, subject to State Use Tax Acts is stated in Paragraphs Nos. 1-240 and 1-250 of Commerce Clearing House's Interstate Sales Tax Service. To the same effect are paragraphs 2-200 to 2-500. In Paragraph 2-600 the treatise shows that "doing business" for use tax purposes is wholly different from "doing business" for other tax purposes. As pointed out above, even "solicitation" by advertisement is sufficient under the decisions of the United States Supreme Court if the seller is within the reach of the State's power.

For this reason, and because the tax is upon an event after interstate commerce is at an end, it would seem clear that registration for the purpose of the use tax would not be a waiver of the protection that the Commerce Clause gives the seller. It would be entirely proper and acceptable for the seller to expressly reserve its rights in that respect and by full and adequate language state that it is registering only for the purpose of that tax, which is laid on an event occurring after interstate commerce has ceased.

It is, therefore, my opinion that the Standard Register Company can constitutionally be required to register and to collect and remit the use tax on its interstate sales for use in this State. If it does not do so, its salesmen in this State may be proceeded against either civilly or criminally, though of course no such steps should be taken until ample prior notice has been given.

RE: INHERITANCE TAXES; ANNUITY CONTRACTS PAYABLE TO SON OF SUBSCRIBER; (1) TAXABILITY WHEN SUBSCRIBER RESERVES (a) RIGHT TO CHANGE BENEFICIARY AND (b) RIGHT TO DEMAND PAYMENT OF CASH SURRENDER VALUE AT ANY TIME; (2) WHETHER POLICY IS "LIFE INSURANCE"

21 August, 1941.

I reply to your letter of yesterday enclosing a letter from Hon. W. B. Rodman, Attorney for the Estate of Eleanor Berry Tayloe.

It appears from Mr. Rodman's letter that on November 18, 1934, Mrs. Tayloe paid to Mutual Life Insurance Company of New York the sum of $5,000.00 for which it issued to her an annuity policy or contract. The policy was payable to her son, David T. Tayloe, then about nine years of age. The policy provided:

> "Mutual Life will pay to David T. Tayloe, the annuitant, a monthly income of $186.30 for ten years (120 monthly payments) and as long after as the annuitant lives, the first payment being payable on the 18th day of November, 1985, if the annuitant be then living; or will pay to the annuitant's Mother, Eleanor B. Tayloe, if living, if not, to annuitant's uncle, John C. Tayloe, the Beneficiary, upon receipt of due proof that the annuitant died before the maturity date, the net cash value of this Contract at the death of the annuitant."

The annuitant, David T. Tayloe, also had the right to surrender the policy and obtain its then cash value, or to borrow upon it, the cash or loan values depending upon how long the policy is previously in effect.

The agreement also contained this provision:

> "Rights of Beneficiary: Anything in this contract to the contrary notwithstanding, prior to the maturity date, annuitant's mother, Eleanor B. Tayloe, one of the beneficiaries may without the consent and to the exclusion of the annuitant or any other beneficiary, receive, exercise, and enjoy every benefit, option, right and privilege conferred by this contract or allowed by the Company."

The questions presented are whether the value of the policy must be included in Mrs. Tayloe's gross estate for inheritance tax purposes, and, if so, whether it is "life insurance" and entitled to the $20,000.00 exemption allowed by Section 2(d) of the Revenue Act.

Since the rights under the policy were created by a contract executed and effective during the life of the decedent, and no transfer occurred by will or the intestacy laws, the question is whether there was an inter vivos gift "intended to take effect in possession or enjoyment at or after" her death, within the meaning of Section 1(3) of the Revenue Act. If such a gift or transfer occurred, the taxable event is the taking effect in possession or enjoyment at death, and the Revenue Act in force at that time governs, particularly where its provisions are identical with those in effect at the date of the policy, as here. It is no matter that the rates under the later act may be higher than those under the former. These propositions, as well as the constitutional validity of death taxes on inter vivos transfers taking effect in possession or enjoyment at death, are established by Moffitt v. Kelly, 218 U. S. 400, 54 L. Ed. 1086; Orr v. Gilman, 183 U. S. 278, 46 L. Ed. 197; Whitney v. State Tax Commr., 309 U. S. 530, 84 L. Ed. 909; U. S. v. Jacobs, 306 U. S. 363, 83 L. Ed. 763;

Carpenter v. Commonwealth, 17 How. 456, 15 L. Ed. 127; Cohen v. Brewster, 203 U. S. 543, 51 L. Ed. 310; Milliken v. U. S., 283 U. S. 15, 75 L. Ed. 809; Klein v. U. S., 283 U. S. 271, 75 L. Ed. 996; Phillips v. Dime T. and D. Co., 284 U. S. 160, 76 L. Ed. 220.

Bullen v. Wisconsin, 240 U. S. 625, 60 L. Ed. 830, holds that where the decedent made an inter vivos transfer but reserved the right to demand the income, to revoke the trust, and to change the beneficiary, the corpus was properly includible in his estate under an act taxing at death gifts intended to take effect in possession and enjoyment at or after death.

Reservation of the income was held to render the corpus of an inter vivos trust taxable at the death of the settlor in Guaranty Trust Co. v. Blodgett, 287 U. S. 509, 77 L. Ed. 763.

The right to revoke was held to have like effect in Saltonstall v. Saltonstall, 276 U. S. 260, 72 L. Ed. 566; Reinecke v. Northern Trust Co., 278 U. S. 339, 73 L. Ed. 410, and Porter v. Commissioner, 288 U. S. 436, 77 L. Ed. 800.

The right of the decedent to demand payment of the cash surrender value, to borrow upon it, and to change the beneficiary are rights so substantial as to make it pretty plain that it was only when those rights ceased at the death of the decedent that the rights of the annuitant really took effect "in possession and enjoyment." As said in some of the cited cases, "death was the generating source of his rights."

Helvering v. Hallock, 309 U. S. 106, 84 L. Ed. 604, held that where the inter vivos transfer reserves a mere right of reverter, that makes the corpus taxable. If that be true, then certainly it is clear that the much greater rights reserved here must have the same effect. See Guaranty Trust Co. v. Comm., 16 B. T. A. 314.

It is, therefore, my opinion that the policy must be included in the gross estate.

I am not able to state what value or amount should be included as the measure of the tax. It would seem that whatever amount the decedent or the annuitant could demand and receive on the date of death would be the value to be taken. If the policy allowed a refund of the premium or part thereof, that would appear to be the amount; or if it does not provide for a refund but only for a certain cash surrender value, that is the amount. Old Colony Trust Co. v. Commr., (CCA 1), 102 F(2d) 380, 22 A. F. T. R. 691; Guaranty Trust Co. v. Commr., 16 B. T. A. 314.

There remains the question whether such a policy is a "policy of life insurance" within the meaning of Section 2(d) of the Revenue Act and entitled to the $20,000.00 exemption there granted.

The maturity of the policy is not dependent upon death, nor is there any risk assumed on the contingency of death. The rights and benefits are not tied to death. The policy is an "annuity contract," not a "policy of life insurance." See Helvering v. Le Gierse, 61 Supreme Ct. 646, Keller v. Commr., 61 Supreme Court 651, and Tyler v. Helvering, 61 Supreme Court 729, holding that a combination of life insurance and annuity contract is not "life insurance" for the death risk in the former is cancelled by the latter.

The first Circuit Court of Appeals considered the very question in Old Colony Trust Co. v. Commr., (CCA 1) F(2d) 380, 22 A. F. T. R. 691, and held such an annuity contract was not life insurance and hence could not take the benefit of the exemption allowed for life insurance. Other decisions so holding are Estate of Roxy M. Smith, 16 B. T. A. 314; Chemical B. and T. Co. v. Commr., 37 B. T. A. 535.

You are, therefore, advised that the policy is not "life insurance" and Section 2(d) of the Revenue Act is inapplicable. The taxable value of the policy should be added to the other property passing to David T. Tayloe, the total of which is taxable subject to the general exemption allowed by Section 3(a).

RE: INCOME TAXES; EXEMPTION OF HOSPITAL SERVICE CORPS

18 August, 1941.

I reply to your letter of June 25 enclosing a letter from the Auditor of the Medical Service Associations, Inc., Durham, N. C., with an affidavit, signed by the Association's Treasurer, to which is appended a copy of the corporate charter. You have also given me the letter written to you by the Auditor of the Company on August 16 containing information as to the operations and business of the Company, together with a copy of the certificate issued to its subscribers or members. All of the foregoing are returned to you herewith.

You request my opinion whether the Association is exempt from income taxes.

An examination of the charter shows the Association to be a non-stock and non-profit corporation organized in 1940 under Chapter 22 of the Consolidated Statutes of this State for the purpose of providing necessary "hospital, nursing, medical and surgical care for its members and holders of certificates issued by it, and their dependents . . . and to collect from holders of certificates, or otherwise as may be determined, from time to time, dues, and to apply the same toward the payment of fees for such services rendered to members and their dependents." It is also authorized to enter into agreements with "hospitals, nurses, physicians, surgeons, obstetricians, and specialists for the providing" of the several services referred to. In addition, the corporation is given other broad and general powers such as are usually contained in corporate charters for the purpose of carrying out the purposes of the organization.

Chapter 338 of the Public Laws of 1941 provides for the regulation of "Hospital Service Corporations" which are defined to be "any corporation heretofore or hereafter organized under the general corporation laws of the State of North Carolina for the purpose of maintaining and operating a non-profit hospital service plan whereby hospital care may be provided by the said corporation or by a hospital with which it has a contract for such care, to such persons who become subscribers to such plans under a contract which entitles each subscriber to certain hospital care." The Act prohibits "foreign or alien hospital service corporations" from doing business in this State.

The Act requires all such corporations, whenever chartered, to obtain a license to do business from the Commissioner of Insurance and provides for the regulation of their business.

Section 14 of the Act provides that "Every corporation subject to the provisions of this Act is hereby declared to be a charitable and benevolent corporation and all of its funds and property shall be exempt from every State, county, district, municipal and school tax or assessment, and all other taxes and license fees, from the payment of which charitable and/or benevolent institutions are now or shall hereafter be exempt." The Section provides, however, that to raise funds to administer the Act such corporations shall, "in lieu of all other taxes," pay an annual franchise tax of "one-third of one per cent of the gross annual collections of membership dues exclusive of receipt from cost-plus plans."

Section 16 authorizes such corporations, as agent of any other corporation "to administer . . . any employer group hospitalization or medical service plan promulgated" by such other corporation "on a cost-plus administrative expense basis."

Section 16 of the Act impliedly prohibits "hospital service corporations" from issuing medical or surgical care certificates or insurance, but it authorizes them to act as the agent of corporations which issue such certificates or insurance. Medical Service Association has not applied for a license under the Act as it does not operate a "hospital service plan" and, therefore, deems itself not subject to the Act. However, Hospital Care, Incorporated, a domestic corporation, has qualified under the Act and Medical Service Association has an agreement or arrangement with Hospital Care, Inc., whereby the latter, as its agent, under Section 16, "administers" on its behalf its medical and surgical service plan. As shown by its form of certificate, this is the only plan operated by Medical Service Association.

Since Medical Service Association does not operate a "hospital service plan" it is not subject to the Act and is not entitled to the exemption from taxation granted by Section 14.

There remains the question whether Medical Service Association is exempt by Section 314 of the Income Tax Article of the Revenue Act. Insofar as pertinent, it provides:

> "Section 314. *Conditional and Other Exemptions.* The following organizations shall be exempt from taxation under this Article:
>
> " . . . .
>
> "3. Cemetery corporations and corporations organized for religious, charitable, scientific, or educational purposes, or for the prevention of cruelty to children or animals, no part of the net earnings of which inures to the benefit of any private stockholder or individual.
>
> " . . . .
>
> 7. Farmers' or other mutual hail, cyclone, or fire insurance companies, mutual ditch or irrigation companies, mutual or cooperative telephone companies, or like organizations of a purely local character the income of which consists solely of assessments, dues and fees collected from members for the sole purpose of meeting expenses. . . ."

If the Association comes under Section 314(3), it must do so as a "charitable" organization, and it would seem to be plain that that is not its nature. Its service is contractual, not charitable. The benefits received by its members are bought and paid for and are received as a matter of right, not as a matter of grace. Such an organization is not a "charitable" corporation.

In State v. Dunn, 134 N. C. 663, the court dealt with the "Love and Union Society," which collected dues from its members and in return gave them sick and burial benefits. It was held that such organizations, though commendable and laudable in purpose, were neither "charitable" nor benevolent," for the benefits provided for were for themselves, for a price, and the purpose was not to bestow gratuities upon those who could not pay for them. This decision was approved in Odd Fellows v. Swain, 217 N. C. 632, 636, where the court intimated that if benefits are paid "as a matter of right rather than as a matter of charity" the corporation would not be a "charitable" corporation.

I think, therefore, the association is not exempted by Section 314(3).

Is it exempted by Section 314(7)?

In McCanless Motor Company v. Maxwell, 210 N. C. 725, 727, it is said that "It has been generally held that exemption from taxation must be strictly construed in favor of the taxing power. . . . No claim to exemption can be sustained unless it is clearly within the scope of the exempting clause'." But this does not mean that a grant of exemption is to be examined in hostility and admitted only grudgingly. As Merrimon, Judge, said in the Freight Discrimination Cases, 95 N. C. 434, 438, the rule of strict construction means "no more than that the court, in ascertaining the meaning of such a statute cannot go beyond the plain meaning of the words and phraseology employed in search for an intention not certainly implied by them. If there is no ambiguity in the words or phraseology, nothing is left to construction. Their plain meaning must not be extended by inference, etc."

The "plain meaning" of Section 314(7) is that if a corporation is to bring itself within the exemption, it must be, first, a "mutual or cooperative" organization, and, second, it must be "of a purely local character."

I assume that under its charter the association is a "mutual or cooperative" corporation.

It would seem, however, that it is not "of a purely local character," for its business is not restricted to Durham or Durham County; it does business and has members throughout the State. It is my opinion that no corporation can bring itself "within the scope of the exempting clause" (McCanless Case, supra) unless it shows that its members and operations are confined to a particular locality. Where its business is not so confined, but on the contrary extends over the State generally, it is not "of a purely local character" and hence is not entitled to exemption under Section 314(7).

You are, therefore, advised that it is my opinion that Medical Service Association is not exempt from income taxes.

RE: USE TAX LIABILITY; OTIS ELEVATOR COMPANY

18 September, 1941.

You have handed me the letter of September 4, 1941, written to you by Mr. T. I. McKnight, of Sims, Handy and McKnight, Chicago, Attorneys for the Otis Elevator Company. In this letter it is contended that the Use

Tax Article of the Revenue Act, redrafted in 1941, does not apply to those who install elevators in this State, and you desire my advice and opinion with respect to the correctness of the contention.

It would seem that the suggestion of Mr. McKnight that Section 427 of the Revenue Act is the only Section which applies to elevator companies is not well founded. That Section is applicable but the Use Tax Article was also intended to apply. The use tax is a complementary tax, the principal purpose of which is to reach transactions insulated by the Commerce Clause from ordinary business license taxes. It is applicable to all transactions to which the Sales Tax Act applies and, likewise, applies to many transactions subject to the tax levied by Section 427.

In the discussions attending the redrafting of the Use Tax Article it was expressly contemplated that the tax would apply to such transactions as are carried on in this State by the Otis Elevator Company. To that end, new definitions were inserted in Section 801; "use" was defined to include "installation" and "affixation to realty"; "sale" to include "any transfer of title or possession, or both of tangible personal property, however effected and by whatever name called; "sales price" to include the fair market values of the property "where a manufacturer, producer or contractor erects, installs, or applies tangible personal property for the account of or under contract with the owner of realty"; "retailer" to include "every manufacurer, producer, or contractor . . . selling, delivering, erecting, or installing or applying tangible personal property for use in this State notwithstanding that said property may be permanently affixed to a building or to realty"; and "tangible personal property" to mean "personal property which may be seen, weighed, measured, felt, touched, or is in any other manner perceptible to the senses."

It would appear to me pretty clear that the breadth and scope of these definitions is abundantly sufficient to cover the business of installing elevators. The suggestion that they apply only to manufacturers of equipment, refrigerators, furnaces, oil burners, air conditioners, ranges, radios, and the like, which are completely manufactured and ready for use, is not well founded. In view of the all-inclusive scope of the definitions, such a limitation would appear to be arbitrary and wanting in reason.

It is said that the Company "does not in any sense or by any stretch of the imagination sell tangible personal property. It enters into a construction contract and each elevator is manufactured for the particular job and will not work elsewhere. There are many cases supporting this view." That might well be true under ordinary definitions of the terms mentioned, but the General Assembly was not content with them. It made its own, and under them the decisions referred to by Mr. McKnight are not in point. For instance, in York Heating and Ventilating Company vs. Flannery, 87 Pa. Super. 19, the court said:

> "The contract in suit was in no sense a contract of sale. It was a construction contract. It would be just as proper to call a contract for the construction of a building, a sale of the stone, brick, cement, wood, etc., which entered into the erection of the building."

Such reasoning would seem clearly inapplicable under a statute which expressly includes manufacturers or contractors who install machinery and equipment, tangible personal property, notwithstanding its permanent annexation to realty. The law of sales, fixtures and accession may not be read into an Act which manifests an express intention to exclude them, particularly a revenue measure.

That the definitions laid down in the Article must be regarded and given effect is shown by the opinion of Justice Cordozo in Fox v. Standard Oil Company, 294 U. S. 87, 79 L. Edition 780, where he said:

> "We are told that the average man if requested to point out to a stranger the store nearest by or even the nearest mercantile establishment would not be likely to think of a filling station as within the range of the inquiry. (Citation) There might be force in this suggestion if the statute had left the meaning of its terms to the test of popular understanding. Instead, it has attempted to secure precision and certainty by rejecting a test so fluid and indeterminate and supplying its own glossary. The goods offered for sale are to be understood as having reference to goods 'of any kind,' and the place at which the sale is made shall include not only places that in the common speech of men would be designated as stores, but, broadly speaking, any mercantile establishment, whether a store or something else. In such circumstances definition by the average man or even by the ordinary dictionary with its studied enumeration of subtle shades of meaning is not a substitute for the definition set before us by the law-makers with instructions to apply it to the exclusion of all others. (Citation) There would be little use in such a glossary if we were free in despite of it to choose a meaning for ourselves."

The United States Supreme Court has said in a number of recent cases that the technicalities and refinements of the law of contracts and property are not to be read into a Revenue Act. For example, in Helvering v. Hallock, 309 U. S. 106, 84 L. Ed. 604, it was said:

> "The law of contingent and vested remainders is full of casuistries . . . The importation of these distinctions and controversies from the law of property into the administration of the estate tax precludes a fair and workable tax system.

It excluded from consideration in tax cases "elusive and subtle casuistries which may have their historic justification but possess no relevance for tax purposes."

There would not seem to be any doubt that the Otis Elevator Company is engaged in the sale of tangible personal property under the very broad terms of the Use Tax Article. The fact that the elevator and machinery are made subject to order and that they are permanently affixed to the realty are immaterial in view of the statuatory provisions referred to. The Article expressly contemplates that manufacturers and contractors shall collect and remit the tax notwithstanding these facts.

In my opinion, the Company is required to register and to collect and remit the tax. Their rights under the Commerce Clause will not otherwise be affected.

RE: INTANGIBLES TAX; DUTY TO MAKE RETURN WHEN NO TAX DUE BY REASON OF DEDUCTIONS

24 September, 1941.

You have shown me the letter written to you by Atlantic Discount Corporation on September 17, in which it is contended that they are not required to file a return for the reason that no tax is due inasmuch as their payables exceed their receivables.

Under Section 708 of the Revenue Act every person or corporation "owning or holding any intangible personal properties defined and classified . . . in this article or schedule, either as principal or as agent, shall make and deliver to the Commissioner of Revenue, in such form as he may prescribe, a full, accurate and complete return for such tax liability."

It is the function of the Department to determine whether a tax is or is not due. It does not lie in the power of owners of intangibles to determine that they are not due any tax and to refuse to make a return on that ground. Returns are required to aid the Department in determining the questions and failure or refusal to make such returns is unlawful.

It is a well-known fact that thousands of persons make income tax returns when the fact is, and the return shows, that no tax is due.

If the contention of the Atlantic Discount Corporation is correct, then it can determine whether they are or are not liable, and that they may not do. The contention is quite clearly without foundation.

RE: SALES TAXES; LIABILITY OF OPTOMETRISTS FOR SALES OF LENSES, FRAMES, ARTIFICIAL EYES AND OTHER LIKE PROPERTY

26 September, 1941.

I have carefully read and considered the brief filed with you by the North Carolina State Optometric Society, in which it is contended, first, that optometrists are not liable for the retail sales tax on lenses, frames, artificial eyes and other like property sold to their patients, and, second, that if there is any sales tax liability, it is upon the suppliers of materials to the optometrists and not upon the optometrist.

In my opinion, neither contention can be sustained.

Both questions have frequently arisen in this and numerous other States during the past few years and it is now settled that optometrists are engaged in the retail sale of tangible personal property within the broad purpose and definitions of the Sales Tax Acts, and that sales to them by suppliers are sales for resale and, hence, not taxable as retail sales.

The rule is well stated in Paragraph 9-350 of Commerce Clearing House's "Interstate Sales Tax Service," as follows:

> "Optometrists and oculists are not liable for the sales tax with respect to receipts from professional services rendered, such as examination of the eyes or ocular care and treatment. However, if optometrists and oculists also sell lenses, frames or other tangible personal property to clients, they incur liability for the tax with respect to such sales separately billed. If the bill rendered to the client is for examination and treatment and glasses, frames, etc., is in one lump sum, the tax attaches to the entire transaction.
>
> "Opticians who ordinarily only manufacture lenses, etc., are liable for the tax with respect to their entire receipts from sales of eye glasses, lenses, etc., fabricated by them, on prescription or otherwise, and sold directly to users or consumers; no deduction for labor, services or other items of cost of production is allowed. Where opticians make and sell eye glasses, lenses, etc., to oculists and optometrists, and the latter resell them to their clients for use, such sales by opticians are sales for resale and do not carry a liability for tax."

The identical arguments set forth in the Society's brief were made in the cases of State Tax Comm. v. Hopkins, 234 Alabama 566, 176 Southern 210; Kamp v. Johnson, 99 California 172, 99 Pacific (2d) 274; and Commonwealth v. Miller, (Pennsylvania), 11 Atlantic (2d) 141, and in each of them the Supreme Courts of the State held the optometrist liable as a retail seller.

Soon after the enactment of our Sales Tax Act, your Department, following the view taken in other states, adopted the following Regulation:

> "10. *Optometrists, Opticians, Oculists, etc.* Sales made by optometrists, opticians, oculists, eye physicians, etc., of tangible personal property, consisting of eyeglasses, frames, artificial eyes, or other optical appliances, or any other tangible personal property, are taxable sales and subject to the three per cent (3%) retail rate of tax when sold to consumers or users.
>
> "The prescription services rendered in examination and the writing of prescriptions for such tangible personal property are not subject to the tax. The rendering of services, in connection with sales of tangible personal property, must be separated on statements of charges made therefor so as to clearly distinguish between the charges for services and the charge made in the sale of tangible personal property."

The foregoing is copied from Regulations VIII, No. 10, page 29, of the 1937 printed edition of the Sales Tax Regulations.

It is, therefore, my opinion that optometrists are retailers and liable for the sales tax on such sales, and that the suppliers of materials to them, while liable for the wholesale sales tax, are not liable for the retail tax, their sales to the optometrists being sales for resale.

RE: GIFT TAXES; PURCHASE OF UNITED STATES SAVING BOND MADE TO PURCHASER AND DAUGHTER AS ALTERNATE PAYEES

4 October, 1941.

I reply to your letter of the 29th with respect to the 1940 gift tax return of Charles P. Stewart, Anson County.

It appears that on January 2, 1940, he purchased and paid for United States Savings Bonds in the sum of $17,500.00 which were registered and issued jointly to himself and daughter, as follows: "Charles P. Stewart or Miss Dee Stewart."

The effect of the transaction is to make the bonds payable alternatively either to Charles P. Stewart or to Miss Dee Stewart. It created no joint tenancy or tenancy in common and gave Miss Stewart no indefeasible right or title. According to your letter, Charles P. Stewart has never delivered the bonds to his daughter nor has he endorsed or assigned the same to her nor permitted her to redeem them and take the proceeds. The question is whether under these facts a gift tax is due.

On June 14, 1941, the Commissioner of Internal Revenue issued a Mimeograph dealing with the application of the Federal Estate and Gift Tax to United States Savings Bonds purchased and registered in certain authorized forms. Mimeograph 5252, 1 Prentice-Hall, Inheritance and Transfer Tax Service, Paragraph 23,859. The question presented by you is ruled on in the following paragraph of this Mimeograph:

> "If 'John Jones' purchases with his separate funds savings bonds and has them registered in his name and that of another individual in the alternative as co-owners, for example, 'John Jones or Mrs. Ella S. Jones', there is no gift for Federal gift tax purposes, unless and until he during his lifetime gratuitously permits 'Mrs. Ella S. Jones' to redeem them and retain the proceeds as her separate property, in which event a gift of the then redemption value of the bonds would be made. Of course, such bonds if not previously redeemed would, on the death of 'John Jones' be includible in his gross estate for estate tax at the full redemption value."

In my opinion, this excerpt is in accordance with the law of this State. The bonds are payable alternatively and Charles P. Stewart might at any time turn them in and obtain their full present value and thus defeat any expectancy or possibility that Miss Stewart might have, particularly since it is stated that he has retained possession of the bonds and never delivered them to Miss Stewart or to any person for her. Under these circumstances, there has been no completed transfer by gift and no gift tax is due. Compare, Estate of Sanford v. Commissioner, 308 U. S. 39, 84 L. Ed. 20; Rasquin v. Humphreys, 308 U. S. 54, 84 L. Ed. 77.

Without attempting to foreclose the point, it would seem that if Mr. Stewart should retain the bonds until his death and Miss Stewart should then be paid the value thereof, she would be subject to an inheritance tax under the Revenue Act then in force. However, if during his life he should take such steps as would make her the owner of the bonds or their proceeds, or part thereof, a gift tax would be due.

RE: INCOME TAXES; EXEMPTION OF FARMERS' MARKETING ASSOCIATIONS

10 October, 1941.

I reply to your letter of the 7th, enclosing the letter written to you by the Treasurer of the Farmers Cooperative Exchange Service, Incorporated, and a copy of their charter. You desire my opinion whether this Exchange is exempt from income taxes in this State.

It appears from the charter that the Exchange is incorporated under the provisions of Chapter 87, Public Laws of 1921, and possesses the broad powers permitted to corporations organized under its provisions. That Chapter is now Sub-Chapter V, Chapter 93, Article XVI, Section 5259(a), et seq., Volume Three of the Consolidated Statutes.

Section 314(9) of the Income Tax Article of the Revenue Act of 1939 is in part as follows:

> "The following organizations shall be exempt from taxation under this article: . . .
>
> "Marketing associations organized under Sub-Chapter five, Chapter Ninety-three, Consolidated Statutes, Article XVI, Section five thousand two hundred fifty-nine (a) and following."

This language is plain and explicit. It leaves no room for construction. The General Assembly has seen fit to exempt from income tax all corporations organized under the Act of 1921. The only requirement or condition is that they be so organized. Inasmuch as the Farmers Cooperative Exchange Service, Incorporated, was so organized, they are exempt from income taxes.

SUBJECT: LIABILITY OF COMMERCIAL BANKS OPERATING PERSONAL LOAN DEPARTMENT FOR PRIVILEGE TAX ON MORRIS PLAN OR INDUSTRIAL BANKS

31 October, 1941.

You inquire whether a commercial bank operating a personal loan department would be liable for the privilege tax imposed by Section 158 of the 1939 Revenue Act on "every person, firm, or corporation engaged in the business of operating a Morris Plan or industrial bank in the State."

An industrial bank is defined in the banking laws (Public Laws 1923, C. 225, Sec. 1; or Sec. 225(2) of Michie's 1939 N. C. Code) as follows:

> "The term 'industrial bank,' as used in this article shall be construed to mean any corporation organized, or which may hereafter be organized, under the general corporation laws of this state, which is engaged in lending money to be repaid in weekly, or monthly, or other periodical installments, or principal sums as a business: Provided, however, this definition shall not be construed to include building and loan associations, or commercial or savings banks."

You will note that the proviso expressly excludes commercial banks from the definition of industrial banks.

There are well-defined distinctions in the law between industrial banks and commercial banks. Different requirements are made for the incorporations of each, and they do not share all the same powers. For example, under the statute prescribing the powers of industrial banks (1923, C. 225, Sec. 6, as amended; or Sec. 225(f) of Michie's 1939 N. C. Code), such banks are empowered by Subsection 3 to charge certain fees for loans to cover expenses of making the loans, including an investigation of the borrower. Commercial banks are not specifically empowered to charge such fees even though they may operate a personal loan department and make installment loans through such department.

Thus, the law has given industrial banks a different status and definition from commercial banks, and I am of the opinion that the General Assembly did not intend by Section 158 of the 1939 Revenue Act to impose the tax therein levied on commercial banks operating a personal loan department. Such commercial banks cannot be said to be operating "Morris Plan or industrial banks," in the accepted meaning of those words, and if the General Assembly had intended their inclusion, it seems to me that more definite wording would have been used.

SUBJECT: COLLECTION OF STATE INCOME TAX AGAINST ESTATE ADMINISTERED IN FOREIGN JURISDICTION WHERE FEDERAL ESTATE TAXES EXCEED VALUE OF ASSETS

27 October, 1941.

You inquire by letter of October 20, with enclosure, as to the steps you should take to collect the balance of income tax due this State where the estate of the decedent is being administered in another state and it appears that the value of the gross estate is so large that the estate taxes will be far in excess of the assets.

If, in fact, it is determined that the estate taxes far exceed the assets, so that nothing will be left to satisfy other claims, I am of the opinion that this State will be unable to collect the balance of tax due, because of the priority given the federal estate taxes by law.

Section 827 of the Internal Revenue Code gives the United States a lien upon the gross estate of the decedent except that such portion of the gross estate as is used for the payment of charges against the estate and expense of its administration, allowed by a court having jurisdiction, shall be divested of such lien. And U. S. C. A., Title 31, Paragraphs 191 and 192, provide that whenever the estate of a deceased debtor, in the hands of the executor or administrators, is insufficient to pay all the debts due from the deceased, the debts due the United States shall be first satisfied, and that every personal representative who pays any debt due by the estate before he pays the debts due the United States shall become answerable personally for the unpaid balance due the United States.

It was held in Bowes v. United States, 127 N. J., Equity 132, that the Federal estate taxes had priority over state inheritance taxes.

Congress may give priority to debts due to the United States, though the debts subordinated are due to a state. See Annotation, 62 A. L. R. 146.

Thus, if the amount of the federal estate taxes exceeds the assets, the collection of the North Carolina income tax would seem impossible, although the claim should, of course, be filed with the personal representatives so that if assets in excess of those necessary to pay the estate taxes are found, the State's claim may be asserted.

RE: BANKRUPTCY; LIABILITY OF TRUSTEE CONTINUING OPERATION OF BUSINESS FOR INCOME TAXES; FORM OF RETURN

4 December, 1941.

You inquire by letter of November 25 as to the liability of a trustee in bankruptcy who continues to operate the bankrupt's business to pay State income taxes, and also whether such trustee should file a return for the full calendar year in which the adjudication of bankruptcy occurred, or only for that part of the year during which he operated the business.

There seems to be little doubt that the several states can impose income taxes on the income of trustees in bankrupty realized from the continued operation of the business of a bankrupt. In 1934, Congress passed the following statute, which is found in 28 U. S. C. A., Sec. 124(a):

> "Any receiver, liquidator, referee, trustee or other officers or agents appointed by any United States Court who is authorized by said court to conduct any business, or who does conduct any business, shall, from and after June 18, 1934, be subject to all State and local taxes applicable to such business the same as if such business were conducted by an individual or corporation: Provided, however, that nothing in this section contained shall be construed to prohibit or prejudice the collection of any such taxes which accrued prior to June 18, 1934, in the event that the United States Court having final jurisdiction of the subject matter under existing law should adjudge and decide that the imposition of such taxes was a valid exercise of the taxing power by the State or states, or by the civil subdivisions of the State or States imposing them."

If, prior to the enactment of this statute, a state tax on the income of an operating trustee was objectionable in that it amounted to a tax on an instrumentality of the United States, Congress, by providing that such trustees shall be subject to state and local taxes, has removed the objection.

Therefore, the only question to be decided in determining whether the North Carolina income tax laws are applicable to income realized by a trustee in bankruptcy from the continued operation of a bankrupt's business is whether the wording of the North Carolina statute is such that it may be construed to embrace income of this type.

In Section 315 of the Revenue Act of 1939, which appears in the Income Tax Schedule, it is provided that:

> "The taxes imposed by this article shall be imposed upon resident fiduciaries having in charge funds or property for the benefit of a resident of this State, and/or income earned in this State for the benefit of a nonresident, and upon a nonresident fiduciary having in charge funds or property for the benefit of a resident of this State . . . ."

Paragraph 4 of Section 2 of the same Act provides:

> "The word 'fiduciary' means a guardian, trustee, executor, administrator, receiver, conservator, or any person, whether individual or corporation, acting in any fiduciary capacity for any person, estate or trust."

Since the State income tax applies to fiduciaries, and since the statutory definition of fiduciaries is broad enough to include trustees in bankruptcy who continue to operate the bankrupt's business, it would seem that such trustees are liable for the tax.

It should be noted that while 26 U. S. C. A., Sec. 52, and corresponding provisions of earlier federal revenue acts requiring trustees in bankruptcy continuing to operate the business to pay income taxes have been given a strict construction (see, for example, Reinecke vs. Gardner, 277 U. S., 239; In re Heller, Hersch and Co., 258 Fed., 208; In re Owl Drug Co., 21 F. Supp. 907), there seems to be a disposition to construe 28 U. S. C. A., Sec. 124(a), making such trustees subject to state and local taxes, much more liberally. The latter statute applies to trustees who "conduct any business." In the case of In re Mid America Co., 31 F. Supp., 601, it was held that this phrase is not confined in meaning to the situation where the trustee in bankruptcy continues to operate the bankrupt's business. It authorizes the collection of state and local taxes incurred by the trustee in any activity in connection with the handling and management of the bankrupt estate.

It should also be noted that while 11 U. S. C. A., Sec. 93, subdivision j, provides that debts owing to a state as a penalty or forfeiture may not be allowed as claims against a bankrupt, in Boteler vs. Ingels, 308 U. S., 57, it was held that penalties for failure to pay taxes incurred by the trustee in the continued operation of the bankrupt's business may be collected by a State under the authority of 28 U. S. C. A., Sec. 124(a).

Taxes based on income resulting from a continued operation of the bankrupt's business seem to enjoy a priority over taxes generally. In 11 U. S. C. A., Sec. 104, preferred claims against a bankrupt estate are listed in the order of their priority. Administrative expenses are in the first class, and taxes owing to the United States or a State or subdivision thereof, are in the fourth class. In Missouri v. Earhart, 111 F (2d) 992, it was held that unemployment compensation taxes accruing to a state as a result of the continued operation of a bankrupt's business by the trustee should be classified as an administrative expense in the first class, and this suggests that income taxes on income received by a trustee as a result of the continued operation of the business should be so classified, and thus have priority over other taxes and preferred claims.

We now turn to a consideration of the period which the trustee's income tax return should cover. When a corporation is adjudicated a bankrupt after having been in business during part of a calendar year and the trustee in bankruptcy continues the operation of the business during the same calendar year, it is not entirely clear whether separate income tax returns for the period before bankruptcy and for the period in which the business is operated by the trustee should be filed or whether there should be a single income tax return.

However, it seems unjust that the bankrupt should, as a result of bankruptcy, lose the benefit of deductions to which he would normally be entitled. If the business suffered losses prior to bankruptcy, in determining the amount of tax it would seem that the bankrupt is entitled to have these losses set off against income realized by the trustee in the further operation of the business. I am thus of the opinion that the tax should be based on the combined income of the bankrupt prior to bankruptcy and of the trustee after bankruptcy, and that a single return should be filed. This conclusion is strengthened by the analogy offered by O. D. 73, C. B. 1919, p. 235, as the same is abstracted in paragraph 17,283 of the Prentice-Hall 1941 Federal Tax Service. That paragraph is as follows:

> "*Period to be Governed by Return.* A receiver should prepare and file a corporate return of annual net income and excess profits for the entire taxable year, including therein the gross income received by the corporation prior to the time of the receiver's appointment and also the gross income received under the supervision of the receiver. . . .

Further, in the case of Mrs. Grant Smith, 26 B. T. A. 1178, in which trustees had been appointed to liquidate the business of a corporation, the Board of Tax Appeals held that a single income tax return should have been filed by the trustees, saying:

> ". . . Where a corporation is dissolved during a particular calendar year and its affairs remain in the hands of liquidating trustees for the remainder of the year, we know of nothing in the applicable Revenue Act and the Commissioner's regulations thereunder which warrants dividing up the calendar year into two taxable periods, viz., the first period covering the time prior to date of dissolution of the corporation and the second period covering from the time when trustees in liquidation took charge to the end of the calendar year."

This conclusion, also finds support in the language of the Court in *The Southern Cross*, 120 F (2d) 466, 467, where Judge Swan observes:

> "By virtue of federal statutes any receiver appointed by a Court of the United States is subject to the same tax liability as the owner would have been had he continued in possession and operation of the enterprise. 28 U. S. C. A., Secs. 124, 124(a). . . ."

Section 124(a), upon which the Court relies, applies to trustees in bankruptcy as well as receivers.

Paragraph 2 of Section 326 of the Revenue Act of 1939 as amended provides:

> "If the taxpayer is unable to make his own return, the return shall be made by a duly authorized agent or by a guardian or other person charged with the care of the person or property of such taxpayer."

This would seem to authorize a return to be made by the trustee for the period of the calendar year prior to bankruptcy during which the business was operated by the bankrupt.

Since taxes based upon the operation of the business by the trustee are held to be an administrative expense, the trustee filing a single return covering both the operation of the business by the bankrupt and by the trustee during the same calendar year should be required to give full and complete information as to the income realized under the trustee's management in order that the portion of the tax for which the State will claim a special priority may be determined. This information may be required pursuant to Section 327 of the Revenue Act of 1939.

RE: LIABILITY OF COMMUNITY HOUSE FOR PRIVILEGE AND SALES TAXES

10 December, 1941.

You inquire by letter of December 5, with enclosures from C. H. Crabtree and Miss Beatrice Cobb, whether a Community House, situated on municipal property, and operated as a non-profit enterprise for the benefit of the people of the city, which employs a hostess and serves meals to various civic clubs and organizations meeting there, using the receipts from the meals to defray the expenses and upkeep of the building, is liable for a privilege tax under Section 127 of the Revenue Act of 1939, and for the sales tax on the meals it serves.

Section 127 of the Revenue Act imposes a tax on "every person, firm, or corporation engaged in the business of operating a restaurant, cafe, cafeteria, hotel, with dining service on the European plan, drug store *or other place where prepared food is sold . . .*" (Underlining added). I am of the opinion that the Community House, by engaging in the activity referred to above, falls clearly within the scope of the underlined words in the statute. There is no exemption in the law that would give the Community House immunity. Where exemptions are intended in the Revenue Act, it is customary for them to be expressly set forth. See, for example, the proviso to Section 127, exempting industrial plants maintaining a non-profit restaurant. As stated in Warrenton vs. Warren County, 215 N. C. 342, "taxation is a rule; exemption the exception, with strict construction applicable to the latter."

Section 406, prescribing exemptions from the sales tax, does not exempt such organizations as the Community House, and I am of the opinion that the Community House would be liable for the sales tax on the meals it serves.

The fact that the Community House is owned by the city and that the receipts are used to defray expenses and pay off obligations on the property does not, in my opinion, place the enterprise beyond the taxes in question. This office has ruled that the Carolina Inn, which is owned by the University and the income of which goes to the support of the University, is subject to Schedule "B" License taxes.

RE: LICENSE TAXES; SOFT DRINK VENDING MACHINES; SECTION 130 OF THE REVENUE ACT

13 December, 1941.

You request my opinion on certain questions which have arisen with regard to the application of Section 130 of the Revenue Act of 1939, as amended by Section 3(h) of Chapter 50 of the Public Laws of 1941. These questions relate to the liability of soft-drink bottlers for the $100.00 license tax imposed by Paragraph (1) of Section 130, and for the $15.00 license tax imposed by Paragraph (2) of Section 130, in connection with the sale of soft-drinks through slot-vending machines.

It appears from conferences held with certain members of the North Carolina Bottlers Association, Inc., and with their counsel, Mr. F. O. Bowman, that slot-vending machines are made available by the bottlers to retailers, by one of the methods hereinafter referred to, in order to promote and stimulate sales of their respective brands of soft-drinks. The machines are so constructed that by the insertion of a coin in a slot in the machine a purchaser may obtain a bottled, iced drink.

A. The $100.00 Tax

There are three general methods by which the bottlers make the machines available to retailers: (1) by sale; (2) by lease for a stipulated rental; (3) by placing the machine with the retailer on certain agreed conditions, but without the payment of a stipulated rental. These three general arrangements must be examined in the light of the provisions of Paragraph (1) of Section 130, which imposes the $100.00 tax on "every person, firm, or corporation engaged in the business of operating, maintaining, or placing on location anywhere within the State of North Carolina, any machine or machines, in which is kept any article of merchandise to be purchased . . ."

(1) *Sale of The Machine:* Where the bottler makes an absolute sale of the machine to the retailer, he obviously is not "operating, maintaining, or placing on location" the machine since he has severed all connection with it, and as to all such machines, is not liable for the $100.00 tax. This is a reiteration of the view expressed in an opinion of this office dated 16 July, 1941 to Mr. F. O. Bowman. You inquire now whether, if the sale is on time, and the bottler sells on a contract securing him against default by retaining title or giving him a lien on the machine until the full purchase price is paid, the view expressed above is altered. I am of the opinion that if the only interest which the seller retains is one for the security of the debt, the situation is essentially the same as where there is an outright sale. However, if the seller retains other interests, or if the "sale" is not bona fide, or if conditions are attached which render the transaction something less than a sale, it is equally clear that the bottler has not released his interest in the machine and might be "operating,

maintaining, or placing on location" the machine. An example of a situation where there is no sale although the retailer pays the bottler the cost price of the machine may be seen in a typical contract submitted to the Department of Revenue by a bottler. This agreement provides that the retailer shall pay a stipulated sum for the use of the machine, or may elect to pay 10 cents per 24 bottle case until the cost price of the machine has been paid, at which time the service charge will be discontinued and the retailer may continue to use the machine without further cost; however, it is expressly provided that title shall remain in the bottler after the cost price is paid. Obviously, no sale has taken place under such an agreement, and it is clearly only a lease.

(2) *Lease of The Machine for a Stipulated Rental:* Where the bottler leases the machine to the retailer, charging the retailer a definite, stipulated sum for the use of the machine, it is probable that the bottler is not "operating or maintaining" the machine within the meaning of the statute, but I am of the opinion that the bottler is "placing on location" the machine. It is important to note that the phrase "placing on location" is introduced by "or" instead of "and". Hence, it is not connected with or dependent on "operating" or "maintaining". To say that the bottler is not "placing on location" the machine would require, in my opinion, a distortion of the plain words of the statute. By leasing, the bottler places the machine on location and has a definite interest in its continued operation. He is enjoying the privilege not only of selling his product through the machine, but is receiving additional consideration in the form of rent. The machine is the bottler's property, placed in a location chosen by him, on terms agreed to by him, and is ultimately subject to his control, removal, or disposal. I believe the legislature intended "placing on location" to cover this situation.

(3) *Placing of Machine with Retailer on Agreed Conditions, but Without Stipulated Rental:* An example of such an agreement may be seen in another typical contract submitted to the Department of Revenue. By this agreement the parties agree that the machine will be "placed in the retailer's establishment; that title will remain in the bottler; that the drinks will be purchased from the bottler at a fixed sum per case, and that a fixed portion of this sum will be used by the bottler for service and maintenance of the equipment." Here, I am of the opinion that the bottler is clearly "placing on location" the machine for reasons already discussed.

While it is impossible to generalize with complete accuracy, it seems to me that any transaction between the bottler and the retailer which falls short of an absolute, clear-cut sale, will probably leave in the bottler such an interest as will bring him within the broad wording "operating, maintaining, or placing on location . . . ." This, I believe, is essentially the conclusion which is expressed in the earlier opinion of this office.

I turn now to a consideration of the question whether the bottler or retailer is liable for the $15.00 tax imposed by subsection (2) of Section 130 in the following language:

> "(2) In addition to the above operator's license, every person, firm, or corporation operating any of the above machines, shall apply for and obtain from the Commissioner of Revenue, what shall be termed a Statewide license for each machine operated and shall pay therefor the following annual tax: . . .

"Slot Drink Vendors . . . . $15.00. ". . . ."

It will be noted at the outset that the statute imposes the $15.00 tax on the person "operating" the machine. The words "maintaining, or placing on location" do not appear. However, a clue to the scope of the term "operating" is found in the phrase "in addition to the annual operator's license." This is a clear reference to the $100.00 license tax imposed in subsection (1). And since that license, levied on persons "operating, maintaining or placing on location," is styled in subsection (2) an "annual operator's license," I am of the opinion that the intent of the statute is that the license referred to in subsection (2) should be paid by the person "operating, maintaining or placing on location" the machines. Against this view, the bottlers point out the provision that "it shall be the duty of the person in whose place of business the machine is operated or located to see that the proper State license is attached in a conspicuous place on the machine before its operation shall commence." However, this provision says nothing about payment for the license, and in terms merely imposes the duty of *attaching or displaying* the license on the machine on the retailer.

Since the intent seems to have been to impose the $15.00 tax on the same person upon whom the $100.00 tax would fall, it necessarily follows that, under the views expressed in the first part of this opinion, if there has been a sale of the machine to the retailer, he would be liable for the $15.00 tax; but if the bottler has leased the machine or placed it on location with the retailer, or is otherwise "operating, maintaining, or placing on location" the machine, the bottler would be liable for the tax.

Of course, there is nothing to prevent the bottler and retailer from agreeing between themselves on which shall pay the $15.00 tax.

RE: TAXES ON GASOLINE SOLD TO A CONTRACTOR OPERATING UNDER A COST-PLUS-A-FIXED-FEE CONTRACT WITH THE FEDERAL GOVERNMENT; EFFECT OF ALABAMA "COST-PLUS" DECISIONS

15 December, 1941.

You inquire by letter of December 9 whether the opinion rendered by this office on December 12, 1940, regarding the applicability of the gasoline road tax to sales of gasoline to a contractor under contract with the federal government on a cost-plus-a-fixed-fee basis, has been modified by the decisions in the recent cases of State of Alabama v. King and Boozer and Curry v. United States, handed down by the United States Supreme Court on November 10, 1941. These decisions, reversing the Supreme Court of Alabama, held that Alabama would constitutionally impose the state sales and use taxes on sales to a "cost-plus-a-fixed-fee" contractor who had contracted with the federal government for construction in an army camp. The reasoning of these decisions is that the mere shifting of the economic burden of the tax to the federal government by the operation of contract is no ground for claiming immunity; that an analysis of the "cost-plus-a-fixed-fee" contracts reveals that the contractor, and not the federal government is the purchaser liable under the statute; that such contractors, despite certain government supervision and control, are not acting as agencies or instrumentalities of the Federal Government; and that thus the legal incidence of the tax is not on the Federal Government and the imposition of the tax does not violate the Federal Government's immunity from State taxation.

In my opinions dated November 29, 1940, and December 12, 1940, I advised you that whether such gasoline was taxable was, at that time, a legal question which had not been decided by the Supreme Court and about which there was considerable difference of opinion, but that the sales under consideration could reasonably be held to be sales to the United States through the contractor as purchasing agent, and, hence, not taxable.

The Alabama decisions now furnish the authority which was lacking at the time my former opinions were written. These decisions remove the basis for the exemption provided for by Section 24(9) of the Gasoline Tax Act, since they make it clear that the "cost-plus" contractor is not the agent of the Federal Government and hence sales to the contractor are not sales "to the United States Government" within the meaning of Section 24(9).

I have been notified that the Louisiana Supreme Court has held in the decision in Standard Oil Co. v. Fontenot, rendered October 17, 1941, that the Louisiana motor fuel tax could be collected on sales to "cost-plus" contractors. I have not yet obtained this decision, but it is summarized as follows in the Tax Administrators News for November, 1941:

> "The Court, in a carefully reasoned opinion, considered the nature of lump-sum, cost-plus-percentage and cost-plus-a-fixed-fee contracts, and concluded that the contractor is not the agent of the government, but an independent purchaser under all three."

I am, therefore, of the opinion that gasoline sold to "cost-plus" contractors with the Federal Government is not sold to the United States, but to the contractor as a private purchaser, and, hence, that it is subject to the gasoline road tax.

RE: EXEMPTION FROM "GASOLINE ROAD TAX" OF GASOLINE SOLD TO ARMY OFFICERS AND ENLISTED MEN THROUGH FORT BRAGG POST EXCHANGE FOR OTHER THAN EXCLUSIVELY GOVERNMENTAL USE

20 December, 1941.

I enclose herewith a copy of a letter dated 25 November, 1941, to Captain J. A. Myatt, of Fort Bragg, and a copy of a letter dated 1 December, 1941, to Mr. Charles F. Conlon, Federation of Tax Administrators. This correspondence reflects the position taken by Captain Myatt with regard to the exemption from the gasoline tax of gasoline sold to Army personnel through the post exchange for other than exclusively governmental use.

I have carefully considered the arguments advanced by the Army authorities in support of their request for tax exemption but I am unable to agree with them.

The essential differences between the position taken by Captain Myatt and the position taken by this office seem to be three:

(1) The Army authorities contend that the Hayden-Cartwright Act, as amended by the Buck Act, does not authorize the imposition on sales through post exchanges of our kind of tax. I must respectfully disagree with this contention in view of the very broad wording of the Buck amend-

ment to the Hayden-Cartwright Act, which specifically permits State taxes "upon, with respect to, or measured by sales, purchases, storage or use of gasoline or other motor vehicle fuel." The Army authorities contend that this wording is limited in application to commodity taxes—i.e., taxes which are required by law to be passed on to the ultimate consumer. This is a limitation which does not appear from the wording and it is a limitation which I cannot believe was intended in view of the known purpose of the Buck Act amendment, which was to broaden the Hayden-Cartwright Act to apply to all types of gasoline taxes and to avoid the construction placed upon that Act before the amendment. See State vs. Ristine, 36 Fed. Supp. 3.

I cannot see that the fact that our tax is not required by law to be passed on to the consumer is a controlling factor. The basic theory of our gasoline tax is that it is levied for the privilege of using the highways of the State. This is evidenced by the fact that the proceeds go to the maintenance of the highways and by the fact that refunds are allowed for non-highway use. It is true that the tax is levied against the distributor but only as a matter of convenience and he is made a collecting agent for the State. While the distributor is not required specifically to collect the tax from those to whom he sells, the practical result is that he does so almost uniformly. Thus, viewed from its practical operation, our gasoline tax is a use tax which is borne by persons using the highways of the State. Therefore, I am of the opinion that this first contention made by the Army authorities is not tenable for two reasons: (a) it involves reading into the Hayden-Cartwright Act as amended a limitation that is not there, and (b) even if the limitation were there, our tax, viewed in its practical operation, is fundamentally like the gasoline taxes of the other states of the Union—that is to say, the first seller or user of motor fuel in the State is the one liable for the tax, while, at the same time, the tax is passed on to the ultimate consumer of the gasoline.

(2) The Army authorities contend that if the gasoline is shipped from an out-of-the-state-refinery into the Fort Bragg Military Reservation, it is not a shipment into the State of North Carolina and hence cannot be taxed under our statute. I have given my views on this contention in the letter dated November 25, 1941 to Captain Myatt.

(3) The Army authorities contend that the tax cannot be levied because in the very nature of things the post exchange cannot be required to put up bond or cannot be subjected to various criminal provisions and that, therefore, from an administrative standpoint it is impractical to apply the tax. However, these objections go to the enforcement and collection of the tax rather than to the liability for the tax and thus they do not seem to meet the point that the State has the power to levy the tax.

I am of the opinion, for the reasons stated in this letter and in the enclosed correspondence, that the tax exemption requested has no legal sanction.

RE: INCOME TAX; TAXATION OF PROCEEDS OF LIFE INSURANCE ENDOWMENT CONTRACT; DEDUCTION OF INTEREST ON LOAN SECURED TO PURCASE A SINGLE PREMIUM ENDOWMENT CONTRACT

23 December, 1941.

You have referred to me an inquiry of Mr. W. H. Gaither relating to the liability for income taxation of the proceeds of a twenty-year single-premium life insurance endowment contract, and to the deductability for income tax purposes of interest paid on a loan secured from a bank to pay a portion of the single premium with which the contract is purchased.

I understand that the contract in question is a combined insurance and endowment contract, purchased by a single premium, providing for life insurance protection to the purchaser until the maturity of the contract on the expiration of twenty years after its issuance, and for the payment to the purchaser of a lump sum at such maturity if he lives until that time. However, under the inquiry made by Mr. Gaither, it is assumed that the purchaser of the contract lives until the expiration of the twenty-year period, and hence we are not concerned with death benefits. The questions which must be answered center around the contract as an endowment contract only.

(1) *To what extent and at what time are the proceeds of the endowment contract, received at the expiration of the twenty-year period, taxable as income of the recipient?* It seems clear that the proceeds of the endowment policy are taxable to the extent of the excess of the proceeds received over the cost of the policy. This is the basic theory of the federal rule (see Section 22(b), Internal Revenue Code; Paul, *Studies in Federal Taxation,* 3rd Series, page 357; Lucas vs. Alexander, 279 U. S., 573; Prentice-Hall Federal Tax Service, Section 8216, et seq.), and applies with like force and logic to the North Carolina income tax law. Although the principle is not expressly stated by our statute, a clear implication that this theory is intended by our law arises from Section 317(2) of the Revenue Act of 1939, as amended, which excludes from the definition of "gross income", and hence exempts from taxation, the following:

> "(b) The amount received by the insured as a return of premium or premiums paid by him under life insurance endowment contracts, either during the term or at the maturity of the term mentioned in the contracts or upon surrender of the contract."

Thus, in determining the taxable income from an endowment contract, so much of the proceeds as represent the cost of purchasing that contract are deducted, and we must necessarily infer from this provision that the proceeds less the cost—i.e., the gain—represent gross income as defined in Section 317.

I am of the opinion that if the taxpayer makes his return on a cash receipts (as contrasted with an accrual) basis, as most taxpayers do, the gain derived from the endowment contract must be returned in the year in which it is received.

(2) *May the interest on a loan secured to pay part of the single premium with which the endowment contract is purchased be deducted on the purchaser's income tax return, and if so, when?*

Section 322 of the Revenue Act of 1939, as amended, provides that in computing net income the following item shall be allowed as a deduction:

> "3. . . . All interest paid during the income year on indebtedness *except interest paid or accrued in connection with the ownership of real or personal property, the current income from which is not taxable under this article. . . .*" (Underlining added).

Since the endowment contract produces *no current income* in the year in which the loan to supplement the premium price is made, the allowance of a deduction of the interest in that year would be a direct violation of the provisions of the quoted section. Therefore, I am of the opinion that the interest could not be allowed as a deduction in the year in which the loan is made.

The question presented is one upon which I have not been able to find any controlling authority. However, after a consideration of the theory upon which the gain of such endowment contracts is included in gross income, and also the probable legislative intent that prompted the enactment of Section 317, subsection 2(b), of the Revenue Act of 1939, as amended, I am of the opinion that while the interest may not be deducted in the year in which the loan is made, it may be viewed as an element in the cost of the contract and hence deducted, along with the return of premiums paid, from the proceeds of the contract upon maturity in determining the gross income that must be returned. As stated above, it seems to me that the General Assembly intended that so much of the proceeds of the endowment contract as are in excess of the cost of the contract should be included in gross income. And, although Section 317, subsection 2(b), refers in terms only to the exemption of that portion of the proceeds representing return of premiums, it reasonably may be construed to exempt also an amount of the proceeds equal to interest paid on a loan secured to pay the premiums. In this view, the interest is a legitimate element of cost, and may be deducted as such in the year in which the proceeds are paid.

RE: CRIMINAL LAW; PRIVILEGE TAXES; PROSECUTION OF OWNER OF HOUSE FOR OPERATION OF MUSIC SLOT MACHINE WITHOUT LICENSE; FAILURE TO DISPLAY LICENSE

14 January, 1942.

In your letter of December 29, 1941, my opinion is requested on the questions raised by the letter of Mr. William W. Pearsall relating to criminal prosecutions for failure to comply with the provisions of the Revenue Act requiring license taxes to be paid for the operation of music machines. Mr. Pearsall states that music machines operating on the coin-in-the-slot principle are being used without licenses in certain houses of a disreputable character in the City of Wilmington. These places are usually private homes rather than ordinary places of business, but they are equipped with an ice box full of soft drinks and have a large room with a slot victrola for dancing. Mr. Pearsall wishes to know whether the owner or occupant of the house may be prosecuted criminally when the music machine is operated without a state, city, or county license. He also wishes to know whether the person on whose premises the machine is operated would be criminally liable if the machine has been licensed but is operated without the license being displayed.

The question of liability under Section 130 of the Revenue Act for the license tax for operation of music machines is discussed at length in an opinion of this office addressed to Mr. H. W. Galloway on April 11, 1941. In that opinion it was concluded that the annual operator's license of $100 is applicable to manufacturers, distributors, or jobbers of such machines, but not to a person who merely keeps and operates one of such machines on his premises. The latter type of person is liable for the $10 tax on each machine imposed by subsection (2) of Section 130. A person is considered to be "operating" a machine and, therefore, liable for the latter tax, if the machine on his premises is under his control and he shares in the profits. It is immaterial that the machine is placed in a private home so long as it is operated for profit.

Section 187 of the Revenue Act imposes criminal penalties upon those who engage in a business without obtaining a license as required by that Act. It is expressly made applicable to taxes levied by counties under authority of the Revenue Act. Subsection (c) provides that it shall constitute a misdemeanor punishable by fine or imprisonment, or both, in the discretion of the court, for any person to "commence to exercise any privilege or to promote any business, trade, employment, or profession, or to do any act requiring a State license under this article without such State license."

If, under the principles set out in this letter and the letter to Mr. Galloway of April 11, 1941, the owner or occupant of the home in which the machine is operated would be liable for the State tax and the machine is operated without the tax being paid, clearly such owner or occupant would be guilty of a misdemeanor and punishable under Section 187, subsection (c). He would be guilty of a similar offense and similarly punishable if the machine were operated without a county license, for Section 130 authorizes the imposition of a county tax, and the criminal sanctions of Section 187 may be invoked with reference to county taxes.

If the owner of a house merely leases space for the machine without having any control over it and without sharing in the profits so as not to be liable for the tax, it is, nevertheless, possible that he may be guilty of a criminal offense under Section 187 when the machine is operated without a license. Under subsection (c) it is a misdemeanor "to promote" a business when the business is taxable and the tax has not been paid. If the owner provides a dance hall, serves drinks, and encourages people to come and use the machine, he would, in my opinion, be promoting the operation of the music machine and guilty of a misdemeanor if the tax is not paid, regardless of whether he is personally liable for the tax. He would be guilty of this offense if the machine were operated without a county license, as well as if it were operated without a State license.

Subsection (c) of Section 190 of the Revenue Act imposes an additional tax of $25.00 for failure to keep a State license conspicuously posted at the place of business for which the license was issued. The effect of this provision is to impose a civil penalty only. I do not believe there would be any criminal liability for failure to keep a license posted. Only persons liable for the tax would be liable for the penalty for failure to post a license. The section, by its terms, relates only to State licenses.

Mr. Pearsall has inquired, also, as to criminal liability for failure to procure a city license. Under subsection 6 of Section 130 of the Revenue Act, cities are authorized to levy license taxes on music machines. However, Section 187, which imposes criminal penalties for failure to pay license taxes, mentions State and county taxes only. Penal statutes are construed strictly, and, therefore, I do not believe this section would make it a criminal offense to operate a business without a city license. It is possible, however, that if the City of Wilmington has an ordinance forbidding the operation of music machines without a city license, a criminal prosecution might be sustained under C. S., Section 4174, which makes it a misdemeanor to violate a city ordinance. The punishment under this section may not exceed a fifty dollar fine or imprisonment for thirty days.

RE: SECTION 161; APPLICATION OF ICE CREAM GALLONAGE TAX

3 January, 1942.

You inquire by letter of December 31 regarding the application of the additional privilege tax on one-half cent per gallon of ice cream levied by Section 161 of the Revenue Act of 1939 as amended.

Section 161 imposes two privilege taxes on every person, firm, or corporation engaged in the business of manufacturing or distributing ice cream at wholesale. The first tax is for a State License for each factory or place where ice cream is manufactured and/or stored for distribution, and is graduated as to amount according to the population of the city or town of location. The second tax is "an additional tax of one-half cent for each gallon manufactured, sold, and/or distributed."

These taxes apply to "ice cream" and "ice cream" is defined by paragraph (b) of the Section as follows:

> "(b) For the purpose of this Section the words 'ice cream' shall apply to ice cream, frozen custards, sherbets, water ices, and/or similar frozen products."

You state that an auditor's report shows that one company has been paying the one-half cent tax only on ice cream sold in gallon lots, and has not been paying the tax on ice cream sold in Dixie cups, sherbets "and other dainties." You inquire whether such a practice complies with the statute.

I am of the opinion that the statute does not place liability for the gallonage tax upon the form or size of containers in which the ice cream is manufactured, sold, and/or distributed, but upon the total gallons actually manufactured, sold, and/or distributed, regardless of the form or size of containers in which such ice cream is made or marketed. The tax is upon total output manufactured, sold and/or distributed, but is computed upon a division of that total output into gallons.

You inquire, further, whether the gallonage tax is applicable to ice cream manufactured in North Carolina to be sold outside the State. I am of the opinion that the tax is clearly applicable to such ice cream. The theory of the taxes in Schedule "B" of the Revenue Act is that they are exacted for the privilege of carrying on the particular business in question, exercising the privilege, or doing the act named. See Section 100 of the Revenue Act of 1939, as amended. And since the tax is on the privilege of manufacturing or distributing ice cream, the fact that some of the products are sold without the state is wholly immaterial. You will note that the gallonage tax attaches to each gallon "manufactured, sold, and/or distributed." The word "sold" is unqualified, and there nowhere appears any exemption as to ice cream sold out of the State.

RE: SECTION 153(1)(e), COUNTY, CITY OR TOWN LICENSE TAX ON SERVICE STATIONS

6 January, 1942.

You inquire by letter of........................., enclosing a letter from the Town of Aberdeen, concerning the amount of license tax authorized by Section 153 of the Revenue Act of 1939, as amended, which cities or towns may levy on service stations.

Paragraph (1) of Section 153 imposes an annual tax on automobile service stations for the privilege of engaging in business, and the amount of the tax is graduated according to the population of the city or town as set forth in the statute. For the purposes of this inquiry, it is necessary to refer only to the first classification, which is as follows:

"In cities or towns of less than 2,500 population................$10.00."

Subdivision (b) of Paragraph (1) provides that "the tax levied in this Section shall in no case be less than five dollars ($5.00) per pump."

Subdivision (e) of Paragraph (1) is as follows:

> "Counties, cities, and towns may levy a license tax on each place of business located therein under this subsection not in excess of one-fourth of that levied by the state."

You inquire whether it is the intent of the statute that a town with a population of less than 2,500 may levy only a tax equal to one-fourth of the $10.00 state tax, regardless of the number of pumps the service station may have, or whether the tax which the town may levy may be affected by the number of pumps.

I am of the opinion that the clear intent of the statute is to allow such a town to levy a tax not over one-fourth of the state tax; and that the state tax in the situation outlined above would be a minimum of $10.00, but would increase by $5.00 for every pump in excess of two. Thus, a station having three pumps would pay to the State a tax of $15.00 or four pumps, $20.00, and so on. It follows that the amount of tax which the town is authorized to levy would also vary according to the State tax, and, therefore, could be affected by the number of pumps if there were more than two.

RE: REFUND ON GASOLINE USED IN VEHICLES OPERATED ON MILITARY RESERVATION

7 January, 1942.

You inquire by letter of December 12 whether a refund of the gasoline tax should be made with respect to gasoline consumer in trucks not operated on the State-maintained highway running through the Fort

Bragg Military Reservation, but operated at least part of the time over other roads and streets within the Reservation.

The statute governing refunds is Subsection 15 of Section 24 of Chapter 145 of the Public Laws of 1931, as amended by Chapter 304 of the Public Laws of 1931, Chapter 211 of the Public Laws of 1933, and Chapter 111 of the Public Laws of 1937 (see Section 2613 (i-15) of Michie's 1939 North Carolina Code). The pertinent portion of that statute is as follows:

> "Any person, association, firm, or corporation, who shall buy in quantities of ten gallons or more at any one time any motor fuels, as defined in this Act for the purpose of use, and the same is actually used, for a purpose other than the operation of a motor vehicle designed for use upon the highways, on which motor fuels the tax imposed by this Act shall have been paid, shall be reimbursed at the rate of five cents per gallon of the amount of such tax or taxes paid under this Act: Provided, however, that motor vehicles designed but not used upon the highways of this State shall be entitled to the refund of gasoline tax as herein provided. . . ."

Under the proviso quoted above, gasoline consumed in vehicles not used *upon the highways of this State* is subject to the tax refund. Hence, the underlined words must be construed with reference to the facts of your inquiry.

The operation in question occurred partially over streets and roads laid out and maintained by the Fort Bragg authorities, and partially over portions of the Reservation not laid out in streets or roads.

The State of North Carolina has ceded exclusive jurisdiction over the territory comprising the Fort Bragg Military Reservation, except as to the right to serve criminal and civil process, as authorized by Section 8059 of the Consolidated Statutes of 1919. Therefore, since the operation in question occurred on lands owned wholly by the Federal Government, and over roads or streets constructed and maintained exclusively by the Federal Government, and in regard to which the State and its subdivisions have no connection, I am of the opinion that the roads, streets and territory over which the operation in question occurred cannot properly be said to be "highways of this state." It follows that the refund should be allowed.

You state, further, that the owner of the trucks referred to above leased the trucks for a stated sum per hour to the general contractor with the Federal Government, furnishing gasoline and drivers. The trucks were then operated under the direction of the general contractor. You inquire whether the refund should be made to the owner of the trucks, to the general contractor, or to the Government.

The refund statute (cited above) provides that any person, association, firm, or corporation, who shall buy motor fuels consumed in the exempted uses, shall be reimbursed at the rate of five cents per gallon on the amount of taxes paid. Thus, the refund goes to the purchaser who pays the tax.

Your question implies the possibility of making the refund to the person ultimately bearing the economic burden of the tax, if that burden has been passed from the immediate purchaser, who in this case was the owner of the trucks, to other parties by contract. However, it is my opinion that the statute does not authorize any such practice. The tax should be refunded to the owner of the trucks as the immediate purchaser of the tax-paid gasoline, and any adjustments arising out of the passing of the economic burden of the tax by contract should be left to the parties.

RE: PAYMENT OF SHERIFF'S FEES FOR SERVICE OF WARRANTS FOR COLLECTION

12 March, 1942.

You inquire whether, when a Sheriff has served tax warrants for collection, and has failed through misunderstanding to collect from the delinquent taxpayers the amount of his fees, the Department of Revenue has any authority to pay these fees.

Section 913(1) of the Revenue Act of 1939, as amended, provides that if any tax is not paid to the Commissioner within thirty days after it is due, the Commissioner shall issue a warrant for collection, directing the Sheriff to levy upon and sell the property of the taxpayer. The Section then provides as follows:

> "The said Sheriff shall, thereupon, proceed upon the same in all respect with like effect and in the same manner prescribed by law in respect to executions issued against property upon judgments of a court of record, *and shall be entitled to the same fees for his services in executing the order, to be collected in the same manner.*" (Underlining added.)

Reference to the general law regarding collection of Sheriffs' fees with respect to executions (C. S. 3908) reveals that the basis of Sheriffs' fees with respect to executions is as follows:

> "Collecting executions for money in civil actions, two and half per cent on the amount collected; and the like commissions for all moneys which may be paid to the plaintiff by the defendant while the execution is in the hands of the sheriff."

Thus, the fees are to be paid from the amounts collected. In my opinion, there is no authority for the payment of such fees by the Department where the Sheriff has failed to add his fees to the amount collected. It is elementary that State funds may not be expended without clear authority and I find no authority to sanction payment of the fees to which you refer.

RE: INCOME TAX; RESIDENTS—INCOME FROM FOREIGN TRUSTS AND PERSONAL SERVICES

19 March, 1942.

I have your letter of February 21, attaching a copy of a letter from this office on the above subject dated May 12, 1938, and a copy of a letter from this office under date of June 4, 1937. It is noted that you consider the two letters as inconsistent and request a clarification.

The income received by a resident of this State from a foreign trust may be taxed in this State, although the income is also taxed in the state in which the trust is located. See Guaranty Company v. Virginia, 83 L. Ed. 16 (1938); Maguire v. Trefry, 253 U. S. 12, and many cases cited in the annotation found in 87 A. L. R. 380. Such income is taxable under Section 310 of the Revenue Act of 1939, unless it is exempted by reason of Section 322(10). This subsection provides for the following exemption:

"Resident individuals and domestic corporations having an established business in another State, or investment in property in another State, may deduct the net income from such business or investment if such business or investment is in a State that levies a tax upon such net income. The deduction herein authorized shall not include income received by residents of this State and domestic corporations from personal services (except as provided in Section 325), stocks, bonds, notes, mortgages, securities, or bank or other deposits or credits, nor in any case shall it operate to reduce the taxable income actually earned in this State or properly allocable as income earned in this State."

The owner of an interest or share in a foreign trust, in my opinion, does not have on that account "an established business in another state or investment in property in another state." The trustee in the foreign state may as such carry on some type of business or may have the assets of the trust estate invested in property in another state which may be real, personal, or intangible property. Such investment, however, would not bring a beneficiary within the meaning of the language employed in this subsection. Such beneficiary has only the equitable interest in the trust which would be properly classified as an intangible.

It is, therefore, my opinion that the income received by a resident individual or domestic corporation from a foreign trust should be required to include such proceeds in gross income, regardless of the character of investments of the trust estate.

The exemption provided by this subsection would apply only to resident individuals and domestic corporations having an established business in another state or investment in property in another state, the title and ownership of which is in the resident taxpayer. This exemption is limited by the further provisions of the section that it will not include the income received from stocks, bonds, notes, mortgages, securities, or bank or other deposits or credits.

RE: LIABILITY FOR PURCHASERS OF BUSINESS FOR SALES TAX WHICH HAD ACCRUED AGAINST THE BUSINESS AT THE TIME OF PURCHASE; FARMERS COOPERATIVE EXCHANGE

3 April, 1942.

You request my opinion concerning the liability of the Farmers Cooperative Exchange for sales tax owed by the Goodwin Poultry and Egg Company on account of its operations prior to the time it discontinued business and its assets were purchased by the Exchange.

Section 416 of the Revenue Act of 1939, as amended, is as follows:

> "The tax imposed by this article shall be a lien upon the stock of goods and/or any other property of any person subject to the provisions hereof who shall sell out his business or stock of goods, or shall quit business, and such person shall be required to make out the return provided for under Section four hundred seven within thirty days after the date he sold out his business or stock of goods, or quit business, and his successor in business shall be required to withhold sufficient of the purchase money to cover the amount of said taxes due and unpaid until such time as the former owner shall produce a receipt from the Commissioner showing that the taxes have been paid, or a certificate that no taxes are due. If the purchaser of a business or stock of goods shall fail to

withhold purchase moneys as above provided, and the taxes shall be due and unpaid after the thirty-day period allowed, he shall be personally liable for the payment of the taxes accrued and unpaid on account of the operation of the business by the former owner."

I am of the opinion that this statute makes the Exchange liable for any sales tax accruing to the State because of the operation of the Goodwin Poultry and Egg Company. The fact that the tax liability was not reported to the purchaser by the Goodwin Poultry and Egg Company is, of course, no ground for avoidance of this liability.

RE: SECTION 132—LIABILITY OF BANK AS SECURITY DEALER

2 April, 1942.

You request my opinion concerning the liability of a commercial bank which operates a trust department for a license or privilege tax levied by Section 132 of the Revenue Act of 1939, as amended, on the business of dealing in securities or engaging in the business of buying or selling securities. You state that the bank in question does not buy or sell or act as agent in buying or selling securities for its depositors or for the public generally; that it does not maintain a place of business for dealing in securities; and that it does not buy stocks, bonds or other securities for any person for a commission, fee or service charge.

I understand that the only securities bought by the bank are for itself or for the trust estates being administered by its trust department, and that it charges no commission fee or service charge for the securities bought in connection with the trust estates.

Upon the facts as stated, I am of the opinion that the bank is not liable for a license or privilege tax as a security dealer.

RE: EXEMPTION FROM GASOLINE TAX OF GASOLINE BOUGHT BY STATE SCHOOL COMMISSION FOR USE IN DELIVERING SCHOOL BUSES

1 May, 1942.

You have requested my opinion whether gasoline sold to the State School Commission for use in the delivery of school buses from body plants to the various county boards of education is exempt from the gasoline tax of six cents per gallon levied by the statutes compiled as Section 2613 (i5) of Michie's 1939 North Carolina Code and the 1941 supplement.

It appears from a conference with Mr. L. J. Sears of the Gasoline Tax Division and with Mr. C. C. Brown of the State School Commission that each year it is necessary for new or replacement school buses to be delivered from plants at several points in the State at which the bus bodies are made to the various counties needing said buses; that in the assembly of the bodies and the delivery of the trucks it is of course necessary that gasoline be provided; that in order to facilitate the distribution of these trucks to the respective counties, the State School Commission purchases with money from the eight months school fund such quantity of gasoline as will be required for this purpose and places this gasoline in the tanks of the school buses under the supervision of the state inspectors at the plants; that the sole use of this gasoline is for the delivery of said trucks; that the State School Commission bills the county boards of education of each county to which a truck or trucks have been delivered for the amount of gasoline consumed in those trucks and the county boards of education reimburse the eight months school fund for their proportionate part of the purchase price of all the gasoline purchased for delivery purposes.

I am of the opinion that the gasoline so purchased by the State School Commission is exempt from the gasoline tax. Chapter 119 of the Public Laws of 1941 was an act to exempt gasoline used in public school transportation from the gasoline tax. It is true that this act provides that the seller of gasoline shall invoice the gasoline sold for public school transportation to the county boards of education and that such sales shall be supported with an official purchase order from the county boards of education. However, Section 3 of that Act is as follows:

> "Sec. 3. It is the intent and purpose of this Act to relieve gasoline used in the public school system of North Carolina from the six cents gasoline tax now imposed by the State and thereby to that extent reduce the cost of public school transportation."

It is, therefore, my opinion that the act referred to in providing for invoices to and official purchase orders from the county boards of education cannot be reasonably interpreted as meaning that the tax exemption should not extend to the gasoline sales under consideration; for, in net effect, the transaction amounts to an advancement of the purchase price of the gasoline for the benefit of the county boards of education, which advancement is reimbursed by the county boards of education. Thus, the county boards of education are the ultimate consumers and purchasers of the gasoline and the fact that the method of payment is indirect does not, in my opinion, remove the transaction from an exempt status. To hold otherwise, would be to ignore the clear intent of Chapter 119.

You should, of course, make such investigation as will satisfy you that the gasoline thus purchased by the State School Commission is in fact used only in public school transportation and is ultimately paid for by the county boards of education.

RE: SECTION 130; FOOD VENDING MACHINES

21 May, 1942.

You request my opinion concerning the proper construction of Sec. 130(2) of the Revenue Act of 1939, as amended by Public Laws 1941, c. 50, s. 3(h), with respect to the exemption applicable to machines "that vend candy containing fifty per cent (50%) or more peanuts." You state that some vending machine operators contend that the quoted provision exempts machines which vend any bars or pieces of candy containing 50% or more peanuts. Under this construction a vending machine containing some bars made up of 50% or more peanuts would be exempt even though the machine also vended other bars containing no peanuts.

I am of the opinion that the General Assembly intended by this section to exempt only those machines which vend bars or pieces of candy, each one of which contains more than 50% peanuts, and that the exemption does not apply if any bar or piece of candy vended by the machine contains no peanuts or less than 50% peanuts. Exemptions from taxation are strictly construed. McCanless Motor Co. v. A. J. Maxwell, 210 N. C. 725; Town of Benson v. Johnston County, 209 N. C. 751; Steadman v. Winston-Salem, 204 N. C. 203. The settled administrative construction of this section by the Department of Revenue has been in accord with the opinion stated above and this construction is entitled to weight. Cannon v. Maxwell, 205 N. C. 420.

RE: REVENUE ACTS, SECTIONS 139 AND 150; LIABILITY OF HOSPITAL OPERATING AS NONPROFIT ORGANIZATION AND RECEIVING AID FROM THE DUKE ENDOWMENT FUND, FOR LAUNDRY AND DRY CLEANING STAMP TAXES

25 May, 1942.

You request my opinion on the question whether a hospital operating as a nonprofit organization and receiving aid from the Duke Endowment Fund is liable for the dry cleaning and laundry stamp taxes levied by Secs. 139 and 150 of the Revenue Act of 1939, as amended.

I am of the opinion that such hospitals are liable for the tax referred to. There is no exemption in the Revenue Act which relieves them of liability for such taxes. It is a well settled rule of law that exemptions from taxation are strictly construed. McCanless Motor Co. v. Maxwell, 210 N. C. 725; Benson v. Johnston County, 209 N. C. 751; Stedman v. Winston-Salem, 204 N. C. 203.

The opinion expressed above is in accord with the administrative policy of the Department of Revenue and this policy is entitled to weight. Cannon v. Maxwell, 205 N. C. 420.

RE: TAXATION; INCOME TAX; LIABILITY OF FOREIGN CORPORATIONS DOING PURELY INTERSTATE BUSINESS

8 June, 1942.

An opinion has been requested from this office in your letter of June 6, 1942, as to whether the D. D. Jones Transfer & Warehouse Company, Inc., of Norfolk, Virginia, should be required to file income tax returns in this state. You state that this company is a common carrier operating in Virginia and North Carolina; that it does a strictly interstate business, no intrastate business being handled in North Carolina; and that its operations consist of loading freight in Norfolk for points in North Carolina and, on return trips, transporting freight from points in North Carolina to Norfolk, Virginia.

From an examination of our income tax laws, and in particular Sections 301, 311, and 312 of the Revenue Act, it seems clear that it was the intention of the legislature to require an income tax to be paid by all foreign corporations doing business in this state. The statute makes no exceptions of foreign corporations doing a purely interstate business so long as they are in fact doing some business in this state. I think it is evident that the D. D. Jones Transfer & Warehouse Company, Inc., is doing business in North Carolina. It collects and delivers freight in North Carolina, uses our highways for the transportation of property, and in all of these operations enjoys the protection of the state government. I conclude, therefore, that under our statute it is required to file income tax returns unless it is exempted from state income taxation under the Federal Constitution.

The Supreme Court of the United States has never directly decided the question whether a company engaged in a purely interstate business is liable for state income taxation. In the past there has been some disposition to regard such a business as being exempt from state income taxation by reason of the Commerce Clause. This view has been influenced by a line of cases holding that a foreign corporation doing a purely interstate business may not be required by a state to pay privilege or license taxes for the privilege of doing such business, the tax constituting a direct burden on interstate commerce.

Cheyney Bros. Co. v. Massachusetts, 246 U. S. 147.
Ozark Pipe Line Corp. v. Monier, 266 U. S. 555.
Sprout v. South Bend, 277 U. S. 833;
26 R. C. L. Secs. 96, 100, pp. 121, 124.

The view that a purely interstate business is exempt from state income taxation has also been influenced by the decision of the United States Supreme Court in Alpha Portland Cement Co. v. Massachusetts, 268 U. S. 203. In this case a foreign corporation's operations in Massachusetts had consisted of solicitation of orders which were to be approved at the home office outside the state and filled by shipments outside the state to purchasers in Massachusetts. The business was of a purely interstate character. A state tax denominated an "excise" was imposed upon all foreign corporations, the amount of the tax being the sum of two items, one of which was "2½ per cent of that part of its net income . . . which is derived from business carried on within the commonwealth." The United States Supreme Court held that this tax was a burden upon interstate commerce and invalid as applied to the foreign corporation under consideration.

There is reason to believe, however, that these authorities are not determinative of the question of the liability of a purely interstate business for a state income as contrasted with a privilege tax. There is a tendency to regard an income tax, in so far as the Commerce Clause is concerned, as more in the nature of a property tax than a privilege tax; and the Alpha Portland Cement Co. case may be distinguished on the ground that although the tax was measured in part by net income it was denominated an excise or privilege tax and also that the part of the tax based on net income was not separable from the other item of the tax which was clearly a burden on interstate commerce. In commenting on the Alpha Portland Cement Co. case, the writer in 39 Harvard Law Review, 396, concludes:

> "It is still undetermined whether the commerce clause will be construed to circumscribe the state's power to levy an income tax, as such, where the foreign corporation does exclusively interstate business. On the one hand, there is the prohibition against excise taxes; on the other, ordinary property taxes are not restricted; although an income tax is perhaps *sui generis*, it is submitted that it more closely resembles a property tax and does not substantially impede interstate commerce."

There is considerable authority, on the other hand, which tends to uphold the validity of state income taxes as applied to purely interstate businesses.

The Supreme Court of the United States has held on a number of occasions that state taxes on the net income from operations in the state of corporations doing both interstate and intrastate business are valid even though part of the income taxed has been derived from interstate commerce.

United States Glue Co. v. Oak Creek, 247 U. S. 321.

Underwood Typewriter Co. v. Chamberlain, 254 U. S. 113.

Atlantic Coast Line RR. v. Daughton, 262 U. S. 413.

Matson Nav. Co. v. State Board of Equalization, 297 U. S. 431.

Furthermore, there are a number of dicta from the United States Supreme Court and other courts which tend to uphold the validity of state income taxes as applied to purely interstate business. For instance, in United States Glue Co. v. Oak Creek, 247 U. S. 321, 328, Justice Pitney, referring to a state income tax, says:

> "Such a tax, when imposed upon net incomes from whatever source arising, is but a method of distributing the cost of government, like a tax upon property, or upon franchises treated as property; and if there be no discrimination against interstate commerce, either in the admeasurement of the tax or in the means adopted for enforcing it, it constitutes one of the ordinary and general burdens of government, from which persons and corporations otherwise subject to the jurisdiction of the States are not exempted by the Federal Constitution because they happen to be engaged in interstate commerce."

In Maxwell v. Kent-Coffey Mfg. Co., 204 N. C. 365, 371, Justice Clarkson observed that:

> "A state may not impose any tax which results in laying a direct burden upon interstate commerce. But, a state may, in levying a general income tax, include within the taxable status so much of net income derived from interstate commerce as is properly apportionable to operations and business within the state."

In McGoldrick v. Berwind-White Coal Mining Co., 309 U. S. 33, Justice Stone says at page 46:

> "Not all state taxation is to be condemned because, in some manner, it has an effect upon commerce between the states, and there are many forms of tax whose burdens, when distributed through the play of economic forces, affect interstate commerce, which nevertheless fall short of the regulation of the commerce which the Constitution leaves to Congress. A tax may be levied on net income wholly derived from interstate commerce."

Most recent pronouncement of the United States Supreme Court on this subject is in Memphis Natural Gas v. Beeler, 86 L. Ed. Adv. Ops. 745, 750, where it is said:

> "In any case, even if taxpayers business were wholly interstate commerce, a nondiscriminatory tax by Tennessee upon the net income of a foreign corporation having a commercial domicile there, cf. Wheeling Steel Corp. v. Fox, supra, or upon net income derived from within the state, Shaffer v. Carter, 252 U. S. 37, 57; Wisconsin v. Minnesota Mining Co., 311 U. S. 452; cf. New York ex rel. Cohn v. Graves, 300 U. S. 308, is not prohibited by the commerce clause on which alone taxpayer relies."

Under these authorities I am of the opinion that the State of North Carolina is justified in requiring foreign corporations engaged exclusively in interstate commerce in this state to file an income tax return if they are doing some business in the state. The office has previously taken this position with regard to income tax liability of such corporations as the Mohawk Carpet Company and the American Telephone and Telegraph Company. Inasmuch as the D. D. Jones Transfer & Warehouse Company of Norfolk, Virginia, is doing business in this state, although the business is interstate in character, I think it should be required to file an income tax return.

RE: TAXATION; PRIVILEGE TAXES; MORRIS PLAN BANKS; CONSTRUCTION OF TERM "RESOURCES" IN SECTION 158 OF REVENUE ACT

12 June, 1942.

I have your letter of May 29, 1942, in which you request an opinion regarding the contents of a letter from the Salisbury Morris Plan Company of Salisbury, North Carolina. The Company seeks advice as to whether in computing the tax on the total resources of the bank under Section 158 of the Revenue Act the gross amount of loans made by the Company should be included as resources, or instead, the gross amount of such loans less the amount paid in by the borrower.

As I understand the operations of Morris Plan banks, when a loan is made, the borrower signs a note for the full amount of the loan, and thereafter he is required to make payments in periodical installments to the bank. These payments are not actually credited as such on the note; but certificates of indebtedness are issued for the payments, and these certificates are pledged as security for the note. When sufficient payments or deposits have been made, the certificates of indebtedness reach an amount equal to the amount of the loan and are then applied to retire the loan. Prior to the retirement of the loan the borrower has no right to withdraw the payments evidenced by the certificates of indebtedness, and, if there is a default in his payment, the amount of the certificate will be applied on the note and he will be liable for the difference. Thus, it appears that while these periodical payments are treated as deposits in the bank, assigned as security for the loan, they are in substance payments on the principal indebtedness. For practical purposes, all that a borrower owes to the bank and all that the bank can realize on a particular note is the face value of the note less the amount of these deposits.

Under the regulations of the Banking Department, a Morris Plan Bank in its balance sheet or financial statement lists as a resource the gross amount or face value of its loan. Account is taken of the payments which have in substance been made on these loans by listing the total amount of these payments or deposits as liabilities. This practice is no doubt proper and expedient for accounting purposes. However, I do not think that the fact that the gross amount of loans is listed as a resource for accounting purposes should be regarded as determinative in ascertaining the total resources of the bank for tax purposes.

Section 158 of the Revenue Act imposes privileges taxes on Morris Plan or industrial banks in this State graduated according to their total resources as of December 31 of the previous calendar year. In my opinion the term "resources" as used in this section refers to the value of the assets of the bank or the amount which they would bring in money if it were liquidated. This is the generally accepted meaning of the term "resources". In 54 C. J. p. 723, the word is defined as follows: "Money or any property that can be converted into supplies; means of raising money or supplies; capabilities of producing wealth or supplying necessary wants; available means or capability of any kind."

If the assets of the bank represented by these loans were reduced to money the most that could be realized from them would be the difference between the gross amount of the loans and the payments that have been made. The value of this difference is, in my opinion, the value for tax purposes of the resources which these loans constitute.

Applying the foregoing principles to the facts outlined in the letter from the Salisbury Morris Plan Company, it seems to me that in computing its liability under Section 158 the sum of $64,033.65, representing deposits on loans, should be deducted from $234,693.75, the gross amount of loans and discounts.

SUBJECT: TAXATION; CHAIN STORE TAX; TWO STORES IN SAME CITY UNDER SAME MANAGEMENT

19 June, 1942.

It appears from the correspondence with Mr. C. S. Lowrimore of Wilmington, North Carolina, that Gregg Brothers is a wholesale and retail hardware business in that city. Originally only one place of business was operated, but, as a result of expansion of business, additional floor space was needed, and this floor space was acquired by purchasing premises in the same city block. As the business is now operated, there are two stores or floor locations which are separated by one store operated by another firm. There is no passage-way connecting the two Gregg Brothers locations. However, there is a single management and there is no separation of the accounts of the two locations.

Gregg Brothers has been assessed with a chain store tax under Section 162 of the Revenue Act, and you have requested my opinion as to whether the business is liable for the tax.

Under Section 162 of the Revenue Act a chain store tax is imposed upon: "Every person, firm, or corporation engaged in the business of operating or maintaining in this State, under same general management, supervision, or ownership, two or more stores, or mercantile establishments. . . ." The fact that the two places of business maintained by Gregg Brothers are under a single management and do not have separate accounts does not exempt the firm from the tax, for the section is expressly made applicable where two stores are operated under the same general management. Furthermore, in my opinion, the requirement that there be two or more stores is satisfied. In 60 C. J., Section 2, page 117, the writer, speaking of the term *store*, says:

> "The noun has a popular, settled, known, and well defined legal signification, well understood by every person, as meaning a building, or room, in which goods of any kind, or goods, wares, and merchandise, are kept for sale . . ."

Since the firm of Gregg Brothers operates under one management two separate buildings in which goods are offered for sale, I conclude that it is liable for the chain store tax.

RE: REVENUE ACT, SECTION 518½; LIABILITY FOR SEPARATE LICENSES OF TWO FOREIGN CORPORATIONS HAVING COMMON OWNERSHIP AND MANAGEMENT

17 June, 1942.

You have requested my opinion regarding a question raised by Messrs. Royall, Gosney and Smith upon the following facts:

Two foreign corporations are engaged in the manufacture of beer, and desire to sell their products to wholesalers in North Carolina. These corporations are owned by the same stockholders, have the same Directors and officers, and are substantially operated as one enterprise. You inquire whether, in view of the common interests of these two corporations, the Department of Revenue would be authorized to issue a joint non-resident license to both corporations and charge a single license fee therefor.

Section 518½ of the Revenue Act provides that "every non-resident desiring to engage in the business of making sales of the beverages described in Section 501 of this Article, to wholesale dealers licensed under the provisions of this Article, shall first apply to the Commissioner of Revenue for a permit so to do." The statute requires the permit and license of "every non-resident." The corporations are separate legal entities and I know of no authority by which the Department would be justified in disregarding this fact.

In my opinion, the legislative intent was that each foreign corporation secure a separate permit or license. If liability for licenses were to be determined by reference to the degree of interlocking control existing between various applicants, a sure and effective administration of the law would be impossible."

RE: INHERITANCE TAXATION OF LAND CONVEYED TO DECEDENT BY HIS WIFE BY DEED VOID FOR FAILURE OF COMPLIANCE WITH C. S. 2515

16 June, 1942.

You request my opinion upon the following matter.

By deed dated 17 December 1926, decedent's wife executed and delivered to decedent a deed purporting to convey certain real estate to him. This real estate consisted of farm land and was not the site of the home of decedent and his wife. The acknowledgment of the execution of this deed did not comply with the provisions of Sec. 2515 of the Consolidated Statutes in that the official taking the acknowledgment did not certify that it appeared to his satisfaction that the wife formally executed such contract, formally consented thereto at the time for her separate examination, and that the same was not unreasonable or injurious to her. The husband dealt with the land as though it was his own and listed it for ad valorem taxes until his death on 23 May, 1940. The wife now contends that the land should not be included within the property of the decedent which was subject to inheritance taxation for the reason that the husband did not have a good title to the property at the date of his death. You inquire whether the wife's contention is correct.

The failure of the official to certify that the conveyance was not unreasonable or injurious to the wife renders the deed void. Bank v. McCullers, 201 N. C. 440. It is true that a deed which is void for lack of compliance with C. S. 2515 is nevertheless good as color of title. Whitten v. Peace, 189 N. C. 298. However, although there is authority to the contrary in other states, (Anno., 74 A.L.R. 144), it seems to be well established in this state that a title by adverse possession cannot be obtained by one spouse against the other during coverture. Kornegay v. Price, 178 N. C. 441; Hancock v. Davis, 179 N. C. 282.

Some of the authorities (for example 30 Corpus Juris p. 581) seem to predicate this rule upon joint occupancy, and the implication may be drawn from them that where there is no joint occupancy, a title by adverse possession may be acquired. However, I am unable to find that this distinction has been made in the North Carolina decisions, and in view of the broad language in Kornegay v. Price, supra, I must advise that the land in question must be excluded from the base upon which the inheritance tax is computed.

RE: TAXATION; INCOME TAX; NONRESIDENT'S INCOME EARNED IN STATE

24 June, 1942.

I have your letter of March 13, 1942, and the letter of Mr. Ralph A. Hankinson, relating to the necessity for income tax returns being filed by Hankinson Speedways, Inc., and by Mr. Hankinson personally.

Mr. Hankinson states that Hankinson Speedways, Inc., has never sponsored any business transactions in North Carolina. If this information is correct, the corporation has done no business in North Carolina and is not required to file income tax returns.

According to his letter, Mr. Hankinson as an individual has been employed by several fairs in North Carolina for the purpose of producing automobile speed programs. Under Section 310 of the Revenue Act, nonresident individuals are liable for a tax on income from business, trades, professions, or occupations carried on in this State. If Mr. Hankinson received a salary or other compensation for his activities in North Carolina in connection with the production of automobile speed programs at fairs, he would be liable for a State tax on such income. He should, therefore, be required to file State income tax returns.

RE: TAXATION; INCOME TAX; EXEMPTIONS; LOCAL BRANCH OF AMERICAN ASSOCIATION OF UNIVERSITY WOMEN

24 June, 1942.

You have asked my opinion by letter of May 27, 1942, as to the income tax liability of the Chapel Hill branch of the American Association of University Women. According to the letter from Mrs. Arthur M. Jordan, which you enclosed, the Chapel Hill branch is a non-profit organization. It receives income in the form of dues from members and money received from entertainments and from the sale of second-hand books. None of the income of the organization inures to the benefit of individual members, and there are no paid officers. This income is used to pay the expenses of speakers, to make contributions to a scholarship fund for women at the University of North Carolina and a fellowship fund administered by the National organization, and for other charitable purposes. Mrs. Jordan did not state whether the organization is incorporated.

In my opinion, this organization is exempted from state income taxation by Section 314 of the Revenue Act. It is, I think, organized for charitable and educational purposes within the meaning of paragraph 3 of that section, which exempts corporations organized for religious, charitable, scientific, or educational purposes. However, if the organization is not incorporated, and this exemption should be construed to be inapplicable to unincorporated associations, it would be exempt under either paragraph 5 or 6. Paragraph 5 exempts civic leagues or organizations not organized for profit and operated exclusively for the promotion of social welfare. Paragraph 6 exempts clubs organized exclusively for pleasure, recreation, and other non-profitable purposes when no part of their income inures to any private stockholder or members.

RE: TAXATION; INCOME TAX; FOREIGN CORPORATION SOLICITING ORDERS IN STATE; JOHNS-MANVILLE SALES CORPORATION

23 June, 1942.

You state in your letter of April 20, 1942, that the Johns-Manville Sales Corporation of New York has filed annual income tax returns in North Carolina indicating that net taxable income has been earned but that none of this income has been prorated to North Carolina, the reasons assigned being that the corporation does not maintain a business office in this State, that it carries no stock of merchandise in its name within the State, and that its activities are limited to the solicitation of orders for merchandise. My opinion is requested as to whether any part of the corporate income should be allocated to North Carolina for income tax purposes.

The answer to your question depends upon whether the corporation may be regarded as "doing business in this State" within the meaning of Sec. 311 of the Revenue Act. For constitutional reasons also it would seem necessary that the corporation's activities in North Carolina amount to "doing business" if the State is to have jurisdiction to tax its income. Hans Rees' Sons, Inc. v. North Carolina, 283 U. S. 123.

If, in fact, the Johns-Manville Sales Corporation of New York has no business office in North Carolina, does not carry a stock of merchandise here, and restricts its activities to solicitation of orders which are accepted at offices outside North Carolina and filled by shipments from points outside the State, I am of the opinion that it is not doing business here and is not liable for a State income tax. Mere solicitation of orders which are accepted outside a state and filled by shipments into the state does not constitute doing business such as to make a foreign corporation subject to service of process. Note (1929) 60 A.L.R. 994, 1031; Note (1936) 101 A.L.R. 126, 133; 23 Am. Jur., Sec. 381, page 380; 17 Fletcher, Cyclopedia of Corporations, Sec. 8482.

Where sales have been made by the solicitation of orders in the manner stated above, it has been held that the income from such sales is taxable in the state where the orders are accepted. Trane Co. v. Wisconsin Tax Comm., 292 N.W. 897 (Wis.); Montag Bros. v. State Revenue Comm. of Ga., 179 S. E. 563 (Ga.); People ex rel. Stafford v. Travis, 231 N. Y. 339, 132 N. E. 109.

It has also been held that such income is not taxable in the state in which the orders are solicited, the solicitation of orders being the only business activity of the corporation in the state. Curlee Clothing Co. v. Oklahoma, 68 P. (2d) 834 (Okla.).

Although, upon the information stated in your letter as having been furnished by the corporation, the Johns-Manville Sales Corporation of New York would appear not to be liable for income tax in North Carolina, you will naturally wish to satisfy yourself that this information is correct. A very little activity in addition to solicitation of orders may be sufficient to render the corporation liable for State income tax. For example, where such orders have been solicited and sales have been made upon consignment, it has been held that the sales are consummated in the State to which merchandise is consigned, and that the corporation is doing business for purposes of income taxation. Chain Belt Mfg. Co. v. Oklahoma, 116 Pac. (2d) 899.

RE: TAXATION; PRIVILEGE TAXES; LOAN AGENCIES OR BROKERS; PERSONS MAKING LOANS ON INSURANCE POLICIES

24 June, 1942.

From the letter of Mr. I. O. Brady, General Counsel of the Durham Life Insurance Company, dated June 4, 1942, it appears that certain persons are engaged in the business of making loans in the City of Asheville and taking assignments of insurance policies as security. You have requested an opinion as to whether these people are liable for the State license tax imposed upon loan agencies and brokers by Section 152 of the Revenue Act.

If a person, firm, or corporation is to be liable under Section 152, three essential facts must appear:

(1) The taxpayer must be "engaged in the regular business of making loans or lending money."

(2) Security must be taken for the repayment of the loans.

(3) An office or established place for the negotiation or transaction of business must be maintained, *or* the taxpayer must advertise or solicit business.

Mr. Brady does not state specifically whether the individuals mentioned in his letter are engaged in making loans as a regular business. It is implicit in his letter that they are, however. You will, of course, wish to satisfy yourself that this is true if a tax is to be assessed under Section 152.

It is clear from Mr. Brady's letter that loans are made and that security for their repayment in the form of assignments of insurance policies is taken. The second essential requirement is, therefore, satisfied.

It is stated that the persons under consideration maintain an office and advertise in the newspapers and over the radio. Thus, the third requirement seems to be satisfied.

If the facts outlined above can be satisfactorily established, I am of the opinion that a tax under Section 152 of the Revenue Act can and should be collected. It is not clear from Mr. Brady's letter whether the persons under consideration are doing business as a firm or separately as individuals. If the former is true, one tax for the firm should be collected. If the latter, and all of the essential facts can be established as to each individual, a separate tax should be collected from each.

RE: TAXATION; PRIVILEGE TAXES; AUTOMOBILE DEALERS; MANUFACTURER'S AGENTS

26 June, 1942.

I have carefully examined the file on the Nash-Kelvinator Sales Corporation, which claims that it is a manufacturer's agent and, therefore, not subject to the license tax on automobile dealers. Mr. R. N. Todd of the Tax Department of the Corporation states that the Nash-Kelvinator Sales Corporation is a subsidiary of the Nash-Kelvinator Corporation, that the Nash-Kelvinator Sales Corporation contracts to dispose of the products of the latter corporation, and that pursuant to contract it wholesales new automobiles and accessories to retail dealers in North Carolina. Upon these facts, I am of the opinion that the Nash-Kelvinator Sales Corporation is a motor vehicle dealer and is liable for the tax imposed by Section 153 of the Revenue Act.

Mr. Todd has stated no facts which in my opinion justify the conclusion that the Nash-Kelvinator Sales Corporation is a manufacturer's agent. In an opinion to the Commissioner of Revenue dated July 18, 1940, this office ruled that a manufacturer's agent was not liable for the tax imposed by Section 133, paragraph 1, of the Revenue Act. The agents involved in that instance were individuals rather than corporation. The sales which they negotiated were made in the name of the manufacturer, who was their principal. Payment was made by the purchasers directly to the principal. On these facts it was concluded that the agents were not engaged in the business of selling on commission within the meaning of the statute. There is nothing, however, in the file on the Nash-Kelvinator Sales Corporation which suggests that its operations were carried on in this fashion.

RE: BANKRUPTCY; BANKRUPT BUSINESS OPERATED BY TRUSTEE; FRANCHISE TAXES

29 June, 1942.

I have examined the file on the Conover Furniture Corporation, and I think that the State unquestionably had a valid claim against the trustee in bankruptcy as liquidating agent of this bankrupt corporation for franchise taxes during the period in which the trustee continued the operation of the business. This claim was based on 28 U. S. C. A., Sec. 124 a, which provides in part: "any receiver, liquidator, referee, trustee, or other officers or agents appointed by any United States court who is authorized by said court to conduct any business, shall, from and after June 18, 1934, be subject to all State and local taxes applicable to such business the same as if such business were conducted by an individual or corporation. . . ." Taxes for which a trustee in bankruptcy becomes liable as a result of continued operation of a bankrupt business are classified as administrative expenses, Missouri v. Earhart, 111 F. (2d) 992 (C.C.A. 8th, 1940), and they constitute preferred claims of the first class under 11 U. S. C. A., Section 104.

Although the State had a valid claim for franchise taxes against the estate of the Conover Furniture Corporation, it appears from the letter of Mr. L. H. Wall dated March 27, 1942, that this claim was disallowed by the referee in bankruptcy and that all of the assets of the bankrupt corporation have been distributed. If so, the order was undoubtedly erroneous. There are some authorities which hold that a trustee in bankruptcy, who has notice of preferred claims and who distributes the assets of the bankrupt without making provision for such claims, is personally liable even though the distribution is made pursuant to an order of the referee. United States v. Barnes, 31 Fed. 705; In re B. A. Montgomery, 17 F. (2d) 404 (N. D. Ohio, 1927). However, these cases have been influenced by an element of negligence on the part of the trustee in failing to bring the preferred claims to the attention of the referee. It is doubtful whether a trustee could be held personally liable if a valid preferred claim were properly presented to the referee and disallowed by him although erroneously.

It seems likely that the State may have lost its right to enforce its claim for franchise taxes by failure to appeal reasonably from the order of the referee disallowing its claim. However, before we definitely decide whether there is any possibility of enforcing the claim, I think we ought to have further information as to the circumstances under which the claim was presented to the referee and as to the notice which was given. It would be helpful also to have a copy of the order of the referee disallowing our claim and of the orders under which the funds of the bankrupt were distributed. This information might be secured by further correspondence with Mr. Wall or, perhaps, by one of our field deputies.

RE: TAX ON GASOLINE PURCHASED BY SCHOOLS FROM LOCAL FILLING STATIONS SERVED BY COMPANIES NOT ON STATE CONTRACT

30 June, 1942.

You have referred to me a letter from Honorable Clyde A. Erwin, State Superintendent of Public Instruction, with reference to the situation hereinafter stated.

A county board of education found it impossible to purchase gasoline from an oil company having the state contract for the sale of gasoline because of the fact that in one section of the county the necessary school buses did not have access to gasoline storage facilities. The county board of education purchased gasoline through a local service station from a company not on state contract. The question raised by Dr. Erwin is whether in paying for this gasoline the county board may deduct the gasoline tax.

Public Laws of 1941, Chapter 119, provided that any person, firm or corporation holding a North Carolina state contract for the sale of gasoline to be used in public school transportation in the State shall invoice the gasoline so sold at the prevailing contract price, less the State tax. The act provides for a definite procedure by which the Department of Revenue may be advised of such purchases. In Section 2 the act provides that when any authorized dealer has already paid the state gas tax but furnishes the Department of Revenue with proper invoices and purchase orders showing that the gas was purchased for use in public school transportation, such dealer shall be entitled to a refund of the tax. However, it is important to note that the statute specifically refers to "authorized" dealer. As I interpret this act, it was the clear legislative intent to confine the tax exemption to those purchases made from companies operating upon state contract. This meaning is reinforced by the provisions of Section 23 of the School Machinery Act of 1939, which provides that "it shall be the duty of the county boards of education and/or the governing bodies of city administration units to purchase all supplies, equipment and materials in accordance with contracts and/or with the approval of the State Division of Purchase and Contract."

It has been suggested that Section 3 of the 1941 Act, which states that "it is the intent and purpose of this act to relieve gasoline used in the public school system of North Carolina from the six cents gasoline tax now imposed by the State and thereby to that extent reduce the cost of public school transportation" indicates a legislative intent to exempt the gasoline bought in this case from the tax. I am unable to agree with this position. In my opinion Section 3 must be read in its context and when so read is limited by the specific reference in Section 1 to a seller holding a state contract for the sale of gasoline.

I, therefore, conclude that the tax is due in the situation outlined in Dr. Erwin's inquiry.

OPINIONS TO COMMISSIONER OF AGRICULTURE

SUBJECT: PURE SEED LAW; LIABILITY FOR TAX AS A WHOLESALE DEALER

24 July, 1940.

I have your letter of July 22, with enclosure from .... Company of Columbia, South Carolina, dated July 16, 1940.

If this concern is engaged in the business of selling seed at wholesale and has sold or offered for sale seed in this State, I see no reason why it would not be liable for the $25.00 inspection fee, as provided in Section 4830 of Michie's N. C. Code, 1939.

As this office has formerly ruled, in a letter dated January 13, 1939, and addressed to your Department, this is an inspection fee and, as such, does not constitute an unlawful interference with interstate commerce and may be applied to interstate shipments. The whole purpose of seed inspection law is to protect the seed buying public and to prevent seed of inferior quality from being brought into the State of North Carolina or exported therefrom. The State of North Carolina uses the funds realized from the inspection fee to defray the expenses of the examination and analysis of seed by the Department of Agriculture. This being true, it seems to me that it would follow that the inspection fee is a reasonable relation to the services granted by the State of North Carolina and that the imposition of an inspection fee on out-of-State wholesale seed dealers who sell to retail dealers in this State could not be successfully assailed in the Courts by such seed dealers.

SUBJECT: HOUSE BILL NO. 498—AN ACT FOR THE RELIEF OF POTATO FARMERS IN THIS STATE

25 March, 1941.

You state that the S. A. L. Railroad Company plans to enter into an agreement with the farmers in Rutherford County for an aggregate production of one acre of Irish potatoes. Under the agreement the railroad will furnish the seed, fertilizer, and insecticide to be used in the production of the potatoes, the purpose being to develop new seed producing areas in North Carolina. The grower will furnish the land and labor, will grow and harvest the potatoes, and deliver them to the railroad platform at Forest City where the crop will be divided on a fifty-fifty basis. The railroad will use their half of the potatoes for experimental planting in another state; the growers to dispose of their half of the crop as they may desire.

You inquire if such an agreement would come within the meaning of House Bill No. 498, passed by the 1941 General Assembly, which requires supply dealers who furnish growers with seed potatoes, fertilizer, and other supplies, to perform services in connection with the gathering of such crops and marketing the same, to guarantee to the grower a return of not less than ten dollars for each bag of seed potatoes planted out of the first proceeds of the sale of the same after they are marketed, as compensation for labor and work done, and equipment used in growing the potatoes.

I do not think that the transaction in the instant case comes within the meaning of the above Act. Under the present plan the supplier of the seed potatoes only furnishes the seed, fertilizer, and insecticide; he enters into no agreement to market the same, nor is there any provision for a division of the sales price thereof after they are marketed. This is a simple agreement whereby the railroad company agrees to furnish potatoes, fertilizer, and insecticide for a division on a fifty-fifty basis of the crop after it is harvested. Thereafter, the grower may dispose of his half of the crop as he so desires, the railroad company, of course, having this same privilege. I do not think that transactions of this nature are within the purview of the Act above referred to.

SUBJECT: FARM MARKETING ACT; CH. 263, P. L. 1941

2 June, 1941.

Since Section 2 of the above Act only requires operators of a livestock market to furnish a bond "acceptable to the Commissioner of Agriculture," I do not think it necessary that a surety bond be furnished; however, this could be done under the Act.

I think the Act would authorize you, if you thought it safe to do so, to accept a personal bond with individual sureties, or you could require any such operator to deposit with you securities of almost any nature which you thought were of sufficient value to cover any liability of such operator under the provisions of the Act.

SUBJECT: AGRICULTURE; FERTILIZER LAWS; REGISTRATION

12 June, 1941.

You inquire as to what credit persons, who have heretofore registered fertilizer or fertilizer material with the Commissioner of Agriculture, will be entitled under the new registration law on account of the unearned or unused portion of the fees heretofore paid.

The North Carolina Fertilizer Law of 1933, as amended by the Legislature of 1937, required that any person acting for himself or as agent to sell or offer for sale within the State any mixed fertilizer or fertilizer material must file with the Commissioner of Agriculture on registration forms supplied by him, a signed statement giving certain information with respect to each brand, grade or analysis. The Act further provides that all manufacturers, dealers or agents applying for registration shall pay to the Commissioner of Agriculture the sum of $5.00 for each separate registration registered with the Commissioner and sets up the quinquennial registration of brands of fertilizer or fertilizer materials, beginning December 1, 1937. Next to the last sentence of Section 4 of the Act is as follows:

> "It is further provided herein that the full registration fee of five dollars shall be levied on all brands of fertilizer or fertilizer materials offered for registration between the effective date and the expiration of any quinquennial period."

The 1941 Fertilizer Act provides for a new registration of brands and requires a registration fee of $2.00 for each grade or brand or name registered, such registration to expire on November 30 of the year in which it is registered. The 1941 law also contains the following proviso:

> "Provided that all persons heretofore registering fertilizer or fertilizer material with the Commissioner of Agriculture and having paid the registration fee required by Chapter 324 Public Laws of 1933 shall be given credit on future registration fees required under this Act for the unearned or unused portion of the fees so paid on a pro-rata basis of the period covered by said fee."

The 1941 Act becomes effective from and after December 1, 1941, which is the end of the fourth year of the five year period beginning December 1, 1937. It is my opinion that the 1933 Act, as amended by the 1937 Act, required the payment of a $5.00 registration fee for the period beginning December 1, 1937 and ending December 1, 1942, and it would have been necessary for each brand to have again been registered after December 1, 1942, and this would be equally true if the brand had been registered on December 1, 1940 instead of December 1, 1937.

It is likewise my opinion that the Legislature, in enacting the 1941 Act, had this in mind and by making the Act effective on December 1, 1941, the end of the fourth year of the five year period beginning December 1, 1937, intended to limit the amount to which any one person is entitled to credit on future registration fees for one particular brand to the sum of $1.00. In other words, on December 1, 1941, the used portion of the $5.00 fee for registration would be $4.00 and the unused portion $1.00. I am sure it was not the intention of the Legislature to allow credit in excess of $1.00 on each brand of fertilizer registered prior to December 1, 1941.

SUBJECT: CO-OPERATIVE ASSOCIATION; TIME AND PLACE OF MEETING

25 July, 1941.

You state that the by-laws of the Growers Peanut Co-operative, Inc., organized under subchapter V of Chapter 93 of the Consolidated Statutes, provide that the annual meeting of the members of the Association shall be held at a place designated in North Carolina; that under the charter of the Association, Edenton is designated as its headquarters.

You inquire if the provisions of the general law relating to co-operatives, particularly C. S. 1168, which provides that meetings of stockholders of every corporation of the State shall be held at the principal office in this State, would apply to the co-operative association in this instance. C. S. 5259(h) provides that such association may under its by-laws provide, among other things, the time, place, and manner of calling and conducting its meetings.

I think this latter statute is controlling, and since the by-laws provide that the annual meeting of the members shall be held at a place designated in North Carolina, it would not be confined to the meeting place designated in the charter.

RE: CREDIT UNIONS; POSTDATED CHECKS AS PAYMENT OF INSTALLMENTS

25 August, 1941.

I have your letter of August 23, with the enclosure from the Oxford Credit Union, relating to postdated checks as payments for installment loans.

There is not, in my opinion, any statute or decision that makes it unlawful for a person to accept a postdated check, either for a past due debt or for a debt that will become due in the future. The question then is: Is such a practice worthwhile?

In my opinion, accepting a postdated check for a debt gives the accepting party no additional rights. The check is merely evidence of the indebtedness, and would be only a promissory note or an additional promise. This is true, I think, when the checks are given, as in your case, for future installments. True, the case to which Mr. Webb refers (State v. Crawford, 198 N. C. 522, 152 S. E. 504), holds that a postdated check, *given for a past due debt,* is not such a representation as will render the drawer liable to a criminal prosecution, if the check is worthless. However, if the giving of a postdated check *for a debt that is due and payable* will not render the drawer liable criminally, if the check is worthless, surely the giving of a postdated check *for a debt that is not yet due,* will not render him liable criminally. In my opinion, this is merely an additional promise on two contingencies, i.e., a promise to pay when the debt is due and when the check is presented, on or after the date on the face of the check. I feel that a criminal prosecution under such circumstances could not be sustained. The same is true where a check is given with the understanding that the same is to be held and presented by the owner at a future date. State v. Tatum, 205 N. C. 784.

In his letter Mr. Webb says that there are cases where the borrowers have moved away and left the payment to the endorsers, and that if he had their checks he "could at least bring them back under the law." If the borrower has not moved out of the state, he could be reached equally as well civilly as criminally, and if he has moved out of the state, he could not be extradited because he has not violated the criminal law.

SUBJECT: DEPARTMENT OF AGRICULTURE; HANDLERS OF FARM PRODUCTS; CONTRACTS

15 December, 1941.

In your letter of December 15, you refer to that provision of Chapter 359, Public Laws of 1941, which provides that no handler of farm products shall enter into any written contract with a producer in this State for the production, delivery or sale of farm products until he files with the Commissioner of Agriculture a true copy of the contract and the same has been examined and approved by the Commissioner. You inquire if in administering Chapter 359, Public Laws of 1941, you would have to take into consideration the provisions of Chapter 354, Public Laws of 1941, which is an Act for the relief of potato farmers in this State.

There is no provision appearing in Chapter 354, Public Laws of 1941, which would have the effect of requiring contracts within the purview of this statute to be examined and approved by the Commissioner and unless persons or corporations who engage in supplying growers of potatoes with fertilizer and other supplies within the meaning of Chapter 354 and by such operations come within the meaning of Chapter 359, your Department would not be concerned with such transactions. Under the provisions of Chapter 354, the Commissioner of Agriculture is not charged with any duty with reference to the administration of the same.

SUBJECT: SALES TAX PAID BY THE FEDERAL GOVERNMENT

27 May, 1942.

You sent me a memorandum from Mr. Randal B. Etheridge, under date of May 16, in which Mr. Etheridge stated that the Federal Government pays the sales tax on all materials in North Carolina except those used for building purposes.

Mr. Etheridge was incorrectly informed about this. The State of North Carolina does not collect any sales tax on any sales made to the Federal Government. It does, however, collect sales and use taxes on sales made to government contractors, except on building materials. Our Sales Tax Act, Section 406(e), exempts sales which we are prohibited from taxing under the Constitution or laws of the United States. It has always been held that no taxes could be directly imposed on the activities of the Federal Government.

OPINIONS TO BUDGET BUREAU

SUBJECT: STATE BUILDING CONTRACTS; CONTRACTORS, SUBCONTRACTORS—WITHHOLDING PAYMENTS DUE CONTRACTORS—LABOR AND MATERIALS

18 October, 1940.

Receipt is acknowledged of your letter of October 8, in which you ask my opinion as to whether the general contractor under a State contract for construction of State buildings or structures is responsible for the bills of the subcontractor, after the contractor has given notice to the vendor that he would not be liable for these bills.

The question submitted by you involves a question as to whether the State could withhold payments due the general contractor on account of sums due under construction contracts. I have reached the conclusion that you would not be entitled to withhold funds from the general contractor under the general provisions of our laws, as the material men, laborers and subcontractors would have no lien on said property constructed under such contract. Our Court has held that a public agency had no right to withhold funds due a contractor on account of claims of laborers and material men.

I am enclosing you copy of a memorandum made in this office on this subject, which I believe will give you fully the law bearing upon it and which I trust you will find of interest.

This opinion is of a general nature, without reference to the provisions of the bond in any particular case given by the contractor, or the terms of the contract between the State and the contractor. It is conceivable that a contract might be entered between the building agency of the State and the contractor, providing and requiring that before payments on the contract would be made, all claims of subcontractors, labor and material men should be paid, and a bond required guaranteeing performance of these conditions. In such case, the law stated generally would be inapplicable and the terms of the particular contract, and the bond given in pursuance thereto, would support State action in keeping therewith.

SUBJECT: HIGHWAY PATROL; APPOINTEES; CONTRACT OF EMPLOYMENT

16 January, 1941.

I have examined the letter of Major Armstrong, dated August 14, 1940, addressed to Mr. Robert O. Leinster of Concord, wherein he states that there will be vacancies on the Patrol and inquired if Mr. Leinster would be available for a call. It is stated in this letter that "all appointees are on probation for a period of ninety days, that is, they have ninety days in which to make good, and, if they have not done so in that period, they will be notified." Mr. Leinster replied to this letter on the bottom of the page, to the effect that he would be available.

On September 5 Major Armstrong wrote Mr. Leinster again, advising that he had been selected for service and that he was to report to Raleigh on the morning of September 16. Mr. Leinster, by telegram on September

7, accepted the offer and reported and was put to work. Sixty days later he was released from duty and now demands payment of an additional month's salary, and you inquire if the letters of Major Armstrong to Mr. Leinster and his replies thereto constitute a contract of employment for ninety days.

I think so. The preliminary letter of Major Armstrong stated that all appointees were given ninety days in which to make good. Mr. Leinster accepted this offer by notation on the bottom of the letter, and, when notified to report to duty, accepted by telegram and reported.

SUBJECT: TEACHERS' AND STATE EMPLOYEES' RETIREMENT SYSTEM; EMPLOYER'S CONTRIBUTIONS; PAYMENT OUT OF UNEMPLOYMENT COMPENSATION ADMINISTRATION FUND COVERING EMPLOYEES OF UNEMPLOYMENT COMPENSATION COMMISSION

16 June, 1941.

You inquire as to whether, in my opinion, payments to cover employer's contributions for employees of the Unemployment Compensation Commission may be made from the Unemployment Compensation Administration Fund.

I am of the opinion that such payments may lawfully be made under the statutes of the State of North Carolina. The Teachers' and State Employees' Retirement Act covers the employees of the Unemployment Compensation Commission. The Retirement Act requires that the Board of Trustees created under the provisions of the Act shall annually prepare and certify to the Budget Bureau a statement of the total amount necessary for the ensuing fiscal year to be paid to the pension accumulation fund and this amount is in reality the employer's contributions. Section 15½ of Chapter 107 of the Public Laws of 1941 provides:

> "The Director of the Budget is authorized, empowered and directed to allocate out of the highway and public works fund, the agricultural fund, and other special operating funds employing personnel, the amount sufficient to meet the contributions necessary to be made in order to comply with the Act creating the State Teachers' and State Employees' Retirement System."

Under the provisions of the Unemployment Compensation Act, as amended by Chapter 108 of the Public Laws of 1941, all moneys in the administration fund which are received from the Federal Government or any agency thereof or which are appropriated by the State of North Carolina must be expended solely for the purposes and in the amounts found necessary by the Social Security Board for *the proper and efficient administration of the Act.* It is further provided that all moneys in this fund shall be deposited, administered and disbursed in the same manner and under the same conditions and requirements as is provided by law for *other special funds* in the State Treasury.

The Unemployment Compensation Administration Fund to my mind is certainly a special operating fund within the meaning of Section 15½ of the Public Laws of 1941 (Chapter 107), and if this is true, the Director of the Budget has the power and authority to allocate out of the fund a sufficient amount to meet the employer's contributions to the Retirement

System covering the employees who are employed under the provisions of the Unemployment Compensation Act.

It is the purpose of the Retirement Act to provide a certain amount of security in old age for all State employees and to promote efficiency in all State departments and institutions. It seems to me that it would aid in the proper and efficient administration of the Unemployment Compensation Act for the employees to have the protection provided by the Teachers' and State Employees' Retirement Act.

I can see no reason why the employer's contributions to the Retirement System for the employees of the Unemployment Compensation Commission may not, under the State Law, be paid from the unemployment compensation administration fund.

SUBJECT: AGRICULTURE; BOOK ON BIRD LORE; PUBLICATION BY LOCAL PRINTER

7 August, 1941.

You state that there has been some data collected by the Department of Agriculture on birds and bird life in this State, and that it is the desire of the Department to have this data published in book form. You state further that a local printer has offered to print this book free of charge to the State, provided that he be permitted to market the same to cover costs of printing, furnishing, of course, the Department of Agriculture with a sufficient number of copies of the book for their needs.

I see no legal objection to this procedure being followed, and it will certainly result in saving the cost of the printing of this work by the State, which, otherwise, it would incur.

RE: LIQUIDATION OF DRY CLEANERS COMMISSION FUND

9 August, 1941.

I have your letter of August 7, wherein you inquire as to what disposition shall be made of the surplus funds remaining in your hands after the payment of all expenses incurred by your department in the liquidation of the Dry Cleaners Commission.

Under Section 2 of Chapter 127, Public Laws of 1941, you will find that the residue of said funds shall be disbursed pro rata in accordance with the amounts paid into the said fund to the respective payees thereof, as shown by records of the Commission. I think this should be followed, regardless of the fact that some of the payees paid these fees into the Commission under protest; that is to say, all who paid any money into the fund should be repaid on a pro rata basis.

SUBJECT: TEACHERS' AND STATE EMPLOYEES' RETIREMENT SYSTEM; CONTRIBUTIONS FROM SPECIAL OPERATING FUNDS

5 September, 1941.

I have given careful consideration to your letter of August 5, and it is my opinion that the conclusions reached therein are based on sound reasoning and that you would be justified in following the course you suggest.

The term "Special Operating Funds Employing Personnel" standing alone might be considered by the Court as meaningless and that to arrive at what the Legislature intended it would be necessary to consider it in connection with the remainder of the language used in Section 15½ of Chapter 107 of the Public Laws of 1941. When so considered, it certainly could be argued that in naming the Highway and Public Works Fund and the Agricultural Fund, the Legislature indicated the general type of fund which should be included within the phrase, "Special Operating Funds Employing Personnel." I am sure that the Legislature, in enacting Section 15½, did not have in mind to include within the provisions of the section the various funds and activities which you conclude in your letter should be exempted from the provisions of this section.

Of course, it is very difficult to draw a line between what should be included and what should not be included under the provisions of this section, but I am sure no difficulty will arise from following the course outlined by you.

SUBJECT: USE OF STATE OWNED AUTOMOBILE

13 May, 1942.

In your letter of May 8, you inquire as to the law relating to the private use of publicly owned motor vehicles.

The statutes relating to this subject are plain and are self-explanatory. They are as follows:

> "4399(a). *Private use of publicly owned vehicle.*—It shall be unlawful for any officer, agent or employee of the State of North Carolina, or of any county or of any institution or agency of the State, to use for any private purpose whatsoever any motor vehicle of any type or description whatsoever belonging to the State, or to any county, or to any institution or agency of the State."
>
> "4399(d). *Publicly owned vehicle to be marked.*—It shall be the duty of the executive head of every department of the State Government, and of any county, or of any institution or agency of the State, to have painted on every motor vehicle owned by the State, or by any county, or by any institution or agency of the State, a statement with letters of not less than three inches in height, that such car belongs to the State, or to some county, or institution or agency of the State, and that such car is 'for official use only'. Provided, however, that no automobile used by any officer or official in any county in the State for the purpose of transporting, apprehending or arresting persons charged with violations of the laws of the State of North Carolina, shall be required to be so lettered."

SUBJECT: STATE EMPLOYEES; PERQUISITES

16 May, 1942.

I have your letter of May 14 wherein you inquire if there is any law which relates to the furnishing of perquisites to the employees of the various institutions.

There is no law relating to this particular subject. This is an administrative matter and perhaps would be governed by policy adopted by the governing board of the state institutions concerned, of course with the approval of the Budget Bureau.

OPINION TO UTILITIES COMMISSION

SUBJECT: MOTOR VEHICLE LAWS; RULES OF THE ROAD; PARKING

17 July, 1941.

I have your note of July 16, to which is attached a letter from Major Armstrong of the Highway Patrol, addressed to the Seashore Transportation Company of New Bern, wherein he advises that he has instructed highway patrolmen that they are to require all motor vehicles, and particularly buses, carrying passengers over the highways of this State, that when stopping to unload or load, to pull completely off the paved portion of the highway before stopping; that a failure to comply with this requirement would be a violation of Section 123 of Chapter 407 of the Public Laws of 1937, and particularly that portion of this section which provides that "in no event shall any person park or leave standing any vehicle, whether attended or unattended, upon any highway unless a clear and unobstructed width of not less than fifteen feet upon the main traveled portion of said highway opposite such standing vehicle shall be left for free passage of other vehicles thereon, nor unless a clear view of such vehicle may be obtained from a distance of two hundred feet in both directions upon such highway . . ."

I do not think that Major Armstrong's interpretation of the law in this instance is correct. The courts of this State have passed upon the question of what is designated as "parking" under this section of the law.

In the case of Stallings v. Transport Co., 210 N. C. 201-203, this Court, quoting from State v. Carter, 205 N. C. 761-763, said:

> " '. . . to "park" means something more than a mere temporary or momentary stoppage on the road for a necessary purpose'."

The Court further said in the Carter case, supra:

> "There was no error in the instruction of the court to the jury as to the meaning of the word 'park' as used in the ordinance. This word is in general use with reference to motor driven vehicles, and means the permitting of such vehicles to remain standing on a public highway or street while not in use. 43 C. J. 613 . . ."

In my opinion, a mere temporary stoppage by a bus upon the highways of this State for the purpose of taking on or discharging passengers would not be considered "parking" within the meaning of the statute referred to above.

OPINIONS TO INSURANCE COMMISSIONER

SUBJECT: (1) DEFINITIONS; "RESIDENCE"; (2) LICENSES; JEWELRY AUCTIONEER; RESIDENCE

5 July, 1940.

You have asked the meaning of "resident" or "residence."

The meaning of the two terms varies with the way in which they are used. The question whether a person is a resident of North Carolina must be determined on the basis of the facts in each individual case.

Clark, C. J., in Watson v. North Carolina R. R., 152 N. C. 215 (1910), wrote the following:

"The word 'residence' has, like the word 'fixtures', different shades of meaning in the statutes (Overman v. Sasser, 107 N. C., 432), and even in the Constitution, according to its purpose and the context. Tyler v. Murray, 57 Md., 441. See cases cited in 7 Words and Phrases, under head 'Residence'; also, 24 A. and E. (2 Ed.), 692; 34 Cyc., 1647. Even in our Constitution, the word 'reside' has a different meaning in the following articles: Article III, sec. 5: 'The Governor shall reside at the seat of the government of this State'. Article IV, sec. 2: 'Every judge of the Superior Court shall reside in the district for which he is elected'. Article VI, sec. 2: 'He shall have resided in the State of North Carolina for two years, in the county six months, and in the precinct or other election district in which he offers to vote, four months next preceding the election'. And in the statutes, the exact shade of meaning depends somewhat upon whether the enactment concerns Suffrage and Eligibility to office; Attachment and Homestead Exemptions; Publication of Summons or Venue; but they all include the idea of permanence.

"Probably the clearest definition is that in Barney v. Oelrichs, 138 U. S., 529: 'Residence is dwelling in a place for some continuance of time, and is not synonymous with domicil, but means a fixed and permanent abode or dwelling as distinguished from a mere temporary locality of existence; and to entitle one to the character of a "resident," there must be a settled, fixed abode, and an intention to remain permanently, or at least for some time, for business or other purposes'. To same effect Coleman v. Territory, 5 Okla., 201; 'Residence indicates permanency of occupation as distinct from lodging or boarding or temporary occupation. "Residence" indicates the place where a man has his fixed and permanent abode and to which, whenever he is absent, he has the intention of returning'. In Wright v. Genesee, 117 Mich., 244, it is said: 'Residence means the place where one resides; an abode, a dwelling or habitation. Residence is made up of fact and intention. There must be the fact of abode and the intention of remaining'. And in Silver v. Lindsay, 42 Hun. (N. Y.), 120: 'A place of residence in the common-law acceptation of the term means a fixed and permanent abode, a dwelling-place of the time being, as contra-distinguished from a mere temporary local residence'."

A part of the above excerpt was quoted in Howard v. Queen City Coach Co., 212 N. C. 201 (1937).

The terms have often been defined by our courts, but as the above discussion probably presents an accurate analysis of their meaning, it should be helpful in deciding any given case.

SUBJECT: MUTUAL FIRE INSURANCE COMPANIES; WHETHER OR NOT CLASSIFICATION OF PROPERTY FOR DIVIDEND PURPOSES AMOUNTS TO A REBATE

18 February, 1941.

I have carefully considered the question presented in your letter of January 28 as to whether a mutual fire insurance company may classify different classes of property and pay one rate of dividend on one classification and a different rate of dividend on a different class.

In studying this problem, I have had the benefit of an excellent brief filed with you by Honorable Chase Brenizer, Attorney for the Hardware Mutual Fire Insurance Company, in which he presents the view that under our statutes, such a procedure would amount to a rebate and, therefore, be illegal.

I note from your letter that the practice has been engaged in by many mutuals for several years on a nationwide basis, and that you have assumed that the practice was permissible; also, that you have proceeded upon the assumption that as to foreign corporations, the laws of the state creating the corporation control its powers with reference to dividends.

My study of the statutes in force in this State lead me to the conclusion that the practice of classifying property for the purpose of dividends is not prohibited.

N. C. Code Ann. (Michie, 1939), Section 6430, was probably designed to prevent licensed insurance agents from paying commissions or subsidies to unlicensed persons to induce them to solicit business for them. It is only a strained construction of this section which makes it applicable to declaration of dividends by mutual insurance companies.

N. C. Code Ann. (Michie, 1939), Section 6351, provides, in part:

> "The directors of a mutual fire insurance company may from time to time, by vote, fix and determine the amount to be paid as a dividend upon the policies expiring during each year."

It is argued that this is the equivalent of a declaration that one dividend rate shall be fixed and that all policyholders shall be paid at this rate. This construction also appears to be strained. It seems more likely that the provision was designed simply to authorize directors to declare dividends and that the problem of classification did not occur to the draftsman.

N. C. Code Ann. (Michie, 1939), Section 6391, forbids the fixing of fire insurance rates which discriminate unfairly between risks of the same hazard and having substantially the same degree of public protection against fire. It is argued that a declaration of a dividend is the equivalent of a return or refund of a part of the insurance premium and amounts to a reduction in the amount of the premium or the insurance rate. It is admitted that business and property may be classified according to risk for the purpose of fixing rates, but it is contended that classification for the purposes of declaring dividends when the factor of risk has already been considered in fixing rates, results in an ultimate rate which is disproportionate to risk and, therefore, discriminatory. The fallacy in this argument is that, if the declaration of dividends is to be considered something entirely divorced from rate-fixing, Section 6391 is not applicable; whereas, if the declaration of dividends is to be regarded as closely related to or a part of the rate-fixing process, and it is admitted that risks may be considered in fixing rates, it is difficult to see why risks may not be considered in declaring the dividend which directly affects the rate.

The only North Carolina case discovered which discusses classification for purposes of dividends is Graham v. Mutual Life Ins. Co. of New York, 176 N. C. 313. The plaintiff sought to have an insurance policy reformed so as to incorporate an agreement as to the dividends to be paid on the plaintiff's policy. The Court said at p. 318:

> "To reform this policy by decreeing Exhibit 2 to be a part of it would give plaintiff an undue advantage over others holding similar policies and would be an illegal discrimination in her favor at variance with our statutes as well as the general principles of law.
>
> "The defendant is a mutual company and is forbidden to discriminate among its policyholders, and any agreement which would result in the payment of larger proportionate dividends to one of its policyholders than to others *in the same class* would be illegal and void." (Italics added.)

Although this decision condemns arbitrary and discriminatory classification, it does seem to constitute judicial recognition that classification of policyholders for the purpose of declaring dividends, when it has a reasonable basis, is valid.

I am retaining the brief filed by Mr. Brenizer with you, which can be found in my file in the event you have need for it at some later time.

SUBJECT: INSURANCE; MUTUAL INSURANCE COMPANY; NON-ASSESSABLE POLICY CONTRACT; ASSESSABILITY OF POLICYHOLDER ON INSOLVENCY OF COMPANY

14 August, 1941.

I have your letter of August 8, in which you inquire concerning the assessability of a policyholder under the following facts:

A mutual fire or casualty insurance company is incorporated under the laws of a State permitting a mutual insurance company to issue a so-called non-assessable policy contract containing the following specific clause:

> "By resolution, adopted by the board of directors of this company, it is hereby understood and agreed that this policy shall, under no circumstances or conditions, be assessed for any purpose whatsoever."

In addition to this clause, the following quotation appears on the face of the policy:

> "A Cash Non-Assessable Mutual Policy."

You ask if, under these circumstances in the event of insolvency of a mutual company, a policy holder with such a non-assessable policy could be assessed any additional premium. I am of the opinion that the policyholder would not be liable for an additional assessment.

Although the Supreme Court of this State has not passed upon this precise question, the decisions in this jurisdiction do hold that the contract, liability, and duty of the company and the policyholders is governed by the charter and by-laws as are authorized by the State creating the mutual company, provided they are reasonable and not in conflict with any principle of public law. Brenizer v. Royal Arcanum, 141 N. C. 409; Duffy v. Fidelity Mutual Life Ins. Co., 142 N. C. 103; Hollingsworth v. Supreme Council, 175 N. C. 615. In the case under consideration, the issuance of a non-assessable policy is permitted by the state creating the mutual company, and the laws of this State also provide that a cash premium non-assessable policy may be issued. C. S. 6351. Under this statute our Court has held that the policyholders in a mutual fire insurance company are not stockholders therein, and are in no way liable for the debts of the company beyond the contingent liability fixed in the policy. Fuller v. Lockhart, 209 N. C. 61. Hence, it is clear that this type of contract is not in violation of any principle of public law recognizable in this State.

The authorities elsewhere are in complete accord in holding, so far as I have been able to determine, that no additional assessment can be recovered by a receiver from a policyholder who has paid a cash premium with the agreement that he would not be liable for an additional assessment on the policy. Osius v. O'Dwyer, 127 Mich. 244, 86 N. W. 831; Green v. Security Mutual Life Ins. Co., 159 Mo. App. 277, 140 S. W. 325; Wetmore v. McElroy, 96 S. C. 182, 80 S. E. 266; Pink v. Georgia Stages, 35 F. Supp. 437; Couch, Cyclopedia of Insurance Law, Sec. 621; Vance on Insurance, 263.

I am, therefore, inclined to the opinion that our Court would follow this line of authority and hold that a policyholder of the type of non-assessable policy described in your letter would not be liable for further assessment thereon.

SUBJECT: MUNICIPALITIES; TORT LIABILITY; FIRE CHIEF'S CAR; PERSONAL LIABILITY

27 October, 1941.

I have your inquiry of October 22 in regard to liability of the City of Greensboro for damage caused by the Fire Chief's car, when it is being used on official business, or in answering an alarm. It appears that this car is owned by the City along with the other equipment used by the Fire Department. You also inquire as to the personal liability of the Fire Chief or his driver.

The decisions of the Supreme Court of this State uniformly hold that a municipality is not liable in damages for injury occasioned by fire trucks and other fire equipment owned by the municipality, when such equipment is being used by the fire department in fire protection work, which is held to be a governmental function. Peterson v. City of Wilmington, 130 N. C. 76; Harrington v. Town of Greenville, 159 N. C. 632; Mabe v. City of Winston-Salem, 190 N. C. 486; Cathey v. City of Charlotte, 197 N. C. 309. I do not believe that this conclusion would be altered by the fact that it is the chief's car which causes the injury or damage instead of a fire truck or other equipment.

I am of the opinion, however, that both the fire chief and his driver would be personally liable for their own negligence in operating this car, when it results in injury to any individual or damage to property. This opinion is supported by McIlhenny v. City of Wilmington, 127 N. C. 146;

Hobbs v. Washington, 168 N. C. 293. In the latter case it was held that the chief of police of the City of Washington was personally liable, although the City was not, for making an unlawful arrest.

The immunity from liability granted to municipalities when exercising a governmental function does not extend to its employees or officers, unless a governmental discretion or judgment is being exercised by the officer. Betts v. Jones, 203 N. C. 590. I do not believe that the operation of the fire chief's car would come within this rule, so as to preclude personal liability.

OPINIONS TO ADJUTANT GENERAL

SUBJECT: STATE APPROPRIATIONS; RENTAL ON NATIONAL GUARD ARMORIES

10 September, 1940.

You inquire of this office if, during the absence of the National Guard for the one year tour of duty ordered by the President, the appropriation authorized by The Appropriations Act of 1939 and set forth in detail in The Budget, 1939-41, for semiannual allowances to organizations under Title III-13, could be legally expended by your Department for the payment of rental on armories during the Guard's absence from this State.

I see no legal reason why this fund could not be expended for this purpose during the Guard's absence. In my opinion, it is just as important to maintain and keep these armories intact for the storage of equipment and supplies while the Guard is away from its home station, as it is while it is present in this State.

I discussed this matter with the Assistant Director of the Budget and he agrees with this interpretation of The Appropriations Act in this regard.

SUBJECT: STATE GUARD; COMPENSATION WHEN CALLED INTO ACTIVE SERVICE

5 December, 1941.

In your letter of December 3, you inquire if any unit or organization of the North Carolina State Guard should be called into active service by order of the Governor in a case of emergency, would the individual officers and men be entitled to compensation for the period of time while they are actually in the performance of their duty in such emergency.

The act providing for the organization of the State Guard is to be found as Chapter 43 of the Public Laws of 1941. Here you will see that when the National Guard of this State has been called into Federal service, the Governor is authorized to organize such part of the unorganized State militia, as a State force for discipline and training, as may be deemed necessary by him for the defense of the State, and to maintain, uniform and equip such military force within the appropriation available. This military force is subject to the call or order of the Governor to execute the law, suppress riots or insurrections, or to repel invasions, to the same extent as is now or may hereafter be provided by law for the National Guard and for the unorganized militia.

Under this act the Governor is authorized to appropriate to the benefit of the State Guard any and all unexpended moneys found by the Governor to be unnecessary for use of the National Guard, in the appropriations made to the National Guard by the General Assembly for the présent or for subsequent fiscal years, and, if found necessary, to make allotment of funds from the Contingency and Emergency Fund in the manner provided by law.

This act also provides that the State Guard shall be subject to the military laws of the State, not inconsistent with or contrary to the provisions of the act itself, with the exception that members of the State

Guard are not exempt from road or jury duty, C. S. 6870; contributing membership is not permitted, C. S. 6871; organization of the State Guard may not own property, C. S. 6872; nor shall allowances be made to the several organizations for certain expenses set out in C. S. 6889, the expenses contemplated in the latter statute being taken care of by Section 7 of the 1941 Act, to the extent that an annual allowance of not more than $600 is required, or so much thereof as may be necessary, to be applied to the payment of armory, rent, heat, lights, stationery, and other expenses.

It has been suggested that Chapter 54 of the Public Laws of 1941 would have the effect of prohibiting the State from compensating individual officers and men for services when called into active duty in the case of emergency by the Governor.

This suggestion is based upon the paragraph in the preamble to the act appropriating funds for the purchase of uniforms for the State Guard, which is in words as follows:

> "Whereas, the personnel selected for service in the Home Guard as aforesaid are to serve without any compensation whatsoever; . . ."

I do not think that the above, taken from the preamble to the Act, would be controlling. It is true that when a statute is doubtful in its meaning, the meaning may be determined by a search elsewhere. Neither the title to an act nor the preamble thereof can be considered when the meaning of the text itself is clear. The text of the act appropriating funds for the purpose of purchasing uniforms for the State Guard is a straight out appropriation for this purpose. The reason for the appropriation as set out in the preamble is no part of the appropriating act itself and cannot be considered. Neither do I think that the preamble to the appropriating act would have the effect of repealing Section 6864 of the Consolidated Statutes, relating to pay of militia when called into active service of the State.

By the enactment of Chapter 43 of the Public Laws of 1941, which provides for the establishing of the State Guard, the General Assembly made inapplicable to the State Guard certain provisions of the general law relating to the National Guard. Referring to C. S. 6889, it will be seen that among other items not permitted to be paid to the State Guard is the provision for payment of so much per drill to the National Guard. It is noted that C. S. 6864 does not appear among the excluded statutes.

From the above, it is my opinion that where the State Guard is called into active service on order of the Governor in case of emergency, the individual members and officers are entitled to compensation in accordance with C. S. 6864.

SUBJECT: APPROPRIATIONS MADE TO STATE GUARD UNITS; SUPERVISION OF FUNDS

2 February, 1942.

You state that a question has arisen in your office as to whether or not the Adjutant General has any authority to prescribe regulations governing the expenditure of funds appropriated or donated to State Guard units from sources other than the State, and you inquire as to what your duties and responsibilities are in connection with the expenditure of such funds, the particular question being raised as to the legality of these funds being expended to the individuals in such units as compensation for drills which they attend.

Under the Act setting up the State Guard, Chapter 43 of the Public Laws of 1941, there is no provision made for drill pay. The organization, as it is now constituted, is purely a volunteer military body and the Act does not contemplate the payment of the individuals for drills which they attend, either from State funds or funds from other sources.

The relation which you hold to the inferior organizations of the State Guards in the State and their commanding officers is that of superior officer. There is no doubt that individuals or subordinate governmental agencies, such as cities and towns, may, if they choose, donate money to individual units of the State Guard, where the purpose for which such donations are made, do not interfere with the discipline or efficiency of the State Guard. For whatever purpose these donations are made, the statute requires a report of them to be made to your office. We think that you necessarily have authority to prescribe regulations governing the expenditure of funds appropriated or donated from sources other than the State, so as to prevent such donations from being made or used for a purpose which would or might deleteriously affect the discipline or efficiency of the unit to which the donation is made. To this extent, at least, we think you, as a superior officer having such matters in charge, have the right and authority to approve or disapprove the expenditure of such funds, and could, in my opinion, prohibit the expenditure of any funds, regardless of their source, to the individual members of such units as compensation for drills attended.

The above is in accord with an official opinion addressed to you by former Attorney General James S. Manning, under date of February 25, 1921.

SUBJECT: ADJUTANT GENERAL'S DEPARTMENT; RIFLE CLUBS; AUTHORITY OF THE STATE TO LEASE RIFLE RANGES

20 March, 1942.

In your letter of March 14, you state that the Charlotte Rifle Club, which is affiliated with the National Rifle Association, has requested that the Adjutant General's Department accept a lease in the name of the State for certain property which the DuPont Powder Company now owns and upon which they propose to construct a rifle range for the use of the Charlotte Rifle Club, the DuPont Powder Company being anxious to lease this property to the State in order that it might be relieved of any liability in case of an accident to persons or property, either upon the range or in its vicinity.

The only act which relates to the subject of the organization of rifle clubs in this State is to be found as Chapter 449 of the Public Laws of 1937. This Act simply authorizes the Adjutant General to detail a commissioned officer of the North Carolina National Guard, or some member of the unorganized militia of the State, to promote rifle marksmanship and to organize and supervise rifle clubs under rules and regulations prescribed by the Adjutant General, the purpose being, as stated in the Act, to so organize such clubs as to make them acceptable for membership in the National Rifle Association.

The General Assembly made an appropriation to the Adjutant General's Department for the biennium 1937-1939, in the amount of $200, to defray the expenses of the officer detailed to this duty. The Act does not authorize the State or your Department to actually construct such ranges, nor does it authorize the acquisition, either by lease or otherwise, of real property for this purpose.

I advise that this Act does not authorize, nor is there any other act which would authorize your Department of the State of North Carolina to accept a lease of real property for this purpose. Before it can be done, there must be some legislative authority for such action on the part of your Department or the State of North Carolina.

OPINIONS TO COMMISSIONER OF LABOR

SUBJECT: WORLD WAR VETERANS; EDUCATIONAL BENEFITS

23 June, 1941.

You state that one David E. Penland, a World War Veteran, is receiving $50.00 per month for service connected arrested tuberculosis and that the rating record of the Veterans Administration shows this veteran to be disabled permanent partial in the amount of 25% by reason of his service incurred condition, and you inquire if a child of this veteran is entitled to educational benefits under Chapter 242 of the Public Laws of 1937, as amended by Chapter 302 of the Public Laws of 1941.

Chapter 302 of the Public Laws of 1941 extends the benefits provided in the 1937 Act to any child whose father was a resident of the State at the time said father entered the armed forces of the United States, and whose father was, prior to his death, or is at the time the benefits of the Act are sought to be availed of, suffering from a service connected disability of 30% or more as rated by the United States Veterans Administration.

Since this veteran is rated as only 25% service connected disability, I do not think that the provisions of the Act would apply in this case, and that a child of this veteran would not be entitled to the benefits extended under the law.

SUBJECT: WORLD WAR VETERANS; EDUCATIONAL BENEFITS TO CHILDREN OF VETERANS—WALLIE BELL

11 July, 1941.

You state that Joseph Bell, a World War Veteran, adopted the two children of one Wallie Bell, who, prior to his death, was not a World War Veteran, and you inquire if this adoption by Joseph Bell would entitle these children to benefits under Chapter 242 of the Public Laws of 1937, as amended.

Running throughout the original Act and all its amendments, the statute providing these benefits refers to the children whose ". . . father was a member of the armed forces of the United States." It is my opinion that the term "father" as used in the statute means the natural father and not the adoptive father of such children, and I do not think, since the natural father was not a World War Veteran, that these children would be entitled to the benefits under the Act, as amended.

SUBJECT: MUNICIPAL ORDINANCES; REGULATION OF OPENING AND CLOSING HOURS ON SATURDAY

22 October, 1941.

In your letter of October 21, you inquire of this office if a municipality may enact a valid ordinance setting the closing hour of business establishments on Saturdays.

The Supreme Court of North Carolina has had occasion to pass upon this question in the case of State v. Ray, 131 N. C. 814. This case holds that an ordinance of a town requiring stores to be closed at 7:30 in the evening was invalid, on the ground that permitting a city or town to pass such an ordinance would be giving it equal power with the Legislature to restrict personal and property rights.

In view of the opinion in this case, I cannot advise you that a municipality could enact a valid ordinance setting the closing hours of mercantile establishments on Saturdays.

OPINIONS TO STATE HIGHWAY AND PUBLIC WORKS COMMISSION

SUBJECT: LEGAL HOLIDAYS; MAY 30

20 August, 1940.

When I wrote to you on July 3, I was inadvertent to the fact that Chapter 212 of the Public Laws of 1935 affected the statute relating to May 30 being a legal holiday, C. S. 3959. As a matter of fact, Michie's Code of 1939 refers to May 30 as a legal holiday, and Chapter 212 of the Public Laws of 1935, but does not contain the proviso of the 1935 Public Act to the effect that May 30 is a legal holiday but that it applies to State and national banks. It is not a legal holiday for any other purpose, nor does it affect any other institutions or agencies.

SUBJECT: HATCH ACT; SOLICITATION OF FUNDS

14 October, 1940.

I received your letter of October 3, in which you ask my views as to the application of the federal statute enacted August 2, 1939, as amended by the Act of July 19, 1940, known as the Hatch law, to a solicitation of funds by you of employees of the State Highway and Public Works Commission for the Democratic Campaign Fund in North Carolina.

After receipt of your letter, I wired the United States Civil Service Commission as follows:

> "PLEASE ADVISE IF CASHIER OF THE STATE HIGHWAY AND PUBLIC WORKS COMMISSION PROHIBITED BY HATCH ACT FROM SOLICITING POLITICAL CONTRIBUTIONS FROM EMPLOYEES OF COMMISSION WHOSE PRINCIPAL EMPLOYMENT IS NOT IN CONNECTION WITH ANY ACTIVITY, IN WHOLE OR IN PART, FEDERALLY FINANCED. PLEASE FORWARD ANY GENERAL RULINGS COVERING THIS SUBJECT."

I received from it a reply as follows:

> "This refers to your telegram received today concerning solicitation of political contributions from employees of the State Highway Commission. Your particular inquiry has to do with status under the Hatch law of the cashier of the State Highway and Public Works Commision. It is impossible to be definite in reply to your inquiry in absence of facts as to the employment status of the cashier. However, the following are interpretations of the Act as developed by the Civil Service Commission and it may be possible for you to apply them to the case in point in such a way as to determine the question.
>
> "In order to be subject to the prohibitions of the Hatch law a State employee must perform functions in connection with an activity or activities financed in whole or in part from Federal funds. Furthermore, such functions must constitute the principal part of the public employment of such a person.
>
> "It is particularly difficult to apply the terms of the Hatch law to administrative officials of State departments, which departments have some activities financed in part by Federal funds and

other activities financed solely by funds from State sources. In State highway departments there ordinarily is such a combination of activities. Speaking generally, highway construction and reconstruction is a jointly financed activity as distinct from highway maintenance, which also generally speaking is not. However, in many States Federal funds are provided for certain highway maintenance projects and these facts have to be taken into account in attempting to fix jurisdiction of the statute.

"In the event that you have not previously received it you may be interested in the inclosed copy of Civil Service Form 1236-A, which contains matters interpretative of the Hatch law in its application to employees of State and local agencies.

"By direction of the Commission:"

You will observe from the second paragraph of this letter that the law referred to would not prohibit the cashier, whose office was mentioned in my wire by way of illustration, from soliciting political contributions, unless he performed functions in connection with an activity financed in whole or in part from Federal funds, and, *furthermore, such functions constitute the principal part of his employment.*

Manifestly, you, as Chairman, and the cashier, as cashier, would perform functions in connection with some of the activities of the Commission which are financed in whole or in part from Federal funds, but such functions would constitute only a minor part, and not a principal part, of such employment. Upon this construction of the statute, the Chairman or the cashier, or other similar official of the Commission, would not be within the prohibitions of the Act. No funds, however, should be solicited or received from any persons paid from Federal relief appropriations. No solicitation should be made on the location of any activity carried on by Federal relief agencies.

For your further information, I am enclosing you Mimeograph Form 1236-A, issued by the United States Civil Service Commission, which has the responsibility for administration of the Hatch law.

SUBJECT: CRIMINAL PROCEDURE; COMMITMENT OF PRISONER IN CAPITAL CASE

28 May, 1941.

Consolidated Statutes 4659 is as follows:

"Upon the sentence of death being pronounced against any person in the State of North Carolina convicted of a crime punishable by death, it shall be the duty of the judge pronouncing such death sentence to make the same in writing, which shall be filed in the papers in the case against such convicted person and a certified copy thereof shall be transmitted by the clerk of the Superior Court in which such sentence is pronounced to the warden of the State's Penitentiary in Raleigh, not more than twenty or less than ten days before the time fixed in the judgment of the court for the execution of the sentence; and in all cases where there is no appeal from the sentence of death, and in all cases where the sentence is pronounced against a prisoner convicted of the crime of rape, it shall be the duty of the sheriff, together with at least one deputy, to convey to the penitentiary at Raleigh such condemned felon or convict forthwith upon the adjournment of the court in which the felon was tried, and deliver the convict or felon to the warden at the penitentiary; provided, that in all cases where an appeal is taken from the death sentence by any person convicted of a crime punishable by death, except the crime of rape, such convicted felon or convict shall not be taken or conveyed to the penitentiary unless in the judgment of the sheriff of the county in which the felon was tried and the solicitor prosecuting the felon, it shall be deemed necessary for the safety and safekeeping of the convicted person or felon during the pendency of the appeal."

From the above, it will be seen that in all cases where no appeal is taken from a death sentence, and in all cases where a person has been convicted of the capital crime of rape, and in those cases where the sheriff and the solicitor who prosecuted a capital case are of the opinion that it is necessary to remove such convicted person to the State Penitentiary to protect him from violence, such convicted convict or felon shall be sent to the State's Penitentiary and there held until such time as he shall be executed according to law. In all other cases, such convicts may be incarcerated in the county jail of the county in which he was convicted until his case has been determined according to law.

SUBJECT: ALLOCATION OF FUNDS; CITIES AND TOWNS

15 October, 1941.

I have examined Chapter 217 of the Public Laws of 1941, and I agree with the conclusion reached by you, as stated in your letter of October 14. Section 2 of the Act is a mandatory requirement as to the basis of apportionment and allocation of the funds appropriated "as between the several cities and towns," and I do not think that you would be justified in ignoring in this calculation towns which have become inactive, although still existing as corporate bodies.

I understand the argument is made that because the cities and towns are authorized to recommend for approval by the State Highway and Public Works Commission the use of such funds, this would make the Act inapplicable to dormant municipalities. I do not believe that this provision would change the main feature and purpose of the Act, which is to provide for the distribution of the funds as between the several municipalities. The municipalities, under Section 3, could only recommend for the approval of the Highway Commission the manner of use of the funds. I do not believe this provision could be given the dominating effect of rendering the Act totally inapplicable to a municipality in which this recommendatory provision would not be effective due to the fact that such municipality is dormant.

SUBJECT: GOVERNOR'S MANSION; FEEDING PRISONERS ASSIGNED THERETO

18 November, 1941.

I am advised by your letter of November 18 as follows:

"It appears there has been a long standing custom of furnishing certain prisoners to the Governor's Mansion for doing work there and, likewise, furnishing the Governor's Mansion food supplies from the State's Prison. I do not know when this custom was originated, nor under what sort of agreement or understanding. It is certainly desirable from an accounting standpoint that the arrangement, if it is to be continued, be made so definite that the records will at all times give a true picture of just what has taken place."

In conference with you today, in addition to the foregoing, I am advised that the amount of food supplies provided from the State's Prison for the prisoners assigned to the Governor's Mansion is upon the basis of the equivalent of thirty cents in value per day for each prisoner. The supplies are valued on the same basis as all prison supplies are valued in keeping prison records.

Chapter 224 of the Public Laws of 1941 reenacts the statute creating the Board of Public Buildings and Grounds, and defines the duties of this Board. The first section of the Act states that the public buildings and grounds referred to in the Act include the Executive Mansion and all public buildings and grounds owned or maintained by the State. Under the Act, the Board is required to assume the custody and control of the Mansion and supervise the care, operation, and maintenance of the building and grounds, and to employ such efficient assistants and laborers as may be necessary for the adequate care, operation, and maintenance of the same. The other duties of the Board of Public Buildings and Grounds with respect to properties committed to its charge are set forth in the Act.

You advise me that the Superintendent of the Board of Public Buildings and Grounds has heretofore been using, and finds it necessary to continue to use, certain prisoners in connection with this work. In conference with me today, you further state that in making up the budget for the Board of Public Buildings and Grounds and the care and maintenance of the Mansion, it was contemplated that prison labor would be used. You advise that certain prisoners have been assigned for this work whose services are not particularly useful or needed elsewhere and whose condition it was believed would be improved by assignment to this particular work. You further advise that the Chairman of the State Highway and Public Works Commission is willing to approve this assignment of prisoners for work on the Mansion and grounds, and authorize an allowance, payable in supplies from the Central Prison, to equalize the cost of the board of these prisoners if they were fed at the Central Prison, and has requested your opinion as to the legality of this course.

In your letter to me, you express the opinion that the arrangement is legal, but before advising the Chairman, you desire the opinion of this office.

Chapter 172, Section 30, Public Laws of 1933 (Michie's Code, Sec. 7748-z), provides that the State Highway and Public Works Commission may furnish to any of the other State departments, State institutions or agencies, upon such conditions as may be agreed upon from time to time between the Commission and the governing authorities of such department, institution or agency, prison labor for carrying on any work where it is practical and desirable to use prison labor in the furtherance of the purposes of any State department, institution or agency. Under this Act of the General Assembly, it seems clear to me that the State Highway and Public Works Commission is expressly authorized to assign to the Board of Public Building and Grounds such prisoners as may be found necessary for use at the Mansion in carrying out the duties required by law of this Board with respect to Mansion property.

It is my understanding that the Prison Department retains control of these prisoners, clothes them, and in the event of sickness, furnishes hospital and medical attention to them; that under the direction of the Prison Department, as a matter of convenience, these prisoners are assigned to quarters in the basement of the Mansion in order to avoid the inconvenience of being hauled back and forth each day.

I am very definitely of the opinion that the State's Prison is fully justified in providing the Board of Public Buildings and Grounds with food from the State's Prison in an amount equivalent to the value of the cost of feeding the average prisoner in the State's Prison. This seems to be the practical and convenient method of handling the feeding of the prisoners assigned to the Mansion, and, in my opinion, is authorized by law. Very clearly, it is not the obligation of the Governor from his own personal funds to feed these prisoners, and it is the obligation of the State to do so.

SUBJECT: TEACHERS' AND STATE EMPLOYEES' RETIREMENT SYSTEM; STATUS OF EMPLOYEES RECEIVING COMPENSATION UNDER WORKMEN'S COMPENSATION ACT

7 February, 1942.

Your first question relates to the status of employees who were drawing compensation under the provisions of the Workmen's Compensation Act for temporary total disability at the time of the enactment of the Teachers' and State Employees' Retirement Act and who have been drawing such compensation continuously since said date.

Subsection 2 of Section 3 of the Teachers' and State Employees' Retirement Act provides:

> "All persons who are teachers or State employees on the date of the ratification of this Act or who may become teachers or State employees on or before July first, one thousand nine hundred and forty-one, except those who shall notify the board of trustees, in writing, on or before January first, one thousand nine hundred and forty-two, that they do not choose to become members of this Retirement System shall become members of the Retirement System."

The word "employee" is defined in Section 1 of the Act as meaning all full-time employees, agents or officers of the State of North Carolina or any of its departments, bureaus and institutions other than educational, whether such employees are elected, appointed or employed.

From an inspection and consideration of the various provisions of the Workmen's Compensation Act which would in any way tend to bear on the question under consideration, it is my opinion that the relationship of employer and employee is not dissolved by an employee becoming disabled to such an extent as to be eligible to draw compensation under the provisions of the Workmen's Compensation Act. This being true, it is my opinion that employees who were drawing compensations under the provisions of the Workmen's Compensation Act for temporary total disability at the time of the ratification of the Teachers' and State Employees' Retirement Act would be eligible for membership in the Retirement System, unless the employer or employee had taken some affirmative action which would tend to sever the relationship of employer and employee.

I am informed that when an employee of the State Highway and Public Works Commission begins to draw compensation for temporary total disability under the provisions of the Workmen's Compensation Act, he is not carried on the pay-roll but the compensation due under the provisions of the Workmen's Compensation Act is paid from a separate fund which is set up to take care of these payments. Section 8(1) (a) of the Teachers' and State Employees' Retirement Act provides that each employer shall cause to be deducted from the salary of each member on each and every pay-roll of such employer for each and every pay-roll period four per centum of his earnable compensation. When an employee is drawing compensation under the provisions of the Workmen's Compensation Act, he is not, to my mind, to be considered as being on the pay-roll, but on the contrary, is to be considered as drawing compensation which is allowed under the provisions of the Workmen's Compensation Act for a specific injury sustained in the manner provided in the Workmen's Compensation Act.

Under the provisions of the Workmen's Compensation Act it is permissible to pay the compensation awarded thereunder in weekly, monthly or quarterly installments, and in certain instances lump sum payments are allowed. When the provisions of the Teachers' and State Employees' Retirement Act are considered in connection with the applicable provisions of the Workmen's Compensation Act, I am led to the conclusion that during the period of time an employee is drawing compensation under the provisions of the Workmen's Compensation Act, no deductions should be made from the compensation of such employee and no payments should be made to the Retirement System.

Your second question relates to the status of employees who have become disabled since the enactment of the Teachers' and State Employees' Retirement Act and who began drawing compensation upon the occurrence of the disability.

For the same reasons hereinbefore set out, it is my opinion that so long as compensation payments are made under the provisions of the Workmen's Compensation Act, no deductions should be made from the compensation of the employee and no payments should be required from the employee to the Retirement System during such period of disability.

In this connection, the question might also arise as to the effect of subsection 3 of section 3 of the Teachers' and State Employees' Retirement Act should a member draw compensation under the provisions of the Workmen's Compensation Act for a period of more than five out of six consecutive years after becoming a member of the Retirement System. The subsection above referred to reads as follows:

> "Should any member in any period of six consecutive years after becoming a member be absent from service more than five years, or should he withdraw his accumulated contributions, or should become a beneficiary or die, he shall thereupon cease to be a member."

It might be argued that the fact that an employee is drawing compensation under the provisions of the Workmen's Compensation Act and is not carried on the employer's pay-roll, he should be considered as absent from the service under the provisions of this subsection. However, it is my thought that when the Legislature placed this provision in the Retirement Act it meant that absence from service should mean something more than a situation of this kind. It is my thought that the term "absent from service" means a severance of the relationship of employer and employee by the voluntary action of either or both parties concerned.

I am, therefore, of the opinion that a member of the Retirement System who draws compensation under the provisions of the Workmen's Compensation Act retains his membership in the Retirement System, and when the period of disability is terminated, such employee would again begin to make contributions to the System. Of course, upon retirement the member's benefits would be less due to the fact that no contributions were made during the period of disability.

I have undertaken to answer these questions so as to do substantial justice both to the employer and the employee, and in so doing it is possible that I have been forced to invoke the rule that the spirit or reason of the law prevails over its letter. It is a true saying and worthy of all acceptation that "The letter killeth but the spirit giveth life."

OPINIONS TO STATE BOARD OF HEALTH

SUBJECT: HEALTH LAWS; SEWERAGE DISPOSAL

20 September, 1940.

You state that the Town officials of Conover, in Catawba County, have prepared and are desirous of adopting a local ordinance requiring that houses available to the municipal sewerage system be connected therewith, the purpose of the ordinance being the elimination of outdoor privies and the improvement of health conditions through the proper disposal of sewerage, and you inquire as to the town authority to pass such an ordinance.

The town has such authority under provision of C. S. 2795. There you will find that the governing body of cities and towns within the city limits are given all the power and authority to make rules and regulations not inconsistent with the Constitution and laws of the State, for the preservation of the health of the inhabitants of the city or town, as to them may seem right and proper.

The provision at the end of this statute, to the effect that "this paragraph shall not apply to any city or town in Catawba County" has application to the first paragraph in the statute. The paragraph to which this refers is that which permits municipalities to establish hospitals. Cities and towns also have this authority under C. S. 7130 and C. S. 7076.

SUBJECT: MERIT SYSTEM; CLASSIFICATION AND COMPENSATION PLAN; RIGHT OF THE STATE BOARD OF HEALTH TO ADOPT

30 October, 1940.

Receipt is acknowledged of your letter of October 23rd, referring to the amendment to Title V of the Social Security Act adopted by Congress in 1939, requiring that any states receiving grants under the Social Security Act should adopt a merit system plan for personnel. You advise that the State Board of Health has under consideration drafts of a rule for a merit system of personnel administration prepared in accordance with instructions from the Children's Bureau of the Federal Department of Labor, as to which you submit me three questions:

1. "First, the requirement of the Children's Bureau is that all personnel employed out of funds allocated to North Carolina by the Children's Bureau must meet the merit system qualifications. It also requires that employees paid out of state funds used for matching Children's Bureau funds must be subject to the merit system rules and regulations. Are we correct in assuming that the State Board of Health has the authority to adopt such rules for its personnel?"

In my opinion your Board would have the right to adopt any system of selection of its administrative personnel which might be considered desirable. There is nothing in the North Carolina statutes which would deal with this question, but in my opinion it is necessarily implied that any State department, in determining the selection of its administrative personnel, may adopt any such rules and regulations which in its opinion would promote efficiency and the best interest of the department.

Such regulations, however, could not conflict with the provisions of our law establishing in the Budget Bureau a Division of Personnel, which is given by this law authority to fix, determine and classify the number of subordinates and employees in any and all departments of the State, and the type and nature of work to be performed by such subordinates and employees, and positions to be filled by such subordinates and employees in said departments, and the further authority to establish and classify the standard of salaries and wages, with a minimum salary rate and a maximum salary rate, etc. I refer you to the law found in Michie's Code of 1939, Section 7521(n), which defines the duties of the Division of Personnel.

2. Your second question is: Would your Board have a right to extend the merit system rule to other employees of the State Board of Health paid out of State Funds and funds from Title VI of the Social Security Act, the 1939 amendment not having had reference to funds received under Title VI?

For the reason stated above, it is my opinion that you could make your merit system rules applicable to all employees of your department. It has always been your privilege to adopt such regulations or set up such standards as you deemed appropriate for determining the selection of personnel employed by your Board as an inherent and necessary function connected with your activities.

3. Your third question is whether or not your Board could provide, without special legislative authority, to make your merit system rules applicable to any or all local health unit employees in North Carolina wherein either State or Federal funds are used within the cooperative budget with a local health unit?

In my opinion you would have no such authority in the absence of legislative enactment expressly giving you this power. Such authority is not given to your Board by Code, Section 7027, and I do not find such power otherwise given to it by statute.

You refer also to the problem of classification and compensation plan affecting the same group of employees, as to which you inquire whether or not the State Board of Health has the authority to adopt a classification system for (a) State employees and (b) local health unit employees?

In my opinion you do not have such authority, as by law this power as to State employees is given to the Division of Personnel by Code, Section 7521(n), to which reference has already been made, and I do not think you would have any such power with reference to employees of local health units.

I received a copy of the Rules and Regulations adopted by the Children's Bureau of the United States Department of Labor which was sent to me in your letter of the 23rd. As requested, I am returning this to you.

SUBJECT: SANITARY DISTRICTS; POWER TO REQUIRE SEWER CONNECTIONS

15 November, 1940.

I have examined the Sanitary District Law, Chapter 100 of the Public Laws of 1927, and I have been unable to find any power conferred by the Act upon the district board to specifically require all persons in said district to connect with sewer lines to residences situated therein, other than subsection (8) of Section 7 of the Act, which gives the board power to formulate rules and regulations necessary for the proper functioning of the works of the district.

This, in itself, does not, in my opinion, confer sufficient authority upon such district boards to enforce rules and regulations in this regard. Cities and towns have such specific authority under C. S. 2806, but I do not think that the provisions of this latter statute would apply to sanitary districts.

SUBJECT: MARRIAGE LAWS; LICENSE; NON-RESIDENTS

2 December, 1940.

Receipt is acknowledged of your letter of November 26, enclosing correspondence from Dr. I. C. Riggin, State Health Commissioner of the State of Virginia.

The question raised relates particularly to the interpretation of Section 4 of Chapter 314 of the Public Laws of 1939, entitled "An Act to require physical examination before issuance of license to marry." This Section provides:

> "Provided that this act shall not apply to applicants for marriage license by non-residents who are residents of a state or states which do not require the provisions of this law."

This office has previously ruled that non-residents should be required to comply with the provisions of the act unless they show the Register of Deeds to whom the application for license is made that their state has no requirements similar to the requirements contained in this Act.

This office further expressed the opinion that this proof could best be made by the certificate of the Secretary of State or the affidavit of some attorney at law of the state of the applicants' residence. I am informed that the State of Virginia now has enacted a law which contains provisions similar to those contained in Chapter 314 of the Public Laws of 1939, and this being true, no Register of Deeds in the State of North Carolina would be authorized to issue a marriage license to residents of the State of Virginia without requiring strict compliance with the provisions of the North Carolina law.

It seems to me that the duty of seeing that the North Carolina law is complied with rests with the Register of Deeds who issues the license to marry rather than the minister or justice of the peace who performs the ceremony.

Section 3 of Chapter 314 provides in part:

> "Any violation of this act, or any part thereof, by any person charged herein with the responsibility of its enforcement shall be declared a misdemeanor and shall be punishable by a fine of fifty dollars ($50.00) or imprisonment for thirty days, or both."

It is difficult for me to see how the parties mentioned in the correspondence you enclosed in your letter secured a license to marry in the State of North Carolina without complying with the provisions of our laws. There surely must have been some misrepresentation made to the Register of Deeds issuing the marriage license. The provisions of our law apply to all applicants for marriage license unless such applicants are able to bring themselves within the provisions of the exception contained in Section 4 of the Act above referred to, and the burden is upon the applicants to show that they are residents of a state or states which do not require substantially the same provisions contained in our law.

SUBJECT: BURIAL PERMITS; REMOVAL FROM GRAVES

17 February, 1941.

Under the statute, C. S. 7092, the body of any person whose death occurs in this State shall not be interred, deposited in a vault or tomb, cremated, or otherwise disposed of or removed from or into any registration district, or be temporarily held pending any further disposition more than seventy-two hours after death, unless a permit for a burial, removal, or other disposition thereof shall have been properly issued by the local registrar.

I know of no law which would prohibit the reinterring of a dead body under a proper permit issued by the registrar of the district, and placing such body in a vault above ground.

SUBJECT: HOTELS AND CAFES; SANITARY MANAGEMENT; SANITARY RATING OF SAME

1 April, 1941.

I have examined House Bill No. 741 in connection with Chapter 186 of the Public Laws of 1921, as amended. The 1921 Act, as amended, relates both to the sanitary inspection of hotels and cafes and to the operation of the same. There are only minor differences in the two Acts. In Section 1 of the 1941 Act, it is provided that no such establishment shall operate which has received a grade less than "C," while the 1921 Act, as amended, provides for a minimum grading of "seventy points" below which no such hotel, cafe or restaurant may be operated. This section also adds to the establishments which come under the Act, tourist homes, tourist camps and summer camps providing food and lodging to the public for pay.

I am of the opinion that the provisions of the 1941 Act relating to this subject are in addition to the 1921 Act, as amended, and until your Board has gotten together and promulgated rules and regulations for the enforcement of the same, you would have authority to proceed under the terms of the former Act. As stated above, apparently the only inconsistency in the two Acts is that the later Act covers more territory, in that it includes specifically more establishments and simply changes the method by which such establishments may be designated as to its sanitary rating. The 1941 Act does not include a number of items mentioned in the former Acts, and, as to these, I think they are still in effect.

SUBJECT: VITAL STATISTICS; REGISTER OF DEEDS; CUSTODY OF CERTIFICATES

21 April, 1941.

I do not think that the records of vital statistics should be taken away from the Register of Deeds' office and filed in the office of the local health officer who is registrar. The statute, 7109, specifically provides that such records shall be deposited and an index kept of the same in the office of the Registrar of Deeds.

SUBJECT: VITAL STATISTICS; DELAYED REGISTRATION OF BIRTHS

11 June, 1941.

You inquire as to whether it is permissible for a Register of Deeds in a county other than the county of the birth of an applicant for a delayed birth certificate, to accept proof, complete the certificate and then direct the Bureau of Vital Statistics to return the duplicate certificate to the county of the birth of the applicant.

From an inspection of Chapter 126 of the Public Laws of 1941 relating to the delayed registration of births, I am of the opinion that the certificate must originate with the Register of Deeds of the county in which the applicant was born. The Act provides that a birth may be registered with the Register of Deeds of the county in which the birth occurred and that each such certificate must be registered in duplicate on forms approved by the State Board of Health and furnished by the State Registrar. The Register of Deeds is required to forward the original and duplicate certificates to the Bureau of Vital Statistics for final approval, and if the certificate complies with the rules and regulations of the State Board of Health and the birth has not been previously registered, the State Registrar is required to file the original and return the duplicate to the Register of Deeds for recording.

It appears to me that the Act clearly contemplates the return of the duplicate to the Register of Deeds who originally prepared the certificate for recording, and as the certificate can only be recorded in the county in which the birth occurred, it would necessarily follow that the Register of Deeds in a county other than the county of the birth of the applicant would have no right under the law to forward the certificate to the Bureau of Vital Statistics. It does not seem to me that it would be necessary for every applicant for a delayed birth certificate to go to the county of his or her birth to apply for the certificate. If the applicant will communicate with the Register of Deeds, I am sure that arrangements could be made to complete the certificate without forcing the applicant to appear in person.

SUBJECT: PRIVY LAWS; SEWERS AND SEWER CONNECTIONS; POWERS OF BOARD OF HEALTH

14 July, 1941.

I have under consideration your letter of July 9, wherein you inquire if the county boards of health have authority to pass a sewer connection ordinance similar to that authorized to cities and towns under C. S. 2806, and make the same county-wide, thereby relieving the city of this authority, under the statute above referred to. You suggest that the county has such authority under the provisions of C. S. 7065. Under this statute the county boards of health are charged with the immediate care and responsibility of the health interests of the county, and they are authorized to make such penalties as in their judgment may be necessary to protect and advance the public health.

The effect of such an ordinance would be to require all persons living in the county who own property which abuts or adjoins a street, alley, or roadway, along which is located a public sanitary sewer which is within two hundred feet of said lot and there is a water line which is within three hundred feet of said lot, to connect with such sewer line.

The statute, C. S. 2805, and following, provides that the governing bodies of municipalities have the power and authority to acquire, construct, maintain and operate a sewerage system within its limits and to extend such system beyond its corporate limits for the purpose of obtaining proper outlets, as well as to permit such persons who reside outside the corporate limits to connect thereto, if, in its discretion, it deems best.

It is also provided under C. S. 2790 that all ordinances, rules and regulations of municipalities, in the exercise of police powers given it for sanitary purposes or for protection of the property of the city, shall apply with equal force to the territory outside the corporate limits within one mile in all directions of the same.

From these latter statutes, it is apparent that the city itself has jurisdiction in matters of this nature, not only to the territory lying within its boundaries, but also to that territory which extends one mile in all directions therefrom, and I do not think that the general power of the county board of health to promulgate rules and regulations regarding the public health of the county would have the effect of ousting the jurisdiction and authority of the municipalities of this State in this regard.

It will be noted that it is not mandatory upon the municipalities under C. S. 2806 that they require sewer connections to be made within their city limits or in that territory extending one mile outside the city limits. The reason for this is obvious. Take, for example, a city which has a sewer disposal plant which is only adequate for the needs of that territory lying within the city limits itself. It then would be impracticable for it to attempt to serve any territory lying outside the city limits, and to say, in addition to this, that the county board of health could, by adopting an ordinance, require landowners outside the city limits to connect to the city sewer would be an absurdity, because it is well settled that no rule or regulation issued by any administrative board would have the effect of overruling and paramounting the law of the State which gives to cities the power and authority to construct, maintain and operate sanitary sewer systems within its city limits and that territory lying within one mile in all directions thereof.

As said in 29 C. J. 248, paragraph 31:

> "Where a board of health acquires its power directly from the state and not from a municipality in which it is located, a municipal council has no power to nullify its orders. But where a section of a statute confers a general power to preserve the public health and another section of the same statute provides that the common council of the municipality shall have the power to regulate and control a specific subject of public health, the power to regulate such specific subject is in the common council and not in the board of health."

It is further said in paragraph 32 of this volume that:

> "Health authorities cannot, by the operation of their rules and regulations, enlarge or vary the powers conferred upon them by the law creating them and defining their powers, and any rule or regulation which is inconsistent with such law or which is antagonistic to the general law of the state is invalid. . . ."

From the above, it is my opinion that the county boards of health do not have authority to pass an ordinance which would be effective county-wide, including that territory inside the cities, and which would have the effect of requiring all property owners situated adjacent to sewer lines to connect thereto, since this authority is by statute vested in the municipalities of this State.

SUBJECT: PUBLIC HEALTH; RIGHT OF COUNTY BOARD OF HEALTH TO ENACT ORDINANCE REQUIRING SCHOOL TEACHERS TO BE X-RAYED EACH YEAR AND THAT THE X-RAYS BE INTERPRETED BY A MEMBER OF THE ROENTGENOLOGICAL SOCIETY

22 July, 1941.

You inquire as to whether, in my opinion, the Wayne County Board of Health has the power to enact an ordinance requiring school teachers of the county who are not tuberculin negative to be X-rayed each year, and that the X-rays be interpreted by a member of the Roentgenological Society.

Under the provisions of C. S. 7065, county boards of health are given the immediate care and responsibility of the health interests of their respective counties and are authorized to make such rules and regulations and impose such penalties as in their judgment may be necessary to protect and advance the public health. The health power may be exercised for the purpose of preventing the introduction and spread of infectious, contagious or communicable diseases. Health regulations are of the utmost consequence to the general welfare and if they are reasonable, impartial, and not against the general policy of the State, they must be submitted to by individuals for the good of the public, irrespective of pecuniary loss. This is so, whether the regulations are made by the Legislature or by an agency delegated by it to act. Such regulations will be sustained if upon a reasonable construction there appears to be some substantial reason why they will promote the public health and if they are reasonably adapted to or tend to accomplish the result sought. However, regulations enacted and promulgated by a subordinate agency must be within the authority conferred upon it and must not conflict with statutory or constitutional rights.

The Legislature of North Carolina provided for a standard health certificate for teachers who propose to teach in the public schools of North Carolina. The statute containing the requirements is C. S. 5556, which provides as follows:

> "Any person serving as county superintendent, city superintendent, teacher, janitor, or any employee in the public schools of the State shall file in the office of superintendent each year, before assuming his or her duties, a certificate from the county physician, or other reputable physician of the county, certifying that the said person has not an open or active infectious state of

> tuberculosis, or other contagious disease. The county physician shall make the aforesaid certificate on a form supplied by the State Superintendent of Public Instruction, and without charge to the person applying for the certification, and any person violating any of the provisions of this section shall be guilty of a misdemeanor and subject to a fine or imprisonment in the discretion of the court."

Thus, it will be seen that the Legislature of North Carolina has laid down the health requirements to be met by teachers before they are entitled to teach in the public schools of the State. The Legislature in effect has said that if the teachers meet the requirements contained in the section above referred to, there is no danger to the children being taught by such teachers from a health standpoint.

There is manifestly a distinction between a statute enacted by the General Assembly and a rule, regulation or ordinance made or adopted by a county board of health under statutory authority. The General Assembly has the power and authority to enact statutes subject only to constitutional limitations, whereas, a county board of health has only such power to make rules and regulations and to adopt ordinances as has been conferred upon it by statute. When the validity of a rule or regulation made by a board of health is challenged upon the ground that the facts found by the board as justification for the same are not true, the finding is not necessarily conclusive, and a person whose rights are injuriously affected by the rule or regulation will be heard by the courts upon his allegation that the facts are otherwise than as found by the board.

It does not appear from your letter the exact form of the ordinance adopted by the Wayne County Board of Health, but I do not believe a county board of health would be justified, in the face of C. S. 5556, in attempting to enforce such an ordinance. Even if it should be assumed, for the sake of argument, that a county board of health has the right to enact an ordinance of the type above referred to, I am of the opinion that the portion of the same which requires that the X-rays be interpreted by a member of the Roentgenological Society is invalid. This portion of the ordinance is discriminatory and would have the effect of placing the fate of school teachers in the hands of the members of one society and to exclude all other members of the medical profession. I am unable to see any justification for this portion of the ordinance.

SUBJECT: HEALTH LAWS; SANITATION INSPECTION; "LUNCH AND DRINK STANDS"; MEANING OF

7 August, 1941.

In your letter of July 30 you ask for my opinion as to the meaning of the expression "lunch and drink stands," which is used in Section 1 of Chapter 309, Public Laws of 1941. You ask specifically whether or not the places you enumerate would have to have lunch facilities, or eating facilities, along with the sale of drinks, in order to come within this law, which contemplates the inspection and grading of the designated establishments for sanitary purposes.

My examination of the act leads me to the conclusion that both of these activities would have to be present in order for the establishment to come within the purview of the law. Each time the expression is used in the act, it is used as words in a series of definitions of the type of establishment to be covered by the law. In each of the series this expression is set off by commas, and the words "lunch and drink stand" are enclosed by commas as one type of establishment to be covered along with the others enumerated in the series.

I believe that the above mentioned usage of this expression is too clear to permit any other construction of the terms used. As a practical matter, however, it would not seem likely that many soft drink or beer establishments would sell drinks without having some lunch or eating facilities.

SUBJECT: HOSPITALS FOR THE INSANE; OPERATIONS ON PATIENTS

3 October, 1941.

In your letter of October 1, you inquire if the staffs of the State hospitals have authority to perform lumbar punctures on patients who are inmates of any of the State hospitals in those cases where the patient refuses to permit such a test to be made, your specific inquiry being as to whether or not the medical staffs of such hospitals may make a spinal puncture without consent of the patient, in order to determine whether or not insanity is due to cerebrospinal syphilis.

You are no doubt familiar with the provisions of C. S. 7221 and C. S. 7222 where you will find the procedure which must be complied with before an operation may be performed on inmates of a penal or charitable hospital of the State. I have considered this statute to determine whether or not a spinal puncture would come within its meaning; that is to say, whether a spinal puncture would be considered an operation within the meaning of this statute.

I am advised that during the past several years the practice of making spinal punctures for diagnostic purposes has become very common, and, even though perhaps more serious than a puncture of the blood stream to make a blood test, it is, in fact, not as serious as an ordinary layman would think; that is, when such puncture is performed by a competent physician and where extreme care and precaution is taken.

My attention has been called to the case of Riss & Co. v. Galloway, 114 P. (2d) 550, a Colorado case handed down in April, 1941. This opinion holds that in a personal injury action in the courts where the defendant claimed that the plaintiff's disability was a result of syphilis and not of a back injury, the plaintiff might not be forced by an order of court to submit to a spinal puncture as this would be an invasion of private rights and beyond the court's authority without his consent, and, further, that it would be under the guise of a physical examination, forcing him to furnish samples of his bodily components to be used for the purpose of a chemical analysis the result of which might have the effect of requiring him to furnish evidence to bolster up his adversary's defense.

I do not think that the opinion in this case is at all analogous to the question presented in your letter. Here you have a patient who is suspected of being afflicted with syphilis in its final stages and in order to determine whether or not your suspicions are well founded, it is necessary to make the spinal puncture in order to make a correct diagnosis and determine whether or not insanity is due to cerebrospinal syphilis or some other type of insanity; that the information thereby made available by a chemical analysis of the fluid extracted from the spinal column would be of great value in determining the course of treatment in such cases.

I do not think that a spinal puncture would come within the meaning of C. S. 7221 and C. S. 7222, referred to above. Our Court has not passed upon the question presented by your letter and I have been unable to find where courts of other jurisdictions have had occasion to consider the exact question presented, but it is my opinion that should the medical staff of the hospital deem it necessary for the best interest of the patient to make the spinal puncture in order to arrive at a correct diagnosis, which would, in turn, enable the staff to prescribe a proper treatment for such patient, our court would not consider it an operation within the meaning of the statute referred to above.

I do not wish to be understood as advising you that in no instance would such a procedure be actionable in the courts for damages in those cases where injury results to the patient or where a patient is injured by such puncture due to carelessness or negligence on the part of the physician who makes the injection, but it is my opinion that in those cases where the staff of any of the State hospitals are of the opinion that such puncture is necessary and for the best interest of the patient in his care and treatment, it could be made without the patient's consent.

SUBJECT: CONTRACTS WITH LOCAL BOARDS OF HEALTH; RIGHT TO REQUIRE COMPLIANCE WITH MERIT SYSTEM

7 November, 1941.

I have your letter of November 6, in which you attached a copy of the form of contract between the State Board of Health and county, city and district health departments for the fiscal year beginning July 1, 1941, and a copy of a letter from Dr. R. A. Herring, Health Officer of the City of High Point, and a memorandum from Mr. J. A. Richbourg, Chairman of the Buncombe County Board of Commissioners. You request me to answer the following specific questions: (1) Do you have a right under the statute and particularly Chapter 378, Public Laws of North Carolina of 1941, to enter into such altered contract agreements for any fiscal year; and (2) does the State Board of Health have any legal right to continue its financial participation to these local units that have indicated they will not sign the contract agreement?

I note that the contract provides in section 1(d) and in section 2 that the county health officer and the members of the staff shall be appointed in conformity with the merit system, as authorized by Chapter 378. You also refer to the provision in section 11 as to salaries and allowances which, to be approved, must conform to the compensation plan approved by the merit system council as provided in said chapter.

Section 13 of Chapter 378 provides that the merit system council appointed under the provisions of the Act has the authority to establish, maintain and provide rules and regulations in cooperation with the State Board of Health for the administration of a system of personnel standards on a merit rating system with a uniform schedule of compensation for all employees of the county, city and district health departments. It is my understanding that, acting under this authority, the merit system council has, with the cooperation of the State Board of Health, established the rules and regulations provided for. This having been done, it is my opinion that in making contracts with local boards of health, you have a right to provide that the local boards of health in the selection and payment of the staff shall comply with the rules and regulations adopted under the authority of this Act. I do not mean to say that it is an essential or necessary part of the contract, but it would seem to be a reasonable requirement, the State Board of Health having cooperated in the establishment of the rules and regulations which are to govern such matters.

There is nothing in the statute which provides that you would have no right to continue financial participation with the local health departments in the event they refuse to cooperate in the plan. It might well be that the State Board of Health would be unwilling to sign the contract and participate in carrying on the health work in the event the local board of health should refuse to sign the contract for this reason.

With reference to the situation at High Point, we had a letter from the City Manager, Mr. E. M. Knox, in which he raised the question as to the effect of the charter provisions of his city on the general act. He argued that the provisions of the charter would prevail for the reason that they were special, whereas the statute was general. We advised Mr. Knox that we would not attempt to express any opinion upon this matter, as we had not had occasion to consider the terms of the charter and the extent to which there was a conflict in the general statute and the charter provisions. It might well be that the two could be harmonized, which would be done by rules of statutory construction if the language permitted it to be done. In that event, both statutes would be given effect.

SUBJECT: MARRIAGE LAWS; PUBLIC HEALTH

24 November, 1941.

I have your letter of November 22, wherein you inquire if registers of deeds of the State would be authorized to accept health certificates issued by army doctors to soldiers who desire to be married.

Under C. S. 6622 physicians and surgeons in the United States Army or Navy are not required to be licensed in this State, and may practice medicine in the discharge of their official duties. I see no reason why registers of deeds should not accept certificates of such doctors. Neither do I see any reason why the State Board of Health should not approve laboratories of the United States Army and Navy and Public Health Service, so that certificates from such laboratories would be acceptable to registers of deeds by applicants for marriage licenses.

SUBJECT: PUBLIC HEALTH; MUNICIPAL ORDINANCES; MILK ORDINANCES; EFFECT OF COUNTY-WIDE ORDINANCE

24 November, 1941.

I have your letter of November 5, 1941. I am sorry that the press of Supreme Court appeals has prevented me from answering your inquiry earlier.

You ask, first, if a County Board of Health has the power under C. S. 7065 to pass a milk ordinance that would apply to both the incorporated and unincorporated communities within the County. I do not believe that it has. Under C. S. 2795, municipal authorities are given authority to adopt ordinances for the protection of the health of the citizens within the city, and "all the power and authority that is now or may hereafter be given by law to the county health officer or county physician, and such further powers and authority as will best preserve the health of the citizens." The empowering language of this section would seem to require that the governing body of each municipality adopt the uniform ordinance separately. This method would be the safest one to pursue, and at the same time would insure the uniformity that is desired throughout the County.

In answer to your second question, I can see no reason why the County Health Officer could not legally enforce a milk ordinance adopted by a municipality within the municipality, if the ordinance which is adopted so provides. I advise you, therefore, that such authority should be included in the ordinance itself.

SUBJECT: PUBLIC HEALTH; BEDDING LAWS; MANUFACTURE AND SALE OF BEDDING

3 December, 1941.

You state that it has come to your attention that a certain person in Concord has a hospital bed with a mattress which was furnished her free of charge by a funeral home; that prior to the time the bed was furnished this person it had been used by an old man who died on it of old age; that the funeral home has given this person permission to use the mattress in her home for her mother, who is an invalid, not having first had it sterilized. You inquire if this is a transaction which would come within the meaning of Section 7251(x), and following, which relates to the manufacture and sale of bedding.

I have carefully examined the bedding law and I am of the opinion that this law has no application to a transaction of this kind. The law in words applies to those cases where a person sells, offers for sale, consigns for sale, or has in its possession with intent to sell, offer for sale, or consign for sale any article of bedding as defined in the act.

SUBJECT: PUBLIC HEALTH LAWS; INSPECTION OF HOTELS, CAFES, RESTAURANTS, ETC.

9 December, 1941.

In your letter of December 8, you inquire as to the State Board of Health's authority to inspect, grade and supervise by rules and regulations the sanitation of restaurants, cafes and eating establishments which are operated at the various State supported public institutions, as well as such establishments which are operated by the private schools of the State.

The Act itself is very broad in this connection. Section 1 of Chapter 309, Public Laws of 1941, empowers and directs the State Board of Health to "prepare and enforce rules and regulations governing the sanitation of hotels, cafes, restaurants, tourist homes, tourist camps, summer camps, lunch and drink stands, and sandwich manufacturing establishments, *and all other establishments where food is prepared, handled and served to the public at wholesale or retail for pay, or where transient guests are served food or provided with lodging for pay.*"

The above quoted portion of the Act appears in all three sections thereof. In my opinion, it is broad enough to cover eating establishments which are carried on not only at State supported schools, but also is broad enough to cover such establishments which are operated at private schools, such as are referred to in your letter. It is my understanding that at all such institutions food is served to persons who present themselves for such service and a charge is made therefor.

While it is true that the general public is not permitted to purchase food in such establishments, they are certainly, to some extent, public eating places and persons who are permitted to purchase food therefrom are entitled to the protection afforded by the Act.

SUBJECT: HEALTH; STATE BOARD OF HEALTH; MATTRESS MANUFACTURERS; INSPECTION OF PLANT

13 December, 1941.

You present to this office a letter from Mr. E. E. Phillips, of the Cotton Belt Mattress Company, wherein he states that in the future your inspectors will be required to have proper credentials presented to the office of his plant and that you will then be permitted to inspect this plant only in the presence of a guide to be furnished by his organization. You inquire if your representatives should present their credentials to the office of this plant and then inspect the same in company with a guide to be furnished by them.

I see nothing improper in your inspectors first presenting themselves at the office of this organization before inspecting the plant; however, I do not think that you would be required to inspect only such portions of the same as would be pointed out to them by the so-called "guide" furnished by them.

SUBJECT: UNIFORM BEDDING LAW; TAXATION

5 January, 1942.

You state that a father and son operate two separate mattress plants in different towns of the State, but that these plants are operated under the same name; that neither of the owners have anything to do with the actual management of the other's plant, and they contend that since both these plants are operated under the same name, they would not be required to secure separate licenses for each plant.

In my opinion, under the statute, Sections 1, 2 and 7 of Chapter 298 of the Public Laws of 1937, a separate license would be required for each of these plants. Section 1 of the Act defines a person as "any individual, corporation, partnership, or association." Section 2 is in part as follows: "Any person desiring to operate a sterilizer shall first secure a license from the State Health Officer . . . Such license shall be kept conspicuously posted in the place of business." Section 7 is in part as follows: "No person . . . shall manufacture mattresses until he has secured a license therefor from the State Board of Health." This section also requires the license to be at the place where such business is carried on.

From the above quoted sections of the law, it is my opinion that a separate license should be required for each of these plants.

SUBJECT: OSTEOPATHS; PRACTICE OF MEDICINE

16 January, 1942.

In your letter of January 14, you state that Dr. S. V. Lewis of Plymouth has requested that you obtain a reference to the law with regard to the practice of osteopathy as it relates to the medical practice act. Dr. Lewis states that there is an osteopath practicing his profession in one of the counties of the State, who some feel may be violating the medical practice law; that this man has been brought before the grand jury for indictment for the illegal practice of medicine a number of times, but that no true bill of indictment has ever been returned.

The law with regard to the practice of osteopathy in this State is to be found as C. S. 6700, et seq. Here you will find that osteopathy is defined for the purpose of that act "to be the science of healing without the use of drugs, as taught by the various colleges of osteopathy recognized by the North Carolina Osteopathic Society, Incorporated.

Under the chapter on the Practice of Medicine, C. S. 6605, et seq., you will find that no person shall practice medicine or surgery, or any of the branches thereof, nor in any case prescribe for the cure of diseases unless he shall have been first licensed and registered so to do in the manner prescribed by the act. The practice of medicine or surgery would, within the meaning of this act, include the diagnosis or attempted diagnosis, the treatment or attempt to treat, the operation or attempted operation on, or prescribe for or administer to, or profess to treat any ailment, physical or mental, or any physical injury to or deformity of another person. This statute also provides that the act shall not apply to, among other things, "the practice of osteopathy by any legally licensed osteopath when engaged in the practice of osteopathy as defined by law * * *."

SUBJECT: MUNICIPAL CORPORATIONS; MERIT SYSTEM; APPLICATION TO CITY HEALTH DEPARTMENT

16 January, 1942.

In your letter of January 15, you submit a copy of a contract relating to public health activities, which the North Carolina State Board of Health proposes to enter into with the counties, cities and towns of the State.

You advise that Mr. R. W. Flack, City Manager of the City of Charlotte, has objected to Sections 2 and 8 of the proposed contract, because these two sections are apparently in conflict with certain charter provisions of the City of Charlotte, and are specifically in conflict with the general law of the State in effect in those cities which have adopted the city manager form of government, in that under this general law and under the charter of the City of Charlotte, as now written, the city manager has the sole authority to employ, direct, and replace any health employees, while the contract itself, under Section 2, provides that the county, city, or district health officer shall have sole authority to employ, direct, and replace all members of the staff of the county, city, or district health departments, such appointments to be made in conformity with the merit system principle as outlined in Chapter 378, Public Laws of 1941, and the rules and regulations adopted by the Merit System Council under this Act.

While I have the highest regard for the opinion of Mr. Flack and have the utmost respect for his ability and his honesty and sincerity in the conclusion he has reached and his objection to this portion of the contract, I cannot wholly agree with his contention that the Merit System, established by Chapter 378 of the Public Laws of 1941, is ineffective in so far as the employees of the City Health Department of the City of Charlotte are concerned, simply because under the charter and under the general law the city manager has the power and authority to hire and fire employees of that department.

Under the rules of statutory construction in this State, a general law does not have the effect of repealing a special or local act, unless the latter is specifically mentioned. However, an exception to this rule is that a special or local act, although not mentioned, may be repealed by a subsequent, inconsistent, general act if the nature and content of the general act is such as to evidence a clear legislative intent that the general act shall be uniformly followed throughout the State, superseding prior local statutes.

The question of the repeal of municipal charter provisions and special acts regulating city health departments does not present itself unless these statutes are actually inconsistent with the power of the Merit System Council and the State Board of Health to set up a system of personnel standards on a merit basis for employees of city health departments. Ordinarily, two different statutes dealing with the same subject matter, if possible, will be construed as *in pari materia* so that effect may be given to both. Given such a construction, the Merit System Law and many local acts will not be found inconsistent. The Merit System Law may have the effect of determining eligibility for employment by a city health department; and, from the list of persons found to be eligible, employees may be chosen in the manner provided by the municipal charter or statutes of local application.

This case is somewhat analogous to the case of Goode v. Brenizer, 198 N. C. 217, where an election was held for the adoption of the Plan D Form of Government on the same day that a private act of the General Assembly was passed which had the effect of modifying certain of the provisions of the general law with regard to this form of government. The Court held that effect must be given to the Act of the General Assembly, the Court stating:

> "The case turns upon the question as to whether Chapter 142 of the Private Laws of 1929 has the effect of modifying C. S. 2900 so as to provide for the election and appointment in case of vacancies of members of the board of school commissioners of the City of Charlotte, according to the provisions of Chapter 78 of the Private Laws of 1923, as amended by the said Act of 1929. We think it does, else said Act would be meaningless, and it is to be presumed that the Legislature intended something by its enactment."

I am of the opinion, from the above, that the power of the city manager under the charter of the City of Charlotte, and under the general law relating to the manager form of government for municipalities, which is in effect in the City of Charlotte, relating to the hiring and firing of employees of the City Health Department, is modified to the extent that the provisions of Chapter 378 of the Public Laws of 1941 are inconsistent therewith; that is to say, the city manager of the City of Charlotte would have authority to hire and to fire such employees, subject, however, to the conditions of and in the manner prescribed by the Merit System Act.

I think that Mr. Flack is correct in his objection to Section 2, as it is now written; however, this section could be amended to meet the situation in the City of Charlotte, by striking out the words "that the county, city or district health officer," and inserting in lieu thereof the words "the city manager."

With regard to Mr. Flack's objection to Section 8 of the proposed contract, which covers travel allowances by such employees, I note from your letter that you have never insisted that this section be carried out; and, since you do not insist on enforcing the provisions of it, I see no reason why it should be included in the contract.

SUBJECT: SANITARY DISTRICTS; STATE BOARD OF HEALTH

2 February, 1942.

I have your letter of January 29, wherein you inquire if the Board of Health may pass a resolution delegating to the Secretary of the Board authority to issue orders from time to time relative to the creation of sanitary districts, under authority of Chapter 100 of the Public Laws of 1927.

This office formerly advised you, under date of 16 December, 1938, that even the failure of the Board to meet and order such hearing might be a technical omission on the part of the Board, and such omission would not, in our opinion, invalidate or void the establishment of a sanitary district. However, I do not think the statute contemplates the delegation of such authority and I cannot advise you that your Board has authority to delegate this power. The statute itself says that the Board shall name a time and place within the proposed district, at which the State Board shall hold a public hearing concerning the creation of a proposed sanitary district.

As you well remember, the bond attorneys, in one instance, would not approve bonds issued where the Board itself had not named the time and place for the hearing. You also remember that the Legislature refused to change the law so as to permit such delegation to the Secretary.

SUBJECT: PUBLIC HEALTH; OSTEOPATHS; PHYSICAL EXAMINATION AND HEALTH CERTIFICATES FOR EMPLOYEES SERVING IN HOTELS AND CAFES

4 March, 1942.

You inquire as to whether, in my opinion, an osteopath is qualified to make a physical examination and execute a health certificate for employees serving in hotels and cafes.

Section 6700 of Michie's N. C. Code of 1939, annotated, defines osteopathy to be the science of healing without the use of drugs, as taught by the various colleges of osteopathy recognized by the North Carolina Osteopathic Society, Incorporated. Section 6706 provides that osteopathic physicians shall observe and be subject to all State and municipal regulations relating to the control of contagious diseases, the reporting and certifying of births and deaths, and all matters pertaining to public health the same as physicians of other schools of medicine, and that such reports shall be accepted by the officer or department to whom the same are made.

It would seem clear that osteopaths are included in the word "physician" as used in the Chapter of Michie's Code entitled "Medicine and Allied Occupations." The health certificate required to be furnished by employees in hotels and cafes is a matter pertaining to the public health, and unless the examination requires the administration or use of drugs, I can see no reason why an osteopath would not be competent to furnish the certificate required.

SUBJECT: VITAL STATISTICS; CERTIFICATION OF CAUSE OF DEATH

20 May, 1942.

In your letter of May 18 you state that a death certificate has been filed with one of your local registrars and that it is incomplete in that the cause of death was not given when it was filed. The coroner has refused to sign the certificate stating the cause of death because the undertaker had removed the body to South Carolina before the coroner had a chance to see it and make an investigation as to the cause of the death. You state it is reported that the cause of the death was due to an explosion of a railway engine but that the deceased was dead before anyone arrived at the scene of the accident. You inquire as to what procedure your Department should take in having this death certificate completed.

The statute, C. S. 7112, provides, among other things, that it shall be unlawful to inter or finally dispose of a dead body of a human being or remove such body from the primary registration district without the authority of a burial or removal permit issued by the local registrar of the district in which the death occurred, or in which the body was found. It seems to me that perhaps the local registrar could, under C. S. 7109, obtain information satisfactory to himself as to the cause of the death and fill in the missing parts.

SUBJECT: VITAL STATISTICS; DELAYED BIRTH CERTIFICATE; DUTIES OF REGISTER OF DEEDS

27 June, 1942.

You inquire as to the duties of a Register of Deeds in registering a delayed certificate of birth.

Section 1 of Chapter 126 of the Public Laws of 1941 provides in part that the State Board of Health is authorized to promulgate rules and regulations under which any birth which has not been registered with the Bureau of Vital Statistics within four years after birth may be registered with the Register of Deeds of the county in which the birth occurred. It further provides that each such birth must be registered in duplicate on the forms approved by the State Board of Health and furnished by the State Registrar, and that the Register of Deeds shall forward the original and duplicate certificate to the Bureau of Vital Statistics for final approval. If the certificate complies with the rules and regulations of the State Board of Health, and has not been previously registered, the State Registrar will file the original and return the duplicate to the Register of Deeds for recording.

It is my opinion that it is the duty of the Register of Deeds to forward the original and duplicate certificate to the Bureau of Vital Statistics for final approval immediately upon same being filed with the Register of Deeds. It is necessary for the Bureau of Vital Statistics, before final approval, to see that the certificate complies with the rules and regulations of the State Board of Health, and that the birth has not been previously registered. This must be done before the duplicate is recorded in the office of the Register of Deeds.

OPINIONS TO LOCAL GOVERNMENT COMMISSION

SUBJECT: BANKS AND BANKING; SECURITY; DEPOSIT OF SECURITY FOR PROTECTION OF DEPOSITS OF LOCAL UNITS OF GOVERNMENT

7 August, 1940.

In your letter of August 6, 1940, you ask for an interpretation of Section 32 of the Local Government Act, as amended. That section provides in part that "any bank or trust company furnishing United States Government bonds, North Carolina State bonds, County or Municipal bonds, as security for such excess deposits (over and above Federal Deposit Insurance), shall deposit said bonds with another bank which has been approved by the Commission as a depository bank for such purposes, the State Treasurer, or the Federal Reserve Bank, and said bonds when so deposited shall be held for the benefit of a unit and subject to the order of the governing body or board of such unit . . ."

Your question is whether a bank maintaining a trust department may place security for protection of unit funds deposited with it with its own trust department; in other words, is the trust department of a bank "another bank" within the meaning of the section above quoted.

Section 216(a), North Carolina Code Annotated, Michie (1939), defines "bank" so as specifically not to include "trust companies not receiving money on deposit." A bank is defined to mean any corporation, etc., "receiving, soliciting, or accepting money or its equivalent on deposit as a business."

You are, therefore, advised that the trust department of a bank is not "another bank" within the meaning of Section 32 of the Local Government Act.

SUBJECT: DAVIE COUNTY DEBT REDUCTION—FISCAL YEAR 1939-40; JERUSALEM TOWNSHIP SCHOOL NOTE

16 October, 1940.

I received from your office a letter from Mr. G. H. C. Shutt, County Treasurer, Mocksville, North Carolina, under date of October 4, attaching copy of the minutes of the action of the Board of Education of Davie County under date of September 17, 1931, extending (time of payment) the note owed by Jerusalem Consolidated Schools to the Bank of Cooleemee. I received, also, the original note, dated September 1, 1932, for $4900, executed by the Davie County Board of Education, payable six months after date to the Bank of Cooleemee, endorsed on the back of which was approval by the Local Government Commission, together with endorsements of various payments. Also attached is the letter of transmittal of this note, with approval by the State Treasurer, Mr. Stedman, under date of September 27, 1932.

Upon consideration of the entire matter, I feel convinced that we would be justified in treating the payment of $1,000 on the principal of this note in September, 1939, as a debt reduction of Davie County, the obligation having been treated and handled by the County as a valid, outstanding debt of the County and approved as such by the Local Government Commission.

SUBJECT: MUNICIPALITIES; BORROWING MONEY FOR NECESSARY PURPOSE—SECURED BY NORTH CAROLINA AND OTHER BONDS OWNED BY THE MUNICIPALITY

7 December, 1940.

Receipt is acknowledged of your letter of December 5, in which you referred to me an inquiry which you have had from a town which has no outstanding bonds, but which has North Carolina and other bonds received by it from the sale of its light and power system. This town, it appears, desires to construct a sewer system with the aid of the W. P. A., and in lieu of issuing bonds, desires to borrow money and secure the loan with the investments above mentioned, which you advise can be done at a lower rate than the rate at which it might sell bonds.

Article VII, Section 7, and Article V, Section 4, of the North Carolina Constitution are limitations upon the power of municipalities to contract debts without popular approval as well as the power to issue bonds. If a city borrowed money for a sewer project, hypothecating municipally owned stocks and bonds as security for the loan, it would be contracting a debt. It has been held that bonds issued to finance a water works and sewerage system are issued for a necessary expense, Burt v. Biscoe, 209 N. C. 70, obviating the necessity of an election on the bond issue as required by Article VII, Section 7. However, the fact that the expenditure is for a necessary expense will not dispense with the necessity of an election under Article V, Section 4, if the constitutional debt limitation is exceeded.

It is questionable whether a municipal corporation has the power to mortgage property. In 3 Dillon, Municipal Corporations (5th ed.), Section 1591, the following comment is made with reference to the power of municipal corporations to mortgage property:

> "Where property charged with no trusts or public uses is held by the corporation without restriction for sale or profit, it may, in the absence of restrictive legislation, mortgage it to secure any debt or obligation that it has the power to create or enter into. The power to mortgage, if not expressly given or denied, would in such case be an incident to the power to hold and dispose of property, and to make contracts."

In North Carolina, municipal corporations are neither expressly granted nor denied the power to mortgage property. However, in the case of Vaughn v. Commissioners, 118 N. C. 636, it was held that the grant to a county of power to mortgage real property could not be implied from the grant of power to sell and convey such property. A different conclusion might be reached with reference to mortgages or pledges of personal property such as stocks and bonds by municipalities. However, the decision in Vaughn v. Commissioners does make the existence of such power doubtful. Furthermore, the restrictions upon the sale of real or personal property by municipalities contained in C. S., Sec. 2688, might be an obstacle to the implication of a power to mortgage from the power to sell.

It is questionable whether a municipality may borrow money to finance a sewer project by executing a note in lieu of bonds.

C. S. 2960, a part of the Municipal Finance Act, provides that no municipality shall: "Borrow money or issue bonds or notes except as provided in this law." The only provisions for borrowing money otherwise than through bond issues contained in the act relate to temporary loans. Section 2932 authorizes borrowing money in anticipation of revenue to meet appropriations for the current fiscal year. Section 2933 authorizes borrowing money to satisfy judgments, to pay or renew certain notes already executed, and to make payments of principal or interest on certain bonds. Section 2934 authorizes borrowing money in anticipation of the sale of bonds, the issuance of which has been duly authorized. These temporary loans are to be obtained by the execution of notes. No other provisions are made in the Municipal Finance Act for borrowing money otherwise than through the sale of bonds.

In the absence of direct statutory authority and in view of the decision in Vaughn v. Commissioners, I entertain the view that the municipality could not borrow money for the purposes as to which you inquire.

SUBJECT: INTOXICATING LIQUOR; WINE AND BEER—PROHIBITING SALE OF ON SUNDAY; MUNICIPAL ORDINANCE

7 May, 1941.

I have your letter of May 6, in which you inquire as to the power of a town board of commissioners to pass and enforce an ordinance prohibiting the sale of beer and wine within the corporate limits of the town on Sundays. You state that there is no special or private Act authorizing such prohibition.

The office has previously ruled, and is still of the same opinion, that a municipality has a right under its police power to adopt valid ordinances prohibiting the sale of wine and beer within the corporate limits of the municipality on Sunday. A municipality would have the power to exercise this police power even in the absence of any special or private Act giving it the authority to do so.

SUBJECT: MUNICIPAL DEBT LIMITATION; ARTICLE V, SECTION 4, OF THE CONSTITUTION; JUDGMENTS FOR DEBTS INCURRED FOR NECESSARY EXPENSES

7 October, 1941.

I have your letter of October 6, in which you submit the following problem:

"A municipality has issued bonds for a necessary expense and the cost of the project is several thousand dollars in excess of the proceeds of the bonds. This excess is represented by accounts payable to certain creditors for construction materials and other items. The governing board of the municipality proceeded with completion of the project without making provision for this excess, the amount of which is greater than two-thirds the debt reduction in any fiscal year in the past and will be for several years to come. These accounts payable have been reduced to judgment and the town desires to issue bonds for liquidation of the judgments without approval of the voters at an election."

In the case of Hallyburton v. Board of Education, 213 N. C. 9, our Court held that the limitation prescribed by Article V, Section 4, as amended, is in addition to other constitutional limitations relating to taxation and that a county may not borrow money even for a necessary expense without submitting the question to a vote, Article VII, Section 7, when its outstanding indebtedness has not been reduced during the prior fiscal year in accordance with that provision of the Constitution. I do not think that because the claim has been reduced to judgment, the constitutional prohibition against issuing the bonds would be changed. It is my opinion that the bonds could not be constitutionally issued, except when authorized by a vote of the people in accordance with the constitutional provision.

SUBJECT: EDUCATION; LITERARY FUND; VALIDITY OF WILSON COUNTY NOTE

23 December, 1941.

Your letter of December 20, 1941, raises certain questions relating to the validity of notes issued by Wilson County to evidence the indebtedness of the County to the Literary Fund in consequence of a loan made by the Literary Fund to the County on January 10, 1941.

The first question is whether it is essential to the validity of the notes that the procedure set out in the Local Government Act, North Carolina Code Section 2492(15) to 2492(17), be followed at the time such notes are issued. The Local Government Act requires ordinarily that when notes of local governmental units are issued, they be sold by the Local Government Commission, after a published notice in a newspaper and after bids have been received by the Commission. This procedure was not followed when the loan was made by the Literary Fund to Wilson County. In my opinion, the statute does not contemplate the necessity of such a published notice and the receipt of formal bids where a loan is made by an agency of the State to another agency of the State. The purpose of the act is to require a published notice and competitive bidding when the securities of local governmental units are being sold to private purchasers, but when the securities are to be taken by an agency of the State under statutory authority, it is to be assumed that the State will give the local unit the most advantageous terms possible, so that this procedure is unnecessary.

I, therefore, advise that the validity of these notes is not impaired by the failure to follow the procedure set out in the Local Government Act.

Your second question is whether the validity of these notes is affected by reason of the failure of the county board of education at the time the loans were obtained from the Literary Fund to follow the procedure set out in the County Finance Act for the authorization of the issuance of bonds or notes by counties.

Consolidated Statutes 1334(43) (Chapter 81, Public Laws of 1927, as amended) was further amended in 1941 by Chapter 266. Here you will find that the County Finance Act, by this amendment, does not govern the method by which any county board of education may borrow money from the special building fund created by Chapter 201, Public Laws of 1925, or from any special building fund of the State created by any law enacted at the Regular Session of 1927, or from the State Literary Fund as provided in Article 24 of Chapter 136, Public Laws of 1923, as amended.

SUBJECT: COUNTY FINANCE ACT; APPLICATION OF FUNDS REALIZED FROM SALE OF BONDS

9 January, 1942.

You inquire as to whether, in my opinion, the proceeds realized from the sale of bonds issued under the provisions of the County Finance Act can be invested in United States Defense Bonds where a part of the construction program cannot be completed due to the inability to secure building material at the present time.

Section 38 of the County Finance Act, being Section 1334(38) of Michie's N. C. Code of 1939, Annotated, provides in detail the purposes for which the proceeds realized from the sale of bonds issued under the provisions of the County Finance Act may be used. There is no provision in this section which, to my mind, would sanction the investment of the unused balance of the proceeds realized from the sale of the bonds in United States Defense Bonds. Therefore, to my mind, such investment would be in direct conflict with the provisions of the section above referred to.

OPINIONS TO STATE BOARD OF ELECTIONS

SUBJECT: ELECTIONS; SPECIAL; TIME FOR CALLING; ADOPTION OF NEW PLAN OF CITY GOVERNMENT

10 August, 1940.

I have your letter in which you state that you wish to call an election in the City of Raleigh on the question of whether or not the City shall have a city manager form of government, on or about October 1, 1940. The authority for calling such an election is contained in Public-Local and Private Laws of 1939, Chapter 234.

You further state that it is the understanding of the Wake County Board of Elections that this election should be held under the following law; Public Laws of North Carolina, 1917, Chapter 136, Part 5, Plan D City Manager.

It appears that it has been questioned as to whether a local election can be held within a certain time of a General Election. You ask my opinion as to whether or not there is any such time limitation so as to prevent October 1, 1940, from being a valid date for holding the election with regard to any laws to the contrary, and whether or not Chapter 136, Part 5, Plan D, of the Public Laws of 1917, is the proper law to base the election on.

I am of the opinion that October 1, 1940, or thereabouts would be a valid date for holding the above mentioned election. Specific statutory authority for calling the election at that time is granted in Section 1 of Chapter 234 of the Public-Local and Private Laws of 1939. Any prior general statutory limitation as to the time of holding a special or general municipal election within a certain time of the General Election would, to the extent it affected this election, be repealed. In Section 3 of the above cited chapter, it is stated that "All laws and clauses of laws which may be in conflict with the provisions of this act are hereby to the extent of such conflict repealed."

An examination of the Constitution of this State does not disclose any provision containing a limitation as to the period of time before or after a general election in which a special municipal election may not be held. Nor do any reasons present themselves to my mind why holding the special election within that length of time of the General Election would be prejudical to the exercise of a full and free vote on the question presented to the voters. There are no decisions in this jurisdiction passing on the point here under consideration. In Loughran v. City of Hickory, 129 N. C. 281, however, it was held that a "special election" held on a regular election day was valid.

There would seem to be no doubt but that the law cited by you is the correct one to base the election on. In Section 1, Chapter 234, Public-Local and Private Laws of 1939, it is in part provided:

> "* * * and at said election there shall be submitted for determination by the qualified voters of the City of Raleigh voting in such election the question of the adoption of a form of government for the City of Raleigh as defined as Plan D in part five of Sub-Chapter sixteen, of Chapter one hundred and thirty-six, of

> the Public Laws of one thousand nine hundred and seventeen, as amended, which plan provides for a mayor, a city council and a city manager."

I am of the opinion that this reference in the authorizing statute is a valid reference to the germane provisions of the general statute setting out the various plans of city government which may be voted on.

Subject: Election Laws; Salaries and Fees; County Boards of Elections

14 August, 1940.

This office has had under consideration the letter from Mr. W. H. McElwee addressed to you under date of July 30, wherein he raises two questions: First, is the county liable for compensation of registrars and judges of elections on days when they have been officially called to a meeting other than on primary and election days.

This question, I think, is answered by an official opinion to you under date of 23 February, 1940, and, for your convenience, I enclose herewith copy of this letter.

The second question relates to an interpretation of Section 126 of the Election Laws, which provides for the placing of ballot boxes in the voting area and a public inspection, in such a manner that the public may view the activities of electors and election officials.

The statute is Section 126 of the Election Laws Pamphlet, which is as follows:

> "Sec. 126 (a-19). *Regulations for voting at polling places.* No person shall, while the polls are open at polling places, loiter about or do any electioneering within such polling-place or within fifty feet thereof, and no political banner, poster, or placard shall be allowed in or upon such polling places during the day of the election. The election officials and ballot boxes shall at all times be in plain view of the qualified voters who are present, and a guard rail shall be placed *not nearer than ten feet nor further than twenty feet from the said election officials and ballot boxes.*"

Following this section is a diagram which illustrates the arrangement of the polling place, and the Act requires that the polling place shall be arranged substantially according to said diagram, or as nearly thereto as the building or other place in which the election is held will permit.

The underscored part of the section requires the guard rail shall not be further than twenty feet from the election officials and ballot boxes. It may be doubted that it would be a reasonable construction of this section to hold the election in a room with closed doors admitting only such number of persons, at a time, "as can be accommodated by the election officials" as suggested in the letter to you. The general public ought not to be prevented from observing the conduct of the election, and should be permitted to come to the "guard rail," provided for in the section.

Subject: Election Laws; Registration Procedure for One Who Will Be Absent During Registration Period

4 September, 1940.

Consolidated Statutes 5961 provides in effect that any citizen of the State not duly registered, but who may be qualified to vote under the

Constitution and laws of this State, and who expects to be absent from the county in which he lives during the usual period provided for registration of voters in the manner there provided, may be permitted to register. You will find here that provision is made for a special registration book for absent electors, which book shall contain separate columns for the name of the elector, name of the precinct in which the elector resides, age, place of birth, race, and precinct in which the elector last resided. The chairman of the county board of elections is charged with the duty to register on this registration book any qualified elector who presents himself for registration at any time other than the usual registration period and who expects to be absent from the voting precinct in which he resides during the usual registration period, if found to be otherwise entitled to register, in the same manner now provided by law for the registration of voters before the precinct registrar in the usual registration period.

This statute further provides that the chairman of the board of elections shall certify to the respective registrars in each of the precincts where such electors reside, the names, age and residence, place of birth, etc., of any electors registered on the said county registration book and thereby entitled to vote in such precincts. Thereafter, the registrar is required to enter these names on the regular registration book for such precinct, marking beside the names of such electors so certified to him by the chairman of the county board of elections the words, "Registered before the chairman of the county board of elections"; and the electors so registered shall be entitled to vote in any election in such precinct in the same manner as if registered by the precinct registrar.

This office has formerly held that the 1939 Registration Act did not repeal the above statute.

SUBJECT: ELECTION LAWS; MAKING COPIES OF LIST OF ABSENT ELECTORS; CHAIRMAN COUNTY BOARD OF ELECTIONS

21 October, 1940.

It is true that the register of applications for absent voters' ballots, under Section 10 of Chapter 159 of the Public Laws of 1939 is a public record and is required to be open to the inspection of any elector of the county at any time within thirty days before and thirty days after any general election, or at any other time when good and sufficient reason may be assigned for such inspection. These records being public records, they are, of course, available during the times specified in the statute for inspection by any elector.

This is somewhat an analogous situation to that presented to our Court in the case of Newton v. Fisher, 98 N. C. 20. Here the Court held that while it is the duty of the register of deeds of a county to permit all persons to inspect the records committed to his custody, he will not be required without payment of his proper fees to allow anyone to make copies or abstracts therefrom. In this case the Court said:

> "It is the duty of the register to keep them open to the inspection and examination of all who may desire to inspect and examine them, and for this there is no fee; it is his duty to furnish copies to all who require them and will pay the fees allowed. Perhaps, in addition to this, so long and so universal has

been the custom, that it may be said to be the right of lawyers, and others needing them, to take such reasonable memoranda as may not interfere with the rights and duties of the register, and we have never known this refused. We know of no law that requires the register, in this respect, to do more."

Speaking further to this question, on page 24 of the opinion, the Court said:

"If he has the right to make abstracts of all the records of 1886, he has the right to make them for all the years; if he has the right to copy or make abstracts of parts of the records, it may be the material parts, he has the right to copy the whole. If it is the right of one, it is the right of all. Once concede the right, and where will it end? The records of this Court, of all the courts, of the executive departments of every public office in the State, would be subject to the same right in every individual in the State, and, aside from the inconvenience, and perhaps intolerable annoyance and loss of just emoluments to public officers, and danger and risk which they might incur in possible injury to the records, affecting public and private rights, make it manifest that such right cannot exist. It is not the right of all—it is not the right of one."

From the language of the opinion in the above case, I do not think that the chairman of the County Board of Elections would be required to permit indiscriminate copying of the registration book referred to in the statute, if, in doing so, his duties as chairman of the board might be unnecessarily interfered with. However, on the other hand, I do not think that the chairman of the board would be justified in absolutely refusing to permit an elector to copy the registration book in a proper case.

SUBJECT: ELECTIONS; WITHDRAWAL OF CANDIDACY; NOMINATION OF NEW CANDIDATE WITHIN THIRTY DAYS OF ELECTION

2 June, 1941.

I received your letter of May 31, advising that Mr. Marshall C. Kurfees, Republican nominee for Congress in the Fifth Congressional District for the unexpired term in the June 14 special election, desires to withdraw his name as a candidate. You also enclosed me a letter from Mr. Jake F. Newell, State Chairman of the Republican Executive Committee, inquiring as to whether or not the Republican Congressional Executive Committee of that District could now name another candidate and have the name of such candidate appear on the official ballot.

I am advised that the ballots for the June 14 special election have already been printed and distributed as required by law.

C. S. 6007 provides that a special election for a Representative in Congress shall be conducted in like manner as regular elections. C. S. 6055(a-8) provides that after the proper officer has been notified of the nomination of any candidate, he shall not withdraw the same unless upon the written request of the candidate so nominated *made at least thirty days before the day of the election.*

The object of this statute is manifest. If the State Board of Elections should fail to comply with it, ballots would be subject at any time to being withdrawn after having been distributed by law, and endless confusion would result. I am of the opinion that you would not, therefore, have a right to recall the ballots which have already been distributed and reprint and redistribute the same, as the withdrawal of Mr. Kurfees was not made at least thirty days before the day of election. It follows, also, that you would not be authorized to recognize any other nomination made by the Republican Executive Committee of the District and for such purpose withdraw and reprint the ballots which have already been distributed.

SUBJECT: ELECTION LAWS; DUTIES OF STATE BOARD OF ELECTIONS

16 July, 1941.

You inquired over the telephone this morning if the State Board of Elections has authority, under the law, to investigate and make rules and regulations concerning the conduct of municipal elections in this State.

The statute, C. S. 5923, et seq., sets forth in detail the duty of the State Board of Elections. Running throughout the law you will find that it contemplates only the supervision of the conduct of State and county elections. Reference is made throughout this statute to "county boards of elections" and the conduct of "primaries and elections."

I understand that in the past the State Board itself has construed this as not applying to municipal elections, and that the State Board has never assumed any jurisdiction over the same. This office sees no reason to disturb the administrative ruling in this regard.

SUBJECT: ELECTION LAWS; REFUND OF FILING FEE

27 April, 1942.

I have tried to find a statute which would permit the refund of the filing fee of the late Rowland S. Pruette, who died after the time for filing had expired and who had no opposition in the primary; however, the only statute which I have been able to find is C. S. 6024 and this does not contemplate any such refund.

I regret to advise, therefore, that you have no authority to authorize the refund in this case.

SUBJECT: ELECTION LAWS; PRIMARY ELECTIONS; ABSENTEE VOTING

13 May, 1942.

You inquire if the provisions of Chapter 346 of the Public Laws of 1941, relating to absentee voting by members of the armed forces of the United States, would apply to qualified electors who expect to be absent from their counties on the day of the primary election and who are engaged in national defense work, as distinguished from membership in the armed forces of the United States.

Section 1 of this Act is as follows:

> "Any qualified voter entitled to vote in the primary of any political party, who on the date of such primary, is in the military, naval, or other armed forces of the United States may vote in the primary of the party of his affiliation in the manner as hereinafter provided."

In my opinion, the language of the above statute would not apply to others than those electors who are actually in service in the military, naval, or other armed forces of the United States, and could not be construed to include national defense workers and other classifications.

OPINIONS TO STATE BOARD OF CHARITIES AND PUBLIC WELFARE

SUBJECT: PLACEMENT OF EUROPEAN CHILDREN IN THIS STATE

27 August, 1940.

The question arises as to the interpretation of Chapter 226 of the Public Laws of 1931, as it applies to the placing in this State of European refugee children.

You have presented to me a press release issued by Honorable Edward J. Shaughnessy, Acting Commissioner of Immigration and Naturalization, No. 345, dated July 14, 1940, wherein is outlined the procedure which will make possible the admission of refugee children from the war zone in whatever numbers shipping facilities and private assurances of support will permit. It will be noted from this press release that the regulations of the Department of State authorized the issuance of visitors' visas to such children, upon a showing of intention that they shall return home upon the termination of hostilities. These regulations provide further that children traveling either upon visitors' visas or quota visas shall file, or have filed for them, a corporate affidavit to the effect that they will not be permitted to become a public charge; that such corporate affidavit shall be given by charitable corporations such as the United States Committee for the Care of European Children.

The release further discloses that the corporate affidavit shall be backed by affidavits in greatly simplified form, to be given such corporations by individuals who agree to care for such children. Further provision is made for a trust fund equal to fifty dollars for each child brought to the United States under such corporate corporation's auspices, and that this fund may be in the nature of an insurance fund to meet all contingencies respecting the care and departure of the children which may arise from individual assurances of support.

The above press release contains a copy of an order duly issued under authority of law by the Commissioner of Immigration and Naturalization, with the approval of the Attorney General, which outlines in Sections 4 and 5 of the order the following:

> "That a corporation not for profit organized for the purpose of assuring the care and support of refugee children, and approved by the Attorney General for such purpose, has given the Attorney General, with such supporting evidence as he may require and in such form as he may require, the following assurances: first, that an identified child or a child for whom provision for identification has been or will be made will not become a public charge; second, that arrangements have been or will be made for the reception and placement of such child in accordance with the standards of the Children's Bureau of the Department of Labor; and third, that the sum of fifty dollars for each such child has been or, upon the initial placement of the child, will be deposited in a trust fund established by and to be used by the corporation to meet all contingencies, not otherwise met or provided for, arising after such initial placement respecting either the care of the child while in the United States or its departure therefrom. Every corporation approved by the Attorney General to act under the provisions of

this rule shall furnish the Attorney General with an affidavit containing an undertaking that the children admitted under the provisions of this paragraph will be under continuous supervision, during the period of their stay in the country, assuring that they are in proper custody and are being cared for in conformity with the standards of the Children's Bureau of the Department of Labor, and a further undertaking to comply with such directions as the Attorney General shall make respecting the admission, care and support, and departure of the children.

"5. Such children, when presenting quota visas, shall not be excludable, as likely to become a public charge, provided either that they would be admissable independently of the provisions of this rule or that the following conditions have been satisfied:

"That a corporation not for profit, approved by the Attorney General as provided in Paragraph 4 of this rule, has given the Attorney General, with such supporting evidence as he may require and in such form as he may require, the following assurances: first, that an identified child or a child for whom provision for identification has been or will be made will not become a public charge; second, that arrangements have been or will be made for the reception and placement of such child in accordance with the standards of the Children's Bureau of the Department of Labor; and third, that the sum of fifty dollars for each such child has been or, upon the initial placement of the child, will be deposited in the trust fund hereinbefore mentioned to be used by the corporation to meet all contingencies, not otherwise met or provided for, arising after such initial placement respecting the care of the child while in the United States. Every corporation approved by the Attorney General to act under the provisions of this rule shall furnish the Attorney General with an affidavit containing an undertaking that the children admitted under the provisions of this paragraph will be under continuous supervision, until they have reached the age of eighteen and for such further period as the Attorney General may require, assuring that they are in proper custody and are being cared for in conformity with the standards of the Children's Bureau of the Department of Labor, and a further undertaking to comply with such directions as the Attorney General shall make respecting the admission, care and support of the children."

You are, of course, familiar with our law with regard to the placing of dependent children in this State, Chapter 226 of the Public Laws of 1931. In Section 1 of this Act, you will find that no person, agency, association, institution or corporation shall bring or send into this State any child for the purpose of *placing him out* or procuring his adoption, without first obtaining the consent of the State Board of Charities and Public Welfare; that such person, agency, or association shall conform to the rules of the Board and shall enter into a written agreement with the Board to remove such child from the State when requested so to do; that it will place the child under written contract approved by the Board; that the person with whom the child is placed shall be responsible for his proper care and training; that the Board will have supervision of the child and the home in which it is placed.

It is further provided in this section that before such child shall be brought or sent into the State for the purpose of placing him in a home, the person, agency, association, institution or corporation so bringing or sending such child shall first notify the State Board of its intention; shall certify to the Board that such child does not have a contagious or incurable disease, is not deformed, feeble-minded, or of vicious character, and shall obtain from the said Board a certificate stating that such home is a suitable home for the child.

Provision is further made in this section that an annual report shall be made to the Board concerning the location and wellbeing of the child, so long as he shall remain in this State and until he shall have reached the age of eighteen years. Section 2 of this Act provides that no child shall be placed in this State until a justifiable and continuous bond, "not to exceed one thousand dollars" be furnished and maintained by the agency bringing the child into this State, guaranteeing the proper fulfillments of the requirements of Section 1 of the Act.

I am of the opinion that the provisions of Section 1 of the Act, above referred to, particularly that portion of it which relates to obtaining the consent of the State Board before a child shall be placed in this State, and those portions which relate to the requirement of the agency bringing the child into this State to place him in a proper home under a proper contract or agreeemnt, and which relate to the supervision of the child by the State Board or its agent, should be complied with.

Those portions which relate to the physical examination of the child before its entry here and the child's condition as it relates to physical deformity or feeble-mindedness, is perhaps taken care of by the order of the Commissioner of Immigration and Naturalization referred to above, and, since the order of the Commissioner providing for a corporate affidavit and the establishment of a trust fund equal to fifty dollars for each child placed here, guaranteeing that such child will not become a public charge, would perhaps be a substantial compliance with our law in this regard, the very purpose of the Act being to prevent the placement in this State of children who are diseased or who might at some future date become public charges.

SUBJECT: OLD AGE ASSISTANCE ACT; RESIDENCE REQUIREMENTS; AID TO DEPENDENT CHILDREN

4 November, 1940.

You state that the residence requirement in the Public Assistance Act is met when a child "has resided in the State of North Carolina for one year immediately preceding the application for aid; or who was born within the state within one year immediately preceding the application; if the mother has resided in the state for one year immediately preceding the birth." You state further that an applicant for aid to dependent children who has resided in this State eight months prior to the birth of a child, made application for aid to dependent children when this child was four months old, and you inquire if this applicant should be granted aid under the Act above referred to.

There is no provision in the Act which specifically takes care of a situation of this kind; however, I am of the opinion that if the mother has resided in this State for the one year period, her child is entitled to assistance.

SUBJECT: ADOPTION LAWS; CONSENT OF PARENTS

17 December, 1940.

It is very difficult, under the recent decisions of the Supreme Court of North Carolina, to determine whether it is possible for an institution such as the Children's Home Society of North Carolina, Incorporated, to give the necessary consent in an adoption proceeding where the parent or parents of the child undertake to release all their rights to the child to such institution.

The case of Ward v. Howard, 217 N. C. 201, holds in effect that the consent of the living parent or proof of the abandonment of the child is necessary to an adoption and must be made to appear to the court as a jurisdictional matter. This would mean that the Court construed the adoption statutes to mean that the consent must be given in the proceeding itself and not at some time prior thereto.

This case was followed by the case of in re: Holder, 218 N. C. 136, in which case the mother of the child in question had undertaken to release her rights to the child to the Children's Home Society of North Carolina, Incorporated. In this case the Court reiterated its holding in the case of Ward v. Howard, and held that the consent of the parent or parents must at least be in fair contemplation of the proposed adoption and that this includes its most essential feature, —the identity of the adoptive parents. The Court in this case further held that under the statute the consent of the parent or parents must appear within and not *dehors* the proceedings, and must have reference to the particular proceeding which would culminate in adoption and that the jurisdiction of the court could not be made to depend upon a blanket release or consent on the part of the parents that the child might be adopted in whatever proceeding might be brought and to whomsoever might apply for the adoption of the child.

The effect of these cases would be to absolutely prohibit the practice heretofore followed by the Children's Home Society of North Carolina, Incorporated, unless the provisions of C. S. 191(4) were not invalidated by these decisions. This statute provides:

> "Parents or guardians necessary parties; release of rights to child.—The parents or surviving parent or guardian, or the person or persons having charge of such child, or with whom it may reside, must be a party or parties of record to this proceeding: Provided, that when the parent, parents, or guardian of the person of the child has signed a release of all rights to the child, the person, agency, or institution to which said rights were released shall be made a party to this proceeding, and it shall not be necessary to make the parent, parents or guardian parties."

The provisions contained in this section were first enacted into law by Chapter 243 of the Public Laws of 1935. The adoption proceeding in the case of Ward v. Howard was instituted in the year 1924, and in the Holder case, 1926. The Court in neither of these opinions referred to the 1935 amendment to the adoption laws and it is entirely possible that it was not the Court's intention to attempt to invalidate the provisions contained in C. S. 191(4). If this is true, this section is still the law in so far as proceedings instituted after the enactment of Chapter 243 of the Public Laws of 1935 are concerned.

Of course, I have no way of telling what the Court would hold as to this section if the question should be squarely presented to it. If C. S. 191(4) is valid, the Children's Home Society of North Carolina, Incorporated, should be made a party in an adoption proceeding instead of the parent if the proper release as contemplated by said section had been secured prior to the institution of the proceeding.

SUBJECT: ADOPTION; FINAL ORDER; AMENDMENT

6 January, 1941.

You state in your letter of January 4 that a child was adopted in 1926 and that the petition and final order provided for the adoption of the child during its minority and not for the life of the child. You further state that the foster parent now desires to adopt the boy for life, and you desire to know whether in my opinion this can be accomplished by a motion in the original adoption proceedings.

I am of the opinion that the desired result could not be accomplished by a motion in the original adoption proceedings. The petition in the adoption proceedings only set out that the petitioner desired to adopt the child during its minority and all the other orders naturally were based on the allegations contained in the petition.

In addition to this, the adoption laws have been changed since 1926. Under these circumstances, it would certainly not be advisable to undertake to change the whole original proceeding by a motion in the cause or amendment. If it is the desire of the foster parent to adopt the minor for life, I am of the opinion that a new proceeding should be instituted.

If the boy involved is over twenty-one years of age, the adoption statute would no longer apply to him and, of course, no adoption proceedings could be instituted by the foster parent.

SUBJECT: ADOPTION OF MINORS; SERVICE OF PROCESS BY PUBLICATION

11 January, 1941.

You inquire as to whether, under the statutes relating to the adoption of minors, it would be permissible to complete service by publication without advertisement in the newspaper.

Section 191(1) of Michie's N. C. Code of 1939 provides in part:

> "That where the parents or surviving parent or guardian of the child whose adoption is sought cannot be found within this State for the service of process, that fact shall be made known to the court either by affidavit or return of the sheriff of the county in which such person or persons were last known to reside. It shall be competent to make such service by publication of summons as provided by section 484, et seq, of the Consolidated Statutes and such person shall be bound in every respect by such service."

Section 485, being one of the sections referred to in Section 191(1), provides in part:

> "The order must direct the publication in one or two newspapers to be designated as most likely to give notice to the person to be served, and for such length of time as is deemed reasonable, not less than once a week for four successive weeks, of a notice, giving

> the title and purpose of the action and requiring the defendant to appear and answer, or demur to the complaint at a time and place therein mentioned; and no publication of the summons, or mailing of the summons and complaint, is necessary."

It seems to me that the primary purpose of the requirement as to the publication would be to give the parents or guardian notice that the adoption proceeding had been instituted. This being true, I am of the opinion that the notice should be published in at least one newspaper as required by Section 485.

SUBJECT: DOUBLE OFFICE HOLDING; COUNTY WELFARE BOARD MEMBER—MAYOR

15 January, 1941.

You inquire if the office of county welfare board member and that of mayor are both offices within the meaning of Article XIV, Section 7, of the Constitution, which prohibits double office holding.

In my opinion, serving on the county board of charities and public welfare would not prohibit a person from also serving as mayor of a town. The membership on the county board of charities and public welfare is acting as a commissioner of public charity. Article XIV, Section 7, of the Constitution has this proviso:

> "Provided, that nothing herein contained shall extend to officers in the militia, justices of the peace, commissioner of public charities or commissioners for special purposes."

The membership on the county board of charities and public welfare comes within this proviso and the holding of such an office does not prohibit the person so holding it from holding another office.

SUBJECT: MERIT SYSTEM COUNCIL; DEFINITION OF TERM "POLITICAL OFFICE"

17 February, 1941.

From the pamphlet which you furnished me some time ago, relative to the rule for a Merit System of Personnel Administration in the State Employment Security and State Public Assistance Agencies issued by the Social Security Board in Washington, it appears that no member of the Merit System Council shall have held political office, shall have been an officer in a political organization during the year preceding his appointment, nor shall he hold such office during his term.

The question here arises as to the eligibility of the Honorable Ben Prince, who is now a member of the State Board of Elections, to serve on this council; the precise question being—is membership on the State Board of Elections a "political office" within the meaning of the rule referred to above.

The State Board of Elections was created by C. S. 5921. It consists of five electors of this State, appointed by the Governor to serve for a four-year term each, not more than three members of the board to be of the same political party. It presently consists of three Democrats and two Republicans, whose duties are outlined in the statute, C. S. 5923, and consists of quasi judicial functions as well as ministerial. It is a public office and under the statute prescribing their duties, among other things, they shall "ascertain and judicially determine and declare" the results of elections in this State.

Black's Law Dictionary defines "political office" as follows: "Civil offices are usually divided into three classes—political, judicial, and ministerial. Political offices are such as are not immediately connected with the administration of justice, or with the execution of the mandates of a superior, such as the president or the head of a department." To the same effect, see 32 Words & Phrases, Last Edition, 807, and cases cited.

I am of the opinion that even though membership on the State Board of Elections is a public office, it is a judicial or ministerial office rather than a political one. Persons are chosen for membership on this board from among the highest type of citizens of this State and we have been very fortunate in having unbiased, fair-minded, public spirited citizens of both political parties to serve on the North Carolina State Board of Elections. Mr. Ben Prince is a gentleman of this character, and, to my own knowledge, has exercised the duties of his office in a manner which has been a credit not only to himself but to the State which he served. Mr. Prince is also especially fitted for membership on the Merit System Council, not only from his natural ability but from his long experience and training in the public service of the State, and I am sure that membership on the State Board of Elections would not, in any way, affect the performance of his duties as a member of the Merit System Council.

SUBJECT: ADOPTION LAWS; JUVENILE DELINQUENTS OR DEPENDENTS; SEPARATING CHILD UNDER SIX MONTHS OLD FROM MOTHER

18 February, 1941.

You inquire as to whether or not, in my opinion, the provisions of C. S. 2151 can be used to evade the provisions of C. S. 4445 relating to the separation of a child six months old from its mother, and the provisions of Sections 1 and 2 of Chapter 226, of the Public Laws of 1931, relating to the placing or adoption of juvenile delinquents or dependents.

C. S. 4445 is a criminal statute and its purpose is to prevent the separation of a child under six monts old from its mother for the purpose of placing such child in a foster home or institution or removing it from the State for such purpose, unless the matter of such separation has been investigated and passed upon by the clerk superior court and the county health officer of the county in which the mother resides or the county in which the child was born.

The purpose of Sections 1 and 2 of Chapter 226 of the Public Laws of 1931 is to prevent children from being brought into the State of North Carolina for the purpose of placing them out or procuring their adoption unless permission is given by the State Board of Charities and Public Welfare and a bond furnished to guarantee proper fulfilment of the requirements of Section 1 of this Act.

I am unable to see how the provisions of C. S. 2151 could be used to defeat the purpose of the two statutes above referred to.

SUBJECT: CELLS; APPROVAL OF PLANS; PROVISION FOR AIR SPACE IN CELLS

19 March, 1941.

Your first question relates as to whether, in my opinion, you should approve plans for a city or county jail which provide for a dark cell.

C. S. 1318 provides that the common jails of the several counties shall be provided with at least five separate and suitable apartments, one for the confinement of white male criminals; one for white female criminals; one for colored male criminals; one for colored female criminals; and one for other prisoners.

After these minimum requirements have been complied with, whether the remainder of the contents of the plans are approved by you is a matter to be determined by you under the rules and regulations laid down by the North Carolina State Board of Health. I am unable to find any provision in the regulations adopted by the State Board of Health which would allow the use of a dark cell in a county or city jail. On the contrary, I find a regulation which requires at least two square feet of window spacing or grating for each prisoner for ventilation and light, and that arrangement shall be made to give an equal distribution of light and ventilation over the whole jail. I cannot, therefore, recommend that you approve plans for a city or county jail which provides for a dark cell.

Your second question relates as to whether the removal of a bunk from a two-prisoner cell would meet the requirements for air space, when sufficient space would not be available if two prisoners were in the cell.

The regulations of the State Board of Health provides for at least five hundred cubic feet of air space for each person. This means that each two-prisoner cell shall have at least one thousand cubic feet of air space, and I do not believe that this method of attempting to meet the requirements would be feasible, as there would be nothing to prevent the authorities in charge of a jail from replacing the extra bunk in the cell immediately upon the departure of the inspector. The statutes, and the regulations adopted by the State Board of Health, are primarily for the benefit of persons who are confined in the county and city jails, and these statutes and regulations should be administered by your Department with this in view.

SUBJECT: ADOPTION LAWS; RECORDATION OF ADOPTION PROCEEDINGS

3 April, 1941.

You inquire as to what portion of the adoption proceedings should be recorded in the office of the Clerk of the Superior Court of the County in which the adoption is made.

Under the provisions of Chapter 243 of the Public Laws of 1935, it is necessary that all papers, except the report upon the condition and the antecedents of the child and consent of natural parents or guardian to the adoption, be recorded in the book or books in which other special proceedings are recorded in the office of the Clerk of the Superior Court in the County in which the adoption is made. This, of course, would include the petition, the interlocutory order and the final order.

SUBJECT: WELFARE LAWS; APPOINTMENT OF COUNTY SUPERINTENDENTS

23 April, 1941.

You inquire as to what course County Welfare Boards should take toward filling the office of County Superintendent of Welfare if the Merit System Council is unable to hold merit examinations and establish a merit system register prior to the expiration of the terms of the present Superintendents.

Under the provisions of Section 4 of Chapter 270 of the Public Laws of 1941, it is provided that on the first Monday in June, one thousand nine hundred and forty-one or as soon thereafter as practical the several County Welfare Boards shall appoint a Superintendent of Public Welfare of the County in accordance with the rules and regulations of the merit system plan adopted by the State Board of Charities and Public Welfare. This section further provides that in making the appointments a County Board may reappoint the Superintendent whose term expires on the 30th day of June, 1941 and who was serving as Superintendent prior to the first day of January, 1940, if such person is certified by the merit system supervisor as having passed the merit system examination on a qualifying basis; or, the Board may appoint any person who was employed by a County Welfare Department prior to January 1, 1940 and who has been promoted to the duties and responsibilities of Superintendent, if such person meets the minimum requirements of the position of Superintendent and shall be certified by the merit system supervisor as having passed the merit system examination; or, the County Board may appoint as Superintendent a person from an open, competitive, or promotional register as certified by the merit system supervisor.

I assume that at the time Chapter 270 of the Public Laws of 1941 was drafted it was thought that the State Board of Charities and Public Welfare would operate under a merit system plan of its own which would be in operation and the examinations given prior to July 1, 1941. The General Assembly, however, under the provisions of Chapter 378 of the Public Laws of 1941 set up a Merit System Council which will have jurisdiction over the employees of several Departments, including the State Board of Charities and Public Welfare. Unless the Merit System Council is able to conduct examinations, certify the results thereof, and prepare an open competitive or promotional register prior to July 1, 1941, it will be impossible for the various County Welfare Boards to elect Superintendents, as no one would be eligible for appointment under the provisions of Chapter 270.

I am, therefore, of the opinion that unless the Merit System Council has been able to take the steps above specified prior to July 1, 1941, the various County Welfare Boards should defer making the appointments until the Merit System Council has been able to complete the necessary portion of its work. Of course, action should be taken as early as possible, but until the Merit System Council is in a position to function, the County Welfare Boards can take no action.

SUBJECT: WELFARE LAWS; COMPENSATION OF MEMBERS OF COUNTY BOARDS

9 May, 1941.

You inquire as to what should be included in the provision for the reimbursement of members of County Welfare Boards for expenses incurred in attendance at official meetings.

It is my opinion that the only items which should be included in the reimbursement of County Welfare Board members for their expenses are transportation from the respective homes of the Board members to and from the place of meeting, together with reasonable subsistence while at the meeting place.

It will be noted that Section 3 of Chapter 270 of the Public Laws of 1941 provides that members of the County Board *may* be reimbursed for expenses incurred in attendance at official meetings. This would not make it mandatory on the governing bodies of the various counties to pay anything. Therefore, the governing bodies should use their good common sense in arriving at a just amount covering transportation and subsistence.

SUBJECT: ADOPTION LAWS; CHANGE OF NAME OF CHILD

10 June, 1941.

You inquire as to whether it is mandatory, under the provisions of Michie's N. C. Code of 1939, Chapter 2 as amended, for a person filing a petition for the adoption of a child to request that the child's name be changed.

Section 191(1) provides that any proper adult person or husband and wife jointly who have legal residence in North Carolina, may petition the Superior Court of the county in which he or they have legal residence or the county in which the child resides, or the county in which the child had legal residence when it became a public charge, or the county in which is located any agency or institution operating under the laws of this State having guardianship and custody of the child, *for leave to adopt a child and for a change of* the name of such child.

Section 197(7) provides in part that for proper cause shown the court may decree that the name of the child be changed to such name as may be prayed in the petition.

These two sections lead me to the conclusion that it was the intention of the Legislature to leave it in the discretion of the petitioner as to whether a change of name should be requested and that the court will be authorized, but not absolutely required, to change the name of the child sought to be adopted.

SUBJECT: MERIT SYSTEM COUNCIL; APPLICATION OF THE ACT

14 June, 1941.

In your letter of June 14 you inquire whether the Merit System council, established by Chapter 378 of the Public Laws of 1941, is a joint merit system established only for the agencies named in the Act, or whether it is an independent State agency as a State civil service organization.

The title to the Act is as follows:

> "An Act to Create a Merit System Council for Certain Departments and Agencies of the State of North Carolina."

In the preamble to the Act we find that it applies only to those agencies which are operated from funds derived both from State and Federal sources, and only the Unemployment Compensation Commission, the State Board of Health, the State Board of Charities and Public Welfare, and the State Commission for the Blind of this State come within the meaning of the Act, and they are specifically named as such therein.

In Section 1 of the Act the Governor of this State is authorized to appoint a Merit System Council which shall be charged with the "impartial selection of efficient government personnel for the State agencies referred to in the preamble to this Act." Running throughout the Act we find that it applies in specific terms only to the agencies named in the preamble to the Act, and to such agencies as may hereafter be charged with the administration of the social security laws in this State.

It is my opinion, reading the Act as a whole and specifically those portions referred to above, that the Merit System Council created thereby is not an independent agency established as a State-wide civil service organization, but is an independent Merit System created by the Legislature of this State only for the agencies named therein.

SUBJECT: WELFARE LAWS; ADOPTION PROCEEDINGS; UNAUTHORIZED PRACTICE OF THE LAW BY COUNTY WELFARE SUPERINTENDENTS OR EMPLOYEES

16 June, 1941.

You inquire as to whether C. S. 198, as amended by Chapter 177 of the Public Laws of 1941, applies to County Superintendents of Public Welfare and members of the staff of County Departments of Public Welfare.

C. S. 198 prior to the 1941 amendment was as follows:

> "No clerk of the superior or supreme court, nor deputy or assistant clerk of said courts, nor register of deeds, nor sheriff, nor justice of the peace, nor county commissioner shall practice law. Persons violating this provision shall be guilty of a misdemeanor and fined not less than two hundred dollars. This section shall not apply to confederate soldiers."

The 1941 amendment defined the phrase "practice law" but did not include any officers or persons other than those set out and enumerated in C. S. 198 prior to the amendment. Therefore, Section 198 as amended would not apply to the class of persons about which you inquire, and this particular section would not prohibit these persons from assisting in filling out forms in connection with adoption proceedings or proceedings for the separation of a child under six months of age from its mother.

However, I wish to call your attention to C. S. 199(a), which makes it unlawful for any corporation or any persons or association of persons except members of the Bar of the State of North Carolina admitted and licensed to practice as attorneys at law, to practice as an attorney or counsellor at law in any action or proceeding in any court in this State or before any judicial body or the North Carolina Industrial Commission or the Unemployment Compensation Commission; to maintain, conduct or defend the same except in his own behalf as a party thereto.

Under the provisions of this section I would not be justified in advising that County Superintendents of Public Welfare and members of the staff of County Departments of Public Welfare would be authorized to assist in filing petitions in adoption proceedings, as this type of work might be technically considered practicing law under the provisions of C. S. 199(a). The same rule would apply to proceedings under C. S. 4445 as to any legal papers which it would be necessary for the applicant to prepare and file in court.

What I have said above would not apply to any documents or papers which the statute requires that County Superintendents of Public Welfare prepare and file in court or any orders which the statute requires County Superintendents of Public Welfare to sign in any legal matters.

SUBJECT: MERIT SYSTEM COUNCIL; SELECTION OF COUNTY SUPERINTENDENT OF MECKLENBURG COUNTY

18 July, 1941.

The Social Security Board is correct in its assumption that the Superintendent of Mecklenburg County Public Welfare is selected and appointed in accordance with the rules and regulations of the Merit System Council. The mere fact that the appointive authority in Mecklenburg County consists of the Mecklenburg County Welfare Board and the Board of County Commissioners of the county does not have the effect of taking the method of selection of the superintendent away from the Merit System Council. The rules and regulations of the Merit System Council merely refer to the "appointing authority" and the fact that the Welfare Board and the County Commissioners of Mecklenburg County constitute this authority does not change the situation in any respect.

I advise also that all vacancies occurring in the board are filled by the "appointing authority," which, in the case of Mecklenburg County, consists of two boards and this fact is immaterial to this question. They have the same power to fill vacancies as they have to appoint, and these two boards acting jointly have the same duty in this regard as do county welfare boards in the other counties of the State.

SUBJECT: AID TO DEPENDENT CHILDREN; ELIGIBILITY OF CHILDREN OF FATHERS IN MILITARY SERVICE

18 July, 1941.

Receipt is acknowledged of your letter of July 15, in which you ask my opinion as to whether or not children of fathers in the military service may be eligible for Aid to Dependent Children under our Act.

The definition of "dependent child" in our Act, Section 35 of Chapter 288, Public Laws of 1937, as amended by Section 1 of Chapter 395, Public Laws of 1939, includes the requirement that the child "has been deprived of parental support or care by reason of the death, physical or mental incapacity, or continued absence from the home of a parent and who has no adequate means of support."

There is nothing in the statute which would exclude the application of such definition to a dependent child whose parent is in the military service of the United States. Therefore, it is my opinion that if the other conditions of the statute are met as to eligibility, a dependent child would not be deprived of the benefits of the Act on account of the fact that the parent's continued absence was due to military service.

SUBJECT: OLD AGE ASSISTANCE; INMATES OF PUBLIC AND/OR PRIVATE INSTITUTIONS; DEFINITION OF PUBLIC INSTITUTION

18 September, 1941.

I have your letter of September 17 with reference to persons receiving Old Age Assistance who are inmates of the Catherine Kennedy Home at Wilmington. You advise that this institution is now receiving $25 per month contribution from the City of Wilmington, and a like amount from New Hanover County, and inquire as to whether or not the receipt of these funds would change the status of the institution from a private one to a public institution.

I would assume that the $50 per month paid by the city and county represents only a small proportion of the cost of operating this institution. I do not believe that these contributions would change the character of this institution from a private to a public one within the purview of Section 6(d) of the Old Age Assistance Act, which makes ineligible for old age assistance an inmate of any public institution.

In the case of Hospital v. Guilford County, 218 N. C. 673, it was held that the Piedmont Hospital, while a nonprofit, benevolent and charitable corporation, was not a public hospital, as it was not supported, maintained and controlled by public authority. The Catherine Kennedy Home, from the information you give me, is not controlled by public authority, although it receives donations from the county and city. Therefore, in my opinion, it could not be properly classed as a public institution.

SUBJECT: ADOPTION PROCEEDING; MEDICAL EXAMINATION; BY WHOM MADE

16 January, 1942.

You inquire as to whether the medical examination made as a part of the investigation in an adoption proceeding may be made by a person other than one licensed to practice medicine or surgery in this State, and particularly whether such examination may be made by an osteopath.

Section 191(3) of Michie's N. C. Code of 1939, Annotated, provides:

> "Investigation of conditions and antecedents of child and of suitableness of foster home.—Upon the filing of a petition for the adoption of a minor child the court shall instruct the county superintendent of Public Welfare, or a duly authorized representative of a child-placing agency, licensed by the State Board of Charities and Public Welfare, to investigate the conditions and antecedents of the child for the purpose of ascertaining whether he is a proper subject for adoption, and to make appropriate inquiry to determine whether the proposed foster home is a suitable one for the child; or the court may instruct the superintendent of public welfare of one county to make an investigation of the conditions and antecedents of the child and the superintendent of public welfare of another county or counties to make any other part of the necessary investigation. The county superintendent or superintendents of public welfare or the duly authorized representative of such agency described hereinbefore shall make a written report of his or their findings, on a standard form supplied by the state board of charities and public welfare, for examination by the court of adoption."

Even though this section provides that the county superintendent of public welfare or the duly authorized representative of the child-placing agency shall make a written report of his or their findings on a standard form supplied by the State Board of Charities and Public Welfare for examination by the court of adoption, it makes no provision governing the competency of persons making the medical examination which forms a part of the investigation. Of course, one of the purposes of the investigation is to determine whether the child is a proper subject for adoption, and in determining this fact it is necessary and proper that a medical examination be made by a person who is competent not only of making the examination but also competent of reaching the proper conclusions based upon the examination.

The statute, Section 6700 of Michie's N. C. Code of 1939, Annotated, defines "Osteopathy" to be the science of healing without the use of drugs, as taught by the various colleges of osteopathy recognized by the North Carolina Osteopathic Society, Inc. Section 6706 provides that osteopathic physicians shall observe and be subject to all State and municipal regulations relating to the control of contagious diseases, the reporting and certifying of births and deaths, and all matters pertaining to public health, the same as physicians of other schools of medicine, and such reports shall be accepted by the officers or department to whom the same are made. Osteopaths are not authorized in this State to administer any treatments requiring the use of drugs.

If the medical examination required by the court before which the adoption proceeding is pending and by the investigating officer or agency is such as to require the use of drugs in any way, only a person who is licensed to practice medicine would be competent to make the medical report. On the other hand, if the examination does not require the use of drugs, and the court and the investigating officer or agency are satisfied with the report from an osteopath, I can see no reason why an osteopath would not be competent to make such report. It seems to me that in its final analysis the question is one of administrative procedure rather than a strict question of law.

SUBJECT: STATE PLAN FOR DISTRIBUTION OF SURPLUS COMMODITIES; WITHDRAWAL OF FUND FROM STATE TREASURY

13 March, 1942.

As requested by you, I have investigated the question as to the setting up of a State Fund to be used as a revolving fund, to be used in the purchase of stamps which would be redeemed by the Federal Government in accordance with the stamp plan for distribution of surplus commodities. In conference with you and Governor Broughton, I expressed the view that the only way I knew of by which this could be done would be by the allotment of the necessary amount from the Contingency and Emergency Fund by the Governor and the Council of State.

Our Constitution, Article XIV, Section 3, provides as follows: "No money shall be drawn from the Treasury but in consequence of appropriations made by law."

I understand that in other jurisdictions the view has been accepted that the money might be used from the State Treasury for the purpose of investing it in stamps inasmuch as the investment was not regarded as an expenditure, but would be represented either in stamps redeemable at par by the Federal Government or in cash. The language, however, of our Constitution, in my opinion, is broad enough to prevent any "withdrawal" of funds from the Treasury unless supported by and in accordance with an Act of the General Assembly.

In the event your Board decides to request the setting up of a State plan for surplus commodities distribution or a plan upon a State level, the proper course would be, in my opinion, to so recommend to the Governor and Council of State. The Governor and Council of State would have to decide whether they would provide the necessary money to create a revolving fund from the Contingency and Emergency Fund.

In conference with you and Governor Broughton, I expressed the opinion that under Section 3 of Chapter 436 of the Public Laws of 1937, the State Board of Charities and Public Welfare was authorized, under rules and regulations adopted by it, to provide for the distribution of surplus commodities, which would include the right to set up a State plan or a distribution upon a State level.

SUBJECT: DIVISION OF PUBLIC ASSISTANCE; AUTHORITY OF STATE BOARD TO ACCEPT FEDERAL FUNDS AND TO EXPEND THE SAME TO MEET ASSISTANCE NEEDS OF CIVILIANS AFFECTED BY ENEMY ACTION

25 March, 1942.

In your letter of March 24, you state that the Public Assistance Regional Representative of the Social Security Board has brought to your attention the following proposal:

> " 'Under the allocation of $5,000,000 to the Administrator of the Federal Security Agency by the President, from his emergency funds, on February 6, the Administrator has allocated to the Social Security Board, on March 23, funds to meet assistance needs of civilians affected by enemy action. The Social Security Board has delegated primary responsibility to the Bureau of Public Assistance for carrying out the purposes intended by this allocation.' "

You state further:

> "The immediate problem is that presented by shipwrecked persons landed on the coast of North Carolina from vessels attacked by the enemy. Miss FitzSimons, Regional Representative, has been requested to make arrangements immediately, under the authority described above, with the State Board of Charities and Public Welfare to provide necessary assistance directly or through local departments to meet the immediate needs of these persons.
>
> "One of the specific requirements with regard to these funds is that Federal funds advanced to the State agency should not be co-mingled with State monies but should be placed in a separate bank account. No restrictive provisions of State law applying to the expenditure of State funds should apply to the expenditures from Federal funds so advanced, the State agency to be free to act within the scope of the authorization and standards provided by the Board."

You inquire if the State Board has authority to receive and expend these funds in the manner set out above.

Section 3 of Chapter 436 of the Public Laws of 1937 is as follows:

> "The State Board of Charities and Public Welfare is hereby fully authorized and empowered to accept donations and gifts of any and all kinds of commodities, services or moneys which may be donated or given by the Federal or State Governments, or by any political subdivision of the State. Such donations shall be used exclusively by said board for relief purposes in this State, and said board is hereby fully authorized and empowered, under rules and regulations adopted by it, to provide for the distribution thereof."

It is my opinion that the above quoted statute is ample authority to proceed to receive and distribute such funds under rules and regulations and for the purpose and in the manner indicated above.

SUBJECT: STATE BOARD OF HEALTH; POWERS AND DUTIES

17 April, 1942.

Under C. S. 7050, the State Board of Health is required to take cognizance of the health interests of the people of the State, to make sanitary investigations and inquiries in respect to the people, employing experts when necessary, investigate the causes of diseases dangerous to the public health, especially epidemics, the sources of mortality, and the effect of location, employments, and conditions upon the public health. They are required to gather this information and distribute the same among the people, with the especial purpose of informing them about preventable diseases.

As to the water situation at the Mansfield Mills near Lumberton, I suggest that if the mill charges the people in the mill village for the water furnished, the State Laboratory of Hygiene would have supervision over this water supply and would be required to analyze the same, charge a tax to the mill, and require the mill to make periodic reports and transmit samples to the State Laboratory for examination.

It seems to me that as far as the State Board of Health is concerned, its only duty is to investigate these matters and if the conditions found are deleterious to the public health, the matters should be reported to the local Board of Health, which has authority under C. S. 7065, and following, to correct the situation.

C. S. 7065 places the immediate care and responsibility of the health interests of their county upon the County Board of Health. They are authorized to make rules and regulations, pay such fees and salaries, and impose such penalties as, in their judgment, may be necessary to protect and advance the public health. C. S. 7066 provides that a violation of rules and regulations so promulgated shall be a misdemeanor and punishable as there prescribed.

SUBJECT: CHILD WELFARE; SEPARATION OF CHILD UNDER SIX MONTHS OLD FROM MOTHER; COUNTY HEALTH OFFICERS; APPOINTMENT

16 May, 1942.

You desire to know how an infant under six months of age may be legally separated from the mother under the provisions of C. S. 4445, when a county does not have a county health officer.

C. S. 4445 makes it unlawful for any person to separate or aid in separating any child under six months old from its mother for the purpose of placing the child in a foster home or institution or with the intent to remove it from the State for such purposes unless consent in writing for such separation is obtained from the Clerk of the Superior Court and the county health officer of the county in which the mother resides or of the county in which the child was born. The section contains certain other provisions which are not necessarily involved in the question under consideration.

C. S. 7064 provides that the chairman of the board of county commissioners, the mayor of the county town and in county towns where there is no mayor the clerk of the superior court, and the county superintendent of schools shall meet on the first Monday in January in the odd years of the calendar and elect two physicians and one dentist who with themselves shall constitute the county board of health.

C. S. 7067 provides that the board of health shall meet on the second Monday of January in the odd years of the calendar and elect either a county physician or a county health officer whose tenure of service shall be terminable at the pleasure of the county board of health and who shall serve thereafter until the second Monday in January of the odd years of the calendar.

It is further provided that if the county board of health fails to elect a county physician or a county health officer within two calendar months of the time set for the election, the secretary of the State Board of Health shall appoint a registered physician of good standing in the county to the office of county physician, who shall serve for the remainder of the two years.

The Supreme Court of North Carolina, in the case of McCullers v. Commissioners, 158 N. C. 75, held that it is the true intent and meaning of the above statute to give the appointment to the State Secretary when the board of health for any reason permits the office to remain vacant for two calendar months from the date fixed by the statute for the election of county physician or county health officer. The Court further said that the public interest requires that this particular office shall have an incumbent to discharge its duties and that it was the intention of the General Assembly to prevent the office being unfilled for a longer period than the time named in the statute.

If there is no county health officer or county physician in the county referred to in your letter, it is the duty of the Secretary of the State Board of Health to make the appointment under the power and authority conferred upon him by the statute. If the provisions of the statute are followed, the question raised in your letter could not arise. It is to be assumed that the Legislature of North Carolina, in enacting C. S. 4445, contemplated that the provisions of C. S. 7067 would be complied with and that there would at all times be a clerk of the superior court and a county health officer in each county who could perform the duties required by the statute.

OPINIONS TO DEPARTMENT OF CONSERVATION AND DEVELOPMENT

SUBJECT: OWNER OF PRIVATE POND CHARGING FOR PRIVILEGE OF FISHING THEREIN

21 August, 1940.

I can see no legal objection to the practice of the owner of a private pond making a charge for the privilege of fishing therein, even though this charge is based on the number of pounds of fish which a person might catch. In my opinion, this could not be construed as a sale of the fish, but, on the other hand, is a basis for a charge for the privilege of fishing in such pond.

SUBJECT: GAME LAWS; USE OF DOGS WHILE HUNTING DOVES

19 September, 1940.

You inquire of this office if it is unlawful for a person to use dogs while hunting doves in season.

Under the provisions of Section 20 of Chapter 486 of the Public Laws of 1935, which is the title for the North Carolina Game Laws, will be found, on page 867 of the Act, that "a person may take game birds and wild animals during the open season therefor with the aid of dogs, unless specifically prohibited by this Act." I have examined the Act and find no provision therein which would prohibit the use of dogs while hunting doves.

As to the Federal law on this subject, I refer you to the United States Department of the Interior, Fish and Wildlife Service, Wildlife Circular 9, issued August, 1940. Here you will find in regulation 3 that migratory game birds (doves are classified as game birds, regulation 1) may be taken in the open season from land or water with the aid of dogs.

From the State Game Laws referred to above, there is no law which would prohibit the taking of doves with the use of a dog, and, unless the Federal regulation has been changed since the issuance of the circular referred to above, there is no Federal prohibition against such practice.

SUBJECT: GAME LAWS; RUNNING OF TRIALS AND TRAINING DOGS; PERIOD; NO SHOTGUNS USED OR GAME TAKEN DURING CLOSED SEASON

7 October, 1940.

I have examined Section 20 of Chapter 486 of the Public Laws of 1939 and I am of the opinion that a person could run trials and train dogs at any time during the year, provided that in conducting such trials or training no shotgun shall be used and no game birds or game animals taken during the closed season.

SUBJECT: CONSTITUTIONAL LAW; RULES AND REGULATIONS ISSUED BY ADMINISTRATIVE BOARDS

7 October, 1940.

In the case of State v. Dudley, 182 N. C. 822, our Supreme Court held that while the legislature may not delegate to a duly legalized administrative board power to make rules and regulations and prescribe the criminal punishment for their violation, it has the power to delegate to such board the power to establish the pertinent facts or conditions, upon the violation of which the statute itself imposes the punishment.

SUBJECT: GRANTS; NAVIGABLE WATERS; SEASHORE PROPERTY AND NON-TIDAL WATERS

1 November, 1940.

In response to your inquiry as to the effect of calls in a grant or deed for property on seashore or on non-navigable waters, I have examined our files with reference to opinions expressed on this subject.

On November 2, 1934, Attorney General Brummitt, in a letter to Mr. J. S. Holmes, State Forester, wrote as follows: "My impression is that Mr. Mish probably owns to the low watermark, unless there is something unusual about the boundary of the property in his grant or deed. State v. Eason, 114 N. C. 787." Mr. Holmes was inquiring about a boundary on Pamlico River, near Washington, North Carolina. His letter did not have reference to seashore property.

The case of State v. Eason, *supra,* contains the following language:

> "It follows, therefore, that a grant to a riparian proprietor, running with a navigable stream, such as the Pamlico River at Washington, from one designated point on its banks to another above or below on the same bank, must be so located as to extend, not *ad filum aquae,* but only to the low-water mark along the margin of the stream."

Under North Carolina statute, Code Section 7540, lands covered by navigable waters are not subject to grant. The question therefore arises whether a beach on the seashore which is flooded at high tide, but dry at low tide, is land lying under navigable water within the meaning of our statute forbidding entry on land lying under navigable water.

Our Supreme Court, in the case of Shepard's Point Land Company v. Atlantic Hotel, 132 N. C. 517, held as follows: The facts were that plaintiff owned lot No. 1, fronting on the ocean, and also grant No. 83, which extended from the ocean front of lot No. 1 to the deep water line. The plaintiff sold lot No. 1 to the defendant, who erected a hotel thereon. Certain appurtenances were constructed extending out over Grant 83, which grant was covered almost entirely by water at high tide, but which was partly exposed at low tide. Plaintiff brought action against defendant for possession of Grant 83. The Court held that Grant 83 to the plaintiff gave it an exclusive right or easement therein as riparian owners to erect wharves, etc., but held that when it conveyed lot No. 1, the abutting land, to the defendants, its easement passed as an appurtenance to lot No. 1.

This case, therefore, appears to hold that a grant for land below the high water mark on the seashore is valid only for wharfage purposes to the riparian owner. See, also, Atlantic and North Carolina Railroad Company v. Way, 169 N. C. 1, and this same case in 172 N. C. 774.

If the grant calls for the sea on beach property, or shoreline on inland tidal waters, it would appear from these decisions that our Court would hold that the grant does not extend beyond the high water mark. I must say, however, that the cases cited are not conclusive on this point, nor do I find any North Carolina decision which puts the question completely at rest.

SUBJECT: CURRITUCK COUNTY GAME LAW; PROSECUTION OF VIOLATORS

18 December, 1940.

You ask my opinion as to whose duty it is to prosecute criminally a licensed guide for unlawfully using a blind in the waters of Currituck County.

In Chapter 160, Public Laws of 1935, creating the Currituck Game Commission, it is provided in Section 19 as follows:

> "Sec. 19. The penalties for a violation of this act shall be as follows:
>
> "(a) The Game Commission upon approval of the Board of Conservation and Development may prosecute and/or revoke the license of anyone who has in its judgment violated any part of this act, or any of such rules and regulations as it may establish, but prior to such revocation, it shall notify the one charged with the violation to appear before the Commission on a given day at a given hour. The Game Commission may revoke the license of any person who violates any of the provisions of this act regulating hunting, or who, while hunting, shall go upon the marshes or lands of any person, firm or corporation without the permission of the owners."

The above quoted section outlines the procedure for prosecution, which I believe answers fully your question. If I can be of any further service, please advise me.

SUBJECT: NATIONAL DEFENSE; LEAVES OF ABSENCE OF STATE EMPLOYEES CALLED INTO FEDERAL SERVICE

11 April, 1941.

Under the provisions of Section 1 of Chapter 121 of the Public Laws of 1941, any elective or appointive State official may obtain leave of absence from his duties for military and naval service for such period of time as the Governor may designate. Such leave shall be obtained only upon application by the official, and with the consent of the Governor. It is further provided here that such official shall receive no salary during the period of leave. This period may be extended upon application to and with the approval of the Governor, if the reason for the original leave still exists, or it may be shortened if the reason unexpectedly terminates.

This is the only law upon the subject that I have been able to find.

SUBJECT: FISH AND FISHERIES; OYSTERS; C. S. 1905

5 May, 1941.

I have had before me for several days a copy of the contract which you enclosed in your letter of April 17, for consideration as to whether or not operations carried on under the terms of such a contract would violate the provisions of C. S. 1905, relating to the limitation upon the number of acres of oyster bottoms in which one person or a group of persons might be interested.

Under the terms of this lease, as I read it and from my conference with Mr. Johnson, President of the Cultivated Oyster Farms, Incorporated, it appears that under this scheme the Cultivated Oyster Farms would first lease from the State the maximum number of acres permitted it by the statute; that is to say, fifty acres. The corporation would then sell for a consideration this fifty acres in units to any person who might be interested. The person so purchasing these units would then lease from the State the number of acres of oyster bottoms which would conform to the number of units which he had purchased from the Cultivated Oyster Farms, and, under the terms of the contract, would turn over the entire supervision to the said corporation, not only the number of acres which he had leased from the State but also that represented by the number of units which he had purchased from the corporation.

Under the terms of the contract the Cultivated Oyster Farms would plant the oysters within the area leased, would cultivate them, patrol the area, harvest the crop of oysters and sell them, and out of the net proceeds from the sale of the entire acreage would pay to the persons who had purchased units an amount equal to ten cents per bushel upon such purchaser's pro rata share of the entire output from the total acreage, based upon the number of units which he had originally purchased from the corporation.

That portion of C. S. 1905 particularly in question provides as follows:

> "But no person, firm or corporation shall severally or collectively hold any interest in any lease or leases aggregating an area of greater than fifty acres. . ."

In my opinion, the operations proposed to be carried out under the lease contract submitted here for consideration would permit the Cultivated Oyster Farms to collectively hold an interest in more than fifty acres, which is the maximum permitted to be held by any person or by any association or collection of persons, and would not only violate the spirit of the law but the actual language employed. I conclude, therefore, that operations carried out under the terms of the lease presented here should not be permitted by your Department.

SUBJECT: COURTS—JUSTICE OF THE PEACE; JURISDICTION; C. S. 4310

22 May, 1941.

In your letter of May 17 you enclose memorandum from Mr. Floyd Jones, Acting District Forester, which raises the question as to the jurisdiction of a Justice of the Peace in cases arising under the provisions of C. S. 4310, as amended by Chapter 258 of the Public Laws of 1941.

A Justice of the Peace would not have jurisdiction to make a final disposition of a prosecution under the provisions of this section, as amended. Under the provisions of C. S. 1481 a Justice of the Peace only has exclusive original jurisdiction of assaults and batteries and affrays where no deadly weapon is used and no serious damage is done, and of all criminal matters arising in the county of the Justice of the Peace where the punishment prescribed by law does not exceed a fine of $50.00 or imprisonment for thirty days. C. S. 4310, as amended, provides that the offender upon conviction under the provisions of this section shall be fined or imprisoned in the discretion of the court. This would deprive the Justice of the Peace of jurisdiction to finally dispose of a case arising under this section.

When a case of this kind comes before a Justice of the Peace, it is the duty of the Justice to determine the question of whether or not there is probable cause and either bind the defendant to the proper court for disposition or dismiss the case for want of probable cause, as the facts may justify.

SUBJECT: GAME AND FISHING LAWS; AQUATIC PLANT FOOD

18 June, 1941.

I have your letter of June 17, wherein you state that a certain person in Currituck County is claiming ownership on certain bottoms of Currituck Sound which at one time may have been islands, but which are now and have for some time been entirely submerged by the waters of the Sound. You further state that this person is gathering and selling aquatic plant foods from these bottoms and has not secured a permit from you in order to gather this food and ship it out of the State, and you inquire if this is a violation of Chapter 135 of the Public Laws of 1935, as amended by Chapter 205 of the Public Laws of 1941.

Section 1 of the 1935 Act, as amended, provides that "the Director of the State Department of Conservation and Development shall have absolute control and authority over all the aquatic plant foods or other water fowl foods growing in the waters of North Carolina. None of the same shall be sold, transported or shipped from the State, except by permission in writing obtained from the Director of the State Department of Conservation and Development."

The second section of this Act provides that the violation of Section 1 thereof shall be a misdemeanor, and that a person convicted thereof shall be fined not less than $100 nor more than $500, or imprisoned not less than ninety days nor more than six months, or both such fine and imprisonment, in the discretion of the Court.

I advise that land entirely submerged by the waters of Currituck Sound are public waters and that no person should be permitted to take such plant food from these bottoms without first securing a permit from your Department, and that any person who does take such food without first having secured a permit, as in the above Act provided, would be guilty of a misdemeanor, and, upon conviction thereof, should be fined or imprisoned in the manner specified in the Act.

SUBJECT: EASEMENTS; HIGHWAYS; TELEPHONE LINES

30 October, 1941.

In your letter of October 29, you state that you have constructed a telephone line along a highway right-of-way over privately owned property, under an encroachment agreement with the Highway and Public Works Commission, but without securing an easement from the owner of the property; that now the owner of the property has demanded compensation for this encroachment upon his property, and you inquire if the fact that the Highway Commission has a right-of-way across this man's property would entitle your Department to construct a telephone line along this highway without first securing an easement from the owner of the property.

Our Supreme Court has held, in the case of Hildebrand v. Telephone Co., 219 N. C. 402 (1941), that a highway right-of-way and a right-of-way of a telephone company, although both are dedicated to public use, are distinct types of easements and the right to use land for the erection and maintenance of telephone poles and wires is not contemplated when land is required for highway purposes, and is not embraced in the easement acquired for this purpose, but constitutes an additional burden upon the land. This case also holds that the owner of land over which a highway is constructed has exclusive right to the soil, subject only to the right of travel by the public and the incidental right of keeping the highway in proper repair for public use, and that the State Highway Commission has no authority to grant a right-of-way to a telephone company as against the owner of the fee simple title to the land.

SUBJECT: FOREST FIRE PROTECTION; CRIMINAL LAW

16 December, 1941.

I note in your letter of December 16 that you have been advised by Judge Paul Edmundson of Goldsboro that in his opinion the use of the word "negligently" in Chapter 258 of the Public Laws of 1941, has the effect of nullifying the entire provisions of the law; and further, that Judge Edmundson is of the opinion that the enactment of the 1941 Act also has the effect of making ineffective the provisions of C. S. 4311(a), which is commonly referred to as the "brush burning permit law."

I have a very high regard for Judge Edmundson's opinion on any question of law, and I do not wish to cast any reflection upon his opinion on the question of law involved here; however, I wish to advance some reasons why I think the 1941 Act, referred to above, is a valid statute, and, further, that it does not repeal, modify or nullify the provisions of C. S. 4311(a).

The portion of the statute involved in this question is as follows:

> "If any person, firm or corporation shall wilfully or negligently set on fire, or cause to be set on fire, any woods. . . . It (this Act) shall not apply in the case of a landowner firing, or causing to be fired, his own open, non-wooded lands, or fields, in connection with farming or building operations at the time and in the manner now provided by law: . . ."

With regard to the validity of the statute, I do not think that the word "negligently" appearing therein has the effect of nullifying it or invalidating it, since there is no question but that this statute is aimed at criminal negligence on the part of any person who shall set fire to woods and fields, and that a person could be convicted under this statute of negligently doing so.

> " 'Criminal negligence,' as element of crime, is gross negligence or reckless disregard of consequences and of rights of others, and not mere failure to exercise ordinary care . . .

> "Where one is charged with a special duty, the non-performance of which involves danger to the safety of others, the failure to perform the duty, even through inattention, is gross and culpable, or, in other words, criminal negligence . . .
>
> "The same negligence, as it affects the individual and the state, is, respectively, 'gross negligence' and 'criminal' or 'culpable negligence'. Between criminal or culpable negligence and negligence merely there is no principle of discrimination. It differs only in degree . . .
>
> " 'Criminal negligence,' within Criminal Code, is reckless disregard of consequences or heedless indifference to rights and safety of others with reasonable foresight that injury would result, being more than ordinary negligence which would authorize recovery in civil action, the words being synonymous with 'culpable negligence'." Words and Phrases, Permanent Edition, Volume 10, page 521.

And again on page 522 of this volume, we find:

> " 'Criminal negligence' is negligence in such circumstances that it imposes an obligation remissible by the state but irremissible by the individual actually damnified by it, and it must be a substantial thing and not a mere casual inadvertence. Negligence is 'criminal' because it constitutes violation of obligations to state, differing from actionable negligence and culpable negligence only as to degree, the culpability of defendant being a fact question for the jury."

I am of the opinion that a person could be convicted and that such conviction could be upheld in the courts for a person who has violated the provisions of the above statute by wilfully or negligently setting fire to woods or fields in the manner and in those cases within the purview of C. S. 4310.

As to the question of whether or not the 1941 Act has the effect of nullifying and making ineffective the provisions of C. S. 4311(a), referred to as the "brush burning permit law," it is my opinion that the wording of the 1941 statute, that it "shall not apply in the case of a landowner firing, or causing to be fired, his own open, non-wooded lands . . . at the time and in the manner now provided by law," has direct reference to the provisions of C. S. 4311(a).

In this latter statute is set out certain times during the year during which areas of woodlands under the protection of the State Forest Service may be burned, "provided the person who desires to burn such lands has first secured a permit from the State Forester or his duly authorized agents, and it is reasonable to believe that the Legislature had this very statute in mind when the above quoted portion of the 1941 Act was placed therein.

Of course, you know any opinion rendered by this office is not binding upon the courts of this State, and the above is purely the advisory opinion of this office to your Department relating to the validity of certain of the criminal laws of the State, concerning forest fire protection work.

P. S.—The law set forth as to criminal negligence is to the same effect as to that which would be found in the case of State v. Agnew, 202 N. C. 755. The opinion in this case and in the cases cited therein differentiates between negligence in civil actions and that in criminal prosecutions.

SUBJECT: FOREST FIRE CONTROL; ACCEPTANCE OF GIFTS BY FORESTRY DIVISION FROM PRIVATE SOURCES

22 January, 1942.

In your letter of January 21, you inquire if the Department of Conservation and Development has any legal authority to accept funds from private corporations, which are to be used by you in the furtherance of fire prevention in the forests of this State, whether publicly or privately owned.

Consolidated Statutes 6122(bb) is in part as follows:

> "The Department of Conservation and Development through the Division of Forestry shall inaugurate the following policy and plan looking to the cooperation with private and public forest owners in this State in so far as funds may be available through legislative appropriation, gifts of money or land, or such cooperation with landowners and public agencies as may be available:
>
> "a. The extension of the forest fire prevention organization to all counties in the State needing such protection."

I think the above statute gives you authority to accept a gift of money to be used for forest fire protection, and that this money should be labeled as a gift from such corporation or private individual and should not be considered as part of the matched funds under the cooperative agreement referred to in your letter.

SUBJECT: FISH AND GAME LAWS; LICENSE TO FISH IN HIAWASSEE RIVER

10 April, 1942.

You inquire as to whether, in my opinion, the fact that the Tennessee Valley Authority has constructed a dam across the Hiawassee River in Cherokee County would prevent the application of Chapter 316 of the Public-Local Laws of 1933, as amended by Chapters 496 and 562 of said Public-Local Laws, as to fishing in the waters impounded by said dam.

Chapter 316 of the Public-Local Laws of 1933, as amended by Chapters 496 and 562, provides that it shall be lawful to fish with hook and line or trot line at any time in the Hiawassee River in Cherokee County, and that no license shall be charged therefor. A dam such as the one constructed by the Tennessee Valley Authority is merely an obstruction to the natural flow of the water of the Hiawassee River. To my mind, this would not be such a change as would authorize the collection of a county license for fishing in the waters impounded by the dam.

OPINIONS TO COMMISSIONER OF BANKS

SUBJECT: FIDUCIARIES; INVESTMENT IN FEDERAL SAVINGS AND LOAN ASSOCIATION CERTIFICATES

30 July, 1940.

You have asked this department to render an opinion on the question whether fiduciaries are authorized by law to invest money in their hands in the certificates of Federal Savings and Loan Associations.

By N. C. Code Ann. (Michie, 1939) Section 4018(b), Trustees, etc., are authorized to invest in the stock of any Federal Savings and Loan Association, upon approval of an officer of the Home Loan Bank at Winston-Salem, etc.

I am informed that the certificates referred to in your letter are what is known as share certificates. Federal Savings and Loan Associations are required to raise their capital only in the form of payments on such shares as are authorized by their charter. 12 U. S. C. A., Section 1464(b). The Secretary of the Treasury of the United States is authorized to subscribe for preferred shares in such associations. *Id.* Section 1464(g). The heading of such section refers to the shares as "preferred stock."

Federal Savings and Loan Associations are mutual organizations and the shareholders are contributors to the capital stock of the corporation. The word "shares" is usually deemed to refer to shares of stock. Black's Law Dictionary.

It is my opinion that the share certificates issued by Federal Savings and Loan Associations and evidencing a right to share in the profits of the association represent shares of stock and are proper investments for fiduciaries under Section 4018(b).

Banks investing its funds, other than trust funds, in Federal Savings and Loan shares would be limited in the amount of their investment by Section 220(c).

It is provided in Section 2492(27) that sinking funds may be invested in shares of a Federal Savings and Loan Association organized under the laws of the United States with its principal office in this State, provided that no such funds may be invested in the shares of a Federal Savings and Loan Association "unless and until authorized by an officer of the Federal Home Loan Bank at Winston-Salem."

This statute would permit sinking loan funds to be invested in the shares of a Federal Savings and Loan Association.

SUBJECT: NATIONAL BANKS; FIDUCIARY AND TRUST BUSINESS; LICENSE TAX

9 August, 1940.

This office has been asked for an opinion as to the liability of a national bank for the license tax required under Section 6377 of the North Carolina Code Annotated (Michie, 1939). Specific inquiry is made as to the Depositors National Bank of Durham, which has been granted full trust powers by the Federal Reserve Board, but which has heretofore handled only three trust matters, all of them comparatively small and producing little income for the Bank.

In 1931, the then Assistant Attorney General, A. A. F. Seawell, wrote an opinion in which he concluded that national banks doing a trust business are liable for the license tax imposed by Section 6377. I have found no authority which would compel the overruling of such a long settled and followed opinion of this office.

Under Section 6377, the license seems to be required before a bank can act in a fiduciary capacity without bond or execute any bond, obligation or undertaking. The statute, apparently, does not contemplate that a bank would have to be engaged in a series of trust transactions before it would be liable for the license tax. It would seem, therefore, that the fact that the national bank under discussion has only handled three trust matters would not affect its liability for the license fee.

SUBJECT: BANKS; LIMITATIONS ON INVESTMENTS—STOCK OF FEDERAL SAVINGS AND LOAN ASSOCIATIONS

10 August, 1940.

Senator J. L. Blythe has requested this office to render an opinion on the following question, which request was concurred in by you:

"Does the 20% limitation on investments and securities set down in Section 220(b) of the North Carolina Code Annotated (Michie, 1939) apply to the purchase of stock of a Federal Savings and Loan Association?"

A similar question is as to the application of Section 220(d).

In Section 220(d) the banks are limited in the amount of loans they may make to any one person, firm or corporation. It seems to me that the purchase of stock is not a loan and, hence, this section would have no application to the purchase of shares of a Federal Savings and Loan Association.

Section 220(b) provides that "The investment of any bonds or other interest-bearing securities of any firm, individual or corporation * * * * shall at no time be more than twenty per cent (20%) of the unimpaired capital and permanent surplus of any bank to an amount not in excess of $250,000; and not more than ten per cent (10%) of the unimpaired capital and permanent surplus in excess or $250,000":

It will be noticed that the limitation is limited to bonds or other *interest-bearing* securities. Interest is generally defined as the compensation allowed by law or fixed by the parties for the use or forbearance or detention of money. Black's Law Dictionary. On the other hand, the return on a stock investment is generally described as a dividend, which is defined by Black as "the share allotted to each of several persons entitled to share in a division of profits or property."

It would seem, then, that shares of a Federal Savings and Loan Association would not be an interest-bearing security within the meaning of Section 220(b). In reaching this conclusion, I am aware of the proviso to Section 220(b) which stipulates that nothing in the section shall be construed to compel any bank to surrender or dispose of any investment in the stock or bonds of a corporation owning lands or buildings occupied by such banks as its banking home if such stocks or bonds were lawfully acquired prior to the ratification of this Act.

This provision would seem to indicate that the Legislature considered stocks to be within the terms of the provision, but Section 220(c) contains an express limitation on the investment in stocks. Section 220(c) affords some ground for argument that Section 220(b) was not intended originally to apply to stocks.

SUBJECT: BANKS AND BANKING; REDUCTION IN CAPITAL STRUCTURE

2 October, 1940.

You state that there is an industrial bank organized with $50,000 capital and $5,000 surplus; that this bank has been very successful and the capital structure is now approximately $105,000, consisting of—

Capital stock	$50,000.00
Surplus	40,000.00
Undivided profits	14,662.11
Reserves	32,121.05

The management of this bank has reached the conclusion that the bank is over-capitalized and they would like to pay the stockholders a substantial dividend by reducing its surplus from $40,000 to $25,000, which is fifty per cent of the capital stock and the minimum required of a new bank. You inquire if the stockholders have authority to do this at a regular meeting, after proper notice, etc.

Under the definition section of the Banking Act, 221(a), "the term 'surplus' means a fund created pursuant to the provisions of this chapter by a bank from its net earnings or undivided profits, which, to the amount specified and by any additions thereto set part and designated as such, is not available for the payment of dividends and cannot be used for the payment of expenses or losses, so long as such bank has undivided profits."

C. S. 221(k) provides in part that the surplus of any bank doing business under the Act shall not be used for the purpose of paying expenses or losses until the credit to undivided profits has been exhausted, but any portion of such surplus may be divided into capital stock; provided, that such surplus shall not thereby be reduced below fifty per cent of the paid in capital of such bank having paid in capital stock of $15,000 or more.

Under the sections quoted, the bank would be required to first utilize the undivided profit account for the payment of dividends before it would be permitted to use any part of the surplus. After the undivided profits have been so applied, the bank, with the approval of the Commissioner of Banks, may be permitted to pay a dividend from its surplus, provided, of course, the surplus is not reduced below fifty per cent of the paid in capital in case of a bank having a paid in capital of $15,000 or more.

"Broadly speaking, the net profit or surplus of a corporation available for dividends includes what remains after deduction from the total gross assets of the corporation of all its capital liabilities and past and current operating expenses. In determining net or surplus profits, due allowance should be made for all applicable items such as depreciation, taxes, interest charges, and insurance premiums; and on the other hand surplus available for dividends may arise not only from operating profits but also from premiums realized on the sale of securities or other capital assets." 18 Corpus Juris Secundum, page 1100, paragraph 462.

Except as the right to declare dividends from surplus as to a bank is restricted by the North Carolina statute hereinbefore referred to, such dividends, in my opinion, may, with the approval of the banking authority, be paid therefrom, subject to the limitation above stated.

SUBJECT: INVESTMENTS; TRUST FUNDS; STOCK IN BUILDING AND LOAN ASSOCIATIONS

15 October, 1940.

Consolidated Statutes 4018(b) provides that "guardians, executors, administrators, Clerks of the Superior Courts and others acting in a fiduciary capacity may invest funds in their hands as such fiduciaries in stock of any building and loan association *organized and licensed under the laws of this State:* Provided, that no such funds may be so invested unless and until authorized by the Insurance Commissioner. Provided further, that such funds may be invested in stock of any Federal savings and loan association organized under the laws of the United States, upon approval of an officer of the Home Loan Bank at Winston-Salem, or such other governmental agency as may hereafter have supervision of such associations."

From the language of the above statute, I am of the opinion that such investments may not be made in shares of stock of any association which is not organized and licensed under the laws of this State.

SUBJECT: BANKS AND BANKING; LOANS BY TRUST DEPARTMENT; INTEREST

23 November, 1940.

Your letter of November 21, 1940, raises the question whether the trust department of a bank may make first mortgage loans at a rate of interest less than six per cent.

I am not aware of any law that would forbid the making of such loans at less than six per cent. It is provided by N. C. Code Ann. (Michie, 1939), Section 2308, that money lent by guardians shall bear compound interest for which the guardian shall account, but no rate of interest is specified. In Sections 4018-4019, regulating investment of trust funds by fiduciaries, no attempt is made to designate a rate of interest which such investments shall yield. Although the law fixes no minimum rate of interest to be required on loans by the trust departments of banks, and although in many cases a rate less than six per cent would often be justified, the bank should be diligent to secure the best possible return on an investment of trust funds, and for lack of diligence might be held liable for mismanagement of the trust estate.

SUBJECT: LIMITATION OF LOANS; DEFINITION OF COMMERCIAL PAPER

30 January, 1941.

I have your letter of January 29 attaching a copy of a letter from Mr. E. S. Booth, Vice-President of the Fidelity Bank of Durham, of January 28, in which he asks your advice as to whether the definition of commercial or business paper found in Code Section 220(k) is to be considered in connection with a limitation of loans provided by Section 220(d).

In my opinion, the term commercial or business paper used in Section 220(d) must be read in connection with the definition of this paper as set out in Section 220(k), and if the paper offered for discount has maturity at the time of discount in excess of ninety days, it would not be relieved of the limitation provided by Section 220(d). Both of these sections are from Chapter 4, Public Laws of 1921, as amended. Therefore, I am of the opinion that the limitation provided by Section 220(d) would apply to the character of paper offered for discount for instalment loans payable over a period running from two months to twenty-four months.

SUBJECT: DRAFTS; NOTIFICATION OF NONPAYMENT

25 February, 1941.

I have your letter of February 24, attaching a letter from Darby Banking Company asking your opinion as to the liability of a collecting bank for failure to wire nonpayment of a draft sent to such bank for collection.

This is in the nature of a private inquiry from this bank, which it would seem that this office should not attempt to answer. Any answer which you or I might give the bank would have no effect in deciding the question if it arose in litigation.

Our statute, C. S. 3119, requires that where a drawee to whom a bill is delivered for acceptance destroys the same or refuses within twenty-four hours after such delivery, or within such other period as the holder may allow, to return the bill accepted or nonaccepted to the holder, he will be deemed to have accepted the same.

RE: LICENSE TAXES; SECTION 148, INSTALLMENT DEALERS; SECTION 152, LOAN OR FINANCE COMPANIES; LIABILITY FOR BOTH TAXES

5 May, 1941.

I have your letter of May 1, 1941, asking for an opinion as to the questions raised by the enclosed letter from the American Discount Company.

The American Discount Company inquires whether it can make loans directly to home-owners under its present "finance company license" without securing a "loan license." I assume that the company has been licensed as an installment paper-dealer under Section 148 of the Revenue Act and wishes to know whether it can engage in the business of making direct loans without being liable for an additional tax under Section 152, which taxes persons, firms, and corporations engaged in the regular business of lending money.

This office has taken the position that a corporation which makes no direct loans but engages only in the business of discounting commercial paper is not liable for the tax imposed by Section 152. However, where direct loans are made, liability is incurred under Section 152. When the same corporation engages in the regular business of discounting paper and making direct loans, it is regarded as being engaged in two businesses, and it must obtain licenses under both sections.

Under these principles and the previous rulings of this office, I am, therefore, of the opinion that the American Discount Company would have to secure an additional license under Section 152 of the Revenue Act if it should engage in the business of making loans directly to home owners in this State.

SUBJECT: FOREIGN BANKS; RIGHT TO DO FIDUCIARY BUSINESS IN NORTH CAROLINA

4 September, 1941.

I have your letter of August 30, attaching a copy of a letter from Mr. William H. Beckerdite, Attorney at Law, of Kannapolis, N. C., under date of August 27, in which Mr. Beckerdite inquires as to the procedure necessary to qualify a foreign bank to occasionally engage in fiduciary business in this State.

Under date of March 7, 1940, the opinion was expressed in a letter to you from this office that our law does not permit a foreign banking corporation to operate a branch bank in this State. If the acts done by a foreign banking corporation amounted to doing business in this State, whether in a fiduciary capacity or as a banking corporation, I am inclined to think that there is no authority granted by our statute for such operation. I am inclined to the opinion that a foreign banking corporation would not have any authority to engage in or carry on any fiduciary business in this State and that our law does not give you any kind of supervision of foreign banking corporations.

SUBJECT: TEACHERS' AND STATE EMPLOYEES' RETIREMENT SYSTEM; MEMBERSHIP; EMPLOYEES ENGAGED IN BANK LIQUIDATION

17 September, 1941.

You inquire as to whether, in my opinion, persons employed under the provisions of Section 218(c) (16), Michie's N. C. Code of 1939, are entitled to membership in the Teachers' and State Employees' Retirement System.

The word "employee" is defined in the Retirement Act as meaning all full time employees, agents or officers of the State of North Carolina or of any of its *departments*, bureaus and institutions other than educational, whether such employees are elected, appointed or employed.

Section 218(c) (16) of Michie's N. C. Code of 1939 provides that the Commissioner of Banks, for the purpose of liquidating banks, shall employ agents, competent local attorneys, accountants and clerks as may be necessary to properly liquidate and distribute the assets of banks which are in liquidation under the provisions of the Banking Act, and shall fix the compensation for all such agents, attorneys, accountants and clerks and shall pay the same out of the funds derived from the liquidation of the assets of such banks.

From a consideration of the section of the Retirement Act defining the word "employee" and the section authorizing the Commissioner of Banks to employ personnel for the purpose of liquidation of such banks, I am of the opinion that the persons employed by you as Commissioner of Banks in the liquidation of banks, would be considered employees of a State department, and if they are employed on a full-time basis, I would consider that they come within the definition of the word "employee" as defined in the Retirement Act and would be entitled to membership in the Retirement System.

SUBJECT: LOANS; LIMITATIONS; NEW HANOVER ABC BOARD

7 October, 1941.

I have your letter of October 6, in which you enclosed a copy of a letter to you from Mr. D. M. Darden, Cashier, dated September 27, inquiring whether C. S. 220(d) provides a limitation which would be applicable to a loan to the New Hanover ABC Board.

The section referred to provides the limitation of loans made to other than a municipal corporation for money borrowed.

The New Hanover ABC Board was created by Chapter 418 of the Public Laws of 1935. Under this Act, the Board is not created as a municipal corporation, but is merely a public agency for the purposes set forth in the Act. I am, therefore, of the opinion that the limitation of loans provided by Section 220(d) would be applicable.

SUBJECT: BANKS; LIMITATION ON LOANS; EXCEPTION AS TO BILLS OF EXCHANGE DRAWN AGAINST EXISTING VALUES

13 October, 1941.

I have your letter of October 10 enclosing a letter from the Wilmington Savings and Trust Company. They advise that in the opinion of their attorney drafts drawn by a customer, payable at a future date for the price of cotton fixed by the drawee and secured by warehouse receipts for the cotton, are bills of exchange within the meaning of the exception provided by C. S. 220(d), providing a limitation on loans and excluding therefrom "the discount of bills of exchange drawn in good faith against actual existing values."

I agree with the Attorney for the Bank that the draft referred to would be a bill of exchange within the definition of C. S. 3108 and within the meaning and purpose of C. S. 220(d), and that the limitation provided as to loans would not be applicable to such paper.

SUBJECT: BANKS AND BANKING; CERTIFICATE OF DEPOSIT; LOANS AND INVESTMENTS BY BANKS

19 May, 1942.

In your letter of May 16, you inquire whether a North Carolina bank has the right to hold a certificate of deposit issued by another bank when the amount involved exceeds the limitations laid down by C. S. 220(b), 220(d), and 225(h).

Generally, a certificate of deposit is issued by a bank only when money is *deposited* with that bank, and, if the placing of the money with the bank amounts to a *deposit*, the transaction does not amount to an investment within the meaning of C. S. 220(b), nor to a loan within the meaning of C. S. 220(d), as to commercial banks, and C. S. 225(h), as to industrial banks. Those sections contemplate only loans and investments by a bank, and not deposits made by one bank in another. American Jurisprudence (7 Am. Jur. section 491) defines a certificate of deposit as follows:

> "A certificate of deposit ordinarily is defined as a written acknowledgment by a bank or banker of the receipt of a sum of money *on deposit* which the bank or banker promises to pay to the *depositor*, to the order of the *depositor*, or to some other person or to his order, whereby the relation of debtor and creditor between the bank and the *depositor* is created." (Italics mine.)

Also, the fact that money delivered to a bank draws interest, does not destroy its character as a deposit. 9 C. J. S. 40.

However, whether the delivery of money by one bank to another and the issuance of a certificate of deposit therefor by the receiving bank amounts to a deposit, a loan or an investment, depends upon the facts of the particular case. Schumacher v. Eastern Bank and Trust Co., 52 F. (2d) 925 (1931). In that case, the Court says, "Equity regards substance and not form, and is not bound by the names which parties may have given their transactions."

The distinction between a loan and a deposit as these words are used in common parlance is as follows:

> "A loan is primarily for the benefit of the bank; a deposit is primarily for the benefit of the depositor. A loan is not subject to check; a deposit ordinarily is. A loan usually arises from the necessities of the borrowing bank; a deposit, from the confidence of the depositor in its strength. A loan ordinarily is sought by the bank for its own purposes; a deposit is ordinarily made by the depositor for purposes of his own." Schumacher v. Eastern Bank and Trust Co., 52 F. (2d) 925 (1931).

Therefore, the only conclusion that can be reached on the facts stated is that while a certificate of deposit is ordinarily issued by a bank only when it receives money *on deposit*, it is quite possible that this instrument could be used in case of an investment or a loan by one bank to another and whether the transaction amounts to a loan, a deposit or an investment depends upon the facts of the particular case.

OPINIONS TO DIVISION OF PURCHASE AND CONTRACT

SUBJECT: OFFICE HOLDING; MEMBER OF BOARD OF AWARD AN EX OFFICIO DUTY

21 January, 1941.

You telephoned me, asking whether or not Senator Clark while serving as a Member of the State Senate would be disqualified under the double office holding restriction of our Constitution from serving as a member of the Board of Award in your Department.

Under Michie's Code, Section 7502(f), Subsection (a), the Advisory Budget Commission has the authority to adopt rules and regulations governing the designation of the Board of Award, composed of members of the Budget Commission, or other regular employees of the State or its institutions, who shall serve without added compensation, to act with the Director in canvassing bids and awarding contracts.

As a member of the Advisory Budget Commission, Senator Clark served in an *ex officio* capacity. Being designated by the Commission to serve on the Board of Award, in my opinion, would be merely an extension of his *ex officio* duties, and serving on that Board in that capacity would not constitute double office holding within the inhibition of our Constitution.

SUBJECT: DIVISION OF PURCHASE AND CONTRACT; PURCHASE OF TECHNICAL SUPPLIES AND INSTRUMENTS

31 March, 1941.

You inquire in your letter of March 28 if rabies vaccine, required to be purchased by the Department of Agriculture in accordance with Chapter 122 of the Public Laws of 1935, as amended, may be purchased by the Department from a specific source of supply rather than on the basis of public bids or quotations as required by the Act creating the Division of Purchase and Contract.

Under the provisions of C. S. 7502(h), certain purchases are excepted from the provisions of the Act. Here you will find that "unless otherwise ordered by the Director of Purchase and Contract with the approval of the Advisory Budget Commission, the purchase of supplies, materials and equipment through the Director of Purchase and Contract shall not be mandatory in the following cases: (a) technical instruments and supplies . . ."

In my opinion, rabies vaccine would come under the head of "technical supplies," and, unless otherwise ordered by the Director of Purchase and Contract under approval of the Advisory Budget Commission, such vaccine may be purchased from a specified source of supply rather than upon the basis of public bids or quotations.

Attention is also called to the fact that under the Rabies Inspection Act, such supplies are purchased by the Department of Agriculture for resale to the county rabies inspectors throughout the State.

SUBJECT: PURCHASE AND CONTRACT; PURCHASE OF SUPPLIES; DUTIES OF DIVISION

15 October, 1941.

In your letter of October 14, you inquire if the Department of Revenue may purchase from one of its employees, either through your Department or through its Commissioner or Assistant Commissioner, certain personal property consisting of office equipment situated in the office of a deputy collector and owned by him.

The duties of the Division of Purchase and Contract are set out in detail in Consolidated Statutes 7502(b), and following. Among other powers and authority of the Director is to canvass all sources of supply and to contract for the purchase of all supplies, materials, and equipment required by the State Government or any of its departments, institutions, or agencies under competitive bidding, in the manner there set forth. You will find also set out under these statutes the requirement that all contracts for the purchase of supplies and equipment made under the provisions of the article shall, wherever possible, be based on competitive bids and shall be awarded to the lowest responsible bidder, taking into consideration the quality of the articles to be supplied, and conformity with standard specifications which have been established and prescribed by the Division, etc.

There are certain exceptions to purchases of supplies and materials for the Department set out in C. S. 7502(h), where you will find that unless otherwise ordered by the Director of Purchase and Contract, the purchase of supplies, materials and equipment, through the Director of Purchase and Contract, shall not be mandatory, in the following instances: (a) Technical instruments and supplies and technical books and other printed matter on technical subjects; also manuscripts, maps, books, pamphlets and booklets for the use of the State Library or any other library of the State, supported in whole or in part by State funds. (b) Perishable articles, such as fresh vegetables, fresh fish, fresh meat, eggs and milk; provided, that no other article shall be considered perishable within the meaning of this clause, unless so classified by the Director of Purchase and Contract, with the approval of the Advisory Budget Commission.

You will also find under this statute that all purchases of articles there named made directly by the departments, institutions and agencies of the State Government shall, wherever possible, be based on at least three competitive bids.

I understand that your Department has adopted standard specifications and has already awarded contracts for equipment and supplies of the nature of the articles proposed to be purchased by the Department of Revenue from one of its employees. I do not think the Act gives you authority to proceed to purchase this equipment in the manner proposed by the Revenue Department.

SUBJECT: DIVISION OF PURCHASE AND CONTRACT; AWARDING BIDS; CHANGING CONTRACTS

23 March, 1942.

In your letter of March 19, you enclose copies of correspondence with Gray & Creech, Incorporated, with whom you have a contract for furnishing several grades of paper. This correspondence discloses that Gray & Creech will no longer be able to fill that grade of paper known as "Mirra" due to causes beyond their control, specifically a request from the War Production Board that this grade of paper be eliminated. You inquire if you have any authority to substitute in this contract a grade of paper which is slightly better and which is slightly more than you have been paying for the grade which is to be eliminated.

I do not think, under the provisions of the Act which created the Division of Purchase and Contract, that any change in this contract could be made. The only method I know by which substitute paper could be bought would be by requesting bids and awarding a contract under the terms of the law which created the Division.

You are familiar, however, with the provisions of C. S. 7502(i) which permits you, as Director of the Division of Purchase and Contract, to purchase equipment and supplies in cases where there is an emergency arising from any unforeseen cause as the present. This, however, would not permit you to change a contract which has already been signed. It would only authorize you to buy such supplies for any department or agency of the State where their individual need might require it.

SUBJECT: CONTRACT WITH GLASCOCK STOVE & MANUFACTURING COMPANY; RIGHT TO CHANGE THE PRICE FIXED BY CONTRACT

24 March, 1942.

I have your letter of March 17 attaching a letter from Glascock Stove & Manufacturing Company, in which they request to increase the price on stoves over the State contract price by reason of the conditions in the industry existing at this time, brought about by war conditions.

I have examined the statute controlling the action of your Board, and regret to state that I find nothing in it which would permit the Board by agreement to vary the prices fixed by contract, let after competitive bidding as required by this law. The only exceptions made in the statute are for emergency purchases, as provided in Code Section 7502(i). This section, however, would not authorize an agreed amendment to the contract changing the price at which the merchandise is to be sold.

SUBJECT: CONTRACT WITH STANDARD OIL COMPANY OF NEW JERSEY; RIGHT TO CHANGE THE PRICE FIXED BY CONTRACT

24 March, 1942.

I have your letter of March 17 attaching thereto copy of a letter dated March 11, 1942, from the Standard Oil Company of New Jersey. On account of the conditions set forth in the letter, the Standard Oil Company is requesting that they be permitted to substitute Esso, a higher grade gasoline, for Standard gasoline provided for in the contract at an increase of one-half cent per gallon.

I regret to state that upon an examination of the statute controlling the activities of your Board, I do not find any authority granted them by this law to change the prices fixed in the contracts let at competitive bidding. The only exception from the requirement as to competitive bidding is found in Code Section 7502(i), in which under certain emergency conditions, purchases are authorized to be made in the open market. This section, however, does not contemplate the amendment of a contract which has been made after public bidding.

OPINIONS TO STATE SCHOOL COMMISSION

SUBJECT: WORKMEN'S COMPENSATION ACT; SCHOOL TEACHERS; PARENT-TEACHERS MEETINGS

21 October, 1940.

There is nothing in the School Machinery Act, the general school law or in the handbook gotten out by the State Board of Education which would have the effect of requiring school teachers, as a part of their duties, to attend parent-teachers meetings. However, I am advised by Dr. Erwin that it is universally considered part of school teachers' duties.

Since there is no statutory provision affecting teachers in this regard, I am rather of the opinion that this is a matter which should be passed on by the Industrial Commission. To that end, I suggest that compensation be denied and that the school teacher who was injured while attending one of these meetings be given the necessary blanks in order that she might make application to the Industrial Commission for a hearing on the question.

SUBJECT: STATE SCHOOL COMMISSION; WHAT CONSTITUTES QUORUM

23 April, 1941.

Receipt is acknowledged of your letter of April 18 asking my opinion as to what constitutes a quorum of the State School Commission. You advise that due to resignations from the Commission, there are at the present only nine members.

The general law on the subject is stated by our Court in the case of Cotton Mills v. Commissioners, 108 N. C. 678, as follows:

> "The courts of this country have generally adopted the common-law principle, that if an act is to be done by an indefinite body, the law, resolution, or ordinance authorizing it to be done is valid if passed by a majority of those present *at a legal meeting*. 1 Dillon, sec. 277(215). Where the law creating a municipal corporation is silent on the subject, the majority of the officers or persons authorized to act constitute the legal body, and a majority of the members of the legally organized body can exercise the powers delegated to the municipality. 1 Dillon, sec. 278(216); Hieskell v. Baltimore, 65 Md., 125; Bomest v. Paterson, 48 N. J. L., 395. The same rules apply to other bodies, whether the two houses of the Legislature or other organized bodies of officers or persons to whom the Legislature has given authority."

We find in the statute no statement as to what will constitute a majority of the State School Commission and, therefore, the general rule stated in the above quotation would be applicable. Under the School Machinery Act, the State School Commission is composed of three *ex officio* members and one member from each Congressional District, which, as you advise, makes a total of either fourteen or fifteen, depending upon whether or not the Twelfth Congressional District is to be counted. In my opinion, it would take a majority of either fourteen or fifteen members to constitute a quorum on the Commission under the general rule above quoted.

SUBJECT: SCHOOL LAW; COMPENSATION FOR INJURIES TO SCHOOL CHILDREN

27 August, 1941.

You submit to me a letter from Mr. E. L. Gavin, Attorney at Law of Sanford, wherein he states as his opinion that, under the terms of Chapter 245 of the Public Laws of 1935, as amended by Chapter 267 of the Public Laws of 1939, in those cases where a school child who is injured or whose death results from injuries received while such child is riding on a school bus to and from the public schools of the State, the guardian or next of kin of such child is entitled to the full $600 provided in the Act. You inquire if this is a correct interpretation in those cases where death occurs as a result of such action.

Section 2 of Chapter 245 of the Public Laws of 1935 is as follows:

> "Sec. 2. The State School Commission is hereby authorized and directed to pay out of said sum provided for this purpose to the parent, guardian, executor or administrator of any such school child who may be injured and/or whose death results from injuries received while such child is riding on a school bus to and from the public schools of the State, medical, surgical, hospital, and funeral expenses incurred on account of such injuries and/or death of such child in an amount *not to exceed* the sum of $600."

In my opinion, the wording "not to exceed the sum of $600" limits the amount of compensation which may be paid in such cases to the actual expenses incurred in an amount up to and not exceeding the sum of $600.

OPINION TO COMMISSIONER OF VETERANS LOAN FUND

SUBJECT: MORTGAGES AND DEEDS OF TRUST; FORECLOSURE; EFFECT ON JUNIOR MORTGAGES

8 January, 1942.

You state that the World War Veterans Loan Fund, or the Commissioner thereof, owns a piece of property which was acquired by the foreclosure of a valid first mortgage, and that at the time of such foreclosure there were standing on record and unpaid certain junior mortgages or deeds of trust. You desire to know what, in my opinion, would be the effect on the junior mortgages or deeds of trust.

The foreclosure of a valid senior mortgage or deed of trust has the effect of cutting off junior liens or encumbrances unless the owner of the equity or redemption himself becomes the purchaser or there are other equities to preserve the junior liens.

The Supreme Court of North Carolina, in the case of Dunn v. Oettinger, 148 N. C. 276 (282), in discussing this question, said:

> "It is settled that a sale of property, pursuant to a power given in the mortgage, in the absence of fraud, is effectual to foreclose the equity of redemption of the mortgage. 'A sale under a mortgage or deed of trust, if valid and free from fraud or unfairness, will extinguish the equity of redemption in the mortgaged premises, leaving him no title or interest of any kind.' 27 Cyc., 1503. The sale also cuts out and extinguishes all liens, encumbrances and junior mortgages executed subsequent to the mortgage containing the power. Ib. This is clearly established by the decision in Paschall v. Harris, 74 N. C., 335."

Therefore, if the foreclosure sale under which you acquired title to the property about which you inquire was properly conducted and was valid in every respect, it is my opinion that the Commissioner of the World War Veterans Loan Fund acquired title to the property free and clear from any demands by the holders of junior mortgages or deeds of trust.

OPINIONS TO STATE COMMISSION FOR THE BLIND

SUBJECT: TAXATION; STATE-OWNED PROPERTY; EXEMPTION

5 August, 1940.

I have your letter of August 3, enclosing copy of a letter from Mr. J. Arthur Henderson, Tax Supervisor of Mecklenburg County, under date of July 22, in which you are advised that Mecklenburg County proposes to list and assess certain real estate owned by the North Carolina State Commission for the Blind, located in that county.

This property is exempt from taxation under Article V, Section 5, of the State Constitution, and by Section 600(1) of the Machinery Act of 1939, which provides in part as follows:

> "The following real property, and no other, shall be exempted from taxation: (1) Real property, if directly or indirectly owned by the United States or this State, however held, * * *."

There has been no decision of our Supreme Court which has held that such property as that referred to is subject to taxation. On the contrary, our Court has held that State-owned property is exempt from taxation, notwithstanding the character of use of such property. Town of Weaverville v. Hobbs, 212 N. C. 684.

I feel quite sure if you will write Mr. Henderson, sending him a copy of this letter, that Mecklenburg County will not insist upon the listing and assessing of this property for taxation. I enclose you an extra copy of this letter which you may send him, if you so desire.

SUBJECT: FREE PRIVILEGE LICENSES; TAXATION; SCHEDULE B; NEEDY BLIND; SALE OF BEER

10 August, 1940.

This office has formerly rendered an official opinion to the State Revenue Department that free privilege licenses may be issued to needy blind, which will entitle such person to sell beer and wine, upon compliance with the statute in this regard, Chapter 53 of the Public Laws of 1933, as amended.

SUBJECT: AID TO THE BLIND; LICENSING OF OPERATORS OF VENDING STANDS LOCATED ON PROPERTY OF STATE, COUNTIES AND MUNICIPALITIES

17 September, 1940.

Under the provisions of Ch. 123, Public Laws 1939, it is necessary that needy blind persons proposing to operate vending stands on property owned by the State of North Carolina or counties and municipalities located therein, secure a license from the North Carolina State Commission for the Blind before the State, county or municipal officials are authorized to permit the operation of vending stands by such needy blind persons in the public buildings or on the public property.

It is left to the discretion of the Commissions or officials having control and custody of the public property as to whether or not the vending stands proposed to be operated by the needy blind persons may be properly and satisfactorily operated without due interference with the use and needs of the property or premises for public purposes. It, therefore, becomes very important, in order that the proper benefits be realized under the provisions of this Act, that there be strict cooperation between the State Commission for the Blind and the Commissions and officials having charge of the public property. I am sure that it was the intention of the Legislature in providing for the licensing of operators of vending stands by needy blind persons on the public premises or property, to cause strict supervision of such operators by the State Commission for the Blind, which in turn would, in reality, mean supervision of the business itself.

SUBJECT: CONTRIBUTIONS TO THE STATE COMMISSION FOR THE BLIND

1 May, 1941.

Since July 1, 1935, the North Carolina State Commission for the Blind has, under authority of law, received contributions from various cities, counties, work shops, and other sources, to provide funds for Aid to the Needy Blind and other purposes, which contributions, when received, have been deposited to the credit of the Commission with the Treasurer of the State of North Carolina.

In my opinion, all such funds so received became, immediately upon deposit with the State Treasurer, State funds, to the same extent as if said funds had been provided by appropriation of the General Assembly. This opinion is in accordance with former opinions furnished by this office upon this and related subjects.

SUBJECT: MERIT SYSTEM COUNCIL; INDEPENDENT AGENCY

14 August, 1941.

I have your letter of August 13, wherein you state that the Social Security Board has requested an interpretation from this office of Chapter 322 of the Public Laws of 1941.

This Act specifically relates to Chapter 53 of the Public Laws of 1935, in that it provides an additional appropriation. However, no mention is made of the amendment to this Act by Chapter 124 of the Public Laws of 1937. The Social Security Board states that since no reference is made to the 1937 amendment in the 1941 Act, the appropriation under the 1941 Act will have to be kept separate and its identity continually maintained, and that the Federal Government will not match these funds.

There is no question in my mind but that the reference to Chapter 53 of the Public Laws of 1935 carries with it all amendments to this Act. Since an amendment becomes a part of the original statute, both are to be construed together as if they constituted one enactment. Crawford, Statutory Construction, Section 303. State v. Moon, 178 N. C. 715; Williamson Real Estate Co. v. Sasser, 179 N. C. 497. And an amended act is to be construed as if the original statute had been repealed, and a new amended act in the amended form had been adopted in its stead. 59 Corpus Juris, Section 647. It therefore follows that "a general reference in one statute to another antecedent one, naturally embraces also its amendments and additions, because all the provisions must be construed together as composing the act (reddenda singula singulis)." See United States v. Woolsey, 28 Fed. Cas. No. 16, 763.

SUBJECT: LEGAL SETTLEMENTS; CHANGE OF SETTLEMENT

24 January, 1942.

In your letter of January 21, you inquire as to the legal settlement of women in this State who are not divorced or legally separated from their husbands, and whose husbands have residence in other states. You also inquire as to the legal settlement of children whose parents are nonresidents of this State, such children now living in this State with their grandparents.

The law of legal settlements in this State is found in Consolidated Statutes 1342. Here you will find that a married woman "shall always follow and have the settlement of her husband, if he have any in the State; otherwise, her own at the time of her marriage, if she had any, shall not be lost or suspended by the marriage, but shall be that of her husband, till another is acquired by him, which shall then be the settlement of both."

From this statute, it is my opinion that this person is not legally settled in this State, but that she has and retains the settlement of her husband.

As to the child of parents who live in Virginia, but who now lives in this State with its grandmother, I advise that under the above statute, "legitimate children shall follow and have the settlement of their father, if he has any in this State, until they gain a settlement of their own; but if he has none, they shall, in like manner, follow and have the settlement of their mother, if she has any."

Since the parents of this child are still living, I do not think that the child could gain a settlement in this State simply by living with its grandmother.

SUBJECT: WORKSHOPS FOR THE BLIND; FAIR LABOR STANDARDS ACT OF 1938; EXEMPTION

19 February, 1942.

I have your letter of February 19, in which you advise me as follows:

"Under Section 5 of Chapter 53, Public Laws of 1935, the Commission is given power to establish and maintain workshops. Since this is the most feasible method of providing employment to the average blind person, five workshops have been established. It has always been the policy of the Commission to work with lay groups. As you know, our Board itself is composed of lay members who serve without compensation. Our Advisory Medical Committee which directs our medical work also serves without compensation and in every phase of our work we have interested lay groups.

"Our workshops are operated on the following basis: In all of the workshops we own the equipment. The foremen receive a salary from the Commission and are on the State pay roll. The Industrial Supervisor who relieves the foremen during vacation and who instructs them in industrial work and helps in apprenticing new workers is paid entirely by the State and

I also have supervision of these shops directly for the Commission. The Commission pays the room and board of workers during their apprenticeship period and from time to time has provided funds for raw materials, furnishing as much as $1,800 at one time to one of the shops. We buy the trucks which operate with State licenses. In the Charlotte Workshop, we own the land and the building. In Greensboro the City of Greensboro gives us a rent free building. In Durham, Winston-Salem and Asheville the cities did not have a usable building and the Lions Clubs of those respective towns are furnishing us a building.

"Just as all of our work has lay sponsorship, we have local citizen boards as sponsors of the workshops to help us sell the product made by the blind, furnish recreation for the blind workers, in some cases to provide raw materials and to help us in operating the shops on a business basis. These lay people, of course, serve without any compensation. When we were organizing these lay groups, the question of responsibility in case of suit came up and since these were citizens holding property and in some cases the sponsors are from Lions Clubs, they did not want to be sued jointly with the State in case a blind person was injured on the machinery or in case of an accident with the truck. We suggested that the local sponsors incorporate informally to exclude themselves and their group from any joint responsibility with the State. I am enclosing a sample incorporation from Charlotte."

You ask my opinion as to whether or not the workshops for the blind, operated as stated in your letter, are subject to the provisions of the Fair Labor Standards Act of 1938.

This Act provides in Section 3(d) as follows:

> "'Employer' includes any person acting directly or indirectly in the interest of an employer in relation to an employee but shall not include the United States or any State or political subdivision of a State, or any labor organization (other than when acting as an employer), or anyone acting in the capacity of officer or agent of such labor organization."

Section 5 of Chapter 53, Public Laws of 1935, provides as follows:

> "That the commission may establish one or more training schools and workshops for employment of suitable blind persons and shall be empowered to equip and maintain the same, to pay to employees suitable wages, and to devise means for the sale and distribution of the products thereof, and may coöperate with shops already established."

As part of its plan for securing local sponsorship and cooperation, the policy has been pursued of giving the workshops established in various cities the name of the sponsoring agency, but such workshop has continued to be maintained and its work carried on as an agency of the Commission. In all cases except one, a Lions Club of the city has sponsored the activity. On account of apprehension of the possibility of personal liability on the part of the members of the club, non-stock, non-profit corporations have been organized through which the Lions Club cooperates with the State Commission for the Blind in carrying on the activity.

Under the statement of facts made by you as to the method of operation and the character of work done in the various workshops for the blind, I am of the opinion that these workshops are in fact and law agencies of the State Commission for the Blind, which itself is a State agency. It follows from this that such workshops for the blind are State activities, authorized to be carried on by the State Commission for the Blind. It, therefore, is my opinion that these workshops are entitled to exemption under Section 3(d) of the Fair Labor Standards Act of 1938.

SUBJECT: PENSIONS; AID TO THE NEEDY BLIND; DATE OF PAYMENT OF BENEFIT

2 June, 1942.

In your letter of the first of June you state that checks to recipients for aid to the needy blind are prepared and mailed out of your office for the current month on or before the 15th of each month. You inquire if your Commission has authority to mail these checks for the current month on or before the 15th, and if the recipient dies after the 15th of the month after the check has been mailed to him, if the proceeds of this check could be used by the next of kin of such recipient or his or her administrator, or by the Clerk of Court, if paid to him, to defray burial expenses which have been incurred by such recipient during the month of his death.

In reply to the first question, I advise that under the statute, C. S. 5126(13), the State Commission for the Blind is authorized to "make all rules and regulations as may be necessary for carrying out the provisions of this Chapter, which rules and regulations shall be binding on the Boards of County Commissioners and all agencies charged with the duty of administering this Chapter." C. S. 5126(18) provides that "after an award to a blind person has been made by the Board of County Commissioners and approved by the North Carolina State Commission for the Blind, the North Carolina State Commission for the Blind shall thereafter pay to such person to whom such award is made the amount of said award in monthly payments, or in such manner and under such terms as the North Carolina State Commission for the Blind shall determine."

Under this latter section of your law, in my opinion the Commission has authority to determine when and in what manner actual payment of benefits under the Act may be made. That is to say, if the Commission has determined that payment of current monthly benefits should, for the best interests of the recipient, be paid on or before the 15th of the month, the latter Section of the statute above quoted authorizes it to do so.

As to the rights of a recipient to these benefits, I wish to refer you to my letter to you of 11 July, 1940. In those cases where a recipient dies after a check has been mailed to him, then it should be distributed by his personal representative or the Clerk of the Court, as the case may be, under the law in effect relating to disbursement of assets of a decedent's estate.

OPINIONS TO GREATER UNIVERSITY

SUBJECT: EDUCATION; GREATER UNIVERSITY; RESIDENCE

29 August, 1940.

You state that a young man has applied for admission to your institution as an in-state student, the facts being that his mother and father were separated when he was only a few years old and the mother was granted custody of the child; that she is now a resident of New Jersey; that the child was born in this State and the father is still living here and has always resided here, and that the child will, while he is in school in this State, reside with his father.

A minor child under our settlement laws remains and has the residence of his father, if living, C. S. 1342, and, under our State law, the father is responsible for the support and maintenance of his minor child, regardless of the fact that the mother and father have been legally separated.

I am of the opinion from the facts in this case that this applicant is entitled to register as an in-state student.

SUBJECT: THE UMSTEAD BILL; CHAPTER 122 PUBLIC LAWS OF 1939; SALE OF SOFT DRINKS, ETC., AT FOOTBALL GAMES

11 September, 1940.

I have your letter of September 10, wherein you suggest two methods by which self-help students at the University might be permitted to sell soft drinks, etc., at football games and other athletic contests, and inquire if either of these methods, if put into effect, would violate the provisions of Chapter 122 of the Public Laws of 1939.

You suggest, first, whether or not it would be permissible to organize a private corporation and permit this private corporation to handle the sale of refreshments at such athletic contests, using, of course, self-help students in this enterprise.

I see no legal objection to this plan, provided, of course, the University is not interested in the sale of such products on some profit-sharing basis. The prohibition contained in the Umstead Act is that units or agencies of the State Government, or any individual employee or employees of any such unit or agency, in his or her or their capacity as such employees, may not engage in the business of selling merchandise in competition with citizens of the State. Self-help students, however, acting as agents of the University in selling soft drinks and things of like nature, would be prohibited from doing so under the very terms of the Act.

You suggest, secondly, a sale of the franchise or "concession rights" by the Athletic Association to the highest bidder after public advertisement, requiring the purchaser of such rights to enter into a contract to employ only self-help students who have been recommended by the Self-Help Office of the University, the University also reserving in the granting of such privilege the right to prescribe the wages to be paid such students and requiring that all details of the business be conducted under the supervision of the University Athletic Department.

It appears to me that the requirement that "all details of the business be conducted under the supervision of the University Athletic Department" might be considered a little too broad in its meaning. It is possible that this language might have the effect of making the enterprise an agency of the University, thereby violating the terms of the Act, if the business is carried on in this manner. I think perhaps the Self-Help Office could designate the self-help students eligible for employment by the owner of such franchise and could, under contract with the owner, prescribe the wages to be paid such students for their services. Just how far the University could extend its supervision over the actual conduct of the sale of such merchandise without becoming actually interested in it, I am not prepared to say. However, great care should be taken that the spirit of the law as it is written would not be violated by such supervision. If your second suggestion is adopted, care should be exercised that the University be not interested in the sale of such merchandise on any profit-sharing basis.

SUBJECT: THE UMSTEAD BILL; CHAPTER 122, PUBLIC LAWS OF 1939; SALE OF SOFT DRINKS, ETC., AT FOOTBALL GAMES

13 September, 1940.

I have your letter of September 10, in which you state that the University wants to comply at all times with the spirit as well as the letter of the Umstead Bill, Chapter 122, Public Laws of 1939; but, on the other hand, you also wish to extend to Selp-Help students at the University all possible aid which they might receive by employment by some organization in the sale of soft drinks, etc., at athletic contests. You suggest two plans by which such aid might be extended to Self-Help students, and inquire of this office if either of these plans would violate the letter and spirit of the law above referred to.

You suggest first: "A Self-Help Students' Corporation, employing no University 'capital' or 'credit,' to operate the 'refreshment concessions'."

In order for a corporation of this nature to be organized, of course, it would require some capital to be advanced from some private source. The corporation would have to be organized with proper officers and directors, who could not, in my opinion, be in any manner connected with the University in the capacity of employees, officers or members of the faculty. The question would also arise as to distribution of shares of stock in such corporation; and if any profit were realized by the corporation in the enterprise, the question would then arise as to the distribution of dividends which might be earned. Then, of course, from a practical standpoint, a corporation organized by such students would, in my opinion, require supervision and control, at least in an advisory capacity, by some member of the faculty, officer or employee of the University. Such a plan would, in my opinion violate the spirit if not the actual letter of the law in this regard.

You suggest second: "The Athletic Association could sell the refreshment franchise to the highest bidder, after public advertisement, requiring the purchaser of such rights to agree to employ only Self-Help students of the University at prescribed wages. This would give our Self-Help students material benefits."

I see no objection to the second suggestion. Under this plan, neither the Athletic Association nor any agency or employee of the University would be involved in the sale of any article of merchandise in competition with private citizens of the State, which is the prohibition contained in the statute, but, on the contrary, would be the granting of the privilege to carry on such an enterprise to a private individual or corporation in this State.

RE: ESCHEATS

20 September, 1940.

Since the provisions of C. S. 962(c) require the Clerk of the Superior Court of every county of the State to require of any bank, wherein he may deposit money placed with him in trust, a corporate surety bond in an amount sufficient to protect such deposits, or in lieu thereof furnish bonds of the United States, North Carolina bonds or bonds of counties and municipalities which have been approved by the Sinking Fund Commission, I am of the opinion that the clerk who fails to do this would be liable on his own official bond, where such failure resulted in a loss of any such trust funds.

SUBJECT: UNIVERSITY OF NORTH CAROLINA; NAVAL RESERVE OFFICERS' TRAINING CORPS; BOND TO COVER ISSUE OF SUPPLIES, EQUIPMENT, ETC.

16 October, 1940.

You inquire if the University of North Carolina has legal authority to execute a bond to cover the issue of supplies, equipment, etc., by the United States Government for the use of the Naval Reserve Officers' Training Corps unit, which is to be established there, to guarantee the safekeeping of such property under the conditions set out in the bond.

The University of North Carolina is a corporation created under C. S. 5782, et seq. It has the power to bargain, sell, grant, alien or dispose of and convey any real or personal property which it may lawfully acquire, and it shall be able and capable in law to sue and be sued in all courts whatsoever and in general may do all such things as are usually done by bodies corporate and politic, or such as may be necessary for the promotion of learning and virtue.

I think, under these broad powers which the University has as a corporation, it has the authority to obligate itself in the manner above described for the purpose there referred to.

It seems to me that a statement from the Secretary of the Board of Trustees that the President of the University is authorized to execute this instrument, the Federal authorities should be satisfied with the execution of the same by Dr. Graham under such authority. At any rate, I would submit it to them in this form.

I return the letter of the Navy Department, along with the bond which has been executed by Dr. Graham on behalf of the University.

SUBJECT: TAXATION OF PROPERTY OWNED BY THE UNIVERSITY OF NORTH CAROLINA USED FOR RENTAL PURPOSES

22 May, 1941.

I have before me a letter to you from Mr. Neal Y. Pharr, Attorney at Law, of Charlotte, North Carolina, with reference to the taxation of property of the University by Mecklenburg County and the City of Charlotte. This letter raises the particular problem as to what the University will do with reference to the taxation of such property in the event it is listed for taxation.

As I have heretofore advised you, there has been no decision of our Court holding that the property of the University held under conditions here involved would be subject to taxation. I think the University would be thoroughly justified in contesting the liability of its property for taxation. There is nothing in recent decisions by our Supreme Court to indicate that State-owned property will be held liable for taxation. The Court has not overruled or questioned the decision in the Weaverville Case, and the recent decisions have not involved State-owned property.

The decisions in the case of Odd Fellows v. Swain and other recent cases involve the exemption of property under the part of Article V, Section 5, of the Constitution which permits the Legislature to exempt such property, but is not mandatory as it is as to property owned by the State and its subdivisions.

I see no reason from the recent decisions of the Supreme Court to think that the decision in the Weaverville Case will be overruled. The only change in the personnel of the Court since that time occurred by the death of Justice Connor. The vacancy caused by his death was filled by appointment of Justice Seawell. As shown by the strong dissenting opinion of Justice Seawell in the Warren County case and other decisions involving this question, the majority of the Court would remain as it was at the time the Weaverville Case was decided.

Under our Constitution, Article V, Section 5, it is provided: "Property belonging to the State or to municipal corporations shall be exempt from taxation."

Justice Connor said in the Weaverville Case: "There is no ambiguity in this language. Its meaning is plain. The language is clear and not subject to judicial construction in order that the policy with respect to taxation in conflict with its provision may be sustained. Property belonging to the State is exempt from taxation because of its ownership, without regard to the purpose for which it was acquired or for which it is owned by the State."

Under this decision, the only question would be whether or not property owned by the University is property belonging to the State. Property belonging to the University is property of the State, in my opinion, to the same extent that property belonging to the World War Veterans Loan Fund involved in the Weaverville Case was considered as State property.

In 2 Cooley, Taxation, (4th ed. 1924), p. 1322, it is stated that: "Public property not subject to taxation unless otherwise provided includes property owned by a state institution but which is in fact and equitably the property of the State. Public property belonging to the State, which is not taxable, include the property of all public departments or institutions of the State supported by taxation or public funds."

In Board of Regents v. Hamilton, 28 Kansas 376, the question presented was whether real property belonging to the Kansas State Agricultural College could be taxed by a county. The property had been acquired by foreclosure of a mortgage given to the college to secure a loan of college funds. After foreclosure the property had been leased and the rent appropriated to the use of the college. Under a Kansas statute all property "belonging exclusively to this State or to the United States" was exempted from taxation. It was held that, although title to the property was taken in the name of the college, it was, nevertheless, state property and exempted, the college being a state institution.

To the same effect is Aplin v. Regents of the University of Michigan, 83 Mich. 467, 47 N. W. 440, where it was held that property owned by the regents of the University in their corporate capacity was State property and exempted from taxation under a statute exempting all public property belonging to the State. The Court said at p. 470 of the official report: "The public property belonging to the State includes the property of all public departments of the State; such as the Michigan University, the Reform School, the School for the Deaf and Dumb, the State Prison, the Asylums, the Agricultural College, the State Normal School, and other public institutions supported by the State through taxation or by funds or property appropriated by public or private generosity for that purpose.".

There is no conflict in this conclusion with what was said by our Court in Odd Fellows v. Swain, 217 N. C. 632. In that case and the subsequent cases of Hospital v. Guilford County, 218 N. C. 673, Harrison v. Guilford County, 218 N. C. 718, Rockingham v. Elon College, 219 N. C. 342, and Guilford College v. Guilford County, 219 N. C. 347, property was involved, the exemption of which is dependent upon the clause in Article V, Section 5, of the Constitution, which reads as follows: "The General Assembly may exempt * * * property held for educational, scientific, literary, charitable, or religious purposes * * *." The majority of the Court in these cases rested their opinion upon that part of the language of the Constitution as follows: "held for educational, * * * purposes." The language as to State-owned property is entirely different—"Property belonging to the State." Resting its decision upon the words "held for educational, scientific, literary, charitable, or religious purposes," the Court held that property belonging to these institutions which was used commercially and not directly employed for educational, scientific, literary, charitable, or religious purposes, but only indirectly by use of the returns therefrom, was subject to taxation. It is entirely clear that the decisions in this line of cases would be rested upon entirely different constitutional language from that involved in the determination of the exemption of State-owned property.

Without discussing the matter in further detail, I am of the opinion that State-owned property, which includes property owned by State institutions, is exempt from ad valorem taxation by our counties and cities.

Recognizing the validity of this position, our Machinery Act, Section 600, provides that real property shall be exempted from taxation if directly or indirectly owned by the United States or this State, however held. There is no authority in the Machinery Act for any county or city to place on the tax books property which under the Machinery Act is exempt from taxation and, therefore, it is my further opinion that any attempt to list such property in violation of the provisions of the Constitution, as well as the Machinery Act, by a county or city would be unauthorized and illegal.

SUBJECT: TAXATION—SCHEDULE "B"; 1c STAMP TAX ON LAUNDRIES

1 July, 1941.

In your letter of the 28th you ask whether or not the linen sent by the University Cafeteria to the Raleigh Linen Supply Company is subject to the one cent stamp tax lexied on laundries by Section 150 of the Revenue Act.

The answer to this question was foreshadowed in my letter to you of May 30, 1940, in which I advised you that the Carolina Inn, operated by the University, was subject to Schedule "B" license taxes. As pointed out in that letter, there is no exemption in the Revenue Act of Schedule "B" taxes and it would seem that, upon the principles set out in my former letter, the University must pay the stamp tax under Section 150.

SUBJECT: TEACHERS' AND STATE EMPLOYEES' RETIREMENT SYSTEM; EMPLOYEES OF EDUCATIONAL INSTITUTIONS; MEMBERSHIP IN SYSTEM

22 July, 1941.

In your letter of July 11, supplemented by your letter of July 17, you present the case of Dr. A. C. Campbell, who is employed as College physician for the North Carolina State College of Agriculture and Engineering of the University of North Carolina, and you desire to know whether Dr. Campbell is eligible to participate in the Teachers' and State Employees' Retirement System.

Under the provisions of Subsection 3 of Section 1 of the Retirement Act, the word "teacher" is defined as meaning any teacher, helping teacher, librarian, principal, supervisor, superintendent of public schools . . . or any *full-time* employee in any educational institution supported by and under the control of the State. In addition to the definition of the word "teacher," this subsection contains the following language:

> "In all cases of doubt, the board of trustees, hereinafter defined, shall determine whether any person is a teacher as defined in this Act."

For the purpose of determining the question of membership in the Retirement System, various groups are included in the definition of the word "teacher" and all the employees of the University of North Carolina are included. Only full-time employees of the University of North Carolina are entitled to participate in the Retirement System. After thoroughly considering all the facts contained in your letters relative to Dr. Campbell, I am unable to see how he could be considered as a full-time employee of the University of North Carolina. However, it is possible that the Board of Trustees of the Retirement System would have the right, under the portion of Subsection 3 of Section 1 above quoted, to determine the status of Dr. Campbell relative to his participation in the Retirement System, and I would recommend that his case be submitted to the Board of Trustees for its consideration.

SUBJECT: N. C. FORESTRY FOUNDATION; SALE OF TIMBER BY; REGULATION, BY STATE AGENCY

29 November, 1941.

I understand that the Williams & McKeithan Lumber Company proposes to enter into an arrangement with the North Carolina Forestry Foundation, Inc., which owns in fee simple about 80,000 acres of timber lands in Jones and Onslow Counties, whereby it proposes to purchase from the Foundation several million feet of standing timber, to be cut and removed in a period of three years, and to acquire from the Foundation an option to make similar purchases periodically in future thereafter, until this Company has acquired, cut, and removed all the merchantable timber standing upon this tract.

You now ask for an opinion upon the question whether there exists in the State of North Carolina, or any department or bureau or political subdivision thereof, the right to supervise, regulate or control the commercial activities of this Foundation which would constitute a limitation upon the right of the Foundation to enter into the proposed arrangement or to carry it out according to its terms, to the same extent and in the same manner as if the Foundation, to all intents and purposes, is a private corporation.

From my knowledge of the charter and by-laws of the Foundation and its methods of operation, I am of the opinion that the Foundation is authorized by law to enter into this arrangement and to carry out the same in all details, free from and public supervision, regulation or control, and to all intents and purposes as if the said Foundation were a private corporation unaffected with the public interest, and doing business solely for its own account and private gain.

I am further of the opinion that if the Foundation should request the North Carolina Utilities Commission to approve the proposed agreement, the Commission would decline to take jurisdiction of such a petition upon the ground that the Foundation is not affected with the public interest or subject to public control.

OPINIONS TO RETIREMENT SYSTEM

SUBJECT: RETIREMENT SYSTEM; MEMBERS ENTITLED TO CREDIT FOR PRIOR SERVICE

28 May, 1941.

You request my opinion as to the proper interpretation of Section 4 of the Teachers' and State Employees' Retirement Act, relative to the requirements to make a member eligible to receive credit for service rendered prior to the establishmnt of the Retirement System.

Subsection (1) of Section 4 provides:

> "Under such rules and regulations as the board of trustees shall adopt each member who was a teacher or State employee at any time during the year immediately preceding the establishment of the System and who becomes a member during the first year of operation of the Retirement System, shall file a detailed statement of all North Carolina service as a teacher or State employee rendered by him prior to the date of establishment for which he claims credit."

Under the above quoted subsection and the other subsections of Section 4, the board of trustees is given considerable latitude on the question of determining the status of a member in so far as it relates to prior service, but there are certain statutory requirements to be met before the board of trustees would be entitled to consider the claim of a member on account of such service. It is my opinion that before a member is entitled to claim credit on account of prior service, he or she must have (1) been a teacher or State employee at some time during the year immediately preceding July 1, 1941, the date of the establishment of the Retirement System, and (2) become a member of the Retirement System during the first year of its operation.

This construction would allow persons who have rendered service in the past to qualify for prior service credit under requirements that can be met by a majority of the persons who should be given consideration on account of having rendered service prior to the establishment of the System.

There is merit in the argument that it was the intention of the Legislature in enacting Subsection (1) of Section 4 to set up two classes of persons who would be entitled to credit for prior service. In order to give this argument the proper foundation, it seems to me to be necessary that the word "and" in line 4 of Subsection (1) be construed as meaning the word "or." The popular use of "or" and "and" is so loose and so frequently inaccurate, that it has infected statutory enactments. While they are not treated as interchangeable and should be followed when their accurate reading does not render the sense dubious, their strict meaning is more readily departed from than that of other words, and one read in place of the other in deference to the meaning of the context. The general rule is that the word "and" in the statute may be read "or" whenever the change is necessary to give the statute sense and effect, or to harmonize its different parts, or to carry out the evident intention of the Legislature. This rule is based on the assumption that the Legislature could not have intended to produce an absurd or unreasonable result or to express itself in terms which would defeat the very objects of the enactment; and consequently when such effects would follow the literal construction of the statute the rule may be resorted to on the theory that the word to be corrected was inserted by inadvertence or clerical error.

I am unable to see how I would be justified in saying that the above rule should be resorted to in construing the section under consideration. It is entirely possible that such a construction would allow persons to claim credit for prior service who were not in the minds of the Legislature as being eligible to receive such benefits. To follow a literal construction of this section would not produce, in my opinion, any absurd or unreasonable result, neither would it tend to defeat the objects of the enactment.

It is, therefore, my opinion that the conclusion above reached is the most logical one, taking into consideration the Retirement Act as a whole.

SUBJECT: TEACHERS' AND STATE EMPLOYEES' RETIREMENT SYSTEM; EMPLOYER'S CONTRIBUTIONS; PAYMENT OUT OF UNEMPLOYMENT COMPENSATION ADMINISTRATION FUND COVERING EMPLOYEES OF UNEMPLOYMENT COMPENSATION COMMISSION

16 June, 1941.

You inquire as to whether, in my opinion, payments to cover employer's contributions for employees of the Unemployment Compensation Commission may be made from the Unemployment Compensation Administration Fund.

I am of the opinion that such payments may lawfully be made under the statutes of the State of North Carolina. The Teachers' and State Employees' Retirement Act covers the employees of the Unemployment Compensation Commission. The Retirement Act requires that the Board of Trustees created under the provisions of the Act shall annually prepare and certify to the Budget Bureau a statement of the total amount necessary for the ensuing fiscal year to be paid to the pension accumulation fund and this amount is in reality the employer's contributions. Section 15½ of Chapter 107 of the Public Laws of 1941 provides:

> "The Director of the Budget is authorized, empowered and directed to allocate out of the highway and public works fund, the agricultural fund, and other special operating funds employing personnel, the amount sufficient to meet the contributions necessary to be made in order to comply with the Act creating the State Teachers' and State Employees' Retirement System."

Under the provisions of the Unemployment Compensation Act, as amended by Chapter 108 of the Public Laws of 1941, all moneys in the administration fund which are received from the Federal Government or any agency thereof or which are appropriated by the State of North Carolina must be expended solely for the purposes and in the amounts found necessary by the Social Security Board for *the proper and efficient administration of the Act*. It is further provided that all moneys in this fund shall be deposited, administered and disbursed in the same manner and under the same conditions and requirements as is provided by law for *other special funds* in the State Treasury.

The Unemployment Compensation Administration Fund to my mind is certainly a special operating fund within the meaning of Section 15½ of the Public Laws of 1941 (Chapter 107), and if this is true, the Director of the Budget has the power and authority to allocate out of the fund a sufficient amount to meet the employer's contributions to the Retirement System covering the employees who are employed under the provisions of the Unemployment Compensation Act.

It is the purpose of the Retirement Act to provide a certain amount of security in old age for all State employees and to promote efficiency in all State departments and institutions. It seems to me that it would aid in the proper and efficient administration of the Unemployment Compensation Act for the employees to have the protection provided by the Teachers' and State Employees' Retirement Act.

I can see no reason why the employer's contributions to the Retirement System for the employees of the Unemployment Compensation Commission may not, under the State Law, be paid from the unemployment compensation administration fund.

SUBJECT: TEACHERS' AND STATE EMPLOYEES' RETIREMENT SYSTEM; EMPLOYEE'S CONTRIBUTION; DEDUCTIONS FROM SALARIES OF MEMBERS AFTER SUCH MEMBERS REACH THE AGE OF SIXTY

27 June, 1941.

You inquire as to whether, under the Teachers' and State Employees' Retirement Act, deductions should be made from salaries of members of the System who have attained the age of sixty years.

In undertaking to answer this question, it is necessary to look first to the provisions of the Act itself in order to ascertain whether there is any language contained therein which would tend to settle the question.

In Subsection 1(a) of Section 8 of the Act the following language is found:

> "Each employer shall cause to be deducted from the salary of each member on each and every payroll of such employer for each and every payroll period four per centum of his earnable compensation."

There is no limitation as to age contained in the provision above referred to and the clear inference seems to be that deductions from the compensation of members will continue so long as membership in the System is retained, regardless of the age of such members.

Subsection 2 of Section 5 provides:

> "Upon retirement from service a member shall receive a service retirement allowance which shall consist of:
>
> (a) An annuity which shall be the actuarial equivalent of his accumulated contributions at the time of his retirement, and
>
> (b) A pension equal to the annuity allowable at age of sixty years computed on the basis of contributions made prior to the attainment of age sixty; and
>
> (c) If he has a prior service certificate in full force and effect, an additional pension which shall be equal to the annuity which would have been provided at the age of sixty years by twice the contributions which he would have made during such prior service had the system been in operation and he contributed thereunder."

Considering the language used in this subsection, it clearly appears that the contribution of the employer stops when the member reaches the age of sixty, but as the service retirement allowance is based in part on an annuity, which is the actuarial equivalent of the accumulated contributions of the member—not at the age of sixty, but at the time of retirement—it is difficult to see any justification for saying that the member's contribution stops at the same time as that of the employer. Considerable argument could be advanced that the Legislature in setting up the Retirement System did not intend to engage in the insurance business, as such, and that the member's contribution should end at the same time as that of the employer.

Of course, the object of all interpretation and construction of statutes is to ascertain the meaning and intention of the Legislature. This meaning and intention must be sought first of all in the language of the statute itself, for it must be presumed that the means employed by the Legislature to express its will are adequate to the purpose and do express that will correctly. A statute must be interpreted literally if the language used is plain and free from ambiguity. This is true even though the court should be convinced that some other meaning was really intended by the law-making power and even though the literal interpretation should defeat the very purpose of the enactment. The explicit declaration of the Legislature is the law.

I am unable to find any language in the Retirement Act which, to my mind, would justify me in concluding that a member of the System should cease to contribute at age sixty if the member continues in service. I am, therefore, of the opinion that deductions should be made from salaries of members of the Retirement System so long as such members continue in active service.

SUBJECT: TEACHERS' AND STATE EMPLOYEES' RETIREMENT SYSTEM; MEMBERSHIP; WITHDRAWAL PRIOR TO JANUARY 1, 1942

1 July, 1941.

You inquire as to whether, in my opinion, a person who was a teacher or State employee on February 17, 1941, or who became a teacher or State employee on or before July 1, 1941, can notify the Board of Trustees of the Retirement System in writing on or before the first payroll period in July that he or she does not wish to become a member, and then any time prior to January 1, 1942 withdraw the notification of withdrawal and continue as a member.

Two groups of persons constitute the membership of the Teachers' and State Employees' Retirement System: (1) All persons who become teachers or State Employees after July 1, 1941; (2) All persons who were teachers or State employees on February 17, 1941 or who became teachers or State employees on or before July 1, 1941, except those who notify the Board of Trustees in writing on or before January 1, 1942 that they do not choose to become members of the Retirement System. The first group become members of the System by operation of the law at the time they become teachers or State employees, and have no right to withdraw from the System so long as they remain in the service. The persons constituting the second group are made members of the System by operation of the law unless they notify the Board of Trustees in writing on or before January 1, 1942 that they do not choose to become members of the System, in which event they would be entitled to have returned to them any amounts deducted from their salaries prior to the time the notification is filed with the Board of Trustees.

It will be noted that the Legislature in making provision for withdrawal from the System by members in the second group used the word "choose." The word "choose" to my mind means to select, to take by way of preference; to "choose" denotes to take or fix upon by an act of the will, especially in accordance with a decision of the judgment. The person who is entitled to withdraw from the System is given until January 1, 1942 in which to exercise his or her will or judgment in making a decision as to whether he or she will take no affirmative action and thereby remain as a member of the System, or take affirmative action and notify the Board of Trustees of his or her withdrawal from the System. If a person entitled to withdraw chooses one course—that of withdrawal—he or she should be bound by such course, and should not be allowed to have recourse to another. When a person notifies the Board of Trustees in writing that he or she does not choose to become a member of the Retirement System, such person is placed in the same position as if he or she had never been in the System and no rights to membership are retained. I am unable to find anything in the Retirement Act which would justify me in concluding that a person has the right to make more than one choice in regard to membership in the System. I am of the opinion that a person who has filed a notice of withdrawal with the Board of Trustees is not entitled thereafter to withdraw such notice of withdrawal and continue as a member of the Retirement System.

SUBJECT: TEACHERS' AND STATE EMPLOYEES' RETIREMENT SYSTEM; ADOPTION OF MORTALITY TABLES FOR OCCUPATIONAL GROUPS

22 July, 1941.

The question has been raised by Dr. Clyde A. Erwin as to the approximate percentage of average compensation the employees who are defined as teachers in the Retirement Act would receive at age sixty.

There seems to be some contention that the rates under the column designated "teachers" in the pamphlet issued by the Board of Trustees, entitled "Information and Questions and Answers about the Retirement System," would apply to all employees who are defined as teachers in the Act, and that the other two rates set out in this pamphlet would apply only to employees who are defined as State employees.

The table referred to in Dr. Erwin's letter is one showing the approximate percentages of average final compensation which will be provided as an annuity at age sixty by contributions of members. The purpose of this table is only to give a rough idea of the benefits under the Retirement System. The actual annuity payable upon the service retirement of a member is found in accordance with Section 5(2-a) of the Act and depends upon actual contribution of the member and the mortality tables adopted by the Board of Trustees in accordance with Section 6(13) for the occupational group to which the member belongs.

The Board of Trustees, in assigning members to the groups to which they belong, will no doubt consider the type of work done by the member rather than whether such member is a teacher or employee, as defined by the Act. I am sure the Board of Trustees will want to adopt different mortality tables for occupational groups, such as teachers, clerical and administrative employees, and laborers and mechanics. The members, whether they be teachers or employees as defined in the Act, should be assigned to the suitable occupational groups in accordance with the type of work done by the members. Each member of the System, whether he or she be a teacher or employee as defined in the Act, will be assigned to an occupational group, and the mortality tables applying to that occupational group will be used in calculating the annuity of such member.

I am unable to see how the fact that the Act divides the members into two classes in so far as participation is concerned would prevent the Board of Trustees from taking the course above set out relative to the adoption of mortality tables and assigning members to suitable occupational groups. I am sure the Board of Trustees of the Retirement System will work these matters out to the satisfaction of all parties concerned.

Subject: Teachers' and State Employees' Retirement System; Earnable Compensation; Deductions from Compensation Paid for Teaching in Summer Schools

23 July, 1941.

You inquire as to whether educational institutions supported by and under the control of the State should be required to deduct four per centum of the compensation paid teachers for teaching in the summer schools conducted by these institutions.

The Retirement Act provides for the deduction from the salary of each member of the system four per centum of his earnable compensation. "Earnable compensation" is defined in the Act as meaning the full rate of compensation that would be payable to a teacher or employee if he worked full normal working time. To my mind, the term "full normal working time" means the full amount of time the employer could require the employee to work under normal conditions. If I am correctly informed, this is applicable to the teaching personnel of educational institutions supported by and under the control of the State, would mean the regular term, and would not include summer schools. Under the present set-up, I am convinced that teaching in summer schools should be considered in the nature of temporary employment rather than a part of the regular employment.

I am, therefore, of the opinion that no deduction should be made from the compensation payable to the teachers teaching in summer schools.

Subject: Teachers' and State Employees' Retirement System; Eligibility of County Welfare Employee to Membership

24 July, 1941.

Receipt is acknowledged of your letter enclosing letter from Mrs. W. T. Bost, Commissioner, State Board of Charities and Public Welfare, in which the question is raised as to whether County Welfare employees are eligible to membership in the Teachers' and State Employees' Retirement System.

I assume from the facts set out in Mrs. Bost's letter that the employees about which she inquires are employed by the various counties of the State and that the State contributes approximately 32% of the administration costs of the County Welfare Departments, which include salaries of County Welfare employees. I also assume that the amount representing the 32% is forwarded to the various counties, deposited with the county treasurers, and distributed by means of county vouchers.

The membership of the Teachers' and State Employees' Retirement System is confined to teachers and State employees. The word "teacher" as defined in the Retirement Act means any teacher, helping teacher, librarian, principal, supervisor, superintendent of public schools or any *full time* employee, city or county superintendent of public instruction, or any *full time* employee of department of public instruction, president, dean or teacher, or any *full time* employee in any educational institution supported by and under the control of the State. The word "employee" as defined in the Act means all *full time* employees, agents or officers of the State of North Carolina or any of its departments, bureaus and institutions other than educational, whether such employees are elected, appointed or employed, with the exception of Justices of the Supreme Court and Judges of the Superior Court.

With these definitions in mind, I am unable to see how County Welfare employees would be entitled to membership in the Teachers' and State Employees' Retirement System.

SUBJECT: TEACHERS' AND STATE EMPLOYEES' RETIREMENT SYSTEM; CONTRIBUTIONS BY MEMBERS ON LEAVE OF ABSENCE

17 September, 1941.

You inquire as to whether, in my opinion, members of the Teachers' and State Employees' Retirement System on temporary leave of absence occasioned by military service or educational leave should be allowed to make contributions to the Teachers' and State Employees' Retirement System on the basis of the salary received by the member at the beginning of such temporary leave of absence.

Section 8(1) (a) provides that each employer shall cause to be deducted from the salary of each member on each and every pay-roll of such employer for each and every pay-roll period four per centum of his earnable compensation. Section 1(16) defines earnable compensation as the full rate of compensation that would be payable to a teacher or State employee if he worked in full, normal working time. It can be readily seen from the sections above referred to and the other provisions of the Teachers' and State Employees' Retirement Act that the employees' contributions are to be deducted by the employer from the compensation of the employees and there appears to be no provision in the Act which would specifically authorize the Board of Trustees of the Retirement System to receive contributions from the members themselves.

Of course, there appears in Section 8(1) (d) authority for a member to redeposit in the annuity savings funds by a single payment an amount equal to the total amount which such member has previously withdrawn as provided in the Retirement Act, and that such amounts, when so deposited, shall become a part of the accumulated contributions of the member in the same manner as if such contributions had not been withdrawn.

As a matter of justice, it seems to me that a member who is on temporary leave in military service or on temporary educational leave should be allowed to keep up his or her contributions to the Retirement System in the same manner as if actually on the job. However, the Board of Trustees of the Retirement System can only receive such contributions from members as the statute creating the Retirement System authorizes and likewise, the employers can only match employees' contributions authorized by the statute. There being extreme doubt as to the right to receive these contributions and the right of the various employers to provide the funds to match same, I would advise that if the Board of Trustees receive these contributions, they be received with the understanding and agreement that if the next General Assembly does not validate such action on the part of the Board of Trustees and authorize same to be matched by the employers, same are to be returned to the various employees making the contributions. I am sure the General Assembly in enacting the Retirement Act did not have in mind educational and military leave of absence.

SUBJECT: TEACHERS' AND STATE EMPLOYEES' RETIREMENT SYSTEM; METHOD OF FINANCING; TEACHERS EMPLOYED BY LOCAL UNITS; ADULT EDUCATION; EMPLOYER'S CONTRIBUTIONS

13 February, 1942.

In your letter of February 6 you enclosed a letter from Mr. J. E. Miller, State Director, Division of Adult Education, which raises the question as to the employer's contribution under the provisions of the Teachers' and State Employees' Retirement Act, where the teachers are employed by county or city boards of education to teach under the provisions of the State adult education program, said teachers receiving half their salaries from State appropriations and half from a county or city appropriation. Of course, as to that portion of the salary paid from the State appropriation there is no question or controversy.

In considering the employer's contributions as to that portion of the salaries of teachers engaged in adult education work which is paid by local units, it is necessary to refer to the provisions of the Retirement Act itself. Section 8(1)(c) of the Act provides that each board of education of each county and each board of education of each city in which any teacher receives compensation from sources other than appropriations from the State of North Carolina shall deduct from the salaries of these teachers paid from sources other than State appropriations an amount equal to that deducted from the salaries of the teachers whose salaries are paid from State funds, and remit this amount to the State Retirement System. It is further provided that city boards of education and county boards of education in each and every county and city which has employees compensated from other than State appropriations shall pay to the State Retirement System the same per centum of the salaries that the State of North Carolina pays, and for the purpose of enabling county boards of education and the boards of trustees of city administrative units to pay the employer's contributions, the tax levying authorities in such city or county administrative units are authorized, directed and empowered to provide the necessary funds therefor.

As to the contributions on the amount above the State salary schedule and term, it is discretionary with the local authorities. Thus, you will see that it is the duty of the county boards of education and boards of trustees of city administrative units to take steps to see that funds are provided for the employer's contributions, at least to the amount based on the State salary schedule and term. It seems to me that the teachers engaged in adult education work are entitled to the same consideration as other teachers engaged in teaching in the school system.

Section 5451(a) of Michie's N. C. Code of 1939, Annotated, provides that the State Board of Education is authorized to provide rules and regulations for establishing and conducting schools to teach adults, and the said schools, when provided for, shall become a part of the public school system of the State and shall be conducted under the supervision of the State Superintendent of Public Instruction. The State Board of Education is given rather broad powers in so far as providing rules and regulations for the establishment of these schools is concerned, and it is possible that Mr. Miller will find the solution to his problem in the powers contained in this section.

Mr. Miller also seems to be puzzled as to whether all the teachers engaged in adult education work are entitled to membership in the Teachers' and State Employees' Retirement System.

The word "teacher" is defined in the Retirement Act as meaning any teacher, helping teacher, librarian, principal, supervisor, superintendent of public schools, or any full-time employee, city or county superintendent of public instruction, or any full-time employee of the Department of Public Instruction, president, dean or teacher, or any full-time employee in any educational institution supported by and under the control of the State. It is further provided that in all cases of doubt the board of trustees shall determine whether any person is a teacher as defined in the Act.

It seems to me that any teacher engaged in adult education work who is paid a full salary on a State rating should be considered a teacher within the meaning of the Retirement Act. If Mr. Miller has any teachers about whom there is some question as to their right to membership in the System, he should present you with a list of these teachers, together with all the pertinent facts in connection with their salaries, working time, etc., in order that you might in turn present the facts to the Board of Trustees for its consideration.

SUBJECT: TEACHERS' AND STATE EMPLOYEES' RETIREMENT SYSTEM—1. AGRICULTURE AND HOME ECONOMICS TEACHERS; PAYMENT OF EMPLOYERS' CONTRIBUTIONS; 2. STATUS OF PERSONS OVER SIXTY YEARS OF AGE WHO ARE PAID NOMINAL SALARIES FOR PERFORMING NOMINAL DUTIES; PRIOR SERVICE; 3. EMPLOYEES OF STATE HIGHWAY AND PUBLIC WORKS COMMISSION; CREDIT FOR WORK IN COUNTY ROAD MAINTENANCE

19 March, 1942.

1. *Status of Agriculture, Home Economics, and Other Teachers Paid Jointly from State, Federal, and Local Funds*

Your first question relates to the status of agriculture and home economics teachers who are paid jointly from State, Federal, and local funds. From the information furnished me, these teachers are elected by the county boards of education or the governing bodies of the city administrative units. Their compensation is paid by means of vouchers issued by the local units, but quarterly the local units are reimbursed for approximately two-thirds of the salaries by the State Department of Public Instruction, and that approximately one-third of these salaries come from State funds and one-third from Federal funds. The amount furnished by the Federal Government is placed in the State Treasury and is paid out by the State to the various local units. You desire to know who should pay the employer's contribution required under the provisions of the Teachers' and State Employees' Retirement Act.

Under the provisions of Section 8(1)(c) of the Teachers' and State Employees' Retirement Act, each board of education of each county and each board of education of each city in which any teacher receives compensation from sources other than appropriations of the State of North Carolina is required to pay to the State Retirement System the same per centum of the salaries that the State of North Carolina pays. It is further provided that where the salary is paid in part from State funds and part from local funds, the local authorities shall not be relieved from providing and remitting the same per centum of the salary paid from local funds as is paid from State funds. It is, therefore, my opinion that the employer's contributions on the one-third of these teachers' salaries paid from local funds should be furnished by the local boards of education from funds provided by the local taxing authorities.

As to the remaining two-thirds of the salaries of these teachers, it is my opinion that the employer's contributions should be paid by the State of North Carolina unless the Federal Government will voluntarily agree to pay the employer's contributions on that portion of the salaries paid from Federal funds. The payment by the State of the employer's contributions on the amount realized from Federal funds can, to my mind, be justified on the ground that these funds are used to supplement a State fund created by the General Assembly of North Carolina to carry on a State function, to-wit: its educational program. The funds furnished by the Federal Government to supplement the State funds go into the State Treasury of North Carolina and are disbursed to the local units along with the proportion paid from State funds provided for by the General Assembly. I am sure that no injuries can be done in handling the matter in the manner above set out.

2. Status of a Person's Prior Service Who Is on Semi-Retirement at the Present Time and Is Over Sixty Years of Age

Your second question relates to the status of several professors and school superintendents who no longer perform regular duties, but who are still being paid a nominal salary for performing nominal duties. You desire to know whether these persons are eligible to membership in the Retirement System, and if so, will their prior service be based on their salaries for their entire period of service or on the salaries received during the five years immediately preceding the date the Retirement System becomes operative.

The word "teacher" as defined in the Retirement Act means any teacher, superintendent, etc., or any full-time employee of the department of public instruction, president, dean or teacher, or any full-time employee in any educational institution supported by and under the control of the State. It is further provided that in all cases of doubt the Board of Trustees of the Retirement System shall determine whether any person is a teacher as defined in this Act. It is my opinion that it would be impossible to lay down a rule which would govern the status of all the persons in the class referred to in your question without allowing membership to some persons who are not entitled thereto, and on the other hand, closing the door to membership to some other persons who should be entitled to membership. It seems to me that the Legislature anticipated this very situation and in order to take care of it, provided that in all cases of doubt the Board of Trustees should determine whether or not such persons are entitled to membership. It is my thought that each case should be considered separately on the facts and evidence presented, and the right to membership allowed or denied on the basis of such facts and evidence.

If a person in this class is found to be entitled to membership in the System, his or her prior service should, in my opinion, be determined by using the actual compensation of the member during the whole period of prior service, if available. If it is impossible to secure the actual compensation received during the whole period of prior service, then it is my opinion that the Board of Trustees would be justified in using the average salary of the member for the five years immediately preceding the date the Retirement System became operative in arriving at the prior service status of the member.

3. Definition of Continuous County Highway Employment Service

Your third question relates to prior service allowed to employees of the State Highway and Public Works Commission who were employed in road maintenance by various counties and road districts from 1921 to 1931.

Subsection (10) of Section 1 of the Teachers' and State Employee's Retirement Act defines the term "prior service" as meaning service rendered prior to the date of the establishment of the Retirement System for which credit is allowable under Section 4 of the Act, with the proviso that persons now employed by the State Highway and Public Works Commission shall be entitled to credit for employment in road maintenance by the various counties and road districts prior to 1931 and subsequent to 1921, where such employment has been continuous. You desire to know particularly what is meant by the word "continuous" as used in the proviso.

The word "continuous" is ordinarily defined as "without break, cessation or interruption; without intervening space of time." I am, therefore, of the opinion that an employee of the State Highway and Public Works Commission, in order to be entitled to credit for prior service under the proviso contained in Subsection (10), must have been employed in road maintenance by a county or road district between 1921 and 1931, and that after such employment there must be no break or interruption in his service. The purpose of this proviso was to take care of persons who were taken into the State's service at the time the Legislature authorized the State Highway and Public Works Commission to take over the maintenance of the county road systems of the various counties of the State and who had rendered uninterrupted service from the time they were hired by the various counties or road districts up to the time the State assumed control of the county roads. Any break in the service, no matter for what length of time, would, to my mind, deprive an employee of the State Highway and Public Works Commission of the right to claim prior service under the terms of the proviso above referred to.

OPINIONS TO DEPARTMENT OF MOTOR VEHICLES

SUBJECT: UNIFORM DRIVER'S LICENSE ACT; AIDING AND ABETTING IN OPERATION OF A MOTOR VEHICLE WHILE INTOXICATED

8 July, 1941.

You inquire in your letter of July 8 if the Department would have authority to revoke or suspend the driver's license of a person who has been convicted of "permitting or allowing the operation of his motor vehicle by an intoxicated driver." I advise that on April 1, 1937 an official opinion of this office to Mr. Maxwell answers this inquiry. It is as follows:

"Inquiry is made as to the authority of the Division of Highway Safety to revoke a driver's license upon conviction of aiding and abetting in the operation of a motor vehicle in violation of the mandatory provisions of Chapter 52, Public Laws of 1935, this being the Uniform Driver's License Act.

"A violation of the provisions of this Act is a misdemeanor and there are no accessories to the crime of the grade of a misdemeanor, and a conviction of aiding and abetting would be the equivalent of a conviction of the crime itself as a principal.

"We are of the opinion, therefore, that the Department would be required to revoke the license of a person who has been found guilty of aiding and abetting in the operation of a motor vehicle in violation of one of the provisions of Section 12, Chapter 52, Public Laws of 1935."

SUBJECT: FINANCIAL RESPONSIBILITY ACT; CHAPTER 116, PUBLIC LAWS 1931

17 July, 1941.

You inquire if, where there is a judgment taken as a result of damages incurred by a plaintiff as a result of an automobile accident in the amount of $30.00 and the court costs of the case amounted to more than $70.00, this is such a judgment as would come within the meaning of Chapter 116 of the Public Laws of 1931 and would require the suspension of the driver's license and registration certificate of the person against whom the judgment was taken.

Section 1 of the above Act is in part as follows:

> "In the event of the failure of any person, firm or corporation to satisfy any judgment which shall hereafter become final, by expiration, without appeal, of the time within which appeal might have been perfected, or by final affirmance, on appeal, rendered against him, by a court of competent jurisdiction in this State, within thirty days thereafter for damages on account of personal injuries, or deaths, or damage to property in excess of $100.00 resulting from the ownership, maintenance, or operation of a motor vehicle . . ."

There is no question but that court costs are a part of any judgment recovered in a civil action. Young v. Connelly, 112 N. C. 646, and C. S. 1228-1231; however, in my opinion, the Act contemplates only "damages on account of personal injuries or deaths, or damage to property in excess of . . ." and would not include the costs incident to the recovery of damages in cases of this kind.

RE: STATE HIGHWAY PATROL; ARREST OF DESERTERS FROM THE ARMY, NAVY OR MARINE CORPS

4 August, 1941.

In your letter of August 1 you state that recently the State Highway Patrol has been requested by Federal officers to arrest deserters from the military or naval forces of the United States, and you desire my opinion whether the members of the Patrol have lawful authority to make such arrest, and, if so, whether a warrant is required. If such authority exists, it must be found in the Acts of Congress. It is not granted by any law of this State.

The question of the power of State and local officers to arrest military or naval deserters was considered by the United States Supreme Court in Kurtz vs. Moffitt, 115 U. S., 487, 29 L. Ed., 458, decided in 1885. In that case Justice Gray said:

> "If a police officer or a private citizen has the right, without warrant or express authority, to arrest a military deserter, the right must be derived either from some rule of the law of England which has become a part of our law, or from the legislation of Congress."

After finding that the law of England had never authorized such arrests, he examined the Acts of Congress and concluded:

> "Upon full consideration of the question, and examination of the statutes, army regulations, and other authorities cited in the elaborate argument for respondents, or otherwise known to us, we are of opinion that by the existing law a peace officer or a private citizen has no authority as such, and without the order or direction of a military officer to arrest or detain a deserter from the Army of the United States. Whether it is expedient for the public welfare and the good of the Army that such authority should be conferred, is a matter for the determination of Congress."

This is, therefore, a direct holding by the United States Supreme Court that Congress has the power to authorize State officers to arrest deserters. Such an enactment by Congress would be valid and binding on the Patrol for the second clause of Article 6 of the Federal Constitution provides that it and the laws made "in pursuance thereof . . . shall be the supreme law of the land."

In 1898 Congress enacted a law which is now Section 1578, Title 10, Army, United States Code, Article of War 106, and is as follows:

> "It shall be lawful for any civil officer having authority under the laws of the United States or of any State . . . to arrest offenders, summarily to arrest a deserter from the military service of the United States and deliver him into the custody of the military authorities of the United States."

With respect to deserters from the Navy or Marine Corps, T. 34, Navy, Sec. 1011, United States Code, provides:

> "It shall be lawful for any civil officer having authority under the laws of the United States or of any State . . . to arrest offenders, to summarily arrest a deserter from the Navy or Marine Corps of the United States and deliver him into the custody of the naval authorities."

The term "civil officer" means all officers of the State other than military officers. See the definition of the term in Words and Phrases, Perm. Ed., and in 11 Corpus Juris, page 797. The State Highway Patrol possesses authority to "arrest offenders'. Michie's 1939 Code, Section 3846(bbb), 3846(ooo). It follows that the Acts of Congress above quoted confer upon the members of the Patrol authority to arrest deserters from the Army, Navy, or Marine Corps, and to arrest them "summarily", that is, without warrant, as held in Re Matthews, (D. C. Ky.) 122 Fed., 248, 260.

This is the conclusion reached by the Supreme Courts of Mississippi, Missouri and Georgia.

The decision of the Missouri Court was handed down in 1909 in State v. Pritchett, 219 Mo. 696, 119 S. W. 386. Referring to the authority of State constables to make such arrests, the court said:

> "In making this arrest, the deceased was not acting as constable, but as agent of the United States, and, he having power under the laws of this State to arrest offenders, he came within that class of persons referred to in the Act of Congress as being authorized to arrest a deserter from the United States Army and he had authority, under said Act, to make the arrest in any part of the State the defendant might be found . . . It is true that under the law of this State the constable had no authority to make the arrest without a warrant therefor, but by the Act of Congress, under which he acted, he was authorized to arrest the defendant without a warrant."

This decision was followed in Boatwright v. State, 120 Miss. 883, 83 So. 311, and the decision in Huff v. Watson, 149 Ga. 139, 99 S. E. 307, is to the same effect. Accord, Re Matthews, (D. C. Ky.), 122 Fed. 248; Army and Navy, 6 Corpus Juris Secundam, Sec. 40, page 427; Arrest, 6 Corpus Juris Secundam, Sec. 5, page 584.

In 1869 the Supreme Court of Maine held that the Federal military officers had authority to arrest deserters and could direct agents to make such arrests, and that therefore the agents could not be liable to the deserted for false arrest. Hickey vs. Huse, 56 Maine 493.

You are, therefore, advised that in my opinion members of the State Highway Patrol have authority to arrest without warrants deserters from the Army, Navy or Marine Corps.

SUBJECT: MOTOR VEHICLE LAWS; REVOCATION OF LICENSE; PERIOD OF

RE: HERMAN CALDWELL OR GILBERT HAROLD CALDWELL, GREENSBORO, N. C.

13 August, 1941.

At your request I have reviewed the file in this matter to determine the correctness of your decision that this party's application for a new driver's license may not be considered until after October 14, 1941.

Mr. Caldwell states that when the Driver's License Act was passed in 1935 he obtained a license under the name of "H. Herman Caldwell" but that as "there was another H. H. Caldwell in Charlotte, we were being confused, therefore, I changed my name to Gilbert Harold Caldwell and secured new license." Your records show that in 1935 "Harold Herman Caldwell, 2133 Kirkwood Avenue, Charlotte, N. C.," applied for and obtained license No. 357576, and that in 1938 "Gilbert Harold Caldwell, 118 Polk Street, Raleigh, N. C.," applied for and obtained license No. 870236. The file submitted to me does not show that in 1938 Mr. Caldwell advised that he was then already licensed under another name. His letters show that he sometimes signs his name "Gilbert Harold Caldwell" and at other times "Gilbert Herman Caldwell."

Under these circumstances, it would seem that the prior license, issued to "Harold Herman Caldwell" should be cancelled. It is clear, I think, that an individual is not entitled to hold two licenses under different names.

The questions involved relate to your revocation of license No. 870236. The facts are that on July 29, 1940, Mr. Caldwell was convicted of driving drunk in the Municipal Court of High Point. The file shows that at the time Judge McRae required Mr. Caldwell to surrender his driver's license and that the license was attached to the warrant when the case was transferred on appeal to the Superior Court of Guilford County. Mr. Caldwell states that as a result of the appeal he obtained a reduction of a four months' sentence to a sentence of sixty days or $50.00 fine, the latter sentence being entered upon a plea of guilty. The conviction on appeal was entered October 14, 1940. Upon receiving a certified record of the conviction from the Clerk, you revoked the defendant's license and notified him accordingly.

This action on your part was expressly required by Section 12 of the Driver's License Act, Chapter 52, Public Laws of 1935, which provides:

> "The Department shall forthwith revoke the license of any operator or chauffeur upon receiving a record of such operator's or chauffeur's conviction for any of the following offenses, *when such conviction has become final:* . . . 2. Driving a motor vehicle while under the influence of intoxicating liquor or a narcotic drug."

Section 18(c) of the Act provides: "For the purpose of this Act, the term 'conviction' shall mean a final conviction." Section 18(d) provides: "Pending an appeal, the court from which the appeal is taken shall make such recommendation to the Department relative to suspension of license until the appeal shall have been finally determined, as it may seem just and proper under the circumstances."

Section 13 provides: "The Department shall not suspend a license for a period of more than one year and *upon revoking a license shall not in any event grant application for a new* license under the expiration of one year." To the same effect is Section 4(b). Section 15 provides that when an operator's license has been revoked, he shall not operate a motor vehicle in this State "until a new license is obtained *when and as permitted under this Act.*" See, also, Section 22.

Under the foregoing provisions, when a license is *revoked* it is not revoked for a year or for any particular period. The effect is the same as if the operator had never had a license, and he may not drive again until a new license has been obtained. He does not have a right to a new license at the end of a year. The Act simply provides that the Department shall not in any event grant application for a new license under the expiration of one year "after such license was revoked." Section 4(b) and 13.

When an operator has been convicted of drunken driving in a lower court and appeals to the Superior Court, a "final conviction" does not occur until his conviction in the upper court. Under Section 12 you are mandatorily required "forthwith" to revoke the licenses of those convicted of drunken driving "when such conviction has become final." Section 18(c) provides that "conviction" means "final conviction". Section 18(d) provides that "pending an appeal, the court from which the appeal is taken shall make such recommendations to the Department relative to *suspension* of license until the appeal shall have been *finally determined*, as it may seem just and proper under the circumstances." In my opinion, it is pretty plain that the term "final conviction" in Section 18(c) is the equivalent of "finally determined" in Section 18(d). It is quite obvious that the latter contemplates and authorizes that a drunken driver may be deprived of his license for more than a year. That result clearly must follow if the lower court recommends suspension of the license pending appeal. It also necessarily follows if the lower court takes up the license or prohibits driving.

The reasons for the provision that you shall not revoke licenses until the case has been "finally determined" on appeal are not far to seek. They were inserted for the benefit of innocent persons who were mistakenly or erroneously convicted in an inferior court. In Section 18(b) the General Assembly recognized that in many cases even the lower court might have doubts about the guilt of offenders and therefore authorized such courts to recommend to you that in such cases the license remain in effect pending the appeal and until "final conviction". You have uniformly followed such recommendations.

It is also not difficult to find the reasons why the Assembly twice (Sections 4(b) and 13) expressly provided that after revocation of license a drunken driver could not receive from you a new license until the expiration of one year after such license was revoked. If the Act authorized or provided that the year should be computed from the first conviction in the lower court, a great premium would be put on appeals. Every guilty and convicted person would have a strong inducement to appeal for it would be certain that he could not be deprived of his license for any longer period even though again convicted. He could afford to gamble on the result though he might have no hope of acquittal. He might even be reasonably certain that he would receive a lesser sentence in the Superior Court, particularly if he there pleaded guilty. That occurred here for Mr. Caldwell pleaded guilty in the Superior Court and his four months sentence was reduced to sixty days and suspended. These undesirable results could be and were avoided by plain and repeated provisions that licenses should not be revoked until the final conviction and a new license should not be granted until one year after revocation. In Section 11(1) the Assembly further provided that you should have power to suspend licenses in such cases and need not wait until final conviction in the Superior Court. In exercising this power, however, you have used reasonable restraint and have not suspended in cases where the lower court made a contrary recommendation or where the licensee has made any kind of reasonable showing of probable innocence or even doubtful guilt.

In this connection I might say that the lower court not only did not recommend that Mr. Caldwell's license remain in effect pending appeal, but itself took up the license and attached it to the warrant. You received no record of his first conviction and took no action until after his final conviction in the Superior Court. That Mr. Caldwell was deprived of license from July 29, 1940, pending his appeal, was due to the action of the Municipal Court of High Point, which had undoubted power to cause its surrender. Your action deprived him of his license only after his final conviction, and your handling of the matter was in strict accordance with the duties and requirements expressly and plainly imposed upon you by the Act. Without violating the law, you could not have taken any other course, nor, as you have advised Mr. Caldwell, can you grant him a new license until after October 14, 1941. The separate action taken by the court cannot have the effect of requiring that the year be computed from July 29, 1940. See State vs. McDaniel, 219 N. C. 763.

RE: UNIFORM DRIVER'S LICENSE ACT; REQUIREMENTS AS TO NON-RESIDENTS

5 September, 1941.

I write you in compliance with your oral request for my opinion on the above subject.

It appears that there are certain motor vehicle operators or chauffeurs from other states who come into this State for purposes of business or pleasure and who intend to stay here for varying periods. Some intend to remain here for definite periods ranging from a few days to one or more years; some intend to remain until certain business projects are completed, which may require from a few weeks to a year or more; while some, with indefinite plans and purposes, but with no intent to remain here permanently, plan to remain for indefinite periods. You ask me to advise you whether such persons are required to obtain operator's or chauffeur's licenses by the Uniform Driver's License Act, Chapter 52, Public Laws of 1935.

Section 29 of the Act plainly provides that "no person" resident or non-resident, shall drive a motor vehicle upon any highway in this State as operator or chauffeur unless licensed as provided in the Act.

Section 1 of the Act defines the term "non-resident" to mean "any person whose legal residence is in some other state than North Carolina or in a foreign country."

Section 3 provides in part as follows:

> "The following persons are exempt from license hereunder: . . .
>
> "(c) A non-resident who is at least sixteen (16) years of age and who has in his immediate possession a valid operator's license issued to him in his home state or country, may operate a motor vehicle in this state only as an operator;
>
> "(d) A non-resident who is at least eighteen (18) years of age and who has in his immediate possession a valid chauffeur's license issued to him in his home state or country, may operate a motor vehicle in this state either as an operator or chauffeur except any such person must be licensed as a chauffeur hereunder before accepting employment as a chauffeur from a resident of this state;
>
> "(e) Any non-resident who is at least eight (18) years of age, whose home state or country does not require the licensing of operators may operate a motor vehicle as an operator only, for a period of not more than ninety (90) days in any calendar year if the motor vehicle so operated is duly registered in the home state or country of such non-resident;
>
> "(f) Any non-resident who is at least eight (18) years of age, whose home state or country does not require the licensing of chauffeurs may operate a motor vehicle as a chauffeur for a period

> of not more than ten days in any calendar year if the motor vehicle so operated is duly registered in the home state or country of such non-resident."

In my opinion, the words "legal residence in some other state," in the definition of "non-resident," mean the state of domicile or the state where such person has his permanent place of abode. This is shown, I think, by the fact that the portions of Section 3 quoted above refer to such person's "home state or country." Therefore, it follows that since all of the several classes of persons referred to above are domiciled in or have their home or permanent place of abode in some other State, and are here only temporarily even though for substantial periods in some cases, all of them are "non-residents" and are entitled to the exemption of Section 3.

However, in view of the all-inclusive requirements of Section 2, all of them are required to become licensed except to the extent that they may be exempted by Section 3.

That Section exempts the following:

Subsection (c) exempts non-resident operators who are sixteen years of age and over who have in their immediate possession a valid operator's license issued to them in their home state or country. This exemption does not apply to non-resident chauffeurs.

Subsection (d) exempts non-residents who are eighteen years of age and over who have in their immediate possession a valid chauffeur's license issued to them in their home state or country. Such persons may drive a motor vehicle in this State under their foreign license, either as operator or chauffeur, but may not act as a chauffeur for a resident of this State without obtaining a chauffeur's license from your Department. There is no time limitation to this and the preceding exemption. They only provide that the foreign license be valid and in accordance with the law of the other state and that the operator or chauffeur retain his domicile there.

Subsection (d) grants a limited exemption to non-residents who are eighteen years of age or over and whose home state or country does not require the licensing of operators. They may drive a car in this State, as an operator, but not as a chauffeur, for not over ninety days in each calendar year if their cars are duly registered in their home state or country. In my opinion, this latter provision is not intended to provide that the non-residents mentioned in this subsection may not operate vehicles which are duly registered under the laws of this State. It does not expressly prohibit such operation, and I do not think any is to be implied. It would seem that the intention was to provide that such non-residents, bringing in their own cars, may drive them in this State for ninety days if such cars have proper local registration. Just why a similar provision was not inserted in subsections (c) and (d) is not apparent. The provision as to foreign registration is not one related to the obvious purposes of the Act, and it is my opinion that a non-resident eighteen years of age or over and whose home state or country does not require drivers to be licensed, may drive a vehicle in this State as an operator if the vehicle is duly registered either in this State or in some other state or country.

Subsection (f) grants a limited exemption to non-resident chauffeurs eighteen years of age or over whose home state or country does not require the licensing of chauffeurs. They may operate a motor vehicle here as a chauffeur, without license, for not more than ten days in each calendar year. For the reasons stated above, it is my opinion that this exemption permits such chauffeurs to operate vehicles registered either in this State or in some other state or foreign country. But, in view of Subsection (d), the ten-day exemption is inapplicable if such chauffeurs operate in the employment of a resident of this State.

I do not think that Subsections (e) and (f) have the effect of amending our laws relating to the registration of vehicles, and if such persons should operate a foreign registered car in this State in violation of Article VI of the Motor Vehicle Act of 1937, as amended by Chapters 99 and 365, Public Laws of 1941, they would be guilty of a crime, but would not necessarily be guilty of a violation of the Driver's License Act.

In closing, I call your attention to the fact that Section 16 of the Act provides that the exemptions and privileges granted non-residents are subject to suspension or revocation for the causes mentioned in Sections 11 and 12 and other Sections of the Act.

Re: Motor Vehicles; Transfer of Title; Transfer to Widow of Late Owner by Allotment as Part of Year's Allowance

9 September, 1941.

You have inquired my opinion as to what proof of title should be required by you in cases where the registered owner of a motor vehicle dies and the vehicle is set off to his widow as part of her year's allowance.

There are three ways in which the allowance may be made—first, it may be set off by the former owner's executor or administrator (C. S. 4113); second, it may be set off by a justice of the peace and two "jurors" as Commissioners (C. S. 4115-16); third, it may be assigned by proceedings in the Superior Court (C. S. 4121, et seq.)

Under all three methods, the allotment must be filed with the Clerk of the Superior Court. Under the first method, whereby it is assigned by the executor or administrator of the deceased, the practice is that a report be filed with the Clerk so that the property allotted may be taken out of the inventory of the estate. Under the second method, C. S. 4116 expressly requires that a copy of the allotment be delivered to the Clerk of the Superior Court who is required to file and record the same. Under the third method, the report of the allotment is required to be returned to the Superior Court, that is, to the Clerk. (C. S. 397.)

It would, therefore, seem that in such cases you should require the widow to present to you either a copy of the allotment duly certified by the Clerk of the Superior Court, or a simple certificate from him that the vehicle has been assigned to the widow as part of her year's support. That you should require the widow to produce such proof of her title is expressly shown by Section 41(b) of the Motor Vehicle Act of 1937, Chapter 407, Public Laws of 1937. No doubt this provision is based on the thought that the transfer ought to be certified by the official who is charged with permanent possession of the record and who has jurisdiction in matters of probate.

RE: MOTOR VEHICLES; TRANSFER OF TITLE; DEATH OF REGISTERED OWNER

9 September, 1941.

I write this letter in compliance with your oral request for my advice with respect to the proof that you should require where title to a motor vehicle is transferred after the death of the former owner.

In such cases, there are two general types of cases usually arising; first, where there is an administration upon the estate, and, second, where there is no administration.

When There Is Administration

When the owner of a vehicle dies, with or without a will, title to all of his personalty passes by operation of law to his executor or administrator, and upon application he is entitled to a new certificate of title upon filing with you a certified copy of his letters testamentary or letters of administration. This is true even though the decedent left a will giving the vehicle to a named beneficiary, for in such case the latter, strictly and technically speaking, derives his title from the personal representative and not from the decedent. If title passes to the executor on death, this is bound to be true. See Prive v. Atkins, 212 N. C. 583, 589; Wills, 69 C. J., Section 2461, page 1150; Executors and Administrators, 24 C. J., Section 710, page 201.

Therefore, where there is an administration, the executor or administrator is entitled to a certificate and the only proof of his right that you should require is a certified copy of his appointment.

When There Is No Administration

In a great many cases, if not the majority, there is no will and no administration. The Statute (Sec. 41(b), Motor Vehicle Act, 1937), does not indicate what proof of title you should require in such cases. It merely states that you may issue a certificate "upon affidavit showing satisfactory reasons therefor."

It would be difficult to attempt to enumerate all of the varying situations that may arise in such cases, or to lay down a general rule that would apply to all of the numerous possible "reasons" that you might properly regard as "satisfactory."

The only thing that can be said with certainty is that when the owner dies, his personalty passes to his next of kin, whether one or more, subject to the rights of creditors, mortgagees, or others who may have liens upon the vehicle. If there is more than one next of kin, then neither is entitled to the vehicle by inheritance to the exclusion of the other.

The two important things required to be shown are: First, that the funeral bill and other debts and charges against the estate have been paid; and, second, who are the next of kin of the decedent.

A good general rule would seem to be this: That you require the foregoing facts to be shown by affidavit, and that the next of kin have agreed on who shall be entitled to the vehicle. This latter point can be covered either by an affidavit or affidavits signed by the widow or widower and all the children or other next of kin, or by an affidavit of the applicant for title accompanied by a written instrument transferring title to the applicant. This instrument should be signed by all of those who are the next of kin of the decedent.

In many instances, the affidavits will show that the estate owes no debts and that, to avoid unnecessary expense, there is to be no administration, and the heirs and next of kin have all agreed on a division and all have consented that the vehicle is to be allotted to the widow or one of the children. On such a showing, it would be proper to issue a certificate to the one designated.

I shall be glad to confer with you with respect to such matters whenever you desire my advice.

In another letter today, I dealt with the case where the car is allotted as part of the widow's year's allowance and it is not necessary to repeat here what I there said.

SUBJECT: AUTHORITY OF DEPARTMENT OF MOTOR VEHICLES TO ISSUE NEW CERTIFICATES OF TITLE COVERING VEHICLES INVOLVED IN PENDING LITIGATION ON ACCEPTING A BOND FROM ONE OF THE PARTIES TO INDEMNIFY PERSONS WHO MAY BE INJURED BY SUCH ISSUANCE

27 October, 1941.

It appears from your letter of October 25, and from conferences and correspondence between your Department and some of the interested parties, that an automobile finance company requests your Department to issue new certificates or title on certain vehicles which it claims it has the right to sell as assignee or certain automobile lien notes discounted by it for the dealer who made the sales, default having been made in the payment of said notes; that the assignments are valid on their face; that litigation is now pending between the finance company and the dealer and that the pleadings filed raise the question of ownership of some of the cars, and of the ownership of the liens on the others; that the finance company has repossessed some of the cars under claim and delivery and wishes to repossess the others so that they may be sold; that, in view of the controverted questions that have arisen between the finance company and dealer, the dealer will not surrender the outstanding certificates of title to the cars, but has placed them in the hands of a general receiver appointed for the dealer with instructions not to surrender them except upon court order or consent of all parties; that the finance company wishes to obtain new certificates so that it can proceed at once with the sale, without having to delay until the next term of court in the latter part of November, or longer, to obtain a court order, so as to save depreciation on the value of the cars and other loss; that it is willing to file a bond sufficient to indemnify any parties injured by the issuance of new certificates without the surrender of the outstanding certificates.

You inquire whether your Department would be authorized to issue new certificates in view of these facts.

The duty of the Department as to the issuance of new certificates of title where there has been a transfer of title to or interest in a vehicle by operation of law is set forth in Public Laws 1937, C. 407, Sec. 41 (Sec. 2621 (227) of Michie's North Carolina Code of 1939). The conditions therein prescribed (aside from proper application and payment of prescribed fees) are two:

"(1) presentation of the last certificate, if available; (2) presentation of such instruments or documents of authority or certified copies thereof as may be sufficient or required by law to evidence or effect a transfer of interest in or to chattels in such cases . . ."

However, in this case a question has been raised by litigation as to whether title or interest has been transferred by operation of law, and the Department is not at this stage justified in relying wholly on the assignments to the finance company, even though they may appear to be valid on their face.

Conceding this proposition, you inquire whether the acceptance of a bond from the finance company to indemnify all parties would give the Department authority to proceed.

I have carefully considered this question, and find no authority for the issuance of new certificates on the acceptance of such a bond. Further, if the suggested procedure were followed, regrettable consequences might result. If the dealer ultimately won the litigation, he could demand the cars themselves rather than the value thereof, and this would involve the loss of the cars in the hands of the innocent purchasers under the sale. These purchasers would be put to inconvenience and possible expense in attempting to recover their loss from the finance company, or to proceed against the bond.

Public Laws 1937, C. 407, Sec. 21 (Sec. 2621 (207) of Michie's North Carolina Code of 1939) provides that a certificate of title shall contain on the face thereof a statement of all liens upon the vehicle. Since the pleadings raise an issue as to the ownership of the liens, the Department could not with certainty comply with this statute in the issuance of new certificates until the litigation is terminated.

In short, I am of the opinion that there is no authority for your Department to accept a bond, and that the acceptance of a bond and the issuance of new certificates could result in serious inconvenience and possible loss to innocent third parties who are entitled to rely on the assumption that the Department will issue new titles only on compliance with the laws of the State.

Something has been said of the equities of the transaction between the finance company and the dealer. This matter is, of course, for the courts to determine.

The outstanding certificates are in the hands of a general receiver appointed for the dealer who held the certificates when the litigation commenced. Any action by the Department with reference to new certificates for the vehicles covered by the certificates in the receiver's hands might be an unwarranted interference with the custody of the court.

It is my view that the Department should issue new certificates only on presentation of a court order or consent of all parties showing a termination of the differences involved.

RE: INTERSTATE HAULERS; COMPUTATION OF PERCENTAGE OF GROSS REVENUE ALLOCATED TO NORTH CAROLINA FOR ROAD TAX PURPOSES

15 January, 1942.

You have referred to me by letter of December 24 a letter from the Horton Motor Lines, Inc., of Charlotte, N. C., inquiring whether the computation system outlined in that letter and hereinafter referred to, complies with the following provision of Section 52 of Chapter 407 of the Public Laws of 1937, as amended. (Section 2621 (238) of Michie's 1939 North Carolina Code.)

> "Franchise haulers shall pay . . . six per cent of the gross revenue derived from such operation . . . Provided, further, that franchise haulers operating between point or points within this state and point or points without this state shall be required to account as compensation for the use of the highway of this State and the special privileges extended such carriers by this State in computing the six per cent tax only on that proportion of the gross revenue earned both within and without this State which corresponds to the proportion of the mileage in this State as compared to the total mileage, . . ."

It appears from the letter referred to, and from a conference with Mr. Frank McClenaghan, Attorney, and Mr. J. A. Sutton, Secretary-Treasurer of the Horton Motor Lines, that the proposed computation system is as follows:

By the use of a punch card machine, a card is punched for each bill of lading showing the originating and ending terminal. By the use of these cards, movements between terminals are segregated, and the entire traffic for each month is broken down into point-to-point amounts. For example, all traffic between Greensboro and Charlotte is stated in one group, all traffic between Baltimore and Greensboro in another, and so on. On intrastate hauls, the total revenue earned in the various intrastate point-to-point classifications is subjected to the six per cent tax. On interstate hauls, each of the point-to-point classifications is divided on the basis of the miles run in North Carolina and the miles run outside of North Carolina between the points in question. The percentage that the miles in North Carolina bears to the total miles between the two points is determined and this percentage of the revenue derived from the total monthly traffic between the two points forms the basis upon which the six per cent tax is paid. The total of the revenue summaries for all point-to-point classifications equals, of course, the total revenue in any one month.

As I construe the statute, all revenue derived from intrastate operation is subject to the six per cent tax; conversely, revenue derived from operation beyond the territorial limits of North Carolina, which does not originate or terminate in the State, or traverse or touch any part of the State, is to be excluded in the computation of revenue subject to the tax. The tax is expressly based on "the use of the highways of this state and the special privileges extended such carriers by this state." Therefore, revenue earned from operations entirely beyond the limits of the state has no proper relation to the tax basis, and would seem to be entirely exempt from the tax for constitutional reasons. It has been suggested that the statute sets up a formula for the allocation to North Carolina for tax purposes of a certain proportion of the carrier's gross revenue, wherever earned, said proportion being determined by the relation of North Carolina mileage to total mileage; and under this interpretation the tax basis would vary as the carrier's over-all revenue varied. However, I am of the opinion that no such formula was intended. The intended basis seems to me to be the taxation of all revenue derived from intrastate hauls at six per cent; the taxation of interstate hauls originating or terminating in North Carolina on the proportion of the revenue earned between terminals in the state and terminals out of the state as the mileage in North Carolina bears to the mileage outside of North Carolina between the respective terminals; and the taxation of interstate hauls traversing (but not originating or terminating in) North Carolina on the proportion of the revenue earned between terminals as the mileage in North Carolina bears to the mileage outside of North Carolina between the respective terminals.

The computation system proposed by the Horton Motor Lines, Inc., complies with this construction of the law.

RE: RELEASE TO ARMY AUTHORITIES OF MILITARY PERSONNEL ARRESTED BY HIGHWAY PATROLMEN FOR MISDEMEANOR UNDER STATE LAWS

20 January, 1942.

You inquire whether you would be authorized to accede to a request by the military authorities at Fort Bragg that whenever a member of the armed forces of the United States is arrested by a State Highway Patrolman for a violation of the laws of North Carolina, which is not a felony, the military authorities be notified and allowed to take the arrested person from the custody of the arresting officer. You state that the reason for this request is that in view of the state of war now existing, the army authorities deem it necessary for expediting troop movements and to avoid delays in carrying out desired operations that military personnel be continuously under the custody of military authorities.

You further state that you have been given assurances by the army authorities that the arrested men thus surrendered to the army would not escape punishment but would be disciplined in accordance with military law, and that a transcript of every such proceeding before the military courts would be furnished to your office. I understand that the contemplated plan is that when a patrolman arrests a soldier for a misdemeanor under state laws, the military authorities would be notified by telegram, and when they sent for the prisoner, he would be surrendered to them. It is not proposed that the patrolmen assume the task of transporting the prisoners to the military post, but merely that they turn them over to the military authorities when the latter call for them.

I am of the opinion that you would be justified in making the arrangement outlined above with the military authorities in view of the fact that a state of war exists. At such a time, the federal power and control over the military personnel is supreme and exclusive. Any trials in state courts of military personnel in war time are permitted only by comity or expediency. See 5 Corpus Juris, "Army and Navy," Section 225.

RE: ARSON OF A MOTOR VEHICLE AS GROUND FOR MANDATORY REVOCATION OF OPERATOR'S LICENSE

23 January, 1942.

You request my opinion on the question whether a conviction of the crime of arson of a motor vehicle constitutes a ground upon which the Department of Motor Vehicles is required to revoke the operator's license of the person so convicted. The answer to this question involves a construction of Section 12 of Chapter 52 of the Public Laws of 1935 (the

Uniform Driver's License Act), which provides that the Department shall revoke the operator's license when it receives a record of a conviction for:

> "3. Any felony in the commission of which a motor vehicle is used."

I have been unable to find a statute dealing specifically with the arson of a motor vehicle. Therefore, I assume you refer to a conviction under C. S. 4245(a), which is as follows:

> "*Willful and malicious burning of personal property.*—Any person who shall willfully or maliciously burn, or cause to be burned, or aid, counsel, or procure the burning of any goods, wares, merchandise, or other chattels or personal property of any kind, whether the same shall be at the time insured, by any person, or corporation against loss or damage by fire, or not, with intent to injure or prejudice the insurer, creditor or the person owning the property, or any other person, whether the same be the property of such person or another, shall be guilty of felony."

I am of the opinion that it was the legislative intent that arson of an automobile should be ground for the mandatory revocation of license. This offense is clearly one in which an automobile is "used." I understand that the administrative practice has followed this view. It is a well-established rule of statutory construction that the settled interpretation given a statute by the officer or agency charged with its administration is entitled to consideration. Hannah v. Board of Commissioners, 176 N. C. 395; Powell v. Maxwell, 210 N. C. 211; Universal Battery Company v. United States, 281 U. S. 580.

RE: NOL PROS ON PAYMENT OF COSTS BY DEFENDANT AS BASIS FOR MANDATORY REVOCATION OF DRIVER'S LICENSE

5 February, 1942.

You inquire by letter of February 4 whether, when a person is charged with an offense which (by virtue of Section 12 of Chapter 52 of the Public Laws of 1935) entails a mandatory revocation of driver's license upon conviction, and the court disposes of the case by a judgment that "costs including solicitor's fees on two counts having been paid, the solicitor for the State takes a nolle prosequi with leave," you are required to revoke the person's driver's license.

The cited statute provides that "the Department shall forthwith revoke the license of any operator or chauffeur upon receiving a record of such operator's or chauffeur's conviction for any of the following offenses when such conviction has become final: . . ." Further, Section 18(c) of the same Act provides that "for the purpose of this article, the term 'conviction' shall mean a final conviction."

Without expressing any opinion on the propriety of requiring the defendant to pay costs on the taking of a nolle prosequi, I am of the opinion that such a disposition of the case does not constitute a "conviction" within the meaning of the statutes, and that you would consequently have no authority to revoke the driver's license of a defendant ordered to pay costs on the taking of a nolle prosequi.

SUBJECT: JUSTICES OF THE PEACE; JURISDICTION TO TRY SPEED CASES

2 March, 1942.

This office has written a number of opinions to the effect that a justice of the peace does not have final jurisdiction in cases where a defendant has been charged with a violation of the speed restrictions set out in the law. The reason for this is that the punishment which may be meted out is greater than that which a justice of the peace is permitted to inflict.

RE: SUSPENSION OF DRIVER'S LICENSE ON CONVICTION OF ONE OR MORE CHARGES OF SPEEDING, OR ON FIRST CONVICTION OF RECKLESS DRIVING

10 March, 1942.

You inquire whether existing laws will permit your Department to suspend for a limited period of time the license of a driver convicted one or more times of the offense of driving a motor vehicle in excess of the speed limit, or to so suspend the license of a driver convicted once of the offense of reckless driving.

Your authority with regard to the suspension of driver's licenses is prescribed by Section 52, Chapter 11, Public Laws of 1935 (Section 2621(160) of Michie's 1939 North Carolina Code). This statute does not set forth, as one of the express grounds which authorizes suspension, conviction of the offense of speeding or the first offense of reckless driving. Thus, one conviction of speeding, or one conviction of reckless driving, with none of the other enumerated conditions existing, would not justify suspension.

You have asked whether suspension is justified on one "or more" convictions of speeding. It is entirely possible that the driver may have been convicted of speeding on several different occasions and that you would be justified in finding on the basis of such convictions that he is an "habitually reckless or negligent driver," or that he is "an habitual violator of the traffic laws;" and in such cases suspension would be specifically authorized by the statute. The question of when conduct has become "habitual" must be weighed in the light of the facts and circumstances of each case. "Habitual" has been given the following definition for legal purposes:

> "*Habitual.* A word of no technical significance, ordinarily applied to things done customarily or from force of habit; accustomed; common; constant; customary; familiar, formed by repeated impressions; formed or acquired by or resulting from habit, frequent use, or custom; ordinary; regular; usual." 29 Corpus Juris, 200.

It is clear that one conviction of speeding or reckless driving would not support a finding that the offender was an habitual one. However, I am of the opinion that three or more convictions of speeding might justify such a finding.

One of the grounds for suspension of license is that the driver is "incompetent to drive a motor vehicle." This refers, of course, to incompetence to drive with safety and due care.

Speeding does not necessarily indicate incompetence, but repeated convictions of speeding might show a lack of judgment, discretion, and regard for the law and the rights of others, which would support a finding of incompetence. However, if facts exist sufficient to justify a finding that the convictions of speeding demonstrate incompetence to drive, it is probable that the same facts would justify a finding that the driver is an habitual offender.

You must, in my opinion, be guided by determining in each case whether the facts reasonably justify the conclusion that one of the statutory grounds for suspension is present.

SUBJECT: CRIMINAL LAW; PASSING SCHOOL BUS; IDENTIFICATION OF DRIVER OF MOTOR VEHICLE

19 March, 1942.

You inquire as to whether, in my opinion, it would be possible to convict a person under the provisions of the statute regulating passing school busses when the only evidence to identify the person is the identification of his license plates.

I assume that the only evidence you would have would be that the automobile plates as identified by the school bus driver or other person were purchased for an automobile registered in the name of the accused. The fact that the accused owned the motor vehicle would be some evidence that he operated it on the occasion in controversy. But, it is my opinion that this fact alone would not be sufficient to sustain a conviction.

The Supreme Court of North Carolina, in the case of State v. Goodson, 107 N. C. 798, held that a full summary of incriminating facts taken in the strongest view of them adverse to the defendant might excite suspicion in the just mind that he was guilty, but that such view was far from excluding the rational conclusion that some other person might be the guilty party.

In the case of State v. Shu, 218 N. C. 387 (389), the Court in refusing to uphold a conviction on circumstantial evidence, said:

> "This evidence tends to show that the automobile of Wade Shu, which the defendant habitually drove, was used by those who committed the offense charged in the bill of indictment, but it fails to connect the defendant personally with the crime. The fact of the unexplained use of the car by two unidentified persons affords no more than a suspicion or conjecture that the defendant was present or actively participated in the offense . . . It all comes to this, that there must be legal evidence of the fact in issue and not merely such as raises a suspicion or conjecture in regard to it."

As was said in the cases above referred to and in various other cases to be found in the Supreme Court Reports of this State, there must be something more than a suspicion or conjecture that the defendant is the guilty party. This being true, to my mind there should be some additional identification of a person other than the mere fact that an automobile used in the commission of a crime is registered in the accused's name.

RE: REFUND OF REGISTRATION FEES TO FRANCHISE HAULERS FORCED TO DISCONTINUE BUSINESS

27 March, 1942.

You inquire by letter of March 23, with enclosures from the Bradley Transit Company and the Petroleum Carrier Corporation, whether there is any authority for your Department to refund to franchise haulers a pro rata unused portion or any other portion of the registration or license fees paid by such haulers who have been forced to cease business because of the submarine menace which has curtailed the shipment of petroleum products to ports from which these haulers operate, or because of other unforeseen conditions which have grown out of the war and the national emergency.

Section 52, Chapter 407, Public Laws of 1937, as amended by Chapter 275, Public Laws of 1939, and Chapter 15, Public Laws of 1941 (Section 2621 (238) Michie's 1939 North Carolina Code and 1941 Supplement), provides that franchise haulers shall pay an annual deposit as of January 1 of each year based on certain fees for various vehicle classifications as set forth in the statute, and in addition thereto six per cent of the gross revenue derived from operation within the State. However, the additional six per cent tax does not apply unless and until, and only to the extent that, such amount exceeds the deposit.

Section 58, Chapter 407, Public Laws of 1937 (Section 2621(244) of Michie's 1939 Code) provides that where the amount of the license exceeds $400.00, half of the payment may be deferred until April 1 upon the execution of a draft approved by the Department. Most of the carriers who have made requests to you for refund paid one-half of the deposit on January 1 and took advantage of this provision for deferment of payment of the remaining half until April 1.

In my opinion the proper construction of these statutes is that the total registration fee is due on January 1 of each year and the deferment until April 1 relates not to the obligation but merely to the time of payment. The whole obligation accrues on January 1.

The only provision relating to refunds which I have been able to find is that contained in Section 64, Chapter 407, Public Laws of 1937, as amended by Chapter 369, Public Laws of 1939 (Section 2621(250)). That provision is as follows:

> "Upon satisfactory proof to the Commissioner that any motor vehicle, duly licensed, has been completely destroyed by fire or collision, or has been junked and completely dismantled so that the same can no longer be operated as a motor vehicle, the owner of such vehicle may be allowed on the purchase of a new license for another vehicle a credit equivalent to the unexpired proportion of the cost of the original license, dating from the first day of the next month after the date of such destruction."

This statute is clearly inapplicable to the facts under consideration and affords no relief for the situation to which you refer. This office has repeatedly ruled that there is no authority to grant refunds for the unused portions of motor vehicle licenses except to the extent authorized by the statute referred to. In the situation under consideration, the law results in regrettable hardship because of the unforeseen events which have made a cessation of business necessary. In this, as in many other situations, the coming of war has brought about conditions which were not anticipated at the time some of our laws were enacted. However, I am of the opinion that you have no authority, under the present law, to grant the refunds in question.

RE: POWER OF JUVENILE COURT WITH RESPECT TO FINING JUVENILE FOR VIOLATION OF MOTOR VEHICLE LAWS

30 March, 1942.

You request my opinion upon the question whether a Clerk of Superior Court, acting as Judge of Juvenile Court, has the authority to impose a fine upon a person under the age of sixteen who has violated the provisions of the Uniform Driver's License Act (Sections 2621(150)-2621(181) of Michie's 1939 Code) prohibiting the operation of a motor vehicle without a license. The offender was prosecuted in Recorder's Court but the matter was transferred to the Juvenile Court.

State v. Burnett, 179 N. C. 735, and State v. Coble, 181 N. C. 554, construing the Juvenile Court Act (C. S. 5039, et seq.), lay down the following general principles with respect to the jurisdiction of juvenile courts:

(1) That the Superior Court has exclusive original jurisdiction in all cases arising under the provisions of the Child Welfare Act, but that there shall be established in each county a Juvenile Court as a separate part of the Superior Court of the district for the hearing of all such matters and causes.

(2) That children under fourteen years of age are not indictable as criminals but in case of delinquency must be dealt with as wards of the State, to be cared for, controlled and disciplined with a view to their reformation.

(3) That children between the ages of fourteen and sixteen, when charged with felonies in which the punishment cannot exceed imprisonment for more than ten years, are committed to the Juvenile Court for investigation, and if the circumstances require it, may be bound over to be prosecuted in the Superior Court at term under the criminal law appertaining to the charge.

(4) That children of fourteen years and over, when charged with felonies in which the punishment may be more than ten years' imprisonment, in all cases shall be subject to prosecution for crimes as in the case of adults.

(5) That in matters investigated and determined by the Juvenile Court, no adjudication of such court shall be denominated a conviction and no child dealt with under the provisions of the Act shall be placed in any penal institution or other place where such child may come in contact with adults charged with or convicted of crime.

Your inquiry does not state whether the offender was over the age of fourteen, but this is not material in this inquiry since the offense of operating of motor vehicle without a license is a misdemeanor. See Section 2621 (151) (g) of Michie's 1939 North Carolina Code.

I am of the opinion that the Juvenile Court has no authority to fine a juvenile found to have been operating a motor vehicle without a driver's license. A fine can be imposed only after a conviction of the offense of operating without a license and as punishment therefor (see Sections 2612(151) and 2621(178) of Michie's 1939 North Carolina Code), and I find no authority under the Juvenile Court Act for treating such a juvenile offender to the same way that an adult offender would be treated. The intent of the Juvenile Court Act is to prevent the indictment, conviction and fine or imprisonment that is applicable to adult offenders, and to apply to the juvenile offenders corrective treatment which is calculated to enable them to see the error of their deeds and avoid repetition of them in the future, without leaving them with the handicap of conviction and punishment as violators of criminal laws.

SUBJECT: UNIFORM DRIVERS LICENSE; ISSUANCE OF RENEWAL LICENSE TO CHAUFFEURS

14 May, 1942.

You inquire if under C. S. 2621(127)(b) the Department has the discretion to either require an examination to be given an applicant for a chauffeur's renewal license, or may waive the examination, should it be satisfied of the proficiency of the applicant for such license. This subsection is as follows:

> "Every chauffeur's license shall expire June 30 of each year and shall be renewed annually upon application and payment of fees required by law, provided that the department may in its discretion waive the examination of any such applicant previously examined under this article."

I think that the wording of the above statute clearly places the discretion in the Highway Safety Division to either require an examination before a license is renewed or waive the examination, if it appears that an examination is not necessary.

SUBJECT: MOTOR VEHICLES; CRIMINAL LAW; OPERATION WITHOUT DRIVER'S LICENSE; OPERATION WITHOUT LICENSE PLATES; PUNISHMENT

28 May, 1942.

My opinion has been requested on certain questions raised in the letter of Mr. A. W. Graham, Jr., Clerk of the Superior Court of Granville County, addressed to Mr. Ronald Hocutt, Director of the Highway Safety Division.

Mr. Graham inquires, first, whether the offense of operating a motor vehicle without obtaining an operator's or chauffeur's license carries a mandatory minimum fine. Persons operating motor vehicles on the highways in this State are required to have operator's or chauffeur's licenses by virtue of N. C. Code Ann. (Michie's, 1939), Section 2621 (151). Subsection (g) of this Section provides that a person operating a motor vehicle in violation of the Section is guilty of a misdemeanor. The punishment is prescribed by Section 2621 (178) and is a fine of not more than $500.00, or imprisonment for not more than six months. The imposition of a fine is not mandatory, for the court, in lieu of imposing a fine, may sentence the defendant to imprisonment for not more than six months. If the court imposes a fine, the amount is discretionary, provided the maximum of $500.00 is not exceeded. There is no minimum fine.

Mr. Graham also inquires whether the offense of operating a vehicle without an operator's or chauffeur's license is within the jurisdiction of a justice of the peace. Under Article IV, Section 27, of the North Carolina Constitution, justices of the peace have jurisdiction of no criminal cases in which the punishment can exceed a fine of $50.00 or imprisonment for thirty days. As the punishment for this offense may exceed that which justices of the peace are authorized to impose, I advise that justices of the peace have no jurisdiction over this offense.

It is stated in Mr. Graham's letter that the offense of operating a motor vehicle without obtaining license plates undoubtedly carries a *mandatory* fine of not less than ten nor more than fifty dollars. This is not correct, for under N. C. Code Ann. (Michie's, 1939), Section 2621 (322), it is within the discretion of the court to imprison the defendant for a term not exceeding thirty days in lieu of imposing a fine.

RE: MOTOR VEHICLES; CRIMINAL LAW; OPERATION WITHOUT DRIVER'S LICENSE; OPERATION WITHOUT LICENSE PLATES; SUSPENDED SENTENCE

19 June, 1942.

I regret that my letter of May 28 did not fully answer the questions which Mr. A. W. Graham, Clerk of the Superior Court in Granville County, had in mind when he wrote to Mr. Hocutt inquiring about the punishment for the offenses of operating a motor vehicle without a driver's license and operating without license plates. When Mr. Graham asked whether certain fines were mandatory upon conviction of these offenses, I assumed that he wished to know whether fines were the only punishments that could be imposed for these offenses, and I answered in the negative since the statutes authorize prison sentences in lieu of fines. It did not occur to me that he was concerned with the power of the court to suspend sentence, for suspended sentences were not mentioned in his letter.

Supplementing my original letter, which I think accurately states the punishment authorized for driving without a driver's license or without license plates, I advise that the court having final jurisdiction over one of these offenses may, in its discretion, upon conviction of a defendant, suspend sentence upon reasonable conditions. The practice of suspending sentence in this State is based upon custom and usage rather than statute. It is recognized and approved by the Supreme Court. State v. Crook, 115 N. C. 760; State v. Tripp, 168 N. C. 150.

The power to suspend sentence for any offenses within their jurisdiction is inherent in all courts unless suspension of sentence for a particular offense is forbidden by statute. Such a provision restricting the power of the court to suspend sentence, for example, was included in Public Laws of 1927, Chapter 148, Section 159, which formerly prescribed the punishment for drunken driving. There is, however, no statutory restriction upon the power of a court to suspend sentence for operating a motor vehicle without a driver's license or without license plates.

Mr. Graham inquires whether sentences for these offenses could be suspended on payment of costs. The Supreme Court has given its approval to sentences suspended on condition that costs be paid by the defendant. State v. Crook, 115 N. C. 760; State v. Hilton, 151 N. C. 687.

I, therefore, advise that such a condition would be reasonable and that suspension of sentence upon this condition would be valid.

A justice of the peace has authority to suspend sentence in a case within his jurisdiction.

OPINIONS TO MERIT SYSTEM COUNCIL

SUBJECT: MERIT SYSTEM COUNCIL ACT OF 1941; COVERAGE; EMPLOYEES INCLUDED; PROBATION OFFICERS; WORKING UNDER DIRECTION OF COUNTY SUPERINTENDENT OF WELFARE

29 July, 1941.

I have your letter of July 28 in which you ask whether or not probation officers appointed for county and city juvenile courts under C. S. 5049, C. S. 5062, and C. S. 5017 are subject to merit system regulations to the same extent "as other employees in county welfare departments."

The Merit System Act, Public Laws of 1941, Chapter 378, Sec. 13, only makes the act applicable to "all employees of the county welfare departments." The officers you inquire about do not appear to be employees of the county welfare departments. Under the provisions of C. S. 5049, the probation officers of the county juvenile courts are appointed by the judges thereof. Their salaries are fixed by the judge and paid by the county commissioners. They take orders from the court and serve under the direction of the judge. C. S. 5051.

It is true that the employment and discharge of these officers must have the approval of the State Board of Charities and Public Welfare, and that they are placed under the supervision of the County Superintendent of Public Welfare, who is the chief probation officer of all juvenile courts in the county. It is also provided that "the State Board of Charities and Public Welfare shall establish rules and regulations pursuant to which appointments under this article shall be made, to the end that such appointments shall be based on merit only." I do not believe, however, that this would have the effect of making them employees of the county welfare department so as to subject them to the provisions of the Merit System Act as are the employees of the welfare departments themselves.

C. S. 5062 provides that assistant probation officers for city juvenile courts are to be appointed by the governing bodies of the cities in which the courts are established.

For the reasons advanced above, I do not believe that these officers are employees of the county welfare departments, and hence would not be covered by the Merit System Act as are the other employees of the welfare departments.

SUBJECT: MERIT SYSTEM COUNCIL; ADMISSION TO EXAMINATIONS

20 August, 1941.

In your letter of August 18 you inquire:

> "1. Is it the intent of the law that only those who have served continuously since January 1, 1940 to the date of the examination shall be considered as employees, or
>
> "2. May the Council decide that people who were employees in good standing on January 1, 1940, and who are employees in good standing at the time of the examination, may take the examination as an incumbent despite the fact that between that time they had resigned and were working for someone else."

Section 8 of Chapter 378 of the Public Laws of 1941, relating to the above subject, is in part as follows:

> "An employee who is certified by the agency as having given satisfactory service continuously for six calendar months preceding January 1, 1940, or any other date or dates as may be required by the federal agencies supervising the expenditure of federal funds through the State agencies affected by this Act, may be admitted to the examination for the position held by him at the time of the passage of this Act, without regard to minimum qualifications of training and experience."

In my opinion, an employee who is certified and has given satisfactory service for six calendar months preceding January 1, 1940, may be admitted to the examination for the position held by him at the time of the passage of the Act, without regard to minimum qualifications of training and experience, unless this date has been changed by the federal agency supervising the expenditure of federal funds.

I also advise that employees who were in good standing on January 1, 1940, and who are employees in good standing at the time of the examination, may take the examination as incumbents, regardless of the fact that at some interval between these times such employees may have resigned and secure employment elsewhere.

SUBJECT: MERIT COUNCIL SYSTEM; COVERAGE; EMPLOYEES INCLUDED

22 January, 1942.

I have your letter of January 16, enclosing me a copy of a resolution passed by the Merit System Council as to the legality of which, under the Merit System Law, you invite my opinion. The resolution enclosed is as follows:

> "RESOLVED: Inasmuch as the Federal regulations governing the Merit System in the Health Department permits the blanketing in of all employees of the Health Department who had served for five years prior to November 1, 1939, the Council hereby provides that all employees of the State Health Department and Local Health Units who have met this Federal requirement may become permanent employees under the Merit System without any examination."

Under Section 8 of Chapter 378 of the Public Laws of 1941, creating the Merit System Council, it is provided that an employee who is certified by the agency as having given satisfactory service continuously for six calendar months preceding January 1, 1940, or any other date or dates as may be required by the Federal agencies supervising the expenditure of Federal funds through the State agencies affected by the Act, may be admitted to the examination for the position held by him at the time of the passage of this Act without regard to minimum qualifications of training and experience.

I take it that Federal regulations governing the blanketing in of employees of the Health Department who had served for five years prior to November 1, 1939 substantially meet the idea involved in our statute.

Under Section 13 of the Act, the Merit System Council is authorized to establish and maintain and provide rules and regulations in cooperation with the State Board of Health for the administration of personnel standards under the Merit rating system with the uniform schedule of compensation for all employees of county, city and district health departments, and no standards are set up with reference to these rules and regulations which are within the range of control by the Council in the adoption of its rules and regulations. I have heretofore advised that in my opinion the only practical limitations upon your authority with respect to these rules and regulations are found in meeting the requirements of the Federal law. As your resolution adopts as its basis the Federal regulations with respect to employees of local health departments, I am of the opinion that you may validly do so.

It is to be noted further that under Section 14 of the Act it is provided that wherever the provisions of any law of the United States or any rule, order or regulation of any Federal agency or authority providing or administering Federal funds for use in North Carolina impose other or higher civil service merit standards or different classifications than are required by the provisions of this Act, then the provisions of such laws, rules and regulations of the United States or any Federal agency may be adopted by the Council as rules and regulations of the Council and shall govern the class of employment and employees affected thereby, anything in this Act to the contrary notwithstanding.

This provision in my opinion fully authorizes the adoption of the resolution blanketing in the employees of the State Health Department and local health employees.

OPINIONS TO STATE AND COUNTY A. B. C. BOARDS

SUBJECT: CRIMINAL LAW; ARREST; BAIL; SECURING FINGERPRINTS

26 September, 1940.

You inquire if it is necessary for an officer who arrests a violator of the liquor laws to accept a bail bond immediately if such bond is tendered, or whether such officer may take the defendant to the county-seat for the purpose of securing his fingerprints.

C. S. 4548(a) provides that upon the arrest, detention or deprivation of the liberties of any person by an officer in this State, with or without warrant, it shall be the duty of the officer making the arrest to immediately inform the person arrested of the charge against him, and it shall further be the duty of the officer making such arrest, except in capital cases, *to have bail fixed in a reasonable sum, and the person so arrested shall be permitted to give bail bond.*

C. S. 7766(g) provides:

> "Every chief of police and sheriff in the State of North Carolina is hereby required to take or cause to be taken on forms furnished by this bureau the fingerprints of every person convicted of a felony and to forward the same immediately by mail to the said bureau of identification. That the said officers are hereby required to take the fingerprints of any other person when arrested for a crime when the same is deemed advisable by any chief of police or sheriff and forward the same for record to the said bureau."

Where an officer arrests a person without a warrant, C. S. 4548 provides that such person shall either immediately be taken before some magistrate having jurisdiction to issue a warrant in the case, or else committed to the county jail, and as soon as may be, taken before such magistrate, who on proper proof shall issue a warrant and thereon proceed to act as may be required by law.

Where a person is arrested on a warrant issued by a magistrate and the amount of bond is not fixed by the magistrate at the time the warrant is issued and delivered to the officer who is to serve same, it is necessary that the arresting officer take steps immediately to have the magistrate fix the amount of bail required in order that the person arrested may have opportunity to post the required bond.

I am of the opinion that the arresting officer would have the right, both in case of a proper arrest without a warrant, and an arrest with a warrant, to take the defendant to the county-seat in order that his fingerprints might be taken, if the officer deemed the taking of such fingerprints advisable.

The main purpose of Section 4548(a) is to prevent persons arrested being deprived of their liberty as a result of delay in affording such persons the opportunity to give a bail bond where the offense charged is a bailable one. Officers in handling these cases should be very careful to see that there is no undue delay in affording persons arrested the right to give bond.

SUBJECT: PURCHASE OF GRAIN ALCOHOL BY DRUG STORES; USE IN COMPOUNDING MEDICINE; RESALE

1 November, 1940.

Please pardon the delay in answering your letter of October 11, which has been due to pressure of an unusual amount of work in this office.

Answering your question, I would say that a drug store purchasing, in good faith, grain alcohol from an A.B.C. store for use in the compounding of medicines, and used in compounding medicines, could resell the same as a part of the medicine so compounded, and would not be violating the prohibition in the A.B.C. Act in offering for sale or resale alcoholic beverages purchased from such store.

SUBJECT: ABC ACT; EXPENDITURE OF FUNDS FOR ENFORCEMENT

8 April, 1941.

Replying to your letter of April 5, I advise that no part of the percentage of profits from liquor sales may be expended by any county alcoholic beverage control board, except for law enforcement as provided in Section 10(o) of Chapter 49 of the Public Laws of 1937. I am of the opinion that law enforcement will not include an additional program to be sponsored in the schools and by civic agencies of such counties, working toward the elimination of the abuses of the use of alcohol.

I further advise that provision is already made in our statute, C. S. 5440(a), whereby the Superintendent of Public Instruction is authorized and directed to prepare or cause to be prepared courses of instruction for the use of all teachers who are paid from public funds to give courses on the subject of alcoholism and narcotism.

SUBJECT: ABC BOARD; HOW TO FIX PRICES FOR THE SALE OF SWEET WINES

22 April, 1941.

You inquire if, since the sale of sweet wines as defined in Chapter 339 of the Public Laws of 1941 has been placed under the supervision and control of the State Alcoholic Control Board, your Board has the authority to fix a minimum sales price for sweet wines in those counties having alcoholic beverage control stores.

It is true that the 1941 Act provides in Section 6 that the provisions of Chapter 49 of the Public Laws of 1937, as amended, apply to fortified wines; however, the State Alcoholic Beverage Control Board is given power under Section 4(c) of Chapter 49 of the Public Laws of 1937 to "approve or disapprove the prices at which the several county stores may sell alcoholic beverages."

This section, in my opinion, applies only to the sale of fortified wines in alcoholic beverage control stores and does not extend the power to fix prices to the sale of sweet wines as defined in the 1941 Act in hotels, grade A restaurants, drug stores and grocery stores. Nothing appears in the 1941 Act which would extend this power to the State Alcoholic Beverage Control Board and I conclude, therefore, that such power does not exist.

SUBJECT: ABC ACT; ISSUANCE OF "ON PREMISES" LICENSE; SWEET WINES

22 April, 1941.

You inquire of this office for an opinion as to whether or not the State Board of Alcoholic Control has authority to determine what constitutes a grade A restaurant within the meaning of Section 6 of Chapter 339 of the Public Laws of 1941.

Consolidated Statutes 2249, and following, as well as Chapter 309 of the Public Laws of 1941, vests in the State Board of Health the supervision and control over the sanitation of hotels, cafes, restaurants and other establishments providing food and lodging to the public for pay. Under these statutes, the Department of Health is authorized to set up standards under which such establishments are graded according to their sanitary and other conditions; and under authority of the above laws, the State Board of Health has instituted a system of inspection of such establishments with grades designated as grades A, B, C, etc. The 1941 Act specifically provides that no such establishment shall operate which receives a grade of less than C.

The Revenue Act, Chapter 158 of the Public Laws of 1939, as amended, provides in Section 509½ that "On Premises" licenses for the sale of unfortified wines shall not be issued to any hotel, cafeteria, cafe or restaurant unless at the time of the application for such licenses such establishment shall have been given a grade A or B rating "by the State Department of Health."

It is true that Section 6 of the 1941 Act does not specifically state that the grade A rating shall be determined by the State Department of Health; neither does it say that such rating shall be given to such establishments by the State Board of Alcoholic Control. In order to arrive at the intention of the Legislature, therefore, it must be taken into consideration that it has been the policy of the State to vest in the State Board of Health the authority to make sanitary gradings of such establishments, and, following this policy, the Board of Health has instituted a system of grading as above indicated.

Construing these statutes in pari materia, it is my opinion that the term "grade A" appearing in Section 6 would be meaningless and of no effect unless the Legislature intended to refer to the grading of restaurants made by the State Board of Health. I conclude, therefore, that the State Board of Alcoholic Control has no legal authority to determine what constitutes a grade A restaurant within the meaning of Section 6 of the 1941 Act.

SUBJECT: CHAPTER 49, PUBLIC LAWS OF 1937; INTOXICATING LIQUOR; SALE IN HOTELS AND CAFES

5 May, 1941.

Chapter 49 of the Public Laws of 1937 permits the sale of alcoholic beverages having an alcoholic content of more than twenty-four per cent only in duly authorized county alcoholic beverage control stores and does not, in my opinion, permit hotels, restaurants or cafes to purchase such alcoholic beverages from A.B.C. stores and then mix the same into cocktails and sell them over the counter or at a table to customers at retail. Such action, in my judgment, would be violative of Chapter 1 of the Public Laws of 1933, commonly called the Turlington Act.

SUBJECT: ABC ACT; PRICE FIXING OF WHISKEY BY STATE BOARD; POWER AND AUTHORITY

5 March, 1942.

In your letter of March 4, you state that a number of the larger counties of the State have requested that your Board give them the privilege of buying whiskey in carload shipments to be delivered to their individual warehouses, thereby saving the fifteen cents bailment charge on each case of whiskey which they now have to pay to your warehouse in Wilson.

You further state that under the rules and regulations issued by your Board, retail whiskey stores in the State have their prices fixed by adding fifty per cent of the actual cost price of the whiskey, including freight and bailment, this being the profit which the stores are entitled to under your regulations. You also state that the fifteen cents bailment charge is uniform throughout the State; that is to say, the charge per case is the same whether the whiskey is delivered to the stores in Wilson where the warehouse is located or to another store in the State which is a considerable distance away.

You inquire if your Board has authority to permit the larger counties in the State to receive their shipments of whiskey direct from the distillery, thereby eliminating from the cost of the same the fifteen cents bailment charge which they now all pay to the warehouse in Wilson.

I think your question is answered by Consolidated Statutes 3411(68) (c), which is as follows:

> "To approve or disapprove the prices at which the several county stores may sell alcoholic beverages and it shall be the duty of said board to require the store or stores in the several counties coming under the provisions of this article to fix and maintain uniform prices and to require sales to be made at such prices as shall promote temperate use of such beverages and as may facilitate policing."

In my opinion, the above statute places the duty upon the State Board to maintain uniform prices throughout the State. Under other pertinent sections of Chapter 49 of the Public Laws of 1937 the Board of Alcoholic Control has supervision over all the system of liquor stores in North Carolina created by the Act. If you were to permit stores in some counties to purchase liquor at a cost less than other counties are able to purchase such beverages, in my opinion, you would defeat the section above quoted and there would not be maintained a uniform price of whiskey throughout the State. Either the price could be lower in the counties which took advantage of their economic position; that is to say, their larger buying power, and could dispense such beverages to the public at a lower price than it could be sold by other stores in the State, or it would permit such larger counties to increase their profits in excess of the fifty per cent writeup which they are now permitted to do under your regulations.

Since the above statute places the duty upon the State Board to approve or disapprove the prices at which the several county stores may sell alcoholic beverages, and also places the duty upon the State Board to require the store or stores in the several counties which come under the provisions of the Act to fix and maintain uniform prices, it is my opinion that the suggested practice by the larger counties is not authorized by law, since such action would defeat the law in this regard.

SUBJECT: INTOXICATING LIQUOR; WINE AND BEER; SALE OF SWEET WINE

10 April, 1942.

Section 6 of Chapter 339 of the Public Laws of 1941 regulates the sale of sweet wines in wet counties in this State and provides that it shall be legal to sell sweet wines, as therein defined, in hotels, grade A cafes, drug stores and grocery stores in such counties, "such sales, however, shall be subject to the rules and regulations of the State Alcoholic Beverage Control Board."

I advise, therefore, that unless a person, firm or corporation complies with your regulations and secures a permit from your office to sell such sweet wines, the Beverage Control Act would be violated.

SUBJECT: DISPOSITION OF CONFISCATED TAX PAID LIQUORS; FORTIFIED WINES

1 May, 1942.

Chapter 339 of the Public Laws of 1941 includes in the definition of alcoholic beverages, within the meaning of Chapter 49 of the Public Laws of 1937, alcoholic beverages of all kinds which shall contain more than fourteen per centum of alcohol by volume.

I advise, therefore, that fortified wines which contain this per centum of alcohol which have been seized and confiscated would come within the meaning of Chapter 12 of the Public Laws of 1939, and that such confiscated fortified wines may be either turned over to the Board of Commissioners to be given to hospitals for medical purposes and/or sold to legalized alcoholic beverage control stores within the State of North Carolina and the proceeds therefrom placed in the school fund of the county wherein such seizure was made.

SUBJECT: FORTIFIED WINES; SWEET WINES

5 May, 1942.

You enclose a letter from Munson G. Shaw Company, Inc., of New York, wherein they inquire if it will be unlawful for them to ship fortified wines into this State which contain and are so labeled more than 20% of alcohol by volume.

Under the definition of fortified wines, such wine is designated as fortified which is an alcoholic beverage made by fermentation of grapes, fruits and berries and fortified by the addition of brandy or alcohol or having an alcoholic content of more than 14% of absolute alcohol, reckoned by volume.

If this is the class of fortified wine which this company wishes to label as containing more than 20%, I see no objection to their doing so. However, if this is a sweet wine; that is to say, a fortified wine as defined in Section 6 of Chapter 339 of the Public Laws of 1941 as "any wine made by fermentation from grapes, fruits or berries to which nothing but pure brandy has been added, which brandy is made from the same type grape, fruit or berry which is contained in the base wine to which it is added," then there is a top limitation upon the amount of absolute alcohol which it may contain of "not more than 20% of absolute alcohol reckoned by volume" and this company would not be permitted to sell and ship into this State sweet wines, as defined in the Act, which contain and are labeled to contain more than 20% of alcohol.

SUBJECT: ALCOHOLIC BEVERAGES; ISSUANCE OF PERMITS TO WINE SALESMEN BY THE STATE BOARD; REVOCATION PERMITS

21 May, 1942.

Section 6 of Chapter 339 of the Public Laws of 1941, which regulates the sale of sweet wines, provides, among other things, that the sale of such wines shall be subject to the rules and regulations of the State Alcoholic Beverage Control Board. Pursuant to the authority granted hereunder to supervise the sale of such wines by rules and regulations of your Board, you advise that you issue permits to salesmen, and you inquire if you have any authority to revoke any such permit to a salesman who, on his own admission, has violated the rules and regulations, and if, after such revocation, such salesman has any right of appeal to the court.

In my opinion, the statute giving you power to promulgate rules and regulations in this regard implies the right to issue permits to persons who engage in the business of selling such wines, and it follows that the power to issue permits carries with it the power to revoke the same for cause. The revocation of such a permit is a discretionary power vested in the Board and no provisoin appearing in the statute which would permit an appeal from the decision of the Board in this regard, I do not think that any salesman who has had his permit revoked has any right of appeal to the courts.

You further inquire if you have any authority to direct the distillers by whom such salesmen are employed to dispense with his services in this State. Section 3 of the above statute amends Chapter 49 of the Public Laws of 1937 so as to include all alcoholic beverages which contain more than 14 per cent alcohol by volume and brings the sale and consumption of such beverages, which include fortified wines as defined in the Act, under the supervision of the State Board of Alcoholic Control. Under Section 4 of the 1937 Act, the State Board of Alcoholic Control has the power to grant or to revoke permits for any person, firm, or corporation to do business in North Carolina in selling alcoholic beverages to or for the use of any county store and to revoke the same for the causes therein set out. Under Subsection (m) of this Section, the State Board is given all powers which may be reasonably implied from the granting of express powers herein named, together with such other powers as may be incidental to or convenient for the carrying out and performance of the powers and duties therein given to the Board. I doubt seriously if you have authority to order a distiller, by whom such salesmen are employed, to dispense with his services in this State. However, you could, under authority of the 1937 Act, since fortified wines come within its provisions, refuse to issue a license to the distiller in this State who refuses to comply with your request that the salesman in question be not employed here as an alcoholic beverage salesman.

OPINIONS TO UNEMPLOYMENT COMPENSATION COMMISSION

SUBJECT: SELECTION OF PERSONNEL; MERIT EXAMINATIONS; CHARACTER OF EXAMINATIONS

8 November, 1940.

You handed me a letter from Mr. Frank T. de Vyver, Supervisor of Merit Examinations, in which he recites that Mr. Mark A. Kollock of Hendersonville, formerly a Senior Interviewer with your Department, has raised several questions on which he desires the opinion of this office.

The three questions submitted indicate that Mr. Kollock contends that the merit examinations which he was required to take did not consist of questions germane to the character of work which he was expected to do. For this reason, it is contended by him, as indicated by the questions, that he is entitled to his position as long as his services are satisfactory, notwithstanding the result of the examination.

It is my opinion that the Commission, acting through the person selected as its agent to submit the examination, would be the judge of the character of the examination to be submitted and in passing upon the examination as taken by any applicant. It would be assumed that the examination submitted would reasonably disclose the capacity of the applicant to acceptably fulfill the duties of the office.

In the absence of arbitrary action on the part of the examining official in submitting an examination on subjects totally different from ones which would reasonably disclose the capacity of the applicant, the administrative functions of the Commission and its examiners will not be inquired into. In other words, in my opinion, the character of the examinations and the methods of passing upon them are clearly administrative duties of the Commission, which would not be interfered with except in the case of gross abuse of administrative discretion.

SUBJECT: MERIT SYSTEM EXAMINATION; STANDARDS AND CLASSIFICATIONS; ATTORNEYS AT LAW; RECOGNITION OF PRIOR MERIT EXAMINATIONS AS TO EMPLOYEES EMPLOYED UPON ADOPTION OF 1941 ACT

2 June, 1941.

I received your letter of June 2, in which you quote from the rules and regulations adopted by the Social Security Board setting up certain standards for a merit system of personnel administration in State Employment Security and State Public Assistance agencies, adopted November 1, 1939, which standards are still in effect, as certified by Mr. M. T. Dickinson, Regional Attorney.

Your firt question is whether or not the Merit System Council, created by Chapter 378 of the Public Laws of 1941, will be permitted under standards set up by it to exempt attorneys at law serving as legal counsel to the Commission, who have not already passed a merit examination.

The standards adopted by the Social Security Board, from which quotation is made in your letter, provide that certain positions may be exempted from the application of the standards. One of the positions mentioned is attorneys serving as legal counsel.

Our statute, Section 14, provides that wherever the provisions of any law of the United States, or any rule, order or regulation of any Federal agency or authority providing or administering federal funds in this State, impose other or higher civil service or merit standards or different classifications than are required by the provisions of this Act, then the provisions of such laws, classifications, rules, or regulations may be adopted by the Council as rules and regulations of the Council and shall govern the class of employment and employees affected thereby, anything in our Act to the contrary notwithstanding.

Under this section, it is my opinion that the North Carolina Merit System Council is empowered and may adopt the same exemptions as to positions as those provided for in the standards adopted by the Social Security Board on November 1, 1939; and if such regulation is adopted by the Merit System Council of this State exempting attorneys serving as legal counsel to your Commission, you could properly recognize the same.

Your second question relates to your right to retain legal counsel to the Commission who have heretofore passed the merit system examination which by law was required of them and who were presently employed at the time of the adoption of the 1941 Act. This Act, in section 5, says that all employees presently employed in the agencies or departments affected by the Act and who have heretofore taken and passed merit examinations under the merit rating system now in effect shall not be required to have further examinations as herein provided. Under this provision, the attorneys at law acting as counsel for the Commission who had theretofore taken and passed the merit examination and who were then in service, are not required to take the second examination and retain their status as merit system employees, to the same extent as though they had taken the merit system examination under the 1941 Act.

SUBJECT: CHAIRMAN UNEMPLOYMENT COMPENSATION COMMISSION; POWERS AND DUTIES

26 June, 1941.

In your letter of June 25, you inquire as to the rights, powers, duties and obligations of the Chairman of the Unemployment Compensation Commission under Chapter 279 of the Public Laws of 1941, with particular regard to such powers and authority which he might exercise in the absence of the presence and approval of the entire Unemployment Compensation Commission.

Under Section 4 of the 1941 Act, Section 11(a) of the original Unemployment Compensation Act of 1936 is rewritten. Here, you will find that the Commission shall meet at least once in each sixty days and may hold special meetings at any time at the call of the Chairman, and it is specifically provided that "the Chairman of said Commission, except as otherwise provided by the Commission, be vested with all the authority of the Commission when the Commission is not in session * * *." In this respect, I advise that under the authority of the above quoted portion of

Section 11(a), in the absence of either a regular or call meeting of the Commission, the Chairman thereof has full authority to act upon any matters which might come before him and which call for immediate decision or action. I do not think that the Chairman of the Board has authority under the Act to adopt rules and regulations which would be effective, without the approval of the Commission.

You further inquire if the Commission, itself, under the Wagner-Peyser Act, Public No. 30-73d Congress, 48 Stat. 113, whereby certain funds are granted to the State to assist in the establishment and maintenance of public employment offices, could act as the State Advisory Council to this organization. This Federal statute provides that the Unemployment Compensation Commission shall name the State Advisory Council, composed of men and women to represent in equal numbers employers, employees, and the public.

It is my opinion that the six members of the Unemployment Compensation Commission appointed by the Governor under the 1941 Act actually do represent employers, employees, and the public in the same manner and to the same extent as required by the Federal law.

Under Section 6 of the 1941 Act, the Unemployment Compensation Commission created thereby "automatically succeeds to all the rights, powers, duties and obligations of the Unemployment Compensation Commission which it succeeded and of the State Advisory Council." Under this section, it is my opinion that the Unemployment Compensation Commission established by the 1941 Act could, with the approval of the Federal authorities, serve as the State Advisory Council under the Wagner-Peyser Act referred to above.

SUBJECT: UNEMPLOYMENT COMPENSATION COMMISSION LAW; COLLECTION OF CONTRIBUTIONS; PRIORITIES

18 July, 1941.

Replying to your letter of July 14, I advise that under the provisions of C. S. 1220 it is my opinion that an officer or tax collector of the State has authority to levy upon, seize and take possession of property belonging to a corporation, or so much thereof as is necessary to pay any taxes, whether State, county or municipal, and it shall be liberally construed in favor of and in furtherance of the collection of such taxes.

I think this statute would be applicable in cases where the taxes are due prior to the receivership. As to the priority of such taxes, I refer you to C. S. 8052(14)(c). Here you will find that in the event of any distribution of an employer's assets pertinent to an order of any court under the laws of this State, including any receivership, contributions then or thereafter due shall be paid in full prior to all other claims, except taxes and claims for remuneration of not more than $250 to each claimant earned within six months of the commencement of the proceedings.

Under these circumstances, I do not think that you have authority to compromise the amount of contributions due by the corporation to which you refer, which is in receivership.

SUBJECT: UNEMPLOYMENT COMPENSATION TAX; COMPROMISE OF TAX CLAIMS IN LITIGATION

31 October, 1941.

In your letter of October 31, you inquire if the Commission, through its Chief Counsel, has authority to compromise a claim for taxes when a suit for the collection of the same has been instituted in the courts of the State.

It is my understanding of the law that in a real contest or litigation where a tax claim is involved in which the issues drawn are close and uncertain, the tax collecting authorities, in order to avoid extended litigation and settle disputed claims, would have the right to settle such claims by compromise. Such a course; that is to say, compromise judgment in a lawsuit by consent of all parties, would be independent of any statute which expressly authorizes a settlement. I do not think that the law would compel litigation to the bitter end of bona fide controversies as to a tax liability when a reasonable adjustment of the same could be obtained.

I wish to call your attention to a note in 61 C. J., under Section 1253, page 973, where you will find the following:

> "In Virginia (1) Code (1904) Sections 702, 702a, relating to the authority of the auditor to make adjustment of old and disputed claims, has no application to a compromise and settlement of a suit for taxes in a court of competent jurisdiction. Commonwealth v. Schmelz, 81 S. E. 45, 116 Va. 62. (2). Where an auditor acting for the commonwealth agrees, with the consent of the Attorney General, to accept the sum awarded by the circuit court, in settlement and discharge of all claims for taxes, the agreement is binding on the commonwealth."

SUBJECT: UNEMPLOYMENT COMPENSATION LAW; STATE TREASURER; BOND FOR FAITHFUL PERFORMANCE OF DUTIES

4 November, 1941.

I have verified by an examination of Section 12 of Chapter 108 of the Public Laws of 1941 that Section 13(a) of Chapter 1 of the Public Laws of 1936, Extra Session, has been amended to the effect that the State Treasurer, instead of giving a separate and additional bond conditioned upon the faithful performance of his duties in connection with the Unemployment Compensation Administration Fund, shall now be liable upon his official bond as State Treasurer and that since the enactment of the 1941 amendment no separate bond is required of the State Treasurer for the faithful performance of his duties in connection with the Unemployment Compensation Administration Fund.

I have not confused this fund with that of the Unemployment Compensation fund and the bond required in this connection under Section 9 of the Act, which was not amended, and I am still advertent to the fact that the Treasurer is still required to give a separate bond in connection with this latter fund.

I see no reason why the bond heretofore given by the State Treasurer in connection with the Unemployment Compensation Administration Fund should not be cancelled. No doubt, the bonding company has a form of cancellation and release which they would like to use and I suggest that you have them furnish one in order that it may be examined by you and some member of this Department, of course, before it is accepted.

SUBJECT: UNEMPLOYMENT COMPENSATION TAX; AUTHORITY OF THE COMMISSION TO PERMIT INSTALMENT PAYMENTS

26 June, 1942.

In your letter of June 25, you state that a number of unemployment compensation taxpayers have requested that they be permitted to pay the delinquent taxes in monthly instalments; that other taxpayers write in and request delays in the payment of the tax which is due for various periods of time from sixty to ninety days, and you inquire if, under the Unemployment Compensation Act, the Commission has authority to permit this practice.

Section 7(a)(1) of the Unemployment Compensation Act is in part as follows:

> "Such contributions shall become due and be paid by each employer to the Commission for the fund in accordance with such regulations as the Commission may prescribe, . . . Contributions shall become due on and shall be paid on or before the 25th day of May following the close of the calendar quarter in which such wages are paid and such contributions shall be paid by each employer to the Commission for the fund in accordance with such regulations as the Commission may prescribe, . . ."

From the above, it is clear that the Act requires that the taxes shall be paid on or before the 25th day of the month following the close of the calendar quarter. The Commission could not, by regulation, change this mandatory requirement of the law.

However, I wish to refer you to Sections 14(a) and (b) of the Act which relate to the collection of contributions. Under these subsections it will be found that contributions unpaid on the date on which they are due and payable, as prescribed by the Commission shall bear interest at the rate of one-half of one per cent per month after such date until payment, plus accrued interest, is received by the Commission. This section also provides that if, after due notice, any employer defaults in any payment of contributions or interest thereon, the amount due shall be collected by civil action to be instituted and prosecuted at the cost of the taxpayer.

It seems to me that under this latter section the Commission could, if they were satisfied in each individual case that there was merit in the case, agree with the taxpayer that those taxes which remained unpaid after the same had become due, no civil action would be instituted by the Commission for a reasonable length of time; provided, interest on such delinquent taxes is included in the amount set out in the statute and for the period during which the relief is granted.

I think also that the Commission could make this same agreement with such taxpayer with regard to the time that the certificate prescribed by Section 14(b) of the Act will be put on record in the office of the Clerk of the Superior Court.

SUBJECT: UNEMPLOYMENT COMPENSATION LAW; CLERK SUPERIOR COURT; SALARIES AND FEES; DOCKETING JUDGMENT

26 June, 1942.

You inquire as to what fees the Clerk of the Superior Court is entitled for docketing a judgment certified to said Clerk by the Unemployment Compensation Commission pursuant to Section 14(b) of the Unemployment Compensation Law. Section 14(b) provides in part as follows:

> ". . . if any contribution imposed by this act, or any portion thereof, and/or penalties duly provided for the nonpayment thereof shall not be paid within thirty days after the same become due and payable, the commission under the hand of its chairman, may certify the same in duplicate and forward one copy thereof to the clerk of the Superior Court of the county in which the delinquent resides or has property, and additional copies for each county in which the commission has reason to believe such delinquent has property located, which copy so forwarded to the clerk of the Superior Court shall be immediately docketed by said clerk and indexed on the cross index of judgment, and from the date of such docketing shall constitute a preferred lien upon any property which said delinquent may own in said county, with the same force and effect as a judgment rendered by the Superior Court. . . ."

It is my thought that a summary tax judgment issued by the Unemployment Compensation Commission is to be considered as an original judgment to be docketed in the counties where the taxpayer's property is located. It is specifically provided that the Clerk of the Superior Court shall immediately docket the judgment and index it on the cross index of judgments. The only acts required of the Clerk of the Superior Court under the provisions of the Unemployment Compensation Law are the docketing and cross indexing. This to my mind would allow the Clerk of the Superior Court to collect a fee for docketing and a fee for cross indexing. It is my opinion that in the absence of a local statute, the above are the only fees to which a Clerk of the Superior Court would be entitled for his services in handling the judgments about which you inquire.

OPINIONS TO PROBATION COMMISSION

SUBJECT: JUDGMENTS; CONFLICT BETWEEN CLERK'S MINUTE DOCKET AND PROBATION JUDGMENT SIGNED BY JUDGE; CORRECTION OF ERROR

24 August, 1940.

I have your letter of August 21, in which you state that in June, 1939, one William Taylor pled guilty to the crime of forcible trespass, and, according to the probation judgment signed by Judge Burgwyn, an eighteen months suspended sentence was imposed on him and he was placed on probation for three years. It appears, however, from an examination of the Clerk's Minute Book, that the minutes of the court stenographer in the Minute Book, which had been signed by Judge Burgwyn, provided for a six months suspended sentence.

The probationer having violated the terms of his judgment, the question now presents itself as to which shall govern, the suspended sentence contained in the Minute Docket, or the suspended sentence contained in the probation judgment signed by the judge.

Under the facts as they now exist in this case, I am of the opinion that the shorter sentence contained in the Minute Docket should be put into effect. Inasmuch as the Minute Docket and the judgment were both signed by the presiding Judge, they are both of equal dignity, and any doubt as between the two should be resolved in favor of the prisoner.

It is very clear, however, that on a proper motion by the Solicitor, and at a proper legal hearing at which the prisoner shall be present, the Court would have the power to amend the Minute Docket so as to make it speak the truth.

State v. Swepson, 84 N. C. 827;
State v. King, 27 N. C. 203;
State v. Craton, 28 N. C. 164;
16 C. J. 1322.

In 1 Freeman on Judgments (5th Ed.), page 322, Section 165, it is stated:

> "All courts have inherent power, independent of statute, to correct clerical errors at any time and to make the judgment entry correspond with the judgment recorded . . . It exists in criminal prosecutions as well as in civil cases."

Until, however, the error or mistake be corrected in the manner mentioned above, I am of the opinion that the suspended sentence contained in the Minute Docket should govern.

SUBJECT: PROBATION LAW; JUDGMENT AND SENTENCE

30 August, 1940.

You state that a court of record of this State sentenced a defendant on one count to serve a term of eighteen months on the roads, five of which were to be served immediately and the balance of thirteen months was suspended, and the prisoner placed on probation for a period of two years at the expiration of the five months prison sentence. You state further that this prisoner has been convicted of a subsequent offense and is now serving a term on the roads, and you inquire if, at the expiration of his present road sentence, you have authority to pray judgment as to the thirteen months remaining on the original sentence resulting from the original indictment.

By enacting Chapter 132 of the Public Laws of 1937, commonly known as the Probation Act, the Legislature was making an effort to avoid the attachment of the stigma of prison sentences to deserving persons who had been convicted, in order that such persons might be rehabilitated and become good citizens of the State, and, by the very terms of the first section of the Act, the General Assembly did not contemplate the actual imprisonment of a person convicted of crime, other than those crimes punishable by death or life imprisonment, in deserving cases, but, on the other hand, intended to provide that the judge of any court of record with criminal jurisdiction might suspend the execution of the sentence and place the defendant on probation, or impose a fine and also place the defendant on probation.

In the case to which you refer in your letter, it is very clear that the judge of the recorder's court in this instance intended to actually provide that the prisoner serve a five months term in prison and at the expiration of that five months term be placed on probation for a term of two years. This, in my opinion, is not a proper exercise of the authority given the judge under the terms of the Probation Act. However, it is the judgment of the court and one in which I think you would be justified in praying the judgment for the balance of the eighteen months in the original sentence after this prisoner has completed his term on the second sentence.

SUBJECT: REVOCATION OF PROBATION; RULES OF EVIDENCE

28 September, 1940.

You state that you have a number of revocation hearings before the judges of the several courts of this State each month, and you inquire if the rules of evidence would apply in presenting evidence of violation of probation by probationers.

As this is a matter which does not involve a jury and which should properly be brought to the attention of the court in order that he might determine whether or not the conditions of probation have been violated, I do not think that the rules of evidence would apply. In my opinion, the court is entitled to all information available with regard to the possible violation of the probation, and in my judgment all evidence could be presented, whether hearsay or otherwise.

SUBJECT: PROBATION; VIOLATION OF; REVOCATION

30 October, 1940.

You state that in 1937, one Gilbert Cheek plead guilty to a charge of larceny; that prayer for judgment was continued, and the defendant was placed on probation by the Recorder's Court of Iredell County for a period of three years; that in October 1938, this defendant left the State after being on probation for approximately eleven months, and that at that time an instanter capias was issued, but service was not had on the defendant; that the defendant has returned to Iredell County, after the expiration of his three-year probation period. You inquire if the court has authority to revoke the probation judgment and impose sentence.

I am of the opinion that since this defendant violated the terms of his probation by departing from the jurisdiction of the court before its expiration, the court has authority to revoke the probation judgment and order this defendant into custody.

SUBJECT: SUSPENSION OF SENTENCE AND PROBATION; PERIOD OF PROBATION OR SUSPENSION OF SENTENCE

19 February, 1941.

You inquire as to whether there is any distinction in the probation Act between superior courts and inferior courts as to the maximum probation period.

Michie's N. C. Code, 1939, Section 4665(4) provides, in part:

> "The period of probation or suspension of sentence shall not exceed a period of five years and shall be determined by the judge of the court and may be continued or extended, terminated or suspended by the court at any time within the above limit."

This particular section was referred to and discussed in S. v. Wilson, 216 N. C. 130.

I am unable to find any reasonable basis for a distinction in the Act between the superior and inferior courts as to the maximum period of probation, and I am of the opinion that the five years maximum applies equally to superior and inferior courts.

SUBJECT: REVOCATION OF PROBATION

7 March, 1941.

You state that you have a person who was placed on probation for a period of two years; that shortly before the expiration date a report was filed by one of your officers with the court citing certain violations of the probation judgment formerly imposed and asking that the court take action on the same. The court did not act upon this report at this time but took the matter under advisement, stating that he would act upon the same after considering it at a subsequent term of court. The case came on for a hearing before the same judge at a subsequent term of court, which convened after the probation period originally imposed had expired, and the court, after considering the same, entered an order extending the period of probation for an additional twelve months from and after the expiration of the original probation period.

I think the court's action in this case was correct. The defendant was reported for a violation of his probation judgment prior to the expiration of the period originally imposed, and the court's action in withholding judgment in the matter to a date subsequent to the expiration of the original period of probation would not, in my opinion, cause him to lose jurisdiction of the matter.

SUBJECT: PROBATION COMMISSION; JUDGMENTS; SUSPENDED SENTENCES

14 June, 1941.

From your letter of June 13 and the original judgment of Judge Burgwyn in the several cases against James A. Watkins, it appears that the Judge sentenced this defendant in cases numbered 1502, 1503, 1504 and 1505, to jail to be assigned to work under the supervision of the State Highway and Public Works Commission for a period of eighteen months; and in other cases, numbered 1506, 1507, 1508, 1509, 1513 and 1515, sentenced the defendant to an additional period of eighteen months, and, according to the judgment, provided that "in each case sentences to run concurrently with the sentences in 1502, 1503, 1504 and 1505."

A special condition was entered in this judgment which provided that the defendant "shall not violate any criminal law during the next five years," perhaps intending to put this defendant under probation at the expiration of the term of the sentence.

I do not think that the judgment as it is written and signed has the effect of placing this defendant on probation at the end of the term he is now serving, because the sentences in 1506, 1507, 1508, 1509, 1513 and 1515 are for the identical term as that meted out in those cases where he was sentenced to the roads, and the judgment provides that they shall run concurrently with that in the cases under which he is now serving the eighteen months term.

In my opinion, this defendant has not been placed on probation but would be subject to his release at the expiration of the service of the term to which he was sentenced in the cases numbered 1502, 1503, 1504 and 1505.

SUBJECT: PROBATION COMMISSION; MODIFICATION OF CONDITIONS; JUDGMENTS

18 October, 1941.

You state in your letter of October 17 that one Robert Hall was convicted of manslaughter in the Superior Court of Cumberland County, and was sentenced to the roads for a period of from three to five years, the sentence to be suspended, however, upon certain conditions, one of which was that the defendant was to pay into the office of the Clerk of the Superior Court of Cumberland County on the first day of each month, for a period of eight years, the sum of $15.00 for the use and benefit of one Texas Howard. You inquire if the court has the authority to modify this condition of the judgment, to the extent that it will enable the defendant to pay into court a lump sum in full settlement of this part of the judgment.

Consolidated Statutes 4665(3) provides: "The court shall determine and may impose, by order duly entered, and may at any time modify the conditions of probation . . ."

I think under this provision the court may, by order, modify this condition and permit the defendant to pay into court a lump sum in final settlement of this condition in the judgment.

SUBJECT: PROBATION COMMISSION; VIOLATIONS OF CONDITIONS OF JUDGMENT

28 October, 1941.

In your letter of October 22 you state that one Charles Jacobs pled guilty on July 9, 1940 in a court of competent jurisdiction to a criminal offense and was sentenced to six months on the roads, which sentence was suspended and this defendant was placed on probation for a period of one year; that in January, 1941, he was convicted of a subsequent offense in the Superior Court of Wake County and was given a one year sentence on the roads; that while serving the sentence on the subsequent conviction the period of probation of one year given him on the first offense expired, and you inquire if the judgment in the first offense may now be prayed, the one year probation period for the first offense having expired while this defendant was serving on the roads as the result of the conviction of the offense committed in January, 1941.

In my opinion the conviction of the subsequent offense having occurred prior to the expiration of the probation period of the first offense, a showing of this fact would be just reason for praying the judgment in the first case, as the conviction of the subsequent offense is a clear violation of the terms of the conditions under which he was placed on probation upon conviction of the first offense, it having occurred during the probationary period placed on him upon conviction of the first offense.

OPINION TO TEXTBOOK PURCHASE AND RENTAL COMMISSION

SUBJECT: TEXTBOOKS; WITHDRAWAL FROM TEXTBOOK RENTAL SYSTEM

21 October, 1941.

I have your letter of October 20. Chapter 301, Public Laws of 1941, provides as follows:

> "Whenever any county or city administrative unit has paid over to the State Textbook Purchase and Rental Commission, in rentals, a sum equal to the price fixed by said Commission for the sale of rental textbooks, said county or city administrative unit may, at its option, with the approval of the Commission, withdraw from the textbook rental system set up under rules and regulations adopted by the Commission, and upon such withdrawal, shall become the absolute owner of all such textbooks for which the purchase price has been paid in full to the said Commission."

Under this law, with the approval of the State Textbook Purchase and Rental Commission, a county or city administrative unit may withdraw from the textbook rental system when the sum paid in equals the price fixed by the Commission for the sale of rental textbooks. The language "under rules and regulations adopted by the Commission" has reference to the textbook rental system set up under such rules and regulations.

Upon application being filed for the withdrawal from the system by any unit, the Textbook Commission could approve the withdrawal as of such date as they found that the unit had paid in a sum equal to the price fixed by the Commission for the sale of the rental books. I believe that in the discretion of the Commission, they could approve the withdrawal retroactively, but not prior to the time that the statute was enacted; that is to say, March 15, 1941.

OPINION TO LIBRARY COMMISSION

SUBJECT: N. C. FAIR TRADE ACT; PURCHASES BY LIBRARY COMMISSION; STATE AGENCIES

14 February, 1941.

You inquire if the North Carolina Fair Trade Act applies to purchases made by the State Library Commission.

This Act is to be found as Chapter 350 of the Public Laws of 1937, otherwise referred to as House Bill No. 435 of the General Assembly of 1937. Under Section 7 of this Act, you will find the following:

> "This Act shall not apply to any prices offered in connection with, or contracts or purchases made by the State of North Carolina or any of its agencies or any of the political subdivisions of the said State."

I advise that under this section of the Act, the North Carolina Fair Trade Act has no application whatsoever to purchases made by your Commission, it being a State agency.

OPINIONS TO BOARD OF EXAMINERS OF PLUMBING AND HEATING CONTRACTORS

SUBJECT: APPLICATION OF CHAPTER 52, PUBLIC LAWS 1931, AS AMENDED, TO TOWNS HAVING INCREASED POPULATION SINCE 1930 CENSUS

19 September, 1940.

You inquire if, under the official census of 1940, the provisions of the Plumbing and Heating Contractors Act apply to plumbing and heating contractors who reside in cities and towns, which, since the 1940 census, would have a population of more than thirty-five hundred, which under the enumeration of 1930 did not come within the Act because the population of such cities and towns did not exceed thirty-five hundred.

Under the original Act, all persons engaged in the plumbing and heating business and holding a State license at that time were not required to take the examination required by the Act, but in 1939 this provision of the original Act was deleted and since the Act as it was originally drawn did not provide for any later census, and the application of the Act to towns which would increase in population during such later census, I am of the opinion that the legislature intended only to make the Act apply to those cities and towns which had a population of more than thirty-five hundred at the time of the ratification of the Act and would not embrace, without an amendment to the Act, plumbing and heating contractors who now live in cities or towns which have a population in excess of thirty-five hundred under the 1940 census.

SUBJECT: PLUMBING AND HEATING CONTRACTOR'S LICENSE; INSTALLATION OF AIR CONDITIONING SYSTEM BY INDEPENDENT CONTRACTOR; INTERSTATE COMMERCE

5 November, 1940.

I have your letter of October 25, in which you state that the Carrier Corporation of Syracuse sold and had installed an air conditioning system for the purpose of comfort cooling in the Colony Theater, Wilmington, North Carolina, before the incident was reported to your Board. It appears that this corporation made a lump sum contract with the Wil-Kin Theater Supply, Inc., of Atlanta, Georgia, for this installation.

You ask whether or not the Carrier Corporation should be required to obtain a license under Chapter 52, Public Laws of 1931, as amended by Chapter 224, Public Laws of 1939, before being allowed to engage in such activities. This law provides that "All persons, firms or corporations, whether resident or nonresident of the State of North Carolina, before engaging in either the plumbing or heating contracting business, or both, as defined in this article, shall first apply to the State Board of Examiners of Plumbing and Heating Contractors for examination and shall procure a license." Michie's N. C. Code, 1939, Section 5168(ww). This section also provides as follows:

> "The requirements of this article shall apply only to persons, firms, or corporations engaged in the business of either plumbing or heating contracting, or both, in cities or towns having a population of more than thirty-five hundred."

I am of the opinion that since the Carrier Corporation installed this machinery itself, it is required by this section to obtain a license to engage in the business of heating and plumbing contracting. Although the air conditioning system was shipped in interstate commerce, its installation was purely a local or intrastate function, and properly formed the basis for requiring a license before being engaged in. Browning v. Waycross, 233 U. S. 16; General Ry. Signal Co. v. Virginia, 246 U. S. 500; American Amusement Co. v. East Lake Chutes, 174 Ala. 526; Peck-Williamson Heating and Ventilation Co. v. McKnight, 140 Tenn. 563, 205 S. W. 419; Annotation, 101 A.L.R. 356.

The Carrier Corporation was the "person, firm, or corporation engaged in the business of either plumbing or heating contracting" within the meaning of our licensing statutes.

SUBJECT: RENEWAL OF EXPIRED LICENSE

18 January, 1941.

I have your letter of January 14. You advise that Sam E. Beck was a partner in the business conducted prior to 1931 under the name of Plumbing and Heating Sales Company, and that as a member of this firm, under Section 12 of Chapter 52, Public Laws of 1931, a license was issued to him and Henry S. Beck to engage in the business of plumbing and heating contracting. The license issued to the Plumbing and Heating Sales Company parnership, of which Sam E. Peck was a member, became dormant in 1933 and the firm went out of business. Thereafter, Sam E. Beck took the examination and received a license for heating contracting. He has now made application for renewal of the license issued to himself as a former member of the Plumbing and Heating Sales Company.

You inquire if the Board is authorized to make such renewal. In my opinion, the Board would be authorized to grant a renewal in accordance with its rules and regulations, as the statute, Michie's Code Section 5168-(xx) expressly authorizes the Board to make renewals of expired licenses.

OPINION TO BURIAL ASSOCIATION COMMISSION

SUBJECT: BURIAL ASSOCIATIONS; PAYMENT OF CASH BENEFITS

17 December, 1941.

In your letter of December 16, you inquire as to the obligation of a burial association to pay benefits to the estate of a member who came to his death while on active duty with the armed forces of the United States, and where all the expenses of the funeral and other incidentals are paid by the Federal Government.

You further inquire as to the obligation of a burial association to the estate of a member who is killed in battle at sea and is buried at sea by the Government.

I do not think there is any provision in the law, Chapter 130 of the Public Laws of 1941, which would authorize one of the burial associations to extend any of the benefits provided for by the Act, because in such cases the services to be performed by the association are for benefits of a funeral in merchandise and service, "with no free embalming or free ambulance service included in such benefits; and in no case shall any cash be paid. That no other free service or any other thing free shall be held out, promised, or furnished in any case."

I have considered Article 10 of the Act, which provides for benefits to be payable to the representatives of the deceased upon certain conditions. This would not be available in instances like the ones presented by you, because the service contemplated by the Act is furnished free of charge to the next of kin or representatives of the deceased, and there is no provision for the payment of cash in lieu of such benefits. In my opinion, Article 10 of the Act would apply only in those cases where the cost of the services contemplated would be borne by the next of kin or by the deceased's representative.

OPINIONS TO RURAL ELECTRIFICATION AUTHORITY

RE: RURAL ELECTRIFICATION; MEMBERSHIP CORPORATION; RIGHT TO EXTEND LINES OUT OF STATE

12 March, 1941.

I have your letter of March 7, in which you advise that a hearing is to be had on Thursday, March 13, at 11:00 o'clock, by a membership corporation asking for permission to extend its lines to serve members outside the State of North Carolina, and request that some member of my staff be present to assist you at that time.

The hearing involves the question as to whether an electric membership corporation organized under the Public Laws of 1935, Chapters 288 and 291, may extend its lines so as to serve out of state members. I wrote a letter on this subject to Mr. Dudley Bagley when he was Chairman of the Rural Electrification Authority, under date of November 16, 1938. If you so desire, you might refer to that letter as expressing the opinion of this office.

I have gone into the subject again, and after doing so, I have reached the conclusion that the opinion then expressed was correct. I am glad to give you a statement of my further thoughts about the matter.

This discussion may be clearer if we deal first with the question, not whether an existing electric membership corporation can extend its lines to serve out of state members, but rather whether such a corporation can be originally formed, under existing North Carolina law, with the partial purpose of serving out of state members. The answer to this question seems in the negative.

The North Carolina statutes on rural electrification are Public Laws 1935, Chapters 288 and 291, as amended, codified by Michie as Sections 1694(1)-1694(28). Chapter 288 sets up the State Rural Electrification Authority; Chapter 291 deals with formation and operations of local electric membership corporations.

Chapter 288 seems clearly to be drawn with the restricted purpose of serving only inhabitants of North Carolina. Section 2 says the purpose of the Rural Electrification Authority is "to secure electrical service for the rural districts *of the State* where service is not now being rendered . . ." and the powers granted by the Act are given "in order to accomplish that purpose." Subsection (i) of Section 2 empowers the Authority "To investigate all applications from communities for the formation of electric membership corporations and determine and pass upon the question of granting the authority to form such corporations; to provide forms for making such applications; and to do all things necessary to a proper determination of the question of establishment of the local electric membership corporations." The standard for approval by the State REA of any application for formation of these corporations is, then, whether it serves the purpose of furnishing electricity to inhabitants *of North Carolina*.

Public Laws 1935, Chapter 291, authorizes the formation of these local corporations, "for the purpose of promoting and encouraging the fullest possible use of electric energy in the rural section *of the state* by making electric energy available to inhabitants *of the state . . .*" So it would seem that these statutes do not contemplate forming corporations for out of state operations. Nor are the general grant of powers in Public Laws 1935, Chapter 291, Section 12, and the specific grant in Section 12 of the same Act inconsistent with this position, because in Section 12 the general powers are granted to the local electric corporation for the "accomplishment of its corporate purpose"; and the specific powers given it by Section 13 are those "necessary or convenient for carrying out the purpose for which it was formed . . ."

The conclusion is that the statutes do not authorize the *formation* of local electric membership corporations for the purpose of serving out of state patrons. See letter to Mr. Dudley Bagley referred to above.

The question presented is, however, whether a presently operating corporation can *extend* its lines out of the state. The answer seems to be the same as that above. Public Laws 1935, Chapter 291, Section 20, allows a local electric membership corporation to "*change any . . . provision*" in its certificate of incorporation simply by filing a certificate in proper form with the Secretary of State. No express power is given to the State REA, anywhere in the 1935 laws, to regulate these charter amendments. But the provisions to Public Laws 1935, Chapter 291, Section 20, restrict the nature of allowable amendments by saying that "no corporation shall amend its certificate of incorporation to embody therein any *purpose*, power, or provisions which would not be authorized if its original certificate, including such additional or changed purpose, power or provisions, were offered for filing at the time a certificate under this section is offered."

My conclusion is that out of state extension of its lines by an electric membership corporation is unauthorized.

After considering my letter of November 16, 1938, and this letter, if you find it necessary, I will be glad to assign some member of my staff to be present at your meeting, provided we are able to get away from the things we are now having to do for the members of the General Assembly.

SUBJECT: JONES-ONSLOW ELECTRIC MEMBERSHIP CORPORATION; RIGHT TO CONSTRUCT A GENERATING PLANT

26 May, 1941.

You have requested my opinion as to whether your Board is authorized under Section 21 of Chapter 291, Public Laws of 1935, to make application for the Jones-Onslow Electric Membership Corporation for a loan or grant from the United States to be used in part for the construction of a generating plant to furnish electric current to its members, including the United States Navy for the Marine base on New River and the proposed Marine air base on Neuse River.

In conference with you, it appears that sufficient electric energy is not available to this membership corporation for the purposes above mentioned, as well as serving its other members, without acquiring and constructing a generating plant. It is understood that the plant to be constructed for this purpose would cost approximately $2,000,000.

After full consideration of the Act, Chapter 291, Public Laws of 1935, I am of the opinion that your Board would be authorized under the Act to make application for such a loan or grant, if you find as a fact that it is necessary or requisite for this membership corporation to construct such a generating plant to accomplish its corporate purpose as authorized by the Act above referred to.

Section 12 of the Act provides that each corporation formed under this Act is hereby vested with all the power necessary or requisite for the accomplishment of its corporate purpose and capable of being delegated by the Legislature. Section 13 of the Act provides that a corporation created under the Act shall have the power to do any and all acts and things necessary or convenient for carrying out the purpose for which it was formed, including but not limited to the powers thereafter enumerated in the section.

I have before me copy of the charter of the Jones-Onslow Electric Membership Corporation, which provides that the corporation shall have the power to generate, manufacture, purchase, acquire and accumulate electric energy for its members, etc. This corporate power of generating electric current, in my opinion, is authorized by the statute, provided it is found by your Board that it is necessary or requisite for the accomplishment of the corporate purpose.

This is a matter which would have to be passed upon in connection with each individual application. To the extent herein stated, the opinion heretofore given by this office as to the right of a membership corporation to generate electric current is modified.

SUBJECT: RURAL ELECTRIFICATION; AMENDMENTS TO CHARTERS OF MEMBERSHIP CORPORATIONS

13 August, 1941.

In your letter of August 12, you inquire if, under the amendment to Chapter 291 of the Public Laws of 1935 by Chapter 260 of the Public Laws of 1941, an electric membership corporation may amend its charter by a vote of less than a majority of its members.

The 1941 amendment to this Act relates only to the powers of the board of directors of membership corporations and does not apply to an amendment to the certificate of incorporation.

Section 20 of the 1935 Act sets forth in detail how a certificate of incorporation of such corporations my be amended. Here you will find in subsection (c) of this section that the certificate of incorporation must be accompanied by an affidavit stating that the authority for the amendment has been approved by "the votes cast in person or by proxy of a majority of the members of the corporation entitled to vote."

This section of the 1935 Act has not been amended, and I advise that in order for a certificate of incorporation to be amended, authority for the same must be obtained from a majority of the members of the corporation entitled to vote.

SUBJECT: MUNICIPAL CORPORATIONS; ELECTRIC MEMBERSHIP CORPORATIONS

14 January, 1942.

In your letter of January 13, you inquire if a municipal corporation which owns and operates an electric generating and distribution system becomes a member of an electric membership corporation, formed under Chapter 291 of the Public Laws of 1935, such action would place the municipality under the supervision of the North Carolina Utilities Commission.

Section 14 of Chapter 291, Public Laws of 1935, provides that whenever an electric membership corporation is formed in the manner there provided, the same is declared to be a public agency and has within its limits the same rights of any other political subdivision of the State.

Under the present law, municipal corporations, which operate electric generation and distribution systems, are not supervised by the Utilities Commission, and our courts have held, in the Johnston County Case, that electric membership corporations formed under this Act do not come under the supervision of the Utilities Commission.

I do not think that the mere fact that a municipal corporation becomes a member of an electric membership corporation would have the effect of giving the Utilities Commission supervision of either the electric membership corporation or the municipality which has become a member thereof.

SUBJECT: CORPORATIONS; ELECTRIC MEMBERSHIP CORPORATIONS; INDIVIDUAL LIABILITY OF STOCKHOLDERS

10 April, 1942.

The question arises as to the individual liability of stockholders in electric membership corporations, created by Chapter 291 of the Public Laws of 1935, in those cases where employees of such electric membership corporations may be killed or injured as the result of an accident arising out of and in the course of their employment.

Under the general corporation laws of this State, stockholders in any corporation are not individually liable for any debts or any recovery which might be had against the corporation, the corporation itself being the legal entity which would be liable in such cases and then only to the extent of the assets of the corporation itself.

Attention is called to Section 5 in the Application for Membership in Electric Membership Corporations. Here you will find that "the applicant, by paying a membership fee and becoming a member, assumes no personal liability or responsibility for any debts or liabilities of the cooperative, and it is expressly understood that under the law, his private property cannot be attached for any debts or liabilities."

Attention is further called to Section 4 of the By-Laws of Electric Membership Corporations. Here it is stated that "private property of the members of the cooperative shall be exempt from execution for the debts of the cooperative and no member shall be individually liable or responsible for any debts or liabilities of the cooperative."

Under the general corporation laws of this State, as stated above, which laws govern electric membership corporations, there would be no individual liability on the part of stockholders in such corporations for any debts or liabilities of the corporation itself and these laws are supplemented by the application for membership which an individual might make, as well as the by-laws of such corporations.

OPINIONS TO STATE HOSPITALS AND INSTITUTIONS

SUBJECT: JUVENILE COURTS; JURISDICTION

6 July, 1940.

It seems from your letter of June 27 that the question raised therein has become moot in so far as the facts in connection with the particular case are concerned, the case already having been disposed of. This being true, I seriously doubt whether a ruling on this particular set of facts would be of any value to you in the future, as the next case might have different facts, at least to such an extent as to make the rule laid down inapplicable.

Under the provisions of Section 5039 of Michie's N. C. Code of 1939, it is provided that jurisdiction of a Juvenile Court over a child, once obtained, shall continue during the minority of the child unless the child be committed to an institution supported and controlled by the State.

Section 5054 provides that any order or judgment made by the Court in the case of any child shall be subject to such modification from time to time as the Court may consider to be for the welfare of each child except that a child committed to an institution supported and controlled by the State may be released or discharged only by the governing body or officer of such institution.

The Supreme Court of North Carolina, in the case of State v. Burnett, 179 N. C. 735, at 740, discussing the exceptions in the Juvenile Court Act relating to children who are committed to State institutions, uses the following language:

> "It may be well to note that the exceptions appearing here as to children committed to a State institution refer only to the action of the Juvenile Court in the premises and for the reason doubtless that it was not considered feasible that rules and discipline of that character should be liable to obstruction or interference by any one of the one hundred or more Juvenile Courts existent throughout the State. But the exemptions referred to create no limitations on the jurisdiction of the Superior Court in these cases which, under the first sections of the act and by virtue of its powers, as a court of general jurisdiction administering both law and equity, may always, on proper application and appropriate writs, make inquiry and investigation into the status and condition of children disposed of under the statute and make such orders and decrees therein as the right and justice of the case may require."

It seems to me from the language used in the statutes and by the Supreme Court of North Carolina that when a child is committed by the Juvenile Court to an institution supported and controlled by the State, that the Juvenile Court would lose its jurisdiction over the child and that such jurisdiction over the custody and control of the child would be transferred to the institution to which it was committed. If such child so committed should be released by the institution to which it was committed on parole and should thereafter, and after becoming sixteen years of age, violate the terms of the parole and commit other crimes, I seriously doubt the right of the Juvenile Court to change the original order committing such child to the State institution and commit it to another State institution. Certainly, the Recorder's Court or Superior Court would have jurisdiction of crimes committed by a child after becoming sixteen years of age.

SUBJECT: OLD AGE INSURANCE; RIGHT TO RECEIVE PAYMENTS TO SON OF INSURED

18 September, 1940.

I received your letter of September 17. I inquired of the Social Security Board office of this City and talked with Mr. R. F. Tate. He advises me that if John Thomas Blanton's father is eligible for Old Age Insurance, his son would receive one-half the amount paid to the father until the son is eighteen years of age.

Under the law, the father is the guardian of the money paid for the minor son and has control of the expenditure of the money. If the father would be willing to pay the money over to your institution for the payment of the maintenance fee of $20 per month, and leave the rest of the money with your institution to provide for his personal needs and comfort, I do not think there would be any legal objection to your receiving the money.

I am sending a copy of this letter to the Social Security Board. In the event it has an opinion contrary to the one expressed in this letter, I am requesting it to write you, sending me a copy of the letter.

SUBJECT: STATE-OWNED PROPERTY; LEASES

19 September, 1940.

You inquire if your Board of Directors has authority to permit certain property owned by your school to be used by the Boy Scouts of your county for the purpose of erecting a cabin on such property, which will be used exclusively by the Girl and Boy Scouts of your county as a camping site.

Of course, the land upon which your school is situated was purchased and is held by the State for the purpose of conducting a School for the Deaf, and should your board find it expedient to lease this property to the organization to be used for the purpose of building a camp site, I think upon compliance with the provisions of C. S. 7524, et seq., this property might be leased to the organization for the purpose desired.

Under these statutes, you will find that the Governor of the State is authorized and empowered to execute a deed under the Great Seal of the State to any lands, the title to which is now vested in the State, for the use of any State institution upon application of the trustees or directors; such deed shall show such conveyance is for the best interests of the institution and shall be approved by the Council of State. If your board should make the recommendation to the Governor and Council of State, showing that it is for the best interests of your institution, I am quite sure that the conveyance would be approved by them.

SUBJECT: INSANE PERSONS AND INCOMPETENTS; HOSPITALS FOR INSANE; FURNISHING INFORMATION TO INSURANCE COMPANY

19 September, 1940.

You inquire if you should furnish information to representatives of an insurance company, as to the physical condition and your opinion of the cause of a patient's injury whom you had under surveillance as a patient at the State Hospital and who died while in your custody.

I am not prepared to say whether or not this opinion of your observation of his condition would be privileged information available only to the patient's family or a personal representative; however, I think the better practice would be to await an order from some court of competent jurisdiction requiring you to give this information to others than members of the deceased's immediate family or any personal representative.

SUBJECT: EDUCATION; MINIMUM AGE FOR ADMISSION, N. C. SCHOOL FOR THE DEAF

8 October, 1940.

You inquire if the North Carolina School for the Deaf would be authorized to admit a deaf child before it has reached its seventh birthday.

I am unable to find any statute which to my mind would authorize the North Carolina School for the Deaf to admit a deaf child before it has reached its seventh birthday. C. S. 5892 contains rules for admission to the North Carolina School for the Deaf. This section places the limit between the ages of eight and twenty-three. C. S. 5764, which was enacted after C. S. 5892, provides that every deaf and every blind child of sound mind in North Carolina, who shall be qualified for admission into a State School for the Deaf or the Blind, shall attend the School for the Deaf or Blind for a term of nine months each year between the ages of seven and eighteen years. This statute, in my opinion, would have the effect of reducing the minimum age limit for a deaf child who applied for admission to your Institution from eight years to seven.

I am in entire accord with your desire to render all possible assistance to deaf children, but unless there is some statute which I have overlooked, it will be necessary that the Legislature of North Carolina change the statute before you would be authorized to admit children under the age of seven years.

SUBJECT: CRIMINAL INSANE; HOSPITALS FOR THE INSANE; RELEASE TO PRIVATE HOSPITALS

15 October, 1940.

You state that one Oscar Thomas Malpass was admitted to the criminal insane department of the State Hospital from the State's Prison, in accordance with the procedure laid down by law in this regard; that he had been sentenced to the State Prison prior to this time for a period of twelve months, and that this sentence will expire on November 11 of this year. You state further that for some time this patient has been confined to his bed; has various delusions, and declines food and it is necessary for you to tube feed him each day. You state that his people are alarmed about his condition and that your staff is also apprehensive about him, and that his family is desirous of having him transferred to a private institution for further care and treatment.

This man was no doubt committed to your Hospital under C. S. 6238. Here it will be found that all convicts becoming insane after commitment to the State's Prison, and the fact being certified as required by law, shall be admitted to the appropriate State Hospital. It is further provided here that in case of the expiration of the sentence of any convict, insane person, while such person is confined to the said hospital, such person shall be kept until restored to his right mind or such time as he may be considered harmless and incurable.

Under C. S. 6227, it is provided that when it is deemed desirable that any inmate of any State Hospital be transferred to any licensed private hospital within the State, the executive committee may so order and a certified copy of the commitment filed at the State Hospital, and the order of the executive committee shall be sufficient warrant for holding such insane person by the officers of such private hospital.

I am of the opinion that the above statutes are sufficient authority for you to release this man to a private hospital. This could be done either on the expiration of his sentence, which is the 11th day of November of this year, or if he is now considered harmless and incurable.

SUBJECT: INSANE PERSONS AND INCOMPETENTS; PARTY NOT TRIED BEFORE COMMITMENT TO HOSPITAL; RESTORATION; RELEASE
RE: SAMUEL STOVALL

25 October, 1940.

From an examination of the judgment against the above named person rendered at the June Term, 1931, of the Superior Court of Halifax County, it appears to me that this defendant was not put on trial at the time he was committed to your hospital. This is in accord with the former letter written by this office to Mr. Edwin Gill, Commissioner of Paroles, dated August 7, 1940.

At that time, Mr. Gill was advised that the hospital authorities would be the judges as to whether Stovall had been restored to his proper mind and that his release would be governed by C. S. 6237. Here, you will find that a person who has been acquitted of a crime because he was incapable of being tried on account of insanity, and who has been committed to a State Hospital as therein provided, upon becoming restored to his right mind, it is the duty of the authorities having the care of such person to notify the sheriff of the county from which he came, who shall order that he appear before the Judge of the Superior Court to be dealt with according to law. This means, of course, that if he had not been tried before he was committed to the hospital because of insanity, upon the restoration of his sanity, such person should be returned to the county from which he came to face trial upon the charges originally preferred against him.

SUBJECT: INSANE PERSONS; RELEASE FROM STATE HOSPITAL ON BOND

18 February, 1941.

I understand from your letter of February 11 that there is a patient in the State Hospital at Morganton whose cousin desires to have him released on bond; that the Board of Directors has consented to his release upon a $5,000 bond, executed by the cousin, with currency or government bonds as security, but that you are in doubt as to whether the bond should be approved by the Hospital authorities or by the Clerk of the Superior Court in Guilford, the County of the patient's residence.

Although it is apparent from the statutory form appearing in N. C. Code Ann. (Michie, 1939), Sec. 6217, and from the reference in Sec. 6218 to a patient released on bond's being "sent back to the proper hospital," that it was intended that patients who have already been committed to hospitals may be released on bond, the statutes make no clear provision regulating the manner of executing and approving the bond in such cases. When a bond is given to secure the release of an insane person before he has ever been committed to a hospital, it is provided in Sec. 6193 that the amount of the bond shall be fixed by the clerk who adjudged such person insane. Sec. 6216 provides that *all* bonds restraining insane persons from committing injuries "shall be transmitted to the clerk of the superior court of the county wherein said insane person is settled, for safekeeping." If the only purpose of transmitting the bond to the clerk is "safekeeping," that is some indication that approval by the clerk is unnecessary. On the other hand, the requirement that the clerk approve the bond when executed before commitment suggests the possibility of a requirement that all bonds be approved by him.

In the absence of a more specific provision in the statute, it seems to me that out of caution it would be wisest to have the bond in this case approved both by the Hospital authorities and by the Clerk of the Superior Court of Guilford County. The Board of Directors having authorized the acceptance of a bond in the sum of $5,000, it will only be necessary now to secure the approval of the Clerk.

As to the form of the bond, it seems to me that the statutory form contained in N. C. Code Ann. (Michie, 1939), Sec. 6217, should be strictly followed. I would, therefore, advise that the bond be prepared in that form, omitting any recital of the intention of the cousin to remove the patient to Kansas. I would further advise that the bond be filed in the office of the Clerk and that it should not be sent to Kansas.

SUBJECT: INSANE PERSONS AND INCOMPETENTS; CRIMINAL INSANE; RELEASE FROM STATE HOSPITAL

5 March, 1941.

After examining the orders and transcripts of testimony in the cases of State v. Saih Hanes and State v. Malcombe Cole, I am of the opinion that neither of these men has been acquitted of the offense with which he was charged. Although there were findings to the effect that the men were insane at the time the offenses were committed, there were no pleas of not guilty and the only evidence received related to the mental condition of the prisoners. The proceedings seem to have been solely for the purpose of determining the capacity of the defendants to plead rather than for the purpose of deciding their guilt or innocence of the charge.

Taking this view of the two cases, I advise that the prisoners have been committed under C. S. 6236 and that they should be released from the hospital according to the procedure contained in C. S. 6240. You should notify the Clerk of the Superior Court of Buncombe County that the men have recovered and are restored to normal health and sanity.

It will be the duty of the Clerk to place the cases against these men upon the docket of the Superior Court of his county for trial, and they should not be discharged without an order from the Court. You should also notify the Sheriff of Buncombe County, and it will become his duty to remove them to the jail of his county.

After these men have been removed from the State Hospital, the provisions of C. S. 6240 should be fully complied with.

SUBJECT: INSANE PERSONS AND INCOMPETENTS

14 March, 1941.

The only provision in the law which would permit you to perform operations on patients in your hospital is to be found as Consolidated Statutes 7221, and following. Here you will find that the medical staff of any penal or charitable hospital or institution of the State is authorized to have any surgical operation performed by competent and skillful surgeons upon any inmate of any such charitable hospital or institution, when, in the judgment of the board created by such statute, such operation would be for the improvement of the mental, moral or physical condition of such inmate.

This statute creates a board, consisting of one representative of the medical staff of the several charitable and penal institutions of the State, and one from the State Board of Health, such representatives to be designated by the governing bodies of the several institutions. An operation could not be performed on a patient without the recommendation of this board; and, it is further provided that such operation should not be performed until the same shall have been affirmed by the Governor and the Secretary of the State Board of Health.

I do not think you would be safe in getting a blanket approval of the parents of a minor child who has been committed to your institution.

SUBJECT: INSANE PERSONS AND INCOMPETENTS; COMMITMENT TO STATE HOSPITAL; CONVICTS FROM STATE PRISON

25 June, 1941.

I have your letter of June 24, in which you ask whether or not a regular commitment by the Clerk of the Court of Wake County is a legal requirement for admitting convicts from State Prison who have become insane to the Criminal Insane Department of the State Hospital. You state that you have been requested by the Prison to accept a patient by transfer without regular commitment papers.

I am of the opinion a regular commitment as required by C. S. 6190, et seq., should be obtained before admission of such patients to the Hospital is allowed. C. S. 6238 provides that: "All convicts becoming insane after commitment to the State Prison, and the fact being certified *as now required by law in the case of other insane persons,* shall be admitted to the hospital designated in Sec. 6236." It would seem that the underscored portion of the above statute refers to a regular proceeding before a Clerk of the Superior Court, at which the patient has an opportunity to be heard and examined, and commitment ordered or denied, as provided by law.

The last part of C. S. 6238 provides that patients transferred from prison under its provisions shall be kept after the expiration of their sentences if they are still insane. To confine them after their sentences have expired, without giving them an opportunity to be heard and the issue of their insanity properly adjudicated, would approach very closely a denial of due process of law guaranteed by the Constitution. In re Boyett, 136 N. C. 415.

For your protection, I advise that a proper commitment be required before convicts of this type are admitted.

SUBJECT: INSANE PERSONS AND INCOMPETENTS; RELEASE FROM STATE HOSPITAL

30 December, 1941.

I have your letter of December 29, enclosing a letter of Mr. Wolfe, Clerk Superior Court of Mecklenburg County, along with a copy of the judgment in the case against Walter Mason.

An examination of the Clerk's letter and the judgment indicates to me that the defendant in this case was actually put on trial for the crime charged. The issue submitted to the jury was, "Was Walter Mason insane and incapable of committing a crime on the 5th of January, 1936, *at which time the State alleges he killed Andy Cheshire?* Answer: Yes." And the record in the Clerk's office discloses the following:

> "Upon the coming in of the Verdict answering the issue 'Yes' as to the defendant's insanity, the Court directs the jury to render a verdict of Not Guilty."

The judgment in this case also discloses, in the second paragraph, "that the said case was tried and the court submitted one issue, which reads as follows: . . ." The judgment then sets out the issue quoted above, as well as the answer of the jury.

This simply means that in those cases where the defendant has actually been put on trial for the crime charged and the jury finds, upon a proper issue being submitted, that at the time of the alleged commission of the crime, the defendant was insane, then the jury should properly render a verdict of not guilty of the crime charged. If, on the other hand, upon the case coming on for trial, it is found upon proper investigation at that time: i.e., at the time of the trial, that the defendant is incapable of entering a plea of guilty or not guilty and the jury so finds, then defendant should be committed to the hospital and held until such time as he may have been restored to sanity. In such cases, your duty would be to comply with C. S. 6037 and notify the sheriff in order that such prisoner may be remanded to the proper court for trial upon the original case and he should be thereupon discharged under C. S. 6240.

The provisions of C. S. 6239 apply to cases where a person has been found not guilty by a jury of the crime with which he is charged, upon the grounds that at the time of the alleged crime he was insane. This person could be discharged from your hospital only under C. S. 6239, and, since the solicitor, upon the calling of the case for trial, announced in open court that the State would not ask for a verdict of a capital crime but of a less degree of crime, this patient can be discharged from your hospital only on an order from the Governor.

SUBJECT: LEGAL SETTLEMENTS; HUSBAND AND WIFE

16 January, 1942.

You state that the Clerk of the Superior Court of Martin County has pending before him a petition to commit one Annie Mae Tucker to the State Hospital as a drug addict, but there is some question as to her legal settlement in Martin County, because, less than a year ago, she was brought into this county by her husband from Virginia and abandoned by him; that she instituted criminal proceedings for nonsupport and he has been sending her money for her support, under an agreement resulting from the criminal proceedings.

Under the statute on legal settlements, C. S. 1342, legal settlements may be acquired in any county so as to entitle the party to be supported by such county only in the manner therein set out. Subsection (1) of this section provides that every person who has resided continuously in any county for one year shall be deemed legally settled in that county. Subsection (2) provides that "a married woman shall always follow and have the settlement of her husband, if he have any in the State; otherwise, her own at the time of her marriage, if she then had any, shall not be lost or suspended by the marriage, but shall be that of her husband, till another is acquired by him, which shall then be the settlement of both."

I advise that if the husband of this woman is legally settled in the State of Virginia and was so at the time he brought his wife into this State, she has no legal settlement here, but she has and follows the settlement of her husband.

SUBJECT: STATE INSTITUTIONS; N. C. ORTHOPEDIC HOSPITAL; TORT LIABILITY; INSURANCE

10 February, 1942.

I am in receipt of your letter of February 6, 1942, in which you inquire concerning the advisability of the Hospital's carrying liability insurance. You state that you have understood heretofore that the Hospital is a State institution and could not be sued.

I am of the opinion that your conclusion is correct, and that the Hospital, being an agency of the State, could not be sued for tort liability, and, consequently, no liability insurance should be carried thereon.

An examination of the pertinent statutes make it clear that the North Carolina Orthopedic Hospital is an agency of the State. C. S. 7252-7254(a). Its operation and maintenance is provided by the State Appropriations Act, subsection V, Section 1, Chapter 107, Public Laws of 1941.

It is well settled in this jurisdiction that an agency of the State can only be sued when expressly authorized to be sued by the State. Moody v. State Prison, 128 N. C. 12; Jones v. Commissioners, 130 N. C. 451; Carpenter v. Atlanta & C. A. L. Ry. Co., 184 N. C. 400, 114 S. E. 693. No authority to sue the North Carolina Orthopedic Hospital has been granted by the Legislature.

SUBJECT: INSANE PERSONS; CONVICTS BECOMING INSANE AFTER COMMITMENT TO STATE PRISON; DISCHARGE; TRANSFER TO FEDERAL HOSPITAL

16 March, 1942.

You state in your letter of March 14 that you have a patient who was committed to the criminal insane department of your Hospital on January 29, 1940, from the State Prison on regular commitment papers in accordance with the statute, and that his term has already expired. You further state that the matter has been taken up by his family with the Government authorities relative to his transfer to a Federal institution. You desire to know whether, in my opinion, you would be authorized to release this patient if accommodations could be found for him in a Federal hospital or institution.

C. S. 6238 provides:

> "All convicts becoming insane after commitment to the State Prison, and the fact being certified as now required by law in the case of other insane persons, shall be admitted to the hospital designated in section 6236. In case of the expiration of the sentence of any convict, insane person, while such person is confined to such hospital, such person shall be kept until restored to his right mind or such time as he may be considered harmless and incurable."

Under the provisions of this section, ordinarily you would not be authorized to discharge a person of the type referred to in your letter unless he was restored to his right mind or unless he should be considered harmless and incurable. The purpose of the statute above referred to is primarily to protect society in general from these unfortunate persons and to afford treatment to such persons with the hope that they may at some future date be restored to their normal faculties. If the Veterans Administration is willing to accept the responsibility for the person referred to in your letter and is in a position to furnish him accommodations in a place where he will not only be given treatment, but will be confined so as to not be dangerous to society as a whole, it is my thought that you would have a right to release him to the Veterans Administration.

SUBJECT: HOSPITALS FOR THE INSANE; AUTOPSIES

4 May, 1942.

C. S. 6785, and following, which provides for the disposition of dead human bodies to the various medical schools in this State, for the purpose of studying anatomy, specifically provides that the Act shall not apply to the dead bodies of persons who are inmates of State Hospitals. The only other statute relating to autopsies which might be applicable is C. S. 5003(1). This statute is as follows:

> "The right to perform an autopsy upon the dead body of a human being shall be limited to cases specially provided by statute or by direction of the will of the deceased; cases where a coroner or a majority of a coroner's jury deem it necessary upon an inquest to have such autopsy; and cases where the husband or wife of one of the next of kin or nearest known relative or other person charged by law with the duty of burial, in the order named and as known, shall authorize such examination or autopsy."

For your information, I suggest that Dr. Parrott, of Caswell Training School, has been in communication with this office relative to this subject and has asked that we assist him in preparing legislation which would permit an examination of the brain of deceased inmates of the State Hospitals, for the purpose of advancing the medical science in this field. This office has this legislation under consideration and will have a bill prepared for the next General Assembly prior to its convening.

SUBJECT: CASWELL TRAINING SCHOOL; DISCHARGE OF PUPILS

15 June, 1942.

You inquire as to the method to be used in discharging a pupil from the Caswell Training School, where such pupil becomes dangerous and a menace to the remainder of the pupils.

Section 5904 of Michie's North Carolina Code, 1939, Annotated, which deals with the discharging of pupils from the Caswell Training School, provides:

> "Any pupil of said school may be discharged or returned to his or her parents or guardian when in the judgment of the directors it will not be beneficial to such pupil, or will not be for the best interests of said school, to retain the pupil therein."

Under the provisions of this Section, upon action of the Board of Directors of the institution finding that it will not be beneficial to the particular pupil, or that it will not be for the best interest of the school for the pupil to remain therein, you would be authorized to discharge the pupil.

MISCELLANEOUS OPINIONS NOT DIGESTED

SUBJECT: STATE-SUPPORTED INSTITUTIONS; TUITION; RESIDENCE OF MINORS

27 September, 1940.

You inquire as to whether or not students under twenty-one years of age, whose parents reside outside the State of North Carolina but own property in North Carolina, should be required to pay the out-of-State tuition rate while enrolled as students in Western Carolina Teachers College.

The courts of our State have held that the residence of a minor is that of his father, if living, and if the father is not living, that of the mother. This is true even when the child is allowed to live away from his parents, receive wages for his work and pay his expenses out of the same, the Court holding that this does not amount to an emancipation unless it is the manifest intention of the parent to release all parental authority and control. Daniel v. Railroad, 171 N. C. 23.

Thus it becomes necessary in the cases referred to in your letter to determine the residence of the parents in order to determine the rate of tuition to be paid by the students.

The Supreme Court of North Carolina has defined "residence" in numerous cases. In the case of Watson v. Railroad, 152 N. C. 215, the Court defines residence as follows:

> "The word 'residence' has, like the word 'fixtures', different shades of meaning in the statutes . . . Residence is dwelling in a place for some continuance of time and is not synonymous with domicil, but means a fixed and permanent abode or dwelling as distinguished from a mere temporary locality of existence; . . . Residence is made up of the *fact* and *intention*. There must be the fact of abode and the intention of remaining."

In the case of Brann v. Haynes, 194 N. C. 571, at page 577, the Court, in discussing the question of residence, says:

> "All the authorities sustain the following statement of the law: Actually ceasing to dwell within a state for an uncertain period without definite intention as to any fixed time of returning constitutes non-residence even though there be a general intention to return at some future time."

In the case of Discount Corporation v. Radecky, 205 N. C. 163, the Court, in defining the word "residence," says:

> "The term 'residence' has no fixed meaning which is applicable to all cases, its definition in a particular case depending upon the connection in which it is used and the nature of the subject to which it pertains."

From the above definitions you can readily see that it is very difficult to lay down a general rule which would be applicable to all cases involving the question of residence. It is possible that each case might prevent facts which of necessity would prevent the application of any general rule which might be laid down. The fact that the parents of a student own property in the State of North Carolina would not within itself make the parents residents of North Carolina. But ownership of property might become one of the elements in determining the residence of the owner of such property. A person might own any amount of property in the State of North Carolina and still be a non-resident. On the other hand, a person can be a resident of the State of North Carolina without owning any property in this State.

When a student under the age of twenty-one years presents himself for registration, it is necessary that you determine whether the permanent home of the parents of such student is in the State of North Carolina or elsewhere. In arriving at a conclusion, you should take into consideration where the parents actually live, whether they are located at such place temporarily or permanently, the intention as to remaining in such locality, and all the other facts and circumstances in connection therewith which would throw any light on the subject. After considering all the facts, if they show that the parents are residents of another State in the sense that they have their permanent home in such State, they are non-residents of this State, and the student should be charged the non-resident tuition rate.

RE: LICENSE TAXES; CITIES AND TOWNS; TOBACCO JOBBERS HAVING NO PLACE OF BUSINESS IN TOWN BUT SELLING AND DELIVERING FROM TRUCKS; SECTION 149, REVENUE ACT OF 1939

24 September, 1940.

In your letter of the 21st you state that out-of-town jobbers, having no place of business in your Town, send their trucks and cars there and make sales to your merchants. The sales are made direct from the trucks or cars and deliveries are made at the time the orders are received. You inquire my opinion whether, under Section 149 of the Revenue Act of 1939, your Town may impose a license tax upon such jobbers. That section authorizes cities and towns to lay a tax, not in excess of the State tax, upon persons "engaged in the business of retailing and/or jobbing cigarettes, cigars, chewing tobacco, snuff, or any other tobacco product."

In my opinion, towns and cities may impose a license tax upon tobacco jobbers engaged in such commerce notwithstanding that they have no local place of business. The tax is upon those retailing or jobbing tobacco, and it is not required that the trade be carried on from a local place of business. Those who sell and immediately deliver from trucks or cars are engaged in the business in the Town fully as much as local wholesalers and jobbers are, and if the frame of your ordinance follows that of the section, the tax is equal and uniform and not discriminatory. Hilton v. Harris, 207 N. C. 465, State v. Bridgers, 211 N. C. 235.

SUBJECT: TAXATION; EXEMPTIONS; PERSONAL PROPERTY SUBJECT TO LEVY

8 October, 1940.

You inquire as to the right of a tax collector to levy on the personal property of a taxpayer where the personal property of the taxpayer is not valued over $300.00.

Prior to the enactment of the Machinery Act of 1939, this office ruled that the property actually exempted from taxation under the $300.00 exemption was also exempt from sale for taxes, but that personal property acquired by the taxpayer after the listing date or after taxes became due was subject to levy. This conclusion was based on the fact that Article V, Section 5, of the North Carolina Constitution authorized the General Assembly to exempt certain personal property to a value not exceeding $300.00, and that the Legislature under the authority granted by this section of the Constitution exempted certain personal property, and in the provision relative to levy provided that all personal property subject to taxation was liable to be seized and sold for taxes.

This provision was never completely interpreted by our Supreme Court, but in the case of Carstarphen v. Plymouth, 186 N. C. 90(1923), the Court by way of dicta says that the tax collector could have levied on any property except that exempted by constitutional and legislative enactment in conformity thereto. And, in the case of Building and Loan v. Burwell, 206 N. C. 359(1934), the Court by way of dicta said the lien for the payment of taxes assessed against personal property attached only from the date of levy thereon, subject to certain exemptions specified in Constitution, Article V, Sections 3 and 5.

The Machinery Act of 1939, Section 1713(c), provides that any personal property of the taxpayer may be levied upon and sold for failure to pay taxes, regardless of the time at which it was acquired and regardless of the existence of debt or creation of mortgages or liens thereon. It will be noted that this section does not refer to property "subject to taxation." The Supreme Court has not, even by way of dicta, discussed or passed upon the provisions of the Machinery Act of 1939 relative to the right of a tax collector to levy on personal property and it is entirely possible that the Court would now hold that even property subject to the $300.00 exemption may be levied upon to collect the taxes assessed against other property of the taxpayer. This, it seems, would be the logical conclusion to be reached under the Machinery Act of 1939, unless the Court regards the Constitution itself as sufficient to prohibit the levy. The constitutional provision is permissive rather than mandatory, and if it does not require the exemption of the property from taxation in the absence of legislative action, it is difficult to see how it could require exemption of such property from levy unless the Legislature provided for such exemption.

SUBJECT: CITY AND COUNTY TAXES; SALE OF TAX LIENS; SALE ADVERTISED ON LEGAL HOLIDAY; POSTPONEMENT TO NEXT BUSINESS DAY

28 October, 1940.

In your letter of the 26th, you state that the Clerk of the Town of Forest City has advertised the sale of tax liens for Monday, November 11, 1940, that being declared to be a legal holiday by C. S. 3959, and you ask whether a re-advertisement is necessary.

In my opinion, a re-advertisement is not necessary to the legality of the sale.

Section 1715(d) of the Machinery Act of 1939, under which the sale is advertised, expressly provides that the sale "may be continued from day to day, if continuance is necessary in order to complete the sales, without further advertisement." See, also, to the same effect C. S. 692, relating to execution and judicial sales, and C. S. 3960, which provides that when the day for doing an act falls on a legal holiday, the act may be done on the next succeeding business day. Section 1715(L) also provides that the tax lien sale shall not be invalidated by "the failure or neglect of the collector to offer any tax lien or real estate for sale at the time mentioned in the advertisement or notice of such sale," nor shall it be invalidated by "failure of the collector to adjourn the sale from day to day, or any irregularity or informality in the order or manner in which tax liens or real estate may be offered for sale."

Under these provisions, it would seem to be clearly within the power of the collector or clerk to appear at the time and place mentioned in the advertisement and give notice that the sale is postponed to the same hour on the next succeeding business day, the 12th. However, it would be advisable for him also to post notice thereof on the courthouse door, as provided in C. S. 692, and I do not think it would be out of order for him to post a like notice at any other place at which the sale is advertised, and to give a short newspaper notice thereof immediately above or below the next advertisement of the sale, these things to be done now and without delay.

SUBJECT: WORKMEN'S COMPENSATION ACT; RIGHTS AND REMEDIES AGAINST THIRD PARTY FOR NEGLIGENCE CAUSING DEATH OF EMPLOYEE

22 January, 1941.

You inquire as to the rights and remedies of the administrator of a deceased employee covered by the provisions of the Workmen's Compensation Act, who was killed in the course of his employment, but by the negligence of a third party.

The rights and remedies about which you inquire are contained in Section 11 of the Workmen's Compensation Act. This section provides:

> "The rights and remedies herein granted to an employee where he and his employer have accepted the provisions of this Act, respectively, to pay and accept compensation on account of personal injury or death by accident, shall exclude all other rights and remedies of such employee, his personal representative, parents, dependents or next of kin, as against his employer at common law, or otherwise, on account of such injury, loss of service, or death: Provided, however, that in any case where such employee, his personal representative, or other persons may have a right to recover damages for such injury, loss of service, or death from any person other than the employer, compensation shall be paid in accordance with the provisions of this Act: Provided, further, that after the Industrial Commission shall have issued an award, the employer may commence an action in his own name and or in the name of the injured employee or his personal representative for damages on account of such injury or death, and any amount recovered by the employer shall be applied as follows: First to the payment of actual court costs, then to the payment of attorney's fees when approved by the Industrial Commission; the remainder or so much thereof as is necessary shall be paid to the employer to reimburse him for any amount paid and or to be paid by him under the award of the Industrial Commission; if there then remain any excess, the amount thereof shall be paid to the injured employee or other person entitled thereto. If, however, the employer does not commence such action within six months from the date of such injury or death, the employee, or his personal representative shall thereafter have the right to bring the action in his own

name, and the employer, and any amount recovered shall be paid in the same manner as if the employer had brought the action.

"The amount of compensation paid by the employer, or the amount of compensation to which the injured employee or his dependents are entitled, shall not be admissible as evidence in any action against a third party.

"When any employer is insured against liability for compensation with any insurance carrier, and such insurance carrier shall have paid any compensation for which the employer is liable or shall have assumed the liability of the employer therefor, it shall be subrogated to all rights and duties of the employer, and may enforce any such rights in the name of the injured employee or his personal representative; but nothing herein shall be construed as conferring upon the insurance carrier any other or further rights than those existing in the employer at the time of the injury to or death of the employee, anything in the policy of insurance to the contrary notwithstanding.

"In all cases where an employer and employee have accepted the Workmen's Compensation Act, any injury to a minor while employed contrary to the laws of this State shall be compensable under this Act the same and to the same extent as if said minor were an adult."

You will note that this section provides that where the employer does not commence an action against the party whose negligence caused the death of the employee within six months from the date of the injury or death, the employee or his personal representative shall thereafter have the right to bring the action in his own name, and any amount recovered is to be paid in the same manner as if the employer had brought the action.

This particular portion of Section 11 of the Workmen's Compensation Act has been passed on by our Supreme Court in the case of Ikerd v. Railroad, 209 N. C. 270. The Court holds in this particular case that if at the expiration of six months from the date of the injury or death the employer has not commenced an action, the employee or his personal representative has the right to institute the action and that the words "and the employer" used in the sentence authorizing the institution of such suits are surplusage and, as such, must be disregarded.

The remainder of the provisions contained in Section 11 are very clear and I am sure you need no explanation thereon.

I am of the opinion that the safest and best method of procedure in cases of this kind would be to file a claim with the Industrial Commission under the provisions of the Workmen's Compensation Act and after the Commission has issued an award, either let the employer commence an action against the third party, or if the employer fails to commence the action within six months from the date of the death of the employee, then the administrator could institute the action in his own name.

You will note that our Court has said in the case of Thompson v. Railroad, 216 N. C. 554, at 556, that the provisions of the North Carolina Workmen's Compensation Act as amended by Chapter 449, Public Laws of 1933, making the remedy against the employer under the Act exclusive, does not appear in the clause relating to suits against third persons. The Court, quoting from the opinion in the case of Brown v. Railroad, 204 N. C. 668, says that manifestly the statute was designed primarily to secure prompt and reasonable compensation for an employee and at the same time permit an employer or his insurance carrier who has made a settlement with the employee to recover the amount so paid from a third party causing the injury to such employee. And, moreover, that the statute was not designed as a city of refuge for a negligent third party.

I also refer you to the recent cases of Mack v. Marshall, Field & Co., 217 N. C. 55, and Sales v. Loftis, 217 N. C. 674. Both these cases discuss the provisions of the Workmen's Compensation Act and particularly Section 11.

SUBJECT: COURTS; SUPERIOR AND JUVENILE; JURISDICTION

23 January, 1941.

Since receiving your letter relating to the question of imprisonment of minors under sixteen years of age charged with felonies and misdemeanors, this office received a call from Honorable J. H. Sample, Director of the State Probation Commission, relative to certain minors under sixteen years of age placed on probation during a recent term of Anson County Superior Court. A conference was arranged with Mr. Sample and the matter was thoroughly discussed. Thereafter Mr. Sample wrote you in detail relative to the conclusions reached at this conference. My answers to the questions raised in your letter will be confined to misdemeanors and felonies less than capital, as I understand you are not interested in the question of jurisdiction in the case of capital felonies.

Your first question is whether the Superior Court has jurisdiction to sentence a defendant under sixteen years of age to imprisonment, either on the roads or in the State's Prison, where such defendant is charged with breaking and entering and larceny.

The two leading cases on the subject of jurisdiction as between Juvenile Courts and the Superior Courts are State v. Burnett, 179 N. C. 735, and State v. Coble, 181 N. C. 554. These cases lay down the following rules:

(1) That the Superior Court has exclusive original jurisdiction in all cases arising under the provisions of the Child Welfare Act, but that there shall be established in each county a Juvenile Court as a separate part of the Superior Court of the district for the hearing of all such matters and causes.

(2) That children under fourteen years of age are not indictable as criminals but in case of delinquency must be dealt with as wards of the State, to be cared for, controlled and disciplined with a view to their reformation.

(3) That children between the ages of fourteen and sixteen, when charged with felonies in which the punishment cannot exceed imprisonment for more than ten years, are committed to the Juvenile Court for investigation, and if the circumstances require it, may be bound over to be prosecuted in the Superior Court at term under the criminal law appertaining to the charge.

(4) That children of fourteen years and over, when charged with felonies in which the punishment may be more than ten years' imprisonment, in all cases shall be subject to prosecution for crimes as in the case of adults.

(5) That in matters investigated and determined by the Juvenile Court, no adjudication of such court shall be denominated a conviction and no child dealt with under the provisions of the Act shall be placed in any penal institution or other place where such child may come in contact with adults charged with or convicted of crime.

Thus, where a child under the age of fourteen years is charged with breaking and entering and larceny, the Superior Court would have no jurisdiction, but the jurisdiction would be in the Juvenile Court. If the child is between the ages of fourteen and sixteen, the matter must be investigated by the Juvenile Court, and if in the opinion of the Juvenile Judge the circumstances require it, the child may be bound over to the Superior Court and tried and sentenced in the Superior Court in the same manner as an adult.

Your second question is whether a child under sixteen years of age, who is charged with a misdemeanor, could be sentenced to serve on the county roads.

Only Juvenile Courts have jurisdiction over minor delinquents under the age of sixteen years who are charged with the commission of misdemeanors, and the Superior Court would have no jurisdiction. Of course, the Juvenile Judge has no right to sentence a child to work on the roads.

Your third question is whether a child who has been before the Juvenile Judge on a number of charges, and the Juvenile Judge finds that he is incorrigible and transfers the case to the Superior Court, may be sentenced by the Judge of the Superior Court to the roads or to the penitentiary.

If the child is less than fourteen years of age, the Superior Court would have no jurisdiction, regardless of the nature of the crime, and the Juvenile Judge would have no authority to transfer such case to the Superior Court. If the child is between the ages of fourteen and sixteen, and charged with a misdemeanor or series of misdemeanors, the Juvenile Judge would have no right to transfer the case to the Superior Court, and if he undertook to do so, the Superior Court would have no jurisdiction. If the child is between the ages of fourteen and sixteen, and charged with a felony, the punishment for which could not exceed imprisonment for more than ten years, the Juvenile Judge would have the right, after investigation, to transfer the case to the Superior Court, and the Superior Court would, under such circumstances, have jurisdiction. If the child is between the ages of fourteen and sixteen, and charged with a felony, the punishment for which could be more than ten years' imprisonment, such child would be subject to prosecution as in the case of an adult.

Your last question is whether a child under sixteen years of age, who comes to the Superior Court charged with a felony or misdemeanor and is given a sentence and placed on probation, may have his sentence put into effect if he later violates the terms of probation.

The answer to this question is contained in my answers to your other questions and in the principles laid down in the cases of State v. Burnett and State v. Coble, supra. If the Superior Court had jurisdiction at the time the original sentence was pronounced, and the child placed on probation, the court would certainly have jurisdiction to put the sentence into effect upon the terms of probation being violated.

SUBJECT: REGISTER OF DEEDS; VACANCY; TIME FOR WHICH FILLED

13 March, 1941.

You inquire as to whether the board of county commissioners of a county filling a vacancy in the office of register of deeds caused by the death of the incumbent who was elected in the general election of 1940 for a term of four years, should fill such vacancy for the unexpired term or until the next general election.

C. S. 3546 provides:

> "When a vacancy occurs from any cause in the office of register of deeds the board of county commissioners shall fill such vacancy by appointment of a successor for the unexpired term, who shall qualify and give bond by law."

I am, therefore, of the opinion that the board of county commissioners should fill the vacancy for the unexpired term instead of until the next general election.

RE: STATE TAXES AND THE NATIONAL DEFENSE; BEER SOLD THROUGH POST EXCHANGES

9 July, 1941.

Vacation has delayed a reply to your letter of June 28, enclosing a copy of the views of The Judge Advocate General of the Army, dated June 27, 1941.

In our opinion of May 2, 1941, rendered to our Commissioner of Revenue, and in my letter to you of May 23, 1941, we expressed the opinion that under the cited decisions of the United States Supreme Court bottlers could not sell beer to Post Exchanges in this State without paying the crown tax levied by our laws. The correctness of that conclusion is shown by the memorandum issued by Acting Attorney General Biddle on June 5, 1941. I do not understand General Gullion to question the soundness of our opinion in that respect. I am led to believe this because the greater part of his opinion consists of a discussion of the questions relating to the purchase by the North Carolina Exchanges of beer from South Carolina Exchanges and its importation into this State and the supposed want of power in the State to deal with such a course of business. That would seem to be in the nature of confession and evasion.

The suggestion that the Exchanges at Fort Bragg and Camp Davis should violate and defeat our laws by such means is entirely contrary to the opinion of Attorney General Jackson, rendered to the War Department and dated August 5, 1939, 39 Ops. Atty. General, 85. That opinion dealt with the question whether the Hawaiian tobacco tax was applicable to sales by or to Post Exchanges. He concluded, as we do, that sales by Post Exchanges were not taxable, but it was his opinion, as it is ours, that a tax on sales to Exchanges was not prohibited by the Constitution, at least, according to Mr. Biddle's memorandum of June 5, 1941, where, as here, the tax is on the bottler or wholesaler and is not required to be passed on. The Supreme Court of the Philippine Islands upheld a similar tax and the United States Supreme Court denied certiorari in 31st Infantry Post Exchange v. Pasedas, 283 U. S. 839.

Mr. Jackson's opinion contains this significant paragraph following a reference to the recent decisions upholding such taxes on sales to State or Federal governments and their instrumentalities:

> *"It is my opinion, therefore, that the War Department should take no part in any effort to prevent the collection of the tax from dealers domiciled in the Territory on sales made by them to such post exchanges."*

The entire Federal policy in recent years has been not only "to take no part in any effort to prevent collection" of such taxes, but to authorize and facilitate such collection. This is shown by the 21st Amendment, the Buck Act, the decisions of the Supreme Court, the opinions of the Attorney General, and the published views of the Department of Justice. Against this settled policy, the War Department seems to have arrayed itself. It appears determined to pay or indirectly bear no State taxes whatsoever, notwithstanding it may be clear that they are of the lawful and constitutional character referred to in Mr. Jackson's opinion of August 5, 1939, and in Mr. Biddle's memorandum of June 5, 1941. Its attitude in such matters has been the subject of discussion and concern in the meetings of the National Association of Tax Administrators Committee on Uniform Sales Taxes, of which I am a member. That Committee has tried to govern itself by the decisions of the United States Supreme Court but has received numerous reports from all over the county that the War Department is steadfastly opposing taxes such as those upheld in the authorities above referred to. It was largely due to its attitude that, in an effort to clarify the situation and obtain an authoritative statement of Federal policy, the Committee conferred with Attorney General Jackson on the subject. The result of that conference was that the memorandum of June 5, 1941, was issued.

I respectfully protest the evasion of our beer law by purchase in South Carolina. I submit it is unseemly and that the War Department ought not to encourage evasive practices merely because the normal course of business would result in the bearing of a lawful and constitutional State tax. The able brief of the Attorney General in the Dravo case pointed out that State taxes are to pay for benefits and services received by the Federal Government and its instrumentalities and that payment for such benefits in the form of non-discriminatory taxes ought to be made, and the Supreme Court so held. It appears to me that such considerations should govern here, particularly since the presence of the troops in this State has substantially increased the costs and expenses of our government in numerous and increasing particulars. I lay it down as a sound proposition that where the Constitution and the authoritatively stated Federal policy permits State taxes, they ought not to be evaded by the War Department.

So far as the law goes, I am entirely convinced that the conclusions set forth in my two former letters are correct and are supported by the authorities cited. Presumably, the Judge Advocate General feels the same way about his opinion. I will therefore do no more than point out that his reliance upon what was said in Collins v. Yosemite Park and Curry Co. with reference to the Federal areas being "in the State" was expressly limited to the regulatory and not the taxing power of the State and is therefore inapplicable. See Rainier National Park Co. v. Martin, 18 Fed.

Supp. 481, Affd. 302 U. S. 661, 82 L. ed. 511. In view of the Buck Act and the other decisions cited in my former letter, there is, I submit, clearly no question of territoriality. As previously pointed out, too, the 21st Amendment has removed any question of the Commerce Clause, notwithstanding the Virginia decision General Gullion relies on, which is inapplicable to the situation here presented.

We earnestly hope that, notwithstanding General Gullion's opinion that the War Department has power to buy in South Carolina, it will conclude not to do so and will take no part in any effort or plan to flout and evade our laws.

SUBJECT: DATE AND PLACE FOR HOLDING BAR EXAMINATIONS; REQUIREMENT AS TO CHANGE

5 November, 1941.

I have your letter of November 4, in which you quote a copy of the resolution passed by the Council of the North Carolina State Bar at the meeting held on October 23, 1941, recommending that a special or extra examination be given either in January or February 1942 on account of conditions brought about by the European war. I note that on behalf of the Board of Law Examiners and at the direction of the Chairman, you request the opinion of this office as to the right of the Board of Law Examiners to hold a special or extra examination as recommended.

Section 10 of paragraph 4 of Chapter 210, Public Laws of 1933, as amended, which you quote, provides as follows: "The examination shall be held in such manner and at such times as the Board of Law Examiners may determine, but no change in the time or place shall become effective within one year from the date upon which the change is determined."

You also refer to and quote Rule 13 adopted by the Board of Law Examiners and approved by the Council, as appears in Volume 208 North Carolina Reports 857, which fixes the time and place of holding bar examinations for the City of Raleigh on the first Tuesday in August in each year. Would providing an extra or special examination amount to a change in the time and place of holding the bar examination? If so, under the quoted section of the law it could not become effective within one year.

The place for holding the special examination would be the same as the place for holding the regular examination. There will be no change in the time and place for holding the August examination. By providing for an examination to be held at some other time and place, providing an additional or extra examination within the year, would, it seems to me, necessarily be a change in the time and place for the examinations. While realizing the good reasons which prompted the resolution for the special or extra examination, it is my opinion that this change could not be made effective within one year of the time at which the change was made without violation of the terms of the statute. If, for instance, it should be decided to hold examinations quarterly during the next year, without changing the date and place for holding the August examinations, it seems clear that there would be a change within the prohibition of the section. Because the change is denominated a special or extra examination and is to occur only once would not, in my view, prevent it from amounting to a change which cannot be made effective within the year. I regret I cannot reach a different conclusion.

It is conceivable that the statute might be so construed as to permit the proposed extra or special examination to be held by considering that the act referred to only changes the dates and places already fixed by the Board, but, in my opinion such construction would be too narrow in view of the broad language of the statute. It might be held that the provisions are directory and not mandatory, and if so held, the special or extra examination would not be invalid, even though held contrary to the provisions of the statute.

SUBJECT: STATE INSTITUTIONS; WESTERN CAROLINA TEACHERS COLLEGE; TORT LIABILITY

30 March, 1942.

You inquire as to whether, in my opinion, Western Carolina Teachers College would be liable for an injury sustained by a student as the result of a locker or lockers located in your new training school building falling on him.

Under the provisions of Section 5839 of Michie's N. C. Code of 1939, Annotated, it is provided that the Cullowhee Normal and Industrial School shall remain a corporation with power to sue and be sued, to make contracts and to exercise all other conporate rights and privileges incident to a public educational institution of the State and necessary to the management of the school.

The name of the institution was later changed to Western Carolina Teachers College. Under the provisions of Section 5842(g) the board of trustees of the Western Carolina Teachers College, and their successors in office, shall hold in trust for the State of North Carolina all the property transferred to them or to be later acquired by them for the purposes of said school.

Section 5842(1) makes provision for setting up and maintaining a practice or demonstration school, and it is made the duty of the board of trustees of Western Carolina Teachers College to furnish buildings, equipment, water and lights for the practice school. I assume that the lockers referred to in your letter were placed in the building pursuant to this section and as a part of the equipment required thereunder.

Ordinarily, governmental agencies of the State are not liable for torts committed by their agents or employees. In North Carolina the non-liability of a State agency for torts is said to be derived from a settled policy of the law against suits of this character as affecting the State. The real question presented is whether Western Carolina Teachers College is such a governmental agency as to come within the rule of non-liability.

Some question has been raised in this respect as to State supported schools, and the case of Hopkins v. Clemson College, 221 U. S. 636, has been relied upon to support the view that they are liable. The Hopkins case was considered by our court in the case of Carpenter v. Railroad, 184 N. C. 400 (405). There it is pointed out that the college was so managing the land of the State as to damage or do away with private property without due process of law, which was contrary to the Constitution. It is also stated that the college was not acting in a governmental capacity. The general effect of the paragraph referred to in the opinion in Carpenter v. Railroad is to leave a question as to whether or not a State school is such a governmental agency that its activities throughout their whole range might be considered in the prosecution of a governmental function.

The principle is firmly established that a State cannot be sued in its own courts or elsewhere unless it has expressly consented to such suit, except in cases authorized by Article XI of the Constitution of the United States or by some provision in the State Constitution. Of course, it is also a well established principle that a sovereign may, if it thinks proper, waive this privilege and permit itself to be made a defendant in a suit by individuals or by another State. It may prescribe the terms and conditions on which it consents to be sued and the manner in which the suit may be conducted, and may withdraw its consent whenever it may suppose that justice to the public requires it.

In the case of Moody v. State Prison, 128 N. C. 12 (14), it is said:

> "But even if such authority was given, it would cover only actions ordinarily incidental in its operation, and would not extend to causes of action like the present. There is a distinct difference between conferring suability as to 'debts and other liabilities for which the State Prison is now liable,' and extending liability for causes not heretofore recognized. Grape Co. v. Commonwealth, 152 Mass., 28. The exemption of the State from paying damages for accidents of this nature does not depend upon its immunity from being sued without its consent, but rests upon grounds of public policy, which deny its liability for such damages."

In the case of Carpenter v. Railroad, supra, the rule is laid down that where a suit is prosecuted against an officer or agent who represents the State in action and liability and the State is the real party whose action would be controlled by the judgment and against which relief is sought, the action is in effect a suit against the State.

In the case to which you refer, the party was injured by the use of equipment which Western Carolina Teachers College is required by statute, as a part of its educational program, to place in a building located on property which, by statute, is held by the board of trustees of the College in trust for the State of North Carolina and to be used in furthering the educational program of the State. It is my thought that under the rule laid down in the case of Moody v. State Prison, supra, the fact that Western Carolina Teachers College is made a corporation and has the capacity to sue and be sued would not within itself make Western Carolina Teachers College liable in tort actions such as that mentioned in your letter. It seems to me that Western Carolina Teachers College, in the performance of its statutory duties above referred to, is as much a governmental agency as was the State Prison Department when it was sued by Moody, or the Highway Commission when it was sued in the case of Carpenter v. Railroad. It seems to me that the education of the children of the State and the training of teachers under the State educational program, undertaken by an agency created for that purpose, should be considered a governmental function.

It seems to me there would be no liability on the part of Western Carolina Teachers College under the circumstances set out in your letter. Even though I am of the opinion that the Institution would not be liable, it is my thought that you should make a thorough investigation as to the manner in which the accident occurred so that you may be prepared in event any court action is taken in the matter.

SUBJECT: OUT-OF-STATE AID TO GRADUATE AND PROFESSIONAL STUDENTS

21 May, 1942.

I received your letter of May 20, with reference to out-of-State aid for graduate and professional students.

Under Chapter 65 of the Public Laws of 1939, the State can provide aid only in cases in which graduate or professional courses at your institution are not offered. See Section 3 of the Act. Therefore, in my opinion, you are correct in your views as expressed in the first paragraph of your letter, and this also provides the answer to the question asked in the second paragraph.

With reference to the third question, the Act provides in Section 3 that the State will pay the tuition and other expenses in such amount as may be deemed reasonably necessary to compensate a resident student for the additional expense of attending a graduate or professional school outside of North Carolina. The provision of the statute as to expenses "reasonably necessary" would vest your Board of Trustees with discretion in determining what expense allowances should be made at the institution which the student attends. Nothing is said in the statute about travel expenses or any other item except tuition. This, therefore, would rest in the sound discretion of the Board of Trustees of your institution.

SUBJECT: CONTRACTORS; LICENSES; CONSTRUCTION AT ARMY CAMPS AND OTHER FEDERAL AREAS

16 June, 1942.

In your letter of June 11, 1942, you state that a large number of contractors are engaged in performing construction contracts for the Federal Government at army camps and on other Federal areas in this State and that many of these contracts involve sums greatly in excess of $10,000.00. You have requested an opinion as to whether the State Licensing Board for Contractors may require these contractors to be licensed under Public Laws of 1925, Chapter 318, as amended, which regulates the practice of general contracting in this State.

It is impossible to give one opinion which will determine the necessity for all such contractors being licensed, as the necessity for compliance with our statute may vary with the character of the work and with the status of the army camp or Federal area where it is being done. However, I will endeavor to state a few general principles which will assist you in applying the law to these contractors.

(1) It is well settled that the mere fact that a contractor is doing work under contract with the Federal Government does not constitute him an instrumentality of the Government. James v. Dravo Contracting Company, 302 U. S. 134, 82 L. Ed. 155; Silas Mason Company v. Tax Commission of Washington, 302 U. S. 186, 82 L. Ed. 187; Atkinson v. State Tax Commission of Oregon, 303 U. S. 20, 82 L. Ed. 621. Therefore, the imposition of

state occupation or privilege taxes on such a contractor or the requirement that he comply with state statutes enacted in the exercise of the police power does not amount to an unconstitutional burden upon the Federal Government. James v. Dravo Contracting Company, 302 U. S. 134, 82 L. Ed. 155; James Stewart and Company v. Sadrakula, 309 U. S. 94, 84 L. Ed. 596.

(2) The status of all army camps and other Federal areas in the State is not necessarily the same. Under Article I, Section 8, paragraph 17, of the United States Constitution, Congress is authorized to exercise exclusive jurisdiction over "all places purchased by the consent of the state in which the same shall be, for the erection of forts, magazines, arsenals, and other needful buildings." Probably most United States lands in North Carolina have been acquired under C. S., Section 8059, by which the State consents to the acquisition by the United States of land, among other purposes, for arsenals and "for any other purposes of the government." This statute cedes to the United States exclusive jurisdiction over lands so acquired, the State reserving jurisdiction only for the service of civil and criminal process. However, land may be acquired by the United States under C. S., Section 8053, under which the State reserves jurisdiction to punish all violations of its criminal law on such lands. Consent to the acquisition of, and exercise of jurisdiction over particular areas by the United States may also be given by special act rather than under the general law. For example, see Public Laws of 1939, Chapter 257, Section 9. Furthermore, although the State may have consented to acquisition of exclusive jurisdiction over a particular area by the United States, such jurisdiction may not be accepted or may be accepted with qualification. Silas Mason Company v. Tax Commission of Washington, 302 U. S. 186, 82 L. Ed. 187; Atkinson v. State Tax Commission of Oregon, 303 U. S. 20; James Stewart and Company v. Sadrakula, 309 U. S. 94, 84 L. Ed. 596. Thus, it is apparent that the relative jurisdiction of the State and Federal Governments over lands acquired by the United States may vary with the particular areas involved.

(3) If exclusive jurisdiction over lands has been ceded by a State to the United States, the State Law, as such, has no application in the territory involved. Furthermore, where there has been a cession of exclusive jurisdiction with minor reservations involving such matters as service of process or collection of taxes, a State has no authority to enforce police regulations in a Federal Area. For example, in Collins v. Yosemite Park and Curry Company, 304 U. S. 518, 82 L. Ed. 1502, it was held that the State of California, having ceded exclusive jurisdiction over a national park reserving the right to collect certain excises, could not enforce police regulations affecting the sale of liquor in the park area. Public Laws of 1925, Chapter 318, providing for the licensing of general contractors, is a police regulation. I am of the opinion that this law has no application in army camps and other Federal areas in this State over which the United States has acquired and accepted exclusive jurisdiction. If a government construction contract is performed *in its entirety* in such a Federal area, the contractor cannot be required to comply with the State Law regulating the practice of general contracting.

(4) Although contracts may call for the construction of buildings or other facilities on property within the exclusive jurisdiction of the United

States, in many instances the contractor will be unable to perform the contract without carrying on more or less extensive operations on property under the jurisdiction of the State. These operations may consist of transportation of materials, storage, disposal of waste, and partial assembly of materials before installation. Where these operations are carried on outside the area within the exclusive jurisdiction of the United States, although in connection with a government contract for construction within a Federal area, I am of the opinion that the contractor is engaged in the practice of general contracting in territory subject to the jurisdiction of the State and should be required to comply with our licensing laws. On this theory, this office has advised the Commissioner of Revenue in an opinion dated May 16, 1941, that a contractor constructing a post office annex on land within the exclusive jurisdiction of the United States but who stored materials on land not owned by the United States, took possession of parts of the city streets and sidewalks, and supervised the work, in part, from his office not on Federal property, was liable for State privilege taxes.

(5) Where a contract calls for the construction of buildings on lands in this State owned or occupied by the United States but over which the State has not ceded jurisdiction, the contractor should be required to comply with the State Laws regulating the practice of general contracting.

OFFICE DIGEST OF OPINIONS

BANKS AND BANKING; JOINT SAFE DEPOSIT BOX

18 October, 1940.

Where a safe deposit box is rented by husband and wife jointly, the wife should not be permitted to open the box after the death of the husband without compliance with Sec. 21½ of the Revenue Act, relative to safe deposit boxes of decedents.

CITIZENSHIP; CONVICTION OF FELONY; REGISTRATION FOR MILITARY DUTY UNDER DRAFT

30 October, 1940.

A person who has forfeited his citizenship by reason of conviction of a felony does not automatically have his citizenship restored by registration for military duty under the 1940 Selective Service Act.

COUNTY PROPERTY; SALES AND RIGHT TO MAKE DONATIONS

14 October, 1940.

Although property which is not required for any county purpose may be sold by a county under C. S. 1297(15), no authority has been granted to the Board of County Commissioners of a county by the Legislature to donate such property to a park commission. An act may be passed by the Legislature authorizing this to be done.

ELECTIONS; ABSENTEE BALLOT AFFIDAVIT; SIGNED BEFORE OFFICER WITH OFFICIAL SEAL

29 October, 1940.

C. S. 5968(f) of the election laws of this State requires the absentee ballot affidavit to be signed before an officer having an official seal, which seal must be affixed. This excludes Justices of the Peace.

ELECTIONS; RESIDENCE; PERSONS WORKING IN DISTRICT OF COLUMBIA

28 October, 1940.

Under our election laws it is provided that a place shall be considered the residence of a person in which his habitation is fixed and to which, whenever absent, he has the intention of returning.

Provision is also made in our election laws for persons who move to the District of Columbia to engage in government service, and such persons are not considered to have lost their residence during the period of this service.

ELECTION LAWS; COUNTY BOARD OF EDUCATION

21 October, 1940.

Names of candidates for membership on the county boards of education should not be placed on the official ballots for general elections. Board members are chosen by the General Assembly from the party nominees designated in primaries.

Election Laws; Absentee Ballots

18 October, 1940.

It is necessary that a voter sign an application for an absentee ballot.

Gambling; Lotteries; Disposition of Money and Tickets upon Conviction

19 October, 1940.

Upon conviction of a defendant of violating the lottery laws, the judge before whom he is tried should make an order disposing of money and tickets seized from the defendant prior to the trial. Pending the trial, the tickets and money should be held for use as evidence against the defendant.

Game Laws; Hunting on Sunday; Revocation of Hunting License

16 October, 1940.

The regulations of the State Board of Conservation and Development forbid hunting of game on Sundays. Under C. S. 2141(27), upon conviction of a person of violating this regulation, the court should require the surrender of his hunting license and forward it to the Department of Conservation and Development. This should be done in case of first offenses.

Garnishment; State Employees

24 October, 1940.

The provisions for attachment and garnishment appearing in the Revenue Act apply only to the collection of delinquent taxes and do not authorize garnishment for the collection of private debts. The wages of State employees are subject to garnishment for delinquent taxes.

Motor Vehicle Laws; Drunken Driving

3 October, 1940.

A person who operates a tractor on the public highways of this State under the influence of intoxicating liquor would violate Sec. 101 of the Motor Vehicle Laws which prohibits drunken driving.

Motor Vehicle Laws; Sirens on Fire Vehicles

5 October, 1940.

It is lawful for members of the volunteer fire departments to use sirens on their privately owned vehicles while attending fires. However, it would be improper for them to use these sirens at any other time.

Municipal Corporations; Municipal Liability in Tort; Jails

1 October, 1940.

A municipal corporation is not liable for the death of prisoners caused by the burning of a city jail if the jail has been properly constructed and there has been no failure to furnish it so as to afford prisoners reasonable comfort and protection from suffering and injury.

MUNICIPALITIES; PURCHASE OF LAND FOR AIRPORT; USE OF SURPLUS FUNDS

23 October, 1940.

The laws of this State authorize the acquisition of land for a municipal airport (Ch. 2 A, Michie's N. C. Code, 1930). A city is permitted to purchase a site with available surplus funds not involving a tax levy or bond issue, without a vote of the people.

SCHOOLS; SCHOOL GROUNDS; PAVING; PAYMENT FROM CAPITAL OUTLAY

5 October, 1940.

A school board has a right to pay a proportion of the cost of paving the street adjoining the school property from the Capital Outlay Funds of the school, if such expenditure is presented in the school budget and approved as required by law.

SELECTIVE DRAFT ACT; WHEN AGE OF 21 YEARS DEEMED ATTAINED

14 October, 1940.

The law recognizes a person to be 21 years of age on the day preceding the twenty-first anniversary of his or her birthday. Therefore, if the anniversary of the birthday of a young man is October 16, 1940, he would become twenty-one years of age on the first moment of the preceding day, and would have to register under the Selective Draft Act.

TAXATION; A. B. C. STORES; FIXTURES

9 October, 1940.

Under the recent decision of Warrenton v. Warren County, 215 N. C. 542, the office of the Attorney General is of the opinion that the stock and fixtures of the A. B. C. Stores are subject to ad valorem taxation.

ATTACHMENT AND GARNISHMENT FOR TAXES

14 November, 1940.

Employees of a lumber manufacturing plant are subject to garnishment of their wages for the payment of delinquent taxes. Such is not a reduction of wages of the employees on the part of the employers.

CLERKS OF SUPERIOR COURT: POWERS AND JURISDICTION OF ASSISTANT CLERK

18 November, 1940.

An Assistant Clerk of the Superior Court is fully authorized and empowered to perform all the duties and functions of the office of Clerk of the Superior Court in the same manner as the Clerk. N. C. Code Ann. (Michie, 1939), Sec. 934(a).

COUNTIES: RIGHT TO USE PROPERTY OF INMATE OF COUNTY HOME FOR REIMBURSEMENT OF COUNTY

15 November, 1940.

A county would be within its rights in having a guardian appointed to receive the proceeds of an insurance policy payable to an insane inmate of the county home, and in having the proceeds of the policy paid by the guardian to the county as reimbursement to the county for the expense of maintaining such inmate.

County License Taxes: Sale of Beer; Half Year License

6 November, 1940.

The county license tax on the sale of beer authorized by Schedule F of the Revenue Act is an annual tax of twenty-five dollars. A county would have no authority to issue quarterly or half-year licenses at less than twenty-five dollars.

Corrupt Practices Act: Reports of Expenditures

18 November, 1940.

Our law, Code Section 6055(a-51), requires a statement of receipts and expenditures by campaign committees before and after general or special elections, but the law does not require such statements to be filed by candidates themselves.

Double Office Holding: County Accountant and Member of County Board of Commissioners

14 November, 1940.

Although it is provided by N. C. Code Ann. (Michie, 1939), Sec. 1334(54), that the duties of county accountant may, in counties where there is no auditor, be conferred upon any county officer except the sheriff, tax collector, etc., a board of county commissioners could not appoint one of its own members as county accountant and provide for extra compensation for his service in this capacity, without violating Section 4388, which prohibits any person elected as commissioner from making any contract for his own benefit.

Double Office Holding: Notary Public and Clerk to Selective Service Board

8 November, 1940.

The office of clerk to the Selective Service Board does not constitute an office within the meaning of Article XIV, Sec. 7, of the Constitution, which prohibits double office holding.

Election Laws: Qualification of Voters; School Teachers

15 November, 1940.

School teachers who remove to a county for the purpose only of teaching, with the expectation of returning to the county of their parents or other relatives during vacation to live and with no intention of becoming permanent residents of the county in which they teach, are not entitled to vote in the county in which they teach.

ELECTION LAWS: MARKING BALLOTS

14 November, 1940.

In case a voter makes a cross mark in the party circle above the name of the Party for some of whose candidates he desires to vote, and then make a cross mark in the voting square opposite the name of any candidates of any other party for whom he wishes to vote, the cross mark in the party circle above the name of a party will cast the elector's vote for every candidate on the ticket of such party, except for offices for which candidates are marked on other party tickets, and the cross marks before the names of such candidates will cast the elector's vote for them. (C. S. 6055(a-28) (2b).)

GAME LAWS: HUNTING OUT OF SEASON; REVOCATION OF LICENSE

20 November, 1940.

A person is not permitted to kill game birds out of season, even on his own premises.

When a person has been convicted of a violation of the game laws, the court in which such conviction is had is required to take up the hunting license of the person convicted and forward the same to the Department of Conservation and Development.

GAME LAWS: NON-RESIDENT; HUNTING ON OWN LAND

18 November, 1940.

Under the hunting laws of this State, any non-resident owning in his own right one hundred acres or more of land in North Carolina may hunt on these lands, subject to the provisions and restrictions of the North Carolina Game Law, without being required to purchase a hunting license.

HOUSE OF REPRESENTATIVES: VACANCIES

8 November, 1940.

A vacancy in the office of Member of the State House of Representatives caused by the death of a member after his election should be filled in a special election called by the Governor. Candidates in such an election may be nominated by the executive committee of the respective political parties in the county where the vacancy occurred.

POLL TAX: ALIENS; ELECTION LAWS

8 November, 1940.

An alien may be required to pay poll tax if he is an inhabitant of this State.

Prior to 1920, the payment of a poll tax was a prerequisite to the right to vote; however, the Constitution was amended in that year to eliminate this requirement.

TAXATION: LICENSE TAXES; REFUND OF INVALID TAX

5 November, 1940.

A municipal corporation has no authority to refund an invalid license tax on taxicabs if the tax has not been paid under protest.

TAXATION: AD VALOREM TAXES; LIEN OF TAXES

5 November, 1940.

The failure of a tax collector to collect ad valorem taxes by levying on the personal property of a taxpayer does not have the effect of discharging the lien of the taxes upon the taxpayer's real property.

TAXATION: SCHEDULE "B"; CHARACTER READING; TAX LIABILITY

19 November, 1940.

There is no tax liability imposed against persons engaged in the practice of character reading by our law. However, there is a possible tax liability against persons engaged in this practice, who, by doing so, actually foretell fortunes either by reading palms or practicing clairvoyance or phrenology.

ADMINISTRATION; NON-RESIDENTS; REMOVAL

3 December, 1940.

An administrator who becomes a non-resident of the State of North Carolina pending his administration of an estate thereby forfeits his right to administer. He may be removed and a new administrator may be appointed without the necessity of notifying such non-resident.

CLERKS OF SUPERIOR COURT; JUDGMENT DOCKETS

22 November, 1940.

It is permissible for a Clerk of the Superior Court to keep as his judgment docket a loose-leaf judgment docket which upon completion may have the pin withdrawn and be securely and permanently locked.

CONSTABLES; JURISDICTION

2 December, 1940.

The powers and duties of a constable are co-extensive with the limits of the county in which he is elected. In exercising the functions of his office he is not confined to the limits of his township.

COUNTIES: NOTICES TO TAXPAYERS; POSTAGE

2 December, 1940.

The postage on notices sent to taxpayers with reference to the collection of taxes is a proper charge against the county. Sheriffs and tax collectors are not required personally to pay such postage charges.

DOUBLE OFFICE HOLDING: JUSTICE OF THE PEACE; NOTARY PUBLIC; COUNTY SURVEYOR

5 December, 1940.

The office of county surveyor and that of notary public are offices within the meaning of Article XIV, Sec. 7, of the Constitution, which prohibits double office holding. The office of justice of the peace is specifically exempt from this constitutional provision.

JUSTICES OF THE PEACE: SERVICE OF CRIMINAL PROCESS ON RIVERS

5 December, 1940.

Under C. S. 4525 a warrant issued by a justice of the peace may be served in any part of the county of such justice and on any river, bay, or sound forming the boundary of that and some other county. Under this section such a warrant may be served upon persons on board a ship in a stream within or forming a boundary of the county, and it makes no difference whether the ship is tied to a dock.

MARRIAGE LAWS: LICENSE; LABORATORY REPORT

21 November, 1940.

Sec. 1 of Ch. 314 of the Public Laws of 1939 requires that the original laboratory report from a laboratory approved by the State Board of Health for making such tests, showing that the Wassermann or any other approved test of this nature is negative, must accompany the required physician's certificate before a marriage license may be issued by a Register of Deeds.

MARRIAGE LAWS: LICENSE; NON-RESIDENT REQUIREMENTS

21 November, 1940.

Non-residents are required to comply with the marriage license act of this state before obtaining a marriage license here, unless they show the register of deeds that their states have no similar requirements. However, if either party to the proposed marriage is a resident of this state, he or she must comply with the requirements of the act, regardless of the residence of the other party.

NOTARIES: SIGNATURE AFTER MARRIAGE

23 November, 1940.

Where an unmarried woman holds a commission as a notary public and she marries before the commission expires, official acts attested in her maiden name are valid.

In such a situation confusion may be avoided by having the commission renewed in the woman's married name. If this is not done, her married name should be appended after the signature in her maiden name.

STATE FLAG: DISPLAY OF; ADVERTISING

25 November, 1940.

Sec. 4500, Michie's N. C. Code of 1939, prohibits desecration of or use of either the American or North Carolina Flag for advertising purposes.

TAXATION: AD VALOREM; POWER OF BOARD OF EQUALIZATION AND REVIEW AFTER FINAL ADJOURNMENT

3 December, 1940.

The Board of Equalization and Review of a county has no right to raise the assessment of property after it has once adjourned finally, without specifying its intention to reconvene.

Taxation: Ad Valorem; Revaluation; Length of Listing Period

21 November, 1940.

The revaluation of property for the year 1941 should be completed by the date set for the final adjournment of the Board of Equalization, which for the year 1941, would be the fourteenth Monday after January 1, 1941.

Taxation: Collection; Attachment and Garnishment

21 November, 1940.

Under Sec. 1713(d) of Ch. 310 Public Laws of 1939, a tax collector could not garnish more than ten per cent of a delinquent taxpayer's wages during any one pay period. He could not garnish at one time ten per cent of such taxpayer's wages for the entire year.

Taxation: Municipal License Taxes; Plumbing Contractors for Federal Post Office

22 November, 1940.

A city may validly levy and collect its privilege license tax from plumbing contractors working on a Federal Post Office in the city. The Supreme Court of the United States has ruled that such a tax is not a burden on the Federal Government, and therefore it is not unconstitutional.

Taxation: Sale and Foreclosure; Costs and Fees

29 November, 1940.

The provision contained in Sec. 7971(228), Michie's N. C. Code of 1939, relative to costs which may be taxed in a foreclosure action instituted against a delinquent taxpayer, which provides: "that the fees allowed any officer shall not exceed one-half the fees allowed in other civil actions," would apply to the fees charged by a Clerk Superior Court as well as to those of the officers serving the process in the action.

Confederate Pensions: Funeral Expenses; County Contribution

29 March, 1941.

Counties are authorized to contribute $30 toward the funeral expenses of the widow of a Confederate Veteran notwithstanding that such person has been receiving old age assistance prior to death.

Counties; County Attorney; Tax Foreclosures

4 March, 1941.

County commissioners have legal authority to appoint an attorney other than the county attorney to handle tax foreclosure suits.

Double Office Holding: Deputy Collector of Internal Revenue and Notary Public

26 March, 1941.

The office of Deputy Collector of Internal Revenue and notary public are both offices within the meaning of the constitutional prohibition against double office holding.

Double Office Holding: Clerk and Treasurer of a Town; Postmaster; Notary Public

17 March, 1941.

The following positions are offices within the meaning of the constitutional prohibition against double office holding: Clerk and Treasurer of a Town, Postmaster, Notary Public.

Marriage Laws

25 March, 1941.

Persons may be legally married in this State when they are eighteen years of age or over without the consent of their parents.

It is not necessary that a person acquire a residence in North Carolina in order to be married here. Blood tests are not required of residents of a state that does not require them of applicants for marriage there.

Municipal Corporations: License Taxes

18 March, 1941.

A person operating a service station in connection with a garage may be required to pay municipal license taxes on both businesses.

Municipal Corporations: Ordinances; Prohibiting Sale of Wine and Beer

20 March, 1941.

Unless authorized to do so by a special statute, a municipal corporation may not prohibit the sale of wine or beer by ordinance.

Necessary Expenses: Bonds for Water Plant

20 March, 1941.

Bonds for an addition to a municipal water plant would constitute an expenditure for a necessary expense of the municipality within the meaning of the Constitution, Article VII, Section 7, and no election would be necessary on this account.

Register of Deeds: Vacancies

13 March, 1941.

When a vacancy occurs in the office of register of deeds, the vacancy should be filled by appointment by the county commissioners for the unexpired term rather than until the next general election.

Schools: Teachers; Notice of Rejection

20 March, 1941.

The School Machinery Act, as now amended, provides for the continuation of a teacher's contract from year to year unless such teacher is notified of his or her rejection by registered letter prior to the close of the school term, subject to the allotment of teachers made by the State School Commission.

SCHOOLS: COUNTY BOARD OF EDUCATION; REMOVAL OF MEMBER FROM COUNTY

7 March, 1941.

Upon removal from the county for which he was elected, a member of the county board of education becomes disqualified to continue in office.

SMALL LOANS: USURY; CRIMINAL OFFENSE

21 March, 1941.

Charging a usurious rate of interest on loans upon "any article of household or kitchen furniture," or "any assignment or sale of wages, earned or to be earned" is a criminal offense in this State.

STATE EMPLOYEES' RETIREMENT SYSTEM: TEACHERS

11 March, 1941.

All persons who were teachers on the date of the ratification of the State Employees' Retirement Act or who become teachers prior to July 1, 1941, except those who notify the board of trustees in writing before January 1, 1942, become members of the retirement system.

TAXATION: AD VALOREM; LIEN ON REAL ESTATE

17 March, 1941.

A county has a lien on a taxpayer's real estate for poll and personal property taxes as well as real property taxes. The taxpayer is not entitled to demand a release of his real estate without paying his poll and personal property taxes.

TAXATION: COUNTY BOARD OF EQUALIZATION AND REVIEW; ADJOURNMENT

20 March, 1941.

If the county commissioners sitting as the Board of Equalization and Review in their county, after holding their first meeting on the day fixed by statute, are absolutely unable to complete their duties with respect to valuation of property by the date fixed for final adjournment by statute, they may find as a fact that such is the case, enter the finding upon their minutes, and adjourn from time to time until the work is completed.

TAXATION: FRANCHISE TAX; MOTOR VEHICLE CARRIERS

6 March, 1941.

Under the Motor Vehicle Act of 1937 counties cannot impose any franchise tax upon "franchise motor vehicle carriers taxed under this Act."

TAXATION: USE TAXES; BUILDING MATERIALS; CONTRACT WITH U. S.

25 March, 1941.

Our revenue laws expressly exempt building materials used in construction work where the contract is with the United States or with the State of North Carolina from the use tax.

County Commissioners: Official Bonds; Filling Vacancy when County Surveyor Fails to File Bond

17 March, 1941.

When a duly elected county surveyor fails to furnish bond at the time required by statute, the county commissioners may declare the office vacant and appoint some other person to fill it.

Courts: Inferior Court; Jurisdiction in Larceny Cases

13 March, 1941.

The effect of S. B. 124 (Public Laws of 1941, Chapter 178) is to make the larceny of property with a value of not more than fifty dollars a misdemeanor. Inferior courts with jurisdiction over misdemeanors would have jurisdiction over larceny in such cases.

Courts: Jurisdiction; Divorce

24 March, 1941.

A statute giving a recorder's court concurrent jurisdiction with the superior court in civil actions arising out of tort or contract when the amount involved does not exceed $500.00 does not confer jurisdiction in divorce cases upon such court.

Double Office Holding: County Fire Warden

17 March, 1941.

The county fire warden is an office within the meaning of the constitutional prohibition against double office holding.

Double Office Holding: Clerk to Local Draft Board

12 March, 1941.

A clerk to a local Draft Board is not an officer within the meaning of the constitutional prohibition against double office holding.

H. B. 793: Regulation of Unfair Practices by Handlers of Farm Products; Effective Date

27 March, 1941.

H. B. 793, which requires handlers of farm products on any basis except a cash basis to obtain a permit from the Commissioner of Agriculture and to give bond, has no application to contracts made before July 1, 1941, the effective date of the Act.

Municipalities: Group Health and Accident Insurance on Employees; Right to Carry

21 March, 1941.

In the absence of legislative authority, a city would have no right to expend money for the purpose of carrying group health and accident insurance for the benefit of its employees. No statute has been found which purports to give such authority.

MUNICIPALITIES: RIGHT TO EXTEND SEWER LINES

1 March, 1941.

Under the State statute, C. S. 2807, municipalities have the right to extend sewer lines outside their corporate limits. This does not require an amendment to the city charter.

MUNICIPAL ELECTIONS: MARKERS

22 March, 1941.

Markers are not allowed in municipal elections.

SCHOOLS: ELECTION OF TEACHERS; NOTICE OF REJECTION

25 March, 1941.

Teachers and principals must be notified prior to the close of the school term if rejected. The school authorities in office at such time are required to take this action.

TAXATION: AD VALOREM; LISTING

17 March, 1941.

The county commissioners have no discretion as to whether property subject to taxation shall be listed. All such property should be listed.

TAXATION: AD VALOREM; PREPAYMENT OF TAXES

24 March, 1941.

Chapter 310 of the Public Laws of 1939 provides that payment of taxes made before the tax books have been turned over to the collector shall be made to such official as the governing body of the taxing unit may designate. There is no provision, however, for the payment of fees for this service.

TAXATION: COUNTY; GARNISHMENT

13 March, 1941.

Under the provisions of Section 1713 of Chapter 310 of the Public Laws of 1939, garnishment proceeding may be instituted against a delinquent taxpayer for the collection of delinquent taxes on either real or personal property.

TAXATION: LICENSE TAXES; COLLECTING AGENCIES

12 March, 1941.

Under the Revenue Act all collecting agencies are required to obtain a State license for engaging in such business.

TAXATION: LICENSE TAXES; VENDING MACHINES

3 March, 1941.

Soft drink vending machines are liable for State and local taxes notwithstanding that they may be located in charitable institutions.

COUNTIES: BOND ISSUES; SUPERVISION OF ELECTION

4 April, 1941.

Special elections on the question of issuing county bonds should be conducted under the supervision of the board of county commissioners.

DOUBLE OFFICE HOLDING: DIRECTOR OF ELECTRIC MEMBERSHIP CORPORATION

3 April, 1941.

A director of an electric membership corporation is not a public officer within the meaning of the constitutional prohibition against double office holding.

ELECTION LAWS: MUNICIPAL ELECTIONS; REGISTRATION

3 April, 1941.

The registration books for a municipal election should be open between 9:00 A.M. and 5:00 P.M. on each day, Sunday excepted, for seven days preceding the day for closing the registration books, and should remain open until 9:00 P.M. on each Saturday during such period. The books should be closed on the second Saturday before such election.

ELECTION LAWS: MUNICIPAL ELECTIONS; REGISTRATION; HOURS

2 April, 1941.

A registrar for a municipal election may revise the registration books of his ward or precinct so that they will show an accurate list of the electors previously registered and still residing in the ward or precinct.

Under Public Laws of 1941, ch. 222, the polls should remain open from 6:30 A.M. to 6:30 P.M.

ELECTION LAWS: MUNICIPAL ELECTIONS; WRITE-IN CANDIDATES

3 April, 1941.

Names of candidates may be written in on an official ballot in a municipal election. If a person whose name has been written in on the ballot receives a majority of the votes cast for an office, he would be elected.

INTOXICATING LIQUORS: ABC ACT; ELECTIONS

2 April, 1941.

A county board of elections is required to call an election on the question of operating liquor stores in a county if requested in writing by the county commissioners to do so or if petitioned to do so by not less than 15% of the registered voters who voted in the last election for governor. The poll books for the last election should be examined in determining whether a petition is signed by 15% of the voters who voted in the last election for governor.

INTOXICATING LIQUORS: COUNTY ABC BOARD; DISPOSITION OF PROFITS

9 April, 1941.

A county ABC Board has no authority to make donations for civic projects from the profits arising from the operation of liquor stores.

MARRIAGE LICENSES: LABORATORY REPORT; NON-RESIDENTS

7 April, 1941.

A register of deeds is not justified in issuing a marriage license unless the physician's certificate presented with the application is accompanied by the original report from a laboratory approved by the State Board of Health showing that the Wassermann or other approved test is negative.

Non-residents who are residents of a state which does not have similar requirements to those of North Carolina may obtain a marriage license in this State without blood tests.

MUNICIPAL CORPORATIONS: RETIREMENT SYSTEM; ELECTION

2 April, 1941.

Counties, cities, and towns may not levy taxes or incur indebtedness to provide a retirement system for employees without approval of a majority of the qualified voters at an election called for that purpose.

PROBATE AND REGISTRATION: FEES; COUNTY BOARD OF EDUCATION

5 April, 1941.

The County Board of Education is not exempt from paying fees to the Clerk of Court and register of deeds in connection with the probate and registration of instruments.

RETIREMENT SYSTEM: QUALIFICATIONS OF TEACHERS

2 April, 1941.

The Act creating the Teachers' and State Employees' Retirement System does change the qualifications required of teachers in the public schools of this State.

RETIREMENT SYSTEM: WHEN PAYMENTS BEGIN

2 April, 1941.

Under the Act setting up the Teachers' and State Employees' Retirement System no payments of benefits are to be made until after July 1, 1942. No employee may be forced to retire solely on account of having reached the age of retirement until after that date.

SCHOOLS: COUNTY SUPERINTENDENT; WHEN ELECTED

7 April, 1941.

The county superintendent of schools should be elected on April 7, 1941, or as soon thereafter as practicable during the month of April.

SLOT MACHINES: LEGALITY OF MACHINES VENDING FREE GAMES

2 April, 1941.

Slot machines which vend free games are illegal under the Flannagan Act.

TAXATION: AD VALOREM; MEETING AND ADJOURNMENT OF COUNTY BOARD OF EQUALIZATION AND REVIEW

5 April, 1941.

If the county commissioners sitting as the county board of equalization and review are absolutely unable within the time fixed by statute to complete their work with reference to valuation of property, they may enter such findings on their minutes and adjourn from time to time until the work is completed.

TAXATION: AD VALOREM; REMEDIES AGAINST PERSONAL PROPERTY

4 April, 1941.

Any personal property belonging to a taxpayer is subject to levy for the collection of delinquent taxes.

TAXATION: MUNICIPAL; APPROVAL BY VOTERS

1 April, 1941.

A municipal ad valorem tax, unless for a necessary expense, must be authorized by a majority of the registered and qualified voters of the city. In a special election on the question of levying a tax, the city may order a new registration.

TAXATION: MUNICIPAL; INSURANCE COMPANIES

9 April, 1941.

Cities and towns are not permitted to impose any tax on insurance companies operating therein except the ad valorem tax on real and personal property.

VITAL STATISTICS: DELAYED BIRTH CERTIFICATES

8 April, 1941.

Public Laws of 1941, ch. 22, authorizes a person born prior to 1910 to petition the clerk of the Superior Court in the county of his residence and in a proceeding before the clerk establish the facts relating to his birth. The Act provides for a hearing, entry of judgment, and certification of the judgment to the State Bureau of Vital Statistics.

A simpler procedure is afforded by Public Laws of 1941, ch. 126, under which a person whose birth has not been registered may be registered with the register of deeds in the county of his birth under rules and regulations promulgated by the State Board of Health.

COMMISSIONER OF PUBLIC TRUST: CONTRACTING FOR HIS OWN BENEFIT

16 April, 1941.

C. S. 4388, which prohibits a commissioner or director of a public trust from making contracts for his own benefit, exempts transactions in regular course of business with banks from its provisions.

Double Office Holding: Fire Chief and Town Commissioner

9 April, 1941.

The positions of fire chief and town commissioner are public offices within the meaning of the constitutional prohibition against double office holding.

Double Office Holding: Member of Board of Trustees of Teachers' and State Employees' Retirement System

10 April, 1941.

A member of the Board of Trustees of the Teachers' and State Employees' Retirement System, who is not an *ex officio* member, is a public officer within the meaning of the constitutional prohibition against double office holding.

Double Office Holding: Membership on Merit System Council and Housing Commission

15 April, 1941.

The positions of member of the State Merit System Council and Commissioner of a Housing Authority are offices within the meaning of the constitutional prohibition against double office holding.

Double Office Holding: Register of Deeds and School Committeeman

10 April, 1941.

The positions of register of deeds and school committeeman are both offices within the meaning of the constitutional prohibition against double office holding.

Election Laws: Municipal Elections; Absentee Voting in Primaries

16 April, 1941.

Under Chapter 346 of the Public Laws of 1941, persons in the military, naval, or armed forces of the United States are entitled to vote by absentee ballot in partisan municipal primaries.

Election Laws: Municipal Elections; Date Candidates Must File

9 April, 1941.

In municipal elections when there is no primary, unless the time in which candidates for office may file is regulated by a special act or charter provision, the governing body should fix a reasonable time before the date of the election in order that sufficient time will be given to print the ballots.

Election Laws: Registration—Bond Issue; Only for that Purpose

19 April, 1941.

A special registration for an election on a bond issue can be used for that purpose only, and cannot be used in regular municipal elections.

GAME LAWS: RUNNING TRIALS AND TRAINING DOGS

12 April, 1941.

A person may run trials and train dogs at any time during the year, provided that in conducting such trials or training, no shotgun shall be used and no game shall be taken during the closed season.

LOTTERIES: "JACK POT" NIGHT

21 April, 1941.

Where the purchaser of a ticket to a theater gets a ticket with a number on it which entitles him to a cash prize, a consideration is paid for the chance of winning the prize, and such constitutes a lottery. If the customer has to have a ticket in order to participate, the violation is clear.

MARRIAGE LAWS: CEREMONY PERFORMED BY ORDAINED MINISTERS

10 April, 1941.

A minister does not have to be licensed by the State to perform the marriage ceremony. Any ordained minister of a religious denomination may legally perform the ceremony if authorized by his church to do so.

MUNICIPAL CORPORATIONS: PAVING ASSESSMENTS

11 April, 1941.

A statute authorizing a municipality to relieve a college from a paving assessment impliedly authorizes the college to be relieved from payment of interest.

MUNICIPAL CORPORATIONS: STREET REPAIRS

16 April, 1941.

Under the North Carolina laws, the board of commissioners of a town is required to keep in proper repair the streets and bridges of the town in the manner and to the extent they deem best.

MUNICIPAL ELECTIONS: TIME FOR HOLDING SAME

16 April, 1941.

It is necessary that an election be held to elect town officers, even if there is no opposition for any of the offices.

MUNICIPAL PRIMARIES: ABSENTEE VOTING

12 April, 1941.

Chapter 346 of the Public Laws of 1941, providing that any qualified voter who is in the armed forces of the United States may vote by absentee ballot, applies only to partisan primary elections, the language being: "may vote in the primary of the party of his affiliation."

PUBLIC OFFICERS: CONTRACTS; MEMBER OF THE BOARD OF SCHOOL TRUSTEES SELLING INSURANCE ON SCHOOL BUILDING

9 April, 1941.

A member of the board of trustees of a city administrative school unit may not sell insurance on school buildings to the board without violating C. S. 4388, which makes it unlawful for a commissioner of a public trust to contract for his own benefit.

PUBLIC OFFICERS: CONTRACTS; SCHOOL COMMITTEEMAN SELLING GASOLINE TO COUNTY BOARD OF EDUCATION

11 April, 1941.

It is not a violation of C. S. 4388, which makes it unlawful for a commissioner of a public trust to contract for his own benefit, for a local school committeeman to sell gasoline to the County Board of Education. A local committeeman has no control by virtue of his office over purchases by the county board.

It would be unlawful for a member of a county board or a trustee of a city administrative unit to make sales to the board of which he is a member.

SALARIES AND FEES: WITNESS FEES

11 April, 1941.

An officer who makes an arrest and serves a warrant is entitled to receive witness fees like any other witness, if he testifies in the case, provided he is not a salaried officer. If a salaried officer, he is not entitled to witness fees.

A state's witness, duly subpoenaed, sworn, and examined, or tendered in two or more cases in the same day, may prove his attendance and collect the usual fees in all cases in which the defendant is taxed with costs. He is not entitled to be paid by the county for attendance in more than one case on any one day.

SCHOOLS: PRINCIPAL; TERM OF OFFICE

11 April, 1941.

There is no statutory provision authorizing the employment of a principal and permitting the employment to be on the basis of a five year contract. Section 7 of the School Machinery Act, as amended, which provides that contracts of employment of teachers or principals shall continue from year to year until notified of rejection prior to the close of the school term, would control.

TAXATION: AD VALOREM; DISCHARGE OF LIEN WHERE REAL ESTATE SUBDIVIDED

11 April, 1941.

The purchaser of a portion of a tract of land to which a tax lien has already attached is entitled to have the purchased portion released from the lien upon payment of a pro-rata portion of the taxes due from the taxpayer who listed the whole tract for taxation.

TAXATION: AD VALOREM; PROPERTY OWNED BY EDUCATIONAL INSTITUTION AND HELD FOR PROFIT

16 April, 1941.

Property owned by an educational institution and held for profit is not exempt from taxation.

TAXATION: SALES TAX; COLLECTION; LEVY ON HOUSEHOLD AND KITCHEN FURNITURE

15 April, 1941.

Household and kitchen furniture is not exempt from levy under an execution for sales tax.

BOND ISSUE FOR SCHOOLS: DEBT LIMITATION; EFFECT OF JUDGMENT

23 April, 1941.

The question of a bond issue for a school building which exceeds the constitutional debt limitation would have to be submitted to a vote of the people, even though a judgment of the Superior Court be rendered requiring such a building to be constructed.

BUILDING AND LOAN ASSOCIATIONS: FINES

23 April, 1941.

Building and loan associations are authorized by statute to assess fines against shareholders who are in arrears in their payments.

COMMISSIONER OF PUBLIC TRUST: PRESIDENT OF CORPORATION; SCHOOL COMMITTEEMAN

24 April, 1941.

A president of a corporation from which a county board of education purchases certain supplies may lawfully serve as a school committeeman, since a school committeeman has no voice whatsoever in the expenditure of funds.

DOUBLE OFFICE HOLDING: EMPLOYEE OF FEDERAL FARM SECURITY BOARD AND TOWN ALDERMAN

21 April, 1941.

An employee of the Federal Farm Security Board, as distinguished from membership on said Board, is not an officer within the meaning of Article XIV, Section 7, of the Constitution, which prohibits double office holding.

DOUBLE OFFICE HOLDING: MAYOR AND JUSTICE OF PEACE

21 April, 1941.

The mayor of an incorporated town may also hold the office of justice of the peace. Section 7 of Article XIV of the North Carolina Constitution excepts justices of the peace from its provisions against double office holding.

DOUBLE OFFICE HOLDING: MEMBER OF HOUSING AUTHORITY; ARMY OFFICER

23 April, 1941.

A member of a housing authority and an army officer are both offices within the constitutional prohibition against double office holding.

DOUBLE OFFICE HOLDING: REGISTER OF DEEDS; SCHOOL COMMITTEEMAN

24 April, 1941.

Both a school committeeman and register of deeds are offices within the constitutional prohibition against double office holding.

DOUBLE OFFICE HOLDING: MISCELLANEOUS

28 April, 1941.

The positions of county superintendent of schools, chairman of the county board of elections, district school committeeman, and president of a rural electrification association are all offices within the meaning of the constitutional prohibition against double office holding.

Membership on a local draft board, membership in an agricultural conservation association, and the position of chairman of the advisory board to registrants under the 1940 Selective Service Act are not offices within the meaning of the constitutional prohibition.

DOUBLE OFFICE HOLDING: SCHOOL TEACHERS; JUSTICES OF THE PEACE

28 April, 1941.

A school teacher is not an officer within the meaning of the constitutional prohibition against double office holding.

A justice of the peace, by reason of a specific exemption in the Constitution, is permitted to hold another office at the same time.

DOUBLE OFFICE HOLDING: TOWN ATTORNEY; SCHOOL PRINCIPAL

25 April, 1941.

The offices of town attorney, principal of high school and principal of grammar school are not offices within the meaning of Article XIV, Section 7, of the Constitution, prohibiting double office holding.

ELECTION LAWS: MARKING BALLOTS

22 April, 1941.

The State election laws provide that if an elector desires to vote for a person whose name does not appear on the ticket, he can substitute the name by writing it in with a pencil or ink in the proper place, and making a cross mark in the blank space at the left of the name so written. A blank space for this purpose should be provided on the ballot.

ELECTION LAWS: MUNICIPAL ELECTIONS; ABSENTEE BALLOTS; FILING FEES

25 April, 1941.

Absentee ballots may not be used in municipal elections.

Unless organized under the Municipal Corporations Act of 1917 or authorized to do so by a special statute, a municipal corporation cannot require filing fees of candidates for municipal office.

ELECTION LAWS: MUNICIPAL ELECTIONS; PRIMARIES; UNOPPOSED CANDIDATES

22 April, 1941.

Where a city charter provides for the selection of candidates for office in partisan primaries, there is no necessity for holding a party primary when the candidates for nomination by the party are unopposed. The names of the unopposed candidates may be printed on the official ballots for the municipal election without a primary.

INSANE PERSONS AND INCOMPETENTS: RESTORATION OF SANITY

21 April, 1941.

The certificate of the superintendent of either of the State Hospitals to the effect that a patient there formerly adjudged insane has been restored to sound mind and memory has the effect of restoring such person to all his rights which he formerly had before he was adjudged insane.

JUSTICES OF THE PEACE: FEES

25 April, 1941.

It is not proper for justices of the peace to charge fees which are lower than those fixed by law.

JUSTICES OF THE PEACE: HOLDING COURT ON SUNDAY

21 April, 1941.

In cases of emergency, there is no reason why a justice of the peace may not hold court on Sunday.

MARRIAGE LAWS: KINSHIP; LICENSE

30 April, 1941.

The laws of this State provide that all marriages between any two persons nearer of kin than first cousins shall be void, and that double first cousins may not marry.

The marriage laws also provide that application for a marriage license must be accompanied by a health certificate before a license can be issued.

MUNICIPALITIES: FRANCHISE TO TELEPHONE COMPANY; RIGHT TO GRANT

24 April, 1941.

A municipality has a right under N. C. laws to grant, but is not compelled to grant a franchise to a telephone company under such reasonable terms as the city may impose, for such length of time not exceeding sixty years, as the city may care to grant it.

TAXATION: AD VALOREM; ADJOURNMENT OF COUNTY BOARD OF EQUALIZATION AND REVIEW

28 April, 1941.

The board of equalization and review of a county has no authority to reconvene after the date fixed by statute for the final adjournment if on that date it enters an order of final adjournment on its minutes or if it fails to enter on its minutes a finding that it is unable to complete its work and an order fixing a definite date for another meeting.

TAXATION: COLLECTION; ATTACHMENT AND GARNISHMENT

30 April, 1941.

The wages of employees of a contractor building a camp for the United States Government are subject to garnishment for delinquent taxes.

TAXATION: SALES AND USE TAXES; BUILDING MATERIALS

23 April, 1941.

Repair parts, supplies for machinery, dynamite, drills and other like supplies used by a highway contractor under contracts with the State or Federal Governments are not "building materials" within the meaning of 427 of the Revenue Act, and hence are subject to the sale or use tax.

VITAL STATISTICS: REGISTER OF DEEDS; CHANGES IN BIRTH AND DEATH CERTIFICATES

25 April, 1941.

The register of deeds is only the custodian of birth and death certificates filed in his office and has no right to change them. Changes in a birth certificate would have to be made through the local register of vital statistics as provided in C. S. 7105, and such changes should be made to appear on the original certificate on file with the State Registrar and also on the copy on file with the register of deeds.

WILLS: PROBATE; TIME LIMIT

21 April, 1941.

There is no limitation upon the time in which a will may be probated in this State. However, the rights of innocent purchasers from the heirs or distributees of the deceased are protected when a will is not offered for probate within two years after his death.

APPEALS: BY THE STATE; PROSECUTION BONDS; COST

30 May, 1941.

When the State appeals in any of the cases permitted under C. S. 4649, no bond on the part of the State is required. The State takes care of the cost of printing the record.

Change of Name: Aliens

28 May, 1941.

The name of an alien may be changed under our statutes regulating change of name in the same manner as that of a citizen of the State.

Constitutional Law: Constitutionality of Statutes

28 May, 1941.

Acts of the General Assembly are presumed to be valid and binding on administrative officials until declared unconstitutional by a court of competent jurisdiction.

Criminal Procedure: Warrants; Withdrawal

28 May, 1941.

A person who has sworn out a warrant before a justice of the peace for a person accused of a misdemeanor may, with the consent of the justice of the peace, withdraw the warrant.

Criminal Procedure: Commitment of Prisoner in Capital Case

28 May, 1941.

In all cases where no appeal is taken from a death sentence, and in capital rape cases, and in those cases where the sheriff and the solicitor who prosecuted the capital case are of the opinion that it is necessary to remove a convicted person to the State Penitentiary to protect him from violence, such convicted felony shall be sent to the State Penitentiary and there held until such time as he shall be executed according to law.

Intoxicating Liquors: Disposal of Confiscated Liquors; Municipal Corporations

29 May, 1941.

A town has no authority to sell confiscated liquor seized within the town limits. Confiscated liquors should be turned over to the county commissioners, and, if sold in the manner authorized by law, the proceeds must be paid into the county school fund.

Justice of the Peace: Jurisdiction; Motor Vehicle Laws

27 May, 1941.

A justice of the peace does not have jurisdiction over the offense of operating a motor truck with a trailer attached, at a greater rate of speed than allowed by law, 55 miles per hour. The punishment for this is beyond that over which a justice of the peace may exercise jurisdiction. A justice of the peace is limited to punishment of a fine of $50.00 or imprisonment for 30 days.

Justices of the Peace: Official Bonds; Premiums

24 May, 1941.

Public-Local Laws of 1941, Ch. 298, which requires justices of the peace in certain counties to furnish bonds, contemplates that premiums for such bonds will be paid by the boards of county commissioners.

INTOXICATING LIQUORS: BEER LICENSES; REVOCATION; JUDICIAL REVIEW

2 May, 1941.

The action of a board of county commissioners in revoking a beer license is not subject to judicial review except on the grounds that the power has been exercised arbitrarily in violation of a constitutional right or that there has been a wilful or gross abuse of discretion.

JUSTICES OF THE PEACE: JURISDICTION; LARCENY

17 May, 1941.

A justice of the peace does not have jurisdiction over the offense of larceny of property of a value less than $50. The punishment for this offense is within the discretion of the court and since this punishment may exceed a fine of $50 or thirty days in jail, the offense is beyond the jurisdiction of a justice of the peace.

MOTOR VEHICLES: NARCOTICS; SODIUM AMYTAL

26 May, 1941.

Sodium Amytal is not a narcotic drug within the meaning of the statute prohibiting operation of a motor vehicle while under the influence of narcotic drugs.

MUNICIPAL CORPORATIONS: REMOVAL OF GARBAGE; LIABILITY FOR INJURY CAUSED BY GARBAGE TRUCK

2 May, 1941.

Municipal corporations are not liable for personal injuries arising out of the exercise of a governmental function of the city. Removal of garbage is a governmental function and, therefore, there is no liability for personal injuries resulting from the operation of a garbage truck.

MUNICIPAL ELECTIONS: ELECTION OFFICIALS; COMPENSATION

23 May, 1941.

Registrars, poll holders, and judges of elections are entitled to receive the same compensation for holding municipal elections as they are entitled to receive for services rendered in county and state elections.

PRACTICE OF LAW: JUSTICES OF THE PEACE

22 May, 1941.

Under Public Laws of 1941, Ch. 177, the term "practice law" is defined so as to include the performance of any legal service for any person, firm, or corporation, with or without compensation, especially including the preparation of deeds, mortgages, wills, trust instruments, reports of guardians, trustees, administrators, or executors, or by the assisting by advice, counsel, or otherwise, in any such legal work.

Justices of the peace are not authorized to practice law, and they may not perform these services.

School Law: Teachers' Contracts; Roman Catholics Teaching in Public Schools

3 May, 1941.

There is no law in this State which prohibits a Roman Catholic teaching in the public schools. Any law which would attempt to prohibit a member of any religious denomination from teaching in the schools would conflict with the constitutional guaranties of religious freedom. N. C. Constitution, Art. I, Section 26.

State Institutions: Liability for Personal Injuries Received by Student

22 May, 1941.

A state institution is immune from legal liability for injuries received by students or other persons, unless there is some contractual liability for hospitalization or medical care, as the State, and its institutions, cannot be sued without its consent.

Attorneys at Law: Justices of the Peace; Practicing Law

7 May, 1941.

The laws of this State provide that a justice of the peace may not practice law. C. S. 198.

Double Office Holding: Member of the State Board of Dental Examiners

20 May, 1941.

The office of member of the Board of Dental Examiners constitutes an office within the constitutional prohibition of double office holding.

Double Office Holding: Alderman; Member of School Board

16 May, 1941.

Membership on a city board of aldermen and a local school board at the same time constitutes double office holding, forbidden by the Constitution.

Intoxicating Liquors: Confiscation of Vehicles; Right of Holder of Unrecorded Lien in Proceeds of Sale

19 May, 1941.

The holder of an unrecorded lien is entitled to have his lien satisfied according to its priority out of the proceeds from the sale of an automobile confiscated for illegal transportation of liquor which remain after the expense of keeping the property, the fee for seizure, and the cost of the sale have been paid.

Justices of the Peace: Official Bonds; Sureties

21 May, 1941.

Under Public-Local Laws of 1941, Ch. 298, which requires justices of the peace in certain counties to furnish bonds, the county commissioners may accept bonds with either corporate or personal sureties.

Motor Vehicle Laws: Horns and Warning Devices

22 May, 1941.

It is unlawful for any vehicle to be equipped with any siren, compression or spark plug whistle, or for any person at any time to use a horn otherwise than as a reasonable warning, or to make any unnecessary or unreasonably loud or harsh sound by means of a horn or warning device. C. S. 2621(274). The statute permits police, fire departments, fire patrol vehicles and ambulances to be equipped with a bell, siren or exhaust whistle of a type approved by the Motor Vehicle Division.

Municipal Corporation: Sale of Property; Notice

16 May, 1941.

The mayor and commissioners of a town may sell municipal property to the highest bidder at public outcry after giving thirty days' notice of such sale. It is not necessary that notice be posted at the courthouse door. Publication of notice at the city hall and at the location of the property would be sufficient.

Municipal Ordinances: Wine and Beer; Prohibiting Sale of

9 May, 1941.

In the absence of any public-local law applicable to a particular county or city, city commissioners could not pass a valid ordinance prohibiting the sale of wine and beer which is legalized under the State-wide law.

Salaries and Fees: Disposition of Fees for Service of Process by Patrolmen

12 May, 1941.

Fees for service of process by a Highway Patrolman which are taxed in the bill of costs against a defendant should be remitted to the general fund of the county in which the said costs are taxed.

School Laws: Special School Elections

19 May, 1941.

The Board of County Commissioners designates the polling places, appoints registrars and judges and canvasses and judicially determines the results of special school elections.

Schools: City Administrative Units; Buildings; Contracts

9 May, 1941.

Where an appropriation has been made for a new school building or an addition to an old building within a city administrative unit, the contract should be let by the school board of the city administrative unit.

Salaries and Fees: Witness Fees for Salaried Policeman

13 May, 1941.

A salaried policeman is not entitled to witness fees where the court before which he testifies is within the territorial boundaries in which the officer can make arrests.

Witnesses: Service of Subpoenas

19 May, 1941.

Subpoenas for witnesses and summons for jurors may be served by telephone or registered mail. C. S. 918.

Clerk Superior Court: Vacancy in Office; Term of Person Elected to Fill

7 June, 1941.

A person elected to fill a vacancy in the office of clerk of the superior court holds office only for the unexpired term of the previous incumbent and not for a complete new term of four years.

Chief of Police: Residence Requirement

14 June, 1941.

C. S. 2646 requires that a chief of police be a qualified voter and resident of the municipality in which he serves.

Constables: Jurisdiction

9 June, 1941.

A township constable may legally serve process, either civil or criminal, anywhere in the county in which his township is situated.

County Fiscal Control Act: Distribution of Funds by County Superintendent Public Welfare

30 June, 1941.

A county superintendent of public welfare is not authorized to retain funds collected by him for reimbursement for hospitalization, home care and board of children, etc., and disburse same for other expenses of like nature without allowing such funds to go through the county treasurer's account.

CRIMINAL LAW: SENTENCE AND PUNISHMENT; MISDEMEANORS

11 June, 1941.

Where a statute provides that punishment for a misdemeanor shall be fine or imprisonment or both in the discretion of the court, the court may sentence a person to imprisonment for any length of time so long as the sentence is not so excessive as to violate the constitutional prohibition against cruel and unusual punishments. A sentence of two years is valid.

DOUBLE OFFICE HOLDING: DISTRICT GAME WARDEN; CITY POLICEMAN

2 June, 1941.

The positions of district game warden and city policeman are both offices within the meaning of the constitutional prohibition against double office holding.

INTANGIBLES TAX: ALLOCATION TO COUNTY FUNDS

9 June, 1941.

The amount apportioned to a county as its share of the intangibles tax collected by the State should be allocated to the various county funds according to the same proportion as that which regulates distribution of ad valorem taxes on tangible property collected in the county.

JUSTICES OF THE PEACE: BOND REQUIREMENT

23 June, 1941.

House Bill No. 239 requiring a justice of the peace to furnish a surety bond conditioned upon proper accounting for funds coming into his hands contemplates either corporate bond or one furnished by one or more solvent individuals.

JUSTICES OF THE PEACE: CRIMINAL LAW JURISDICTION

14 June, 1941.

A justice of the peace has no final jurisdiction in cases where a person is charged with a violation of the speed laws of the State, because the punishment is over 30 days imprisonment or $50.00 fine, and is therefore greater than that which may be meted out by a magistrate.

MUNICIPAL CORPORATIONS: OFFICERS; INDUCTION

12 June, 1941.

In the absence of a local statutory provision, newly elected municipal officers should be inducted into office as soon as practicable after the election. It is not necessary that the commencement of their terms be delayed until the beginning of the fiscal year.

MUNICIPAL CORPORATIONS: HOUSING AUTHORITIES; BUILDING PERMITS

14 June, 1941.

A housing authority erecting a building within a city must obtain a building permit from the city, but the city is not permitted to charge a fee for the issuance of the permit.

School Law: City Administrative Units; Appropriations for High School Band

26 June, 1941.

A city administrative school unit is authorized to provide in its budget an appropriation for the purchase of musical instruments for a high school band.

Taxation: Municipal; Right to Release Industry from

7 June, 1941.

Board of town commissioners does not have the authority to release an industry from taxation for a period of ten years in order to encourage the industry to locate in that town.

Wine and Beer: License to Sell; Naturalization

24 June, 1941.

In order for a person to be entitled to sell wine and beer at retail, he must be a citizen and resident of the State. Public Laws, 1939, Section 511(5), Ch. 158. Therefore, a foreigner who has not been naturalized would be ineligible to receive a license to sell wine and beer.

Uniform Drivers License Act: Revocation of License; Acquittal on Charge of Drunken Driving

27 June, 1941.

The acquittal of a motorist on a charge of operating an automobile while intoxicated does not preclude the State from revoking such motorist's operating license. There are no civil or property rights involved in an automobile drivers license. It is merely a privilege extended which may be withdrawn by the State for cause in the interest of public safety upon the highways.

Commissioner of Public Trust: Trading for His Own Benefit

18 June, 1941.

C. S. 4388, which provides that a public official may not make a contract by virtue of his office for his own benefit, would make it unlawful for a Town Board to purchase supplies from a wholesale corporation of which one of its members is general manager.

Coroner: Fees

18 June, 1941.

Under C. S. 3905 a coroner is entitled to $5.00 for holding an inquest, and, if he is necessarily engaged more than one day, he is entitled to $5.00 for each additional day.

Criminal Law: Lotteries; "Prosperity Night"

2 June, 1941.

The fact that the winner at a "prosperity night" at a theater is chosen by name rather than by number does not keep the scheme from being a violation of our lottery laws.

Double Office Holding: Membership on A.B.C. Board; Postmaster

19 June, 1941.

Membership on a county A. B. C. Board and holding the office of postmaster are both offices within the meaning of Art. XIV, Section 7, of the Constitution, which prohibits double office holding.

Double Office Holding: Member of Recreation Commission

9 June, 1941.

A member of a municipal recreation commission is an officer within the meaning of the Constitutional provision against double office holding.

Election Laws: Poll Tax; Qualification of Voters

2 June, 1941.

Payment of poll tax is not a condition precedent to the right to vote in this State.

Justice of the Peace: Jurisdiction

6 June, 1941.

A magistrate does not have final jurisdiction in cases where a person is charged with operating a motor vehicle without a driver's license. A Justice of the Peace has jurisdiction only in those cases where the punishment does not exceed $50.00 fine or thirty days in jail.

Marriage: First Cousins

6 June, 1941.

Persons who are first cousins may be legally married in this State, but marriages between persons nearer of kin are void.

Municipal Corporation: Tax Ordinances; Publication

14 June, 1941.

There is no general statutory requirement that a municipal privilege tax ordinance be published in a newspaper.

Municipal Corporation: Taxation; Business Outside Corporate Limits

13 June, 1941.

Municipal corporations are not permitted to levy a license tax upon businesses which are operated outside the corporate limits.

School Law: Teachers; Discrimination on Account of Marriage

3 June, 1941.

The provision of the School Machinery Act which provides that no rule may be made in the employment of teachers which discriminates with respect to marriage applies to teachers paid from county funds as well as to those paid from State funds.

TAXATION: MUNICIPAL LICENSE; MORE THAN ONE BUSINESS

20 June, 1941.

A person who operates a garage and in connection therewith a service station is liable for the license tax on both these businesses.

TAXATION: PROPERTY BOUGHT WITH COMPENSATION INSURANCE

11 June, 1941.

Real property bought with the proceeds of compensation insurance received by a veteran from the Federal Government is subject to ad valorem taxation.

UNAUTHORIZED PRACTICE OF LAW: NOTARY PUBLIC; SURVEYOR; DRAWING DEEDS AND OTHER LEGAL INSTRUMENTS

2 June, 1941.

The practice of a notary public or a county surveyor drawing deeds and other legal instruments would be a violation of Chapter 157 of the Public Laws of 1931, which prohibits the unauthorized practice of law.

COUNTIES: COUNTY FISCAL CONTROL; TRANSFER OF APPROPRIATIONS

10 July, 1941.

Funds appropriated by the county commissioners for "poor and health" purposes may not be used for any other purpose than that designated in the appropriations resolution.

COUNTIES: MUNICIPAL CORPORATIONS; MEETINGS OF COMMISSIONERS

24 July, 1941.

Meetings of county commissioners and of commissioners of municipalities are required to be open to the public.

ELECTIONS: MUNICIPAL; MARKING BALLOT

21 July, 1941.

An elector placing a cross mark only after one name on a ballot containing six other names, would not have the effect of voting six ballots for the one candidate opposite whose name he had placed the cross mark. This would amount to only one ballot being cast for the person after whose name the elector places the mark.

INTOXICATING LIQUORS: BEER; ISSUANCE OF LICENSE

7 July, 1941.

The Machinery Act of 1939 provides that it shall be mandatory that the governing body of a municipality or county issue licenses to sell beer to any person applying for the same when such person shall have complied with the requirements of the article.

Marriage Law: County Performed in

10 July, 1941.

A minister or officer would not be authorized to perform a ceremony of marriage in one county on a license issued by the Register of Deeds of another county. However, if the marriage is performed in one county on a license from another, such would not invalidate the marriage, but would subject the officer performing the ceremony to the penalty of the statute prohibiting him from performing such ceremony.

Motor Vehicles: Licenses: Refund of Truck Licenses

17 July, 1941.

Where pursuant to contract with a general contractor the Federal Government exercises its right to purchase trucks being used by the contractor, the contractor is not entitled to a refund of the license taxes paid to the State on the trucks or to use the license plates on other trucks.

Motor Vehicles: License; Purchase of by Non-Resident

14 July, 1941.

The reciprocity agreement between this State and Tennessee provides that if a resident of either is stationed in the other for a period in excess of sixty days under circumstances that require him to live there and engage in a gainful occupation, then he must purchase motor vehicle plates.

Slot Machines: Operated by Club

3 July, 1941.

The fact that a country club intends to operate slot machines, the proceeds of which are to be used for the upkeep of the club house, would not have the effect of making legal the operation of slot machines outlawed by the Flanagan Act.

Taxation: Revaluation

18 July, 1941.

The county commissioners of a county which has postponed its revaluation and reassessment of real property during 1941 have the authority to revalue and reassess such property in 1942.

Taxation: Poll Tax; Soldiers

15 July, 1941.

A person called into military service who was an inhabitant of a county at listing time is liable for the poll tax levied by the county at that time.

Taxation: Poll Tax; Residence

11 July, 1941.

A highway patrolman who is stationed in one county but who retains his residence and votes at his original home should list and pay his poll tax in the county of his residence. State employees whose duties require them to remove from one county to another do not acquire a new legal residence in the absence of an intention on their part to do so.

TAXATION: SALES AND USE TAXES; BUSINESS MACHINES

19 July, 1941.

Under the Sales Tax Act leases by a person engaged in the business of leasing or licensing the use or consumption of tangible personal property for a consideration are taxable. A transaction in which a business machine company leases a machine to a client in this State is taxable either under the Sales Tax Act or the Use Tax Act, which complements it.

WINE LAW

29 July, 1941.

Sweet wines may be sold in wet counties in drug stores, grade A cafes, grocery stores, and hotels, which have qualified as sweet wine dealers under the 1941 Wine Law.

CLERKS OF THE SUPERIOR COURT: COMMISSIONS; FUNDS PAID INTO COURT ON JUDGMENT

25 July, 1941.

Under C. S. 3903, clerks of the superior court are not entitled to commissions on funds placed in their hands on judgments. Where the amount of a judgment in a wrongful death action brought by an administrator is paid to the clerk and is distributed by him, he is not entitled to commissions on this amount.

CRIMINAL LAW: CARRYING CONCEALED WEAPON

7 July, 1941.

A person who carries a weapon in the glove compartment of an automobile with the door to the compartment closed may be convicted of carrying a concealed weapon under C. S. 4410. The weapon need not be actually on the person of the defendant if it is within his reach and control.

CRIMINAL LAW: ADVERTISING SCHEME; LOTTERY

12 July, 1941.

An advertising scheme whereby a drug store issues a ticket each day to a customer making a purchase, containing a question thereon, and if the customer's ticket is drawn and he is able to answer the question, he receives the amount of a "jack pot," which is built up by adding $5.00 a day thereto, constitutes a lottery.

DEPARTMENT OF CONSERVATION AND DEVELOPMENT: QUALIFICATIONS OF EMPLOYEES; GAME PROTECTORS

28 July, 1941.

The Board of Conservation and Development has authority to make rules and regulations relating to the qualifications of game protectors.

A regulation requiring applicants for the position of game protector to be between the ages of 22 and 40 years is reasonable and valid.

JUVENILE COURTS: EXCLUSION OF GENERAL PUBLIC; PUBLIC INSPECTION OF RECORDS

26 July, 1941.

The judge of a juvenile court has authority to exclude the general public and admit only persons directly interested in the case to a hearing or trial before him. He may also withhold records from indiscriminate public inspection when it is for the best interest of the child concerned.

MORTGAGES: DEEDS OF TRUST; CANCELLATION BY AGENT

3 July, 1941.

A person who attempts to cancel a deed of trust as agent or attorney for the trustee named in such deed of trust should have a power of attorney from the trustee and this power of attorney should be properly recorded.

PUBLIC OFFICERS: DEPUTY SHERIFFS; RESIDENCE REQUIREMENT

7 July, 1941.

A person who has been a resident of this State for less than one year would not be eligible for appointment as a deputy sheriff.

REGISTER OF DEEDS: INDEXING; NAME OF CORPORATION

7 July, 1941.

Names of corporations, whether public, municipal, or private, should be indexed according to the corporate name of such corporation as it appears in the charter.

SALARIES AND FEES: CONSTABLES

21 July, 1941.

A constable is within his rights in demanding his fees in advance for summoning jurors in a civil action before a justice of the peace.

TAXATION: AD VALOREM; FARM PRODUCTS IN HANDS OF PRODUCERS

9 July, 1941.

A county may not collect ad valorem taxes for the year 1941 on crops grown in 1940 and owned by the producer on January 1, 1941.

TAXATION: AD VALOREM; UNPAID TAXES, 1929 AND 1940

8 July, 1941.

Taxes for the years 1929 and 1930 which remain unpaid may be collected by foreclosure proceedings under the Machinery Act.

TAXATION: MUNICIPALITIES; TAXI-CABS

11 July, 1941.

Municipalities may not levy a license tax in excess of one dollar per vehicle on taxi-cabs operated within their limits and resident therein.

TAXATION: MUNICIPAL; SALE OF WINE

8 July, 1941.

Under C. S. 2677, which is the general law permitting cities and towns to levy a tax on trades and professions, by proper ordinance a municipality may levy a privilege license tax on persons engaged in the business of selling sweet and fortified wines in wet counties.

TAXATION: COUNTIES; LICENSE TAX ON FISHING GUIDES

18 July, 1941.

There is no general statute authorizing counties to impose license taxes on fishing guides.

CITIZENSHIP: RESTORATION

12 August, 1941.

Application for the restoration of citizenship to a person who has been convicted of a felony and whose citizenship was thereby forfeited should be made by a petition to the Superior Court of the county of his conviction. The Governor of North Carolina has no authority under the law or the Constitution to restore a person's citizenship.

COSTS: DISTRIBUTION; CASE IN WHICH PLAINTIFF NONSUITED

11 August, 1941.

In a case in which the plaintiff is nonsuited and adjudged to pay the costs, the costs should first be applied to paying the defendant's witnesses and costs, in preference to plaintiff's witnesses and costs.

COURTS: JUSTICE OF THE PEACE; JURISDICTION

11 August, 1941.

It would not be proper for a deputy sheriff to arrest a person charged with a crime in which such deputy is a witness and then have the matter brought before himself as a justice of the peace to pass upon the guilt or innocence of the defendant.

COURTS: JUSTICE OF THE PEACE; SENTENCE; IMPRISONMENT

1 August, 1941.

The laws of this State authorize a justice of the peace in proper cases to sentence a defendant who has been convicted in his court to thirty days in the county jail to be assigned to work the roads under the supervision and control of the State Highway and Public Works Commission.

INTOXICATING LIQUORS: WINE AND BEER; SUNDAY LAWS

21 August, 1941.

Municipalities may, under their police power, prohibit the sale of wine and beer on Sundays, by passing an ordinance to this effect.

MARRIAGE LAWS: DIVORCE AND ALIMONY

26 August, 1941.

Under the laws of this State, in order for a person to obtain a divorce the plaintiff to the divorce action must have resided in the State of North Carolina for a period of at least one year. An absolute divorce may be granted upon a showing that the parties to the action have been living separate and apart for a period of at least two years.

MARRIAGE LAWS: LICENSE; PERIOD OF TIME BEFORE MARRIAGE

11 August, 1941.

There is no statutory time required in this State which must expire before a person may get married after he has received a marriage license.

MOTOR VEHICLE LAWS: RESIDENTS REQUIRED TO HAVE NORTH CAROLINA PLATES

7 August, 1941.

The Motor Vehicle Laws of this State prohibit a bona fide resident of this State from using any registration plate or plates of another state upon his automobile. In interpreting these laws the resident and not the domicile of a car owner should control.

MUNICIPALITIES: CORPORATE EXISTENCE

18 August, 1941.

The fact that a town has not been an active municipal corporation for a period of twenty years would not have the effect of vacating its charter.

PARDON AND PAROLE: REVOCATION; AFTER EXPIRATION OF SENTENCE

6 August, 1941.

The Governor and Paroles Commissioner have the authority to revoke a parole after the term of the original sentence has expired and to require the prisoner to complete his sentence.

POSTDATED CHECKS

25 August, 1941.

Accepting a postdated check for a debt gives the accepting party no additional rights. The check is merely evidence of the indebtedness, and would only be a promissory note or an additional promise. The representation contained in a postdated check is not such as will render the drawer liable to a criminal prosecution.

TAXATION: MUNICIPAL; PRIVILEGE; DOGS

2 August, 1941.

Under empowering state laws a municipality would have a right to levy a tax on the privilege of keeping a dog therein.

TAXATION: AD VALOREM; IMPROVEMENTS SINCE JANUARY 1

1 August, 1941.

Real property should be assessed and valued for purposes of 1941 taxes as of January 1, 1941. There is no authority for changing the valuation of property for this purpose as of result of improvements made since January 1.

TAXATION: MUNICIPALITIES; LICENSE TAX ON ICE CREAM MANUFACTURERS

2 August, 1941.

Municipalities are authorized to levy a privilege license tax not in excess of one-fourth the tax levied by the State on ice cream manufacturers within their corporate limits.

TAXATION: POLL TAX; LISTING; ENLISTED MEN

14 August, 1941.

An enlisted man who is an inhabitant of a county at tax-listing time would be required to list for poll tax in that county.

TAXATION: EXEMPTIONS; HOUSING AUTHORITY PROPERTY

29 August, 1941.

Property owned by housing authorities organized under Chapter 456 of the Public Laws of 1935, as amended, is specifically exempt from taxation.

TAXATION: COLLECTION; FAILURE TO LEVY FOR PRIOR YEARS

20 August, 1941.

The fact that the operator of a pool room failed to pay his taxes for the years 1938, 1939, 1940 and 1941 and no levy on the property for this tax has been made would not bar the right of a town to collect the tax for these years.

VETERANS: EXEMPTIONS; COUNTY PEDDLERS' TAX

5 August, 1941.

County Commissioners may exempt disabled veterans from payment of peddlers' tax .

CLERK SUPERIOR COURT: ENTRY OF JUDGMENTS; CIVIL ACTIONS

30 August, 1941.

A Clerk of the Superior Court would not be authorized to sign a judgment on a day other than Monday, where the judgment is based on a motion to dismiss the action for failure to file a complaint.

Debtors' Names: Publication of; Minors

21 August, 1941.

There is no law which would prohibit a merchant from posting the names of his debtors upon a signboard in front of his place of business. This is true whether the debtor is a minor or of age.

Double Office Holding: Registrar of Vital Statistics; School Committeeman

1 August, 1941.

A Registrar of Vital Statistics and a School Committeeman are both officers within the prohibition contained in Article XIV, Section 7, of the Constitution of North Carolina, relative to double office holding.

Intoxicating Liquors; Mixed Drinks; Cafes

16 August, 1941.

It would be a violation of the prohibition laws of this State for a restaurant to serve wine mixed with whiskey to its patrons.

Justices of the Peace: Mayor's Courts

28 August, 1941.

The mayor of every city or incorporated town is constituted an inferior court and as such court has the jurisdiction of a justice of the peace in all criminal matters arising under the laws of the State, or under the ordinances of such city or town.

Municipal Elections: Vacancy; Commissioners

18 August, 1941.

In case of a vacancy after the election in the office of town commissioners, the other members of the town board may fill it until the next election.

Salaries and Fees: Payment of Fees of Arresting Officer; County

29 August, 1941.

In a case where the defendant is sentenced to the roads for a period of thirty days by a justice of the peace, the arresting officer and justice of the peace could not collect their fees from the county.

School Law: Teachers; Distribution

8 August, 1941.

Under the School Machinery Act the district committee has the authority to distribute teachers who have been allotted to a school district where there is more than one school in the district.

Taxation: Municipal; Refunds

8 August, 1941.

The laws of this State do not grant express authority to local governing bodies to make tax refunds, for any reason whatever, when the taxes have been paid without protest.

Taxation: Listing and Assessing

11 August, 1941.

The Machinery Act empowers the county commissioners to assess and list any property for any preceding years it escaped taxation, not exceeding five, in addition to the current year.

Taxation: Poll; Amount; Municipalities

22 August, 1941.

A municipal poll tax of three dollars would be invalid although the charter of a municipality provides that this amount may be levied. The charter provision would conflict with Article V, Section 1, of the North Carolina Constitution, which provides that the poll tax levied by cities and towns shall not exceed one dollar.

Taxation: Ad Valorem; Prepayment; Commission of Collector

2 August, 1941.

Officials selected to take prepayments of taxes, would not be entitled to commissions on the amounts paid to them.

Taxation: Ad Valorem; Liquor Stock in A. B. C. Stores

22 August, 1941.

The liquor stock in a county A.B.C. store operated in a town is subject to ad valorem taxation by the town.

Costs: Criminal Cases; Officers' Benefit Fund

10 September, 1941.

In every case in which a defendant is convicted in any of the criminal courts of the State, he is required to be taxed with a one dollar fee for the Officers' Benefit Fund, which is a part of the costs. This item should be collected when the defendant pleads guilty.

Counties: Compensation of County Welfare Board

20 September, 1941.

Members of the County Board of Welfare may be reimbursed by the county for expenses incurred in attending official meetings. Reimbursement is permitted but not required under Public Laws, 1941, Ch. 270, Sec. 3. If the county decides to pay the expenses of the board, these expenses should be limited to the cost of transportation to and from the place of meeting, together with reasonable subsistence at the place of meeting.

COURTS: JUSTICES OF THE PEACE; JURY TRIALS

5 September, 1941.

A person is always entitled to a jury trial before a justice of the peace, if demanded before the trial begins and a deposit is made as required by statute.

CRIMINAL LAW: DRUNKEN DRIVING; OWNER PERMITTING ANOTHER TO DRIVE

18 September, 1941.

It is possible for a person in charge of an automobile, who requests and permits a person under the influence of liquor or other intoxicant to operate the automobile, such party at the time riding with the driver in an intoxicated condition, and knowing that the operator was intoxicated, to be convicted of drunken driving.

CRIMINAL PROCEDURE: PLEA OF NOLO CONTENDERE; REVOCATION OF HUNTING LICENSE AFTER

29 September, 1941.

A plea of *nolo contendere* in a criminal prosecution is the equivalent of a conviction for the purpose of giving the court power to punish the defendant. When a defendant pleads *nolo contendere* to a charge of violating the game laws, the court is required to compel the surrender of his hunting license and to forward it to the Department of Conservation and Development.

ELECTION LAWS: TERM IN FEDERAL PENITENTIARY NO BAR TO VOTING

30 September, 1941.

A conviction and sentence of a person to the Federal Penitentiary does not deprive him of the right to vote in this State.

LIBRARIES: STATE AID TO COUNTIES

3 September, 1941.

Funds allocated to a county by the North Carolina Library Commission, under Public Laws of 1941, Ch. 93, for the promotion of public library service, constitute a supplement to any appropriations made by the county. The funds may not be used to reimburse the county for what it has spent.

MUNICIPAL CORPORATIONS: APPROPRIATIONS TO HOME GUARD; SURPLUS FUNDS

15 September, 1941.

An appropriation to the Home Guard for the purpose of buying shoes is for a public purpose, and surplus funds could be appropriated therefor without a vote of the people.

MUNICIPALITIES: TAX COLLECTORS; DELEGATION OF AUTHORITY

11 September, 1941.

A municipal tax collector does not have the authority to delegate his duties as tax collector to a member of the police department who is not under bond for this purpose.

MUNICIPAL CORPORATIONS: ORDINANCES; REGULATION OF TAXI CABS

30 September, 1941.

A municipal corporation has no authority by ordinance to prescribe qualifications for drivers of taxi cabs in addition to those prescribed for operators of automobiles and chauffeurs by the Uniform Drivers' License Act. It may not require the payment of any tax or fee for the operation of a taxi cab in excess of the license fee of $1.00 per year which it is authorized to collect under the motor vehicle laws.

SALARIES AND FEES: WITNESS FEES FOR SALARIED POLICEMEN

29 September, 1941.

Under C. S., Sec. 3893, a policeman who is paid a salary is precluded from collecting fees as a witness in criminal courts sitting within the territory in which he serves as an officer.

TAXATION: MOTOR VEHICLE LICENSE; NON-RESIDENTS; RECIPROCITY

11 September, 1941.

The length of time when a visitor from one state to another state is allowed to remain before he is required to purchase state license plates is governed by reciprocal agreements between the several states and is not the same in all instances.

TAXATION: MUNICIPAL CORPORATIONS; DOGS

15 September, 1941.

Municipal corporations have authority to levy an annual privilege tax fixed at a reasonable amount on the ownership of dogs.

TAXATION: AD VALOREM; REDUCTION IN VALUATION OF PROPERTY AFTER LOSS BY FIRE

10 September, 1941.

When a portion of property listed for taxation on January 1 is subsequently destroyed by fire, there is no authority to reduce its valuation for the year in which it is listed so as to reflect the loss. The valuation of the property must be determined as of January 1, the listing date. There is authority for an adjustment of the valuation of property destroyed or damaged by tornado, cyclone, hurricane, or other wind or wind-storm, but the statutes do not provide for such an adjustment in case of fire.

Costs: Witness Fees in Criminal Cases

20 September, 1941.

When the defendants in criminal cases pay the costs, witnesses may prove their attendance and collect fees for every case in which they are witnesses, although several cases may be tried on the same day. If the county pays the costs, a witness is not entitled to collect from the county witness fees in more than one case for any one day.

Counties: Profits from A. B. C. Store; Appropriation for Airport

19 September, 1941.

Funds representing a county's share in profits from an A. B. C. store may lawfully be used to finance the construction of a public airport. The profits from the A. B. C. Store constitute surplus funds which may be expended for a public purpose even though the expenditure is not included in the annual county budget. A public airport is such a purpose.

Counties: Bond Issues; Application of Proceeds

20 September, 1941.

When a bond issue has been approved by the voters of a county, the proceeds may not be used for any purpose other than that specified in the order authorizing the bonds, except that any part of the proceeds not applied to or not necessary for such purpose may be applied to the payments of the principal and interest of said bonds.

Courts: Utilities Commission; Witnesses

11 September, 1941.

The Utilities Commission has the same authority to subpoena witnesses as does the Superior Court.

Double Office Holding: Town Clerk; Assistant Police Judge

29 September, 1941.

The office of town clerk and that of assistant police judge are both offices within the meaning of Article XIV, Section 7, of the Constitution, which prohibits double office holding, and one person cannot hold both these offices at the same time.

Election Laws: Absentee Ballots; Soldiers

23 September, 1941.

No absentee ballots may be used in a special election. Provision is made, however, for members of the armed forces of the United States to vote by absentee ballot in primary elections, upon compliance with the provisions of the 1941 law in this regard.

LABOR LAWS: MAXIMUM HOURS LAW; REGISTERED PHARMACIST

5 September, 1941.

The provisions of the Maximum Hours of Labor Law of this State do not apply to a registered pharmacist, whether a man or woman, who is employed in a retail drug establishment. A registered pharmacist is exempt under the professional classification section.

MUNICIPAL CORPORATIONS: SALE OF WINE AND BEER

2 September, 1941.

The commissioners of a town do not have authority to refuse to issue beer and wine licenses for the retail sale of these beverages directly across the street from a school. The Beverage Control Act, however, does prohibit their sale within fifty feet of a church building in an incorporated town during church services.

MUNICIPALITIES: TORT LIABILITY

5 September, 1941.

The maintenance and acts of the police and fire departments are governmental functions, and municipalities are not liable for injuries arising from the exercise and performance of these municipal functions.

MUNICIPAL CORPORATIONS: CONTRACT TO EXTEND AND PAVE STREET

23 September, 1941.

A municipal corporation has authority to enter into a contract to extend and pave one of its streets.

TAXATION: FORECLOSURE PROCEEDINGS

9 September, 1941.

Chapter 181 of the Public Laws of 1933 bars the collection of taxes for 1926 and prior years in counties not exempted from this act. When taxes for certain years have been declared by statute to be barred and uncollectible, the lien for the same is lost.

TAXATION: SPECIAL TAX DISTRICTS; LIABILITY FOR SCHOOL TAX WHEN CHILDREN ATTEND SCHOOL IN ANOTHER DISTRICT

12 September, 1941.

A person who owns real property within the limits of a special tax district is liable for school taxes levied in the district even though his children attend school in another district.

TAXATION: POLL TAX; EXEMPTION ON ACCOUNT OF MILITARY SERVICE

8 September, 1941.

County commissioners have authority to exempt persons from the payment of poll tax on account of indigency, but they do not have authority to exempt anyone solely on the ground that he has been drafted into the armed forces of the United States.

Taxation: Collection; Discharge of Tax Lien; Mortgagees

27 September, 1941.

When a taxpayer owns two or more parcels of land, a mortgagee or other person interested in one of the parcels has a right to have one tract or parcel released upon payment of the taxes on the parcel sought to be released, with interest and penalties thereon, plus a proportionate part of the personal property and poll tax owned by the taxpayer, with interest and penalties thereon, and a proportionate part of the costs allowed by law.

Taxation: Exemptions; World War Veterans; Scrap Tobacco

3 September, 1941.

There is no law which would have the effect of permitting disabled World War Veterans to secure free licenses to engage in the business of dealing in scrap tobacco.

Counties and County Commissioners: Appropriations; State Guard

7 October, 1941.

County commissioners have the authority to make appropriations for the support of the various units of the State Guard.

Game Laws: Game Wardens; Appointment of

21 October, 1941.

There is no statutory authority for county commissioners to employ game wardens. This authority rests in the Director of the Department of Conservation and Development.

Game Laws: Hunting without License; Revocation

29 October, 1941.

A person who is apprehended while hunting without having his hunting license on his person at the time may be convicted of hunting without license, although he produces his license at the trial, which he had purchased at least a month prior to his apprehension.

Judgments: Judgment Docket; Entry of Name of Attorney or Collection Agency

13 October, 1941.

It is permissible for the judgment docket of the superior court to contain the name of the attorney of record for the plaintiff. However, there is no provision in law and the clerk of the superior court has no authority whatsoever to insert the name, telephone number, and address of a collection agency acting as agent for the plaintiff.

MUNICIPAL CORPORATIONS: REFUND OF TAXES

15 October, 1941.

Municipal corporations have no authority to refund taxes which have not been paid under protest.

MUNICIPAL CORPORATIONS: TAXICABS; ORDINANCE REQUIRING BOND OR LIABILITY INSURANCE

October 6, 1941.

A municipal ordinance requiring operators of taxicabs engaged in the business of transporting passengers for hire over the streets of the city to file a bond or liability insurance policy with the city clerk is valid. Such an ordinance is applicable to operators of taxicabs from an adjacent town if they habitually use the city streets by bringing passengers to and from the city.

PUBLIC HEALTH: SCHOOLS; CERTIFICATES OF VACCINATION FOR SMALLPOX

3 October, 1941.

The laws of this State provide that the board of health of any town, city or county shall have authority to require children attending the public schools to present a certificate of immunity from smallpox, either through recent vaccination or previous attack of the disease.

TAXATION: COLLECTION; TRANSFER OF PERSONAL PROPERTY AFTER LISTING

14 October, 1941.

A lien on personal property for nonpayment of taxes arises to a municipality or county only upon a levy thereon. When no levy has been made before a sale of personal property by the municipality for taxes for prior years, the purchaser at such sale obtains a good title, free from taxes for the year of the sale.

ATTORNEYS: WORLD WAR VETERANS; RIGHT TO PRACTICE LAW

20 October, 1941.

There is no authority for a World War Veteran being permitted to practice law without passing the bar examination.

COUNTIES: POOR RELIEF; CONTROL OF FUNDS

11 October, 1941.

In the administration of county funds for poor relief other than funds for old age assistance and aid to dependent children, an initial determination of whether an applicant is entitled to assistance is made by the county superintendent of public welfare. The action of the superintendent is subject to review by the county commissioners.

CRIMINAL LAW: SECURING FINGERPRINTS; AUTHORITY TO TAKE

17 October, 1941.

C. S. 7766(g) has the effect of authorizing sheriffs and chiefs of police to take the fingerprints of any person charged with any crime, however small, should they deem it advisable, even though such person is not even suspected of having committed another crime.

CRIMINAL PROCEDURE: PRELIMINARY EXAMINATION; WAIVER

1 October, 1941.

A person accused of crime may waive the right to any preliminary examination before a magistrate and consent to be bound over to the Superior Court without it.

DOUBLE OFFICE HOLDING: TOWN ALDERMAN AND SOLICITOR OF RECORDERS COURT

22 October, 1941.

The position of assistant solicitor of a Recorders Court and that of a town alderman are both offices within the meaning of Article XIV, Section 7, of the Constitution, which prohibits double office holding and one person may not hold both these offices at the same time.

MUNICIPAL CORPORATIONS: ORDINANCES; TERRITORIAL LIMITATIONS

14 October, 1941.

A municipality may not enact a valid ordinance forbidding the sale of wine and beer on Sunday in territory outside its corporate limits unless clearly authorized to do so by a special act of the legislature. Ordinarily, municipal powers may not be exercised beyond the corporate limits.

MUNICIPALITIES: PAVING ASSESSMENTS; PAYMENT; REMISSION

13 October, 1941.

Under C. S. 2715 the governing board of a municipality may correct, cancel, or remit any assessment for a local improvement and remit, cancel or adjust the interest or penalties on any such assessment.

MUNICIPAL TAXATION: PHOTOGRAPHERS

6 October, 1941.

The 1941 General Assembly amended the Revenue Act so as to prohibit cities and towns from levying a tax upon those persons engaged in the business of photography.

NOTARY PUBLIC: JURISDICTION

8 October, 1941.

A notary public has full power and authority to perform the functions of his office in any and all counties of the State, and full faith and credit is required to be given to all of his official acts wherever they are made.

SCHOOL LAW: COMPULSORY ATTENDANCE OFFICER; SUPT. OF PUBLIC WELFARE

27 October, 1941.

In cases where the county or city unit has failed to employ compulsory attendance officer, the superintendent of public welfare serves in that capacity.

TAXATION: AD VALOREM; FORECLOSURE; RESALE BY COUNTY

31 October, 1941.

When a county purchases property at a tax foreclosure sale, it may resell the property to any person at a price approved by the county commissioners. Whether the former owner will be given an opportunity to redeem the property is a matter within the discretion of the commissioners.

TAXATION: PEDDLERS; FARM PRODUCTS; RAISED ON OWN PREMISES

27 October, 1941.

Under our revenue laws no peddlers or itinerant merchants tax may be levied against persons, firms or corporations, or their bona fide agents, who sell farm products raised on their own premises.

UNITED STATES LANDS: MILITARY RESERVATIONS; JURISDICTION OF CORONER

27 October, 1941.

A county coroner has no jurisdiction to hold inquests relating to deaths occurring upon a Federal military reservation in this State.

TAXATION: AD VALOREM; LIMITATION OF RATE

31 October, 1941.

There is no statute which prohibits a board of county commissioners from fixing the tax rate of a county at over $2.00 on each $100.00 valuation.

COMMISSIONER OF PUBLIC TRUST: TRADING FOR HIS OWN BENEFIT

5 November, 1941.

A member of a local city council who is the owner of a fire insurance company would violate the act prohibiting a commissioner of a public trust from trading for his own benefit, should his company sell fire or liability insurance to the city, even though the rate be the same in all companies bidding.

CRIMINAL PROCEDURE: STATUTE OF LIMITATIONS; NOL. PROS. "WITH LEAVE"

6 November, 1941.

A criminal prosecution is instituted within the time required by the two year statute of limitations for misdemeanors if the bill of indictment is returned within two years after the commission of a crime.

A nolle prosequi "with leave" is not the equivalent of an acquittal and does not necessarily terminate proceedings upon an indictment. At a subsequent term the solicitor may have a capias issued for the defendant and have him tried on the original bill of indictment. It will be immaterial if the trial takes place more than two years after the commission of the crime if the bill of indictment has been seasonably returned.

Criminal Procedure: Indictment; Waiver of Indictment for Felony

10 November, 1941.

A person cannot be tried for a felony in this State except upon a bill of indictment. A bill of indictment for a felony cannot be waived.

Criminal Procedure: Arrests; Fingerprinting

21 November, 1941.

A chief of police or sheriff has authority, if he deems it advisable, to take the fingerprints of a person arrested for the commission of a crime.

Double Office Holding: Tax Collector; Town Commissioner

5 November, 1941.

If one person served as tax collector of a county and at the same time held office as a town commissioner, he would violate the provisions of Article XIV, Section 7, of the Constitution, prohibiting double office holding.

Game Laws: Hunting License; Non-Residents; Minors

19 November, 1941.

The Game Laws of this State do not permit the minor child of a non-resident to exercise the privilege of hunting game under his father's license.

Judgments: Statute of Limitations; Alimony

19 November, 1941.

When a judgment for alimony without divorce provides for the payment of alimony in periodical instalments, the ten year statute of limitations begins to run against each instalment separately as it becomes due. It does not commence to run against an instalment before it is due.

Monopolies and Trusts: Milk Price Fixing

3 November, 1941.

An agreement of competitive milk companies to fix the price of milk is in violation of the common law against the unlawful restraint of trade and commerce, and constitutes a crime.

MUNICIPAL CORPORATIONS: BORROWING MONEY; MORTGAGES

12 November, 1941.

In North Carolina, municipal corporations are neither expressly granted nor denied the power to mortgage property. However, the Supreme Court has held that the grant to a county of power to mortgage real property could not be implied from the grant of power to sell and convey such property.

MUNICIPALITIES: ORDINANCES; OPENING AND CLOSING OF MERCANTILE ESTABLISHMENTS

7 November, 1941.

A municipality may not enact a valid ordinance fixing the opening and closing hours of business establishments. The Supreme Court has said that to permit a town or city to pass such an ordinance would be giving it equal power with the Legislature to restrict personal and property rights.

PUBLIC OFFICES: OFFICIAL BONDS; PAYMENT OF PREMIUMS BY COUNTY

5 November, 1941.

It is not mandatory that county commissioners pay the premiums on official bonds of county officers. However, in their discretion, the Commissioners may do so.

TAXATION: INTANGIBLES TAX; ALLOCATION TO COUNTIES AND MUNICIPALITIES; DISTRIBUTION

17 November, 1941.

Money allocated to counties and municipalities from the intangibles tax should be distributed among the various county and municipal funds as are other ad valorem taxes.

WORKMEN'S COMPENSATION: APPLICABILITY TO SCHOOL TEACHERS

21 November, 1941.

The Workmen's Compensation Act applies to all school employees paid from State school funds, including teachers. It is also applicable to school teachers paid from local funds.

CRIMINAL LAW: ARRESTS; AIR RAID WARDENS; SPECIAL POLICE

29 December, 1941.

Persons volunteering to serve as air raid wardens cannot be clothed by a municipality with the power to make arrests unless they are sworn in as special police. They may be made special policemen and serve without pay, and, if this procedure is followed, they can make arrests while on duty.

Criminal Procedure: Fines Collected by Mayors; School Fund

18 December, 1941.

Fines collected by mayors, like other fines, are required by the Constitution, Article IX, Sec. 5, to be faithfully appropriated for education. They should be paid into the county school fund to be used for the support of the public schools.

Double Office Holding: Local Rationing Board

24 December, 1941.

A member of a Local Rationing Board is probably an officer but he would be considered a commissioner for a special purpose during the emergency and, therefore, not disqualified to hold another office by Article XIV, Sec. 7, of the North Carolina Constitution.

Double Office Holding: Oyster Inspectors

29 December, 1941.

An oyster inspector is a public officer within the meaning of the constitutional prohibition against dual office holding.

Hospitals and Asylums: Insane Persons; Expenses of Patient at State Hospital

17 December, 1941.

Patients other than indigent patients are required to bear the expense of their care and treatment in any of the State Hospitals. Upon the death of such a patient an action may be brought against his estate by the hospital for his support and maintenance.

Justices of the Peace: Jurisdiction; Disposing of Mortgaged Property

22 December, 1941.

A justice of the peace does not have final jurisdiction over the offense of disposing of mortgaged property, the punishment for the offense being greater than that which can be imposed by a justice of the peace.

Municipal Corporations: Governing Body; Mayor; What Constitutes Quorum

22 December, 1941.

The mayor of a town presides over meetings of the commissioners of the town, and, in case there is a tie, he may vote. He is not a member of the board of commissioners for the purpose of determining whether there is a quorum. A majority of the board constitutes a quorum.

Municipal Corporations: Ordinances; Blackouts

22 December, 1941.

Under the general powers granted to municipalities by C. S., Secs. 2673 and 2787, municipal corporations may enact ordinances regulating blackouts.

MUNICIPAL CORPORATIONS: SPECIAL POLICE, GUARDING CITY WATER SUPPLY

22 December, 1941.

Under C. S., Sec. 2790, the police power of a municipal corporation extends to rights-of-way and other property which constitutes a part of the city water system even though located outside the city limits. Special police may be employed to guard such property.

MUNICIPAL CORPORATIONS: TORT LIABILITY; INJURIES CAUSED BY AUTOMOBILE OF

29 December, 1941.

A municipal corporation is not liable in tort for personal injuries caused by the operation of an automobile by its city manager.

MUNICIPAL CORPORATIONS: WATER SYSTEM; RATES

23 December, 1941.

A municipal corporation may charge different rates for furnishing water and sewerage service within and without the corporate limits.

MUNICIPAL CORPORATIONS: WORKMEN'S COMPENSATION; PRISONERS

23 December, 1941.

Prisoners sentenced to work out a fine upon city streets are not employees of the city within the meaning of the Workmen's Compensation Act.

TAXATION: AD VALOREM; EFFECT OF TRANSFER OF PROPERTY AFTER LISTING

30 December, 1941.

Property transferred to a church for parsonage purposes after the tax listing date and during a taxing year remained liable for the full amount of the taxes for that year. The lien of taxes attaches to real property as of the listing date and is not impaired by a subsequent transfer.

TAXATION: AD VALOREM; FORECLOSURE; OFFICERS' FEES

30 December, 1941.

An officer serving process in a tax foreclosure action has no right to demand that the county pay his fees in advance.

TAXATION: USE TAX; MEDICINES

30 December, 1941.

The exemption of medicines from the North Carolina Use Tax applies only to medicines sold under a doctor's prescription.

AD VALOREM TAXATION: EXEMPTION OF PROPERTY OWNED BY VETERANS LOAN FUND

3 January, 1942.

Property owned by the World War Veterans Loan Fund is exempt from ad valorem taxation.

Ad Valorem Taxation: Exemptions; Property Owned by World War Veterans Loan Fund

5 January, 1942.

Property owned by the World War Veterans Loan Fund which has been rented to an individual under a lease option agreement, would be exempt from ad valorem taxation until the option has actually been taken up and the deed made by the Commissioner to the proposed purchaser.

(1) Ad Valorem Taxation: Attachment and Garnishment. (2) Double Office Holding: List-taker and Assessor, and Tax Collector

2 January, 1942.

(1) Tax Collector may garnish wages of taxpayer to the extent of ten per cent of such compensation.

(2) Holding the office of list-taker and assessor and that of a tax collector is prohibited by the double office holding prohibition of Article XIV, Sec. 7, of the Constitution.

Criminal Procedure: Waiver of Bill of Indictment on Appeal; Misdemeanor Involving Fraud, Deceit or Malice; C. S. 4610

6 January, 1942.

It is not necessary to find a bill of indictment upon which to try defendant charged with the commission of a misdemeanor containing the "element of fraud, deceit or malice" where the case has been appealed or transferred to the Superior Court from an inferior court having exclusive jurisdiction of the offense.

Justices of the Peace: Illegal Practice of Law

5 January, 1942.

A justice of the peace may not draw up contracts, chattel mortgages, or fill in warranty deed blanks without violating the terms of C. S. 198, as amended.

Marriage Laws: Kin Nearer than First Cousins

2 January, 1942.

Persons nearer of kin than first cousins may not legally be married in North Carolina. C. S. 2495.

Member of Board of Aldermen Acting as City Treasurer; Compensation

2 January, 1942.

C. S. 4388, which prohibits a commissioner of a public trust contracting for his own benefit, would prohibit the board of aldermen paying one of its members a salary for serving as city treasurer.

Municipal Appropriations for Other than Necessary Expenses

7 January, 1942.

No municipality shall make an appropriation of money except as provided by statute. There is statutory authority for making appropriations for public libraries.

Schools: Local Supplements; Elections; Expenses

6 January, 1942.

The expenses of an election on the question of voting a supplement under the provisions of Section 14 of the School Machinery Act should be paid by the county.

Taxation: Poll Tax; Municipal Taxation

5 January, 1942.

Under the Constitution, counties may levy a poll tax not in excess of $2.00, and municipalities may levy a poll tax not in excess of $1.00.

Teachers' and State Employees' Retirement System: Eligibility of Persons Employed by County for County Health Department Work

5 January, 1942.

County health workers paid by the county and under direct supervision of the county board of health are not entitled to membership in the Teachers' and State Employees' Retirement System.

Unemployment Compensation Law: State Treasurer; Bond for Faithful Performance of Duties

2 January, 1942.

The North Carolina State Treasurer is not required to have a separate bond for the Unemployment Compensation Administration Fund, but is liable on his official bond for this Fund.

World War Veterans Loan Fund: Powers of Acting Commissioner

5 January, 1942.

In the absence of the Commissioner, the Acting Commissioner of the World War Veterans Loan Fund has ample authority to execute deeds for that office.

Municipal Corporations: Ordinances; Operation of Business Establishments on Sunday

21 January, 1942.

Municipal corporations have authority to regulate the operation of business establishments on Sunday and may require them to remain closed on that day.

ADMINISTRATION OF ESTATES: DECEASED TEACHER'S SALARY CHECK

21 January, 1942.

A deceased teacher's salary check could not be endorsed, nor could the proceeds thereof be distributed, until there is an administration upon his estate.

ARREST FEES: STATE HIGHWAY PATROLMEN

9 January, 1942.

Arrest fees in those cases where a State Highway Patrolman makes the arrest, should be paid into the general fund of the county in which the cost of such fee is taxed.

COM'R. OF PUBLIC TRUST CONTRACTING FOR OWN BENEFITS; MEMBER BOARD OF EDUCATION SELLING INSURANCE ON SCHOOL BUILDINGS

19 January, 1942.

Since the school laws require the board of education to contract for insurance on county school property, a member of the board of education could not, in his capacity as insurance agent, insure such property without violating the provisions of C. S. 4388, which prohibits a director of a public trust from contracting for his own benefit.

CRIMINAL PROCEDURE: WARRANTS; STATUTE OF LIMITATION

12 January, 1942.

In North Carolina there is no statute which limits the time in which a criminal warrant may be executed after it has been issued. Once issued, a warrant which has not been returned to the officer issuing it remains in force until executed.

DOUBLE OFFICE HOLDING: BUILDING INSPECTOR; TOWN COMMISSIONER

16 January, 1942.

A building inspector appointed under the provisions of C. S. 2741 is a public officer, and a town commissioner could not serve in such capacity and at the same time hold his office as town commissioner without violating Article XIV, Section 7, of the Constitution which prohibits double office holding.

JUSTICES OF THE PEACE: BAIL; SHERIFFS

21 January, 1942.

After a city prisoner has been committed to a county jail and his bond fixed by a Justice of the Peace, the sheriff or jailer has no authority to release such prisoner upon his own recognizance, or to reduce the bond fixed by the Justice of the Peace.

Marriage: Waiting Period after Application for License

14 January, 1942.

There is no statutory waiting period after application for license to marry which must elapse in North Carolina before license may issue or the ceremony can be performed. However, a physician's health certificate and a laboratory report on blood tests must be produced before license can issue.

Marriage: Common Law Marriages

15 January, 1942.

Common law marriage is not recognized in North Carolina.

Municipal Corporations: Board of Commissioners; Vacancies on Board

24 January, 1942.

Where it is not provided otherwise in a municipal charter, vacancies on the board of commissioners may be filled until the next election by the other commissioners, under authority of C. S., Sec. 2629.

Municipal Corporations: Public Funds; Appropriation of to Private Corporations

14 January, 1942.

Town commissioners of a municipality cannot legally make a donation from town funds to a privately owned corporation, to be used by the private corporation for advertising purposes.

Municipal Ordinances: "Blackout Ordinance"

29 January, 1942.

Under C. S. 2787 and similar empowering statutes, authorizing municipalities to pass such ordinances as are expedient for maintaining and promoting the peace, good government and welfare of the city and the morals and happiness of its citizens, a city would have the authority to pass a "blackout" ordinance.

Municipal Corporations: Elective Membership Corporations

14 January, 1942.

The fact that a municipal corporation becomes a member of an electric membership corporation would not give the Utilities Commission supervision of either the electric membership corporation or the municipality which has become a member thereof.

School Law: Sale of Property; Disposition of Funds

27 January, 1942.

Funds realized from the sale of school property in one district need not be spent or used in the same district, but could be used anywhere in the county.

Taxation: Ad Valorem; Listing Pledged Property

9 January, 1942.

When personal property has been pledged or pawned as security for a debt, the pledgor is considered the owner, and he is the proper person to list the property for taxation.

Taxation: Failure to List Property and Polls

16 January, 1942.

The effect of failure to list property and polls for taxes during the regular listing period is that when they are eventually listed the taxes with penalties become immediately due. A wilful failure to list property or to list for poll taxes constitutes a misdemeanor, and a failure to list within the required time is *prima facie* wilful.

Taxation: License Tax; Liability for Tax of Person Buying from Farmer, Storing, then Selling It

31 January, 1942.

Persons who buy cotton in their own name, becoming owners of the cotton, and later sell the cotton at a profit, are not required to purchase a license tax under Section 133(1) of the Revenue Act, as this Act only applies to buying and selling cotton "on commission." Persons selling cotton in excess of five thousand bales per annum, however, would be taxable as cotton merchants under another section of the Revenue Act.

Vital Statistics: Amendments to Birth Certificates

20 January, 1942.

Amendments to birth certificates to supply omitted names, dates, etc., must be authorized in the office of the Bureau of Vital Statistics; when, upon sufficient evidence being presented, such an amendment is allowed, the register of deeds of the county where the certificate is recorded should be notified in order that he may change his records.

Constables; Service of Process

16 February, 1942.

Process directed to a constable may be served by him in any township in the county in which he holds office.

Costs: Collection; Responsibility of Clerk of Court and Sheriff

16 February, 1942.

The primary responsibility for collecting court costs in criminal actions rests with the clerk of court. It becomes the duty of the sheriff to make such collections only when process has been issued to him for their collection by the clerk of the superior court or the judge.

CRIMINAL LAW: FAILURE TO PAY TAXI FARE

13 February, 1942.

There is no State law which makes it a criminal offense to fail to pay taxi fare.

CRIMINAL PROCEDURE: WARRANTS; WITHDRAWAL

18 February, 1942.

Neither the clerk of the superior court, the clerk of an inferior court, nor the prosecuting witness has authority to withdraw a criminal warrant. Such action must be sanctioned by the court itself.

ELECTIONS: CANDIDATES; NOMINATION BY CONVENTION

25 February, 1942.

Where it is provided by special act that candidates for office in a particular county shall be nominated by convention rather than by primary, it is not necessary for candidates to pay filing fees or to sign a writing obligating themselves to support party candidates, as would be required of candidates for nomination by primary.

GOVERNOR: SPECIAL POLICE; GUARDS FOR COUNTY AIRPORT

13 February, 1942.

The Governor has no authority to appoint special police or guards with power of arrest to guard a county airport.

JUSTICES OF THE PEACE: JURISDICTION

2 February, 1942.

A justice of the peace does not have jurisdiction to try any person charged with the violation of a Federal statute.

MOTOR VEHICLES: LICENSE PLATES; IMPROPER USE

6 February, 1942.

The penalty for use of an automobile license plate on a vehicle other than that on which use of the plate is authorized is the revocation and cancellation of the license plate. The Department of Motor Vehicles has no discretion in such matters, revocation being mandatory when such an improper use is established.

MOTOR VEHICLE LAWS: SPEED RESTRICTIONS

4 February, 1942.

The only absolute speed limit for vehicles in North Carolina is sixty miles per hour. However, operation of a motor vehicle at a speed in excess of the other rates mentioned in C. S., Sec. 2621(288), constitutes prima facie evidence of operation at a speed greater than that which is reasonable and prudent, which is forbidden by law.

MUNICIPAL CORPORATIONS: ORDINANCES; REGULATION OF BARBER SHOPS

25 February, 1942.

Municipal corporations are authorized by Public Laws of 1939, Ch. 164, to enact ordinances regulating the opening and closing hours of barber shops.

OATHS: ADMINISTRATION; USE OF BIBLE

24 February, 1942.

Under C. S., Sec. 3189, when an oath is administered in a judicial proceeding, the party taking the oath is required to lay his hand upon the Bible in token of his engagement to speak the truth. However, under Sec. 3190, if he has conscientious scruples against taking a book oath, he may be excused from laying his hands upon the Bible and be permitted to take the oath by uplifted hand.

TAXATION: AD VALOREM; DEDUCTION OF INDEBTEDNESS ON STOCK OF MERCHANDISE

16 February, 1942.

A merchant listing his stock of merchandise for ad valorem taxation is not entitled to deduct indebtedness owed on the goods from the valuation.

TAXATION: AD VALOREM; EXEMPTIONS; LIVESTOCK

20 February, 1942.

Livestock is not exempt from ad valorem taxation under subsection 12 of Section 601 of the Machinery Act, which exempts "all cotton, tobacco or other farm products owned by the original producer" from taxation for the year following that in which it has been grown.

TAXATION: GASOLINE TAX; REFUNDS

13 February, 1942.

A seller of gasoline is not entitled to a refund of gasoline tax because gasoline which he sells is used for purposes other than operation of motor vehicles on the highways. The consumer is the proper person to make application for a refund.

TAXATION: INCOME TAX; TEACHERS; DEDUCTION FOR RETIREMENT

14 February, 1942.

Teachers in computing their State income tax are not entitled to deduct the portion of their salary which is placed to their credit in the retirement system.

TAXATION: POLL TAX; LIMITATION

2 February, 1942.

Municipalities may, by proper ordinance, levy a poll tax not in excess of $1.00 upon each male inhabitant resident in such municipality between the ages of twenty-one and fifty years.

Taxation: Privilege Taxes; Municipal Taxation of Taxicabs

13 February, 1942.

A municipality may not impose privilege taxes for operation of taxicabs in excess of one dollar per vehicle.

Double Office Holding

12 March, 1942.

A tax list-taker and a school committeeman are both officers within the meaning of Article XIV, Section 7, of the Constitution of North Carolina, which prohibits double office holding.

Double Office Holding: Policeman and Deputy Sheriff

19 March, 1942.

The Supreme Court of this State has held that the office of a city policeman and that of a deputy sheriff are both offices within the meaning of Article XIV, Section 7, of the Constitution, which prohibits double office holding.

Elections: Primaries; Residence Requirement for Candidate for County Office

23 March, 1942.

A person, if otherwise qualified, may be a candidate for nomination for a county office in a primary election if he has been a resident of the county for four months preceding the primary election.

Guardian and Ward: Investment of Trust Funds

13 March, 1942.

There is no statutory authority which would allow a guardian to turn over stock in Federal Building & Loan Associations to the Clerk of the Superior Court, thereby entitling him to have his bond reduced in the amount of the money paid for the stock certificates.

Intoxicating Liquors

17 March, 1942.

County A.B.C. boards have authority to discontinue a liquor store within a municipality.

Marriage Laws: License

19 March, 1942.

Under our laws no minister is permitted to perform a marriage ceremony between two persons until there has been delivered to him a license for the marriage of said persons, signed by the Register of Deeds of the county in which the marriage is intended to take place.

Motor Vehicle Laws: Driver's License; License Plates; Seizure by Highway Patrolman

6 March, 1942.

A highway patrolman has no authority to take up an automobile driver's license unless it has been suspended or revoked by the Division of Motor Vehicles and he has been ordered by the Department to take it up.

A patrolman has authority to take up automobile license plates for revocation and cancellation if the operator of a motor vehicle admits that they have been improperly used. If improper use is denied, the plates should not be taken up by a patrolman until such improper use has been judicially ascertained.

Municipalities: Sunday Laws; Wine and Beer

19 March, 1942.

Under its general police power, a municipality has authority to fix the hours of, and to actually prohibit, the sale of merchandise on Sunday, including wine and beer.

Municipal Corporations: Ordinances; Privilege Taxes

24 March, 1942.

Municipal corporations may impose privilege taxes upon trades and professions, and the payment of such taxes may be enforced through the imposition of reasonable penalties, provided by ordinance, for non-payment.

Primary Elections: Change in Party Affiliation

30 March, 1942.

The election laws of this State provide that no registered elector shall be permitted to change his party affiliation for a primary or second primary after the close of the registration period.

Public Officers: Leave of Absence

10 March, 1942.

Under the laws of this State, any elective or appointive county official may obtain leave of absence from his duties for military or naval service.

Sheriffs: Practicing Attorney

24 March, 1942.

The laws of this State provide that no person shall be eligible to the office of sheriff who is a practicing attorney. This would not prevent, however, a practicing attorney from becoming a candidate for the office of sheriff. If such candidate was successful and elected, he could not, after qualifying, engage in the practice of law.

TAXATION: AD VALOREM; EFFECT OF SALE OF REAL PROPERTY AFTER LISTING DATE

26 March, 1942.

A person who owns real property on January 1 of each year, the listing date for ad valorem taxation, is liable for the taxes on the property for that year, and the taxes are a lien on the property from the listing date. A sale of the property after the listing date does not extinguish the liability for taxes of the person who owned the property as of that date, nor is the tax lien impaired. If the parties to the contract of sale agree to prorate the taxes for the year, the contract is enforceable as between the parties although not binding upon the taxing unit. Any scheme of proration satisfactory to the parties may be agreed upon.

COUNTIES: APPROPRIATIONS FOR STATE GUARD

4 April, 1942.

Boards of county commissioners are authorized to make appropriations for the support of the State Guard.

CRIMINAL LAW: OBTAINING MEALS AT BOARDING-HOUSES, ETC., WITHOUT PAYING THEREFOR

4 April, 1942.

Persons obtaining entertainment at boarding-houses, etc., without paying therefor, violate the criminal laws only if the boarding-house, etc., is licensed and held out as such. If the boarding-house, etc., is not so licensed, there is no violation of the criminal law unless the obtaining of the entertainment amounts to obtaining property by false pretenses.

CRIMINAL PROCEDURE: WARRANTS; CAPIAS

3 April, 1942.

A court is not justified in issuing a capias for the arrest of a person who has been notified by an officer to appear in court and has failed to appear unless a warrant has previously been issued for the defendant and he has given bond to appear in court and failed to appear.

DIVORCE: CONFLICT OF LAWS; FOREIGN DIVORCES

2 April, 1942.

The courts in North Carolina do not recognize as valid divorce decrees obtained in other states against North Carolina defendants when the defendants have not been personally served with process and make no appearance in the state where the decree is granted.

DOUBLE OFFICE HOLDING: COUNTY ATTORNEY

2 April, 1942.

A county attorney is not a public officer within the contemplation of the constitutional prohibition against double office holding.

DOUBLE OFFICE HOLDING: TOWNSHIP CONSTABLE AND CITY POLICEMAN

8 April, 1942.

One person cannot hold the office of township constable and city policeman at the same time.

ELECTION LAWS: PRIMARIES; CANDIDATES; PERSONS IN ARMED FORCES OF UNITED STATES

2 April, 1942.

A person in the armed forces of the United States is eligible to be a candidate for nomination for public office in a primary election.

ELECTRIC MEMBERSHIP CORPORATIONS: LIABILITY OF STOCKHOLDERS AS INDIVIDUALS

10 April, 1942.

The stockholders of an electric membership corporation are not individually liable for the death of an employee of such corporation arising out of and in the course of the employment.

MARRIAGE: AGE; WAITING PERIODS AFTER ISSUANCE OF LICENSE

7 April, 1942.

A person over eighteen may enter into a marriage contract without the consent of his or her parents.

There is no waiting period which must elapse before the marriage must be performed, after the issuance of the license.

MUNICIPAL CORPORATIONS: PUBLIC UTILITIES; FRANCHISES; CONDITIONS

2 April, 1942.

Telephone and electric companies and other public utilities may be required to have franchises to operate within a municipality. A municipal corporation may attach reasonable conditions to the granting or renewal of a franchise.

MUNICIPAL CORPORATIONS: REGULATION OF BUSINESS HOURS OF MERCANTILE ESTABLISHMENTS ON SATURDAYS AND SUNDAYS

7 April, 1942.

Municipal corporations have no authority to regulate the opening and closing hours of mercantile establishments on Saturdays. They may regulate the opening and closing hours of such establishments on Sundays.

SCHOOLS: ELECTION OF PRINCIPAL; APPROVED BY COUNTY SUPERINTENDENT OF SCHOOLS AND COUNTY BOARD OF EDUCATION

3 April, 1942.

A person is not duly elected principal of a school until his election by the district school committee has been approved by both the county board of education and the county superintendent of schools.

TAXATION: AD VALOREM TAXATION; EXEMPTIONS

9 April, 1942.

There is no provision in the 1939 Machinery Act which has the effect of exempting mercantile establishments operated by churchs from ad valorem taxation.

TAXATION: PRIVILEGE TAXES; SECURITY DEALERS; BANKS

2 April, 1942.

A commercial bank which does not buy or sell securities as agent for its depositors or for the public and only purchases securities for itself or for a trust department which it maintains, is not required to be licensed or to pay a state privilege tax as a security dealer.

TAXATION: SALES TAX; LIEN; SALE OF BUSINESS

3 April, 1942.

The State has a lien for sales tax against the stock of goods of a business. If the business is sold, the lien is enforceable against the purchaser although he is not aware of the indebtedness for sales tax of the seller.

COUNTIES: USE OF DEBT SERVICE FUNDS FOR OTHER PURPOSES

14 April, 1942.

The Board of County Commissioners have no right to use any portion of the debt service fund of the county for the purpose of sponsoring victory gardens.

DOUBLE OFFICE HOLDING: DEPUTY SHERIFF; COUNTY GAME WARDEN

14 April, 1942.

A county game warden cannot hold the office of deputy sheriff without violating Article XIV, Sec. 7, of the Constitution, prohibiting double office holding.

DOUBLE OFFICE HOLDING: DRIVER'S LICENSE EXAMINER

10 April, 1942.

The office of driver's license examiner is not a public office within the meaning of Article XIV, Sec. 7, of the Constitution, prohibiting double office holding.

DOUBLE OFFICE HOLDING: MAYOR; MEMBER CIVILIAN DEFENSE COUNCIL; MEMBER DRAFT BOARD

13 April, 1942.

The Mayor of a town may also be a member of a Selective Service Draft Board or of a local Civilian Defense Council without violating Article XIV, Sec. 7, of the Constitution, prohibiting double office holding.

DOUBLE OFFICE HOLDING: MEMBER BOARD OF EDUCATION; FARM COMMITTEEMAN

15 April, 1942.

A farm committeeman may be appointed to the county board of education without violating Article XIV, Sec. 7, of the Constitution, prohibiting double office holding.

ELECTION LAWS: QUALIFICATION OF ELECTION OFFICIALS

13 April, 1942.

A member of a local draft board is not eligible to serve as an election official.

MUNICIPAL CORPORATIONS: WATER AND SEWER CONNECTIONS

13 April, 1942.

A municipality is not required, as a matter of law, to furnish water and sewer connections to citizens whose homes or business establishments are not located on or near any sewerage line.

SCHOOLS AND SCHOOL LAWS: KINDERGARTENS; USE OF CURRENT TAXES TO ESTABLISH

15 April, 1942.

None of the proceeds of a tax levied for the current operation of public schools can be used to establish kindergartens.

TAXATION: AD VALOREM TAXATION; EXEMPTIONS; LANDS HELD BY CITY FOR PUBLIC PURPOSE

12 April, 1942.

Land which a city purchases for using as a cemetery but later decides to use as a water shed, but as yet has not been used as either, but is being held for the purpose of establishing one or the other of these uses, is not subject to ad valorem taxation by the county.

TAXATION: MUTUAL INSURANCE COMPANIES; OFFICE FURNITURE AND FIXTURES; AD VALOREM TAXATION

14 April, 1942.

A mutual insurance company is required to list its office furniture, fixtures and equipment for ad valorem taxation.

TAXATION: POLL TAX; MUNICIPAL CORPORATIONS

11 April, 1942.

The Constitution, Article V, Sec. 1, limits the amount of poll tax which municipalities may levy to $1.00.

TEACHERS' AND STATE EMPLOYEES' RETIREMENT SYSTEM: COMPULSORY RETIREMENT; AGE LIMIT

14 April, 1942.

The employer has nothing to do with the retirement of a member under the provisions of the Retirement Act until the member becomes sixty-five years of age. Up until that time, the question of retirement on account of age is purely in the discretion of the member himself.

CLERK SUPERIOR COURT: COSTS; PROCESS TAX; CAVEAT TO WILL; SPECIAL PROCEEDING

24 April, 1942.

A caveat to a will is not a civil action; therefore, the Revenue Act of 1939 does not authorize the inclusion in the bill of costs of the process tax of $2.00 which is levied at the time of suing out the summons in a civil action, or the docketing of an appeal in the Superior Court from an inferior court.

The tax may not be included in the bill of costs when a special proceeding is transferred to the civil issue docket.

CRIMINAL PROCEDURE: CONFISCATED WEAPONS; DISPOSITION

27 April, 1942.

Under C. S., Sec. 4410, it is mandatory that weapons which have been condemned and ordered confiscated in a municipal court be destroyed.

CRIMINAL PROCEDURE: FINES; DISPOSITION

30 April, 1942.

All fines imposed and collected in the court of a justice of the peace must be paid into the county school fund. The justice of the peace has no right to withhold the fines. Where they are imposed for violations of municipal ordinances, the municipal corporation is not entitled to the fines.

DOUBLE OFFICE HOLDING: CLERK OF A.B.C. BOARD

18 April, 1942.

A clerk employed by a county A.B.C. board is not a public officer within the meaning of the constitutional prohibition against double office holding.

DOUBLE OFFICE HOLDING: MEMBER OF SCHOOL BOARD; COUNTY COMMISSIONER

16 April, 1942.

One person cannot hold the office of county commissioner and be a member of a local school board at the same time.

ELECTIONS: ABSENTEE VOTING BY MEMBERS OF THE ARMED FORCES

24 April, 1942.

Members of the armed forces home on furlough, may make application for and receive an absentee ballot, but the same must be taken by him to his commanding officer for verification before it is delivered to the chairman of the board of elections.

The Act allowing members of the armed forces to use absentee ballots applies only to those in the armed forces and not to persons who have been notified that they will be called but who have not been inducted.

ELECTIONS: WITHDRAWAL OF CANDIDATES; REFUND OF FILING FEE

16 April, 1942.

A candidate for public office may withdraw upon his written request, if the request is made at least thirty days before the date of election. There is no provision in the statute for a refund of the filing fee which is paid by the candidate.

JUSTICES OF THE PEACE: CONCEALED WEAPONS

24 April, 1942.

Justices of the peace are not exempted from the provisions of C. S., Sec. 4410, which forbids the carrying of a concealed weapon.

MOTOR VEHICLES: BICYCLES; TRAFFIC LAWS

17 April, 1942.

The statutory regulations governing the operation of motor vehicles on the highways of the State apply to the operation of bicycles unless these regulations by their nature can have no application. Bicycles, like automobiles, should be driven on the right-hand side of the road.

POOR RELIEF: HOSPITALIZATION; COUNTY COMMISSIONERS

29 April, 1942.

The commissioners of a county are authorized to provide by taxation for the maintenance of the poor and to do everything expedient for their comfort and well ordering.

PUBLIC ADMINISTRATORS: OFFICIAL BONDS; SURETIES

27 April, 1942.

The bond of a public administrator may be signed by three or more personal sureties or by a corporate surety.

PUBLIC OFFICERS: CONTRACTS; MEMBER OF BOARD OF ELECTIONS CONTRACTING FOR PRINTING BALLOTS

29 April, 1942.

By reason of C. S., Sec. 4388, which makes it a misdemeanor for a commissioner of a public trust to contract for his own benefit, it is unlawful for a member of a county board of elections to contract to print ballots for a primary election in his private printing establishment.

SCHOOL LAW: APPOINTMENT OF LOCAL COMMITTEES; CALL OF MEETINGS

17 April, 1942.

The School Machinery Act of 1939 provides in Section 7 that at the first regular meeting in April, 1939, and biennially thereafter the county boards of education shall appoint school committees for the districts in their counties, consisting of not more than five nor less than three persons, who shall serve for terms of two years. After appointments have been made for a particular biennium, a county board of education has no authority during the biennium to increase the size of a district committee by appointing new members.

Calling meetings of a district committee is primarily the responsibility of the chairman of the committee. However, a meeting called by any member would be a legal meeting if notice were served on all members and a quorum were present.

A person who is not a member of the school committee or who has been placed on the committee without authority of law has no right to call a meeting of the committee.

TAXATION: AD VALOREM TAXATION; ATTACHMENT AND GARNISHMENT

16 April, 1942.

The remedies of attachment and garnishment may be used to collect taxes due on real property.

TAXATION: AD VALOREM; FORECLOSURE STATUTE OF LIMITATIONS ON JUDGMENTS

17 April, 1942.

There is no statute of limitations which runs against a judgment obtained by a county in a tax-foreclosure action.

COUNTIES: BLACKOUT ORDINANCES

2 May, 1942.

Boards of county commissioners are not authorized to enact blackout ordinances for their respective counties.

CRIMINAL PROCEDURE: BASTARDY; JUVENILES

6 May, 1942.

The juvenile court alone has jurisdiction over a proceeding against an infant under sixteen years of age accused of failure to support his bastard child.

INTOXICATING LIQUORS: UNFORTIFIED WINE; CAFE WITH C RATING

7 May, 1942.

A cafe which has been given a C rating by the State Board of Health is not eligible to receive a license to sell unfortified wines.

MUNICIPAL CORPORATIONS: CHANGE OF PLAN OF GOVERNMENT; ELECTION

5 May, 1942.

A municipal corporation may not adopt the city manager plan of government without submitting the question to a vote of the city in a special election.

Municipal Corporations: Unsafe Buildings; Criminal Law

27 May, 1942.

When a building within a municipality has been condemned as being unsafe and dangerous to life and, because of the character of the building, a permit cannot be issued for its repair, the owner may be prosecuted criminally under C. S., Sec. 2774, if he refuses to tear it down.

Public Officers: Contracts; Mayor and Aldermen Selling Land to City

5 May, 1942.

It is not proper for the mayor or any of the aldermen of a municipal corporation to sell property to the corporation, for C. S., Sec. 4388, makes it a misdemeanor for a commissioner of a public trust to contract for his own benefit.

Public Officers: Contracts; Purchase of Airport Authority Bonds by Member of Authority

2 May, 1942.

Under C. S., Sec. 4388, making it a misdemeanor for a commissioner of a public trust to contract for his own benefit, it would not be proper for a member of a local airport authority to purchase bonds of the authority when they are sold through the Local Government Commission. There would be no objection to the members purchasing such bonds after they have been originally sold and are in the hands of a third person.

School Law: School Bus Accidents; Compensation to Pupils

4 May, 1942.

Under Public Laws of 1935, Ch. 245, the only school children entitled to compensation for injuries in school bus accidents are those injured while actually riding in a school bus to and from school. A child who is struck by a bus while outside waiting for it to turn around is not covered by the statute.

State Employees: Participation in Politics

6 May, 1942.

There is no State law which prohibits participation in politics and elections by school teachers and other State employees paid from State funds.

Taxation: Ad Valorem; Change in Valuation after Adjournment of Board of Equalization and Review

6 May, 1942.

After the Board of Equalization and Review of a county has completed its work of fixing valuations of property for taxation and has adjourned, there is no authority for the Board to reopen the case of a taxpayer who claims a decrease in the value of his property as the result of a forest fire.

TAXATION: AD VALOREM; LISTING PERSONAL PROPERTY; PERSONS IN MILITARY SERVICE

7 May, 1942.

The fact that a person is serving in the armed forces of the United States does not exempt him from the requirement that his personal property be listed for taxation annually in the county of his residence.

TAXATION: AD VALOREM; MUNICIPAL CORPORATION ORGANIZED AFTER JANUARY 1

5 May, 1942.

A municipal corporation incorporated after January 1 during a particular year may not levy property taxes for the year during which it is incorporated, January 1 being the date as of which property is to be listed and on which the tax lien attaches.

TAXATION: AD VALOREM; PROPERTY LISTED UNDER BUSINESS NAME; TAX LIEN

4 May, 1942.

When an individual lists personal property under a business name and the business is not incorporated, the taxes against the property constitute a lien upon the real property of the owner listed by him individually.

CRIMINAL LAW: SLOT AND PIN BALL MACHINES

23 May, 1942.

All slot and pin ball machines are illegal if the operator or user has a chance to make varying scores or tallies upon which wagers can be made.

DOUBLE OFFICE HOLDING: OFFICER OF STATE GUARD

9 May, 1942.

An officer of the State Guard is probably a public officer, but he is not precluded from holding another public office for Article XIV, Section 7, of the Constitution, forbidding dual office holding, exempts officers of the militia from its operation.

ELECTION LAW: PRIMARIES; PARTICIPATION BY REPUBLICANS IN DEMOCRATIC PRIMARY

20 May, 1942.

The fact that there are no local Republican candidates in a primary election does not authorize Republicans to vote in the Democratic Primary. The only way that a member of one political party may participate in the primary of another party is by taking an oath, prior to the primary election and while the registration books are open, to support the nominees of the party in whose primary he desires to vote.

Executors and Administrators: Commissions; Widow's Year's Allowance

15 May, 1942.

An executor is not entitled to receive commissions on amounts paid out as widow's year's allowance.

Guardian and Ward: Commissions; Funds for Maintenance of Ward

15 May, 1942.

A guardian is entitled to receive commissions on funds paid out for the maintenance and support of his ward.

Municipal Corporations: Ordinances; Requiring Photographers to Give Security for Performance of Contracts

25 May, 1942.

A municipal corporation has no statutory authority to enact an ordinance requiring transient photographers to deposit a sum of money with the City Clerk as security for the faithful performance of contracts made with residents of the corporation.

Prison-Made Goods: Sale

25 May, 1942.

Under C. S., Section 4468(a), the sale of prison-made goods of any nature or description is forbidden in North Carolina. It is immaterial whether the goods are manufactured within or without the State.

State Highway Patrol: Receipt of Reward by Member of Patrol

25 May, 1942.

It is not unlawful for a member of the State Highway Patrol to receive a reward offered for the apprehension of a criminal.

Taxation: Ad Valorem; Municipal Property not Used for Governmental Purpose

9 May, 1942.

Property owned by a municipal corporation and used by an individual for the manufacture of shirts is subject to county ad valorem taxation although the municipal corporation receives no compensation for the use of the property.

Taxation: Ad Valorem; Taxes for 1926 and Prior Years

26 May, 1942.

Under Public Laws of 1933, Chapter 181, Section 7, ad valorem taxes for 1926 and prior years were barred and rendered uncollectable.

TAXATION: INCOME TAX; DEDUCTIONS; PAYMENTS TO EMPLOYEES IN MILITARY SERVICE

22 May, 1942.

Payments by an employer to former employees during their military service are deductible as business expenses on the employer's North Carolina income tax return.

TAXATION: PRIVILEGE TAXES; SALES TAX; LIABILITY OF MUNICIPAL CORPORATION

12 May, 1942.

A municipal corporation which operates a municipal park and public stadium at which beer, tobacco products, and candy are sold by the corporation, is liable for the State license tax for the sale of beer, the State license tax for the privilege of selling tobacco products, and the State sales tax on account of the sale of tobacco products and candy.

TAXATION: SALES TAX; VETERANS

22 May, 1942.

A veteran is not exempt from payment of sales tax on furniture which he purchases, even though the purchase money is a part of his disability compensation from the Federal Government.

REPORT OF THE DIRECTOR OF THE BUREAU OF INVESTIGATION TO THE ATTORNEY GENERAL FOR THE YEARS JULY 1, 1940 TO JULY 1, 1941; JULY 1, 1941 TO JULY 1, 1942

Since the creation of the State Bureau of Investigation on July 1, 1939, as a Division of the Department of Justice, there has been one change affecting the Bureau's status. Chapter 157, Public Laws of 1941, amended the original Act by discontinuing the allotment of one-half of the monies received from costs assessed in criminal cases for the maintenance of the Bureau. In lieu thereof the Bureau was placed on an appropriation basis effective July 1, 1941.

On July 1, 1940, the personnel of the Bureau consisted of the Director, Assistant Director, seven Special Agents and technical assistants, one photographer, one budget officer and two stenographers, or a total of thirteen persons. There has been no change in the number of persons during the present biennium.

During this period every effort has been made to exhaust our resources and facilities in the investigation of major crimes following requests for assistance from the law enforcement agencies. We have endeavored to respond to all requests made upon the Bureau coming within its jurisdiction.

The laboratory facilities have been expanded for the analysis of the evidences of crime. The Firearms Identification Section has examined some 312 exhibits. More than 700 document exhibits have been examined. Experiments have been conducted in the use of the psychograph (lie detector). One of our Agents has just completed special training in the use of this device, enabling us to be better prepared in the interrogation of suspects.

The Fingerprint Identification Section has greatly expanded during this biennium. A large percentage of our requests have involved fingerprint examinations.

The use of photography in criminal investigations has further demonstrated its adoption as being indispensable. The photographing of fingerprints, the scenes of crimes, and photostatic copies of evidence average up to about 5,000 photographs per year.

We are compiling a forged and worthless check file, having circularized the law enforcement agencies, banks, and Merchant's Associations for their cooperation in collecting all data bearing on this subject. Our files containing typewriter standards have been brought up to date so that we now have complete records of all makes of typewriters in common use.

It will be noted that during the year 1941-42 the Bureau has assisted the Federal agencies in reporting some seventy-three different subjects suspected of subversive activities.

Of the 531 miscellaneous cases handled during the biennium very little investigation was necessary; however, proper attention was given each subject and filed for reference.

The officers and agents of this Bureau have received the wholehearted cooperation of the executive departments, the law enforcement agencies, and the law abiding citizens of the State.

The following classification of crime has been adopted by the Bureau and all cases received and investigated have been assigned thereunder:

CRIME CLASSIFICATION

A. *Assault*	1. Simple Assault
	2. A. D. W. with Intent to Kill
	3. Assault with Intent to Commit Rape
	4. All Others
B. *Burglary—Breaking and Entering*	1. First Degree (occupied)
	2. Second Degree (unoccupied-safecracking)
E. *Embezzlement—Fraud*	1. Embezzlement
	2. Forgery
	3. Worthless Checks
	4. Extortion
	5. All Others
H. *Homicide*	1. First Degree Murder
	2. Second Degree Murder
	3. Manslaughter
L. *Larceny*	1. Auto
	2. All Others
R. *Robbery*	(person)
S. *Sex Offenses*	1. Rape
	2. Abortion
	3. Adultery and Fornication
	4. Bastardy
	5. Bigamy
	6. Buggery
	7. Incest
	8. Prostitution
	9. Seduction
	10. All Others
M. *Miscellaneous*	1. Arson
	2. Bribery
	3. Buying or Receiving Stolen Property
	4. Conspiracy
	5. Perjury
	6. Possession Burglar Tools
	7. Trespass
	8. Unlawful Use or Possession Explosives
	9. Weapons
	10. Abandonment and Non-support
	11. Escape
	12. Abduction
	13. Poisoning
	14. Resisting Arrest
	15. Riot
	16. Anonymous Letters
	17. Pure Food and Drug Laws
	18. Prohibition Laws
	19. Motor Vehicle Laws
	20. Gambling and Lottery
	21. Parole Violation
	22. Probation Violation
	23. Election Laws
	24. All Others

The following statement shows new, old, and miscellaneous cases investigated and closed for each month during the period from July 1, 1940 to July 1, 1941:

	NEW CASES		OLD CASES		MISCELLANEOUS CASES
	Investigated	*Closed*	*Investigated*	*Closed*	*Investigated and Closed*
July	33	14	18	4	11
August	32	18	20	12	27
September	32	14	26	15	29
October	26	14	23	11	23
November	18	10	14	7	15
December	27	16	11	4	20
January	29	13	16	10	25
February	20	9	19	9	13
March	28	19	14	2	24
April	30	19	10	5	22
May	25	12	15	6	18
June	32	26	11	5	28
Totals	332	184	197	90	255

July 1, 1940 to July 1, 1941

The following statement shows the number of requests received by counties and the classification of the types of crime investigated therein:

Counties	Assault	Burglary	Embezzlement	Homicide	Larceny	Robbery	Sex Offenses	Misc.	Totals
Alamance		2	4	3				1	10
Alexander			1						1
Alleghany	1								1
Anson				1		1			2
Ashe									0
Avery								2	2
Beaufort		1	1	1		1		1	5
Bertie	1	2				1			4
Bladen	2	1		1	1		1		6
Brunswick									0
Buncombe									0
Burke		4		1		1			6
Cabarrus		1		1					2
Caldwell									0
Camden									0
Carteret		1						2	3
Caswell									0
Catawba		1	1	1		1		1	5
Chatham		1	1			1			3
Cherokee									0
Chowan	1	1			2	1		1	6
Clay									0
Cleveland		2							2
Columbus	1							1	2
Craven		1		3			1		5
Cumberland	1	1	1	1	1	2		2	9
Currituck							1	1	2
Dare									0
Davidson		2	1	1	1			2	7
Davie				1					1
Duplin		9	1	1					11
Durham		1			1				2
Edgecombe			1	1	1			1	4
Forsyth			1			1	3		5
Franklin		6		1	1			2	10
Gaston		1		1					2
Gates									0
Graham									0
Granville									0
Greene									0
Guilford			1	2				3	6
Halifax		6	1	1		1		1	10
Harnett		7	1			1			9
Haywood									0
Henderson									0
Hertford									0
Hoke		3						1	4
Hyde									0
Iredell	1								1
Jackson		1							1
Johnston	1	6	2	1	4	1			15
Jones									0
Lee	1	1	1	1		1		1	6
Lenoir		1		2				1	4

Counties	Assault	Burglary	Embezzlement	Homicide	Larceny	Robbery	Sex Offenses	Misc.	Totals
Lincoln		1		1					2
Macon									0
Madison									0
Martin		4	1						5
McDowell		2		1					3
Mecklenburg			1			1		1	3
Mitchell	1		1	3				1	6
Montgomery	2	1						2	5
Moore		18		1		1		1	21
Nash								2	2
New Hanover	1		2					2	5
Northampton		2		1					3
Onslow									0
Orange		1	1			1			3
Pamlico		1			1				2
Pasquotank		1	1						2
Pender		1		4	1				6
Perquimans			1						1
Person		4	1						5
Pitt	1		3			1			5
Polk									0
Randolph		1	2						3
Richmond		2	1						3
Robeson	3	5		1		1		3	13
Rockingham			1						1
Rowan	1								1
Rutherford		1	1		2				4
Sampson	1	1			1	2		1	6
Scotland		1							1
Stanly	1								1
Stokes		1							1
Surry		1							1
Swain									0
Transylvania									0
Tyrrell									0
Union		2	1	1					4
Vance		1			1				2
Wake	1	1	4	2	2	4		3	17
Warren		4						1	5
Washington		1						1	2
Watauga		1			1				2
Wayne		1		1					2
Wilkes		1	1	1	1				4
Wilson				1				1	2
Yadkin		1				1		1	3
Yancey				1					1

July 1, 1940 to July 1, 1941

The following statement shows the number of requests received by counties and from what sources requests were made:

Counties	Sheriff's Depts.	Police Depts.	Highway Patrol	Solicitors	Judges	Executive Depts.	Coroners	Misc.	Totals
Alamance	3	4	1	2					10
Alexander						1			1
Alleghany								1	1
Anson	1	1							2
Ashe									0
Avery				2					2
Beaufort	1	1	1					2	5
Bertie	3			1					4
Bladen	6								6
Brunswick									0
Buncombe									0
Burke	4	2							6
Cabarrus	1			1					2
Caldwell									0
Camden									0
Carteret	3								3
Caswell									0
Catawba	1	3				1			5
Chatham	3								3
Cherokee									0
Chowan	1	5							6
Clay									0
Cleveland	2								2
Columbus				1		1			2
Craven	2	1		1				1	5
Cumberland	1	1	5	1				1	9
Currituck	1			1					2
Dare									0
Davidson	5				1			1	7
Davie	1								1
Duplin	5	3		1		1		1	11
Durham		2							2
Edgecombe	2	2							4
Forsyth	1	1		1				2	5
Franklin	6	2	2						10
Gaston	2								2
Gates									0
Graham									0
Granville									0
Greene									0
Guilford		3			1	2			6
Halifax	5	4	1						10
Harnett	2	6	1						9
Haywood									0
Henderson									0
Hertford									0
Hoke	1	3							4
Hyde									0
Iredell	1								1
Jackson	1								1
Johnston	3	8	1	1				2	15
Jones									0
Lee	2	3				1			6
Lenoir	1	2						1	4

Counties	Sheriff's Depts.	Police Depts.	Highway Patrol	Solicitors	Judges	Executive Depts.	Coroners	Misc.	Totals
Lincoln	1	1							2
Macon									0
Madison									0
Martin	2	2	1						5
McDowell	3								3
Mecklenburg			1			1		1	3
Mitchell	5			1					6
Montgomery	4	1							5
Moore	6	14					1		21
Nash	1	1							2
New Hanover	1	1		3					5
Northampton	1	1					1		3
Onslow									0
Orange	2	1							3
Pamlico	2								2
Pasquotank	1	1							2
Pender	6								6
Perquimans	1								1
Person		3	1			1			5
Pitt	2	3							5
Polk									0
Randolph		1				2			3
Richmond	1	2							3
Robeson	8	3	1			1			13
Rockingham		1							1
Rowan	1								1
Rutherford	2	2							4
Sampson	5		1						6
Scotland	1								1
Stanly		1							1
Stokes	1								1
Surry		1							1
Swain									0
Transylvania									0
Tyrrell									0
Union	2	1		1					4
Vance		1	1						2
Wake	2	6			1	4	1	3	17
Warren	3	1						1	5
Washington		1	1						2
Watauga		1						1	2
Wayne	1	1							2
Wilkes	2			1		1			4
Wilson	1	1							2
Yadkin	2			1					3
Yancey	1								1

The following statement shows the volume of latent fingerprint work in the Identification Section for each month during the period from July July 1, 1941:

	1940									1941	
	July	*Aug.*	*Sept.*	*Oct.*	*Nov.*	*Dec.*	*Jan.*	*Feb.*	*Mar.*	*April*	*May*
Examinations Requested	24	18	18	10	7	16	13	10	15	13	15
Examinations Completed	24	18	18	10	6	16	13	10	15	13	15
Identifications Effected	1	3	0	1	4	1	4	1	0	2	3
Latents Received											
(a) Photographs	0	1	0	0	0	0	20	0	1	0	0
(b) Lifts	3	6	0	0	1	3	0	0	8	6	0
Fingerprints of Suspects Rec'd.	40	22	24	7	1	23	18	18	8	14	35
Fingerprints for Elimination	6	3	0	0	18	32	7	7	5	23	20
Identification to Suspects	1	3	0	1	1	0	3	1	0	3	3
Cases Involving Identification to Suspects	1	3	0	1	1	0	3	1	0	3	3
Identifications for Elimination	0	0	0	0	3	1	0	0	0	5	3
Physical Articles Received for Examination	18	26	9	15	5	30	16	12	18	15	30
Latents Developed on Phys. Articles	44	75	56	62	50	142	30	48	74	60	13
Negatives Made	229	220	160	77	117	118	72	71	68	79	42
Photographs Printed	101	174	160	62	33	16	64	36	492	135	77
Enlargements Made	51	54	75	111	157	91	95	86	97	240	19
Photostats Made	42	22	50	36	22	23	6	24	0	17	30

he following statement shows the volume of work performed by the Firearms and tioned Document Examiner; also the Medico-Legal examinations and the Psycho- ı tests made for each month during the period July 1, 1940 to July 1, 1941:

	1940						1941						
	July	*Aug.*	*Sept.*	*Oct.*	*Nov.*	*Dec.*	*Jan.*	*Feb.*	*Mar.*	*April*	*May*	*June*	*Total*
rms Exhibits ıined	16	8	43	19	8	17	8	6	7	0	0	17	149
ment Exhibits ıined	29	17	56	51	47	16	23	19	27	53	82	38	458
:o-Legal ıinations	6	1	6	5	0	6	6	2	2	3	3	3	43
ıograph	0	0	0	0	3	0	0	0	7	0	0	0	10

The following statement shows new, old, fifth column, and miscellaneous cases investigated and closed for each month during the period from July 1, 1941 to July 1, 1942:

	New Cases		Old Cases		Fifth Column	Miscellaneous Cases
	Investigated	*Closed*	*Investigated*	*Closed*		*Investigated and Closed*
July	26	14	10	3	2	39
August	30	20	10	1	1	27
September	22	12	15	4	2	22
October	25	15	13	3	0	23
November	35	15	15	6	1	23
December	37	23	6	3	13	19
January	24	17	15	4	7	23
February	19	10	7	2	14	13
March	29	19	6	2	10	25
April	30	9	5	2	12	19
May	27	12	14	7	6	28
June	16	9	9	2	5	15
Totals	320	175	125	39	73	276

July 1, 1941 to July 1, 1942

The following statement shows the number of requests received by counties and the classification of the types of crimes investigated therein:

Counties	Assault	Burglary	Embezzlement	Homicide	Larceny	Robbery	Sex Offenses	Misc.	Totals
Alamance		10		2	2			1	15
Alexander									0
Alleghany									0
Anson		1				1		1	3
Ashe									0
Avery									0
Beaufort		2		1					3
Bertie		3		1				1	5
Bladen		3						1	4
Brunswick									0
Buncombe			1					1	2
Burke								1	1
Cabarrus				2				1	3
Caldwell								1	1
Camden									0
Carteret		1		1					2
Caswell					1				1
Catawba							1		1
Chatham	1				1				2
Cherokee									0
Chowan				1	1		1	1	4
Clay									0
Cleveland				1	1	1		1	4
Columbus				1					1
Craven				1				2	3
Cumberland	1	1	1	6	1			1	11
Currituck		1				1			2
Dare				1					1
Davidson		4		1		1			6
Davie								1	1
Duplin	1	4	1	1	1				8
Durham				2				1	3
Edgecombe		2	1						3
Forsyth				4				1	5
Franklin		4			1			3	8
Gaston		2		1	1				4
Gates									0
Graham									0
Granville									0
Greene									0
Guilford			3	1				5	9
Halifax		7		1				2	10
Harnett		9	1					2	12
Haywood								3	3
Henderson				3			2		5
Hertford									0
Hoke								1	1
Hyde									0
Iredell	1	3						1	5
Jackson									0
Johnston		6		3	1			2	12
Jones									0
Lee		1			1			2	4
Lenoir	1	1		1					3

Counties	Assault	Burglary	Embezzlement	Homicide	Larceny	Robbery	Sex Offenses	Misc.	Totals
Lincoln		2		1			1		4
Macon									0
Madison									0
Martin		4	2						6
McDowell		1		2					3
Mecklenburg								1	1
Mitchell		1						1	2
Montgomery		6	1	1	1			2	11
Moore		13				1			14
Nash		4	1		1	1		1	8
New Hanover									0
Northampton	1	6		1		1			9
Onslow			2						2
Orange	1	2			1				4
Pamlico									0
Pasquotank			2	1					3
Pender			1	1	1			1	4
Perquimans			1						1
Person	1	2	2						5
Pitt								2	2
Polk									0
Randolph	1	1							2
Richmond		2		1					3
Robeson		4			1	1		3	9
Rockingham			1					2	3
Rowan									0
Rutherford				1					1
Sampson		5		2					7
Scotland		2							2
Stanly				1				1	2
Stokes		1							1
Surry			1		1				2
Swain									0
Transylvania								2	2
Tyrrell		1			2				3
Union									0
Vance		2						2	4
Wake		2	7	2	3			3	17
Warren		3							3
Washington									0
Watauga								1	1
Wayne	1			1				1	3
Wilkes		1							1
Wilson		1							1
Yadkin	1	1			1				3
Yancey									0

July 1, 1941 to July 1, 1942

The following statement shows the number of requests received by counties and from what sources requests were made:

Counties	Sheriff's Depts.	Police Depts.	Highway Patrol	Solicitors	Judges	Executive Depts.	Coroners	Misc.	Totals
Alamance	7	7		1					15
Alexander									0
Alleghany									0
Anson	3								3
Ashe									0
Avery									0
Beaufort	2	1							3
Bertie	4		1						5
Bladen	4								4
Brunswick									0
Buncombe						2			2
Burke	1								1
Cabarrus	2	1							3
Caldwell						1			1
Camden									0
Carteret	1						1		2
Caswell	1								1
Catawba	1								1
Chatham	2								2
Cherokee									0
Chowan	1	3							4
Clay									0
Cleveland	2	2							4
Columbus						1			1
Craven	1			1		1			3
Cumberland		1	1			1		8	11
Currituck				2					2
Dare				1					1
Davidson		6							6
Davie	1								1
Duplin	5		1	1				1	8
Durham		1		1				1	3
Edgecombe	1	2							3
Forsyth		2				1		2	5
Franklin	4	1	2			1			8
Gaston	4								4
Gates									0
Graham									0
Granville									0
Greene									0
Guilford	1	4			1		3		9
Halifax	3	5	1					1	10
Harnett	6	5						1	12
Haywood						3			3
Henderson	3					1	1		5
Hertford									0
Hoke	1								1
Hyde									0
Iredell	5								5
Jackson									0
Johnston	5	6				1			12
Jones									0
Lee	3	1							4
Lenoir	2	1							3

Counties	Sheriff's Depts.	Police Depts.	Highway Patrol	Solicitors	Judges	Executive Depts.	Coroners	Misc.	Totals
Lincoln	4								4
Macon									0
Madison									0
Martin	5	1							6
McDowell	3								3
Mecklenburg		1							1
Mitchell	2								2
Montgomery	9					1		1	11
Moore	8	6							14
Nash	7		1						8
New Hanover									0
Northampton	8	1							9
Onslow								2	2
Orange	2	1	1						4
Pamlico									0
Pasquotank	3								3
Pender	4								4
Perquimans	1								1
Person	2	1				1		1	5
Pitt			1			1			2
Polk									0
Randolph	1		1						2
Richmond	1	2							3
Robeson	6	3							9
Rockingham		2	1						3
Rowan									0
Rutherford	1								1
Sampson	7								7
Scotland	1	1							2
Stanly	2								2
Stokes	1								1
Surry		1				1			2
Swain									0
Transylvania						2			2
Tyrrell	3								3
Union									0
Vance		2	1					1	4
Wake	3	1		1	1	7	2	2	17
Warren	2	1							3
Washington									0
Watauga		1							1
Wayne	1							2	3
Wilkes				1					1
Wilson		1							1
Yadkin	3								3
Yancey									0

atement shows the volume of latent fingerprint work performed Section for each month during the period from July 1, 1941 to

ι								1942			
Aug.	*Sept.*	*Oct.*	*Nov.*	*Dec.*	*Jan.*	*Feb.*	*Mar.*	*April*	*May*	*June*	*Total*
16	9	10	21	17	7	8	9	11	8	18	144
16	9	10	21	17	7	8	9	11	8	18	144
0	3	2	1	3	0	0	4	1	2	4	23
2	0	0	3	5	0	8	10	0	0	0	28
5	5	4	0	3	3	5	6	0	8	5	44
22	17	30	8	28	22	10	30	8	21	18	227
23	10	2	24	49	13	8	5	12	10	14	197
0	3	2	1	3	1	0	3	1	2	4	20
0	3	2	1	3	1	0	0	0	0	0	10
7	4	0	3	10	1	1	0	2	1	4	36
27	19	18	30	14	8	10	30	56	40	47	308
93	90	54	98	164	27	18	33	97	60	0	825
210	229	81	100	123	39	83	216	65	165	189	1610
0	37	336	0	34	6	21	272	14	113	112	945
199	116	91	86	192	75	67	162	112	118	92	1415
6	2	51	36	54	12	85	97	79	75	28	529

The following statement shows the volume
and Questioned Document Examiner; also the
Psychograph tests made for each month during
1, 1942:

	1941					
	July	*Aug.*	*Sept.*	*Oct.*	*Nov.*	*Dec.*
Firearms Exhibits Examined	17	16	4	9	19	28
Document Exhibits Examined	8	0	23	42	27	21
Medico-Legal Examinations Made	4	2	1	3	4	3
Psychograph Tests	0	0	0	0	0	0

TOTAL TYPES OF CRIMES INVESTIGATED IN VARIOUS COUNTIES:

	1940-41	1941-42
Assault	22	11
Burglary	125	132
Embezzlement	42	29
Homicide	45	51
Larceny	22	24
Robbery	26	8
Sex Offenses	6	5
Miscellaneous	44	60
	332	320

TOTAL REQUESTS FROM LAW ENFORCEMENT AGENCIES:

	1940-41	1941-42
Sheriff's Depts.	142	166
Police Depts.	110	75
Highway Patrol	19	12
Solicitors	20	9
Judges	3	2
Executive Depts.	17	26
Coroners	3	7
Miscellaneous	18	23
	332	320

BRIEF SUMMARY
of
IMPORTANT CASES INVESTIGATED
PERIOD

July 1, 1940 to July 1, 1941.

State v. Ed Shew, et al.;
Sinclair Adams, Victim, Murder

In March, 1941, Hon. Avalon E. Hall, Solicitor of the Seventeenth Judicial District, requested the assistance of the Bureau in connection with the fatal assault on a negro man named Sinclair Adams of Wilkes County which occurred on January 13, 1941.

An Agent was assigned and immediately conferred with Sheriff C. T. Doughton of Wilkes County. It developed that three suspects; Ed Shew, Mutt Shew, and Ivey Williams had been apprehended and held for questioning. Ed Shew, white, age 22 years, a brother of Mutt Shew, age 19 years, told Agent that he alone was responsible for the death of Sinclair Adams. That he in company with Adams had purchased some liquor and after they had several drinks they got into a fight and he knocked the negro down and kicked him in the head.

A homemade "black jack" was found at the scene of the fight which was thought to contain blood. This was analyzed by the Bureau Toxicologist and it was found that the substance was rust and grease rather than blood.

Ed Shew, Mutt Shew, and Ivey Williams were indicted for murder and tried in the Superior Court of Wilkes County at the March, 1941, term. Ed Shew and Ivey Williams were found guilty and were sentenced to from eight to ten years in the State's Penitentiary by Judge F. Don Phillips. Mutt Shew was sentenced to four months in the County Home.

State v. Lester Morris;
Belton's Laundry, Victim, Safe Robbery

Following a request from the Chief of Police of Mount Airy, N. C., it was disclosed that on the night of June 8, 1940, Belton's Laundry had been broken into and the iron safe blown open by high explosives. The victim reported the loss of $536.00 in cash, one check for $75.00, Liberty Bonds in the amount of $1,100.00, Building & Loan stock valued at $2,500.00, personal notes in the amount of $8,000.00 and other valuable papers, in addition to two diamond rings valued at $750.00.

An intensive investigation was conducted at the scene of the crime and a description of all suspicious characters secured, among them being one Lester Morris. Morris was arrested in Hartsville, S. C., the latter part of August, 1940, at which time he had in his possession a small pocket knife with the little blade broken off. The broken blade, which matched perfectly with the knife taken from Morris, was found at the Belton's Laundry immediately following the safe blowing. When Morris was confronted with these facts he admitted that it was his knife and that he was guilty of the crime. He further stated that he would get the bonds and the diamond rings, which were later recovered and delivered to the owner.

Morris was tried in the Superior Court of Surry County, Dobson, N. C., September 16, 1940, where he entered a plea of guilty and was sentenced by Judge J. A. Rousseau to serve twelve years in the State's Penitentiary.

State v. H. C. Warren, et al.;
Samuel N. Welsh, Victim, Theft of Auto

At the request of Sheriff C. C. Tart of Sampson County an investigation was made in connection with the theft of an automobile belonging to Samuel N. Welsh. It developed that the victim's automobile had been found abandoned near Roseboro, N. C. A fingerprint examination was made and latent fingerprints secured and photographed. A comparison of the latent fingerprints was made with those obtained from the Prison Department of H. C. Warren, and they were found to be identical with the fingerprints secured from the car.

At the August, 1940, term of Superior Court of Sampson County the defendant Warren was found guilty and sentenced to State's Penitentiary to from two to three years. Two other defendants, Mearnie Carter and Wallie V. Parker, who were suspected of being involved in this crime were found not guilty.

State v. George "Crip" Smith, et al.;
Numbers Racket, Wilmington, N. C.

Following urgent requests from the law enforcement agencies, including the grand jury of New Hanover County, Special Agents were assigned to that County to investigate an organized numbers racket. This investigation was instituted in September, 1940, and resulted in the arrest of thirty-five persons who were engaging in this racket in Wilmington and New Hanover County.

It developed that this racket was headed up by one George "Crip" Smith, who resided in another section of the State but made periodical trips to Wilmington in administering his operations through local subordinates. Most of the suspects were negroes who spent the major part of their time selling numbers, collecting, and paying off. These persons loitered around questionable places, which were presumed to be engaged in other types of business. Due to their extensive operations it was necessary that all of our Special Agents with the assistance of the Sheriff of New Hanover County, his deputies, and the State Highway Patrol, make a wholesale raid on these persons. On December 4, 1940, twenty-nine arrests were made in little more than one hour's time. Since some of the "big shots" were not in Wilmington at the time of the raid they were picked up a few days later and held for trial. On December 13, 1940, thirty-four of these parties were found guilty of violating the lottery laws through participation in the numbers racket, having been given fines ranging from $100.00 to $2,000.00 and road sentences up to six months by Judge Alton A. Lennon in the Recorder's Court of New Hanover County. County Solicitor H.

Winfield Smith was assisted by Hon. David Sinclair, District Solicitor, in prosecuting these defendants.

George "Crip" Smith, who later was apprehended and tried, was given a fine of $2,000.00 and cost, with two six-month road sentences, for conspiracy in operating a lottery.

Among the several defendants appealing to the Superior Court was one Missouri Galloway, a negress known as the numbers "czarina," who was given the maximum penalty of six months in jail and fined $1,000.00 by Judge John M. Burney, after a jury took only ten minutes to confirm the Recorder's Court conviction.

State v. Joseph Calcutt, et al.;
Slot Machines, Gambling Devices;
Violation of Flannagan Act

On September 10, 1940, Sheriff N. F. Turner of Wake County communicated with the Director informing him that Hon. Wm. Y. Bickett, Solicitor of the Seventh Judicial District, had requested him to arrange a conference relative to an investigation involving the unlawful operation of slot machines and other gambling devices. At this conference with the Solicitor and Presiding Judge it was divulged that an extensive investigation had been conducted several months prior thereto at the request of another Superior Court Judge in Cumberland County relative to the unlawful operation of slot machines and gambling devices. Following this conference further investigation was made and among those indicted was one J. N. Finch, representative of the Vending Machine Company, who was found guilty and sentenced to twelve months on the roads. In addition he was placed on probation for three years thereafter under a one year suspended sentence. One H. E. Laing, trading as the Capital Amusement Company, was sentenced to eight months on the roads and also placed on probation for three years under a one year suspended sentence.

Joseph Calcutt, through counsel, submitted to the charges of violation of the Flannagan Act and was sentenced by Hon. R. Hunt Parker, the Presiding Judge in the Superior Court of Wake County, to one year on the roads and given two years suspended sentence, and fined $10,000.00 and cost.

Calcutt's appeal to the Supreme Court resulted in the confirmation of the decision of the Superior Court.

State v. Charles L. Abernathy, Jr.;
Violation of Election Laws

In May, 1940, just prior to the date of the State Primary, Hon. W. A. Lucas, Chairman of the State Board of Elections, requested assistance in connection with certain election law irregularities in the Third Congressional District which had been reported to him.

Agents were assigned and they conducted an extensive investigation in that district. It was disclosed that Charles L. Abernathy, Jr., a candidate for Congress from the Third Congressional District, had come into possession of official ballots which he was distributing in violation of the State Election Laws.

After several continuances Abernathy was tried in the Superior Court of Wayne County at the April, 1941, term. He was found guilty of violating the election laws and sentenced by Judge Q. K. Nimocks. Abernathy was given a thirty day jail sentence, which was suspended, and he was placed on probation for five years and required to pay the cost of court.

Following an appeal, the North Carolina Supreme Court upheld the conviction on the charges of election law violations at the October, 1941, term.

State v. Harold J. Rundt;
Wade H. Lefler, et al., Victims—
Embezzlement, Fraud and Forgery

On March 24, 1941, Sheriff Ray Pitts and Hon. Wade H. Lefler, Clerk of the Superior Court of Catawba County, requested the assistance of the Bureau in connection with the embezzlement of certain trust funds from the Clerk's office. They reported that on March 20, 1940, a man who introduced himself as S. L. Rollins came to the Clerk's office with affidavits and credentials from the Clerk of Superior Court of Durham County, indicating that he was the duly qualified administrator of the estate of R. P. Cline. The document bore the genuine seal of the Clerk of the Superior Court of Durham County and as a result $297.00 was delivered to Rollins. Mr Lefler was somewhat suspicious and upon communicating with the Clerk of Superior Court of Durham County found that the document in question had been forged and the seal of his office had been illegally impressed thereon.

Investigation developed that this Rollins' real name was Harold J. Rundt. That this man had been operating in Georgia, Florida, and South Carolina before arriving in this State. That he had executed similar frauds on some one-half dozen other Clerks of Court in North Carolina.

The Bureau secured the best possible description of this man and his methods of operation, thereafter circularizing the Clerks of Court in all of the surrounding States. On April 9, 1941, Rundt entered the courthouse at Warrenton, Va., and after contacting the Clerk of the Court there with his usual letters of introduction he was identified by the Clerk from a circular letter from this Bureau giving his description. He was detained and the Sheriff of that County communicated with this Bureau. It was ascertained that it would not be necessary to extradite him. Agents were sent to Warrenton and Rundt was returned to the custody of Sheriff Pitts of Catawba County.

Since there were several indictments pending he was first tried in Alamance County May 13, 1941, and sentenced to from three to five years in the State's Prison by Judge Hubert E. Olive. On July 9, 1941, he was tried and sentenced in Wake County to five years in State's Prison by Judge C. Everett Thompson. On July 31, 1941, he was tried in the Superior Court of Mecklenburg County and sentenced to from four to six years and from two to four years, to run consecutively following sentences previously given.

Detainers have been filed by the States of Alabama, Georgia, and South Carolina, in each State of which Rundt is wanted on similar charges at the completion of his prison terms in North Carolina.

State v. Florence Holmes and Tom Melvin; Irby Holmes, Victim, Murder

On September 16, 1940, Sheriff Paul Garrison of Wayne County requested the assistance of the Bureau in connection with the slaying of Irby Holmes, which occurred on or about January 1, 1940, on the outskirts of Goldsboro, N. C.

Investigation developed that Holmes was engaged in operating a taxicab business in and around Goldsboro. After a thorough investigation the facts disclosed that Mrs. Florence E. Holmes, the wife of the victim, had persuaded a negro man by the name of Tom Melvin to commit the murder. Melvin had requested Holmes to take him out in the country in his taxicab. After having Holmes drive him to an isolated spot, Melvin struck him over the head with a hammer and left him lying beside his car. Melvin then returned to Goldsboro by foot. Melvin had borne a good reputation in Goldsboro, having been employed by a local florist firm over a long period of years. Following his arrest he confessed to having committed the crime and explained in detail the circumstances leading up to its commission. He stated that Mrs. Holmes had told him that her husband carried considerable life insurance and that if he would commit the crime she would pay him well for his services as soon as she was able to collect the insurance.

Mrs. Holmes and Tom Melvin were tried in the Superior Court of Wayne County for murder. Melvin was convicted of murder in the first degree and was sentenced to be executed by lethal gas; while Mrs. Holmes entered a plea of accessory before the fact and was sentenced to life imprisonment by Hon. Henry L. Stevens, Judge Presiding.

Upon appeal to the Supreme Court the judgments in the lower court were affirmed.

Laucy McGee, Victim; Suspicious Death

Laucy McGee, a resident of Hamlet, N. C., and for many years an employee in the shops of the Seaboard Railway Company was scheduled to report for duty at an early hour on the morning of June 15, 1940. Since he did not report on scheduled time the company sent a messenger boy to his home at about 2:30 a.m. Mrs. McGee informed the boy that her husband had left home at about 2:00 a.m. to go to work. The messenger boy went around to the back of their home and saw the body of McGee lying mid-way between the house and the garage. The Hamlet Police Department was immediately notified and upon examination it was discovered that McGee had been shot through the chest and had been dead for some time.

The Hamlet Police Department instituted a prompt investigation and arrived at the conclusion that McGee had committed suicide since they found his revolver partly wrapped in a cloth lying in his garage. They were unable to find any motive for foul play. The authorities, therefore, closed the case, regarding same as suicide.

Later on relatives of the deceased indicated that some threats had been made against the victim and that they felt he had been robbed and murdered.

The Chief of Police of Hamlet communicated with the Bureau welcoming further investigation. Likewise, Gov. Clyde R. Hoey received a letter from a prominent citizen of Hamlet requesting further investigation, which he referred to the Bureau.

The investigation disclosed that the deceased had been warned by his employers about the excessive use of intoxicants. Further, that the deceased carried an accident policy providing double indemnity in the event of a violent death. The family arranged to have the body exhumed and the bullet removed therefrom. A careful ballistics examination of the bullet removed from McGee's body disclosed that the bullet was fired from his pistol.

No evidence of foul play was discovered and after a very careful investigation all facts were revealed to the relatives and the local law enforcement agencies, who expressed their appreciation for the services rendered.

State v. Mrs. W. J. Blanchette
and James Devore Cahoon

On April 17, 1941, a male infant's body was found in the Trent River about one mile from New Bern, N. C. At the request of Sheriff R. B. Lane and Coroner U. W. Daugherty of Craven County an investigation was instituted. It was disclosed that a new born male infant's body had been found wrapped in a woman's old fashioned petticoat and a pair of men's striped pajama trousers. The body had been placed in a small wood box in which there were also three small pieces of scrap iron. The body when found was in a well preserved state and appeared to be normal in every respect.

Further investigation disclosed that a widow woman by the name of Mrs. W. J. Blanchette, who lived at Bridgeton about two miles from New Bern, was known to have been in a pregnant condition prior to March 9, 1941. That on or about that date she had lost several days from her work as a W. P. A. employee. That when she returned to her work there was a noticeable difference in her physical appearance. It was further disclosed that one James Devore Cahoon had been keeping company with Mrs. Blanchette. The petticoat in which the child's body was found was identified as having been worn by Mrs. Blanchette. Upon being confronted with these facts Mrs. Blanchette admitted having given birth to the child found in the Trent River but declared that it had been born dead. Cahoon admitted placing the baby in the box and throwing it in the Trent River on the morning of March 30, 1941.

On June 4, 1941, in the Superior Court of Craven County, Mrs. W. J. Blanchette and James Devore Cahoon pled guilty to concealing the birth of and disposing of an infant's body. Hon. J. Paul Frizzelle, Judge Presiding, sentenced these defendants to from three to five years each in the State's Penitentiary.

State v. Woody L. Graham;
Margaret Clayton, Victim,
Criminal Assault

On May 1, 1941, the victim, a twelve year old white girl, was left alone at her home by her parents who were engaged in night work in Fayetteville, N. C. At about 11:00 o'clock she awoke and found a man in her bedroom. She screamed and the man put his hand over her mouth and struck her several times, and left her after she fell to the floor during the struggle.

One suspect, Woody L. Graham, colored, age twenty-six, upon being examined and questioned it was discovered that he had some reddish substance under his fingernails. He first told the officers that the substance was ketchup and later said it was blood from meats he had handled in the kitchen of a hospital where he was employed. The substance was removed from his fingernails and after being analyzed by the Bureau Toxicologist it was found to be human blood.

A fingerprint examination of the victim's bed was made and latent prints were lifted from the bed post. A comparison of these prints was made and they were positively identified as those of Woody Graham.

Woody Graham was tried and found guilty in the Superior Court of Cumberland County at the May, 1941, term and sentenced to life imprisonment by Judge W. H. S. Burgwyn.

State v. James DeGraffenreid;
Waddell Chavis, Victim, Murder

At the request of Hon. Wm. H. Murdock, Solicitor of the Tenth Judicial District, an investigation was instituted in connection with the fatal shooting of one Waddell Chavis, colored, on March 16, 1941, near Mebane, N. C.

It developed that the victim, in company with two other colored men and three colored girls, went for a ride in an automobile which James DeGraffenreid was driving. All of the parties were drinking throughout the afternoon and early part of the night. Chavis and DeGraffenreid got into an argument over one of the girls and after the three girls had been returned to their homes DeGraffenreid, in company with Chavis drove to Tom Holt's house, where DeGraffenreid had a room. DeGraffenreid got out of the car and stated that he was going to his room to change his clothes. In about five minutes he returned from his room with a shot gun and without any warning leveled it at Chavis and shot him.

DeGraffenreid claimed that he shot Chavis in self-defense. James Lee Hester, the third man in the car, was very reluctant to talk about the facts; however, he finally admitted that he was an eye witness to the killing and with the statements of the three colored girls DeGraffenreid was found guilty of murder in the second degree in the Superior Court of Alamance County at the May, 1941, term. He was sentenced to the State Penitentiary to from twelve to fifteen years by Judge Hubert E. Olive.

State v. Bascum Smith;
Brunt Smith, Victim, Assault
With a Deadly Weapon

At the request of Sheriff H. M. Clark of Bladen County an investigation was instituted in connection with the assaulting of Brunt Smith with a deadly weapon. After an exhaustive investigation it developed that Bascum Smith, eighteen year old son of the victim, had been conducting himself in a rather queer manner. An investigation of his activities on the night of the shooting of his father disclosed that he had taken his father's car and attempted several places to get gasoline. It was also learned that he owned a .32 caliber pistol and that his father was shot with a .32 bullet.

Bascum Smith was then apprehended and questioned relative to his activities and conduct on the night of the shooting. He finally admitted in the presence of the Sheriff, his deputies, and our Agents that he had shot his father because he would not let him have the family automobile for use as he desired. Bascum Smith made a complete confession, giving a signed statement of the facts.

Bascum Smith was held for trial in the Superior Court of Bladen County at the March, 1941, term. He was sentenced by Judge Q. K. Nimocks to two years on the roads, sentence being suspended on condition of good behavior.

State v. John Monroe Wilson;
Fred Sutton, Victim, Murder

The body of Fred Sutton, sixty-one year old white man, was found where he had been murdered in a service station owned by the Loftin Oil Company where he was employed as a night watchman. The cash register had been robbed of approximately $35.00. The body was discovered at about 4:00 a. m. on January 10, 1941. This crime was committed about a mile and one-half from Kinston on Highway No. 55. Following a request for assistance an Agent of this Bureau immediately instituted an investigation and in cooperation with the sheriff and police several suspects were held for questioning.

An axe was found lying near the counter where the body lay. On the "eye" of the axe was a quantity of congealed blood and also crushed particles of glass. The axe was retained and processed for fingerprints. Two sets of fingerprints were developed on the painted portion of the axe handle. These fingerprints were compared with those of one of the suspects, John Monroe Wilson, and found to be identical. When confronted with these facts Wilson confessed to the crime and the other suspects were released.

Wilson was tried at the January, 1941, term of the Superior Court of Lenoir County, where he was found guilty of second degree murder and sentenced to from 20 to 25 years in the State Penitentiary by Judge C. Everett Thompson.

State v. Sammy Davis;
Louis Gaylor, Victim, Murder

On November 24, 1940, Louis Gaylor, a resident of Kinston, N. C., and a plumber by trade, was last seen at an early hour on that morning.

Since he had mysteriously disappeared the law enforcement officers of Lenoir County requested the assistance of the Bureau.

An intensive investigation was instituted and several suspects held for questioning. Gaylor's body was found in the Neuse River three weeks after he disappeared.

The evidence developed that Sammy Davis, son-in-law of the deceased, and one Harold Howard in company with Gaylor had been on a drinking spree and that Gaylor had some liquor which the other two men wanted. That they finally persuaded Gaylor to go to the Neuse River bridge where they all took a drink and then pushed Gaylor over the bridge into the river while he was in an intoxicated state.

Davis and Howard were bound over to the Superior Court of Lenoir County for trial at the January, 1941, term. Davis entered a plea of guilty of murder in the second degree and Howard was acquitted by the jury. Davis was sentenced to from 15 to 20 years in the State Penitentiary by Judge C. Everett Thompson.

State v. W. T. Satterfield;
Edenton Peanut Company, Victim, Larceny

In September, 1940, the Police Department of Edenton, N. C., requested the assistance of the Bureau in connection with the larceny of peanut bags to the value of approximately $1,000.00.

Investigation developed that at various times from the fall of 1939 to the date of the request that the Edenton Peanut Company had lost various quantities of empty peanut sacks, most of which had been baled in bundles of fifty. Early in July, 1940, six hundred sacks had been taken on one night. It was discovered that 4,000 of the missing sacks were stored in the Leary Brothers Warehouse at Edenton, N. C. These sacks were identified as belonging to the Edenton Peanut Company by the lot numbers stenciled on them; further, they had been stored there by one W. T. Satterfield.

After a very careful investigation in cooperation with the Police Department it was found that several negroes had been employed by W. T. Satterfield to steal the sacks on various occasions and under varying conditions. These negroes finally confessed to their participation in this crime and as a result were bound over to the Superior Court of Chowan County.

On December 10, 1940, James "Buddy" Lawrence, Charles Bonner and Lloyd Norfleet, the three negro defendants, pled guilty but judgment was withheld by Judge W. C. Harris until the defendant Satterfield was tried. In the March, 1941, term of Superior Court Satterfield was placed on trial and entered a plea of guilty of larceny and receiving. Judge Henry L. Stevens sentenced Satterfield to the State Penitentiary to from 3 to 5 years, this sentence being suspended upon payment of $600.00 to the Edenton Peanut Company to reimburse it for the stolen sacks and payment of the court costs. Norfleet, Bonner and Lawrence, who entered pleas of guilty at an earlier term of court, were each sentenced to two years in the State Penitentiary, suspended upon the payment of the cost of court.

State v. G. I. Westcott;
Gambling Devices, Slot Machines

In April, 1940, Hon. Chester Morris, Solicitor of the First Judicial District, requested the assistance of the Bureau in connection with the gambling in Dare County, especially by means of slot machines. At various times the Agents secured evidence disclosing violations under State Laws relative to this subject in Dare County. In August, 1940, Westcott's place was visited and sufficient evidence secured showing illegal operation of slot machines. In October, 1940, the Solicitor obtained a search warrant and Agents in company with the Sheriff of Dare County found in the loft of the defendant's farm house a large quantity of pin board and various types and models of gambling machines.

At the May, 1941, term of the Superior Court of Dare County this defendant submitted to a charge of the violation of the Flanagan Act and was sentenced by Judge Henry L. Stevens to twelve months on the roads, suspended upon the payment of $300.00 and cost, and upon condition that he refrain from any form of gambling and that he not violate any of the laws of the State of North Carolina for said period.

State v. William Dudley Emerick and
Enoch Arden Osburn; Mrs. Eloise K.
Horner, Victim, Violation of Security Laws

On April 23, 1941, Hon. Thad Eure, Secretary of State, requested the assistance of the Bureau for the purpose of investigating suspicious persons in Oxford, N. C., who were engaged in dealing in stocks and securities without having a State license. Mr. Eure stated that he had received a complaint from Mrs. Eloise K. Horner of Oxford, N. C., in which she had advised that a Mr. Wm. Dudley Emerick had come to her home and proposed swapping her oil royalties for Tidewater Power Company stock. That she had delivered the shares of Tidewater stock to Emerick and held his receipt but that he had not delivered the securities in exchange therefor.

When Mr. Eure and our Agent arrived in Oxford, N. C., the Police Department had apprehended Emerick at the home of Mrs. Horner where he was in the act of presenting Mrs. Horner with a check for her Tidewater Power stock. Emerick was then interviewed and stated that he was living in Asheville, N. C., with a Mr. Enoch Arden Osburn. An examination of the portfolio which Emerick had with him disclosed pictures of oil wells in Oklahoma, deeds for oil lands in Mexico, and various and sundry other papers which proved this man to be engaged in a fraudulent business.

A warrant was sworn out by Mr. Eure and Emerick and Osburn were placed under arrest. At a special hearing on April 25, 1941, in the Recorder's Court of Person County these defendants were bound over to Superior Court and placed under bond of $500.00 each.

Further investigation disclosed that these parties had secured the names and addresses of the holders of Tidewater Power stock, many of whom had been approached by Emerick and Osburn with flattering offers of exchange of bogus stock for securities. It was further learned that these parties were engaged in similar fraudulent schemes in various parts of the United States.

At the July, 1941, term of the Superior Court of Granville County neither Emerick nor Osburn answered to their names when called for trial. It was learned that these parties had been convicted in the Federal Court in Kentucky and were serving sentences in the Federal Penitentiary; also, that the Kentucky authorities were holding further warrants and a detainer had been placed against them upon their release from the Federal Penitentiary.

United States v. Bonnie Earl Jackson;
United States Post Office, Cameron, N. C.
and United States Post Office, Carthage, N. C.,
Victims, Robbery

At the request of Sheriff C. J. McDonald of Moore County an investigation was instituted in connection with the breaking and entering of the Post Office at Cameron, N. C., on August 17, 1939 and at Carthage, N. C., on August 25, 1939.

Latent fingerprints were secured in the Post Office and identified as those of Bonnie Earl Jackson. This defendant was tried on September 9, 1940, in the United States Court at Rockingham, N. C., and upon learning that his fingerprints had been identified entered a plea of guilty. He was sentenced to the Federal Penitentiary by Judge Johnson J. Hayes to a term of five years.

State v. Charlie Frank Swain;
Roper High School, Victim, Burglary

Corporal T. B. Brown of the State Highway Patrol stated that the Washington County Superintendent of Schools had called upon him on several occasions about the breaking and entering of the school lunch room at Roper, N. C. That the last time the lunch room was broken into, which was on or about November 14, 1940, a printed note had been left as follows: "Thanks very much for the food, we enjoyed it." Corporal Brown stated that he had some suspects and that he wanted to have a handwriting comparison made.

Our Document Examiner went to Plymouth, N. C., where Corporal Brown and Chief of Police Snell of Roper, N. C., brought in a suspect by the name of Swain. Additional standards of handwriting were procured from Swain which satisfied our Examiner of Questioned Documents that Swain had written the note left in the school. Swain made a complete confession after being confronted with the reasons why the Examiner was satisfied he had written the note. He gave a signed statement that he had entered the Roper High School lunch room on the night of November 14, 1940, when he left the note in question.

Swain was bound over to the Washington County Court where he was sentenced to one year on the roads.

BRIEF SUMMARY
of
IMPORTANT CASES INVESTIGATED
PERIOD
July 1, 1941 to July 1, 1942.

State v. C. W. Sneed, et al.;
State Department of Revenue,
Victim, Embezzlement

On February 10, 1942, Gov. J. Melville Broughton requested that the Bureau communicate with Hon. Wm. Y. Bickett, Solicitor of the Seventh Judicial District, and institute an investigation into certain irregularities in the Department of Revenue which had been called to his attention by the Solicitor.

An intensive investigation was conducted, numerous employees interviewed, and various audits checked, which disclosed that certain employees on varying occasions had collected funds from taxpayers which had not been credited to their accounts in the Revenue Department. The Solicitor was kept advised from time to time of the progress of the investigation, and full cooperation was received from the Solicitor and the staff of the Revenue Department.

Following indictments and trials in the Superior Court of Wake County at the April, 1942, term the following defendants plead guilty to a charge of embezzlement and were sentenced as follows: Lee C. Taylor to not less than one year nor more than three years in State's Prison, Charles C. Huitt to not less than one year nor more than three years, and C. W. Sneed to not less than eighteen months nor more than four years. The defendant Rodney Warner, after a plea of nolo contendere, was sentenced to State's Prison for a period of not less than one year nor more than three years. The defendants Harry Howard and R. L. Ward, Jr., submitted pleas of not guilty of embezzlement and not guilty of aiding and abetting Sneed in embezzling; however, they were both found guilty and Howard was sentenced to State's Prison for a period of not less than one year nor more than three years, sentence on the second count to run concurrent with the first; and Ward was found guilty on three counts and sentenced to State's Prison for a period of not less than two years nor more than four years on the first count, and on the second and third counts sentences to run concurrent with the first. The defendant F. B. Drake submitted a plea of not guilty to the charge of embezzlement and also a plea of not guilty of aiding and abetting Sneed in embezzling. Drake was found not guilty on the embezzlement charge but was found guilty on the charge of aiding and abetting Sneed. Drake was ordered to pay a fine of $200.00 and cost and prayer for judgment was continued for a period of two years upon condition that this subject not violate any of the laws of the State of North Carolina for a period of two years, and further that he secure gainful employment.

Judge F. Don Phillips presided at this special term of Wake County Superior Court at the request of Governor Broughton.

State v. F. C. Bonner, et al.;
Ira L. Godwin, Victim, Murder

Ira L. Godwin, 51 year old filling station operator, was shot to death about 10:30 o'clock on the night of April 4, 1942. He resided about three miles southeast of Whiteville in Columbus County and was one of the most substantial citizens of that community. His wife had left the filling station and gone to their home about fifty yards away shortly after 10:00 p.m. She expected her husband to close the station and come home shortly thereafter. As he did not come to his home within a reasonable time she returned to the station and found her husband's body lying back of the counter riddled with bullets, and he had a $10.00 bill clutched in his right hand. His wallet containing a considerable amount of money was missing.

The Bureau was called upon to make a ballistics examination and Governor Broughton directed that the Bureau institute an intensive investigation. It was found that Godwin had been shot six times and his body contained both .22 and .32 caliber bullets. Several local suspects were detained and questioned, all of whom were able to give satisfactory alibis. After following various clues it was learned that Ollin Fowler carried a .22 caliber pistol and that an associate of his carried a .32 caliber pistol; further, that they had been suspected of stealing an automobile near the South Carolina line on or about the time this murder occurred. Our Agent contacted the law enforcement officers of South Carolina and with their cooperation apprehended Fowler. When confronted with the facts Fowler confessed to firing the .22 caliber pistol at the merchant and further stated that one F. C. Bonner fired a .32 caliber pistol. The body of Godwin was exhumed and at the autopsy both .22 and .32 caliber bullets were removed.

Fowler and Bonner made a further statement that Lonnie Melton Todd and Joe McDaniel also participated in this crime. These individuals made the further confession that they had stolen four automobiles at various times in Marion County, South Carolina, and that one of these automobiles was used on the night of the Godwin murder. They also admitted that they participated in several other robberies in both North and South Carolina.

At the May, 1942, term of the Superior Court of Columbus County these defendants were tried for the murder of Ira L. Godwin. F. C. Bonner, age 19; and Melton Todd, age 28, both soldiers stationed at Fort Bragg, N. C.; and Ollin Fowler, age 18, of Dufort, S. C., were convicted of murder in the first degree and sentenced to death in the gas chamber by Judge C. Everett Thompson. The fourth defendant, Joe McDaniel, age 16, was found guilty as accessory after the fact of murder and was sentenced to from five to seven years in the State's Penitentiary.

State v. Coy Harris, et al.;
Cy Winstead, Victim, Mob Violence

During the late afternoon of August 14th, 1941, Sheriff M. T. Clayton apprehended one Cy Winstead, colored, charged with rape upon the person of one Pauline Dunn, a young white woman residing in Person County. Winstead was placed in the Person County jail at Roxboro, N. C., about 7:00 p.m. About 10:00 o'clock that night a crowd began gathering around the Person County Courthouse with the alleged intention of taking Winstead from the custody of the Sheriff and lynching him. The crowd became more boisterous and the Sheriff barricaded himself with other local officers in the Courthouse and called for the assistance of the State Highway Patrol. The crowd continued to gather and started throwing rocks and bottles, breaking windows in the Courthouse, and occasionally shooting in the front and rear doors of the Courthouse. During the early morning hours the crowd became more violent and the Sheriff called for assistance from the Durham City Police and the State Bureau of Investigation. It was not until the Sheriff and other officers, along with the State Highway Patrolmen, resorted to the use of tear gas that the mob began to disperse, enabling the officers to remove Winstead to the State Penitentiary in Raleigh for safe keeping.

Gov. J. Melville Broughton then directed the State Bureau of Investigation to make a thorough investigation in order to ascertain the identity of the persons responsible for this violence.

After an intensive investigation Agents of the Bureau appeared before the Grand Jury of the Superior Court of Person County, at which time ten men were indicted on a misdemeanor charge in connection with the attempted lynching of Cy Winstead. At the April, 1942, term of the Superior Court of Person County nine of the ten men accused entered pleas of not guilty. The tenth defendant had joined the United States Army and was not available. During the trial the presiding judge directed verdicts of acquittal for three of the defendants and a non-suit was granted for another. The five remaining defendants were convicted upon the charges of assembling unlawfully. Judge R. Hunt Parker sentenced Coy Harris and A. P. Spriggs to eighteen months on the roads; and P. I. Holt, Johnnie Holt, and Willie Atkin to twelve months each.

State v. W. H. Smith, et al.;
G. & M. Motor Transfer Company,
Victim, Robbery and Arson

During the early hours on the morning of June 22, 1941, when a G. & M. Motor Transfer Company truck loaded with cotton piece goods was en route north being driven by one Howard Brown and Bristol Ayers, a relief driver, it was ordered stopped on the highway near Stokesdale, N. C., by a group of unknown men.

The tires on the truck were shot down forcing the truck to stop, and the drivers were then pulled out of the truck cab. They were placed in an automobile by unknown parties and carried to Greensboro where they were turned loose. Before the drivers could return to their truck some fifteen miles away the truck and the contents, estimated to the value of $15,000.00, had been destroyed by fire.

Shortly after this occurrence Gov. J. Melville Broughton requested that the Bureau institute an investigation in connection with this crime. Agents were immediately assigned and it developed that on several occasions prior to this incident assaults had been made on various trucks operating within the State in addition to threats of violence against non-union drivers. Reports had been made by drivers that they had been shot at from ambush while operating their trucks on the State Highways. The drivers of the G. & M. Motor Company truck were at first hesitant to assist in identifying any of their assailants for fear of being done bodily harm.

After an intensive investigation by the Agents in cooperation with the State Highway Patrol, and other law enforcement officers, several of the assailants were identified and apprehended. They admitted their participation in this crime and implicated several others which resulted finally in the indictment of ten individuals.

At the September, 1941, term of the Superior Court of Guilford County six of those participating in this crime were found guilty and sentenced by Judge J. A. Rousseau to from three to nine years in the State's Penitentiary.

On an appeal to the North Carolina Supreme Court the judgments entered against these defendants were confirmed.

State v. Solomon Guffey;
LeRoy Scoggins, Victim, Murder

On January 25, 1942, one LeRoy Scoggins, white, age about forty-two, was found dead near a small stream just outside the city limits of Rutherfordton, N. C. Scoggins' skull had been badly fractured, his jawbone broken, and there was a large gash across the left side of his neck which had severed his jugular vein. Scoggins was last seen alive leaving a filling station around 8:00 p. m. on the night of January 25th. One Sol Guffey was seen leaving the filling station shortly thereafter and returned about 10:00 p. m., at which time he drank several bottles of beer. He was arrested for public drunkenness at about 10:30 p. m. and it was noticed that he had what appeared to be blood on his coat.

Sheriff C. C. Moore requested the assistance of the Bureau and an analysis was made of the substance from Guffey's coat, which was found to be human blood of the same type as that of the victim. When Guffey was confronted with the facts developed he stated that he had an argument over a half gallon of liquor. This argument resulted in a fight which led to the brutal killing of Scoggins. Guffey admitted using a club which he hid after the crime and later revealed its whereabouts.

Guffey was tried in the May term of Superior Court of Rutherford County. He was found guilty and sentenced to from twenty-two to twenty-three years in the State's Prison by Judge H. Hoyle Sink.

United States v. Hub Parker, et al.;
Pisgah National Forest, Haywood
County, Incendiarism

During the month of April, 1942, a number of forest fires broke out in the Pisgah National Forest, which comprises some 600,000 acres of timber land. These fires spread out over a distance of approximately fifteen miles making it necessary to close Pisgah National Forest for more than thirty days to the public. It was estimated that approximately 15,000 acres of timber land was destroyed.

All of the resources of the United States Forestry Service and Game Wardens located in Western North Carolina, in company with the North Carolina State Guards, were called to active duty to assist in fighting the forest fires which had spread into four counties in that section.

Gov. J. Melville Broughton directed the State Bureau of Investigation to make an intensive investigation into the origin and cause of these fires. It developed that fires had originated in about ten different sections of the forest counties. In the instant case it was disclosed that one Hub Parker, age about 46, from time to time had been violating the Game Laws and had had trouble with the Game and Forest Wardens. That he had employed one Nelcey L. Reece, age 17, to set out fires in Haywood County. That some twenty-one fires had been set out in one section by these parties. When confronted with the facts resulting from the investigation Reece admitted his participation in the unlawful acts.

Parker and Reece were tried in the United States District Court at Asheville on May 17, 1942. Both were found guilty of intentionally setting forest fires in the Pisgah National Forest. Judge E. Yates Webb sentenced Parker to seven years in the Federal Prison. Reece was given a suspended sentence upon condition that he enter the United States Army in lieu of the prison sentence.

Two young boys were apprehended in Henderson County where they were tried in the County Court and given suspended sentences to the Stonewall Jackson Training School. Three individuals were apprehended in Transylvania County where they have been bound over to the Superior Court and now await trial. One young boy was apprehended and tried in the Haywood County Court. He was found guilty and given a suspended sentence to the Stonewall Jackson Training School. Investigation disclosed that in a section of Haywood County known as the Big East Fork Section numerous reputable citizens had been fishing and fires in that section were most likely started accidentally.

It is the opinion of the Forest Wardens that the apprehension and prosecution of the several parties involved in these fires will prevent the further violation of the Forestry Laws regulating the preservation of the National Forest.

North Carolina State Highway Commission; Mysterious Explosion of Ferry Barge, Cape Fear River, Bladen County

On Sunday morning, March 1, 1942, at approximately 9:00 a. m., a barge owned and operated by the North Carolina State Highway Commission on the Cape Fear River about 25 miles southeast of Elizabethtown, near Kelly, connecting North Carolina highways 53 and 87, mysteriously exploded killing the operator, one W. H. Russ.

At the request of Sheriff H. M. Clark of Bladen County an Agent of this Bureau immediately instituted an investigation in company with Mr. A. M. McLamb, District Supervisor of Roads and Bridges, and Mr. G. W. Moore, Construction Engineer of the State Highway Commission. Careful investigation and examination at the scene of the explosion revealed that the flat top barge measured some 45 feet in length. That it was driven by a V-8 gasoline motor located in the inside under deck of the barge. That there was no ventilation under the deck for gas fumes to escape other than the exhaust from the engine. The relief operator of the barge admitted that oil and gasoline had collected in the hull of the barge and that on the day prior to this explosion the gasoline line became clogged, it being necessary to disconnect the line and considerable gas ran out of the line onto the bottom of the barge.

At the conclusion of the investigation our Agent in company with the engineers for the State Highway Commission satisfied the Sheriff and Coroner of Bladen County that the explosion was due to the accidental ignition of the gasoline in the hull of the barge.

State v. Henry Harper;
Mrs. Clyde White, Victim,
Attempted Criminal Assault

On August 1, 1941, the victim, Mrs. Clyde White, age 24 years, was assaulted at her home by an unknown negro man while she was sitting on her back porch peeling peaches. The victim was struck on the head three times, also on her shoulder, and her right hand and fingers were injured. From the meager description Mrs. White was able to give one Henry Harper, a 25 year old negro man, was suspected of having attacked her. Harper had a bad criminal record and had just been released from the roads on Monday before the crime occurred on Friday. Harper was unable to give a satisfactory alibi as to his whereabouts when this crime was committed. Mrs. White was able to identify Harper as being the same size and color as the man who attacked her.

Harper was tried in the Superior Court of Iredell County at the November, 1941, term where he was found guilty of a charge of secret assault with intent to kill. Harper was sentenced to from 15 to 20 years in State's Prison by Judge A. Hall Johnson.

State v. Joseph Ellis;
Bessie Brewer, Victim, Murder

At the request of Chief of Police J. A. Massey of Smithfield, N. C., Agents were assigned to assist in apprehending the murderer of Mrs. Bessie Brewer. Upon Agents arrival in Smithfield immediately following the request, it was disclosed that Mrs. Brewer had been found murdered in her home at about 3:30 p. m. on January 19, 1942.

Mrs. Brewer was Superintendent of the Salvation Army at Smithfield. About a week prior to her death she had permitted a young man named Joseph Ellis to become a guest in her home. While the Agents were making a preliminary investigation information was received that Ellis had come to Raleigh from Smithfield and surrendered to the Raleigh Police Department. Ellis was removed to Smithfield where our Agents in cooperation with the Smithfield officers secured a complete written confession. It was disclosed that this young man had hoboed around the eastern section of the country and that he had been addicted to the use of dope. Further, that he had a criminal record in his home State of New Jersey.

Ellis was tried and found guilty at the March term of the Superior Court of Johnston County. He was sentenced to thirty years in the State's Prison by Judge Clawson Williams.

Pattie Hill and Dr. Louis N. Gallego, Subjects;
State of North Carolina, Victim, Fraud

Hon. T. W. Bruton, Assistant Attorney General, requested the Bureau to assist the State Treasurer's office in recovering monies paid through error. He advised that the State Treasurer's office had instructed the Wachovia Bank to mail an interest check on a North Carolina bond to one Pattie Hill at Asheville, N. C. It developed that the interest check should have been directed to one Pattie Hill of Ansonville, N. C. When Pattie Hill of Asheville received the check she got a colored doctor named Louis N. Gallego to identify her at the Wachovia Bank in Asheville, paying him $5.00 for introducing her at the Bank where she got the check cashed.

An Agent in company with the Assistant State Treasurer interviewed these parties in Asheville. Their attention was called to the seriousness of having cashed the check knowing it not to be the property of Pattie Hill. They then persuaded these parties to reimburse the State and on November 19, 1941, Pattie Hill with the cooperation of Dr. Gallego raised the money and reimbursed the State in the amount of $216.00.

State v. Robert Bridges;
Roy Byrd, Victim, Murder

Roy Byrd, operator of a cafe on the highway near Fort Bragg, N. C., some seven miles from Fayetteville, was fatally shot on the night of January 8, 1941. Several parties had been drinking in the cafe and had become quite boisterous. Byrd had ordered them out and a short time thereafter he was shot.

Robert Bridges, one of the participants, was overheard to have made the remark that if he had a revolver he would go back and kill Byrd. One of the parties sold Bridges his revolver for $10.00. A ballistics examination of the .32 caliber revolver which had been purchased by Bridges, along with a bullet removed from Byrd's body, disclosed that the fatal bullet had been fired from Bridges' pistol.

Robert Bridges was indicted, tried, and found guilty and sentenced to 30 years in the State's Prison by Judge Q. K. Nimocks in the Superior Court of Cumberland County at the November, 1941, term.

State v. Jake Patterson;
Noah Patterson, Victim, Murder;
Alva Patterson, Victim, Assault

On the night of July 15, 1941, between the hours of 8:00 p.m. and 9:00 p.m., Noah Patterson and his wife Alva Patterson were assaulted in their home in Cleveland County, near Patterson Springs, N. C., by unknown party or parties. Noah Patterson died the following day in the Shelby Hospital from wounds inflicted by a sharp edged instrument. Alva Patterson was severely bruised and she was carried to the Shelby Hospital for treatment.

Assistance was requested by Sheriff J. R. Cline of Cleveland County and Agents were immediately assigned to cooperate with him in the investigation. It developed that Noah Patterson, the deceased, was seventy-four years of age and that his wife was only about thirty-five years of age. That Noah Patterson was addicted to the use of liquor and that he had a rather violent temper, having on several occasions severely beaten his wife. It was also learned that Jake Patterson, a man of low mentality and a brother of Alva Patterson, had learned that Noah Patterson had beaten his wife upon several occasions. Jake Patterson had threatened to kill Noah Patterson if he attacked his sister again.

Alva Patterson at first stated that she did not know who had attacked her and her husband. That someone had entered their home and taken money, and when she came to she was in the hospital and learned that her husband was dead. Later on Alva Patterson admitted that her husband was assaulting her and that she began screaming. A short while thereafter Jake Patterson came into their home with an axe under his coat and proceeded to attack her husband. That she had been badly bruised in the attack made upon her by her husband prior to that time.

Jake Patterson was tried and found guilty of murder in the second degree at the October, 1941, term of the Superior Court of Cleveland County. He was sentenced to from 8 to 10 years in State's Prison by Judge Wilson Warlick.

State v. Jesse Manning;
Paul Best, Victim, Murder

Paul Best, 67 year old store clerk, was fatally assaulted in his store room at Windsor, N. C., about 11:00 a. m., on July 8, 1940.

At the request of Sheriff F. M. Dunstan of Bertie County an investigation was instituted which resulted in the arrest of one Jesse Manning, 28 year old lumber mill employee, and Sammy Gilliam, a local colored man. These parties had been seen loitering around the store shortly before Best's body was found. About ten days after this crime was committed Manning made a confession of his participation in this crime and implicated Sammy Gilliam. Gilliam denied any participation in the crime and later on Manning admitted that Gilliam did not participate in the crime.

Manning was tried in the Superior Court of Bertie County at the August, 1941, term. He was found guilty of murder in the first degree and was sentenced to death in the gas chamber by Judge J. J. Burney. Due to Manning's low mentality Governor Broughton commuted the death sentence to life imprisonment.

State v. Charlie Shaw;
Mrs. Jean Sawyer, Victim, Rape

Mrs. Jean Sawyer lived alone about ten miles from Currituck, N. C., in an old plantation home since her husband had been interned in the State Insane Asylum for about two years. On June 15, 1941, during the night time Mrs. Sawyer reported to the law enforcement authorities that a negro man had hoisted a ladder to her bedroom window where he entered and criminally assaulted her.

Sheriff L. L. Dozier of Currituck County requested the assistance of the Bureau in an effort to secure latent fingerprints for comparative purposes. An Agent was immediately assigned and he secured fingerprints from the ladder and window sill which were compared with the suspect, one Charlie Shaw. Also, a bed sheet taken from the bed occupied by Mrs. Sawyer at the time of the attack was analyzed by the Bureau Toxicologist, who reported that upon examination the spots were revealed to be human blood. The Toxicologist also reported that the large yellow stain on the sheet was examined and spermatozoa were found. Mrs. Sawyer was able to identify Shaw as having been her assailant.

Shaw was indicted and found guilty of both rape and burglary at the September term of the Superior Court of Currituck County. He was sentenced to death in the gas chamber by Judge J. Paul Frizzelle. On April 2, 1942, Governor J. M. Broughton commuted to life imprisonment the death sentence imposed upon Charlie Shaw in view of the mental condition of the prosecutrix, who was at that time a patient at the State Insane Asylum.

State v. Herman Allen;
Mrs. Ruth Lee Allen, Grady Lee,
and Cap Raynor, Victims, Murder

At the request of Sheriff Kirby L. Rose of Johnston County our Firearms Identification Examiner was asked to cooperate in connection with the investigation into the fatal shooting of three persons in his county on January 8, 1942, by Herman Allen.

Two empty sixteen-gauge shotgun shells were found at the home of Cap Raynor and one near the barn of Grady Lee, two of the victims. Shortly after the apprehension of Herman Allen he made a complete confession concerning the triple killing, in which a sixteen-gauge shotgun had been used.

Allen was tried at the February, 1942, term of the Superior Court of Johnston County where he was found guilty of murder in the first degree and sentenced to death by Judge Jeff D. Johnson.

State v. Charles B. Davis;
Wm. Roberson, Victim, Burglary

Unknown parties entered the home of Wm. Roberson in Northampton County on the night of September 19, 1941, stealing a trunk containing money and other personal property of the victim. Shortly thereafter the trunk was recovered in an isolated part of the County.

Sheriff J. C. Stephenson of Northampton County requested the assistance of the Bureau in securing fingerprints from the trunk. An Agent was assigned and after processing the trunk he was able to get several latent prints. The Sheriff had several suspects, all of whom were eliminated except one Charles B. Davis. When Davis was apprehended his fingerprints were found to be identical with those secured from the trunk.

Davis was indicted, tried, and found guilty in the Superior Court of Northampton County at the October, 1941, term. He was sentenced to from 2 to 3 years in State's Prison by Judge R. Hunt Parker.

State v. Delbert Lewis;
Mrs. Emma Lewis, Victim, Murder

On September 6, 1941, the body of Mrs. Emma Lewis was found in her bed at her home in Marion, N. C., she apparently being the victim of a brutal murder. Mrs. Lewis' feet had been bound together with strips of cloth and her elbows had been bound behind her back. A make-shift cloth rope was bound about her neck three times and tied in a knot, and rags had been tied over her nose and mouth. Her death evidently was due to suffocation as there was no knife or bullet wounds. The bed on which Mrs. Lewis was found had not been disarranged.

Upon the request of Sheriff Grady Nichols, Agents were assigned to cooperate with him in connection with the investigation of this mysterious crime.

Delbert Lewis, the husband of the victim, upon being interviewed, claimed that he had left their home at about 6:00 a. m. for his work and that his wife was in good health and spirits. That he worked on during the day and upon returning to his home that afternoon when he called for his wife she did not answer him. That he went to the kitchen where he left groceries and then went out and talked to some neighbors. Later on he went back to his home and when he went to the bedroom he found his wife's body lying on the bed bound and tied with cloth sheets. He then ran out and called for help stating that someone had murdered his wife, following which the law enforcement officers were notified. Lewis' reputation bore some suspicion and his activities were carefully checked. Since there had been no motive for anyone else having committed the crime, Lewis was taken into custody and after considerable questioning finally admitted that he was guilty. It was disclosed that he had spent some time in an asylum about fifteen years prior to the date of this crime.

Lewis was tried in the Superior Court of McDowell County at the June, 1942, term. He entered a plea of guilty of murder in the second degree and was sentenced by Judge H. Hoyle Sink to serve 29 to 30 years in State's Prison.

CRIMINAL STATISTICS

REPORT OF DIVISION OF CRIMINAL AND CIVIL STATISTICS

The report of the Division of Criminal and Civil Statistics for the biennium ending July 1, 1942, represents a summarization and limited analysis of all cases reported by the Clerks of the Superior Courts and of various courts of record below the Superior Courts, as required by the provisions of Chapter 315 of the Public Laws of 1939.

The criminal cases covered by this report total 192,490 for the biennium, 27,796 cases having been disposed of by our Superior Courts, and 164,694 cases in various municipal and county courts of record.

It should be noted that this marked increase over the total of 73,493 for the preceding biennium does not reflect a corresponding increase in crime throughout the State, but is largely due to the extension of the work of the department to include reports from the various municipal and recorders courts. As a matter of fact, the total number of criminal cases disposed of in the Superior Courts of the one hundred counties during the biennium ending July 1, 1940, was 25,281, as compared with 27,796 for the biennium just passed, this representing an increase of only 2,515, so that it is apparent that the greatly increased volume of criminal cases handled by this Department during the last biennium represents in large measure an increase in cases reported, rather than an increase in cases tried.

It will be recognized that the filing of these reports by the clerks of the various courts calls for considerable painstaking work, particularly in the larger counties, and that the work of this Division in analyzing and coördinating these reports has increased in proportion to the increased number of cases handled. Moreover, it is obvious that the value of this work depends not only upon the accuracy, but upon the adequacy of the information gathered, as any comprehensive picture of the functioning of the various courts must necessarily be based upon figures which are not only accurate in themselves but comprehensive in their scope.

The language of the statutes creating and enlarging this Department requires it to collect and correlate information in civil and criminal law administration throughout the State, and, while we feel that this expansion of the work of the Department is absolutely essential to the value of the data collected, we have been careful to require of the Clerks only such information as has a direct and definite bearing on the functioning of the various courts.

The statistics upon which this report is based have recently been made available to the Commission on Judicial Districts, and form the factual basis of that Commission's report to the General Assembly, as well as furnishing the only available current figures upon which a further consideration of the problem of a more efficient administration of the work of our lower courts could be based. The value of these statistics and the accuracy of conclusions drawn from them will, in our opinion, increase from year to year as the data accumulate and the picture of the functioning of the courts becomes more and more complete. Aside from this prospective value, these figures, for the last biennium, will provide a very definite basis for whatever action may become necessary in the light of the recent constitutional amendment providing for the creation of solicitorial districts.

During the last biennium, this Department has begun the collection of information on the handling and disposition of civil cases in the Superior Courts, with special attention to the condition of the civil dockets in the several counties, and while the information already in hand is interesting and significant, it is not yet considered sufficiently complete to justify a general summarization. It is, in our opinion, highly important that this particular phase of the work of this Department be continued and extended, as these figures must of necessity form the basis of any well-considered change in the administrative procedure of our civil courts, just as the data on criminal cases should govern any proposed change affecting the administration of the criminal laws.

Taken as a whole, these statistics reflect the activities of the courts of record throughout the State, and present a composite picture of the functioning of these courts. Taken in detail, these figures furnish the only available factual basis for any proposed readjustment of the judicial districts, or for any such changes in civil or criminal procedure as may be considered desirable in the public interest.

The following table of averages, based on cases reported for the calendar year 1941, should be of particular interest in connection with any proposed revision of the present Judicial Districts:

Average Population—per county, 1940, 35,716, plus; per district, 170,077.

Average Weeks of Criminal or Mixed Courts Calendared in 1941, including Special Terms—per county, 5 plus; per district, 28 plus.

Average Number of Criminal Cases Disposed of in Superior Court, 1941—per county, 145 plus; per district, 695 plus.

Average Number of Criminal Cases Reported from Inferior Courts of Record, 1941—per county, 924 plus; per district, 4,403 plus.

Average Number of Weeks Civil or Mixed Court Calendared, 1941, including Special Terms—per county, 9 plus; per district, 46 plus.

Average Number of Hours Consumed in Trial of Civil Cases, 1941—per county, 129 plus; per district, 618 plus.

Average Number of Civil Cases Disposed of, exclusive of Divorce, 1941—per county, 74 plus; per district, 355 plus.

Average Number of Divorce Cases Tried, 1941—per county, 40 plus; per district, 193 plus.

Average Total of All Civil Cases Disposed of, 1941—per county, 115 plus; per district, 548 plus.

FIRST JUDICIAL DISTRICT

IN SUPERIOR COURT

Offense	JULY 1, 1940—JULY 1, 1941															
	CONVICTIONS								OTHER DISPOSITIONS							
	White		Negro		Indian		Unclassified		White		Negro		Indian		Unclassified	
	M	F	M	F	M	F	M	F	M	F	M	F	M	F	M	F
Assault	2		5						1							
Assault and battery											1					
Assault with deadly weapon	2		17	1							3					
Assault on female	1		1						1							
Assault with intent to kill	1		5								2					
Assault with intent to rape			2						1							
Drunk and disorderly	5		2						7		2				1	
Possession—illegal whiskey			3	1							2					
Possession for sale—sale			2	1												
Manufacturing—possession of material for			2													
Transportation																
Violation liquor laws																
Driving drunk	13		1	1					4		2				1	
Reckless driving	3		5						5		1					
Hit and run	2		1							1						
Speeding									1							
Auto license violations			1													
Violation motor vehicle laws			1						1							
Breaking and entering	7		11													
And larceny			1													
And receiving	1		4						1							
Housebreaking and receiving			7													
Storebreaking																
Larceny			11						1		9					
Larceny and receiving	2		6	2					3		3					
Larceny by trick and device			1								1					
Temporary larceny																
Murder—first degree									1							
Murder—second degree			4	1												
Manslaughter			1	1					2							
Burglary—first degree																

Offense	JULY 1, 1941—JULY 1, 1942															
	CONVICTIONS								OTHER DISPOSITIONS							
	White		Negro		Indian		Unclassified		White		Negro		Indian		Unclassified	
	M	F	M	F	M	F	M	F	M	F	M	F	M	F	M	F
Assault	3		5						4		2					
Assault and battery																
Assault with deadly weapon	5		14	1					3		1					
Assault on female	3		6						2		1					
Assault with intent to kill			3													
Assault with intent to rape	1		1						1							
Drunk and disorderly	17		4						4		1					
Possession—illegal whiskey																
Possession for sale—sale	1		2													
Manufacturing—possession of material for																
Transportation									1							
Violation liquor laws			2	1												
Driving drunk	17		8				1		2		3				3	
Reckless driving	2		3						5		2					
Hit and run	2															
Speeding	1															
Auto license violations		1	1						1	1						
Violation motor vehicle laws	1								1							
Breaking and entering	2		5						1							
And larceny	1		5						1							
And receiving			2						4		1					
Housebreaking and receiving																
Storebreaking			1													
Larceny	8		12	2					4		1					
Larceny and receiving			2								1					
Larceny by trick and device																
Temporary larceny	1															
Murder—first degree			2								1					
Murder—second degree			2													
Manslaughter			3						1		3					
Burglary—first degree			1													

Larceny and receiving
Larceny by trick and dev
Temporary larceny
Murder—first degree
Murder—second degree
Manslaughter

Burglary—second degree																		1													
Abandonment	1								1							1								2		1					
Affray	2		2	1														1													
Arson												1																			
Bigamy																		1						1							
Carrying concealed weapon																		1	1												
Conspiracy	3								2															4							
Cruelty to animals																		1													
Disorderly conduct			4	1																											
Disorderly house																	1														
Disposing of mortgaged property																1														2	
Embezzlement	3								4							1								1							
Failure to list tax											1																				
Fish and game laws	4								4							1														2	
Forcible trespass			3																												
Forgery	2		3						1							1		2													
Fornication and adultery									2	2																					
Gaming and lottery laws	1		1						3									2													
Health laws																		1													
Injury to property																						1				1					
Municipal ordinances																		1												1	
Non-support	4		1						2		3					2								4		3					
Non-support of illegitimate child			1																					1							
Nuisance			1																					1		1					
Perjury	1		5																			1		1							
Rape									1																						
Receiving stolen goods																		2	1												
Resisting officer			1													1		1													
Robbery	1								1		1				1	2															
Slander																		1													
Trespass			1						3		1							1				1									
Worthless check	1								4		1				1	1								2							
False pretense	1		1												1									1		4					
Slot machine laws	1								1															1							
Miscellaneous	3		3						5	1		3				4		1						3		1					
Totals	67		121	10					63	4	33	4			5	80	2	101	6			4		57	1	28				8	

Convictions	198
Nolle pros.	56
Acquittals	42
Other dispositions	11

Convictions	193
Nolle pros.	53
Acquittals	26
Other dispositions	15

SECOND JUDICIAL DISTRICT
IN SUPERIOR COURT

Offense	JULY 1, 1940—JULY 1, 1941 CONVICTIONS	JULY 1, 1940—JULY 1, 1941 OTHER DISPOSITIONS	JULY 1, 1941—JULY 1, 1942 CONVICTIONS	JULY 1, 1941—JULY 1, 1942 OTHER DISPOSITIONS Unclassified F
Assault				----
Assault with ddly weapon				----
Assault on female				----
Assault with intent to kill				----
Assault with intent to pa				----
Assault—secret				----
Drunk and disorderly				----
Possession—illegal whiskey				----
Possession for sale				----
Manufacturing—possession of material for				----
Transportation				----
Vion liquor laws				----
Driving drunk				----
Reckless driving				----
Hit and run				----
Speeding				----
Auto ie violations				----
Vtion otor hle ls				----
Breaking and entering				----
And ny				----
And receiving				----
Housebreaking				----
And larceny				----
And receiving				----
eny				----
Larceny and ing				----
eny from the person				----
Larceny by trick and device				----
Larceny of ai				----
Temporary by				----
Murder—first degree				----
Murder—second degree				----
Manslau hter				----

Abandonment	3								2	2							1										1					
Affray			1	1					1			3					1		1						2						1	1
Arson	1		1									1																				
Bigamy																			2						1							
Carrying [illegible]ed [illegible]n			2	2					3		2																1					
[illegible]			1																													
Conspiracy																											1					
Disorderly conduct			1						1								2								3							
Disorderly house									1						1				1													
Disposing of mortgaged property									1																							
Embezzlement	2			1					1								1		1						1							
Escape			1																													
Failure to list tax															1																	
Fish and game laws	1		2	1					4		1														1							
Forcible trespass	11		8						1								5	2	1								1					
Forgery	10		2						3								9		2						2	1	2	1				
Fornication and adultery			1								1	1					1		1	1												
Gaming and [illegible]ry laws	5		5								13	1							1								4					
[illegible]th laws																											1					
[illegible]			1														1															
[illegible]nry to property	2								3		1														1			1				
Municipal [illegible]es	1								1																3							
Non-support	9		1						4		3						3										1				3	
Non-support of [illegible]mate child			1						1										1						1						2	
Perjury											2						1														1	
[illegible]ion																	1		2							2					2	
Rape																									1		3					
Receiving stolen goods	3		5	1					1		5																1					
Resisting [illegible]r			2						3	4					1										2		2	1				
Robbery	3		9														2		5								5	1				
Seduction			1																						2		1					
Trespass			3						1								2								5							
[illegible]ss check	7		3						3		1					1	7															
False [illegible]e			4						1		3								1						3						1	
Carnal [illegible]e, etc.			4						1								1		2								1				1	
Crime again ts [illegible]e			2																								1				1	
Miscellaneous	2		4						7		1					1	8								2		2					
Totals	232	1	290	13					158	14	122	15			14	3	160	4	156	14					110	8	96	15			23	1

Convictions	536
Nolle pros	221
Acquittals	91
Other dispositions	14
	862

Convictions	334
Nolle pros	180
Acquittals	63
Other dispositions	10
	587

THIRD JUDICIAL DISTRICT

IN SUPERIOR COURT

Offense	JULY 1, 1940—JULY 1, 1941																JULY 1, 1941—JULY 1, 1942															
	CONVICTIONS								OTHER DISPOSITIONS								CONVICTIONS								OTHER DISPOSITIONS							
	White		Negro		Indian		Unclassified		White		Negro		Indian		Unclassified		White		Negro		Indian		Unclassified		White		Negro		Indian		Unclassified	
	M	F	M	F	M	F	M	F	M	F	M	F	M	F	M	F	M	F	M	F	M	F	M	F	M	F	M	F	M	F	M	F
Assault	6	2	6								2								2								1					
Assault with deadly weapon	8		16	2					4		3				1		8		12	2					2		2					
Assault on female	1		2	1													1		2						1		1					
Assault with intent to kill	1		7	1					1										15								1					
Assault with intent to rape			1								1								2													
Assault—secret																											1					
Drunk and disorderly	6	1	4	2					1																2							
Possession—illegal whiskey			1								1								3													
Possession for sale	1		2	2							4						2	1	3	2							1					
Manufacturing—possession of material for	1																		2													
Transportation	4		3																1													
Violation liquor laws	1		1								2						1		1													1
Driving drunk	8		4						4		3								2						3		1					
Reckless driving	1		1								1								2						6	1						
Hit and run	3		5														1		3						1		1					
Speeding	1																															
Auto license violations																			1													
Violation motor vehicle			2																						1							
Breaking and entering	3		13						1		1						2		9						2		1					
And larceny	17		17								6						5		6						4		1					
And receiving	9		2						1		2						3		6								1					
Housebreaking and larceny			2																1								1					
And receiving											1																					
Storebreaking																			1													
Larceny	7		21	2					2		7	3					4		13						2		2	1				
Larceny and receiving	1		2																5	1							1					
Larceny from the person			1								1								5								1					
Larceny of automobile			4						1		2				1		7		5								1					
Murder—first degree			1						3		1	1					3		4						1		2					
Murder—second degree	1		7								1						1		8								1					
Manslaughter	1		3						1			1					4		10	2							2	1				
Burglary—first degree																			2													

Larceny from the person
Larceny of automobile
Murder—first degree
Murder—second degree
Manslaughter
Burglary—first degree

Burglary—second degree			4																												
Abandonment		1							1								1														
Affray			2																7												
Arson															1				1												
Bigamy			3						1		1	1					2		2												
Burning other than arson	1																														
Carrying concealed weapon			2								1						1		3						1						
Conspiracy	7		1														7														
Disorderly conduct	1																		4												
Disorderly house										2																					
Disposing of mortgaged property	3								1																						
Embezzlement	2		1						2		2								1						1		1				
Escape																			1								2				
Failure to list tax	17		24				1	3	143	2	121				81	5	17		34						77		56			20	
Fish and game laws	1																														
Forcible trespass	1		3								3								13	1											
Forgery	5		4								2						7		5						1		1				
Health laws	1																														
Incest			2																1												
Injury to property	2			1					2								1								1						
Non-support	2		1						2		1						2														
Non-support of illegitimate child			3						1		3								3												
Perjury	2	3																													
Prostitution			1																1												
Rape	1		3																2						1						
Receiving stolen goods	1		5	3							1	1					1		7	2							1	1			
Removing crops																									1						
Robbery	1		3						1								1		2								2			1	
Seduction			3						1		3						1		4								1				
Trespass			2								2								1						1						
Usury			1																												
Worthless check	1								1	1																					
False pretense	1		3						1								2														
Carnal knowledge, etc.			3						1		3						1		3						2		1				
Crime against nature			1																												
Slot machine laws	3								1																						
Miscellaneous	2		3						2		2						1			1					2						
Totals	136	7	206	14					180	5	184	7			84	5	87	1	221	11					113	1	88	3			21	1

Convictions	363
Nolle pros.	418
Acquittals	38
Other dispositions	9

Convictions	320
Nolle pros.	190
Acquittals	27
Other dispositions	10

FOURTH JUDICIAL DISTRICT
IN SUPERIOR COURT

JULY 1, 1940—JULY 1, 1941

Offense	Convictions White M	Convictions White F	Convictions Negro M	Convictions Negro F	Convictions Indian M	Convictions Indian F	Convictions Unclassified M	Convictions Unclassified F	Other Dispositions White M	Other Dispositions White F	Other Dispositions Negro M	Other Dispositions Negro F	Other Dispositions Indian M	Other Dispositions Indian F	Other Dispositions Unclassified M	Other Dispositions Unclassified F
Assault	8	2	4								1					
Assault with deadly weapon	20	1	11						2		4	1				
Assault on female	6										1					
Assault with intent to kill	4		16	1								1				
Assault with intent to rape			1						1							
Assault—secret			3						1							
Drunk and disorderly	5	1														
Possession—illegal whiskey	1		1													
Possession for sale	3	1	4													
Manufacturing—possession of material for	6		4						2							
Transportation			1													
Violation liquor laws	6	1	2						3		1					
Driving drunk	21		3						6		2					
Reckless driving	9		2						4		4					
Hit and run	2		1													
Auto [illegible]			1													
Violation motor vehicle laws	1								1							
Breaking and entering	1		2													
And larceny	8		19						3		7					
Housebreaking	2		1													
And larceny	8		22						3	1	2					
Storebreaking	12		3								1					
And [illegible]ry	1		3						2							
Larceny	16	1	12						9		5					
Larceny and receiving			1													
Larceny from the person	2		1													
Larceny of automobile	6		8						1		3					
Petty larceny																
Murder—first degree			3						1	1	6					
Second degree	1	1	7	1												
Manslaughter	2	1	6	2					3		2					
Burglary—first degree											1					

JULY 1, 1941—JULY 1, 1942

Offense	Convictions White M	Convictions White F	Convictions Negro M	Convictions Negro F	Convictions Indian M	Convictions Indian F	Convictions Unclassified M	Convictions Unclassified F	Other Dispositions White M	Other Dispositions White F	Other Dispositions Negro M	Other Dispositions Negro F	Other Dispositions Indian M	Other Dispositions Indian F	Other Dispositions Unclassified M	Other Dispositions Unclassified F
Assault	5		*10	1					5		2					
Assault with deadly weapon	21		12	2					5		2				1	
Assault on female	6		2						2							
Assault with intent to kill	4		20	2			1		3		4					
Assault with intent to rape	1		2						1							
Assault—secret				1												
Drunk and disorderly	1		2						1							
Possession—illegal whiskey	3		4							1	1					
Possession for sale	1	1	1													
Manufacturing—possession of material for	3		3													
Transportation			1													
Violation liquor laws	20	1	8	5												
Driving drunk	19		2						8		1					
Reckless driving	1		3						6							
Hit and run	2		1													
Auto [illegible]																
Violation motor vehicle laws																
Breaking and entering	7		3								1					
And larceny	9		2						4		1					
Housebreaking	2		1													
And larceny	19		24						3		3					
Storebreaking																
And [illegible]ry																
Larceny	15	2	26						3		3					
Larceny and receiving	4		5						1		1				2	
Larceny from the person			2													
Larceny of automobile	15		5						1							
Petty larceny			1													
Murder—first degree	2		1						1		6	1				
Second degree	1		4								2					
Manslaughter	6	1	3						5							
Burglary—first degree			1													

Abandonment	8								2								3								4		1					
Affray																									1							
Arson																									1							
Bigamy	1																								1							
Burning other than arson	1			1					1																							
Carrying concealed weapon																	1		2													
[illegible]cy	1										1																					
Disorderly conduct	1																3												1			
Disposing of mortgaged property	1								1																1		1					
[illegible]ion of [illegible]ion laws	1																															
Embezzlement									4						1		4		2						5							
Escape	2																															
Forcible trespass	3																2		3				1									
Forgery	4		4									1					26	2	3												1	
Fornication and adultery	1	1	1																	1					1							
Gaming and lottery laws	3								2																							
Health laws																	1								1							
Incest																	1															
Injury to property	1										1								1									1				
Non-support	4		2						1								1								2		1					
Non-support of illegitimate child	2								1		2						2		1													
[illegible]									1	1																						
[illegible]ion				1													1	1														
Rape											1								1													
Receiving stolen goods	3		2	1					1		1						4		1						1							
Removing crop																	1								1							
Resisting officer	2	1							1								1		1													
Robbery	4		8								2						5		8						2		5					
Seduction	2																1		1													
Trespass			2						1																1							
Worthless checks			1						1								3															
False pretense	4			1					1								1		1						3							
Carnal knowledge, etc.	1		1						1								1		2						1							
Crime against nature	1		2								1						1															
Slot machine laws							55																									
Miscellaneous	5								1				4				5	1							1		1	1				
Totals	207	11	165	8			55		62	3	49	3	4		1		235	9	176	12			2		76	1	36	3	1		4	

Convictions	446
Nolle pros	64
Acquittals	43
Other dispositions	15
	568

Convictions	434
Nolle pros	67
Acquittals	32
Other dispositions	22
	555

FIFTH JUDICIAL DISTRICT

IN SUPERIOR COURT

JULY 1, 1940—JULY 1, 1941

Offense	Convictions White M	Convictions White F	Convictions Negro M	Convictions Negro F	Convictions Indian M	Convictions Indian F	Convictions Unclassified M	Convictions Unclassified F	Other Dispositions White M	Other Dispositions White F	Other Dispositions Negro M	Other Dispositions Negro F	Other Dispositions Indian M	Other Dispositions Indian F	Other Dispositions Unclassified M	Other Dispositions Unclassified F
Assault	11		2						8							
Assault and battery			1													
Assault with deadly weapon	11		18	1					6		3					
Assault on female	3		5								1					
Assault with intent to kill	1		3						2							
Assault with intent to rape	3		3													
Assault—secret	1		1													
Drunk and disorderly	2								2							
Possession—illegal whiskey	2		2								2					
Possession for sale	3		6	2							4					
Manufacturing—possession of material for			2													
Transportation	1		1													
Violation liquor laws	6		8						2		2					
Driving drunk	24		4						3		2					
Reckless driving	4		4						8		3					
Hit and run	6		1													
Auto [illegible]									1							
Breaking and entering	8		27						1		3					
And larceny	10		6						1							
And receiving	1															
Larceny	12		58						7		11					
Larceny and receiving																
Larceny from the person			1													
Larceny of automobile			1													
Murder—first degree																
Murder—second degree	1		9	1							4					
Manslaughter	4		5	1					2							
Burglary—second degree			3													

JULY 1, 1941—JULY 1, 1942

Offense	Convictions White M	Convictions White F	Convictions Negro M	Convictions Negro F	Convictions Indian M	Convictions Indian F	Convictions Unclassified M	Convictions Unclassified F	Other Dispositions White M	Other Dispositions White F	Other Dispositions Negro M	Other Dispositions Negro F	Other Dispositions Indian M	Other Dispositions Indian F	Other Dispositions Unclassified M	Other Dispositions Unclassified F
Assault	3		2						3							
Assault and battery																
Assault with deadly weapon	4		19	2												
Assault on female	4		4													
Assault with intent to kill	2		7	1					3							
Assault with intent to rape	1		4						1		2					
Assault—secret	2															
Drunk and disorderly																
Possession—illegal whiskey																
Possession for sale			2													
Manufacturing—possession of material for																
Transportation																
Violation liquor laws	7		1	3							3					
Driving drunk	16		8						8		3					
Reckless driving	2		5						2							
Hit and run	1		2													
Auto [illegible]	2	1							1							
Breaking and entering	3		22								5					
And larceny	5		5								3					
And receiving																
Larceny	12		18	2					6		8					
Larceny and receiving	2		4													
Larceny from the person																
Larceny of automobile	1															
Murder—first degree	1															
Murder—second degree	1		6	1												
Manslaughter	1		1						1							
Burglary—second degree			2													

Abandonment	4		1						4								1		2						1							
Arson																											1					
[illegible] other than arson	2								1										1								1					
Carrying concealed [illegible]			3						1								3		6						1		1					
Conspiracy									2	1																						
[illegible]ty to animals			1																													
Disorderly conduct	1		1																													
Disturbing [illegible] [illegible]hip																	1															
Embezzlement	2								2								1								1		1					
Fish and [illegible]									1																		1					
F[illegible]	3										1																					
Forgery	2																1		1													
Fornication and [illegible]			2																													
Gaming and [illegible]	9		3																								1					
Injury to property									1		1																1					
[illegible]	2		2								1						1								1							
[illegible]rt of [illegible] child			1								2						1		2													
Nuisance	2																															
Receiving stolen goods			3																1													
Resisting officer	1																		1						1							
[illegible]bbery	2		2																12						1		5					
Seduction									3		1						1		1													
Slander																											1					
Trespass	1		1						2								2		1						3							
Worthless [illegible]	10								12	1	2						5										2					
False pretense	1								3																1		2					
Carnal knowledge, [illegible]	1		1						1																							
Crime against nature																	1															
Slot machine [illegible]									10																							
Kidnapping									1																							
Miscellaneous	1	1							5	1																	1					
Totals	158	1	192	5					92	3	43						88	1	140	9					35		42					

Convictions	356
Nolle pros	85
Acquittals	40
Other dispositions	13
	494

Convictions	238
Nolle pros	44
Acquittals	21
Other dispositions	12
	315

SIXTH JUDICIAL DISTRICT

IN SUPERIOR COURT

JULY 1, 1940—JULY 1, 1941

Offense	CONVICTIONS White M	White F	Negro M	Negro F	Indian M	Indian F	Unclassified M	Unclassified F	OTHER DISPOSITIONS White M	White F	Negro M	Negro F	Indian M	Indian F	Unclassified M	Unclassified F
Assault		1							2		1					
Assault with deadly weapon	13		18	2					2		10					
Assault on female			2						1		1					
Assault with intent to kill			9	1							2					
Assault with intent to rape			2						1		2					
Assault—secret				1												
Drunk and disorderly	2		4						2							
Possession—illegal whiskey	3	1	2	1					3		3					
Possession for sale	3		13	1					2		2					
Manufacturing—possession of material for	4		5						3		1					
Transportation									5		1					
Violation liquor laws		1														
Driving drunk	11		4						1		2					
Reckless driving	2								6		4					
Hit and run	1		1								1					
Speeding																
Auto license laws			1													
Violation motor vehicle laws																
Breaking and entering	1		7										1			
And larceny	3		5													
And receiving											1					
Housebreaking			2													
And larceny	2		4								1					
And receiving	1															
Storebreaking																
And larceny									2							
And receiving	4		6						2		1					
Larceny	8	1	8						7	1	6	2				
Larceny and receiving	3		4						1		3					
Larceny from the person	1		2													

JULY 1, 1941—JULY 1, 1942

Offense	CONVICTIONS White M	White F	Negro M	Negro F	Indian M	Indian F	Unclassified M	Unclassified F	OTHER DISPOSITIONS White M	White F	Negro M	Negro F	Indian M	Indian F	Unclassified M	Unclassified F
Assault											2					
Assault with deadly weapon	14		21	2					7		5				1	
Assault on female	1		1						2							
Assault with intent to kill	5		7						4		5					
Assault with intent to rape	1		1								2					
Assault—secret	1								1							
Drunk and disorderly	3															
Possession—illegal whiskey	4		5						2							
Possession for sale	6		9	2					3		4	1				
Manufacturing—possession of material for	3		5						2							
Transportation	1		1													
Violation liquor laws																
Driving drunk	41		7						15				1			
Reckless driving	11		4						5		1					
Hit and run	1		3													
Speeding	1															
Auto license laws	3								1							
Violation motor vehicle laws			3													
Breaking and entering	1		3						2							
And larceny	14		6								4		1			
And receiving																
Housebreaking																
And larceny									3		2					
And receiving											1					
Storebreaking	3								3							
And larceny			2						1							
And receiving																
Larceny	11		19	1					9		20		2			
Larceny and receiving	4		2	1					3		2					
Larceny from the person	1		5	1					1		2					

Larceny of automobile	1																8		5						3							
Temporary larceny	2																3								1		1					
First degree									3		4	2													7		2					
Murder—second degree	3		7	2													4		2	1												
Manslaughter			2						4		2						5		1						3							
Burglary—first degree			1																3						2							
Burglary—second degree			3																3													
Abandonment	3								2																6							
[illegible]																	1															
Affray			1								2																					
Bigamy																				1	1						1					
Burning other than arson									1																1							
Carrying concealed weapon	3		2						1										5								1					
Conspiracy																									2							
Disorderly conduct	1		1						1																							
Disorderly house																				1												
Disposing of mortgaged property									1								2								1							
Disturbing religious worship			1																													
Embezzlement	2								2								2								2							
Escape																			1													
Failure to list tax									71		26																					
Fish and game laws										1																						
Forcible trespass	1								1								4		4						1							
Forgery	9		6						1	1	1						4								1		2					
Fornication and adultery			1																						1		2	1				
Gaming and lottery laws																			2													
Incest									1		1														1							
Injury to property																	4		1								2					
Municipal ordinances																									1							
Non-support	1								2		1						1								5							
Non-support of illegitimate child	1		1																1						2		2					
Nuisance			1								1																					
Official misconduct									1																							
Prostitution			2															3														
Rape									1		1						2								1							
Receiving stolen goods	1								1										1								2					
Removing crop											1																					
Resisting officer	1								1		1						1		3													
Robbery	1										2								3								2					

SIXTH JUDICIAL DISTRICT—(Continued)

IN SUPERIOR COURT

JULY 1, 1940—JULY 1, 1941

Offense	CONVICTIONS								OTHER DISPOSITIONS							
	White		Negro		Indian		Unclas-sified		White		Negro		Indian		Unclas-sified	
	M	F	M	F	M	F	M	F	M	F	M	F	M	F	M	F
Seduction	1								2		1					
Trespass	1								2		1					
Worthless check									1							
False pretense	1								2		2					
Carnal knowledge, etc.	2		1						1		2					
Kidnapping																
Miscellaneous	3		1						5		1					
Totals	100	4	130	8					148	3	92	4	1			

JULY 1, 1941—JULY 1, 1942

Offense	CONVICTIONS								OTHER DISPOSITIONS							
	White		Negro		Indian		Unclas-sified		White		Negro		Indian		Unclas-sified	
	M	F	M	F	M	F	M	F	M	F	M	F	M	F	M	F
Seduction									1							
Trespass									1							
Worthless check	4		1						1							
False pretense	1		4						3							
Carnal knowledge, etc.									2		1					
Kidnapping	1		2						1							
Miscellaneous	1		2						4		2	1				
Totals	178	3	148	10	1				118		70	3	4		1	

JULY 1, 1940—JULY 1, 1941

Convictions	242
Nolle pros	52
Acquittals	69
Other dispositions	127
	490

JULY 1, 1941—JULY 1, 1942

Convictions	340
Nolle pros	123
Acquittals	58
Other dispositions	15
	536

SEVENTH JUDICIAL DISTRICT

IN SUPERIOR COURT

Offense	JULY 1, 1940—JULY 1, 1941																JULY 1, 1941—JULY 1, 1942															
	CONVICTIONS								OTHER DISPOSITIONS								CONVICTIONS								OTHER DISPOSITIONS							
	White		Negro		Indian		Unclassified		White		Negro		Indian		Unclassified		White		Negro		Indian		Unclassified		White		Negro		Indian		Unclassified	
	M	F	M	F	M	F	M	F	M	F	M	F	M	F	M	F	M	F	M	F	M	F	M	F	M	F	M	F	M	F	M	F
Assault	1		2																1	1					1							
Assault with deadly weapon	10		25				5		1						2		4		12				1		2		1					
Assault on female	1		7																								1					
Assault with intent to kill	4		8				4				1				1				5								2				1	
Assault with intent to rape	1		3																													
Assault—secret			1																													
Drunk and disorderly	3		1														1	1														
Possession—illegal whiskey	1		2				1								3		1		4	4											1	
Possession for sale																	1											1				
Manufacturing—possession of material for			1														3															
Transportation			1																													
Driving drunk	7		2				2		3		1						5		3				1		3		1				1	
Reckless driving	7		2				1				2				3		4	1	2													
Hit and run	1		2																1													
Violation motor vehicle laws			1														1		3												1	
Breaking and entering	2		1				2												3													
And larceny			5				3																									
And receiving	7		1				4								2				1													
Housebreaking																	1		5													
And larceny	6		20				5				1				1		7		29								12					
Storebreaking and larceny																	2		7						1		5					
Larceny	2		7	1				1									2	1	6						1							
Larceny and receiving	23		34	3			5		10		2				6		16		10						6	1	3				2	
Larceny from the person	1						1										1		9								2				1	
Larceny of automobile	1		2														9		17								2					
Petty larceny	1																1										1					
Murder—second degree	2		1	2			2										1		9													
Manslaughter	4		12	1			2								1		1		2	1					3			1			1	
Burglary first degree																											1					

Abandonment	3						1										2		1													
Abduction	1																															
Arson																											2					
Bigamy	1	1	1														1															
[illegible]ing concealed weapon			1				2												1								1					
[illegible]cy									3																							
[illegible]lty to animals																	1															
Disorderly [illegible]	1	3	1				2	1		3																						
Disorderly house	1																	2								3	1					
Disposing of mortgaged property	3		1				1		1						1		1															
Violation of [illegible]ion laws	1	3									2														1							
Embezzlement	1		1												1		12		5	1					3						1	
Escape	1								1																							
[illegible]ire to list tax							349								195																1	
Forcible trespass	2		2				1										4		2													
Forgery	26	5	10	5											1		13		2				1		1		1					
Fornication and adultery		1																							1	1						
Incest																	1										1					
Non-support	2																1								2							
Non-support of [illegible]e child	1																2		1												1	
Nuisance																									1							
Perjury															6																	
Rape															1										1							
Receiving [illegible]en goods	8		2				5	1	8										7													
Resisting officer			1														1		1													
Robbery	3		11				2											1	10						1		6					
Worthless ch[illegible]ck	9														1		2		1								1					
False pretense	1		2												2		2		7												1	
[illegible]al [illegible]ge, [illegible]	1		3												1		1		1													
Crime against nature	5																															
Slot [illegible]ine laws	1						129	1	1						23	3	1								2						1	
Revenue act violations							11								1																	
[illegible]			5				9	1							5		1										1	1			1	
Totals	157	13	182	12			549	5	28	3	9				257	3	107	6	168	7			3		30	5	45	3			14	

Convictions	918
Nolle pros	282
Acquittals	13
Other dispositions	5
	1,218

Convictions	291
Nolle pros	84
Acquittals	7
Other dispositions	6
	388

EIGHTH JUDICIAL DISTRICT

IN SUPERIOR COURT

Offense	JULY 1, 1940—JULY 1, 1941																JULY 1, 1941—JULY 1, 1942															
	CONVICTIONS								OTHER DISPOSITIONS								CONVICTIONS								OTHER DISPOSITIONS							
	White		Negro		Indian		Unclassified		White		Negro		Indian		Unclassified		White		Negro		Indian		Unclassified		White		Negro		Indian		Unclassified	
	M	F	M	F	M	F	M	F	M	F	M	F	M	F	M	F	M	F	M	F	M	F	M	F	M	F	M	F	M	F	M	F
Assault	6		1						2	1	1						6								2		1					
Assault with deadly weapon	4		23	3			1		6		6				1		10	1	12						9		6	2				
Assault on female	4		9						5		4						7		4						1		1					
Assault with intent to kill	3		11						2		2	1					3		12								3					
Assault with intent to rape			1								1				1				5						1							
Assault—secret																			1													
Drunk and disorderly	18	1	4						15								21								8		1					
Possession—illegal whiskey	2		4																5	1					1	1	1					
Possession for sale	5		4						3		1	1					1		6	1					1		3	1				
Manufacturing—possession of material for	4		2								2						1		2						4							
Transportation	2		14	2					3										3													
Violation liquor laws			3						2		5	3					3		10	5					1		7	5				
Driving drunk	15		4						15		6						9		1						11		4	1			1	
Reckless driving	2		3		1				4		2						3		1						4		2					
Hit and run	4		3								1						2		4	2							1					
Speeding																											1					
Auto license violations	1								1		1						1								1							
Violation motor vehicle laws																			1						2			1				
Breaking and entering	7		14						2				2						4													
And larceny	5		8						3								4								2		2					
And receiving	18		1														1										1					
Housebreaking																			4						1		1					
And larceny	1																1		1								5	1				
And receiving	22		16						1		8								1								1					
Storebreaking	2		2														1		2													
And larceny																			3						2							
And receiving	10	1	4														3		21						1		4					
Larceny	8		11						2								2		7						7	2	3	2				
Larceny and receiving	13		4	1													5		4	2					3		3					

Larceny from the person												2																				
Larceny by trick and device	4																															
Larceny of [illegible]	6		6														11		5						5							
Temporary larceny			1														1															
Murder—first degree			2								5				2		3								1		4					
Murder—second degree	1		10						1		2	2							4	1							2					
Manslaughter	1		4	2							1						1		5	3					3		3				1	
Burglary—second degree			2														1		3								3					
Abandonment	3								3								1		1						2							
Abduction																											1					
Affray									1											1												
Arson			1																	1					2		1					
Bigamy	1		1							1									1	2							1				1	
[illegible] other than [illegible]									3																							
Carrying [illegible] weapon			1																													
[illegible]cy	4	1							1																							
Disorderly [illegible]	3								2		1						2		1						1		1					
Disorderly [illegible]																	2		4								1					
Disposing of mortgaged property																	1								1							
Embezzlement									1								1		1						2							
Escape																			1													
Fish and game laws									1																3							
Forcible [illegible]	2								1	1							7		9						1							
Forgery	5		4						3		3						8		4	1					1		1					
Fornication and [illegible]									1			1					1	1	2	1					1	1	3	1				
Gaming and lottery laws			2	2															1													
Health laws																	1			1												
I[illegible]st																	1															
Injury to property	1		1						1		1						1										3					
[illegible]al ordinances																	1								1							
Non-support	1														2		2		2						3							
Non-support of illegitimate child																	2															
Nuisance		1		1					1		1						2									1						
[illegible]ial misconduct																									1							
Perjury			2						5			2					1										1					
[illegible]ion																	1	7	2	9					1		2	2				
[illegible]pe			1								1														1		1					
Receiving stolen goods	7		5							2		2					4		10						1							
Resisting [illegible]	1								1										1				1		2							
Robbery	7		18	2	4				4		5				1				12						5		3					

EIGHTH JUDICIAL DISTRICT—(Continued)

IN SUPERIOR COURT

Offense	JULY 1, 1940—JULY 1, 1941																JULY 1, 1941—JULY 1, 1942															
	CONVICTIONS								OTHER DISPOSITIONS								CONVICTIONS								OTHER DISPOSITIONS							
	White		Negro		Indian		Unclas-sified		White		Negro		Indian		Unclas-sified		White		Negro		Indian		Unclas-sified		White		Negro		Indian		Unclas-sified	
	M	F	M	F	M	F	M	F	M	F	M	F	M	F	M	F	M	F	M	F	M	F	M	F	M	F	M	F	M	F	M	F
Seduction	1								1																							
Slander	1		1																													
Trespass											1														1	3						
Vagrancy									1	1	1															3						
Worthless check	2								1								3															
False pretense	1										2								1						5							
Carnal knowledge, etc.	1		1																						1							
Crime against nature	1																		2													
Slot machine laws	1								1																							
Kidnapping																	2															
Miscellaneous	2		2						4		1						4	1	1						1		6	1				
Totals	213	4	211	13	5		1		104	14	57	14	2		7		149	10	187	31			1		108	11	88	17			3	

	July 1, 1940—July 1, 1941
Convictions	447
Nolle pros.	69
Acquittals	77
Other dispositions	52
	645

	July 1, 1941—July 1, 1942
Convictions	378
Nolle pros.	93
Acquittals	112
Other dispositions	22
	605

NINTH JUDICIAL DISTRICT

IN SUPERIOR COURT

Offense	JULY 1, 1940—JULY 1, 1941																JULY 1, 1941—JULY 1, 1942															
	CONVICTIONS								OTHER DISPOSITIONS								CONVICTIONS								OTHER DISPOSITIONS							
	White		Negro		Indian		Unclassified		White		Negro		Indian		Unclassified		White		Negro		Indian		Unclassified		White		Negro		Indian		Unclassified	
	M	F	M	F	M	F	M	F	M	F	M	F	M	F	M	F	M	F	M	F	M	F	M	F	M	F	M	F	M	F	M	F
Assault	6		5	3	4				6		8	2					7		6	2	1				5	1	5	1			1	
Assault and battery	1																															
Assault with deadly weapon	14	2	14	3	11		1		7		8	2	9	2			14	1	21	2	14				4	1	4	1		2	1	
Assault on female	3		5						1		1						5		2						3							
Assault with intent to kill	5		7						3		5						4		5	1							4					
Assault with intent to rape	2		4						1		1						1		1								2		1			
Assault—secret			1						1		1										1								1			
Drunk and disorderly	10		3						3	1			3				1		1								1					
Possession—illegal whiskey	5		2	2	3	1											1	1	4		5								1			
Possession for sale	2										2		2																			
Manufacturing—possession of material for			2		2	1											1				1				1							
Transportation																			1													
Violation liquor laws	2		2	1	3				1	1	1		1				8								1		1					
Driving drunk	14		1				1		5		2						11		3				1		5	1	1				2	
Reckless driving	7		2				1		3								4		1						1		3				2	
Hit and run	3		1						1		1							1	1								2					
Speeding																											1					
Auto lice[illegible] [illegible]ns																	1		2													
[illegible]ion [illegible]or vehicle laws	3		1		3				2										1												1	
[illegible]ing and entering	8		8		1				2		2				1	1	8		15		1				1		3		1		1	
And larceny	8		23						2		15		2				7		23		4						1		3			
And receiving			2						1																							
Housebreaking	1		1																													
And [illegible]y											1								1													
Storebreaking and larceny																	3															
And [illegible]ng			1																													
Larceny	25	1	23	3	1		2	1	9	1	17				4		22		28	3	8				12		12		1			
Larceny and [illegible]ng	2		3	1							4		2		1		6		4						1							
[illegible]ny from the person	1											1					1		1						1							

NINTH JUDICIAL DISTRICT—(Continued)

IN SUPERIOR COURT

Offense	JULY 1, 1940—JULY 1, 1941																JULY 1, 1941—JULY 1, 1942															
	CONVICTIONS								OTHER DISPOSITIONS								CONVICTIONS								OTHER DISPOSITIONS							
	White		Negro		Indian		Unclassified		White		Negro		Indian		Unclassified		White		Negro		Indian		Unclassified		White		Negro		Indian		Unclassified	
	M	F	M	F	M	F	M	F	M	F	M	F	M	F	M	F	M	F	M	F	M	F	M	F	M	F	M	F	M	F	M	F
Larceny by trick and device	1		1	1							2														1							
Larceny of automobile	10		4									2							1						1		3					
[illegible]			1														1		4								1					
Murder—first degree									9		3	2			3		1		1						5		1					
Murder—second degree	2		8	3	5				1								2		9	2	3				1		1					
Manslaughter	8	1	8	1	3				2		2		1		1		3		10		1				3	1	6		1	1		
Burglary—first degree			1																						1		1					
Burglary—second degree	1		3																5		4											
Abandonment	5								2								3								2	1			1		1	
[illegible]																	1															
Affray									1																							
Arson									3								1								1		4					
Bigamy	2	1		1	1				1								3		1						2							
Bribery															1																	
Burning other than arson					2								1																			
Carrying concealed weapons	1		3		1				1		1						2		1								2					
Conspiracy																	3				8								1			
Cruelty to animals			1								1																					
Disorderly conduct									1								1															
Disorderly house									2	1		3				1	2	1	1						1							
Disposing of mortgaged property	1								2																							
Disturbing religious worship			1																													
Embezzlement	1								3						1										4						1	
Escape	1																		1													
Fish and game laws	1								6								5									4						
Forcible trespass	4	1	6				1		1						1	1	7		6													
Forgery	7		4		1				1		1	1					2		4						2							
Fornication and adultery	1	2	2	1	3				3				1	1		1			1								1	1				
Gaming and lottery laws	6																1															
Injury to property											3						2		1								3		1			

Municipal [redacted]s							1		1																							
Non-support	3				1																				1						1	
Non-support of illegitimate child	3						1		1								4		1													
[redacted]			1						1																							
Perjury	2				1								1				3								1							
Prostitution		1															3	5			3	5			2	1		1				
Rape									1				1														2					
Receiving stolen goods	2										2						1		1		4											
Removing crop																					1						1					
Resisting officer			1	1	2																				1							
Robbery	9		16		2				3		5		1				13		16	1	3				3	1	3	1			1	
Seduction	2		1						1		1				1								1								1	
Trespass	1								1		1		1												1	1					1	
Vagrancy	1																															
Worthless check									4						4												1					
False [redacted]	3								1								4				1				2		1		1		2	
[redacted]nal knowledge, etc.	1		1		1				1						1				2										1			
Crime against nature	2								3								2		1													
Slot machine laws	3								6								1															
Miscellaneous	5				1				5				2		1		1		2			1					1					
Totals	211	9	174	21	52	2	8	1	116	4	91	13	28	3	20	4	177	9	190	11	63	6	2		70	12	72	5	14	3	16	

Convictions	478
Nolle pros	115
Acquittals	105
Other dispositions	59
	757

Convictions	458
Nolle pros	73
Acquittals	92
Other dispositions	27
	650

TENTH JUDICIAL DISTRICT

IN SUPERIOR COURT

Offense	JULY 1, 1940—JULY 1, 1941																JULY 1, 1941—JULY 1, 1942															
	CONVICTIONS								OTHER DISPOSITIONS								CONVICTIONS								OTHER DISPOSITIONS							
	White		Negro		Indian		Unclas-sified		White		Negro		Indian		Unclas-sified		White		Negro		Indian		Unclas-sified		White		Negro		Indian		Unclas-sified	
	M	F	M	F	M	F	M	F	M	F	M	F	M	F	M	F	M	F	M	F	M	F	M	F	M	F	M	F	M	F	M	F
Assault			5						1	1	12						2		2	1					2		2					
Assault and battery	1		2						2	3							2		2								2					
Assault with deadly weapon	13		28	4					6		11						10		14	1	1				2		6	2				
Assault on female	3		9								3						3		1						2							
Assault with intent to kill	5		7						1		1								6						2		2					
Assault with intent to rape	2		1						1								1		4								2					
Assault—secret	1																								2		1					
Drunk and disorderly	15		2	2					4								8	2	1	1					1							
Possession—illegal liquor	3		7	1													5	1	10	2					1			1				
Possession for sale	6		2						10	1	6	3					5		9	1					4	1	3	1				
Manufacturing—possession of material for	1								1		1						1		1													
Transportation			4						1								1										1					
Violation liquor laws	1								3		1																					
Driving drunk	38	2	7						13								30		3						10		2					
Reckless driving	9		8						11			1					4		2						13		3					
Hit and run	3		4						2		1						1															
[illegible]	1	1															1															
Auto license violations																	1															
Violation motor vehicle laws	1								2		1						3								2							
Breaking and entering	7		2						8	1							3		4						3		1					
And larceny	11		10						6								3		11	1					1							
And receiving																	3								1							
Housebreaking			2								1								3													
And larceny	2	1	2								1						4		16													
And receiving	2		3								1																					
Storebreaking			2														1		2													
And larceny	1		6								8	2					6		5													
And receiving	4		11								1								2								2					

Larceny	44		27	2					16	3	4	2					25	1	23	1			1		3		7	1				
Larceny and receiving			3																													
Larceny from the person			4						1								3		5						2		5	3				
Larceny by trick and device																			1													
Larceny of [illegible]	3		3						4								5		2						2							
Temporary larceny			1								1								1						2							
Murder—first degree	1									1	6						1								1		1					
Second degree	1		3														2		4													
Manslaughter			6	4					4								1		7	1					7	1	2					
Abandonment									2								1															
Affray			2	1							1								2						1							
Arson				1					1																		1					
Bigamy																	2		1													
Bribery																			1													
Burning other than arson																									2							
Carrying concealed weapon	4		2						3										1													
Conspiracy									1	1																						
[illegible]	1		3														6								9							
Disorderly house	1										1								1	3							1					
Disturbing religious worship	1																															
Embezzlement	2		1									1					5		1						1							
Escape	1										1								1													
Failure to list tax																	7		12								1					
Forcible trespass	3		3														2		1								1					
Forgery	24	1	6														3		13	42							1					
Fornication and adultery	3	1																														
Gaming and lottery laws	1		2						1		1								2								1					
Health laws	1																															
Incest																									1							
Injury to property	1	1	2						1			1					1		2						4		1					
Municipal ordinances																	1		1	1					3							
Non-support	1		4						1					8		1									2		1					
Non-support of illegitimate child	1		4								1						2		3								1					
Nuisance		1								1																						
Perjury	1		1						1																1							
Prostitution		1	1						1			2					1															
Rape									1		1								1								1					
Receiving stolen goods	2		3														3		1						1	2						
Resisting officer	4																		1													

TENTH JUDICIAL DISTRICT—(Continued)

IN SUPERIOR COURT

JULY 1, 1940—JULY 1, 1941

Offense	CONVICTIONS White M	White F	Negro M	Negro F	Indian M	Indian F	Unclassified M	Unclassified F	OTHER DISPOSITIONS White M	White F	Negro M	Negro F	Indian M	Indian F	Unclassified M	Unclassified F
Robbery	5		6						3		1					
Seduction																
Slander																
Trespass		1	3													
Vagrancy	1															
Worthless heck	4								6							
False [illegible]e									6		2					
[illegible]al [illegible]e, etc.			3						1							
[illegible]e against nature			1						1							
Slot machine a[illegible]s	3		1						1							
[illegible]s	3	2	7	1					4	3	2					
Totals	247	12	226	16					132	15	71	12				

JULY 1, 1941—JULY 1, 1942

Offense	CONVICTIONS White M	White F	Negro M	Negro F	Indian M	Indian F	Unclassified M	Unclassified F	OTHER DISPOSITIONS White M	White F	Negro M	Negro F	Indian M	Indian F	Unclassified M	Unclassified F
Robbery	2		5						1		5					
Seduction			2													
Slander	1								1		1					
Trespass			2						3							
Vagrancy																
Worthless heck									3							
False [illegible]e	3	1							4							
[illegible]al [illegible]e, etc.	2		1						2							
[illegible]e against nature																
Slot machine a[illegible]s									1							
[illegible]s	3		4						12	1	1	1				
Totals	188	5	201	55	1		1		115	5	59	9				

July 1, 1940—July 1, 1941

Convictions	501
Nolle pros	120
Acquittals	67
Other dispositions	43
	731

July 1, 1941—July 1, 1942

Convictions	451
Nolle pros	73
Acquittals	83
Other dispositions	32
	639

ELEVENTH JUDICIAL DISTRICT

IN SUPERIOR COURT

Offense	JULY 1, 1940—JULY 1, 1941																JULY 1, 1941—JULY 1, 1942															
	CONVICTIONS								OTHER DISPOSITIONS								CONVICTIONS								OTHER DISPOSITIONS							
	White		Negro		Indian		Unclassified		White		Negro		Indian		Unclassified		White		Negro		Indian		Unclassified		White		Negro		Indian		Unclassified	
	M	F	M	F	M	F	M	F	M	F	M	F	M	F	M	F	M	F	M	F	M	F	M	F	M	F	M	F	M	F	M	F
Assault	7		1						4								3	2	2													
Assault with deadly weapon	10	1	23	4					1			2					7		12	4					2		3					
Assault on female	5		3								2						1		6								1					
Assault with intent to kill	2		15	3							2	1							1	2					1							
Assault with intent to rape	3		4																2													
Drunk and disorderly	3																7	1	1	1												
Possession for sale																	1															
Manufacturing—possession of material for	2																		1								1					
Violation liquor laws	42	6	30	7					11		4						19	2	35	9					6	1	10					
Driving drunk	31		9						5								16		6						2	1						
Reckless driving	12		4						4		1						10		7	1					6		1					
Hit and run	3								1								3		3						1							
Speeding	2																3		1						1							
Auto license [illegible]																	2															
Violation motor vehicle laws	2		2														2		1													
Breaking and entering	12		3								1						3															
And larceny	20		2														1															
Housebreaking			4														1		2													
And larceny																	2															
And entering	2		33	7					2		1						6		28	1							2					
Storebreaking	2		2								1						1		1													
And larceny																	1		1													
And entering	13		37	1					1		3						28		47	1					1		3					
Larceny	24	2	35	1					2		4	1					18	1	29	3					6		4	1				
Larceny and receiving									5								1		1													
Larceny from the person	2		4	1						1	6						2		15	5												
Larceny by trick and device	1																															
Murder—first degree									2																	1						
Murder—second degree	3		10	3													1		4													
Manslaughter	4		2	1					3								3		3						4	1		1				
Burglary—second degree			6																3													

Abandonment																	1															
Arson									1																							
Bigamy	1		1	1													2		2	1												
Carrying concealed weap on	2		2	1					2								4		2													
Conspiracy									2																							
Disorderly [illegible]duct	1																															
[illegible]dy h[illegible]e		2	4						2								3		3	3							1					
Disturbing religious worship	1																															
Embezzlement	5		3						1		2						5		2						3			1				
Fish and game laws									3																							
Forcible [illegible]ss	1		1														1															
Forgery	20		3														15		5						1							
Fornication and adultery		2	5	2													1	1	3	2												
[illegible]ing and [illegible]ry [illegible]s	3	1	17	1							2						8		20						2		2	1				
[illegible]st										1																						
[illegible]ury to property	3																															
Municipal ordinances																	1										4					
Non-support	7		5						2								7		2								2					
Non-support of illegitimate child	7		7														5		3								3					
Nuisance	2																		1	1							1					
Perjury									4																							
Prostitution			1														1	2	2								1					
Rape									1										2													
Receiving stolen goods	1		2						1								2	2														
Resisting officer	2		1								1						3		2													
Robbery	5		5	2													3		11	1							2					
Seduction	1																3															
Trespass											1																					
Vagrancy	1	1	1							3	1						1		2	1					1			2				
False [illegible]e	5	3	2														4	3	3	2						1						
Carnal [illegible]e, etc.	1																1															
[illegible]e against [illegible]e	1		3						1										1													
Slot machine laws	4																															
[illegible] [illegible]ous	2		2	2													5	2	6	3					1		1					
[illegible]ls	283	18	294	37					61	5	32	4					218	16	284	41					38	5	42	6				

Convictions	632
Nolle pros	11
Acquittals	67
Other dispositions	24
	734

Convictions	559
Nolle pros	26
Acquittals	45
Other dispositions	20
	650

Offense	JULY 1, 1940—JULY 1, 1941																JULY 1, 1941—JULY 1, 1942															
	CONVICTIONS								OTHER DISPOSITIONS								CONVICTIONS								OTHER DISPOSITIONS							
	White		Negro		Indian		Unclassified		White		Negro		Indian		Unclassified		White		Negro		Indian		Unclassified		White		Negro		Indian		Unclassified	
	M	F	M	F	M	F	M	F	M	F	M	F	M	F	M	F	M	F	M	F	M	F	M	F	M	F	M	F	M	F	M	F
Assault	1		1								1						3		1													
Assault with deadly weapon	13	1	23	10					1		5						14		9	6					3		4					
Assault on female	6		12						1		2						10		6													
Assault with intent to kill	1		3	1					2						1		2		9	1					1		3					
Assault with intent to rape	1		1						1								6		1								1					
Drunk and disorderly	38		8	2					2						1		28	2	11	1					3							
Possession—illegal [illegible]	1		1						1								3		1													
Possession for sale	5	1	8	2					2		4	1					2		4	3					2		1					
Manufacturing—possession of material for	1																															
Transportation	1		1						1								2		3													
Violation liquor laws	9		5	2					2	1	1						16	1	3	3									2			
Driving drunk	20		1												1		19		1						2							
Reckless driving	20	1	9						14		1						10	1	7						4		1					
Hit and run	4		5								5						7		1						1							
Speeding																	2		2													
Auto license violations																	1								2							
Violation motor vehicle laws			4								1						3		1						1							
Breaking and entering	15		15						1	1	3	1					33		23						2		5					
And larceny	34		29	1					3		7	1					15		20	2							4					
And receiving	40	1	30	1					1		5						32		28								1					
Larceny	11		12		1				4		1	2					17		8	4					3	1	1					
Larceny and receiving	29	2	40	3					5		3						22		8	3					4	1						
Larceny from the person	2	3	5	1					1	1	1						5	1	6						3	2	1	1				
Larceny by trick and device	1	1															1															
Larceny of automobile	7		1						1		2						5		6						3							
Petty larceny	4		1						1								2															
Murder—first degree																											3	1				
Murder—second degree	1		6	3							1								1	2												
Manslaughter	9		8						9		2						10		8	4					4		2					
Burglary—first degree											1																					
Burglary—second degree	3																		4													
Abandonment	6								1								7		1													
Abduction																									2							

Affray			3	1															1													
Arson			1																													
Bigamy	2																4		1	3												
Burning other than arson			2						1								5								3							
Carrying ded we p nao	4		1														4										1					
cy	3	1	5						10		4						18								4							
lly conduct	4																2		2	1					1							
Disorderly house			2																	1												
Disposing of mortgaged property	1		7																													
Embezzlement	19		1						2		1						8								2							
Escape	2		1								1						2		3						1							
Forcible trespass	13		4						1		2						16	1	1													
Forgery	18		8														33	1	4						2							
Fornication ard	3	2	2								1						2		1									1				
Gaming and ry laws	1		6	2					2								1		3	2												
Injury to property	2	1															4		1													
Municipal ordinances																	2								1							
Non-support	9								1		1						6		3								1					
Non- port of illegitimate child	3								3								3		2													
le																	4															
Perjury	1																															
Prostitution	1																1	1														
Rape			1								1														4							
Receiving stolen goods	11		8	1							1						1		1	1												
Resisting officer	1			1							1									1												
R bbery o	4		10						4		1						14		9	1					5	1	3					
Seduction									1																							
Trespass	2																															
Vagrancy			2														1	3	1													
Worthless che k	8								2								3		1													
False pe	10		4						1								14										1					
Carnal knowledge, etc.	1		2														1						1				2					
Crime against ture			3																						1							
Slot machine aws	25								1																							
Kidnapping																	1															
Miscellaneous	1	1							1		1						7	1	1						2							
Totals	432	14	302	31	1				84	3	61	5			3		436	13	209	37					66	5	35	3	2			

Convictions	780
Nolle pros.	60
Acquittals	62
Other dispositions	34
	936

Convictions	695
Nolle pros.	30
Acquittals	59
Other dispositions	22
	806

THIRTEENTH JUDICIAL DISTRICT

IN SUPERIOR COURT

Offense	JULY 1, 1940—JULY 1, 1941																JULY 1, 1941—JULY 1, 1942															
	CONVICTIONS								OTHER DISPOSITIONS								CONVICTIONS								OTHER DISPOSITIONS							
	White		Negro		Indian		Unclassified		White		Negro		Indian		Unclassified		White		Negro		Indian		Unclassified		White		Negro		Indian		Unclassified	
	M	F	M	F	M	F	M	F	M	F	M	F	M	F	M	F	M	F	M	F	M	F	M	F	M	F	M	F	M	F	M	F
Assault	2		2		2				1								3		1	1					5		3					
Assault and battery																											1					
Assault with deadly weapon	18		9	2	1		2		3		3						14		12	1	2				2		2					
Assault on female	1		4						1								3		5						1							
Assault with intent to kill		1	7	2					3								1		4	1												
Assault with intent to rape	1										2						1								2		2					
Assault—secret											1																					
Drunk and disorderly	6		5		2				1								2		6						1		2					
Possession for sale			1																2													
Manufacturing—possession of material for	1																1		1						1		1					
Transportation																			1								1					
Violation liquor laws	1		4						1		3						2		3													
Driving drunk	8		5														16		5						3		3					
Reckless driving	1										1	1					3	1	3						2		1					
Hit and run			2														3		2						2							
Speeding							1																									
Auto license violations																	2															
Violation motor vehicle laws	2		3						2		1						1		1								1					
Breaking and entering	14		11						10		3								4								3					
And larceny	18		8		1		3										4		9								1					
And receiving	1		4								2						5		8						1		1					
Larceny	8		8								2						10		6		1				1							
Larceny and receiving	20		16						8		4						7		15						4		6	1				
Larceny from the person																			1													
Larceny of automobile	5				1														1													
Temporary larceny									1	1	2																					
Murder—first degree																			1						3		1					
Murder—second degree	4		6	1															12													
Manslaughter	2		11	2					6		4						4		4						13		6					
Burglary—first degree																									1							
Burglary—second degree			3																2													

Abandonment																	1		1													
Affray			1																													
Arson			1						1								1								2							
Bigamy		2			1												2								1							
Bribery																											2					
Carrying concealed weapon	2																1		2													
Cruelty to animals											1																					
Disorderly conduct	1																															
Disposing of mortgaged property									1																							
Embezzlement	1								4			1					1		1													
Escape	3				2																											
Fish and game laws	5																2															
Forcible trespass	4				1												5															
Forgery	8		3						2	1							5		2						2		1					
Fornication and adultery	1									1									2	1					3			1				
Gaming and lottery laws																			2													
Health laws									1																							
Incest											1																					
Injury to property			1		2				1																1							
Non-support	4		2														6		1						2		2					
Non-support of illegitimate child			1						1																		1					
Perjury			1	3													2															
Rape	1																		1								4					
Receiving stolen goods							1		3		2						1															
Resisting officer			1														1								5		2					
Robbery	6										1	1					1		1								7					
Seduction																	1															
Trespass	4		2		1				1																		1	1				
Worthless check																	5								1							
False pretense			1								1						2	1	1						1							
Carnal knowledge, etc.			1														1								1		1					
Crime against nature			3														1															
Miscellaneous	3								1		5	1													1		2					
Totals	156	3	127	10	14		7		53	3	39	4					121	2	123	4	3				62		58	3				

Convictions	317
Nolle pros	38
Acquittals	44
Other dispositions	17
	416

Convictions	253
Nolle pros	56
Acquittals	53
Other dispositions	14
	376

FOURTEENTH JUDICIAL DISTRICT
IN SUPERIOR COURT

Offense	JULY 1, 1940—JULY 1, 1941 CONVICTIONS	JULY 1, 1940—JULY 1, 1941 OTHER DISPOSITIONS	JULY 1, 1941—JULY 1, 1942 CONVICTIONS	JULY 1, 1941—JULY 1, 1942 OTHER DISPOSITIONS Unclassified F
Assault				----
Assault with deadly weapon				2
Assault on female				----
Assault with intent to kill				----
Assault with intent to rape				----
Assault—secret				----
Drunk and disorderly				----
Transportation				----
Violation liquor laws				----
Driving drunk				1
Reckless driving				1
Hit and run				----
Speeding				----
Auto license violations				1
Violation motor vehicle laws				----
Breaking and entering				----
And larceny				----
And receiving				----
Housebreaking and larceny				----
And receiving				----
Storebreaking and larceny				----
And receiving				----
Larceny				----
Larceny and receiving				----
Larceny from the person				----
Larceny of automobile				----
Temporary larceny				----
Murder—first degree				----
Murder—second degree				----
Manslaughter				----
Burglary—first degree				----
Burglary—second degree				----
Abandonment				----

Abandonment
Abduction
Affray

Bigamy	1	1													1		3								2	1	1					
Burning other than arson	1																										1					
Carrying concealed weapons	4		14						1		3				2		3		11												4	1
[illegible]cy	7	1							4																		1	1				
Disorderly conduct	1		1						6						1				1						1			1				
Disorderly house																		1							1			1				
Disposing of mortgaged property	2								1		1				1		1										1				1	
Disturbing religious worship									2																							
[illegible]nt	3		2						3		1	1			2		7		6						9						2	
Escape																															1	
Fish and game laws															2																	
Forcible trespass	2	1	3						1						1		2		3												1	
Forgery	4		3	1			1				1						8		1	1												
Fornication and adultery	4	2																									1					
Gaming and lottery laws			1						2						2		2								2							
Health laws																									1							
Incest			1														1								2							
Injury to property	5	1	4	1					8	1	2	1			2			2	2	2					2							
[illegible]al [illegible]s																	4															
[illegible] [illegible]pt	27		7				1		11		2				6		22		7						8						10	
Non-support of [illegible] child									1						1		1						1				1				2	
N[illegible]	1		1														1								1						1	
Perjury											1	1			1										1							
[illegible]tion		2		2					4	4		3					1	1														
Rape									1						1		1								4							
Receiving stolen goods	1		14	2							3				1		4		11	2					3			2			2	
Resisting officer	3		1														1		1						1	1						
Robbery	9		12	1					2		11	1					9		29	1					7		16	4			3	1
Seduction									2						1										1							
[illegible]ss	3		4														2								2							
[illegible]y										1										2								1				
[illegible]ss [illegible]k	1	1			1				1						2		2								3						1	
False pretense	6		1				1								3		6		1						1	1					3	
Carnal [illegible], etc.	1		1								2				1				1								1					
[illegible] against nature			1												1		2		1						1							
Slot machine laws	1								1																2							
[illegible]ing																			1													
Miscellaneous	10		1						10						3		2		1						4						1	
Totals	397	16	348	39	1		5		230	12	122	18			146	2	368	16	283	45			5		225	15	117	33			172	7

Convictions	806
Nolle pros	194
Acquittals	173
Other dispositions	163

Convictions	717
Nolle pros	325
Acquittals	185
Other dispositions	59

FIFTEENTH JUDICIAL DISTRICT

IN SUPERIOR COURT

Offense	JULY 1, 1940—JULY 1, 1941																JULY 1, 1941—JULY 1, 1942															
	CONVICTIONS								OTHER DISPOSITIONS								CONVICTIONS								OTHER DISPOSITIONS							
	White		Negro		Indian		Unclassified		White		Negro		Indian		Unclassified		White		Negro		Indian		Unclassified		White		Negro		Indian		Unclassified	
	M	F	M	F	M	F	M	F	M	F	M	F	M	F	M	F	M	F	M	F	M	F	M	F	M	F	M	F	M	F	M	F
Assault	14								7		2						6		2													
Assault with deadly weapon	26	1	15	3					12	1	5	1					16		10	5					1		6	2				
Assault on female	5		4						2		1						11		2						6							
Assault with intent to kill	6		7	1					3								1		2													
Assault with intent to rape	2		1						1								2		2						1							
Drunk and disorderly	17		1						3		1						19								2							
Possession illegal whiskey	5		3						4								4		1													
Possession for sale	16		12						4			1					6	1	4						2							
Manufacturing—possession of material for	14		2						5		1						14		2						3		1					
Transportation	21		8						11								17		5													
Violation liquor laws	5		1	3					3			1					7		4				1		2		1					
Driving drunk	185	2	30						19		2						226	8	30	1			7		43		6				1	
Reckless driving	14	1	4						6								21	1	1						7							
Hit and run	4	1	4						3		1						7		1						7							
Speeding	1																1															
Auto license violations	5		1														8		1						1		1					
Violation motor vehicle laws	5		1	1													1															
Breaking and entering	22		11						3	1	2						10		8						4		2					
And larceny	12		17						2		2						15		17						1		3					
And receiving	3		5						3		2						9		2													
Housebreaking and receiving																	5															
Larceny	25	1	12	1					14		9						37	2	17	2					8	1	8	1				
Larceny and receiving	8	1	5	2					8		1						7	1							2							
Larceny from the person	2																1															
Larceny by trick and device																	1															
Larceny of automobile	2								1								2		4						1							
Temporary larceny																	1															
Murder—first degree									1		1																1					
Murder—second degree	1		11	1													1		3	2												
Manslaughter	12		1						6		4						8		7	2					3	1						
Burglary—second degree			1																1													

Abandonment	3																5								2							
Abduction	2								3																							
Arson											1						2											1				
Burning other than arson											2																					
Carrying concealed weapon	5		2						2		1						9		2						3		1					
Disorderly conduct	1								2								3															
Disorderly house		3									1																					
Disposing of mortgaged property	4																1								1							
Embezzlement	4								3								1		1						1			1				
Escape																	1															
Fish and game laws	2								2																							
Forcible trespass	5		1						1								10	1	1						2							
Forgery	15	1	6						2								7		1													
Fornication and adultery											1	3					1	1	2	1												
Gaming and lottery laws	4		5																2													
Incest	1								1								2															
Injury to property			1								1																					
Non-support	15	1	2						12		1						20		1						11		3					
Non-support of illegitimate child	5		3						3								6															
Nuisance											1																					
Perjury	1																3		1													
Prohibition	7	1							2																							
Rape																	1															
Receiving stolen goods			1														2	1								1						
Resisting officer	2		2						1								2								2							
Robbery	5	1	5	1					1		1	2					2								2		3					
Seduction									2																							
Trespass	2								2								2															
Worthless checks	8								2			1					3								1							
False pretense	2		4						3	2		1					2		1								1					
Carnal knowledge, etc.			1														1		1													
Offense against nature																	1															
Miscellaneous	5		1						3	1	2						5		1						5		1					
Totals	530	14	191	13					168	5	46	10					556	16	140	13			8		124	3	38	5			1	

Convictions	748
Nolle pros.	158
Acquittals	55
Other dispositions	16
	977

Convictions	733
Nolle pros.	130
Acquittals	33
Other dispositions	8
	904

Offense	JULY 1, 1940—JULY 1, 1941																JULY 1, 1941—JULY 1, 1942															
	CONVICTIONS								OTHER DISPOSITIONS								CONVICTIONS								OTHER DISPOSITIONS							
	White		Negro		Indian		Unclassified		White		Negro		Indian		Unclassified		White		Negro		Indian		Unclassified		White		Negro		Indian		Unclassified	
	M	F	M	F	M	F	M	F	M	F	M	F	M	F	M	F	M	F	M	F	M	F	M	F	M	F	M	F	M	F	M	F
Assault	1		1								1						5		3													
Assault with deadly weapon	13		10	1					6		4						19	1	7						5		4					
Assault on female	3		4						2		2						4		2													
Assault with intent to kill			1																													
Assault with intent to rape	4		2						1								2		1						4							
Assault—secret																	1															
Drunk and disorderly	25	2									1						19		1						3	1	1					
Possession—illegal whiskey									1								2															
Possession for sale																	2															
Manufacturing—possession of material for	1																1															
Violation liquor laws	19		1						3								19	4	5	4							3	1				
Driving drunk	79		4						3								59								6		2					
Reckless driving	10								5								3								1		1					
Hit and run	1	1							1								1															
Speeding																	1															
Auto license violations																	2								2							
Violation motor vehicle laws	4	1							2										2						6							
Breaking and entering	8		11						3								11		2													
And larceny	26	1	11						4		1						21		8						3							
And receiving	9		3								1						2															
Larceny	36	4	11	3					9	1	1						38	2	12						7	1	2					
Larceny and receiving	13		2						1		2						6	1	2						7		1					
Larceny from the person	1		1								4																					
Larceny by trick and device	1																															
Larceny of automobile	7																7		1													
Temporary larceny	2		1														2								1	1						
Murder—first degree			1						3	1		1														1						
Murder—second degree	3		6	1													5		5													
Manslaughter	11		8						4								10		5						4		1					
Abandonment	6		1						1								4								3							
Abduction									2																							
Affray																	1															
Arson			1																													

...iy									1								3	1	1							2						
Burning ...ther than arson																	1															
Carrying ...ed weapon	2										1						1															
...pt	4																															
...cy	2																1								1							
...lty to ...mals																			1													
Disorderly ...duct																	4															
Disorderly house		1															1	2														
Disposing of mortgaged ...perty																									2							
...ing religious worship	2								1																							
Embezzlement	3								2								5								3							
Escape																	1															
Fish and game laws	1																															
Forcible trespass	5			1													3								1							
Forgery	15		6							1							11	3	9						4	1						
Fornication and adultery	2	2							1								3	1								1						
Health laws																	2								4							
Incest			1																													
Injury to property	3	2		1																												
Non-...pport	11		2														9								6							
Non-support of illegitimate child	3		1														19		2						2							
Perjury																	1								3							
...ution																	1	2														
Rape																			1													
Receiving ...len goods	1		1														3		4						1							
Resisting officer	7								2								2		1													
...y	6		1																													
Seduction	1		1														1															
...s	8										1																					
...cy																	1	1							1							
...s ...ck	5																1								2							
False pretense	3								1		1						5		1						2							
Carnal ...ge, etc.																									1							
...e ...ast ...e	1																2		2													
Slot machine ...	2																															
Miscellaneous	9								1		2	1																				
Totals	379	14	93	7					60	3	22	2					328	18	78	4					85	8	15	1				

Convictions	493
Nolle pros	38
Acquittals	44
Other dispositions	5
	580

Convictions	428
Nolle pros	70
Acquittals	30
Other dispositions	9
	537

SEVENTEENTH JUDICIAL DISTRICT
IN SUPERIOR COURT

Offense	JULY 1, 1940—JULY 1, 1941																JULY 1, 1941—JULY 1, 1942															
	CONVICTIONS								OTHER DISPOSITIONS								CONVICTIONS								OTHER DISPOSITIONS							
	White		Negro		Indian		Unclassified		White		Negro		Indian		Unclassified		White		Negro		Indian		Unclassified		White		Negro		Indian		Unclassified	
	M	F	M	F	M	F	M	F	M	F	M	F	M	F	M	F	M	F	M	F	M	F	M	F	M	F	M	F	M	F	M	F
Assault	8	1	1						3								6								5							
Assault with deadly weapon	12	2	1						4	1							12		3						12		1				1	
Assault on female	6								2		1						3								5							
Assault with intent to kill	2		2						1	1	10						2															
Assault with intent to rape																	2										1					
Drunk and disorderly	5	1							4								3								5							
Possession—illegal whiskey	3		1																													
Possession for sale	2																															
Manufacturing—possession of material for	1																															
Transportation	3								1																							
Violation liquor laws	26	4	2						3	1	2						51	3	11	1					23		7	2			1	
Driving drunk	31		1						7		1						68		5				1		9		2				1	
Reckless driving	2		1						1	1							5	1	3						7							
Hit and run	1		1														1								1							
Speeding									1																							
Auto license violation																	3								1							
Violation motor vehicle laws	37		6						10		1						20	1							11		4					
Breaking and entering	11		4						5								8	2	5						4							
And larceny																	4	1	4						2							
And receiving	1																2								6							
Housebreaking	2		2								2						2															
And ...ing	1								4								44	6								1						
Larceny	11		5						12	2	1						4		2						8	1	2	1				
Larceny and receiving	7		4								1						11		2						6		1					
Larceny of automobile																	1															
Murder—first degree									3																4							
Murder—second degree	3		1														2															
Manslaughter	5	1							8								8	1	2						4		1					
Burglary—second degree	1																															
Abandonment	12								1								8								7		1					
Abduction																									1							

Affray	5	1	4						4		1	1					5		1	1								1				
Bigamy																	1															
Carrying concealed weapon	7		3						1								5								2		1					
Cruelty to animals																									2							
Disorderly house	1			1														1														
Disposing of mortgaged property	4								1																2							
Disturbing religious worship																									1							
Embezzlement									3								1															
Escape																	2															
Forcible trespass	6								2								5								4							
Forgery			1								1						3								1							
Fornication and adultery	3	1							4	2							1	1							1	1						
Gaming and lottery laws									5																							
Health laws																									1							
Incest																	1															
Injury to property	1																2								3							
Municipal ordinances																									6							
Non-support	8								2		1						5		1						2							
Non-support of illegitimate child	2		2						1								2								1							
Nuisance	1								1																1							
Official misconduct																									5							
Prostitution		2	1						2	2															1							
Rape			1						2																1							
Receiving stolen goods	1		2						1																							
Resisting officer	2																6	1							2							
Robbery	1								2																							
[illegible]er																	2															
Trespass									1																							
Worthless check									1								2								2							
False pretense	1								1								1	1							3							
Slot machine laws																	10	2														
Miscellaneous	2		1						5								2								2	1						
Totals	238	13	47	1					109	10	22	1					326	21	39	2			1		164	4	21	3			3	

Convictions	299
Nolle pros	85
Acquittals	21
Other dispositions	36
	441

Convictions	389
Nolle pros	148
Acquittals	28
Other dispositions	19
	584

EIGHTEENTH JUDICIAL DISTRICT
IN SUPERIOR COURT

	JULY 1, 1940—JULY 1, 1941		JULY 1, 1941—JULY 1, 1942	
Offense	CONVICTIONS	OTHER DISPOSITIONS	CONVICTIONS	OTHER DISPOSITIONS
		Negro \| Indian		Unclassified
				F
Ault				
Ault with dally spon				
sault on female				
Ault with intent to kill				
Assault with intent to rape				
Drunk and disorderly				
Possession—illegal diey				
Possession for sale				
Manufacturing—possession of				
material for				
Gun				
Vi lati liquor laws				
Driving drunk				
Rbis ing				
Hit and run				
Speeding				
Auto ribe vi lati ns				
Vi lation ator vehicle laws				
Breaking and eaig				
Ard larceny				
Storebreaking				
Larceny				
Larceny and ing				
Larceny from the person				
Larceny of automobile				
glary l ary				
Murder—first degree				
nd degree				
Manslaughter				
Burglary—second degree				
Abandonment				
Affray				
Arson

Burning other than arson		1							1																							
Carrying concealed weapon	5		2						2								6		4						2		1					
Cruelty to animals																									1							
Disorderly conduct			2						1		2																					
Disorderly house																	1			1												
Disposing of mortgaged property									1								1								2							
Disturbing religious worship																									3							
Embezzlement	1								6								2								2							
Food and drug laws																									1							
Fish and game laws									2								2															
Forcible trespass	9		1														5		2													
Forgery	3		1						5								7								3			3				
Fornication and adultery	2	2							2	3							6	3							2	3						
Gaming and lottery laws	4																10															
Health laws									2																							
Incest	1		1																													
Injury to property	3		2						1								1	1							1							
Municipal ordinances																									1							
Non-support	10								1								10		1	1					2							
Non-support of illegitimate child	3		2						2		1						3								1		1					
Nuisance		1								2																						
Prostitution																			1													
Rape									2																							
Receiving stolen goods	1		2									1							1													
Resisting officer	1		2								1								2						2		1					
Robbery	9		6									1					3		3													
Seduction									2																1							
Trespass	3								3								7		2													
Vagrancy	1									2																						
Worthless check	5								3																							
False pretense									6								11								4							
Carnal knowledge, etc.	2																															
Crime against nature	1																2															
Slot machine law																			1													
Miscellaneous	4		4						2		1						1	1	1						5		1					
Totals	405	12	113	8				2	120	16	41	2					367	12	108	21			1		113	5	32	7				

Convictions	536
Nolle pros	128
Acquittals	21
Other dispositions	30
	715

Convictions	509
Nolle pros	124
Acquittals	23
Other dispositions	10
	666

NINETEENTH JUDICIAL DISTRICT
IN SUPERIOR COURT

Offense	JULY 1, 1940—JULY 1, 1941 CONVICTIONS	JULY 1, 1940—JULY 1, 1941 OTHER DISPOSITIONS Indian sified	JULY 1, 1941—JULY 1, 1942 CONVICTIONS	JULY 1, 1941—JULY 1, 1942 OTHER DISPOSITIONS Unclassified F
Asult				----
Assault and battery				----
Assault with adly apon				----
Asult on female				----
Asult with intent to kill				----
Assault with intent to ape				----
Drunk ard disorderly				----
Possession—illegal biy				----
Possession for sale				----
Manufacturing—possession of				
mal for				----
fin				----
Vion qlior laws				----
Driving drunk				----
Reckless driving				----
Hit ard run				----
Auto die violations				----
Mti n tor vehicle laws				----
Big ard entering				----
And larceny				----
Ard ing				----
Housebreaking				----
And larceny				----
Storebreaking				----
Larceny				----
ary ard receiving				----
Larceny from the pen				----
Irany by trk ard cide				----
Larceny of hile				----
Temporary larceny				----
Murder—first degree				----
Murder—second degree				----
Manslaughter				----

Arson	1								1																3							
Bigamy	2																								2	1	1					
Bribery																	1															
Burning other than arson	2																															
Carrying [illegible]	5			1					1								4								6							
[illegible]pt																	1															
Conspiracy		1							2	1																						
[illegible]lty to [illegible]mals																	1															
[illegible]ly conduct									1			1					1		1	1												
[illegible]ly house	1	1								4							3		4													
Disposing of mortgaged property	1										1						1								1							
Embezzlement									6		1						1								7		4				1	
Escape																	2								1							
Forcible [illegible]	4		1						2	1							9	2							2							
Forgery	7		1	1					8								4								3							
Fornication and adultery	2	1							3	1																	1	1				
Gaming and [illegible]ry laws																	3		1						1							
[illegible]th laws									2								5	3							1	1						
Incest									1																							
[illegible]jury to property		1							1								1		1													
Municipal ordinances									1								5								3						1	
Non-support	11								6		1								2						6		1					
Non-support of illegitimate child	6								7								4								1							
Perjury									1																							
Prostitution																	2	2														
Rape									1		1						1								1		1					
Receiving stolen goods	4		3						2								9		3													
Resisting officer	3								1			1																				
[illegible]bb[illegible]y	3	1	6						5		1						3		3	1					5		6					
Seduction									3		1						1								2						1	
[illegible]der										1																						
[illegible]ss									1		1				1		2								2	1						
Vagrancy		2																1							4							
[illegible]ss check	2								1																2							
False pretense			3						6								3		1						7	1	2				1	
Carnal [illegible]ge, [illegible]et																	1								1						2	
[illegible]ne against nature																	1								2							
Slot machine laws	3								2	1																						
Miscellaneous	13	2	1	1					15			1			2			2							10	2						
Totals	323	20	83	10					193	16	39	10			4		288	14	68	8	1				178	16	44	3			10	

Convictions	436
Nolle pros	183
Acquittals	71
Other dispositions	8

Convictions	379
Nolle pros	176
Acquittals	59
Other dispositions	16

TWENTIETH JUDICIAL DISTRICT

IN SUPERIOR COURT

Offense	JULY 1, 1940—JULY 1, 1941																JULY 1, 1941—JULY 1, 1942															
	CONVICTIONS								OTHER DISPOSITIONS								CONVICTIONS								OTHER DISPOSITIONS							
	White		Negro		Indian		Unclassified		White		Negro		Indian		Unclassified		White		Negro		Indian		Unclassified		White		Negro		Indian		Unclassified	
	M	F	M	F	M	F	M	F	M	F	M	F	M	F	M	F	M	F	M	F	M	F	M	F	M	F	M	F	M	F	M	F
Assault	11		1		1	1			7	1							14	1	2				1		6	1						
Assault with deadly weapon	20	1	4	3					10	1							26	1	3						15	4			1			
Assault on [illegible]fle	2								2																1							
Asult with intent to kill	1								1										1													
Assault with intent to rape																			1						2							
Drunk and disorderly	7	1		1					3								19	1			1				3							
[illegible]ion																	1															
Violation liquor laws	60	2	4						14	2							27	3	1						16	5						
Driving drunk	181	2	2		1				9								124	2	5						9							
Reckless driving	17								11								10								12							
Auto license [illegible]	1																3								1							
[illegible]ion [illegible]tor vehicle laws	3																															
B[illegible]king and [illegible]nt[illegible]ri[illegible]	2	2							3								3	1	2													
And [illegible]ny	6								1								6															
And receiving	2								4								1															
Housebreaking									1																							
And [illegible]ing	2								4								2								2							
[illegible]y	21	1	3						15	3			1				24	2	2						9							
Larceny and [illegible]ing	3																1															
Larceny of [illegible]ile																	2															
[illegible]ry [illegible]																	1															
Murder—first degree									2	1															2		4					
Murder—second degree	5																4															
Manslaughter	6				1												2	1	1													
Burglary—second degree																			1													
Abandonment	14		1		2				5	1							15		1		1				6							
Affray	14	2															17	2	1						3	1						
[illegible]									5								1		1													
Bigamy	1																															
Burning other than arson																									1							
Carrying [illegible]aled weapon	8				1				3								8		1						8							

[illegible]cy									2																							
Disorderly conduct										2		1													3							
Disorderly house	1	2							2	3								1														
Disposing of mortgaged property																									1							
Disturbing [illegible] worship	2								2								2															
Embezzlement	2																															
Escape	4		1														11	1							2	2						
Fish and game laws	2								1								2															
Forcible trespass	7								1								1															
Forgery	3				1				2				2				3		4													
Fornication and adultery	2	1							3	3															3	3						
[illegible] and [illegible] laws									8																4		1					
Incest									1	1																						
Injury to property	4																6								1							
Municipal ordinances									1																2							
Non-support	7								3								11		1													
[illegible] f illegitimate child	1		1								1						3								1							
Nuisance	1								1	1															2	2						
Perjury	1									1																						
Prostitution																	1															
Rape									1																							
Receiving stolen goods	2																1															
Resisting officer	4		1						1								3								4							
Seduction	1								1								1															
Slander																									1							
Trespass	6	3							1																3							
Worthless [illegible]																	1															
False [illegible]	7								6	1							2		2						7							
Slot machine laws	1																															
Miscellaneous	3								3																2		1					
Totals	448	17	18	4	7	1			140	21	1	1	3				359	16	31		2		1		132	18	6		1			

Convictions 495
Nolle pros 116
Acquittals 27
Other dispositions 23

661

Convictions 409
Nolle pros 112
Acquittals 28
Other dispositions 17

566

TWENTY-FIRST JUDICIAL DISTRICT

IN SUPERIOR COURT

Offense	JULY 1, 1940—JULY 1, 1941															
	CONVICTIONS								OTHER DISPOSITIONS							
	White		Negro		Indian		Unclassified		White		Negro		Indian		Unclassified	
	M	F	M	F	M	F	M	F	M	F	M	F	M	F	M	F
Assault	10	1	14						1		2					
Assault with deadly weapon	26		30	3					3	1	13					
Assault on female	7		9						3		2					
Assault with intent to kill	1															
Assault with intent to rape																
Drunk and disorderly	14		8					1			1					
Possession—illegal whiskey	6		2						2							
Possession for sale	1															
Manufacturing—possession of material for	6								1							
Transportation	4		8						2							
Violation liquor laws	51	5	28	5			3		10	2	6	4			4	
Driving drunk	73	1	15				1		10	1					2	
Reckless driving	14		7						9							
Hit and run	3															
Auto license violations	2		1						2	1						
Violation motor vehicle laws	6		2													
Breaking and entering	11		1						1		1					
And larceny	6		4													
And receiving	6		3								2					
Housebreaking			2													
And receiving	5															
Larceny	21		23	1			1		7		7	1				
Larceny and receiving	12		1													
Larceny from the person	3	1	1	4					1							
Larceny of automobile	2															
Temporary larceny																
Murder—first degree			1													
Murder—second degree	4			1												
Manslaughter	6		4	1					1		2					
Burglary—first degree											1					
Burglary—second degree	1															

Offense	JULY 1, 1941—JULY 1, 1942															
	CONVICTIONS								OTHER DISPOSITIONS							
	White		Negro		Indian		Unclassified		White		Negro		Indian		Unclassified	
	M	F	M	F	M	F	M	F	M	F	M	F	M	F	M	F
Assault	16		7	3					3							
Assault with deadly weapon	28		18	3					7	1	2					
Assault on female	5		3								2					
Assault with intent to kill	2			1					1							
Assault with intent to rape	1															
Drunk and disorderly	19	1	8						1		1					
Possession—illegal whiskey	2		1													
Possession for sale				1					1							
Manufacturing—possession of material for	5		5								1					
Transportation	4		3								1	1				
Violation liquor laws	28	2	25	4					5		1	2			1	
Driving drunk	66	1	13						6		2					
Reckless driving	18		4						4		3					
Hit and run	2		2													
Auto license violations	3															
Violation motor vehicle laws	2		1						1							1
Breaking and entering	1		2													
And larceny																
And receiving	1								1							
Housebreaking																
And receiving	3		7													
Larceny	16	1	10	1					4	2	11					
Larceny and receiving	5		6						5		1					
Larceny from the person			2													
Larceny of automobile																
Temporary larceny	2															
Murder—first degree																
Murder—second degree	1		2	1							1					
Manslaughter	5	1	4						4		3					
Burglary—first degree											1					
Burglary—second degree			1													

Abandonment	2		1						2								5		2	1					3		1					
[illegible]																			1													
Affray			1						1																1							
Arson																		1														
[illegible] other [illegible] arson			1																3													
Carrying [illegible] weapon	2		9	1					1								1		6	1							1					
[illegible]cy																	2								2	1	1					
Cruelty to animals									1								1								1							
[illegible]ly conduct	2																															
Disorderly [illegible]	1									1																						
Disposing of mortgaged [illegible]	2		2																1													
Disturbing religious worship									1																							
Embezzlement	1																								2							
Escape	1		4																													
F[illegible] and game [illegible]	1								3								1															
Forcible [illegible]	10		1	1											2		2		3								1					
Forgery	1																2								1							
Fornication and [illegible]										1		1					1									1						
[illegible]g and [illegible]ry [illegible]	1		1														1		6													
I[illegible]t	1								1																							
Injury to property	1																								1							
[illegible]-support	7		3						3		1						7		7						2		1					
Non-support of [illegible] child			1						2								3		2						1		1					
[illegible]e	2																2		1						1							
Prostitution			1	1																												
Receiving [illegible]en goods	2		2																													
Resisting officer	1																4															
Robbery	5						3																									
[illegible]r		1																														
[illegible]s	2		3								1														1							
[illegible]s c[illegible]k									1								1															
False [illegible]	1		2														1		1						1		1					
Carnal knowledge, [illegible]	2		1								1						1															
[illegible] against [illegible]	1																															
[illegible] [illegible] [illegible]	2	1																														
Miscellaneous	4		3						2								1			2					2							
Totals	356	10	200	18			8	1	71	7	40	6		8			272	7	157	18					62	5	37	3			1	1

Convictions	593
Nolle pros	48
Acquittals	79
Other dispositions	5
	725

Convictions	454
Nolle pros	39
Acquittals	51
Other dispositions	19
	563

ALPHABETICAL LIST OF CRIMES IN SUPERIOR COURTS

Offense	July 1, 1940—July 1, 1941		July 1, 1941—July 1, 1942	
	Convictions	Other Dispositions	Convictions	Other Dispositions
Assault	232	119	171	95
Assault and battery	5	6	6	3
Assault with deadly weapon	753	288	694	260
Assault on female	183	65	139	52
Assault with intent to kill	222	81	170	69
Assault with intent to rape	59	26	54	34
Assault—secret	12	10	8	7
Drunk and disorderly	451	123	316	119
Possession—illegal whiskey	81	25	83	15
Possession for sale	124	63	96	40
Manufacturing—possession of material for	72	18	73	18
Transportation	90	27	59	6
Violation liquor laws	526	189	462	167
Driving drunk	1,098	266	1,071	328
Reckless driving	245	158	228	162
Hit and run	88	27	75	35
Speeding	11	11	18	14
Auto license violations	20	8	46	17
Violation motor vehicle laws	124	50	67	51
Breaking and entering	377	87	278	63
And larceny	432	66	298	60
And receiving	175	44	118	24
Housebreaking	21	5	24	4
And larceny	91	15	154	46
And receiving	120	22	113	9
Storebreaking	27	3	18	5
And larceny	14	15	30	9
And receiving	95	8	102	11
Larceny	855	324	760	288
Larceny and receiving	343	113	230	98
Larceny from the person	54	30	83	33
Larceny by trick and device	13	3	4	1
Larceny of automobile	97	30	140	28
Temporary larceny	17	7	28	11
Murder—first degree	15	100	22	78
Murder—second degree	194	19	129	11
Manslaughter	216	92	201	121
Burglary—first degree	2	3	9	9
Burglary—second degree	33	----------	34	3
Abandonment	107	53	96	63
Abduction	4	5	3	4
Affray	49	18	52	21
Arson	11	18	12	21
Bigamy	28	7	44	20
Bribery	----------	1	2	2
Burning other than arson	14	11	10	9
Carrying concealed weapon	112	33	104	39
Contempt	5	----------	1	----------
Conspiracy	37	37	39	19

ALPHABETICAL LIST OF CRIMES IN SUPERIOR COURTS

Offense	July 1, 1940—July 1, 1941		July 1, 1941—July 1, 1942	
	Convictions	Other Dispositions	Convictions	Other Dispositions
Cruelty to animals	2	3	5	4
Disorderly conduct	40	26	35	21
Disorderly house	22	25	44	10
Disposing of mortgaged property	33	15	10	17
Disturbing religious worship	8	6	3	4
Violation of election laws	5	2	----------	1
Embezzlement	64	60	80	63
Escape	24	3	28	9
Failure to list tax	394	646	70	155
Food and drug laws	----------	----------	----------	1
Fish and game laws	21	31	13	11
Forcible trespass	140	25	147	15
Forgery	280	45	285	41
Fornication and adultery	62	44	44	38
Gaming and lottery laws	87	42	64	19
Health laws	2	5	14	10
Incest	9	9	9	5
Injury to property	51	34	38	29
Municipal ordinances	2	3	17	26
Non-support	180	77	154	89
Non-support of illegitimate child	67	35	85	26
Nuisance	17	13	12	13
Official misconduct	----------	1	----------	6
Perjury	25	26	13	9
Prostitution	26	20	63	15
Rape	8	21	13	27
Receiving stolen goods	126	40	100	19
Removing crop	----------	1	2	3
Resisting officer	53	21	44	29
Robbery	226	65	198	119
Seduction	15	28	19	11
Slander	3	1	4	4
Trespass	59	31	25	32
Vagrancy	11	7	14	12
Worthless check	69	60	46	22
False pretense	80	60	98	72
Carnal knowledge, etc.	39	18	26	22
Crime against nature	29	7	20	6
Slot machine laws	236	52	15	7
Kidnapping	----------	1	7	1
Revenue act violations	11	1	----------	----------
Miscellaneous	140	160	124	90

Convictions	10,620	Convictions	8,962
Other dispositions	4,499	Other dispositions	3,715
Total	15,119	Total	12,677

GRAND TOTAL 27,796

FIRST JUDICIAL DISTRICT

INFERIOR COURTS

Offense	JULY 1, 1940—JULY 1, 1941																JULY 1, 1941—JULY 1, 1942															
	CONVICTIONS								OTHER DISPOSITIONS								CONVICTIONS								OTHER DISPOSITIONS							
	White		Negro		Indian		Unclassified		White		Negro		Indian		Unclassified		White		Negro		Indian		Unclassified		White		Negro		Indian		Unclassified	
	M	F	M	F	M	F	M	F	M	F	M	F	M	F	M	F	M	F	M	F	M	F	M	F	M	F	M	F	M	F	M	F
Assault	44	3	95	16					10	2	30	4					46	3	105	10			15	1	20		24	10				
Assault and battery																	5		34	8			5	1	1		15	3				
Assault with deadly weapon	14		65	10					2		18	5			1																	
Assault on female	5		19						1		2						3		9				3		3		2					
Assault with intent to kill											3																4					
Drunk and disorderly	258	2	79	4			6		4		1						200	10	195	11			33	3	17		10				10	
Possession—illegal whiskey	2		21	7								1					2		10	3			1		2		3					
Possession for sale			1	5													2		1				1				5	1				
Manufacturing—possession of material for																			1								3					
[illegible]ation	2		2														1		4						1		1				1	
Violation liquor laws	1	1	7	1					4		3	2					5		18	4												
Driving drunk	43		17				3		1								79		25				14		17	1	4				1	
Reckless driving	57	3	40	1			2		10	1	6				1		104	2	61	1			18		32		16	1			9	
Hit and run	8	1	6						1		1						3		6				1		4		2					
Speeding	116	5	33				2		3		1						179	3	46	2			6	2	2						1	
Auto license violations	31	3	24				3		4	2	1						38	11	52	7			6	1	1						5	
Violation motor vehicle laws	85	1	88	1			4		12		2				1		92	6	124	2			18	1	9		6				1	
Breaking and entering			1						2		5								1						2		5					
Ard [illegible]			1																								3					
Housebreaking																									2							
Larceny	8		37	1					5		20						15		51	3			2		2		23	1			2	1
Larceny and receiving			1																1													
Larceny of automobile	2		1								1														1		1					
[illegible]	2		1								2						2															
Murder—first degree											3																4					
Manslaughter									2		1														3		1					
Burglary—second degree																											1					
Abduction																	7	2	6	2			6		1		1	2				
Affray	15		16	3			4		5	1	4	1																				
Carrying concealed weapon	3		12						1		2						1		13						1		1					

[illegible]pt	3	1															1			1												
Cru lty to animals			1														1								1							
Disorderly conduct	17		33	11					1		6						8		33	5			3		2	1		2			1	
Disorderly houso																	1															
Disposing of mortgaged property	1	1	1								1				1		1															
Disturbing rel igus worship			2								1								1													
Embezzlement																	1															
Failure to list tax	8		16														16		64				2		1		5					
Fish and game laws	17								1		2						9								4							
Forcible trespass			1																													
Forgery									1		2						1										3					
Fornication and [illegible]			1	1														3	4				3	5			1					
Gaming and lottery [illegible]	3		17	1													2		3				3		1		3					
H alth laws																			4								1					
Injury to [illegible]y	5		10						1		1						1		3					1	1							
Mi ipal ordinan e	55	7	18						3		2						198	23	46	5					1	2	3					
Non-supp ot	9		21						2		3						8		9				1		3		2				1	
N n- [illegible]t of [illegible]e child			1						2										7													
[illegible]																				1												
Perjury											3																					
Prostitution			3	2					1	1							2	1	2	1									1			
Rape											2														2		1					
Receiving [illegible]n g ds			12	1							8						1		1								5					
Re [illegible]ing [illegible] p																			2													
Resisting [illegible]r	2		6								2						1		10				1									
Seduction											1																					
[illegible]ss	14		19	3					5		1	1					5		13				5		2		4		2		1	
Vagrancy									1		1				1																	
Worthless ch [illegible]k	28		4														15		2						1						1	
False pretense			4								2								9	2			2		1		8					
Slot [illegible]ine laws	22		2																													
Miscellaneous	19	5	19	2					4		4						16	1	22						2		2	1				
Totals	899	33	758	70			24		89	7	48	5			4		1072	65	998	68			149	15	143	4	173	21	3		34	1

Convictions	1,784
Bound over	39
Other dispositions	114
	1,937

Convictions	2,367
Bound over	51
Other dispositions	328
	2,746

SECOND JUDICIAL DISTRICT

INFERIOR COURTS

Offense	JULY 1, 1940—JULY 1, 1941																JULY 1, 1941—JULY 1, 1942															
	CONVICTIONS								OTHER DISPOSITIONS								CONVICTIONS								OTHER DISPOSITIONS							
	White		Negro		Indian		Unclassified		White		Negro		Indian		Unclassified		White		Negro		Indian		Unclassified		White		Negro		Indian		Unclassified	
	M	F	M	F	M	F	M	F	M	F	M	F	M	F	M	F	M	F	M	F	M	F	M	F	M	F	M	F	M	F	M	F
Assault	16		57	15					9	1	26	6					18	3	35	13					10	2	27	5				
Assault and battery	1		1	2					1		4	1					3		7	2					3		9	7				
Assault with deadly weapon	20	2	87	17					12	2	33	3					15	1	72	20					11	3	25	4				
Assault on female	13		46						2		22						17		26						10		22					
Assault with intent to kill																											1					
Assault with intent to rape																											2					
Drunk and disorderly	490	21	331	42			2		13		8						297	13	148	22					21	1	8	2				
Possession—illegal whiskey	8		13	2													3		14						1							
Possession for sale	4		7	1					2		3						6	1	2						4		1					
Manufacturing—possession of material for	5		4						1		4						9		7						3		1					
[illegible]	4		5						2		1																					
Violation liquor laws	34	3	96	28					29	1	19	4					28		99	21			3		10	1	26	5			4	
Driving drunk	95	1	31						22		4				1		91	3	51	3			1		30		10				2	
Reckless driving	49	1	42	1					33	1	14	1					54	3	38				1		28	1	17					
Hit and run			2						2		1						2		2						3		1					
Speeding	47		11				2		2								110	1	11	1					6							
Auto license violations	20	1	17	1					4		2						29	4	25	2					3		6				1	
Violation motor vehicle laws	31	6	37	2					11	1	7						122	7	66	4					14		6					
Breaking and entering			3						2		1						2		2						11		2					
And larceny																											6					
Housebreaking and larceny																											1					
Larceny	10		37	6					5		18	1			1		13	2	36	2					18		17	7				
Larceny and receiving	8	2	77	8					1	1	10						8	2	47	3					2		32	2				
Larceny from the person			1																	1							5	4				
Larceny of automobile																			1													
Temporary larceny																									4		1					
Murder—first degree																											1	2				
Abandonment	9		6						7		6						8	1	11						8		4					
Affray	10		36	21					1		10	5					20		28	7					7		8	1				
Bigamy																											2					

Carrying concealed weapon	7	1	21						1		6						6		23	2					3		7	1				
Contempt																									1							
Cruelty to animals									1		1						1		3													
Disorderly conduct	21	2	36	22					4	1	10	3					25	2	20	6					7	3	10	3			1	
Disorderly house			1	1					1	2	1								1						2		1	1				
Disposing of mortgaged property									2								1															
Disturbing religious worship			2																													
Embezzlement																				1					2		1					
Escape			1														1		5	2												
Failure to list tax	10		3				25		10		2				123		14	1	40						2							
Fish and game laws	3								6								2		1						1							
Forcible trespass	4		2						1	1									1													
Forgery																			2						6		2					
Fornication and adultery	1	1	10	10					3	2	1	2					1	1	2	2					1		1	1				
Gaming and lottery laws	16		130	2			2		4		7						4		70	1					2		3					
Health laws	3			1							1						6	1	15	14					2							
Injury to property	3		10	2					1		4	2					2		9	1					1	3	4					
Municipal ordinance	12		5						2		1						43	2	28						4							
Non-support	20		20						9		5						16	1	32						15		13					
Non-support of illegitimate child	3		28						4		10						2		14						7		8					
Perjury																											1					
Prostitution	2	1	1	1						1							1	15	1	7					1			2				
Receiving stolen goods			5								2	1					3								1							
Removing crop			1						2																1							
Resisting officer	2		4								3						9		4								4					
Robbery											1								2								7	2				
Seduction									1																							
Slander											2																					
Trespass	6	1	27						4		1						3		17	3					4	1	4					
Vagrancy	3	4	13	1						1	1								5	3					1		1					
Worthless check	14	1	1						16						1		5								2	1	1					
False pretense	2	19							3		4								2						5		2					
[illegible]	6		10						7		2						18	7	9	3					10	2	2	1				
Totals	1012	67	1278	186			31		243	15	258	29			126		1018	71	1034	146			5		288	18	313	48			8	

Convictions	2,574
Bound over	5
Other dispositions	666
	3,245

Convictions	2,274
Bound over	66
Other dispositions	609
	2,949

THIRD JUDICIAL DISTRICT

INFERIOR COURTS

JULY 1, 1940—JULY 1, 1941

Offense	Convictions White M	Convictions White F	Convictions Negro M	Convictions Negro F	Convictions Indian M	Convictions Indian F	Convictions Unclassified M	Convictions Unclassified F	Other Dispositions White M	Other Dispositions White F	Other Dispositions Negro M	Other Dispositions Negro F	Other Dispositions Indian M	Other Dispositions Indian F	Other Dispositions Unclassified M	Other Dispositions Unclassified F
Assault	48	3	84	6					28		44	3	1			
Assault with deadly weapon	36	2	119	16					17	2	35	6				
Assault on female	10		34						3		5					
Assault with intent to kill	1															
Assault—secret	1															
Drunk and disorderly	69	9	47	2					5		9					
Possession—illegal whiskey	3		18	1					2		2	2				
Possession for sale	13	3	27	8					5		9					
Manufacturing—possession of material for	3		14	1					1		3					
[illegible]on	3		9								2					
Violation liquor laws	17	1	102	5					5	1	15	3				
Driving drunk	138	2	122	1			1		38	1	11					
Reckless driving	54	2	71						29	3	23	2			1	
Hit and run	3		4	1					3		1					
Speeding	9	1	5													
Auto license violations	18	2	33	1					6		3					
Violation motor vehicle laws	8		6								2					
Breaking and entering	2		2	1												
And larceny																
And receiving			2						5							
Larceny	28	1	73						21		39	4				
Larceny and receiving																
Larceny from the person			1													
Larceny by trick and device	2															
Larceny of automobile			1						1							
Murder—first degree											1					
Manslaughter																
Abandonment	4		11						8		5					
Affray	3		34	4					2		5					
Carrying concealed weapon	7		44	1					1		3					
Conspiracy									1							

JULY 1, 1941—JULY 1, 1942

Offense	Convictions White M	Convictions White F	Convictions Negro M	Convictions Negro F	Convictions Indian M	Convictions Indian F	Convictions Unclassified M	Convictions Unclassified F	Other Dispositions White M	Other Dispositions White F	Other Dispositions Negro M	Other Dispositions Negro F	Other Dispositions Indian M	Other Dispositions Indian F	Other Dispositions Unclassified M	Other Dispositions Unclassified F
Assault	50	3	74	5					14	1	14	10				
Assault with deadly weapon	18	6	116	12					11	1	34	4				
Assault on female	14		24						5		7					
Assault with intent to kill			4													
Assault—secret																
Drunk and disorderly	72	5	52	2					8	3	5					
Possession—illegal whiskey	4	1	28	1					1		7					
Possession for sale	1		14	9					2	1	5	3				
Manufacturing—possession of material for	5		9						5		8					
[illegible]on	7		15	1					3		6					
Violation liquor laws	8	1	51	1					2		10					
Driving drunk	167	3	139	2					25		12					
Reckless driving	63		80						31	1	27				1	
Hit and run	4		4						2		2					
Speeding	56		19				1		4		1					
Auto license violations	29	1	84	1					6	1	4				1	
Violation motor vehicle laws	13		14						10		4					
Breaking and entering			2								1					
And larceny			3													
And receiving	1		3						2	1	1					
Larceny	18		60	9					10		21	1				
Larceny and receiving			1								6	1				
Larceny from the person																
Larceny by trick and device																
Larceny of automobile																
Murder—first degree																
Manslaughter											2					
Abandonment	7		4	2					1		4					
Affray	8		41	2					1		6	2				
Carrying concealed weapon	9		37								4	1				
Conspiracy																

Cruelty to animals	2																								2							
Disorderly conduct	4		7	3					3		5						2	5	12						6	2	4				1	
Disorderly house	1	1								2															1							
Disposing of mortgaged property										1							1		1						1		1					
Disturbing religious worship			1								3						5		4								2					
Embezzlement			1						1										1													
Escape	3		1																3								2					
Failure to list tax																	2										2					
Fish and game laws	1								2										2													
Forcible trespass			9						3	1							1		6	1							1					
Fornication and adultery	1	2	7	5					2	2	4	6					2		4	3					2	2						
Gaming and lottery laws	5		5								5						4		4						4		5					
Health laws	1		1	7							1																					
Injury to property		1	4						4								4		2						1		2					
Municipal ordinances	3		5	1					2		1						5		7													
Non-support	24		16						11		14						33		8						10		9				1	
Non-support of illegitimate child	1		8						6		11						2		12						1		12					
Nuisance	1								1		1						1															
Perjury																				1												
Prostitution	3	1								1							1			1												
Rape																											2					
Receiving stolen goods			3	1					3		1	2					1		3						2	1						
Removing crop	1																										1					
Resisting officer	8	1	10	2					3		2	1				1	6		8								3					
Robbery									1																1							
Seduction			1								1																1					
Slander				1					1																							
Trespass	8		6	1				1	1		4	1					14		9	1					2	1	6					
Vagrancy	2																															
Worthless check	3		2								1						10								1		1					
False pretense	3	1	3						1		1						1		4								2					
Carnal knowledge, etc.									1		2														1		3					
Slot machine laws	3																5		1													
Revenue act violations																	1															
Miscellaneous	10	3	3	3					8		1						12		8						9	1						
Totals	568	36	956	72			1	1	235	14	275	30	1		1	1	667	25	977	54			1		187	16	250	22			4	

Convictions	1,634
Bound over	10
Other dispositions	547
	2,191

Convictions	1,724
Bound over	12
Other dispositions	467
	2,203

FOURTH JUDICIAL DISTRICT
INFERIOR COURTS

Offense	JULY 1, 1940—JULY 1, 1941 CONVICTIONS Unclassified	JULY 1, 1940—JULY 1, 1941 OTHER DISPOSITIONS White	JULY 1, 1941—JULY 1, 1942 CONVICTIONS	JULY 1, 1941—JULY 1, 1942 OTHER DISPOSITIONS Unclassified F
Aslt				2
Aslt and btry				----
Assault with deadly : wep				----
Aslt on female				----
Asult with intent to kill				----
Assault with int nt to rape				----
Assault—secret				----
Drunk and disorderly				----
Possession—illegal whiskey				----
Possession for sale				3
Manufacturing—possession of mtal for				----
Transportation				----
Vion qlior laws				----
Driving drunk				3
Reckless driving				1
Hit and run				----
Speeding				----
Ato license dis				----
Vion motor vile laws				----
Breaking and entering				----
And larc ny				----
And receiving				----
Housebreaking				----
And larceny				----
Storebreaking and lany				----
deny				----
deny and ing				----
Larceny from the person				----
Larceny of automobile				----
Temporary rly				----
Murder—first dee				----
Manslaughter				----

Manslaughter
Burglary—second degree
Abandonment
Affray

Carrying concealed weapon	12		18	2			18	1			5				6		14		29				2		5		4				2	
Contempt				1															1													
Conspiracy											2	1																				
Cruelty to animals																									2							
Disorderly conduct	11		15	2	2		8		5		4				7	1	7	1	23	8			2	2	2	4	9	3				
Disorderly house	1	1					1												1								1					
Disposing of mortgaged property	2		1												1		2								1							
Disturbing religious worship			1	3							2								4													
Embezzlement									1		1								1								2				2	
Escape	2		5				1		1								4		4	2												
Failure to list tax			2														1															
Fish and game laws	4						2		3						3										2							
Forcible trespass	5		1						1								6		6						3							
Forgery									10		1																					
Fornication and adult[illegible]ry	1		3	1			1	1	1	1	1	1			1	1	6	4	4	3							1	1				
Gaming and [illegible]tery laws	6		23				21	6	5		1				6	1	7		17	2			8	1	9		23	4			1	
Health laws	1								1								1								1			1			1	
Injury to [illegible]ty	7	1	3				7		5						1		14		9				1		3		2				1	
[illegible]al [illegible]es	9		3	1					4		3						9		8		1				2		2	2			1	
Non-support	32		17				10		12		6				15		42		22	1			4		11		7				2	
Non-support of illegitimate child	3		11				16		2		3				9		5		20				4		3		9				1	
Nuisance																									2	1					1	
Perjury									1										1													
Prostitution	5	5	3	4			6	4							1	2	1	1	14	18			1	1		3	6	7			1	
Rape											3																1					
Receiving stolen goods			1				3	1	1								1	1									2					
Removing crop	2								2																1						1	
Resisting officer	3		4				2								2		6		11								4					
Robbery																			2						4		6					
Seduction									1		3														2							
Slander	1																		1													
Trespass	18		22	1					4		3						20		16	2					12	1	5	1			2	
Vagrancy																	1		3					2								
Worthless check	7		1				2		4						4		8	4	4				2									
[illegible]alse [illegible]se	2		1						6		1	1			2		1								1		2				2	
Carnal [illegible]e, etc.			1								1																					
Slot [illegible]ine laws	4	1					1								3		6															
R[illegible]venue act [illegible]							1																									
Miscellaneous	2		4				2		9			1					5		5				2		1		1				1	
Totals	1080	27	868	76	11	1	468	89	250	9	167	24	1		215	25	1230	38	1093	149	3		122	28	364	23	271	44	1		75	9

Convictions
Bound over 7
Other dis[illegible]ositions

Convictions 2,663
Bound over 59

FIFTH JUDICIAL DISTRICT

INFERIOR COURTS

JULY 1, 1940—JULY 1, 1941

Offense	Convictions White M	Convictions White F	Convictions Negro M	Convictions Negro F	Convictions Indian M	Convictions Indian F	Convictions Unclassified M	Convictions Unclassified F	Other Dispositions White M	Other Dispositions White F	Other Dispositions Negro M	Other Dispositions Negro F	Other Dispositions Indian M	Other Dispositions Indian F	Other Dispositions Unclassified M	Other Dispositions Unclassified F
Assault	11		31	5					5	1	1					
Assault and [battery]																
Assault with deadly weapon	6	1	65	20					5		23	5				
Assault on [female]	3		11								2					
Assault with intent to kill																
Drunk and disorderly	5		7								1					
Possession—illegal whiskey	52	1	48	4												
Possession for sale																
Manufacturing—possession of material for	1		5													
Transportation			6													
Violation liquor laws	1	1	10	11					3	1	5					
Driving drunk	46	1	23						14		1					
Reckless driving	15		21						14	3	9	1				
Hit and run	1															
Speeding	2															
Auto license	11	1	7													
Violation motor vehicle laws	7		2						1							
Breaking and entering			1								1					
Larceny	8	1	70	8					5		16					
Larceny and receiving																
Temporary larceny	2								1							
Manslaughter									2		1					
Abandonment	1		5	1					3		1					
Affray	6								1							
Carrying concealed [weapon]	6		10						1		4					
Cruelty to animals									2							
Disorderly conduct	2	1	14	4							4					
[illegible]	1															
Disposing of mortgaged property			1													
Disturbing religious worship			2													

JULY 1, 1941—JULY 1, 1942

Offense	Convictions White M	Convictions White F	Convictions Negro M	Convictions Negro F	Convictions Indian M	Convictions Indian F	Convictions Unclassified M	Convictions Unclassified F	Other Dispositions White M	Other Dispositions White F	Other Dispositions Negro M	Other Dispositions Negro F	Other Dispositions Indian M	Other Dispositions Indian F	Other Dispositions Unclassified M	Other Dispositions Unclassified F
Assault	17	2	20	4					4		2					
Assault and [battery]	3															
Assault with deadly weapon	17	1	55	9					7		25	2				
Assault on [female]	2		4						1		5					
Assault with intent to kill									1							
Drunk and disorderly	65	2	56	2			3		3		1					
Possession—illegal whiskey	2		10	1			1				3	2				
Possession for sale	1		3	3			1				2					
Manufacturing—possession of material for			1													
Transportation			2								2					
Violation liquor laws	13	3	26	19					6		7	3				
Driving drunk	92	3	40						20		2				2	
Reckless driving																
Hit and run			2						1							
Speeding	44	1	5						2							
Auto license	15	1	15						1		1					
Violation motor vehicle laws	4		2						3		1					
Breaking and entering		1	1								1					
Larceny	21		68	2					7		12					
Larceny and receiving			1													
Temporary larceny																
Manslaughter																
Abandonment	5		4				1		2		2					
Affray	1	1	6	3						2						
Carrying concealed [weapon]	6	1	11				1		1		4					
Cruelty to animals			1													
Disorderly conduct			12	2							2					
[illegible]			1	1												
Disposing of mortgaged property																
Disturbing religious worship																

Manslaughter
Abandonment
Affray
Carrying concealed weapon ... 10 ... 4
Cruelty to animals ... 2
Disorderly conduct ... 2 ... 1 ... 14 ... 4 ... 4 ... 2
Disorderly house ... 1 ... 1
Disposing of mortgaged property ... 1
Disturbing religious worship ... 2

Escape																			2													
Fish and game laws	7		1																						2							
Forcible trespass			2																1													
Fornication and adultery			3	2								1							1	1							1					
Gaming and lottery laws			3														1		13								4	1				
Injury to property	3		3						1		1						11		3								1					
Municipal ordinances	2		3														1															
Non-support			7						1	1	3						5		8				1				3					
Non-support of illegitimate child	1		4						1		4								1								1					
[illegible]	5	1															6	1	2													
[illegible]ion			1	1														1														
Receiving stolen goods			1								2								1													
Removing crop									2																		1					
Resisting officer	5		4	1													4		3				1		2		1					
Trespass	2		1	1					1		2						2		9	3					1		2	2				
Vagrancy	2	1															1	3	1													
Worthless check	13		4						8								5		1								2	1				
False pretense	1		3								1																1	1				
Carnal knowledge, etc.			1																													
Slot machine laws			2																2	1												
Miscellaneous	2		4						2								8		3						1							
Totals	230	9	386	58					73	6	82	7					353	21	397	51			9		65	2	89	12			2	

Convictions 683
Bound over 9
Other dispositions 159

851

Convictions 831
Bound over 4
Other dispositions 166

1,001

SIXTH JUDICIAL DISTRICT

INFERIOR COURTS

Offense	JULY 1, 1940—JULY 1, 1941																JULY 1, 1941—JULY 1, 1942															
	CONVICTIONS								OTHER DISPOSITIONS								CONVICTIONS								OTHER DISPOSITIONS							
	White		Negro		Indian		Unclas-sified		White		Negro		Indian		Unclas-sified		White		Negro		Indian		Unclas-sified		White		Negro		Indian		Unclas-sified	
	M	F	M	F	M	F	M	F	M	F	M	F	M	F	M	F	M	F	M	F	M	F	M	F	M	F	M	F	M	F	M	F
Assault	17	2	13	4					8	2	5	11					11	1	19	5					8	1	5	3				
Assault and battery	1		1	1						1	2	1							1						2	1						
Assault with deadly weapon	38	2	95	30					29	3	61	15	1		1		32	2	73	23					14	2	38	18				
Assault on female	32		47						19		24				2		18		34						9		13					
Assault with intent to kill	1								3		2								1						2		1	1				
Assault with intent to rape											2																					
Assault—secret																									1							
Drunk and disorderly	393	21	259	34	1		1		37	1	16	3			1		461	31	272	24	1				56	4	15	2				
Possession—illegal whiskey	6		5						1						1		5		4													
Possession for sale	37	5	69	13					14	2	16	3	1				4		9	5					2		3	2				
Manuacturing—possession of material for	26		24		1				1		9		1				4		1													
Transportation	17	1	27		1				4		7						6		7	1					2		1	1				
Violation liquor laws	10	2	39	22			1				9	1					15	1	33	17						1	5	3				
Driving drunk	88		43	1	1		1		23	2	6		2		1		63	1	23						8							
Reckless driving	48	3	31	1					43	3	9	1			2		70	1	22						16	2	9	2				
Hit and run	2		3						1	1							1		1						1		1					
Speeding	17		15	1					1								65		6						4		2					
Auto license laws	47	4	40	2	3		1		2		1						36	3	37	2					10		2					
Violation motor vehicle laws	22		17						8		5						27		18						9	1	2					
Breaking and entering			1				1				1								1						1		9					
And larceny			7						13		17														5		4					
Storebreaking and entering												1																				
Larceny	14		54	3	1				13	2	23	5					13		50	3					12	1	30	4				
Larceny and receiving	5	1	6						6		4	1			1		3		13	1					3		1					
Larceny from the person											3	1													1	1	3	2				
Larceny by trick and device			1						1		1														1		1	1				
Larceny of automobile									1		1						1		1						2		5					
Petty larceny			3		1						1								2						2							
Burglary—first degree											2																					
Abandonment	14		11						12	1	8				1		9		7	1					8		1					
Affray	8	2	13	4			1		3	2	4	3					6		15	7							7	2				
Carrying concealed weapon	3		32		1				3		2		1		1		6		19								3					

Cruelty to animals														
Disorderly conduct	13	6	37	13					15	5	16	9		
Disorderly house		1	4	5					1	2				
Disposing of mortgaged property	2		1						1		2			
Disturbing religious worship			3								3	3		
Embezzlement									1		1			
Escape		1	1						1					
Failure to list tax														
Fish and game laws	7						1		3					
Forcible trespass	6		8	1					3		2			
Forgery									4		2			
Fornication and adultery		2	3	2					3	2	3	4		
Gaming and lottery laws	1		12							2				
Health laws	1		1	1					1					
Incest	1	1												
Injury to property	7		14	1					6		6	1		
Municipal ordinances	9	1	11						9	6				
Non-support	24		15						14	1	12			
Non-support of illegitimate child	5		7		1				1		7			
Nuisance	6	2	4	2					3	1		1		
Perjury														
Prostitution	5	6	8	7					3	3				
Rape									1		1			
Receiving stolen goods			1								1			
Removing crop									2					
Resisting officer	8	1	5						3	1	3	1		
Robbery									1		2			
Seduction						1			2					
Trespass	2		5	2					4		2			
Vagrancy	1	1	2	3					1	1				
Worthless check	20	1	1						23		1			
False pretense									3		3			
Carnal knowledge, etc.											1			
Crime against nature											1			
Slot machine laws	8													
Kidnapping													1	
Miscellaneous	9		5						10		4			
Totals	981	66	1004	153	11	1	7		365	44	314	65	7	

Convictions	2,223
Bound over	47
Other dispositions	768
	3,038

Convictions	2,100
Bound over	51
Other dispositions	588
	2,739

SEVENTH JUDICIAL DISTRICT

INFERIOR COURTS

Offense	JULY 1, 1940—JULY 1, 1941															JULY 1, 1941—JULY 1, 1942							
	CONVICTIONS								OTHER DISPOSITIONS							CONVICTIONS	OTHER DISPOSITIONS						
	White		Negro		Indian		Unclassified		White		Negro		Indian			Unclassified	White		Negro	Indian		Unclassified	
	M	F	M	F	M	F	M	F	M	F	M	F	M			F	M	F	M	M	F	M	F
Assault	15	2	25	5					9	1	10	3					4		3			1	
Assault and battery	55	7	85	5					19	1	15						14		12				
Assault with deadly weapon	42	4	196	59			3		24	6	44	12					22	1	41				
Assault on female	21		30				1		8		9						5		9				
Assault with intent to kill	5		1						2		5						2		3				
Assault with intent to rape											1								1				
Assault—secret									1														
Drunk and disorderly	1223	76	589	71			7	2	34	3	8	1					23		8			2	
Possession—illegal [illegible]	23		148	60			2		5	2	21	13					7		23			1	
Possession for sale	5		19	3			8		3	1	3	2					3	1	7			1	
Manufacturing—possession of material for	9		13				1		2		1	1					3		3				
Transportation	2		13	1					2								1		1				
Violation liquor laws																							
Driving drunk	145	3	52	2			15		25	1	7						28		4			1	
Reckless driving	68	4	54	1			11		53	2	18	1					40	1	12				
Hit and run	7		8				1		5		3						1	1	2				
Speeding	308	7	71	1			26		5		3						9		2			1	
Auto [illegible]	64	5	44	6			10		3		11						1		3			1	
Violation motor vehicle laws	41	4	39	1			3		8		8						2		3				
Breaking and entering	1		4						3		9								4				
And larceny									2		2								5			1	
And receiving	1		2								10						6		13				
Larceny	51	6	137	40					12	3	39	13					28	1	28				
Larceny and receiving	5		19						2		18	2					1		6				
Larceny from the person	1		1	1					1	1	7	1							4				
Larceny by trick and device	1																						
Larceny of automobile	5		3						2		1						4		3				
Temporary larceny	3		2																				
Murder—first degree											3	1					6		1				
Manslaughter											1												
Burglary—first degree									3		1								1				
Burglary—second degree																							
Abandonment	20		14						11		2						4						
Affray	18	3	26	7					6		9						5		1				

Burglary second degree
Abandonment
Affray

Bigamy									1																							
Carrying [illegible]ed [illegible]	12	1	42	7							4				1		9	1	28	1			3		4		3					
[illegible]lty to [illegible]als			1						1	1									3						1							
[illegible]ly conduct	41	7	68	24					11	3	6	3					57	10	68	20			3		11		8	4				
Disorderly [illegible]se	6	3	9						2	2	5						13	11	5	5					6	4		2				
Disposing of mortgaged property	6		6	1					2		1						2		3													
[illegible]urbing [illegible]gious [illegible]			1																1													
Embezzlement	2								2		2														6		5					
Escape																		2	3													
Fish and [illegible] laws	3								1								7		1						1							
Forcible trespass	3		9								1						5		9								1	1				
Forgery	1								6		1														13		1	2				
Fornication and adultery	3	3	6	6							1						4	4	10	9					1	1	1					
Gaming and [illegible]ry laws	11		61				3		6		7						30		51	1					3		3					
Health laws			3	2							4	2															1					
Injury to property	23	2	20	6					10		8						9	1	18	4			1		5							
Municipal [illegible]es	48	1	19	1					14	1	5	2					132	7	60	2					11	1	4					
Non-support	27		26						15		9						19		26						9		5					
[illegible]-support of illegitimate child	4		11						1		3						2		7						1		3					
[illegible]le	82	3	22	6					1								89	7	10	13							1					
Perjury																									1							
Prostitution	6	7	15	16					1			1					2	2	2	2					7		2					
Rape									1			1													1		1					
Receiving [illegible]en goods	3		1						4			2							8						5		4	1				
Removing crop	1		1						1																							
Resisting officer	11		14	3					1		2						20	2	13	2					3							
[illegible]bbery											7								1								19					
Seduction																									1							
[illegible]der				1																												
[illegible]ss	48	4	54	3			1		6		6	1					21	4	41	2					3		4					
Vagrancy	32	27	54	6						1	13						32	20	27	16					4	4	4	1				
[illegible]ss [illegible]	30	4	3						6								15	9	1						4	1						
False pretense	2		9						4		2				1		1		4						4		5					
Carnal knowledge, etc.									1		2						1								1		2					
C[illegible]e [illegible]t nature									2																							
Slot [illegible]ine laws	2						1		1								6		10	2					1							
Revenue act [illegible]											1																					
Miscellaneous	34	4	19	1					10	1	3						23	2	14	2					2							
Totals	2580	187	2069	346			93		361	30	362	62			9		2317	164	1781	324			63		328	16	280	50			9	

Convictions	5,275	Convictions	4,649
Bound over	83	Bound over	132
Other dispositions	741	Other dispositions	551

EIGHTH JUDICIAL DISTRICT

INFERIOR COURTS

JULY 1, 1940—JULY 1, 1941

Offense	Convictions: White M	Convictions: White F	Convictions: Negro M	Convictions: Negro F	Convictions: Indian M	Convictions: Indian F	Convictions: Unclassified M	Convictions: Unclassified F	Other Dispositions: White M	Other Dispositions: White F	Other Dispositions: Negro M	Other Dispositions: Negro F	Other Dispositions: Indian M	Other Dispositions: Indian F	Other Dispositions: Unclassified M	Other Dispositions: Unclassified F
Assault	12	2	7		2		89	68	5		4				101	12
Assault and battery	1							1							60	7
Assault with deadly weapon	31	2	61	12	2		109	114	18	2	17	1			300	20
Assault on female	17		23				26		3		8				13	
Assault with intent to kill			2	2				1	4							
Assault with intent to rape															3	
[illegible]et			1						1		1					
Drunk and disorderly	70	3	28	2	1		877	695	6		1				45	4
Possession—illegal whiskey	34	1	19					1	4		2					
Possession for sale	24	5	21	9	1				17	2	8					
Manufacturing—possession of material for	18		10						14		4					
[illegible]n	13		11						5	2	5	2				
Violation liquor laws	12	1	20	6			61	36	3	1	5	1			84	19
Driving drunk	91		41	1	1		69	56	24		3				38	2
Reckless driving	49	1	20				65	21	16	1	3				58	2
Hit and run	3		3				8	3	1						19	2
Speeding	35	1	7				91	61	2						5	
Auto license violations	106	1	32		1		87	42	18		2				39	7
Violation motor vehicle laws	125	2	24				94	33	8		1				13	1
Breaking and entering															7	
And larceny									2						2	
And receiving															19	1
Housebreaking							1				1				3	1
And larceny															1	
And receiving								1							41	
Storebreaking							1								2	
And larceny							1									
And receiving															26	
Larceny	17		41	4	1		7	2	12		9	1			6	1
Larceny and receiving			1				61	25			1	1			67	3
Larceny from the person							1								3	2

JULY 1, 1941—JULY 1, 1942

Offense	Convictions: White M	Convictions: White F	Convictions: Negro M	Convictions: Negro F	Convictions: Indian M	Convictions: Indian F	Convictions: Unclassified M	Convictions: Unclassified F	Other Dispositions: White M	Other Dispositions: White F	Other Dispositions: Negro M	Other Dispositions: Negro F	Other Dispositions: Indian M	Other Dispositions: Indian F	Other Dispositions: Unclassified M	Other Dispositions: Unclassified F
Assault	7	4	5	1			35	8	4		2	4			90	3
Assault and battery																
Assault with deadly weapon	32	1	48	12			77	22	14	1	11	3			231	24
Assault on female	11		16				59		10						152	
Assault with intent to kill							4	1	1		2				14	1
Assault with intent to rape							1		1							
[illegible]et																
Drunk and disorderly	51	4	20				780	61	7		4	1			656	4
Possession—illegal whiskey	14		8	1					3						2	
Possession for sale	23	5	16	6					16	1	10	2				
Manufacturing—possession of material for	13		9						3							
[illegible]n	9		10				1		3		2				2	
Violation liquor laws	1		15				20	5	2		10				123	8
Driving drunk	59		25				32	3	31	1	2				108	
Reckless driving	40		29				45	1	18	1	7	1			99	2
Hit and run	2		2				2								28	1
Speeding	34		4				339	9	5		3				117	1
Auto license violations	57	3	16	2			81	8	4	2	1				106	1
Violation motor vehicle laws	75		18				75	1	12		1				114	1
Breaking and entering			1				1								5	
And larceny										1	3					
And receiving			1						1						8	
Housebreaking															6	
And larceny							1		1						1	
And receiving							1								2	
Storebreaking															1	
And larceny																
And receiving							1								34	
Larceny	5		29	6			2		7	1	14				15	
Larceny and receiving			1				20	1	1						86	7
Larceny from the person							1								4	1

Larceny by trick ard device								1							1	1									1						5	
Irany of automobile							3	1			1				14								1		1						24	
ry larceny							1	3							1																4	
Murder—first degree							2																								8	2
er																									1							
Burglary—first degree															1																13	
Burglary—second degree																							1									
Abandonment	2		4	1			3	3	4						10		3		4				1		2		2				18	1
Abduction															1																	
Affray	2			1			47	35							19	1	3			2			27								52	2
Arson															1																	
Bigamy											1				1																1	1
Carrying dod w ap n	5		12				17	7	6		1				8		6	1	19				19		3	3	2				27	
dpt	1						1										1		1				1									
Conspiracy															3																	
lty to animals															1		1															
lly duct	5	3	1	4			78	113							23	4	9	3	6	1			96	26	3		2				146	6
Disorderly house							1	2							1	1			1	1			1		1						13	
g of mortgaged property	3						1		4		1						1								2							
Disturbing religious worship			5						6							1															3	
Embezzlement															2										1						7	
Escape							9	4									2		1				6	3							10	
Fhire to list tax								2							4								4								2	
Fish ard ame laws	2						1	2							1		4								7							
Forcible trespass	1			1			3	1	1		1												1								1	
Forgery															2																13	
Fornication and adultery	2	2	2	1			23	32	3	1	1	2			4				3	1			34	30	4	1	4	4			66	17
ing ard ry :	9		10				45	48			1				18	2			1				50				5				62	
Health laws							6	1							6								9	1							46	3
Injury to property	2		2				12	6	2		1				15	3	2		4				12	2	7	1					17	2
Municipal ies			1				336	138							24	1							282	12			1				1317	1
Non-support	12		14				19		5		4				44		9		8				1		5		4				58	
Non-support of illegitimate			2						4		1				1												1				1	
:	2							1							3	1			1					1			1				6	
Perjury															4	2															2	
Prostitution								4										1					9	36							77	21
Rape											1				9																16	
Receiving len gds			2				1								9								1				1				10	1
Removing crop									4		1	1					2								1							
Resisting officer	2		2				11	17							6		2		4				28	2	1		3				21	1
Robbery			1				9				1				21																31	
Seduction															1												1					

EIGHTH JUDICIAL DISTRICT—(Continued)

INFERIOR COURTS

Offense	JULY 1, 1940—JULY 1, 1941																JULY 1, 1941—JULY 1, 1942															
	CONVICTIONS								OTHER DISPOSITIONS								CONVICTIONS								OTHER DISPOSITIONS							
	White		Negro		Indian		Unclassified		White		Negro		Indian		Unclassified		White		Negro		Indian		Unclassified		White		Negro		Indian		Unclassified	
	M	F	M	F	M	F	M	F	M	F	M	F	M	F	M	F	M	F	M	F	M	F	M	F	M	F	M	F	M	F	M	F
Slier							1		1	2					1	1									1		2	3			1	1
Trespass	7	1	5		1		9	7	6		1				11		8	1	6				4	1	10		2				22	
Vagrancy	1		1				7	2							71	11							5								125	4
Worthless check	2		3				18	18	9						3		6						11	1							14	1
False pretense	1						1	1	5		1				1										8		4				9	
Carnal knowledge, etc.															6																2	
Crime against nature															1																4	1
Slot machine law	1						2								2																	
Kidnapping																											1	1			2	
Revenue act violations															1																	
Miscellaneous	1		3				16	9	6						12	2	5		2				24	8	3		2				49	3
Totals	721	25	442	44	10		2331	1618	229	11	93	9			1324	115	497	23	334	33			2206		243	13	110	19			4309	122

Convictions	5,191
Bound over	305
Other dispositions	1,476
	6,972

Convictions	3,083
Bound over	301
Other dispositions	4,515
	7,899

NINTH JUDICIAL DISTRICT

INFERIOR COURTS

JULY 1, 1940—JULY 1, 1941

Offense	CONVICTIONS								OTHER DISPOSITIONS							
	White		Negro		Indian		Unclassified		White		Negro		Indian		Unclassified	
	M	F	M	F	M	F	M	F	M	F	M	F	M	F	M	F
Assault	96	9	184	28	19	1	1		44	7	52	13	11			
Assault with deadly weapon	3	1	8	1	5						4		1	2		
Assault on female	9		7		2				2		1					
Assault with intent to kill																
Assault with intent to rape																
Drunk and disorderly	95	7	75	8	98	2	3		14		5	3	13		1	
Possession—illegal whiskey	2		11	5	6	3					3	2	1			
Possession for sale			6	2							1		1			
Manufacturing—possession of material for			3		7	1							1			
Transportation	5		3		1											
Violation liquor laws	82	5	110	64	5				12	3	16	7	1			
Driving drunk	196	6	34		5				51	3	9					
Reckless driving	134	4	52	1	2		1		85	4	34		1			
Hit and run	3		2						5							
Speeding	199	5	37		2		1		5		1		1			
Auto license violations	164	5	42	1	2				15		8		1			
Violation motor vehicle laws	39	1	19		5				3		6		4			
Breaking and entering											1		1			
And larceny																
Larceny	45		79	10	7	1			18		22	5		1		
Larceny and receiving			3								1	1				
Larceny from the person	1															
Larceny by trick and device	1															
Larceny of automobile	2		6													
Petty larceny	1															
Burglary—first degree																
Burglary—second degree																
Abandonment			1		1				2	1	1	2				
Abduction												1				
Affray	12		14	7	1				1		6		1			
Arson													1			
Carrying concealed weapon	15		24		2				4		7		1			

JULY 1, 1941—JULY 1, 1942

Offense	CONVICTIONS								OTHER DISPOSITIONS							
	White		Negro		Indian		Unclassified		White		Negro		Indian		Unclassified	
	M	F	M	F	M	F	M	F	M	F	M	F	M	F	M	F
Assault	93	11	140	34	20	1			36	2	36	11	7			
Assault with deadly weapon	6	2	38	12	6				3		13	1				
Assault on female					1						3		1			
Assault with intent to kill	1		1								2		1			
Assault with intent to rape			1		1											
Drunk and disorderly	128	13	182	9	70	7	1		9	2	4	1	1			
Possession—illegal whiskey	1		9	5	9	3					4					
Possession for sale	1		1	2	2							1				
Manufacturing—possession of material for			1		4	1							1			
Transportation			1										1			
Violation liquor laws	123	11	166	59	40	4			12		15	5	5			
Driving drunk	155	7	45	1	9			1	22	1	7		1			
Reckless driving	101	3	67	2	5				45	1	21		1			
Hit and run	8		3		1											
Speeding	399	14	60	1	1				17		1	1				
Auto license violations	69	5	29		4				3	1	4					
Violation motor vehicle laws	94	3	19		14				19	2	6		3			
Breaking and entering																
And larceny	1		4									1				
Larceny	40		104	26	2				17		22	7	4			
Larceny and receiving																
Larceny from the person																
Larceny by trick and device																
Larceny of automobile																
Petty larceny			2								2					
Burglary—first degree			1													
Burglary—second degree			4													
Abandonment	4		6						3		1					
Abduction																
Affray	2		10	4	3				1		5	2				
Arson																
Carrying concealed weapon	6	1	25	1	4				2							

Contempt	1				1																											
[illegible]lty to animals											1		2						1	2							1					
Disorderly conduct	10	2	11	6	2				4	1	2	3					8		10	1					1	1		1		1		
Disorderly [illegible]e	6	11							2	5									1						5	1	2	4				
Disposing of mortgaged property	1		2														2		3													
Disturbing religious worship			1	1	2						2								3								1					
Embezzlement									1																1							
Escape			3														1															
Failure to list tax	6	1	2							1	1						2		4						1							
Fish and game laws	2				1		1		1								7								1							
Forcible [illegible]ss	8		6						8	1	3						4		3						1							
Forgery																	-1															
Fornication and adultery	2	2	1	1					3	2	3	3					5	4	3	5							1	2				
Gaming and [illegible]ry laws	40	1	10						11		3						6		11								1	2				
Health laws			11	10	1	1						1						1														
Injury to [illegible]	4		2	1	4						2		1				10	5	2	1	3						4		2	1		
Municipal [illegible]s	4		1						3	1	1						1		2						11							
Non-support	15	1	4						7	1	4		3				13		5		2				2		2					
Non-support of illegitimate child			3						1		1								4						1		1					
Nuisance	7								8								4		1	2					4			1				
Official misconduct	1								1																							
Prostitution	5	8	1						4	3							11	45	9	47	1				7	13	5	26		1		
Rape													1														1					
Receiving stolen goods			1								1		1				1		3		3	1			1		2		1			
Removing crop									1																							
Resisting officer	7		5	1	4				1		2						4		9		1				2							
Robbery											1																1					
Seduction									1																							
Slander									2	1							2		1													
Trespass	10		12	1	3				8	1	6	2	1		1		11		15	3	1				8		2		2			
Vagrancy	5	21	10	1					2			3					2	29	6	13		1			1	1		3				
[illegible]ss check	15		1		4				8	1	2		3				7		1						3		1					
False pretense	2	1	2						4				1				1	2	1	1	1						3					
Carnal knowledge, etc.			1								1																					
[illegible]e against [illegible]re																											1					
Slot [illegible]ine laws	11		1							2																						
[illegible]us	6	11	4						19		3	1					9	10	8	1					2	3	3		3			
Totals	1272	102	815	149	192	9	7		361	38	217	47	53	3	2		1344	166	1025	232	208	18	1	1	241	28	178	69	34	3		

Convictions	2,546
Bound over	5
Other dispositions	716

Convictions	2,995
Other dispositions	553
	3,548

TENTH JUDICIAL DISTRICT

INFERIOR COURTS

Offense	JULY 1, 1940—JULY 1, 1941																JULY 1, 1941—JULY 1, 1942															
	CONVICTIONS								OTHER DISPOSITIONS								CONVICTIONS								OTHER DISPOSITIONS							
	White		Negro		Indian		Unclassified		White		Negro		Indian		Unclassified		White		Negro		Indian		Unclassified		White		Negro		Indian		Unclassified	
	M	F	M	F	M	F	M	F	M	F	M	F	M	F	M	F	M	F	M	F	M	F	M	F	M	F	M	F	M	F	M	F
Assault	9	1	33	3					7	1	3	1					5		19	2					4	1	2	4				
Assault and battery	108	6	217	28	1				19	5	40	15					120	11	209	21					31	5	36	7			1	
Assault with deadly weapon	70	5	284	35					31	2	98	13			1		57	4	250	55					26	5	77	26			1	
Assault on female	10		19						1		1						11		8						5							
Assault with intent to kill	1		2						4		13	2							4	1							12				1	
Assault with intent to rape									2		2				1												3					
Assault—secret											1																					
Drunk and disorderly	1184	73	611	80				1	37	1	10	1					285	67	545	65					54	3	10	2			1	
Possession—illegal whiskey	53	2	132	46					4		28	22					47	4	87	27					6		10	7				
Possession for sale	9		28	14					4		11	1					14	3	23	16			1		1	2	1				1	
Manufacturing—possession of material for	2		20	4							3						7		14								4					
Transportation			5						1		1						6		2	1												
Violation liquor laws	4								1								9									1	2					
Driving drunk	84	3	40	1					18		5						112	4	46				1		18	1	5					
Reckless driving	146	8	102						92	2	51	1	1				211	14	126	1					116	12	49	1			2	
Hit and run	8	1	8		1				5		5						18	3	13						4	1	6					
Speeding	575	17	161	4					18								403	6	162	1					4							
Auto license violations	107	16	95	9					9	6	8	5					62	5	73	4					17	1	12					
Violation motor vehicle laws	369	24	155	4					22	1	10	1					298	20	136	7			2	2	8	2	5					
Breaking and entering	1								1			1													1		1					
And larceny									1																		1					
And receiving	1																															
Housebreaking											1														1		1					
And larceny									1		4														3		10	1				
And receiving									2		8																					
Storebreaking									3																		2					
And larceny											3								2						5		9					
And receiving									3		7																					
Larceny	67	6	146	19					30	5	41	8			1		69	13	115	15					32	7	41	6				
Larceny and receiving																			1													
Larceny from the person			2						3	3	10	1							3						2	3	9	2				

Larceny by trick and device									1								2		1	1							1	1				
Larceny of [illegible]			4						1		3														1							
Petty larceny	4		8						1		1	1					1		2								3					
Murder—first degree											6	2													2		5	1				
Manslaughter									7		1														8	1	3				1	
Burglary—first degree																									1		3					
Abandonment	13		4						2								5		2						6		1					
Abortion									2		1																					
Affray	26	1	37	7					5		9	3					46	1	27	8					6	1	6	4				
Arson																											1					
Bigamy									1																		1					
Carrying concealed weapon	14		50	3					3		10						4		42	1					1		5				1	
[illegible]		1															1															
Cruelty to animals			1								1						1															
Disorderly conduct	80	7	86	34					7		10	4					106	20	89	38					11	4	7	3				
Disorderly house	9	4	1	3							1	1					3	4	3	6					1	1	3	3				
Disposing of mortgaged property	9	1	9	1					2		2	1				1	1		6	1					5	1	2					
Disturbing religious worship			1								4																					
Embezzlement									1	1															5		3					
Escape	10	5	9	8							1	1					10	3	3	7			1		1	1						
Fish and game laws																	1		1						2							
Forcible trespass	22	4	28	3					3		2	1					18	5	27	3					4		4	2				
Forgery	2								21		2																14					
Fornication and adultery	3	3	2	2					1	1	1	1					3	3	9	9					3	3	7	6				
Gaming and lottery laws	56	1	201	6					73		17	1					63		159	13			1		9		13	2				
Health laws	2		4														12	1	5	1			1					1				
Injury to property	37	4	38	5					12		6	2					41	2	34	6					17	1	7					
Municipal ordinances	1374	173	206	29			15		199	27	49	6					363	43	144	9			6	2	70	9	25	7			10	1
[illegible]	42		25						15		9						43		27						18		9					
Non-support of illegitimate child	6		47				2		3		17						3		48				1				23				1	
[illegible]	24	18	2						6	3	3	3					25	22	5	1					1	5	2	1				
Perjury																									1		2					
Prostitution	5	11	10	10					3	1							12	16	8	8					1		3	1				
Rape											2																4					
Receiving stolen goods									1		3						1		3	2							4					
Removing crop									1																							
Resisting officer	15		11	1					2	1	1						24	3	8	1					3		1					
Robbery									5		9	1													3		7					
Seduction	1								2																1		1					
Trespass	47	2	47	2					5		6	1					52	2	31		1				7	2	9	4				
Vagrancy	10	17	4						3	5	3						12	7	7	2						4	1					
Worthless check	14	1							4								14	3	1					2	5		1					

TENTH JUDICIAL DISTRICT—(Continued)

INFERIOR COURTS

JULY 1, 1940—JULY 1, 1941

Offense	Convictions: White M	White F	Negro M	Negro F	Indian M	Indian F	Unclassified M	Unclassified F	Other Dispositions: White M	White F	Negro M	Negro F	Indian M	Indian F	Unclassified M	Unclassified F
False pretense	1								2		2					
Carnal knowledge, etc.											3					
Crime against nature									1		3					
Slot machine laws	11		1						2	1	1					
Kidnapping																
Revenue act violations																
Miscellaneous	29	6	29	2					11	2	11	2				
Totals	4674	421	2925	363	2		17	1	727	68	564	103	1		3	1

JULY 1, 1941—JULY 1, 1942

Offense	Convictions: White M	White F	Negro M	Negro F	Indian M	Indian F	Unclassified M	Unclassified F	Other Dispositions: White M	White F	Negro M	Negro F	Indian M	Indian F	Unclassified M	Unclassified F
False pretense	10	1	15	1					6	2	5					
Carnal knowledge, etc.											1					
Crime against nature									4		1					
Slot machine laws	6										1					
Kidnapping											1					
Revenue act violations	2															
Miscellaneous	47	2	26	3					15	2	7	3				
Totals	3666	292	2571	337	1		14	4	556	81	505	95			20	1

1940–1941	
Convictions	8,403
Bound over	145
Other dispositions	1,322
	9,870

1941–1942	
Convictions	6,885
Bound over	142
Other dispositions	1,116
	8,143

ELEVENTH JUDICIAL DISTRICT

INFERIOR COURTS

JULY 1, 1940—JULY 1, 1941

Offense	Convictions White M	Convictions White F	Convictions Negro M	Convictions Negro F	Convictions Indian M	Convictions Indian F	Convictions Unclassified M	Convictions Unclassified F	Other Dispositions White M	Other Dispositions White F	Other Dispositions Negro M	Other Dispositions Negro F	Other Dispositions Indian M	Other Dispositions Indian F	Other Dispositions Unclassified M	Other Dispositions Unclassified F
Assault	24	4	42	26					6	3	14	13				
Assault and Battery																
Assault with deadly weapon	26	1	214	60					12	2	71	24				
Assault on female	37		195	1					18		52	1				
Assault with intent to kill			1								7					
Assault with intent to rape											2					
Drunk and disorderly	539	43	448	58					7	1	4	1				
Violation liquor laws	116	7	392	191					16	4	34	22				
Driving drunk	90	3	30	1					10	1						
Reckless driving	39	9	32	1					122	12	37	1				
Hit and run	1		1													
Speeding	732	24	137	5					4		1					
Auto license violations	62	12	67	6			1									
Violation motor vehicle laws	19	2	15									1				
Breaking and entering																
And receiving											2	1				
Housebreaking											2	1				
And entering			1						20		15					
Storebreaking																
And entering									4		27					
Larceny	19	1	67	31					20	1	54	5				
Larceny from the person																
Larceny by trick and device																
Larceny of automobile									2		2					
Murder—first degree		1									5	1				
Murder—second degree									1							
Manslaughter									3		2					
Burglary—first degree											1					
Abandonment																
Affray																
Bigamy									2		1	1				
Carrying concealed weapon	5		12	1					2	1	4					

JULY 1, 1941—JULY 1, 1942

Offense	Convictions White M	Convictions White F	Convictions Negro M	Convictions Negro F	Convictions Indian M	Convictions Indian F	Convictions Unclassified M	Convictions Unclassified F	Other Dispositions White M	Other Dispositions White F	Other Dispositions Negro M	Other Dispositions Negro F	Other Dispositions Indian M	Other Dispositions Indian F	Other Dispositions Unclassified M	Other Dispositions Unclassified F
Assault	79	12	84	65					21	4	33	29				
Assault and Battery										1						
Assault with deadly weapon	48	4	324	125					30	4	116	57				
Assault on female	79		291						15		79					
Assault with intent to kill	1		1							2	4					
Assault with intent to rape											1					
Drunk and disorderly	875	70	869	159					14	3	2					
Violation liquor laws	194	18	580	408					24	6	59	36				
Driving drunk	191	6	46	1					10	1	1					
Reckless driving	75	3	56	2					232	33	84	5				
Hit and run	1		1						2		1					
Speeding	1039	21	270	6					12		2	1				
Auto license violations	107	18	124	7					3		1					
Violation motor vehicle laws	88	4	63						5	1	3					
Breaking and entering	1															
And receiving																
Housebreaking	1								1		1					
And entering				1					9		34	3				
Storebreaking									1		3					
And entering									32		100	1				
Larceny	63	2	152	38					36	6	58	33				
Larceny from the person											5	1				
Larceny by trick and device			1													
Larceny of automobile									1			1				
Murder—first degree									2	1	8	1				
Murder—second degree																
Manslaughter									9		5	1				
Burglary—first degree											3					
Abandonment	2								1		1					
Affray	6															
Bigamy											2					
Carrying concealed weapon	13		37	3							3	1				

Con[illegible]pt		1						1									1	1		1												
Disorderly conduct	2		2	1													1		7	2												
Disorderly house	2		2	2								1							1	5						1		2				
Disposing of mortgaged property			2																								1					
Disturbing religious [illegible]ship			3								1	1																				
Embezzlement									2																11		1	1				
Failure to list tax	300	15	92	5					2		4																					
F[illegible]cible [illegible]s																	2		1													
Forgery									14		1	1													20		4	1				
Fornication and adulte[illegible]ry	4	2	96	104							5	4					11	10	279	261							11	9				
[illegible]ing and [illegible]ery [illegible]s	35	1	385	47					5		21	5					115	2	873	68					6		46	11				
Health [illegible]s			17	12							1						3		39	31					1		2					
[illegible]st									1	1																						
[illegible]ury to property	12	1	34	5					2		8	3					26	3	56	14					7		19	1				
Municipal [illegible]es	206	13	81	8					3		6						545	31	279	24				1	18		7	1				
Non-support	35		44						15		24						58		93						30		43					
Non-support of illegitimate child	1		29						5		6						3		33						5		8					
Nuisance	37	7	54	37					10	4	6	6					50	18	96	91					13	11	17	18				
Perjury																			1													
[illegible]ion	10	5	20	20							2	3					11	13	32	37					5	3	2	3				
Rape									1																1		2					
Receiving stolen goods			4	3								1					1		13	3					1		1					
Resisting officer	1		4	3													9		15	7					3	1	1					
Robbery									7		4	1															13	1				
Seduction									1																14							
Trespass	15	1	22	5					3	1	1						20	1	46	8					5	1	6	1				
Vagrancy	6	31	32	7					1	2	7	1					12	28	42	16					3	6	11	4				
Worthless check				1					1			1																				
False [illegible]se									6	2	6	1							2						4	2	3	2				
Carnal knowledge, [illegible]te									1																		1					
Crime against nature											2																1					
Slot machine laws									2																							
Revenue act violations																			1	1							1					
Miscellaneous	32	7	38	18					5	2	7						49	22	46	20					9	3	11	7				
Totals	2407	191	2615	659			1	1	336	37	449	101					3780	288	4854	1404				1	606	60	821	232				

Convictions	5,874
Bound over	170
Other dispositions	753
	6,797

Convictions	10,327
Bound over	341
Other dispositions	1,378
	12,046

TWELFTH JUDICIAL DISTRICT

INFERIOR COURTS

JULY 1, 1940—JULY 1 1941

Offense	CONVICTIONS								OTHER DISPOSITIONS							
	White		Negro		Indian		Unclassified		White		Negro		Indian		Unclassified	
	M	F	M	F	M	F	M	F	M	F	M	F	M	F	M	F
Assault	18	1	11	4					14	2	8	3				
Assault with deadly weapon	25	4	64	27					10	2	19	5				
Assault on female	29		55	1					12		13					
Assault with [illegible]tent to kill									2							
Assault with [illegible]tent to [illegible]																
Assault—secret																
Drunk and disorderly	759	54	202	20			2		8	1		1			3	1
Possession—illegal whiskey	16	2	17	14					1		3	2				
Possession for sale	6	2	12	14					2		5	3				
Manufacturing—possession of [illegible]al for	3									1						
Transportation																
Violation liquor laws	68	3	8	9					3	1	4	2				
Driving drunk	75	6	9						9		1				1	
Reckless [illegible]g	102	1	33						86	13	11				6	
Hit and run	11	1	7				1		4		5					
Speeding	335	29	47				4		1						1	
Auto [illegible]ise violations	47	5	29				1		9	1	5				1	
Violation [illegible]tor [illegible]ile laws	16		6						2							
[illegible]g and [illegible]ing											3					
A[illegible]d larceny	10		4	1											1	
And receiving																
Larceny	6		21	1					1	1	2	3				
Larceny and receiving	16	1	10	3					47	2	18	2			2	
Larceny from the person										2	3					
Larceny by trick and d[illegible]vice											2					
Larceny of automobile	2										2					
Temporary larceny	1		2						3							
Murder—first degree											2	3				
Manslaughter									3		1					
Burglary—first degree									2		3					
Abandonment	20		7						7		2					

JULY 1, 1941—JULY 1, 1942

Offense	CONVICTIONS								OTHER DISPOSITIONS							
	White		Negro		Indian		Unclassified		White		Negro		Indian		Unclassified	
	M	F	M	F	M	F	M	F	M	F	M	F	M	F	M	F
Assault	64	7	38	17					15	8	9	5				
Assault with deadly weapon	78	6	188	76					37	4	57	15			3	
Assault on female	96		127				2		29		27				4	
Assault with [illegible]tent to kill			1	3					1		7					
Assault with [illegible]tent to [illegible]									2		2					
Assault—secret			1													
Drunk and disorderly	1211	103	366	48			2		25	3	2	3			2	1
Possession—illegal whiskey	31	3	33	16					3		2					
Possession for sale	22	6	79	46					8	1	14	16			1	
Manufacturing—possession of [illegible]al for	1		1						1							
Transportation	8		6						7		1					
Violation liquor laws	55	1	14	4					1	1	9	1				
Driving drunk	189	4	29				1		11		2				1	
Reckless [illegible]g	228	15	86	2			1		188	20	33				13	
Hit and run	37		18						12		7					
Speeding	533	17	111				31		3		1					
Auto [illegible]ise violations	122	9	77	4			4		13	1	9	2			1	
Violation [illegible]tor [illegible]ile laws	50	4	20						7		3					
[illegible]g and [illegible]ing	1	1							10	1	16					
A[illegible]d larceny	1		4													
And receiving			1						34		30					
Larceny	43	2	88	18					9	2	18	3			1	
Larceny and receiving	13	2	42	3					25	2	13	4				
Larceny from the person	1			1					8	3	13	6				
Larceny by trick and d[illegible]vice																1
Larceny of automobile	1		2						6		5					
Temporary larceny	8		5													
Murder—first degree									2		6	2				
Manslaughter									7	1	2					
Burglary—first degree									2		5					
Abandonment	44		18	1					12		5				3	

Affray	27	2	9	4					21	5	3						57		29	17					17	1	9	3				
Arson			1								1																					
Bigamy																									1		1	1				
Carrying [illegible]	3	1	11						2	3		1					7		24	3					4		3					
Contempt																	7		7	1					1							
Conspiracy																									1		2					
[illegible]lty to animals									1								1								1							
Disorderly conduct	26	5	21	10					7		1	2					68	17	95	33					17	3	10	6			1	1
Disorderly house												1					4		1	1					2							
Disposing of mortgaged property	3		3						5		1						5		5													
[illegible]ing religious worship			1																													
Embezzlement	2		2						2								9		4						5		1					
Escape	6		6												4		18	1	11	6			1		1		2	1			3	1
Fish and game laws	1																2															
Forcible trespass	2		3						1								12	1	10	2					2	1	2					
Forgery											3														21							
[illegible]on and adultery	3	4	9	8													5	5	22	18							3	3				
Gaming and [illegible]ry laws	16		45	6					1		2						87		54	5					16		1					
Health laws	1		2	1					1								5	2	11	6					1		1	1				
Injury to property	11		11	1					4	2	1						17	3	23	2					17		6					
[illegible]al [illegible]rdinances	68	3	14						5	1	1				1		287	20	100	2			3	1	41		9	1			1	
Non-support	30	1	11						12		6						78		60	2					29		13				4	
Non-support of illegitimate child	2		7						2		1						5		10						2		3					
[illegible]	3																5		2							1	2					1
Perjury											3																1					
Prostituti[illegible]n	5	10	6	7					2		2	2					26	31	6	5					4	1	1					
Rape									2																3		4					
Receiving stolen goods	3								2		2						2		1	1							2					
Removing crop																									1							
Resisting officer	4		2						1								15	1	6	2					3		2				1	
Robbery				1							6														6		12					
Trespass	16		6	2					1								21	1	31	2					5	1	1				2	
Vagrancy	5	2	8	3						2	3						21	21	10	3					7	12	9	1			7	
[illegible]ss [illegible]k	9	2							3								57	3	1				1		3							
False pretense	2																2								4		1					
Carnal knowledge, etc.																											1					
Slot [illegible]ine [illegible]																	4															
Miscellaneous	13	2	12	1					11		3	1			1		52	4	37	1					6	3	8	1			8	
Totals	1826	141	734	138			6		320	39	151	31			21	1	3716	290	1915	351			46	1	699	70	408	75			56	5

Convictions	2,845
Bound over	41
Other dispositions	522

Convictions	6,319
Bound over	210
Other dispositions	1,103

THIRTEENTH JUDICIAL DISTRICT

INFERIOR COURTS

Offense	JULY 1, 1940—JULY 1, 1941																JULY 1, 1941—JULY 1, 1942															
	CONVICTIONS								OTHER DISPOSITIONS								CONVICTIONS								OTHER DISPOSITIONS							
	White		Negro		Indian		Unclassified		White		Negro		Indian		Unclassified		White		Negro		Indian		Unclassified		White		Negro		Indian		Unclassified	
	M	F	M	F	M	F	M	F	M	F	M	F	M	F	M	F	M	F	M	F	M	F	M	F	M	F	M	F	M	F	M	F
Assault	26	1	26	7			10	2	9	4	11	1	4		8		26	2	22	5					9		10	4				
Assault and battery			2	1					2		1						8	1	4						1		2					
Assault with deadly weapon	38	1	101	19	1		10	2	30	1	23	7			5		45	8	98	26					20	3	25	12				
Assault on female	24		42				2		6		5				1		14		14						6		7					
Assault with intent to kill			5						2	1	5					1	1		9	1					5		4					
Assault with intent to rape											1																					
Assault—secret									1		1						1		1						1							
Drunk and disorderly	342	6	205	11	1		128	1	16		7				2	1	234	2	146	12			1		5	2	2	1				
Possession—illegal whiskey	6		16	2			6		3		2						4		7								1					
Possession for sale	6	5	22	4			18	3			4	1			1	1	23	1	26	15					4		5	2				
Manufacturing—possession of material for	7		4		1		4		3						2		15		9	1					3							
Transportation	5		8	1			7		1		3						13	1	18	1					1		1					
Violation liquor laws	58	1	75	7					12	1	14	3					24	1	52	7					1		3	1				
Driving drunk	182	3	88	2	1		21	1	22		5				3		250	5	76	2					32	1	4					
Reckless driving	76	1	55		1		4		22		10				3		138	3	58	1					25	2	18					
Hit and run	7		3				1		7		1						3		9						2							
Speeding	25		9				23		4						1		301	8	51						8		4					
Auto license violations	34	2	35		1		18	2	6		4				4		54	1	22						2	1	3					
Violation motor vehicle laws	113	2	57	1	2		36		18		11				1		92		28	1					9		3					
Breaking and entering			2						6		7						2		2						3		6					
And larceny											5				2																	
And receiving			3						1		5						2										9					
Larceny	6		26	3			19		16		13		3	3	15		13		19	3					3	1	15	1				
Larceny and receiving	21	1	39	7					9		16						11		47	6					14		15	6				
Larceny from the person											1						2															
Larceny of auto	1								1										1						3		1					
Temporary larceny	2								1		1						5		3								1					
Murder—first degree											3														2							
Murder—second degree											1																					
Manslaughter									5		1														1							
Abandonment	11		6						5		1						15		5	1					10	1	3					
Affray		1	5	7			1	1			5						4		6	1					4	1	2					
Arson									1																							
Bribery											2																					

Burning other than arson																	2		1													
Carrying concealed weapon	18		24	3			7		3	1	4				2		17		30	2					4	1	6					
Cheat	1																1		1	1												
Cruelty to animals			1						1										2						1		1					
Disorderly conduct	8		11	8			5		3		2						10		20	8					1		3					
Disorderly house									1																2			2				
Disposing of mortgaged property	1		1								1						3		2						3			1				
Disturbing religious worship			4				2				3				1				1						1		4					
Violation of election laws																			1													
Embezzlement																									1							
Escape	11						1		1								9															
Fish and game laws			1						2								2															
Forcible trespass	6		3				1		3		2						4		3						1		3					
Forgery									4		2														1							
Fornication and adultery	3	5	5	7					4	3	3	1					1	3	6	4							5	3				
Gaming and lottery laws	4		23				10				5				1		2	2	10													
Health laws			5	11					2	2		5							12	12							2	2				
Incest											1																1					
Injury to property	2		4				1		1		1	1					7	1	2								1					
Municipal ordinances	8		5	1			3		6	1		2					1		1													
Non-support	31		21				1		11	1	10				1		24		26	1					12		5	1				
Non-support of illegitimate child	2		7				1		1		3				1		5		4						3		4					
Nuisance											1																					
Perjury																											1					
Prostitution	2			1						1							5	4	1	5						11	1					
Rape									1						1												1					
Receiving stolen goods	6		2						1		4				1				1								3	2				
Removing crop									1											1					2	1						
Resisting officer	9	1	8						2								7	1	9						2							
Robbery									5		1								1						2							
Seduction			1																						1		1					
Trespass	11		8				6		4	1	3		2		4	1	9		8						5	2	1					
Vagrancy																			2							5						
Worthless check	10						1		1		1						2		1								2					
False pretense	2		1				1	1	2																1		4					
Carnal knowledge, etc.									2																3		1					
Slot machine laws	5								1								2															
Kidnapping									2																							
Miscellaneous	4	1	4	1					4	2	2	1			1		7	1	10						4		2	1				
Totals	1134	31	973	106	8		348	13	278	19	218	22	9	3	61	4	1420	45	888	117			1		224	32	196	39				

Convictions	2,613
Bound over	48
Other dispositions	566

Convictions	2,471
Bound over	27
Other dispositions	464

JULY 1, 1940—JULY 1, 1941

Offense	Convictions White M	Convictions White F	Convictions Negro M	Convictions Negro F	Convictions Indian M	Convictions Indian F	Convictions Unclassified M	Convictions Unclassified F	Other Dispositions White M	Other Dispositions White F	Other Dispositions Negro M	Other Dispositions Negro F	Other Dispositions Indian M	Other Dispositions Indian F	Other Dispositions Unclassified M	Other Dispositions Unclassified F
Assault	123	15	104	34					76	18	47	54				
Assault with deadly weapon	73	6	199	57					86	11	137	46				
Assault on female	34		42						44		28					
Assault with intent to kill	8	1	8						19		21	1				
Assault with intent to rape									1		1					
Assault—secret	1															
Drunk and disorderly	4181	309	1584	174					73	9	33	3				
Possession—illegal whiskey	1	1														
Transportation																
Violation liquor laws	226	31	101	60					40	5	29	19				
Driving drunk	279	5	64						92	3	9					
Reckless driving	155	19	36						53	3	23					
Hit and run	28	1	9						11		10	1				
Speeding	704	31	113	6					19		3					
Auto license violations	180	8	68	6					56	2	9	1				
Violation motor vehicle law	104	3	34	2				1	13	1	1					
Breaking and entering	2		2						1		1	1				
And larceny									9		2	1				
Housebreaking									1							
And larceny			1						8	1	27	1				
Storebreaking																
And larceny	1								21		30					
Larceny	111	9	205	64					74	13	73	26				
Larceny and receiving	1								1		26					
Larceny from the person	2								2		1					
Larceny by trick and device																
Larceny of automobile	5		4						17		6					
Temporary larceny	5		2													
Murder—first degree									3		17	3				
Manslaughter									4		3					
Burglary—first degree											3					
Abandonment	19		17						8		6					
Abduction									1							
Affray	50	3	34	18					18		8	8				
Arson											1					
Bigamy		1							1							

JULY 1, 1941—JULY 1, 1942

Offense	Convictions White M	Convictions White F	Convictions Negro M	Convictions Negro F	Convictions Indian M	Convictions Indian F	Convictions Unclassified M	Convictions Unclassified F	Other Dispositions White M	Other Dispositions White F	Other Dispositions Negro M	Other Dispositions Negro F	Other Dispositions Indian M	Other Dispositions Indian F	Other Dispositions Unclassified M	Other Dispositions Unclassified F
Assault	85	8	66	29					52	7	34	6				
Assault with deadly weapon	51	4	121	55					68	7	109	63				1
Assault on female	45		59						58		57					
Assault with intent to kill									1		2					
Assault with intent to rape									2		1					
Assault—secret																
Drunk and disorderly	2973	309	1157	191					71	20	27	10				
Possession—illegal whiskey																
Transportation			1													
Violation liquor laws	137	14	81	73					49	7	16	16				
Driving drunk	255	6	62						74	2	10					
Reckless driving	145	4	47						44	2	24					
Hit and run	13		6						10	2	7					
Speeding	738	18	161	2			1		35	3	13					
Auto license violations	76	7	37						23	2	5					
Violation motor vehicle law	93	3	37	1					11		5					
Breaking and entering			6						3		1					
And larceny									1							
Housebreaking																
And larceny	2		1						11		40	11				
Storebreaking			1													
And larceny									19		19					
Larceny	57	2	130	24					57	9	69	13				
Larceny and receiving	22	1	74	20					26		43	8				
Larceny from the person									1		4					
Larceny by trick and device											1					
Larceny of automobile	2		2						2		6					
Temporary larceny	2		1						2							
Murder—first degree									3		24	8				
Manslaughter									6	1	1					
Burglary—first degree									1		2					
Abandonment	25	1	8						8		5					
Abduction																
Affray	35	6	25	24					7	3	8	5				
Arson											1					
Bigamy									5							

Bribery																	1															
Carrying ([illegible]aled [illegible]apon	27	2	82	8					15		14	1					29	2	45	12					10		12	1				
[illegible]	1		2	4																												
[illegible]cy	5	1		2					9	1		1													4		2	1				
[illegible]elty to [illegible]mals	2								1																							
Disorderly [illegible]duct	84	15	56	30					39	11	12	10					80	19	73	36					28	7	10	3			1	
Disorderly house	2	2		4					4			1					2	2	2													
Disposing of mortgaged property	2	1	2								2						1		2								1					
[illegible]ing religious [illegible]ip	1		3																3	1												
Embezzlement	2								7		2	1					1		2						9		9					
Escape	4	1	2														1	1	1													
Fish and game [illegible]ws	2	1	1								4								9						7							
Forcible trespass	2		2														2		4						2		4					
Forgery	2								19		3	1													10		2	1				
Fornication and [illegible]ry	2	2	3	1					1	1		3					4	1	2	2					3	3						
Gaming and [illegible]y [illegible]ws	100		158	5					13		19	3					101	1	156	10					5		9	4				
Health laws	3	1	9	2					3	1		1					12	3		4					1							
Injury to [illegible]erty	66	10	33	11					22	3	12	2					20	1	25	4					11	4	11	2				
[illegible]al [illegible]ds	1991	205	245	11					47	13	8						969	104	307	21			2		111	9	22	1				
Non-support	15		15						9		5						25	1	8						8		5					
[illegible]ice	1		3	1					4	1	1	3					1		3						3	1						
Perjury										1							1								1							
Prostitution	27	25	15	15					10	10	3						41	62	12	13					9	10	3	1				
Rape									3		3														1	2	2					
Receiving [illegible]en [illegible]ds	16		12	3					16		7	5					6		9						7		5					
Resisting [illegible]	23	1	8	11					9		3						14	2	8	7					2		1					
Robbery			1						10	1	2	2					1								19		61	4				
Seducti n											2																					
[illegible]der									1		1						1															
e [illegible]s	39	5	28	1					32	2	8	1					16		16						5	1	3	2				
Vagrancy	9	16	1	2					3	4							19	21	1	6					4	6	2	2				
Worthless check	27	6	1						9	2	4						17		4						6		3					
False [illegible]ense	4		2						7	1		1													8							
[illegible]e against nature			2						1		1																1					
Slot [illegible]ine [illegible]ws	9								1								13		1						7							
Kidnapping																											1					
Revenue act violations	56	2	5	1					5		3						2		2													
Miscellaneous	176	4	32	10					29	2	5	1					47	1	24	2					15		5	1				
Totals	8993	743	3350	543				1	1081	120	697	202					6183	604	2752	537			3		946	108	708				1	1

Convictions	13,630
Bound over	317
Other dispositions	1,783

Convictions	10,079
Bound over	72
Other dispositions	1,692

FIFTEENTH JUDICIAL DISTRICT

INFERIOR COURTS

JULY 1, 1940—JULY 1, 1941

Offense	Convictions White M	Convictions White F	Convictions Negro M	Convictions Negro F	Convictions Indian M	Convictions Indian F	Convictions Unclassified M	Convictions Unclassified F	Other Dispositions White M	Other Dispositions White F	Other Dispositions Negro M	Other Dispositions Negro F	Other Dispositions Indian M	Other Dispositions Indian F	Other Dispositions Unclassified M	Other Dispositions Unclassified F
Assault	13		27	9						1	9	2				
Assault and battery	1		1													
Assault with deadly weapon	38	3	99	24					7		13	2				
Assault on female	39		39						8		6					
Assault with ... to ...	1															
Drunk and disorderly	84	3	31	10					3							
Possession—illegal ...	50	4	22	5					2							
Possession for sale	7	2	6	1												
Manufacturing—possession of material for	6		1							1						
Transportation	28	4	14	2					3							
Violation liquor laws	7	1	3						2							
Driving drunk	187	6	28						6			1				
Reckless driving	50	1	18						13	1	1					
Hit and run	6		3						4							
Speeding	17		3						2							
Auto ... violations	10		8						1		1					
Violation motor vehicle laws	3		2						1							
Breaking and entering	1															
And larceny																
And ...																
Larceny	32		33	5					7	1	5					
Larceny and ...			1													
Larceny from the person																
Larceny by trick and device																
... of ...																
...ry ...	2								5	1	1					
Manslaughter																
Burglary—first degree																
Abandonment	3			1					1							
Affray	3		4													
Arson																

JULY 1, 1941—JULY 1, 1942

Offense	Convictions White M	Convictions White F	Convictions Negro M	Convictions Negro F	Convictions Indian M	Convictions Indian F	Convictions Unclassified M	Convictions Unclassified F	Other Dispositions White M	Other Dispositions White F	Other Dispositions Negro M	Other Dispositions Negro F	Other Dispositions Indian M	Other Dispositions Indian F	Other Dispositions Unclassified M	Other Dispositions Unclassified F
Assault	55	13	29	2					17	4	1	7			3	
Assault and battery																
Assault with deadly weapon	85	6	173	48			1		30	6	47	8			2	1
Assault on female	51		48						26		13				2	
Assault with ... to ...	1								1							
Drunk and disorderly	677	23	317	34			8	1	8	1	2				3	1
Possession—illegal ...	23	2	14	1								1				
Possession for sale	17	1	31	8					1		1					
Manufacturing—possession of material for	4		1													
Transportation	40	4	13	5					3	1		1				
Violation liquor laws	74	8	37	15			1		3	1	1					
Driving drunk	425	10	77	3			6		33		1				4	
Reckless driving	273	12	65				7		93	3	15				7	1
Hit and run	33	2	9	1					5		2				1	
Speeding	579	12	81	3			5	1	13	2					6	
Auto ... violations	66	2	39	1			2		11		1					
Violation motor vehicle laws	74	3	34	2					13	1	5				2	
Breaking and entering	1		3						5			1			1	
And larceny									2							
And ...	7		4						14		2	1			3	
Larceny	49	2	58	14			1		14		18	6			1	1
Larceny and ...	96	10	58	13					16	4	13	3			4	1
Larceny from the person			2	2							1	1				
Larceny by trick and device			1						1							
... of ...									2							
...ry ...											1					
Manslaughter									1	1						
Burglary—first degree											1					
Abandonment	24		10						12	1					4	
Affray	7		13	6			1		4		1	3				
Arson											1					

Bigamy									1								1								2							
Carrying concealed weapon	4		17						2		1	1					26	1	33	4					3	1	1					
Cruelty to animals																									1							
Disorderly conduct	3	1	7														21	5	20	6			4		3	1	2					
Disorderly house																	4		1	2												
Disposing of mortgaged property	6		4						3								4	1							2		2					
Disturbing religious worship	1		3								1						4		1													
Embezzlement																									1							
Escape																	3		4	1												
Fish and game laws																	17										1					
Forcible trespass	10		6														19	1	12	3					2		3				1	
Forgery																			1													
Fornication and adultery	4	4	5	5					2								9	7	4	2					1	1	1	1				
Gaming and lottery laws	24		44	1					11		5	2					109	1	98	10					4		2					
Health laws			3	4														1	34	42					1							
Injury to property	2		6						1								9		5						6		1					
Municipal ordinance	3	1	3														8		7						1		1					
Non-support	57		22						10		3						104		24						32	1	10				3	
Non-support of illegitimate child	2		3								1						2		4				2		2		2				1	
Nuisance																		1														
Perjury																									2		1					
[illegible]ion	1	1															5	5	4	4					2	1	1	1				
Rape																									1							
Receiving stolen goods																			6						2							
Removing crop																	1															
Resisting officer	4		3	1													16	1	15	1					2							
Seduction																									3							
Slander																									1							
Trespass	7		5	3													35	1	24						3	2	1	1				
Vagrancy																	10	6	6	1					1							
Worthless check	2								1		1						8															
False pretense	2								1								5		1						1							
Carnal knowledge, etc.									1																2							
Crime against nature																									1		1					
Slot machine laws	1		1																													
Revenue act [illegible]																	1															
Miscellaneous	5		4	1					1								16		3				1		6		1					
Totals	726	31	479	72					94	4	47	8					3103	142	1425	234			39	2	416	32	158	35			48	5

Convictions	1,308
Other dispositions	153
	1,461

Convictions	4,945
Bound over	35
Other dispositions	659

Offense	JULY 1, 1940—JULY 1, 1941																JULY 1, 1941—JULY 1, 1942															
	CONVICTIONS								OTHER DISPOSITIONS								CONVICTIONS								OTHER DISPOSITIONS							
	White		Negro		Indian		Unclassified		White		Negro		Indian		Unclassified		White		Negro		Indian		Unclassified		White		Negro		Indian		Unclassified	
	M	F	M	F	M	F	M	F	M	F	M	F	M	F	M	F	M	F	M	F	M	F	M	F	M	F	M	F	M	F	M	F
Assault	42	13	16	14				2	11	3							66	11	5	5					11	2	3	1				
Assault and battery	1																															
Assault with deadly weapon	52	2	32	3					26	2	13	3					91	2	42	13					42	8	12	5				
Assault on female	19		6						9								23		5						15		5					
Assault with intent to kill			1						2																1		1					
Assault with intent to rape									3																3							
Drunk and disorderly	268	21	28	2				2	28	4	3	1					387	14	71	18					17	5	2					
Possession—illegal whiskey	50	5	7	3					6		1	1					33	2	6	2					6							
Possession for sale	8		/ 5						3	2							14	5	4	1					3		2					
Manufacturing—possession of material for	9																6															
Transportation	5																7	5								1						
Violation liquor laws	79	4	19	11					15		2						30	1	21	7					5	2	6	1				
Driving drunk	125	1	14						21								130	4	20						18							
Reckless driving	114	4	15	2					36	2	4	1					92		14						40	4	5					
Hit and run	13		1						6								6								2							
Speeding	15		2						3								65		10				1		2							
Auto license violations	38	4	5						4	1	1						37	2	9	1					4							
Violation motor vehicle law	17	1	1						6								11		2						4							
Breaking and entering	4								5																1		2					
And larceny	2								3		2						6		1						2		1					
And receiving									4																2							
[illegible]y	54	3	14						18	1	5	1					46		19	3					13	1	7					
Larceny and receiving	2		4						1								1		1						2							
Larceny from the person									2	1							1															
Larceny of automobile									1								2		1													
Temporary larceny	1		3														5															
Murder—first degree									3																1		2					
Manslaughter									4		1														2							
Abandonment	21	2	2						5		1						8		1						2							
Abduction																									1							
Affray	17	3	3						4	3	2						17	2	1	1					10	2						3
Bigamy									1																	1						
Burning other than arson									2																							

Carrying concealed weapon	11		3	1					4		2						5	1	7						1		1					
Conspiracy									1																4							
Cruelty to animals									2																							
Disorderly conduct	7		1	1					5			2					3	1		3					2	4						
Disorderly house	1	2	1						1									2							1	1						
Disposing of mortgaged property	1								1								2		2						2							
Disturbing religious worship	1																1															
Violation of election laws	2																															
Embezzlement									4								1								2							
Escape	3																6															
Fish and game laws	6																1								4							
Forcible trespass	10		2						3		1						7								2	1						
Forgery									2	2															5		3					
Fornication and adultery	6	5	3	5					1	1	1	1					4	2	3	3					1	2						
Gaming and lottery laws			3	1					2								6		6													
Health laws																	8		1						2			1				
Injury to property	10		2						3	1							9		1						10		2					
Municipal ordinances	12		1						5		2						5								3							
Non-support	48		6						18		4						34	1	5						15		2					
Non-support of illegitimate child	12		2						4		1						3		5								1					
Nuisance									1								1								1							
Perjury																									1	1						
Prostitution	1	2															2	2														
Rape									1																1							
Receiving stolen goods	3	1	3						2	1	1						2								2		1					
Resisting officer	5		2						3								7		2						1							
Robbery											1						1		1						2							
Seduction	1																															
Slander																										2		1				
Thefts	11	2	5					1	7	2	3						11		2						9	5						
Vagrancy	1	4							2	1								3														
Worthless check	11		1						2								3								1							
False pretense	5		1						18								2		1						4		1					
Carnal knowledge, etc.			1								1																					
Crime against nature																									1							
Slot machine laws	2								3								1															
Kidnapping									1																							
Miscellaneous	15		3	8					5	1	1						7	2							7	3						
Totals	1141	79	218	51				5	333	28	52	10					1216	57	274	57			1		293	45	59	9				3

Convictions	1,494
Bound over	28
Other dispositions	395

Convictions	1,605
Bound over	26
Other dispositions	383

SEVENTEENTH JUDICIAL DISTRICT
INFERIOR COURTS

Offense	JULY 1, 1940—JULY 1, 1941																JULY 1, 1941—JULY 1, 1942															
	CONVICTIONS								OTHER DISPOSITIONS								CONVICTIONS								OTHER DISPOSITIONS							
	White		Negro		Indian		Unclassified		White		Negro		Indian		Unclassified		White		Negro		Indian		Unclassified		White		Negro		Indian		Unclassified	
	M	F	M	F	M	F	M	F	M	F	M	F	M	F	M	F	M	F	M	F	M	F	M	F	M	F	M	F	M	F	M	F
Assault	2		1														26	1	1	1							1					
Assault and battery																	1		2						1		3					
Assault with deadly weapon			1																3	1												
Assault on female																	1		3						1							
Drunk and disorderly	5		1														35		12								2					
Possession—illegal whiskey	1		1														5		2													
Possession for sale																	2		2													
Transportation	1																1		3													
Driving drunk			1						1								3		3						3							
Reckless driving																	2	1	1													
Hit and run																	1															
Auto license violations																		1	1	1												
Violation motor vehicle laws																	2								1		1					
Larceny																	3	2							1							
Larceny of automobile											1																					
Murder—first degree																											1					
Manslaughter																											2					
n [illegible]nt	1																		1													
Affray																			1													
Carrying concealed weapon																	1															
Disorderly conduct			1																													
Fish and game laws																	3															
Injury to property																	1															
Municipal ordinances																	1		1													
Non-support																			2													
Non-support of illegitimate child																	1															
Nuisance																										1						
Prostitution																			1	1												
Receiving stolen goods																	1		2													
Trespass	1		1														1		3									1				
Totals	11		7						1		1						91	5	44	4					7	1	10	1				

Convictions 18 Convictions 144

EIGHTEENTH JUDICIAL DISTRICT

INFERIOR COURTS

Offense	JULY 1, 1940—JULY 1, 1941																JULY 1, 1941—JULY 1, 1942															
	CONVICTIONS								OTHER DISPOSITIONS								CIONVICTONS								OTHER DISPOSITIONS							
	White		Negro		Indian		Unclassified		White		Negro		Indian		Unclassified		White		Negro		Indian		Unclassified		White		Negro		Indian		Unclassified	
	M	F	M	F	M	F	M	F	M	F	M	F	M	F	M	F	M	F	M	F	M	F	M	F	M	F	M	F	M	F	M	F
Assault	23	1	6	1					14	1	6	2					19		6	3			1	1	21	6	16	3				
Assault and battery																	1															
Assault with deadly weapon	14	2	34	3			1		40	2	27	8			3		35	2	26	12			5	1	28		36	17			1	
Assault on female	8		4						4								8		1				3				1					
Assault with intent to kill	1								1	1																						
Assault with intent to rape									1		1																1					
Drunk and disorderly	170	17	72	10			3		34	2	11	1			2		213	8	54	13			2		23	5	12	4				
Possession—illegal whiskey	8	2	3																													
Possession for sale	4		1									1					4		5													
Manufacturing—possession of material for	11	2	2						1								2	1							1							
Transportation	9	1	2						1	1	4						3	3					3		1							
Violation liquor laws	47	2	13	2					23	11	4				1		55	4	31	6					15	3	11	6				
Driving drunk	156	5	18				1		25		4				1		161	2	23				20	1	23		5					
Reckless driving	44		8						32	4	5				1		61	1	18				5		30	6	13	1				
Hit and run	13		3						2								4		1							1	1					
Speeding	4								1								30		4				1		5		1					
Auto license violations	19	1	8						1	1							27	3	6				5	1	2		2					
Violation motor vehicle laws	6		2						3								7	1	4				1		6						1	
Breaking and entering	2	2									1								2						3		2					
And larceny									8						1		2								9	2	3					
And receiving																									1							
Larceny	19	2	8	1			1		10	3	8	3			1		33	2	16	13					24	1	18	3				
Larceny and receiving	1																1						1									
Larceny by trick and device	1								1																							
Larceny of automobile	1																															
Temporary larceny	1		2						1																							
Murder—first degree											2														4	2						
Manslaughter									1																							

[illegible]ent	2	1							3								15	1	3				2		3							
Affray	7								4		2	2							4					1	1		1					
[illegible]son																									3							
Bigamy																									3	1						
Carrying [illegible] [illegible]	7		4	1					3		4						7		4				1		2		1					
[illegible]																							1									
[illegible]y to [illegible]ands																			1													
[illegible]ly [illegible] [illegible]lt	7	3	7	3					6	1	3	3					2	1	6	2					8		6	3				
Disorderly house										2	1						2			2					7							
[illegible]ing of [illegible]ed [illegible]ty	6								6		3				1		1								2	2						
Disturbing religious [illegible]ship	4								3								1		1													
Embezzlement	6								2										1													
Escape	1								1																							
Fish and game [illegible]s	2								2								2								4							
[illegible]le [illegible]s	2	1	2						7						1		7		3				1		3		3					
Forgery	1								4		1														2		2					
Fornication and adultery	4	2	1	1					2	2							1	1	2						5	1	4	2				
[illegible]g and [illegible]ry laws			6														4		5								2					
[illegible]lth laws			1	2							1						3			1					2			2				
[illegible]									1		1																					
Injury to property	4								7	2	2	1			1		6		3	2			1		1		1					
Municipal [illegible]s									2		1														5		1					
Non-support	17		1						10		1						28		3				4		11		5					
Non-support of illegitimate child	4		1						3								2						2		1							
N [illegible]	3	3							1								2	2							1	2						
Prostitution			1															2							2	2						
Rape									1		1														2							
Receiving [illegible] goods																	1			3							2					
Removing [illegible]																	1															
[illegible]ing [illegible]r	10		7	1					3		2						4	2	1	1			1		1		1	1				
Robbery											3																					
Trespass	4		4						10	1	7				1		4	1	5	1					5	3						
Vagrancy	3	4							1	2							10	5	3						1	1						
[illegible]ss [illegible]k	15		3				1		7		1				4		3		2						1							
False [illegible]se									14		2				2		1		1						4							
[illegible]e [illegible]st [illegible]e									2																1							
Miscellaneous	11	3	1						7	1	1						7		2						8	1	3					
Totals	682	54	225	25			7		316	36	111	21			20		780	42	247	59			60	5	285	39	154	42			2	

Convictions	993
Bound over	77
Other dispositions	427
	1,497

Convictions	1,193
Bound over	57
Other dispositions	465
	1,715

TWENTIETH JUDICIAL DISTRICT

INFERIOR COURTS

JULY 1, 1940—JULY 1, 1941

Offense	Convictions White M	Convictions White F	Convictions Negro M	Convictions Negro F	Convictions Indian M	Convictions Indian F	Convictions Unclassified M	Convictions Unclassified F	Other Dispositions White M	Other Dispositions White F	Other Dispositions Negro M	Other Dispositions Negro F	Other Dispositions Indian M	Other Dispositions Indian F	Other Dispositions Unclassified M	Other Dispositions Unclassified F
Drunk and disorderly	450	28	30	4	3											
Transportation																
Violation liquor laws	2	1	1	1												
Driving drunk	9		1													
Reckless driving	9		3													
Speeding	2															
Larceny	2															
Affray	3															
Carrying concealed weapon	1		1													
Disorderly house			2													
Forcible trespass	2															
Gaming and lottery laws																
Injury to property																
Municipal ordinances																
Resisting officer	1															
Trespass																
[illegible]		1														
Totals	481	30	38	5												

Convictions 554
Other dispositions
554

JULY 1, 1941—JULY 1, 1942

Offense	Convictions White M	Convictions White F	Convictions Negro M	Convictions Negro F	Convictions Indian M	Convictions Indian F	Convictions Unclassified M	Convictions Unclassified F	Other Dispositions White M	Other Dispositions White F	Other Dispositions Negro M	Other Dispositions Negro F	Other Dispositions Indian M	Other Dispositions Indian F	Other Dispositions Unclassified M	Other Dispositions Unclassified F
Drunk and disorderly	383	28	51	1							1					
Transportation	1															
Violation liquor laws																
Driving drunk	6															
Reckless driving	10	1				1										
Speeding	4	1	1													
Larceny																
Affray	3	1	2	1												
Carrying concealed weapon	2		1													
Disorderly house																
Forcible trespass																
Gaming and lottery laws	26															
Injury to property	1															
Municipal ordinances	3															
Resisting officer	2															
Trespass	3	1														
[illegible]		13								1						
Totals	444	45	55	2		1				1	1					

Convictions 547
Other dispositions 2
549

TWENTY-FIRST JUDICIAL DISTRICT

INFERIOR COURTS

Offense	JULY 1, 1940—JULY 1, 1941																JULY 1, 1941—JULY 1, 1942															
	CONVICTIONS								OTHER DISPOSITIONS								CONVICTIONS								OTHER DISPOSITIONS							
	White		Negro		Indian		Unclassified		White		Negro		Indian		Unclassified		White		Negro		Indian		Unclassified		White		Negro		Indian		Unclassified	
	M	F	M	F	M	F	M	F	M	F	M	F	M	F	M	F	M	F	M	F	M	F	M	F	M	F	M	F	M	F	M	F
Assault	22	4	13	8					3		4	1					25	7	16	5					6	1	4					
Assault with deadly weapon	26	1	57	10					10	1	26	4					32	2	50	15					12		21	3				
Assault on female	21		32						12		9	1					27		32						1		2					
Assault with intent to kill	1										1	1																				
Drunk and disorderly	546	11	267	29	1				22	1	9						813	14	244	27					19		4	1				
Possession—illegal whiskey	44	2	11	1					3		3	1					19	1	8	1					3		2					
Possession for sale	5		5	1					3	1	2	1													4	2	1					
Manufacturing—possession of material for	1		4														3		1						1		1					
Transportation	10		7						1		1						4		2													
Violation liquor laws	13	1	30	4					1		15	8					16	1	30	10					3	1	8	4				
Driving drunk	119	1	31						8		2						136	3	26						15		3					
Reckless driving	57	2	37	1					19	1	6						67	1	38						19	1	6	1				
Hit and run	3		2						1								5		2						4							
Speeding	17		12						1		2						120	1	35						4		1					
Auto license violations	51	4	25	1					4		4						23	6	22						3		2					
Violation motor vehicle laws	11		7						9	1	4						6	1	5							1						
Breaking and entering									3																1		1	1				
And receiving																									1							
Larceny	10		7						5			2					18		3						3		2					
Larceny and receiving	12	4	49	7					3		11	2					11		25	4					2		6	1				
Larceny from the person																			1													
Larceny of automobile	1																2		1													
Temporary larceny			1																													
Murder—first degree											1	1															1					
Manslaughter									1																3		2					
Abandonment	17		5						3		1						15		13	1					3		2					
Affray	4	2	5	2					7		2						9		10	4					2		1					
Bribery																											1					
Carrying concealed weapon	9	1	9	2					2		7						7		10								3					
Cruelty to animals																	1															
Disorderly conduct	16		16	10					3	1	6	3					28	5	27	16					3	1	3	1				

Disorderly house	1																		2													
Disposing of mortgaged property	3		1														1		1													
Disturbing religious worship			1																													
Embezzlement									1																							
Escape	3		3	1															1						2		1					
Fish and game laws																	1															
Forcible trespass	2	1	1	2													1		4	1					1		2					
Forgery									1																1							
Fornication and daltery	2	3															1	1														
Gaming and lttery alws	6		6						4								3		2						2		1					
Injury to property	4		2								1						8								3							
Municipal ales	5	1	1						2		1						11		7						1							
Non-support	17		10	1					5		1						9		15						5		2	1				
Non-support of illegitimate child	4		16								3						2		6								1					
Nie	2		2														1		4								1					
Bion			1														1	1	4	2												
Receiving stolen goods	7		3	1					1																1							
Removing crop																	1										1					
Resisting officer	4		3	1					2		1						4		3													
Robbery										1																						
ndler																				1												
Trespass	4									1		1					4		14						4		1					
Vagrancy			1								1								1													
dHess hek	8		1						1								7		1								1					
False pretense	1	1	1						1			1													6							
Slot machine lws																	2	1							1							
Revenue act violations																	6		4	2					4		2					
Miscellaneous	20		2	1					3																							
Totals	1109	39	687	83	1				145	8	124	27					1450	45	670	89					143	7	90	12				

Convictions 1,919
Other dispositions 304

2,223

Convictions 2,254
Bound over 3
Other dispositions 249

2,506

ALPHABETICAL LIST OF CRIMES IN INFERIOR COURTS

Offense	July 1, 1940—July 1, 1941		July 1, 1941—July 1, 1942	
	Convictions	Other Dispositions	Convictions	Other Dispositions
Assault	1,918	884	1,974	805
Assault and battery	527	197	499	137
Assault with deadly weapon	3,246	1,634	3,438	1,684
Assault on female	1,041	372	1,287	622
Assault with intent to kill	42	109	35	80
Assault with intent to rape	1	24	4	20
Assault—secret	5	6	3	3
Drunk and disorderly	19,599	592	19,327	1,273
Possession—illegal whiskey	1,182	163	824	135
Possession for sale	628	165	756	197
Manufacturing—possession of material for	268	57	167	47
Transportation	275	56	261	62
Violation liquor laws	2,505	567	3,025	583
Driving drunk	3,359	569	4,074	651
Reckless driving	2,251	1,241	2,962	1,660
Hit and run	207	109	254	119
Speeding	4,187	90	6,591	301
Auto license violations	1,950	276	1,938	291
Violation motor vehicle laws	1,811	214	2,081	352
Breaking and entering	33	66	36	107
And larceny	27	77	27	55
And receiving	9	49	20	129
Housebreaking	1	13	1	12
And larceny	1	47	4	100
And receiving	2	86	2	48
Storebreaking	1	5	1	7
And larceny	2	56	2	52
And receiving	----------	68	1	167
Larceny	1,930	866	2,135	906
Larceny and receiving	401	261	587	356
Larceny from the person	11	49	17	87
Larceny by trick and device	7	8	9	14
Larceny of automobile	42	59	23	69
Temporary larceny	54	14	52	20
Murder—first degree	----------	63	----------	102
Murder—second degree	----------	2	----------	----------
Manslaughter	----------	47	----------	66
Burglary—first degree	----------	16	----------	34
Burglary—second degree	----------	1	6	1
Abandonment	308	149	370	154
Abduction	----------	6	----------	1
Affray	714	208	704	233
Arson	----------	6	----------	6
Bigamy	1	11	1	24
Bribery	----------	2	1	1
Burning other than arson	----------	2	3	----------
Carrying concealed weapon	685	161	685	144
Contempt	20	----------	29	2
Conspiracy	8	19	----------	14

ALPHABETICAL LIST OF CRIMES IN INFERIOR COURTS

Offense	July 1, 1940—July 1, 1941 Convictions	July 1, 1940—July 1, 1941 Other Dispositions	July 1, 1941—July 1, 1942 Convictions	July 1, 1941—July 1, 1942 Other Dispositions
Cruelty to animals	8	16	19	13
Disorderly conduct	1,233	300	1,411	421
Disorderly house	94	41	101	75
Disposing of mortgaged property	86	46	55	30
Disturbing religious worship	49	35	31	11
Violation of election laws	2	----------	1	----------
Embezzlement	15	38	22	77
Escape	105	10	130	27
Failure to list tax	487	147	357	74
Fish and game laws	69	30	75	37
Forcible trespass	188	51	211	54
Forgery	6	110	8	129
Fornication and adultery	462	103	860	203
Gaming and lottery laws	1,681	264	2,320	280
Health laws	132	34	307	81
Incest	2	5	----------	1
Injury to property	481	177	479	197
Municipal ordinances	5,380	474	4,098	1,722
Non-support	783	371	971	436
Non-support of illegitimate child	257	123	225	109
Nuisance	341	73	482	102
Official misconduct	1	1	----------	----------
Perjury	----------	14	5	15
Prostitution	342	61	650	268
Rape	----------	36	----------	55
Receiving stolen goods	104	86	89	72
Removing crop	6	19	8	16
Resisting officer	289	64	358	71
Robbery	12	112	9	204
Seduction	5	16	1	27
Slander	4	13	6	12
Trespass	617	193	622	212
Vagrancy	367	149	486	256
Worthless check	314	134	247	68
False pretense	83	118	74	118
Carnal knowledge, etc.	4	23	1	19
Crime against nature	2	14	----------	17
Slot machine laws	91	19	63	10
Kidnapping	----------	4	----------	6
Revenue act violations	65	10	22	7
Miscellaneous	755	158	435	159

	1940–1941		1941–1942
Convictions	64,181	Convictions	69,455
Other dispositions	13,434	Other dispositions	17,624
Total	77,615	Total	87,079

GRAND TOTAL ---- 164,694

TABLE ONE

Sections in Michie's N. C. Code and Consolidated Statutes Cited or Construed in Biennial Report.

Consolidated Statutes	Page	Consolidated Statutes	Page	Consolidated Statutes	Page
191(3)	277	2621(227)	337	4830	209
191(4)	268, 269	2621(238)	122, 339, 344	4941	124
191(l)	269, 274	2621(244)	344	4945	124
197(7)	274	2621(246)	122	5003(1)	387
198	275, 428, 455	2621(250)	344	5006	52
199(a)	275, 276	2621(274)	429	5008	52
216(a)	255	2621(288)	133, 460	5011	52
218(c)(16)	295	2621(288)(d)	132	5017	348
220(b)	291, 292, 296	2621(322)	122, 347	5039	379
220(c)	290, 292	2629	458	5049	348
220(d)	291, 294, 296	2673	453	5051	348
220(h)	296	2688	256	5054	379
220(k)	293, 294	2715	449	5062	348
221(k)	299	2774	471	5126(13)	308
225(2)	177	2779	21	5126(18)	308
225(f)	177	2787	453, 458	5168(ww)	371
397	335	2790	242, 454	5168(xx)	372
485	269, 270	2795	237, 248	5255	120
692	391, 392	2805	242	5259	120
870	20	2806	239, 242	5259(a)	176
918	430	2807	415	5259(h)	211
934(a)	406	2932	257	5394	21
962(6)	311	2934	257	5416	80, 96
980	20	2960	257	5440	90, 92
1013(a)	59	3119	294	5440(a)	352
1062	20	3176	46	5451(a)	324
1065	20	3288	134	5470(a)	78
1113	134	3411(68)(c)	354	5513	85
1131	63	3484	53, 54	5534	85
1131(2)	58	3485	53	5537	92
1143	20	3546	396	5556	243, 244
1168	211	3846	40	5596	75
1181	134	3846(bbb)	330	5730	76, 99
1181(b)	131			5734	99
1185	20	3846(fff)	145	5749(a)	99
1187	20	3846(ooo)	50, 330	5749(g)	99
1218	63	3893	145, 444	5754(1)	21
1220	360	3903	436	5757	76, 93
1224(a)	57	3908	193	5758	76
1224(f)	57	3924(i)	62	5764	381
1297(15)	404	3959	230, 391	5782	311
1318	272	3960	392	5786	71
1334(43)	258	3971	60	5839	399
1334(54)	407	4018	293	5842(1)	399
1334(64)	74	4018(b)	290, 293	5863	96
1342	306, 309, 386	4019	293	5892	381
1342(1)	386	4113	335	5893	381
1342(2)	386	4115	335	5904	388
1694(1)-(28)	374	4116	335	5919	41
1715(l)	392	4121	335	5921	270
1905	285	4174	190	5923	264, 270
2141(27)	405	4245(a)	341	5961	261
2151	271	4310	285, 288	5968(f)	404
2244	353	4311(a)	287, 288	5975	41
2304(q)	21	4388	407, 418, 421	6007	43, 263
2308	293		457, 469, 471	6008	43
2379	20	4399(a)	217	6012	40
2492(15)-(17)	258	4399(d)	217	6024	264
2492(27)	290	4410	436, 468, 469	6046	20
2495	455	4445	271, 276, 281	6055(a-8)	263
2515	202, 203	4468(a)	473	6055(a-28)(2b)	408
2567-73	20	4500	410	6055(a-51)	407
2613(i-5)	195	4525	410	6056	65
2613(i-15)	192	4548(a)	351	6057	65
2621(150)-(181)	345	4556(d)	20	6058	65
2621(151)	345	4610	455	6062	65
2621(151)(g)	345, 346	4649	425	6122(bb)	289
2621(160)	342	4659	231	6124	20
2621(178)	345, 346	4665(3)	367	6168	51
2621(187)(w-1)	133	4665(4)	366	6173	51
2621(207)	338	4828	20	6216	383

TABLE ONE (Continued)

Consolidated Statutes	Page	Consolidated Statutes	Page	Consolidated Statutes
6217	382, 383	7050	280	7508
6218	382	7064	281	7521(n)
6227	382	7065	241, 243,	7524
6236	383, 384		248, 280	7524(a)-7524(e
6237	39, 382	7066	280	7525
6238	381, 384, 387	7067	281	7534(k)
6239	39, 385	7076	237	7534(o)(1)
6240	383, 385	7092	240	7540
6351	220	7105	425	7554
6377	290, 291	7109	241, 253	7587
6391	220	7112	253	7588
6430	220	7130	237	7636
6524	20	7221	245, 384	7694
6525	20	7222	245	7748(z)
6605	250	7251(x)	248	7757
6622	247	7252-7254(a)	386	7766(g)
6625	20	7331	48	7880(167)
6700	250, 252, 278	7334	48	7971(3)
6706	253	7343(d)	48	7971(228)
6785	387	7343(k)	48	7976
6864	225	7502(b)	299	7979(a)
6870	225	7502(f)(a)	298	8052(14)(c)
6871	225	7502(h)	299	8053
6889	225	7502(h)(a)	298, 299	8059
7027	238	7502(1)	300	

TABLE TWO

Public Laws Cited or Construed in Biennial Report

Year	ch. No.	Sec.	Page
1879	98		71
1913	102		68
1915	144		120
1917	136		260
1921	4		294
1921	4	221(a)	292
1921	87		176
1921	186		240
1923	136		258
1923	136	60	91
1923	225	1	177
1923	225	6	177
1925	155		21
1925	201		258
1925	275	10	65
1925	318		401
1927	81		258
1927	100		238, 252
1927	100	7(8)	239
1927	149		60
1929	120	11	392, 393
1929	120	21	124
1929	143		73
1929	218	8	145
1931	52		371
1931	52	12	372
1931	60	32	255
1931	116		144, 328
1931	116	1	328
1931	145	24(15)	192
1931	157		434
1931	226	1	266, 271
1931	226	2	267, 271
1931	304		192
1933	1		354
1933	40		145
1933	53		304
1933	172	30	233
1933	181		446
1933	181	7	473
1933	210		398
1933	211		192
1933	324		210, 211
1933	324	4	210, 211
1933	562		90
1933	562	26	50
1935	11	52	342
1935	52		125, 328
1935	52	1	333
1935	52	3	334
1935	52	3(c)	333, 334
1935	52	3(d)	333, 334, 335
1935	52	3(e)	333, 335
1935	52	3(f)	333, 334, 335
1935	52	4(b)	331, 332
1935	52	11	47
1935	52	11(1)	332
1935	52	12	47, 331, 340, 341
1935	52	12(3)	341
1935	52	13	47, 331, 332
1935	52	15	331
1935	52	16(b)	155
1935	52	18	155
1935	52	18(a)	155
1935	52	18(b)	332
1935	52	18(c)	331, 332, 341
1935	52	18(d)	331, 332
1935	52	22	331
1935	52	29	333
1935	53		305
1935	53	5	306
1935	135		286
1935	160	19	284
1935	212		230
1935	243		268, 272
1935	245		302, 471
1935	245	2	302
1935	288		374
1935	288	2	374
1935	288	2(1)	374
1935	291		374, 376, 377
1935	291	12	375, 376
1935	291	14	377
1935	291	20	375, 376
1935	291	21	375
1935	340		21
1935	371	315	121
1935	371	315(d)	121
1935	371	317(1)	110
1935	371	318(4)	121
1935	455		89
1935	456		149, 440
1935	486	20	282
1936	Ex. Ses. 1	7(a)(1)	362
1936	Ex. Ses. 1	14(a)	362
1936	Ex. Ses. 1	14(b)	362, 363
1937	49		352, 353, 355
1937	49	3	356
1937	49	4	356
1937	49	4(c)	352
1937	49	10(o)	352
1937	111		192
1937	124		305
1937	127	122(b)	151
1937	127	315	121
1937	127	315(d)	121
1937	127	317(1)	110
1937	127	318(4)	121
1937	127	322(7)	131
1937	132		365
1937	242		228
1937	288	35	276
1937	298	1	249
1937	298	2	249
1937	298	7	249
1937	313		54
1937	349		70
1937	350		370
1937	353		91
1937	407	2(2)	147
1937	407	15	122
1937	407	21	338
1937	407	41	337
1937	407	41(b)	335, 336
1937	407	52	339, 344
1937	407	52(b)	122
1937	407	58	344
1937	407	60	122
1937	407	64	344
1937	407	123	218
1937	407	137	122
1937	414		156, 159
1937	436	3	280
1937	449		226
1939	6		70
1939	12		355
1939	52	11(a)(8)	46
1939	52	18(b)	46
1939	65		401
1939	65	3	401
1939	91		21
1939	96	5	42
1939	122		309, 310
1939	158	1	134, 162
1939	158	1(3)	126, 167
1939	158	1(7)	115
1939	158	2(d)	135, 167, 169
1939	158	2(4)	179
1939	158	7	108

TABLE TWO (Continued)

Sec.	Page
7(d)	116
7(g)	119
11	125, 134
21½	404
00	191
27	181
30	182, 189
30(2)	189, 196
30(6)	190
32	195
33(1)	206, 459
39	197
48	294
49	390
50	197
52	205, 206, 294
53	206
53(1)	191
53(1)(b)	191
53(1)(e)	191
58	177, 200
61	190
61(b)	190
62	201
87	189, 190
87(c)	189
90(c)	189
01	137
03	136
03(3)	136
10	134
01	197
10	193, 203
11	197, 204
12	135, 197
14	170, 204
14(3)	170, 171, 204
14(5)	204
14(6)	204
14(7)	124, 170, 171
14(9)	120, 176
15	179
17	135, 187
17(2)(a)	150
17(2)(b)	150, 187, 188
17(2)(d)	149
22(3)	150, 188
22(5)	135
22(9)	123, 124
22(10)	193
23(c)	150
23(h)	146
24(1)(b)	156
26(2)	181
27	181
06	181
16	194
27	172
01	202
09½	353
11(5)	432
18½	202
04	149
08	174
01	172
13(1)	193
19	125
10	262
	65
	21
	402
	302
	344
	415
02	108
00(1)	304

Year	ch. No.	Sec.	Page
1939	310	601(12)	461
1939	310	1105	158
1939	310	1105(5)	157
1939	310	1105(7)(d)	157
1939	310	1108(6)	158, 159
1939	310	1401	107
1939	310	1713	415
1939	310	1713(c)	391
1939	310	1713(d)	411
1939	310	1715(d)	391
1939	314	1	410
1939	314	3	239
1939	314	4	239
1939	358		51, 86
1939	358	5	75, 90, 100
1939	358	7	79, 82, 84,
			92, 93, 101,
			103, 104,
			105, 421
1939	358	9	75, 77
1939	358	12	81, 82, 84,
			91, 92, 93,
			101, 104, 105
1939	358	14	83, 456
1939	358	15	74, 78, 84
1939	358	15(a)	83
1939	358	15(c)	73
1939	358	19	95
1939	358	20(1)	95
1939	358	22	82
1939	358	28	96
1939	369		344
1939	389		156, 159
1939	395	1	276
1939	398		21
1941	15		344
1941	22		418
1941	25		18, 84, 320, 321
1941	25	1	234
1941	25	1(3)	314
1941	25	1(10)	326, 327
1941	25	1(16)	322
1941	25	2	105
1941	25	3(2)	234
1941	25	3(3)	235
1941	25	4	316, 326
1941	25	4(1)	316
1941	25	5	97
1941	25	5(1)(b)	105
1941	25	5(2)	318
1941	25	5(2)(a)	320
1941	25	6(13)	320
1941	25	8(1)(a)	235, 318, 322
1941	25	8(1)(c)	84, 323, 325
1941	25	8(1)(d)	322
1941	25	13	97, 105
1941	28		21
1941	35		16, 32
1941	36		55
1941	43		224, 225, 226
1941	43	7	225
1941	50	3(h)	182
1941	50	30(h)	196
1941	54		225
1941	93		85, 443
1941	99		335
1941	107		215
1941	107	1	386
1941	107	15½	215, 217, 317
1941	108		215, 317
1941	108	12	361
1941	119		196, 207
1941	119	1	208
1941	119	2	207
1941	119	3	196, 208
1941	121	1	284

TABLE TWO (Continued)

Year	ch. No.	Sec.	Page	Year	ch. No.	Sec.	Page
1941	126		241, 418	1941	270	4	273
1941	126	1	253	1941	279		359
1941	127	2	216	1941	279	6	360
1941	130		373	1941	301		369
1941	130	10	373	1941	302		228
1941	157		70	1941	309		353
1941	158		98, 99	1941	309	1	244, 248
1941	177		275, 427	1941	322		305
1941	178		414	1941	338		169
1941	204		164	1941	338	14	170
1941	204	1(b)	161	1941	338	16	170
1941	217		232	1941	339		352, 355
1941	217	2	232	1941	339	6	352, 353, 356
1941	217	3	232	1941	346	1	264
1941	222		416	1941	354		212
1941	224		21, 233	1941	359		212
1941	246		156, 159	1941	365		335
1941	246	2	156, 159	1941	368		210, 211
1941	258		285, 287	1941	378		246, 251,
1941	260		376				274, 358
1941	263	2	210	1941	378	8	349
1941	266		258	1941	378	13	246, 348, 349
1941	270	3	274, 442	1941	378	14	350, 359

TABLE THREE

North Carolina Constitution Cited or Construed in Biennial Report.

ARTICLE	SECTION NUMBER	PAGE
I	6	71
I	26	89, 428
II	13	41
III	5	219
III	6	39, 46
III	13	19
III	14	17, 21
IV	2	219
IV	27	346
V	1	442, 467
V	3	131, 391
V	4	256, 258
V	5	304, 312, 313, 391
VI	2	219
VII	7	87, 89, 256, 258, 412
IX	1	88
IX	2	88
IX	3	88
IX	5	453
XI	7	51
XIV	3	278
XIV	7	45, 49, 74, 270, 407, 409, 422, 423, 433, 445, 449, 451, 453, 455, 462, 466, 467, 472

INDEX

A

B

D

E

F

G

H

I

N

O

P

R

S

U

V

W

Lightning Source UK Ltd.
Milton Keynes UK
UKHW011342100219
336964UK00010B/724/P

9 781331 152873